California Special Education Programs
A Composite of Laws

Education Code—Part 30, Other Related Laws,
and California Code of Regulations—Title 5

Twenty-fourth Edition 2002

Covering Laws Enacted During 2001

Prepared by the
Special Education Division
California Department of Education

Publishing Information

California Special Education Programs: A Composite of Laws
(Twenty-fourth edition) was prepared by Paul D. Hinkle, Consultant,
Special Education Division, California Department of Education, and was
published by the Department, 721 Capitol Mall, Sacramento, California
(mailing address: P.O. Box 944272, Sacramento, CA 94244-2720). Any
questions regarding the document should be addressed to the Special
Education Division at 515 L Street, Room 270, Sacramento, CA 95814.
The Division can also be contacted at (916) 445-4613.

Distributed under the provisions of the Library Distribution Act and
Government Code Section 11096.

ISBN 0-8011-1557-4

Ordering Information

Copies of this publication are available for $20 each, plus shipping and
handling charges. California residents are charged sales tax. Orders may be
sent to the California Department of Education, CDE Press, Sales Office,
P.O. Box 271, Sacramento, CA 95812-0271; FAX (916) 323-0823. See the
order form at the back of the book for complete information on payment,
including credit card purchases, or call the Sales Office at (800) 995-4099.
Prices on all publications are subject to change.

Parents of children with a disability are eligible to receive one complimentary copy, subject to availability. To receive a complimentary copy, fill out
and submit the order form.

An illustrated *Educational Resources* catalog describing publications,
videos, and other instructional media available from the Department can be
obtained without charge by writing to the address given above, by calling
the Sales Office at (916) 445-1260, or by visiting the Department's Web
site *<http://www.cde.ca.gov/cdepress>*.

CALIFORNIA
DEPARTMENT
OF
EDUCATION

721 Capitol Mall

Sacramento

CA 95814

Phone: (916) 657-4766

Fax: (916) 657-4975

DELAINE EASTIN

State Superintendent of Public Instruction

January 2002

Dear Parents, Teachers, Administrators and All Others
    Interested in the Education of Individuals with Exceptional Needs:

24th Edition — CALIFORNIA SPECIAL EDUCATION PROGRAMS: A COMPOSITE OF LAWS

This document contains changes to the *Education Code* enacted by the California Legislature during the first year of the 2001-02 Regular Session affecting programs for individuals with exceptional needs. Among the major changes are provisions pertaining to the composition of the individualized education program team and the role of the regular education teacher; rights of foster parents; and fiscal provisions implementing the settlement of the 20-year-old special education state-mandated claims issue. New provisions providing grants for the establishment of Family Empowerment Centers on Disability and for improving monitoring of special education programs operated by the Department of Youth Authority are also in this volume. As in prior editions, this document includes state special education statutes, provisions of the *California Code of Regulations*, Title 5 (Education), and related laws and regulations impacting special education programs.

This document is also available in a PDF format that can be printed or downloaded from the Internet at the California Department of Education's Web site < *http://www.cde.ca.gov/spbranch/sed/*> and is available in a searchable database at < *http://www2.otan.dni.us/laws_search/lawsrch.taf*>. Additional copies of the Composite of Laws can be ordered by calling CDE Press at 1-800-995-4099.

During 2002 the California Department of Education will once again sponsor legislation in an attempt to bring state special education law into alignment with the federal Individuals with Disabilities Education Act (IDEA), including bringing the discipline provisions into conformity with federal law. This year Congress will also be focusing on federal special education issues as IDEA is reauthorized. Full funding of Part B of IDEA, program accountability, overrepresentation of minorities in special education, and the shortage of qualified personnel will be among the issues.

As in the past two years, quality assurance and focused monitoring will continue to be the thrust of our department to monitor local educational agency compliance with state and federal laws and regulations governing special education so that adjustments can be made to prepare our children to reach their full potential. Focusing on outcomes for individuals with exceptional needs, rather than on the processes, is one of our major goals.

Within the Special Education Division, we have a Procedural Safeguards Referral Service to provide easy access to technical assistance information and resources for parents, teachers, school districts, advocates, and others about procedural safeguards regarding our students with disabilities. You may call 1-800-926-0648 for procedural safeguards assistance, or you may call (916) 445-4613 for general assistance or information. You may also contact professional staff in the Focused Monitoring and Technical Assistance regional units by county or special education local plan area assignment by accessing the listing at <*http://www.cde.ca.gov/spbranch/sed/fmtacnt.htm*>.

I thank all of you for your hard work in serving children with special needs, and I look forward to our continued efforts this year.

Sincerely,

Delaine Eastin

DELAINE EASTIN
State Superintendent of Public Instruction

TABLE OF CONTENTS

EDUCATION CODE - PART 30 - SPECIAL EDUCATION PROGRAMS

| CALIFORNIA CODE OF REGULATIONS - TITLE 2 - ADMINISTRATION |

CALIFORNIA EARLY INTERVENTION SERVICES ACT
(Government Code - Title 14)

CALIFORNIA CODE OF REGULATIONS - TITLE 17 - PUBLIC HEALTH

DIVISION 2. STATE DEPARTMENT OF DEVELOPMENTAL SERVICES
CHAPTER 2. EARLY INTERVENTION SERVICES

SUBCHAPTER 1. GENERAL PROVISIONS

SUBCHAPTER 2. PROGRAM AND SERVICE COMPONENTS

SUBCHAPTER 3. INDIVIDUALIZED FAMILY SERVICE PLAN

SUBCHAPTER 4. SERVICE COORDINATION AND INTERAGENCY AGREEMENTS

SUBCHAPTER 5. PROCEDURAL SAFEGUARDS

BUDGET ACT OF 2001-2002

FOREWORD

EDUCATION CODE – PART 30

CALIFORNIA CODE OF REGULATIONS – TITLE 5

SPECIAL EDUCATION PROGRAMS

This twenty-fourth edition of *California Special Education Programs – A Composite of Laws* covers Part 30 (commencing with Section 56000) of the Education Code relative to special education programs and includes Chapters 3 (commencing with Section 3000) and 5.1 (commencing with Section 4600) of Division 1 of Title 5 of the California Code of Regulations relative to special education for children and youth with disabilities and uniform complaint procedures.

This document also includes Part 32 (commencing with Section 59000) of the Education Code covering the statutes governing the State Special Schools and Centers and the regulations implementing Chapter 26.5 of Division 7 of Title 1 of the Government Code, "Interagency Responsibilities for Providing Services to Handicapped Children." The interagency regulations, Chapter 1 (commencing with Section 60000) of Division 9 of Title 2 of the California Code of Regulations, begin on page G-1. The composite also contains selected provisions of the Education Code, Health and Safety Code, Government Code, Welfare and Institutions Code, noncodified sections, and the 2001-02 Budget Act that have a direct impact on special education and related services for individuals with exceptional needs. This edition includes public health regulations of Title 17 that implement the California Early Intervention Services Act. The Act appears in Title 14 of the Government Code, which is also included in this edition.

Part 30 of the Education Code was rewritten in 1980, primarily by Senate Bill 1870 (Rodda), (Chapter 797), which became law on July 28, 1980. This legislation repealed all former special education categorical programs and Education Code sections pertaining to the Master Plan for Special Education program that were in effect on January 1, 1980. It also restructured and added code sections implementing the Master Plan for Special Education statewide. Since the passage of SB 1870, 134 separate legislative measures have modified California's special education statutes.

The California Code of Regulations, Title 5, governing special education was originally adopted to implement the Master Plan and became effective in March 1981. The State Board of Education adopted substantive amendments on December 11, 1987, and they became operative on April 20, 1988. Regulations governing behavioral interventions for special education pupils were approved in 1996. In December 1998 the State Board of Education adopted regulations pertaining to resource specialist caseload waivers. The State Board adopted regulations in 1999 pertaining to nonpublic, nonsectarian schools and agencies.

During 2001, 12 legislative bills were chaptered into law amending, adding, or repealing special education provisions under Part 30 of the Education Code.

The measures are as follows:

Senate Bill 505 (Perata)	- Chapter 536 – Statutes of 2001 October 5, 2001
Senate Bill 511 (Alpert)	- Chapter 690 – Statutes of 2001 January 1, 2002
Senate Bill 662 (Committee on Judiciary)	- Chapter 159 – Statutes of 2001 January 1, 2002
Senate Bill 735 (Committee on Budget and Fiscal Review)	- Chapter 891 – Statutes of 2001 October 14, 2001
Senate Bill 982 (O'Connell)	- Chapter 203 – Statutes of 2001 August 13, 2001
Senate Bill 1105 (Margett)	- Chapter 405 – Statutes of 2001 January 1, 2002
Senate Bill 1191 (Speier)	- Chapter 745 – Statutes of 2001 October 12, 2001
Assembly Bill 303 (Dickerson)	- Chapter 551 – Statutes of 2001 January 1, 2002
Assembly Bill 306 (Frommer)	- Chapter 736 – Statutes of 2001 January 1, 2002
Assembly Bill 804 (Committee on Education)	- Chapter 734 – Statutes of 2001 October 11, 2001
Assembly Bill 992 (Papan)	- Chapter 215 – Statutes of 2001 January 1, 2002
Assembly Bill 1539 (Pavley)	- Chapter 629 – Statutes of 2001 January 1, 2002

Senate Bill 505 (Perata), an urgency measure, added Chapter 8.5 (commencing with Section 56867) to Part 30 of the Education Code to intensify monitoring of special education programs at the Department of Youth Authority, also known as the California Youth Authority (CYA). The new chapter does the following:

➢ Specifies that the California Department of Education (CDE) is responsible for monitoring the CYA for compliance with state and federal laws and regulations regarding special education.
➢ Requires CDE and the California State University (CSU) to enter into an interagency agreement under which the Center for the Study of Correctional Education, located on the CSU, San Bernardino campus, provides CDE with technical assistance regarding compliance with state and federal laws and regulations regarding special education at the CYA.
➢ Requires CDE to prepare an interagency agreement in consultation with CSU, San Bernardino, and the superintendent of education for the CYA.
➢ Specifies that the interagency agreement shall require the center to provide designated services to the Special Education Division of CDE.

The technical assistance to be provided shall reflect existing or subsequently adopted standards for state and federal compliance. SB 505 specifies that reviews conducted shall include, but not be limited to, assessments of the following special education services for wards at the CYA with exceptional needs:

1. Identification and assessment of wards with exceptional needs.
2. Parent notification, consent, and participation.
3. Individual education plan development and content, including behavior intervention and transition plans.
4. Assessment of ward progress.
5. Provision of services in the least restrictive environment maximizing inclusion.
6. Services to pupils who are not proficient in English.
7. Observance of procedural safeguards and compliance with state and federal law.

Anticipating the enactment of SB 505, the Budget Act of 2001, approved by the Governor on July 26, 2001, appropriated $250,000 in federal funds under the Individuals with Disabilities Education Act (IDEA) for allocation by CDE to the CSU, San Bernardino, Center for the Study of Correctional Education. Those funds were allocated for monitoring of the special education program and technical assistance to the program at the CYA.

Senate Bill 511 (Alpert) added Chapter 4.3 (commencing with Section 56400) to Part 30 of the Education Code, entitled "Family Empowerment Centers on Disability." The measure requires CDE to award grants for establishing centers in each of the 32 regions in the state established under the Early Start Family Resource Centers that are operated by the State Department of Developmental

Services for the purpose of extending services to communities not receiving services. The legislative intent of the new law is spelled out in Section 56400. To the extent feasible, the new law aims to accomplish the following actions:

> Ensure that children and young adults with disabilities are provided a free and appropriate public education in accordance with applicable federal and state law and regulations.
> Ensure that children and young adults with disabilities receive the necessary educational support and services they need to complete their education.
> Offer parents and guardians of children and young adults with disabilities access to accurate information, specialized training, and peer-to-peer support in their communities.
> Ensure that parents, guardians, and families of children and young adults with disabilities are full participants in their child's education, school reform, and comprehensive systems change efforts.
> Build upon existing local and regional service delivery systems to improve, expand, and offer coordinated technical assistance to the network of existing resources available for parents, guardians, and families of children and young adults with disabilities.

Section 56402 requires CDE to award grants that establish Family Empowerment Centers on Disability no later than February 15, 2002, in the first year of operation and in subsequent years (to the extent funding is available) no later than February 15 of that year. A noncodified section of SB 511 provided CDE with an appropriation of $2,372,000 in federal IDEA funds for establishing the centers.

Senate Bill 662 (Committee on Judiciary), among numerous other amendments, made technical, nonsubstantive amendments to Sections 56045 and 56845 of Part 30 of the Education Code.

Senate Bill 735 (Committee on Budget and Fiscal Review), an urgency measure, added Section 56836.095 to Part 30 of the Education Code, pertaining to special education funding computations for 2001-02 fiscal year, listing the order in which specified computations are to be made. The bill also added two other sections to Part 30 of the Education Code. Section 56836.158, pertaining to the computation of special education funding for increasing the statewide target amount per unit of average daily attendance (ADA), specified the computation and distribution of funding. Section 56836.159, pertaining to the computation of special education funding for providing a permanent adjustment for each special education local plan area (SELPA), specified the method the Superintendent of Public Instruction shall use in computing a permanent adjustment.

Senate Bill 982 (O'Connell), an urgency measure, added Sections 56836.156 and 56836.157 to Part 30 of the Education Code, providing funding for special education in settlement of a contested state mandate claims issue of 20-year standing known as (1) Riverside County Superintendent of Schools et al. CSM-3986 on remand from the Superior Court of Sacramento County, No. 352795, and (2) Long Beach Unified School District, CSM-3986A (consolidated with the Santa Barbara County Superintendent of Schools, SB 90-3453).

The measure provided for more than $1.5 billion over a ten-year period for local educational agencies to implement the settlement of special education mandated cost claims that resulted from state special education laws that exceeded federal special education mandates as determined by the Commission on State Mandates. The Governor and the parties to the special education mandate settlement agreed to the terms in October 2000.

Specifically, SB 982:

> Requires the Superintendent of Public Instruction to increase the annual state funding entitlement for special education by $100 million, appropriated in the measure, starting with the 2001-02 fiscal year. The bill declares that the $100 million increase in special education funding shall be used to meet the costs of any state-mandated programs or services and shall be considered to have fully met any such costs. It further requires that any costs identified by the Commission or any other mandates shall have priority for use of the funding. The measure also declares that the $100 million is not intended to fund any mandates that may result in the future from amendments to special education law that are enacted subsequent to July 1, 2000.

> Provides for the annual appropriation of $25 million "on a one-time basis each fiscal year" from the General Fund to local educational agencies for each of ten years from 2001-02 through 2010-11 (a total of $250 million). This funding is to be distributed as an equal amount per pupil in average daily attendance in 1999-2000. The $25 million for fiscal year 2001-02 is appropriated from the General Fund in this measure.

> Appropriates $270 million from the General Fund on a one-time basis in lieu of specific previous year mandated cost claims and in full satisfaction of those claims made by the Riverside County Superintendent of Schools, the Long Beach Unified School District and the Santa Barbara County Superintendent of Schools. The funds shall be allocated as follows:

1. $10,800,000 to county offices of education to be distributed on the basis of the county office special education pupil counts of December 1999.
2. $2,700,000 to SELPAs to be distributed on the basis of the statewide special education pupil count of December 1999, with each SELPA's share being determined by that portion of the statewide count that is in the SELPA's area.
3. $6,000,000 to the Riverside County Office of Education.
4. The remaining $250,500,000 to all school districts on the basis of their ADA for the 1999-2000 year. The ADA of county superintendent-run programs, adult education, and regional

occupational centers and programs is not included in the distribution.

➢ Excludes from the settlement any costs associated with a specific claim (CSM-4464) that is pending normal review and was filed by the San Diego Unified School District, the San Joaquin County Office of Education, and the Butte County Office of Education.

➢ Further stipulates that the one-time $25 million appropriation may not be made in any year in which the Proposition 98 guarantee of K-14 funding is governed by Test 3. Such an event means that state revenues may not be growing adequately to provide the inflation adjustment required by Test 2.

(*Historical Note*: The Santa Barbara County Superintendent of Schools and the Riverside County Superintendent of Schools first filed test claims for costs mandated by state special education laws in 1980 and 1981. Seventeen areas in the test claim alleged that state law exceeded the federal mandate. These and subsequent mandated cost claims were denied on the argument that all special education mandates emanate from the federal law and, therefore, were not reimbursable under state law. The claimants sought a remedy through the state courts, which remanded the case to the Commission on State Mandates with instructions to determine "which, if any portions of the State's special education programs exceed federal mandate, and whether such portions are to any extent unfounded." On November 20, 1998, the commission determined that the test claim legislation constituted a partial, reimbursable state-mandated program within the meaning of Section 6 of Article XIIIB of the California Constitution for the following eight special education program areas:

1. Maximum age limit
2. Community advisory committee
3. Governance structure
4. Enrollment caseloads (both resource specialists and language, speech, and hearing specialists)
5. Extended school year
6. Interim placements
7. Resource specialist program (excluding maximum caseloads)
8. Written parental consent

On June 5, 2000, the commission determined that the mandates were unfunded, and it adopted parameters and guidelines for filing claims. The California Department of Finance had prepared to go to court to contest the commission's decisions on the basis that any state mandates were well funded by state special education appropriations, which far exceed federal funding. To avoid the costs and uncertainty of continued litigation, claimants and the state agreed to settle.

Senate Bill 1105 (Margett) repealed and then added Section 56341, regarding the composition of the individualized education program (IEP) team, including the role of the regular education teacher, to align Part 30 of the Education Code with the federal IDEA. It provides that at least one regular education teacher of the pupil (if the pupil is, or may be, participating in the regular education environment) shall be on the IEP team. It specifies that if more than one regular education teacher is providing instructional services to the individual with exceptional needs, one regular education teacher may be designated by the district, special education local plan area, or county office to represent the other regular education teachers.

Section 56341 also provides that the regular education teacher of an individual with exceptional needs shall, to the extent appropriate, participate in the development, review, and revision of the pupil's IEP, including assisting in the determination of appropriate positive behavioral interventions and strategies for the pupil and supplementary aids and services, and program modifications or supports for school personnel that will be provided for the pupil, consistent with the Code of Federal Regulations. The IEP team member representing the local educational agency shall, in addition to being qualified to provide or supervise the provision of specially designed instruction to meet the unique needs of the individual with exceptional needs, be knowledgeable about the availability of resources of the local educational agency. It also provides that, at the discretion of the parent, guardian, or the district, special education local plan area, or county office of education, other individuals who have knowledge or special expertise regarding the pupil shall be included on the IEP team. This would include related services personnel, as appropriate. The section says the determination of whether the individual has knowledge or special expertise regarding the pupil shall be made by the party who invites the individual to be a member of the IEP team. The section also specifies transition services participants.

SB 1105 also added Section 56341.1 to Part 30 of the Education Code, specifying what the IEP team shall consider in the development of the IEP, including the strengths of the pupil and the concerns of the parents or guardians for enhancing the education of the pupil; the results of the initial assessment or most recent assessment of the pupil; and, as appropriate, the results of the pupil's performance on any general state or districtwide assessment programs. Other special considerations are also listed. The new section also specifies that the IEP team shall revise the IEP, as appropriate, to address among other matters, any lack of expected progress toward the annual goals and in the general curriculum, where appropriate; the results of any reassessment conducted pursuant to Section 56381; information about the pupil provided to, or by, the parents or guardians; the pupil's anticipated needs; and other factors specified in the development of the IEP.

Senate Bill 1191 (Speier), an urgency measure revising or deleting certain reporting requirements for state and local agencies, amended Section 56885 of Part 30 of the Education Code to eliminate a Department of Finance report to legislative committees regarding amounts of funds that should be transferred between state agencies for interagency services to individuals with exceptional needs. (*Historical Note*: Chapter 9 [commencing with Section 56875] of Part 30, of which Section 56885 is included, has never been implemented since its enactment in 1980.)

Assembly Bill 303 (Dickerson) added Section 56213 to Part 30 of the Education Code to authorize a necessary small special education local plan area that receives less funding than it did in the prior year because of declining enrollment to claim an amount equal to 40 percent of the reduction in addition to the current year funding.

Assembly Bill 306 (Frommer) added Section 56351.5 to Part 30 of the Education Code to permit a school district, special education local plan area, or county office of education to reinforce Braille instruction using a Braille instructional aide who meets specified criteria. The measure also amended Section 56352 to permit local educational agencies to provide pupils who have low vision with the opportunity to receive assessments to determine the appropriate reading medium or media, including Braille instruction.

Section 60061 of Part 33 of the Education Code was also amended to delete the provision that requires a publisher or manufacturer to provide computer diskette versions of print material if they are made available to any other state. Instead the law would require computer files or electronic versions of each state-adopted literacy title to be provided within 30 days of request by the state and computer files or other electronic versions of nonliterary titles, including science and math, to be provided when the technology to convert those materials is available.

The Legislature stated the following in findings and declarations in AB 306:
  "(a) This state is in need of more credentialed teachers who are able to teach Braille to visually impaired pupils.
  "(b) It is vitally important for visually impaired individuals to learn Braille. There is a direct correlation between Braille literacy and the level of employment and education attained by people who are visually impaired and blind.
  "(c) This state should ensure that visually impaired pupils are able to read at the same level as their peers."

Assembly Bill 804 (Committee on Education), a "technical" cleanup measure containing an urgency clause, made nonsubstantive amendments to Sections 52026 (definition of individuals with exceptional needs); 56200 (pertaining to local plans); 56207 (transfer of programs); 56391 (participation in graduation ceremony and related activities); 56836.02 (apportionments for school districts and county offices of education) of Part 30 of the Education Code. The measure also:
  ➤ Amended Section 56029, defining referral for assessment. The measure expands the list of persons allowed to make a referral to include a "guardian" and a "foster parent of the individual, consistent with the limitations contained in federal laws."

- Added Article 3.7 (commencing with Section 56055) to Chapter 1 under the heading of "Foster Parents" providing that:
  - A foster parent, except as provided in subdivision (b) of Section 56055, shall, to the extent permitted by federal law, including, but not limited to, Section 300.20 of Title 34 of the Code of Federal Regulations, have the rights related to his or her foster child's education that a parent has under Title 20 (commencing with Section 1400) of the United States Code and pursuant to Part 300 (commencing with Section 300.1) of Title 34 of the Code of Federal Regulations.
  - The foster parent may represent the foster child for the duration of the foster parent-foster child relationship in matters relating to identification, assessment, instructional planning and development, educational placement, reviewing and revising an individualized education program (IEP), if necessary, and in all other matters relating to the provision of a free appropriate public education of the child. Notwithstanding any other provision of law, this representation shall include the provision of written consent to the IEP, including nonemergency medical services, mental health treatment services, and occupational or physical therapy services pursuant to this chapter. The foster parent may sign any consent relating to IEP purposes.
  - A foster parent exercising rights relative to a foster child under this section may consult with the parent or guardian of the child to ensure continuity of health, mental health, or other services.
  - Subdivision (b) of Section 56055 specifies that "a foster parent who has been excluded by court order from making educational decisions on behalf of a pupil shall not have the rights relative to the pupil set forth in subdivision (a)."
  - [*Cautionary Note*: Section 300.20(b)(1) and (b)(2) of Title 34 of the Code of Federal Regulations states that a foster parent may act as a parent under Part B of the IDEA if "(1) The natural parents' authority to make educational decisions on the child's behalf has been extinguished under State law; and (2) The foster parent—(i) Has an ongoing, long-term parental relationship with the child; (ii) Is willing to make the educational decisions required of parents under the Act; and (iii) Has no interest that would conflict with the interests of the child."]
- Amended Section 56366.1, pertaining to nonpublic, nonsectarian school application for certification by striking subdivision (b) that read: "Unless the board grants a waiver pursuant to Section 56101, a nonpublic, nonsectarian school or agency shall file an application

for certification between January 1 and June 30." The amendment permits applications for certification to be filed year-round.

➢ Repealed Section 56044 providing that state funds may not be allocated to offset any federal funding intended for individuals with exceptional needs and withheld from a local educational agency due to the agency's noncompliance with federal law. (*Note*: This language is still contained in subdivision (c) of Section 56845.)

<u>Assembly Bill 992</u> (Papan) amended Section 56366.3 of Part 30 of the Education Code to remove the prohibition against a nonpublic, nonsectarian school hiring someone who is or was an employee of a contracting school district, special education local plan area, or county office of education within the last 365 days.

<u>Assembly Bill 1539</u> (Pavley) added Sections 56435 and 56449 to Part 30 of the Education Code allowing the transfer of information, with the permission of the parent or guardian, about an infant, toddler, or preschooler, to the public school, from the previous school year, deemed beneficial to the pupil and the teacher, including, but not limited to, development issues, social interaction abilities, health background, and diagnostic assessments, if any.

The measure contains findings and declarations of the Legislature in a new Article 13.5 (commencing with Section 8282) of Chapter 2 of Part 6 of the Education Code that "the state makes a substantial, annual investment in preschool, infant and toddler, and schoolage child development programs for eligible families. It is in the best interests of children and their families, and the taxpayers of California, to have information about the development and learning abilities of children developed in these settings, health and other information transferred to, or otherwise available to, the pupil's elementary school."

NO MORE "SUNSET" REVIEWS FOR SPECIAL EDUCATION

Assembly Bill 379 authored by Assembly Member Lou Papan, an urgency measure, became law on July 16, 2001, repealing Section 62000.8 of Part 34 of the Education Code, the 22-year-old law requiring periodic sunset reviews of special education programs. Although AB 379 did not amend Part 30 of the Education Code, it certainly had an enormous impact on special education laws. The measure became Chapter 64, Statutes of 2001.

The general sunset review provisions were enacted in 1979 "to provide state leadership and assistance for school and curricular improvement as well as state support to aid in meeting the unique educational needs of specified groups of students." In enacting these provisions, including Section 62000.8, the Legislature specified its intent to "assure a thorough review of programs. . .so that they most effectively, efficiently, and economically meet the needs of pupils and improve schools." The Legislature always contended that the purpose "was not to remove resources from students with special needs or to cease efforts to improve schools."

One of the first categorical programs scheduled for evaluation and termination (sunset) on June 30, 1981, were programs of "special education for physically handicapped, educationally handicapped, mentally retarded, severely mentally retarded, and individuals with exceptional needs." The latter disability descriptor was first added by the Master Plan for Special Education in 1974 (AB 4040, Chapter 1532, Statutes of 1974) and today is defined in Section 56026 of Part 30 of the Education Code. The first sunset report on special education programs was dated March 24, 1980. The last and final sunset report was dated January 2001.

The section repealed by AB 379 required the special education program to sunset on June 30, 2001. When an educational program sunsets under the evaluation and sunsetting provisions of the laws, the specific categorical program ceases to be operative under state laws and regulations, but funding continues for the general purposes of that program as specified in the provisions relating to the establishment and operation of the program. AB 379 was sponsored by the California Department of Education.

HIGHLIGHTS OF THE BUDGET ACT OF 2001-2002

Budget items for special education programs and State Special Schools and Centers for fiscal year 2001-02 may be found on pages J-1 through J-8. Senate Bill 739 (Chapter 106, Statutes of 2001), the Budget Act of 2001-2002, provided special education programs with a 3.87 percent cost-of-living adjustment (COLA). Budget Item 6110-161-0001, in part, provided a General Fund appropriation for special education programs in the amount of $2,602,658,000 (which includes the COLA), including $68,662,000 for the Early Education Program, minus $14,395,000 reimbursements for the Early Education Program (Part C). The budget allocated $49.2 million to fund statutory growth and allocated $122,866,000 for COLAs for special education program growth, low-incidence disabilities, nonpublic school/licensed children's institutions (NPS/LCIs), program specialist and regionalized services, and regional occupational centers and programs.

The budget also provided $55.9 million in additional aid to equalize special education funding rates among school districts and county offices of education for 2001-02. This amount is expected to fully fund the equalization requirement of Assembly Bill 602 (1997) (i.e., that all special education local plan areas [SELPAs] with ADA below the statewide target funding rate reach the statewide target). The budget also provided up to an additional $48.9 million to provide funding increases to SELPAs with the lowest ADA rates. In addition, the budget provided $5.9 million for a special disabilities adjustment, which will continue through the 2002-03 fiscal year. The NPS/LCI funding was capped at $120.2 million for the 2001-02 fiscal year. As mentioned earlier, SB 982 made several augmentations to the Budget Act as a part of the special education mandated cost claims settlement.

A $12 million appropriation from the General Fund was provided through Budget Item 6110-485-0001, on a one-time basis, to cover deficiencies in the 2000-01 funding of special education.

Budget Item 6110-161-0890 provided a total of $664,818,000 for special education programs from the federal Individuals with Disabilities Education Act.

PART 30. SPECIAL EDUCATION PROGRAMS

CHAPTER 1. GENERAL PROVISIONS

Article 1. Intent

56000.   The Legislature finds and declares that all individuals with exceptional needs have a right to participate in free appropriate public education and that special educational instruction and services for these persons are needed in order to ensure them of the right to an appropriate educational opportunity to meet their unique needs.

- Free Appropriate Public Education

It is the intent of the Legislature to unify and improve special education programs in California under the flexible program design of the Master Plan for Special Education. It is the further intent of the Legislature to assure that all individuals with exceptional needs are provided their rights to appropriate programs and services which are designed to meet their unique needs under the Individuals with Disabilities Education Act (20 U.S.C. Sec. 1400 et seq.).

- Unify and Improve Programs

- Assure Rights to Appropriate Programs and Services

It is the further intent of the Legislature that nothing in this part shall be construed to abrogate any right provided individuals with exceptional needs and their parents or guardians under the Individuals with Disabilities Education Act (20 U.S.C. Sec. 1400 et seq.). It is also the intent of the Legislature that nothing in this part shall be construed to set a higher standard of educating individuals with exceptional needs than that established by Congress under the Individuals with Disabilities Education Act (20 U.S.C. Sec. 1400 et seq.).

- Standard of Educating

It is the further intent of the Legislature that the Master Plan for Special Education provide an educational opportunity for individuals with exceptional needs that is equal to or better than that provided prior to the implementation of programs under this part, including, but not limited to, those provided to individuals previously served in a development center for handicapped pupils.

- Provide Educational Opportunity

It is the intent of the Legislature that the restructuring of special education programs as set forth in the Master Plan for Special Education be implemented in accordance with provisions of this part by all school districts and county offices during a two-year transitional period commencing with fiscal year 1980-81, with full implementation to be

- Full Implementation

completed by June 30, 1982.

56000.5. (a) The Legislature finds and declares that:

(1) Pupils with low-incidence disabilities, as a group, make up less than 1 percent of the total statewide enrollment for kindergarten through grade 12.

- Low-Incidence Disabilities

(2) Pupils with low-incidence disabilities require highly specialized services, equipment, and materials.

(b) The Legislature further finds and declares that:

(1) Deafness involves the most basic of human needs--the ability to communicate with other human beings. Many hard-of-hearing and deaf children use an appropriate communication mode, sign language, which may be their primary language, while others express and receive language orally and aurally, with or without visual signs or cues. Still others, typically young hard-of-hearing and deaf children, lack any significant language skills. It is essential for the well-being and growth of hard-of-hearing and deaf children that educational programs recognize the unique nature of deafness and ensure that all hard-of-hearing and deaf children have appropriate, ongoing, and fully accessible educational opportunities.

- Deafness

(2) It is essential that hard-of-hearing and deaf children, like all children, have an education in which their unique communication mode is respected, utilized, and developed to an appropriate level of proficiency.

- Unique Communication Mode

(3) It is essential that hard-of-hearing and deaf children have an education in which special education teachers, psychologists, speech therapists, assessors, administrators, and other special education personnel understand the unique nature of deafness and are specifically trained to work with hard-of-hearing and deaf pupils. It is essential that hard-of-hearing and deaf children have an education in which their special education teachers are proficient in the primary language mode of those children.

- Trained Personnel

(4) It is essential that hard-of-hearing and deaf children, like all children, have an education with a sufficient number of language mode peers with whom they can communicate directly and who are of the same, or approximately the same, age and ability level.

- Language Mode Peers

(5) It is essential that hard-of-hearing and deaf children have an education in which their parents and, where appropriate, hard-of-hearing and deaf people are involved in determining the extent, content, and purpose of programs.

- Parental Involvement

(6) Hard-of-hearing and deaf children would benefit from an education in which they are exposed to hard-of-hearing

- Role Models

and deaf role models.

(7) It is essential that hard-of-hearing and deaf children, like all children, have programs in which they have direct and appropriate access to all components of the educational process, including, but not limited to, recess, lunch, and extracurricular social and athletic activities.

- Access to Educational Process

(8) It is essential that hard-of-hearing and deaf children, like all children, have programs in which their unique vocational needs are provided for, including appropriate research, curricula, programs, staff, and outreach.

- Vocational Needs

(9) Each hard-of-hearing and deaf child should have a determination of the least restrictive educational environment that takes into consideration these legislative findings and declarations.

- Least Restrictive Environment

(10) Given their unique communication needs, hard-of-hearing and deaf children would benefit from the development and implementation of regional programs for children with low-incidence disabilities.

- Regional Programs

56001. It is the intent of the Legislature that special education programs provide all of the following:

(a) Each individual with exceptional needs is assured an education appropriate to his or her needs in publicly supported programs through completion of his or her prescribed course of study or until the time that he or she has met proficiency standards prescribed pursuant to Sections 51215 and 51216.

- An Education Appropriate to Needs

(b) By June 30, 1991, early educational opportunities shall be available to all children between the ages of three and five years who require special education and services.

- Between Ages 3 and 5 Years

(c) Early educational opportunities shall be made available to children younger than three years of age pursuant to Chapter 4.4 (commencing with Section 56425), appropriate sections of this part, and the California Early Intervention Service Act, Title 14 (commencing with Section 95000) of the Government Code.

- Ages Birth to 3 Years

(d) Any child younger than three years, potentially eligible for special education, shall be afforded the protections provided pursuant to the California Early Intervention Services Act, Title 14 (commencing with Section 95000) of the Government Code and Section 1439 of Title 20 of the United States Code and implementing regulations.

- Protections for Children Younger Than 3 Years

(e) Each individual with exceptional needs shall have his or her educational goals, objectives, and special education and related services specified in a written individualized education program.

- Written Individualized Education Program (IEP)

(f) Education programs are provided under an approved local plan for special education that sets forth the elements of the programs in accordance with this part. This plan for special education shall be developed cooperatively with input from the community advisory committee and appropriate representation from special and regular teachers and administrators selected by the groups they represent to ensure effective participation and communication.

- Local Plan Development

(g) Individuals with exceptional needs are offered special assistance programs that promote maximum interaction with the general school population in a manner that is appropriate to the needs of both, taking into consideration, for hard-of-hearing or deaf children, the individual's needs for a sufficient number of age and language mode peers and for special education teachers who are proficient in the individual's primary language mode.

- Maximum Interaction

(h) Pupils be transferred out of special education programs when special education services are no longer needed.

- Pupils Transferred Out

(i) The unnecessary use of labels is avoided in providing special education and related services for individuals with exceptional needs.

- Avoid Unnecessary Use of Labels

(j) Procedures and materials for assessment and placement of individuals with exceptional needs shall be selected and administered so as not to be racially, culturally, or sexually discriminatory. No single assessment instrument shall be the sole criterion for determining placement of a pupil. The procedures and materials for assessment and placement shall be in the individual's mode of communication. Procedures and materials for use with pupils of limited English proficiency, as defined in subdivision (m) of Section 52163, shall be in the individual's primary language. All assessment materials and procedures shall be selected and administered pursuant to Section 56320.

- Assessment Procedures and Materials

(k) Educational programs are coordinated with other public and private agencies, including preschools, child development programs, nonpublic nonsectarian schools, regional occupational centers and programs, and postsecondary and adult programs for individuals with exceptional needs.

- Coordination of Educational Programs

(l) Psychological and health services for individuals with exceptional needs shall be available to each schoolsite.

- Psychological and Health Services

(m) Continuous evaluation of the effectiveness of these special education programs by the school district, special education local plan area, or county office shall be made to ensure the highest quality educational offerings.

- Continuous Program Evaluation

(n) Appropriate qualified staff are employed, consistent

- Qualified Staff

with credentialing requirements, to fulfill the responsibilities of the local plan and positive efforts are made to employ qualified disabled individuals.

(o) Regular and special education personnel are adequately prepared to provide educational instruction and services to individuals with exceptional needs.

- Prepared Personnel

Article 2. Definitions

56020. As used in this part, the definitions prescribed by this article apply unless the context otherwise requires.

- Application of Article

56021. "Board" means the State Board of Education.

- Board

56022. "County office" means office of the county superintendent of schools.

- County Office

56023. "Day" means a calendar day.

- Day

56024. "Department" means the Department of Education.

- Department

56025. "District" means school district.

- District

56026. "Individuals with exceptional needs" means those persons who satisfy all the following:

- Individuals with Exceptional Needs (1)

(a) Identified by an individualized education program team as a child with a disability, as that phrase is defined in subparagraph (A) of paragraph (3) of Section 1401 of Title 20 of the United States Code.

- Identified by IEP Team

- Federal Definition Citation

(b) Their impairment, as described by subdivision (a), requires instruction, services, or both, which cannot be provided with modification of the regular school program.

- Impairment Requires Special Instruction and Services

(c) Come within one of the following age categories:

- Age Categories

(1) Younger than three years of age and identified by the district, the special education local plan area, or the county office as requiring intensive special education and services, as defined by the State Board of Education.

- Younger Than 3 Years

(2) Between the ages of three to five years, inclusive, and identified by the district, the special education local plan area, or the county office pursuant to Section 56441.11.

- Between 3 and 5 Years

(3) Between the ages of five and 18 years, inclusive.

- Between 5 and 18 Years

(4) Between the ages of 19 and 21 years, inclusive; enrolled in or eligible for a program under this part or other special education program prior to his or her 19th birthday; and has not yet completed his or her prescribed course of study or who has not met proficiency standards prescribed pursuant to Sections 51215 and 51216.

- Between 19 and 21 Years

(A) Any person who becomes 22 years of age during the months of January to June, inclusive, while participating in a program under this part may continue his or her participation in the program for the remainder of the current fiscal year,

- Twenty-two Years of Age (January to June, Inclusive)

including any extended school year program for individuals with exceptional needs established pursuant to regulations adopted by the State Board of Education, pursuant to Article 1 (commencing with Section 56100) of Chapter 2.

(B) Any person otherwise eligible to participate in a program under this part shall not be allowed to begin a new fiscal year in a program if he or she becomes 22 years of age in July, August, or September of that new fiscal year. However, if a person is in a year-round school program and is completing his or her individualized education program in a term that extends into the new fiscal year, then the person may complete that term.

- Twenty-two Years of Age (July to September, Inclusive)

(C) Any person who becomes 22 years of age during the months of October, November, or December while participating in a program under this act shall be terminated from the program on December 31 of the current fiscal year, unless the person would otherwise complete his or her individualized education program at the end of the current fiscal year.

- Twenty-two Years of Age (October, November, or December)

(D) No school district, special education local plan area, or county office of education may develop an individualized education program that extends these eligibility dates, and in no event may a pupil be required or allowed to attend school under the provisions of this part beyond these eligibility dates solely on the basis that the individual has not met his or her goals or objectives.

- IEP Cannot Extend Eligibility Date

(d) Meet eligibility criteria set forth in regulations adopted by the board, including, but not limited to, those adopted pursuant to Article 2.5 (commencing with Section 56333) of Chapter 4.

- Eligibility Criteria

(e) Unless disabled within the meaning of subdivisions (a) to (d), inclusive, pupils whose educational needs are due primarily to limited English proficiency; a lack of instruction in reading or mathematics; temporary physical disabilities; social maladjustment; or environmental, cultural, or economic factors are not individuals with exceptional needs.

- Not Individuals with Exceptional Needs

56026.2. "Language mode" means the method of communication used by hard-of-hearing and deaf children that may include the use of sign language to send or receive messages or the use of spoken language, with or without visual signs or cues.

- Language Mode

56026.5. "Low incidence disability" means a severe disabling condition with an expected incidence rate of less than one percent of the total statewide enrollment in kindergarten through grade 12. For purposes of this

- Low Incidence Disability

definition, severe disabling conditions are hearing impairments, vision impairments, and severe orthopedic impairments, or any combination thereof. For purposes of this definition, vision impairments do not include disabilities within the function of vision specified in Section 56338.

56027. "Local plan" means a plan that meets the requirements of Chapter 3 (commencing with Section 56200) and that is submitted by a school district, special education local plan area, or county office.

56028. "Parent" includes any person having legal custody of a child. "Parent," in addition, includes any adult pupil for whom no guardian or conservator has been appointed and the person having custody of a minor if neither the parent nor legal guardian can be notified of the educational actions under consideration. "Parent" also includes a parent surrogate. "Parent" does not include the state or any political subdivision of government.

56029. "Referral for assessment" means any written request for assessment to identify an individual with exceptional needs made by any of the following:

(a) A parent or guardian of the individual.

(b) A teacher or other service provider of the individual.

(c) A foster parent of the individual, consistent with the limitations contained in federal law.

56030. "Responsible local agency" means the school district or county office designated in the local plan as the entity whose duties shall include, but are not limited to, receiving and distributing regionalized services funds, providing administrative support, and coordinating the implementation of the plan.

56030.5. "Severely disabled" means individuals with exceptional needs who require intensive instruction and training in programs serving pupils with the following profound disabilities: autism, blindness, deafness, severe orthopedic impairments, serious emotional disturbances, severe mental retardation, and those individuals who would have been eligible for enrollment in a development center for handicapped pupils under Chapter 6 (commencing with Section 56800) of this part, as it read on January 1, 1980.

56031. "Special education" means specially designed instruction, at no cost to the parent, to meet the unique needs of individuals with exceptional needs, whose educational needs cannot be met with modification of the regular instruction program, and related services, at no cost to the parent, that may be needed to assist these individuals to

- Local Plan

- Parent

- Referral for Assessment (2)

- Responsible Local Agency

- Severely Disabled

- Special Education (Specially Designed Instruction)

benefit from specially designed instruction.

Special education is an integral part of the total public education system and provides education in a manner that promotes maximum interaction between children or youth with disabilities and children or youth who are not disabled, in a manner that is appropriate to the needs of both.

— Integral Part of Public Education

— Maximum Interaction

Special education provides a full continuum of program options, including instruction conducted in the classroom, in the home, in hospitals and institutions, and in other settings; and instruction in physical education, to meet the educational and service needs of individuals with exceptional needs in the least restrictive environment.

— Full Continuum of Program Options

Individuals with exceptional needs shall be grouped for instructional purposes according to their instructional needs.

— Grouped for Instructional Purposes

56032. "Individualized education program" means "individualized family service plan" as described in Section 1436 of Title 20 of the United States Code when individualized education program pertains to individuals with exceptional needs younger than three years of age.

— Individualized Education Program

56033. "Superintendent" means the Superintendent of Public Instruction.

— Superintendent

56034. "Nonpublic, nonsectarian school" means a private, nonsectarian school that enrolls individuals with exceptional needs pursuant to an individualized education program, employs at least one full-time teacher who holds an appropriate credential authorizing special education services, and is certified by the department. It does not include an organization or agency that operates as a public agency or offers public service, including, but not limited to, a state or local agency, an affiliate of a state or local agency, including a private, nonprofit corporation established or operated by a state or local agency, or a public university or college. A nonpublic, nonsectarian school also shall meet standards as prescribed by the superintendent and board.

— Nonpublic, Nonsectarian School

56035. "Nonpublic, nonsectarian agency" means a private, nonsectarian establishment or individual that provides related services necessary for an individual with exceptional needs to benefit educationally from the pupils' educational program pursuant to an individualized education program and that is certified by the department. It does not include an organization or agency that operates as a public agency or offers public service, including, but not limited to, a state or local agency, an affiliate of a state or local agency, including a private, nonprofit corporation established or operated by a state or local agency, a public university or college, or a

— Nonpublic, Nonsectarian Agency

public hospital. The nonpublic, nonsectarian agency shall also meet standards as prescribed by the superintendent and board.

Article 3. General Provisions

56040. Every individual with exceptional needs, who is eligible to receive educational instruction, related services, or both under this part shall receive such educational instruction, services, or both, at no cost to his or her parents or, as appropriate, to him or her.

- Free Appropriate Educational Instruction and Services

56041. Except for those pupils meeting residency requirements for school attendance specified in subdivision (a) of Section 48204, and notwithstanding any other provision of law, if it is determined by the individualized education program team that special education services are required beyond the pupil's 18th birthday, the district of residence responsible for providing special education and related services to pupils between the ages of 18 to 22 years, inclusive, shall be assigned, as follows:

- Residency Requirements

(a) For nonconserved pupils, the last district of residence in effect prior to the pupil's attaining the age of majority shall become and remain as the responsible local educational agency, as long as and until the parent or parents relocate to a new district of residence. At that time, the new district of residence shall become the responsible local educational agency.

- Nonconserved Pupils

(b) For conserved pupils, the district of residence of the conservator shall attach and remain the responsible local educational agency, as long as and until the conservator relocates or a new one is appointed. At that time, the new district of residence shall attach and become the responsible local educational agency.

- Conserved Pupils

56041.5. When an individual with exceptional needs reaches the age of 18, with the exception of an individual who has been determined to be incompetent under state law, the local educational agency shall provide any notice of procedural safeguards required by this part to both the individual and the parents of the individual. All other rights accorded to a parent under this part shall transfer to the individual with exceptional needs. The local educational agency shall notify the individual and the parent of the transfer of rights.

- Age 18 and Transfer of Rights

56042. Notwithstanding any other provision of law, an attorney or advocate for a parent of an individual with

- Conflict of Interest

exceptional needs shall not recommend placement in a nonpublic, nonsectarian school or agency with which the attorney or advocate is employed or contracted, or otherwise has a conflict of interest or from which the attorney or advocate receives a benefit.

56043. The primary timelines affecting special education programs are as follows:

(a) A proposed assessment plan shall be developed within 15 calendar days of referral for assessment, not counting calendar days between the pupil's regular school sessions or terms or calendar days of school vacation in excess of five schooldays from the date of receipt of the referral, unless the parent agrees, in writing, to an extension, pursuant to subdivision (a) of Section 56321.

(b) A parent shall have at least 15 calendar days from the receipt of the proposed assessment plan to arrive at a decision, pursuant to subdivision (c) of Section 56321.

(c) A parent shall be notified of the individualized education program meeting early enough to ensure an opportunity to attend, pursuant to subdivision (b) of Section 56341.5.

(d) An individualized education program required as a result of an assessment of a pupil shall be developed within a total time not to exceed 50 calendar days, not counting days between the pupil's regular school sessions, terms, or days of school vacation in excess of five schooldays, from the date of receipt of the parent's written consent for assessment, unless the parent agrees, in writing, to an extension, pursuant to Section 56344.

(e) Beginning at age 14, and updated annually, a statement of the transition service needs of the pupil shall be included in the pupil's individualized education program, pursuant to subdivision (a) of Section 56345.1.

(f) Beginning at age 16, or younger, and annually thereafter, a statement of needed transition services shall be included in the pupil's individualized education program, pursuant to subdivision (b) of Section 56345.1.

(g) A pupil's individualized education program shall be implemented as soon as possible following the individualized education program meeting, pursuant to Section 3040 of Title 5 of the California Code of Regulations.

(h) An individualized education program team shall meet at least annually to review a pupil's progress, the individualized education program, including whether the annual goals for the pupil are being achieved, the

- Primary Timelines

- Proposed Assessment Plan

- Parent Arrives at a Decision

- IEP Meeting Notification

- IEP Development

- Statement of Transition Service Needs

- Statement of Transition Services

- IEP Implementation

- Annual IEP Meeting

appropriateness of the placement, and to make any necessary revisions, pursuant to subdivision (d) of Section 56343, subdivision (a) of Section 56380, and Section 3068 of Title 5 of the California Code of Regulations.

(i) A reassessment of a pupil shall be conducted at least once every three years or more frequently, if conditions warrant a reassessment and a new individualized education program to be developed, pursuant to Section 56381.

- Reassessment

(j) A meeting of an individualized education program team requested by a parent to review an individualized education program pursuant to subdivision (c) of Section 56343 shall be held within 30 calendar days, not counting days in July and August, from the date of receipt of the parent's written request, pursuant to Section 56343.5.

- Request for Review of IEP

(k) The administrator of a local program under this part shall ensure that the pupil is immediately provided an interim placement for a period not to exceed 30 calendar days whenever a pupil transfers into a school district from a school district not operating programs under the same local plan in which he or she was last enrolled in a special education program pursuant to Section 56325.

- Interim Placement Upon Transfer

(l) The parent shall have the right and opportunity to examine all school records of the child and to receive copies within five calendar days after a request is made by the parent, either orally or in writing, pursuant to Section 56504 and Chapter 6.5 (commencing with Section 49060) of Part 27.

- Pupil Records

(m) Upon receipt of a request from an educational agency where an individual with exceptional needs has enrolled, a former educational agency shall send the pupil's special education records, or a copy thereof, within five working days, pursuant to subdivision (a) of Section 3024 of Title 5 of the California Code of Regulations.

- Pupil Records; Former Educational Agency

(n) The department shall:

(1) Have a time limit of 60 calendar days after a complaint is filed with the state education agency to investigate the complaint.

- Complaints

(2) Give the complainant the opportunity to submit additional information about the allegations in the complaint.

(3) Review all relevant information and make an independent determination as to whether there is a violation of a requirement of this part or Part B of the Individuals with Disabilities Education Act (20 U.S.C. Sec. 1400 et seq.).

(4) Issue a written decision, pursuant to Section 300.661 of Title 34 of the Code of Federal Regulations.

(o) A prehearing mediation conference shall be scheduled within 15 calendar days of receipt by the superintendent of the request for mediation, and shall be completed within 30 calendar days after the request for mediation, unless both parties to the prehearing mediation conference agree to extend the time for completing the mediation, pursuant to Section 56500.3.

- Prehearing Mediation Conference

(p) Any request for a due process hearing arising from subdivision (a) of Section 56501 shall be filed within three years from the date the party initiating the request knew or had reason to know of facts underlying the bases for the request, pursuant to subdivision (j) of Section 56505.

- Due Process Hearing Statute of Limitation

(q) The superintendent shall ensure that, within 45 calendar days after receipt of a written due process hearing request, the hearing is immediately commenced and completed, including any mediation requested at any point during the hearing process, and a final administrative decision is rendered, pursuant to subdivision (a) of Section 56502.

- Due Process Hearing Completion

(r) If either party to a due process hearing intends to be represented by an attorney in the due process hearing, notice of that intent shall be given to the other party at least 10 calendar days prior to the hearing, pursuant to subdivision (a) of Section 56507.

- Notice of Attorney Representation

(s) Any party to a due process hearing shall have the right to be informed by the other parties to the hearing, at least 10 calendar days prior to the hearing, as to what those parties believe are the issues to be decided at the hearing and their proposed resolution of those issues, pursuant to paragraph (6) of subdivision (e) of Section 56505.

- Due Process Hearing Issues

(t) Any party to a due process hearing shall have the right to receive from other parties to the hearing, at least five business days prior to the hearing, a copy of all documents, including all assessments completed by that date, and a list of all witnesses and their general area of testimony that the parties intend to present at the hearing, pursuant to paragraph (7) of subdivision (e) of Section 56505.

- Copy of Documents; List of Witnesses; General Area of Testimony

(u) An appeal of a due process hearing decision shall be made within 90 calendar days of receipt of the hearing decision, pursuant to subdivision (i) of Section 56505.

- Appeal of Due Process Hearing Decision

(v) When an individualized education program calls for a residential placement as a result of a review by an expanded individualized education program team, the individualized education program shall include a provision for a review, at least every six months, by the full individualized education program team of all of the following pursuant to paragraph

- Residential Placement Review

(2) of subdivision (c) of Section 7572.5 of the Government Code:

(1) The case progress.

(2) The continuing need for out-of-home placement.

(3) The extent of compliance with the individualized education program.

(4) Progress toward alleviating the need for out-of-home care.

56045. (a) The superintendent shall send a notice to the governing board of each local education agency within 30 days of when the superintendent determines any of the following:

- Noncompliance Notification of Members of Governing Board (3)

(1) The district, special education local plan area, or county office is substantially out of compliance with one or more significant provisions of this part, the implementing regulations, provisions of the Individuals with Disabilities Education Act (20 U.S.C. Sec. 1400 et seq.), or the implementing regulations.

(2) The district, special education local plan area, or county office fails to comply substantially with corrective action orders issued by the department resulting from focused monitoring findings or complaint investigations.

(3) The district, special education local plan area, or county office fails to implement the decision of a due process hearing officer for noncompliance with provisions of this part, the implementing regulations, provisions of the Individuals with Disabilities Education Act (20 U.S.C. Sec. 1400 et seq.), or the implementing regulations, which noncompliance results in the denial of, or impedes the delivery of, a free and appropriate public education for an individual with exceptional needs.

(b) The notice shall provide a description of the special education and related services that are required by law and with which the district, special education local plan area, or county office is not in compliance.

- Notice Content

(c) Upon receipt of the notification sent pursuant to subdivision (a), the governing board shall at a regularly scheduled public hearing address the issue of noncompliance.

- Address Issue of Noncompliance at Governing Board Hearing

56048. The superintendent shall review the information and calculations submitted by special education local plan areas in support of all apportionment computations described in this part. The review shall be conducted on the data submitted during the initial year of apportionment and for the first succeeding fiscal year only. Adjustments to any year's

- Superintendent Review of Information and Calculations

apportionment shall be received by the superintendent from the special education local plan area prior to the end of the first fiscal year following the fiscal year to be adjusted. The superintendent shall consider and adjust only the information and computational factors originally established during an eligible fiscal year, if the superintendent's review determines that they are correct.

Article 3.5. Surrogate Parents

56050. (a) For the purposes of this article, "surrogate parent" shall be defined as it is defined in Section 300.515 of Title 34 of the Code of Federal Regulations.

- Surrogate Parent Definition

(b) A surrogate parent may represent an individual with exceptional needs in matters relating to identification, assessment, instructional planning and development, educational placement, reviewing and revising the individualized education program, and in other matters relating to the provision of a free appropriate education to the individual. Notwithstanding any other provision of law, this representation shall include the provision of written consent to the individualized education program including nonemergency medical services, mental health treatment services, and occupational or physical therapy services pursuant to Chapter 26.5 (commencing with Section 7570) of Division 7 of Title 1 of the Government Code. The surrogate parent may sign any consent relating to individualized education program purposes.

- Representation

(c) A surrogate parent shall be held harmless by the State of California when acting in his or her official capacity except for acts or omissions which are found to have been wanton, reckless, or malicious.

- Liability Protection

(d) A surrogate parent shall also be governed by Section 7579.5 of the Government Code.

- Also Governed by Section 7579.5 of Government Code

Article 3.7. Foster Parents

56055. (a) (1) Except as provided in subdivision (b), a foster parent shall, to the extent permitted by federal law, including, but not limited to, Section 300.20 of Title 34 of the Code of Federal Regulations, have the rights related to his or her foster child's education that a parent has under Title 20 (commencing with Section 1400) of the United States Code and pursuant to Part 300 (commencing with Section 300.1) of Title 34 of the Code of Federal Regulations. The foster

- Rights of Foster Parents When Natural Parents' Authority to Make Educational Decisions Has Been Extinguished (4)

parent may represent the foster child for the duration of the foster parent-foster child relationship in matters relating to identification, assessment, instructional planning and development, educational placement, reviewing and revising an individualized education program, if necessary, and in all other matters relating to the provision of a free appropriate public education of the child. Notwithstanding any other provision of law, this representation shall include the provision of written consent to the individualized education program, including nonemergency medical services, mental health treatment services, and occupational or physical therapy services pursuant to this chapter. The foster parent may sign any consent relating to individualized education program purposes.

(2) A foster parent exercising rights relative to a foster child under this section may consult with the parent or guardian of the child to ensure continuity of health, mental health, or other services.

— Foster Parent May Consult with Natural Parent or Guardian

(b) A foster parent who had been excluded by court order from making educational decisions on behalf of a pupil shall not have the rights relative to the pupil set forth in subdivision (a).

— Foster Parent Excluded by Court Order from Making Educational Decisions

Article 4. Substitute Teachers

56060. A noncredentialed person shall not substitute for any special education certificated position.

— Noncredential Substitutes Prohibited

56061. A person holding a valid credential authorizing substitute teaching may serve as substitute for the appropriately credentialed special education teacher as follows:

— Substitute Teacher Qualifications

(a) Except as provided in subdivisions (b) and (c), the employer shall not employ an inappropriately credentialed substitute teacher for a period of more than 20 cumulative school days for each special education teacher absent during each school year.

— Number of Days

(b) Upon application by the district or county office, the superintendent may approve an extension of 20 school days in addition to those authorized by subdivision (a).

— Extension of 20 School Days

(c) Only in extraordinary circumstances may additional number of days be granted beyond the 40 school days provided for by subdivisions (a) and (b). Such additional days shall be granted in writing by the superintendent. The superintendent shall report to the board on all requests

— Beyond 40 School Days

granted for an additional number of days pursuant to this subdivision.

56062. The employer shall use the following priorities in placing substitute teachers in special education classrooms:

(a) A substitute teacher with the appropriate special education credential or credentials.

(b) A substitute teacher with any other special education credential or credentials.

(c) A substitute teacher with a regular teaching credential.

56063. The employer shall be responsible for seeking, and maintaining lists of, appropriately credentialed substitute teachers. The employer shall contact institutions of higher education with approved special education programs for possible recommendations of appropriately credentialed special education personnel.

- Substitute Teacher Priorities

- Employer Maintains Lists

NOTE

(1) Education Code Section 56026 was amended by Assembly Bill 804, Chapter 734, Statutes of 2001.

(2) Education Code Section 56029 was amended by Assembly Bill 804, Chapter 734, Statutes of 2001.

(3) Education Code Section 56045 was amended by Senate Bill 662, Chapter 159, Statutes of 2001.

(4) Article 3.7 (commencing with Section 56055) was added to Chapter 1 of Part 30 of the Education Code by Assembly Bill 804, Chapter 734, Statutes of 2001.

(Note: Education Code Section 56044 was repealed by Assembly Bill 804, Chapter 734, Statutes of 2001.)

CHAPTER 2. ADMINISTRATION

Article 1. State Board of Education

56100. The State Board of Education shall do all of the following:

(a) Adopt rules and regulations necessary for the efficient administration of this part.

- Adopt Rules and Regulations

(b) Adopt criteria and procedures for the review and approval by the board of local plans. Local plans may be approved for up to four years.

- Approve Local Plans

(c) Adopt size and scope standards for determining the efficacy of local plans submitted by special education local plan areas, pursuant to subdivision (a) of Section 56195.1.

- Adopt Size and Scope Standards

(d) Provide review, upon petition, to any district, special education local plan area, or county office that appeals a decision made by the department that affects its providing services under this part except a decision made pursuant to Chapter 5 (commencing with Section 56500).

- Provide Review of Department Decisions

(e) Review and approve a program evaluation plan for special education programs provided by this part in accordance with Chapter 6 (commencing with Section 56600). This plan may be approved for up to three years.

- Review and Approve Program Evaluation Plan

(f) Recommend to the Commission on Teacher Credentialing the adoption of standards for the certification of professional personnel for special education programs conducted pursuant to this part.

- Recommend Adoption of Professional Standards

(g) Adopt regulations to provide specific procedural criteria and guidelines for the identification of pupils as individuals with exceptional needs.

- Adopt Specific Procedural Criteria for Identification

(h) Adopt guidelines of reasonable pupil progress and achievement for individuals with exceptional needs. The guidelines shall be developed to aid teachers and parents in assessing an individual pupil's education program and the appropriateness of the special education services.

- Adopt Reasonable Pupil Progress and Achievement Guidelines

(i) In accordance with the requirements of federal law, adopt regulations for all educational programs for individuals with exceptional needs, including programs administered by other state or local agencies.

- Adopt Title 5 Regulations

(j) Adopt uniform rules and regulations relating to parental due process rights in the area of special education.

- Adopt Rules and Regulations on Due Process Rights

(k) Adopt rules and regulations regarding the ownership and transfer of materials and equipment, including facilities, related to transfer of programs, reorganization, or restructuring of special education local plan areas.

- Adopt Rules and Regulations on Ownership and Transfer of Materials and Equipment

56101. (a) Any district, special education local plan area, county office, or public education agency, as defined in Section 56500, may request the board to grant a waiver of any provision of this code or regulations adopted pursuant to that provision if the waiver is necessary or beneficial to the content and implementation of the pupil's individualized education program and does not abrogate any right provided individuals with exceptional needs and their parents or guardians under the Individuals with Disabilities Education Act (20 U.S.C. Sec. 1400 et seq.), or to the compliance of a district, special education local plan area, or county office with the Individuals with Disabilities Education Act (20 U.S.C. Sec. 1400 et seq.), Section 504 of, the Rehabilitation Act of 1973 (29 U.S.C. Sec. 794), and federal regulations relating thereto.

- State Board Waivers

(b) The board may grant, in whole or in part, any request pursuant to subdivision (a) when the facts indicate that failure to do so would hinder implementation of the pupil's individualized education program or compliance by a district, special education local plan area, or county office with federal mandates for a free, appropriate education for children or youth with disabilities.

- Whole or Partial Waiver

Article 2. Superintendent of Public Instruction

56120. The superintendent shall administer the provisions of this part.

- Administer Special Education Law

56121. The superintendent shall grant approval of the organization of the local plans within each county.

- Grant Approval of Organization of Local Plans Within Each County

56122. The superintendent shall establish guidelines for the development of local plans, including a standard format for local plans, and provide assistance in the development of local plans. The purposes of such guidelines and assistance shall be to help districts and county offices benefit from the experience of other local agencies that implement programs under this part, including, but not limited to, reducing paperwork, increasing parental involvement, and providing effective staff development activities. To the extent possible, all forms, reports, and evaluations shall be designed to satisfy simultaneously state and federal requirements.

- Establish Local Plan Development Guidelines

56123. The superintendent shall review and recommend to the board for approval, local plans developed and submitted in accordance with this part.

- Review and Recommend to State Board on Local Plans

56124. The superintendent shall promote innovation and improvement in the field of special education at the public and nonpublic, nonsectarian school, district, county, and state levels.

- Promote Innovation and Improvement

56125. The superintendent shall monitor the implementation of local plans by periodically conducting onsite program and fiscal reviews.

- Monitor Local Plan Implementation

56126. The superintendent shall encourage the maximum practicable involvement of parents of children enrolled in special education programs.

- Encourage Maximum Parent Involvement

56127. The superintendent shall make recommendations in the areas of staff development, curriculum, testing and multicultural assessment, and the development of materials for special education programs.

- Make Recommendations

56128. The superintendent shall prepare for board approval, as necessary, any state plan required by federal law in order that this state may qualify for any federal funds available for education of individuals with exceptional needs.

- Prepare State Plan

56129. The superintendent shall maintain the state special schools in accordance with Part 32 (commencing with Section 59000) so that the services of those schools are coordinated with the services of the district, special education local plan area, or the county office.

- Maintain State Special Schools and Coordinate Services

56130. The superintendent shall develop in accordance with Sections 33401 and 56602, an annual program evaluation plan and report of special education programs authorized under this part for submission to the board.

- Develop Annual Program Evaluation Plan

56131. The superintendent shall apportion funds in accordance with Chapter 7.2 (commencing with Section 56836) and approved local plans.

- Apportion Funds

56132. The superintendent shall assist districts, county offices, and special education local plan areas in the improvement and evaluation of their programs.

- Assist in Improvement and Evaluation of Local Programs

56133. The superintendent shall provide for the mediation conference prescribed by Sections 56502 and 56503 and the state hearing prescribed by Section 56505.

- Provide Mediation Conference and State Hearing

56134. The superintendent shall perform the duties prescribed by Chapter 4.5 (commencing with Section 56452).

- Promote Career and Vocational Education

56135. (a) The superintendent shall be responsible for assuring provision of, and supervising, education and related services to individuals with exceptional needs as specifically required pursuant to the Individuals with Disabilities Education Act (20 U.S.C. Sec. 1400 et seq.).

- Assure Provision of and Supervise Education and Relate Services Required by Federal Law

(b) Nothing in this part shall be construed to authorize the superintendent to prescribe health care services.

- Excludes Prescription of Health Care Services

56136. The superintendent shall develop guidelines for each low incidence disability area and provide technical assistance to parents, teachers, and administrators regarding the implementation of the guidelines. The guidelines shall clarify the identification, assessment, planning of, and the provision of, specialized services to pupils with low incidence disabilities. The superintendent shall consider the guidelines when monitoring programs serving pupils with low incidence disabilities pursuant to subdivision (a) of Section 56836.04. The adopted guidelines shall be promulgated for the purpose of establishing recommended guidelines and shall not operate to impose minimum state requirements.

- Develop Low Incidence Disability Guidelines

56137. The superintendent shall develop, update every other year, and disseminate directories of public and private agencies providing services to pupils with low-incidence disabilities. The directories shall be made available as reference directories to parents, teachers, and administrators. The directories shall include, but need not be limited to, the following information:

- Develop and Disseminate Directories

(a) A description of each agency providing services and program options within each disability area.

(b) The specialized services and program options provided, including infant and preschool programs.

(c) The number of credentialed and certificated staff providing specialized services.

(d) The names, addresses, and telephone numbers of agency administrators or other individuals responsible for the programs.

Article 3. County Offices

56140. County offices shall do all of the following:

- Duties

(a) Initiate and submit to the superintendent a countywide plan for special education which demonstrates the coordination of all local plans submitted pursuant to Section 56200 and which ensures that all individuals with exceptional needs residing within the county, including those enrolled in alternative education programs, including, but not limited to, alternative schools, charter schools, opportunity schools and classes, community day schools operated by school districts, community schools operated by county offices of education, and juvenile court schools, will have access to appropriate special education programs and related services. However, a county office shall not be required to submit a countywide plan when all the districts within the county elect to submit a

- Countywide Plan

single local plan.

(b) Within 45 days, approve or disapprove any proposed local plan submitted by a district or group of districts within the county or counties. Approval shall be based on the capacity of the district or districts to ensure that special education programs and services are provided to all individuals with exceptional needs.

- Approve or Disapprove Proposed Local Plan

(1) If approved, the county office shall submit the plan with comments and recommendations to the superintendent.

- Submit Approved Local Plan to State Superintendent

(2) If disapproved, the county office shall return the plan with comments and recommendations to the district. This district may immediately appeal to the superintendent to overrule the county office's disapproval. The superintendent shall make a decision on an appeal within 30 days of receipt of the appeal.

- Return Disapproved Plan to District

(3) A local plan may not be implemented without approval of the plan by the county office or a decision by the superintendent to overrule the disapproval of the county office.

- Local Plan Implementation Approval

(c) Participate in the state onsite review of the district's implementation of an approved local plan.

- State Onsite Review

(d) Join with districts in the county which elect to submit a plan or plans pursuant to subdivision (c) of Section 56195.1. Any plan may include more than one county, and districts located in more than one county. Nothing in this subdivision shall be construed to limit the authority of a county office to enter into other agreements with these districts and other districts to provide services relating to the education of individuals with exceptional needs.

- Join with Districts to Submit Plan

(e) For each special education local plan area located within the jurisdiction of the county office of education that has submitted a revised local plan pursuant to Section 56836.03, the county office shall comply with Section 48850, as it relates to individuals with exceptional needs, by making available to agencies that place children in licensed children's institutions a copy of the annual service plan adopted pursuant to subdivision (g) of Section 56205.

- Make Information Available to Other Agencies Placing Individuals in LCIs

Article 3.5. Charter Schools

56145. Individuals with exceptional needs attending charter schools pursuant to Part 26.8 (commencing with Section 47600) shall be served in the same manner as individuals with exceptional needs are served in other public schools.

- Service to Individuals in Charter Schools

56146. It is the intent of the Legislature that local plans for special education local plan areas, adopted pursuant to Chapter 2.5 (commencing with Section 56195), shall provide for federal funds available under Part B of the Individuals with Disabilities Education Act (20 U.S.C. Sec. 1400 et seq.) to individuals with exceptional needs enrolled in charter schools.

- Federal Funds for Individuals Enrolled in Charter Schools

Article 4. Juvenile Court Schools

56150. Special education programs authorized by this part shall be provided, pursuant to Section 48645.2, for individuals with exceptional needs who have been adjudicated by the juvenile court for placement in a juvenile hall or juvenile home, day center, ranch, or camp, or for individuals with exceptional needs placed in a county community school pursuant to Section 1981.

- Programs for Adjudicated Individuals

Article 5. Licensed Children's Institutions and Foster Family Homes

56155. The provisions of this article shall only apply to individuals with exceptional needs placed in a licensed children's institution or foster family home by a court, regional center for the developmentally disabled, or public agency, other than an educational agency.

- Application of Article

56155.5. (a) As used in this article, "licensed children's institution" means a residential facility that is licensed by the state, or other public agency having delegated authority by contract with the state to license, to provide nonmedical care to children, including, but not limited to, individuals with exceptional needs. "Licensed children's institution" includes a group home as defined by subdivision (g) of Section 80001 of Title 22 of the California Code of Regulations. As used in this article and Article 3 (commencing with Section 56836.16) of Chapter 7.2, a "licensed children's institution" does not include any of the following:

- LCI Definition

(1) A juvenile court school, juvenile hall, juvenile home, day center, juvenile ranch, or juvenile camp administered pursuant to Article 2.5 (commencing with Section 48645) of Chapter 4 of Part 27.

(2) A county community school program provided pursuant to Section 1981.

(3) Any special education programs provided pursuant to Section 56150.

(4) Any other public agency.

(b) As used in this article, "foster family home" means a family residence that is licensed by the state, or other public agency having delegated authority by contract with the state to license, to provide 24-hour nonmedical care and supervision for not more than six foster children, including, but not limited to, individuals with exceptional needs. "Foster family home" includes a small family home as defined in paragraph (6) of subdivision (a) of Section 1502 of the Health and Safety Code.

56156. (a) Each court, regional center for the developmentally disabled, or public agency that engages in referring children to, or placing children in, licensed children's institutions shall report to the special education administrator of the district, special education local plan area, or county office in which the licensed children's institution is located any referral or admission of a child who is potentially eligible for special education.

- Referring/Placing Agencies

(b) At the time of placement in a licensed children's institution or foster family home, each court, regional center for the developmentally disabled, or public agency shall identify all of the following:

- Identify Responsible Individual

(1) Whether the courts have specifically limited the rights of the parent or guardian to make educational decisions for a child who is a ward or dependent of the court.

(2) The location of the parents, in the event that the parents retain the right to make educational decisions.

(3) Whether the location of the parents is unknown.

(c) Each person licensed by the state to operate a licensed children's institution, or his or her designee, shall notify the special education administrator of the district, special education local plan area, or county office in which the licensed children's institution is located of any child potentially eligible for special education who resides at the facility.

- LCI Operators

(d) The superintendent shall provide each county office of education with a current list of licensed children's institutions in that county at least biannually. The county office shall maintain the most current list of licensed children's institutions located within the county and shall notify each district and special education local plan area within the county of the names of licensed children's institutions located in the geographical area of the county covered by the district and special education local plan area. The county office shall notify the director of each licensed children's institution of

- Superintendent Shall Provide Current List

the appropriate person to contact regarding individuals with exceptional needs.

56156.4. (a) Each special education local plan area shall be responsible for providing appropriate education to individuals with exceptional needs residing in licensed children's institutions and foster family homes located in the geographical area covered by the local plan.

- Educational Responsibility

(b) In multidistrict and district and county office local plan areas, local written agreements shall be developed, pursuant to subdivision (f) of Section 56195.7, to identify the public education entities that will provide the special education services.

- Local Written Agreements

(c) If there is no local agreement, special education services for individuals with exceptional needs residing in licensed children's institutions shall be the responsibility of the county office in the county in which the institution is located, if the county office is part of the special education local plan area, and special education services for individuals with exceptional needs residing in foster family homes shall be the responsibility of the district in which the foster family home is located. If a county office is not a part of the special education local plan area, special education services for individuals with exceptional needs residing in licensed children's institutions, pursuant to this subdivision, shall be the responsibility of the responsible local agency or other administrative entity of the special education local plan area. This program responsibility shall continue until the time local written agreements are developed pursuant to subdivision (f) of Section 56195.7.

- No Local Agreement

(d) This section shall apply to special education local plan areas that are submitting a revised local plan for approval pursuant to Section 56836.03 or that have an approved revised local plan pursuant to Section 56836.03.

- Application of Section

56156.5. (a) Each district, special education local plan area, or county office shall be responsible for providing appropriate education to individuals with exceptional needs residing in licensed children's institutions and foster family homes located in the geographical area covered by the local plan.

- Educational Responsibility

(b) In multidistrict and district and county office local plan areas, local written agreements shall be developed, pursuant to subdivision (f) of Section 56195.7, to identify the public education entities that will provide the special education services.

- Local Written Agreements

(c) If there is no local agreement, special education services for individuals with exceptional needs residing in licensed children's institutions shall be the responsibility of the county office in the county in which the institution is located, if the county office is part of the special education local plan area, and special education services for individuals with exceptional needs residing in foster family homes shall be the responsibility of the district in which the foster family home is located. If a county office is not a part of the special education local plan area, special education services for individuals with exceptional needs residing in licensed children's institutions, pursuant to this subdivision, shall be the responsibility of the responsible local agency or other administrative entity of the special education local plan area. This program responsibility shall continue until the time local written agreements are developed pursuant to subdivision (f) of Section 56195.7.

(d) This section shall not apply to any special education local plan area that has a revised local plan approved pursuant to Section 56836.03. This section shall apply to special education local plan areas that have not had a revised local plan approved pursuant to that section.

(e) This section shall become inoperative on July 1, 2003, and, as of January 1, 2004, is repealed, unless a later enacted statute, that becomes operative on or before January 1, 2004, deletes or extends the date on which it becomes inoperative and is repealed.

56156.6. If the district in which the licensed children's institution or foster family home is located is also the district of residence of the parent of the individual with exceptional needs, and if the parent retains legal responsibility for the child's education, Sections 56836.16 and 56836.17 shall not apply.

56157. (a) In providing appropriate programs to individuals with exceptional needs residing in licensed children's institutions or foster family homes, the district, special education local plan area, or county office shall first consider services in programs operated by public education agencies for individuals with exceptional needs. If those programs are not appropriate, special education and related services shall be provided by contract with a nonpublic, nonsectarian school.

(b) If special education and related services are provided by contract with a nonpublic, nonsectarian school, or with a licensed children's institution under this article, the terms of

Marginal notes:

- No Local Agreement
- County Office Responsibility
- District Responsibility
- Responsibility of the Responsible Local Agency
- Application of Section
- Repeal Clause; Inoperative 7-1-03
- Residence of Parent
- First Consider Public Options
- Contracts

the contract shall be developed in accordance with the provisions of Section 56366.

56159. If a district, special education local plan area, or county office does not make the placement decision of an individual with exceptional needs in a licensed children's institution or in a foster family home, the court, regional center for the developmentally disabled, or public agency, excluding an education agency, placing the individual in the institution, shall be responsible for the residential costs and the cost of noneducation services of the individual.

- Residential Costs/Noneducation Services

56162. Individuals with exceptional needs placed in a licensed children's institution or foster family home by a court, regional center for the developmentally disabled, or public agency, other than an educational agency, prior to the effective date of this article, shall be considered residents of the geographical area of the local plan in which the licensed children's institution or foster family home is located, for special education and related services pursuant to the provisions of this article.

- Residency; Location of LCI or FFH

56163. A licensed children's institution which provides nonsectarian educational programs for individuals with exceptional needs shall be certified by the department as prescribed by subdivision (c) of Section 56366.

- Certification

56164. This article shall not apply to programs operating in state hospitals and juvenile court schools.

- Exclusion

56165. This article shall not apply to individuals with exceptional needs placed in a licensed children's institution pursuant to Section 56365.

- Exclusion

56166. The board shall adopt rules and regulations to implement the provisions of this article.

- Rules and Regulations

56166.5. This article shall become operative July 1, 1982.

- Operative Date

Article 5.5. Public Hospitals, Proprietary Hospitals and Other Residential Medical Facilities

56167. (a) Individuals with exceptional needs who are placed in a public hospital, state licensed children's hospital, psychiatric hospital, proprietary hospital, or a health facility for medical purposes are the educational responsibility of the district, special education local plan area, or county office in which the hospital or facility is located, as determined in local written agreements pursuant to subdivision (e) of Section 56195.7.

- Educational Responsibility

- Local Written Agreements

(b) For the purposes of this part, "health facility" shall have the definition set forth in Sections 1250, 1250.2, and

- Health Facility Definition

1250.3 of the Health and Safety Code.

56167.5. Nothing in this article shall be construed to mean that the placement of any individual with exceptional needs in a hospital or health facility constitutes a necessary residential placement, as described under Section 300.302 of Title 34 of the Code of Federal Regulations, for which the district, special education local plan area, or county office would be responsible as an educational program option under this part.

- Placement Not Educational Program Option

56168. (a) A public hospital, state licensed children's hospital, psychiatric hospital, proprietary hospital, or a health facility for medical purposes located either within and outside of this state that did not provide special education to individuals with exceptional needs who satisfy the criteria set forth in paragraph (2) of subdivision (c) of Section 56026 pursuant to a waiver granted under Section 56366.2 for the 1994-95 schoolyear, is ineligible for certification as a nonpublic, nonsectarian school pursuant to Section 56034 and Sections 56365 to 56366.5, inclusive, to provide special education to individuals with exceptional needs. Districts, special education local plan areas, or county offices shall have until September 1, 1994, to find an appropriate alternative placement for any children currently served in one of these programs.

- Hospitals Ineligible for Certification as Nonpublic School

(b) The district, special education local plan area, or county office in which the hospital or health facility is located has the educational responsibility for individuals with exceptional needs who reside in these facilities.

- Educational Responsibility

(c) A hospital or health facility is eligible for certification as a nonpublic, nonsectarian agency pursuant to Section 56035 and Sections 56365 to 56366.5, inclusive, to provide designated instruction and services to individuals with exceptional needs whether the child attends a public or nonpublic school or is enrolled in both a public and nonpublic school program as specified in Section 56361.5.

- Hospitals Eligible for Certification as a Nonpublic Agency

56169.5. This article shall not apply to programs operating in state hospitals.

- Exclusion

56169.7. If any provision of this article, or the application thereof to any person or circumstances, is held invalid by an appellate court of competent jurisdiction, the remainder of the article, and the application of the provision to other persons or circumstances, shall not be affected thereby.

- Severance Clause

Article 5.6. Children Enrolled in Private Schools

56170. As used in this part, "private school children with disabilities" means children with disabilities enrolled by a parent in private elementary and secondary schools or facilities, other than individuals with exceptional needs placed by a district, special education local plan area, or county office in a nonpublic, nonsectarian school pursuant to Section 56365.

56171. Districts, special education local plan areas, and county offices shall locate, identify, and assess all private school children with disabilities, including religiously affiliated schoolage children, who have disabilities and are in need of special education and related services residing in the jurisdiction of the district, special education local plan area, or county office in accordance with Section 56301.

56172. The district, special education local plan area, or county office shall make provision for the participation of private school children with disabilities in special education programs under this part by providing them with special education and related services in accordance with the provisions of this article.

56173. To meet the requirements of Section 56172, each district, special education local plan area, or county office shall spend on providing special education and related services to private school children with disabilities enrolled by a parent in private elementary and secondary schools, an amount of federal state grant funds allocated to the state under Part B of the Individuals with Disabilities Education Act (20 U.S.C. Sec. 1400 et seq.) that is equal to a proportionate amount of federal funds made available under the Part B grant program for local assistance.

56174. The district, special education local plan area, or county office shall not be required to pay for the cost of education, including special education and related services, of a child with a disability at a private school or facility if the district, special education local plan area, or county office made a free appropriate public education available to the child and the parent of the child elected to place the child in the private school or facility.

56175. If a parent of a child with a disability, who previously received special education and related services under the authority of the district, special education local plan area, or county office, enrolls the child in a private

- Definition of Private School Children with Disabilities

- Obligation to Locate, Identify, and Assess All Private School Children with Disabilities

- Make Provision for Participation of Private School Children with Disabilities

- Federal Grant Funds; Proportionate Amount

- Not Required to Pay Cost of Education at Private School if LEA Made a Free Appropriate Public Education Available

- Exception When Free Appropriate Public Education Not Made Available

elementary or secondary school without the consent of or referral by the district, special education local plan area, or county office, a court or a due process hearing officer may require the district, special education local plan area, or county office to reimburse the parent for the cost of that enrollment if the court or due process hearing officer finds that the district, special education local plan area, or county office had not made a free appropriate public education available to the child in a timely manner prior to that enrollment in the private elementary or secondary school.

56176. The cost of the reimbursement described in Section 56175 may be reduced or denied in the event of any of the following:

- Reasons for Reducing or Denying Reimbursement

(a) At the most recent individualized education program meeting that a parent attended prior to removal of the child from the public school, the parent did not inform the individualized education program team that they were rejecting the placement proposed by the district, special education local plan area, or county office to provide a free appropriate public education to the child, including stating his or her concerns and the intent to enroll the child in a private school at public expense.

(b) The parent did not give written notice to the district, special education local plan area, or county office of the information described in subdivision (a) at least 10 business days, including any holidays that occur on a business day, prior to the removal of the child from the public school.

(c) Prior to the parent's removal of the child from the public school, the district, special education local plan area, or county office informed the parent of its intent to assess the child, including a statement of the purpose of the assessment that was appropriate and reasonable, but the parent did not make the child available for the assessment.

(d) Upon a judicial finding of unreasonableness with respect to actions taken by a parent.

56177. Notwithstanding the notice requirement in subdivision (a) of Section 56176, the cost of reimbursement may not be reduced or denied for failure to provide the notice in the event of any of the following:

- Exceptions

(a) The parent is illiterate and cannot write in English.

(b) Compliance with subdivision (a) of Section 56176 would likely result in physical or serious emotional harm to the child.

(c) The school prevented the parent from providing the notice.

(d) The parent had not received notice of the due process hearing rights under Chapter 5 (commencing with Section 56500).

Article 7. Community Advisory Committee

56190. Each plan submitted under Section 56195.1 shall establish a community advisory committee. The committee shall serve only in an advisory capacity.

- Committee Serves Only in an Advisory Capacity

56191. The members of the community advisory committee shall be appointed by, and responsible to, the governing board of each participating district or county office, or any combination thereof participating in the local plan. Appointment shall be in accordance with a locally determined selection procedure that is described in the local plan. Where appropriate, this procedure shall provide for selection of representatives of groups specified in Section 56192 by their peers. Such procedure shall provide that terms of appointment are for at least two years and are annually staggered to ensure that no more than one half of the membership serves the first year of the term in any one year.

- CAC Appointments

56192. The community advisory committee shall be composed of parents of individuals with exceptional needs enrolled in public or private schools, parents of other pupils enrolled in school, pupils and adults with disabilities, regular education teachers, special education teachers and other school personnel, representatives of other public and private agencies, and persons concerned with the needs of individuals with exceptional needs.

- CAC Composition

56193. At least the majority of such committee shall be composed of parents of pupils enrolled in schools participating in the local plan, and at least a majority of such parents shall be parents of individuals with exceptional needs.

- Parent Majority

56194. The community advisory committee shall have the authority and fulfill the responsibilities that are defined for it in the local plan. The responsibilities shall include, but need not be limited to, all the following:

- CAC Responsibilities

(a) Advising the policy and administrative entity of the district, special education local plan area, or county office, regarding the development, amendment, and review of the local plan. The entity shall review and consider comments from the community advisory committee.

(b) Recommending annual priorities to be addressed by the plan.

(c) Assisting in parent education and in recruiting parents and other volunteers who may contribute to the implementation of the plan.

(d) Encouraging community involvement in the development and review of the local plan.

(e) Supporting activities on behalf of individuals with exceptional needs.

(f) Assisting in parent awareness of the importance of regular school attendance.

CHAPTER 2.5. GOVERNANCE

Article 1. Local Plans

56195. Each special education local plan area, as defined in subdivision (d) of Section 56195.1, shall administer local plans submitted pursuant to Chapter 3 (commencing with Section 56200) and shall administer the allocation of funds pursuant to Chapter 7.2 (commencing with Section 56836).

- SELPA Shall Administer Local Plans and Allocation of Funds

56195.1. The governing board of a district shall elect to do one of the following:

- Local Plan Options

(a) If of sufficient size and scope, under standards adopted by the board, submit to the superintendent a local plan for the education of all individuals with exceptional needs residing in the district in accordance with Chapter 3 (commencing with Section 56200).

- Sufficient Size and Scope

(b) In conjunction with one or more districts, submit to the superintendent a local plan for the education of individuals with exceptional needs residing in those districts in accordance with Chapter 3 (commencing with Section 56200). The plan shall include, through joint powers agreements or other contractual agreements, all the following:

- Multidistricts

(1) Provision of a governance structure and any necessary administrative support to implement the plan.

- Governance Structure

(2) Establishment of a system for determining the responsibility of participating agencies for the education of each individual with exceptional needs residing in the special education local plan area.

- Education Responsibilities

(3) Designation of a responsible local agency or alternative administrative entity to perform functions such as the receipt and distribution of funds, provision of administrative support, and coordination of the implementation of the plan. Any participating agency may perform any of these services required by the plan.

- RLA/Administrative Entity

(c) Join with the county office, to submit to the superintendent a local plan in accordance with Chapter 3 (commencing with Section 56200) to assure access to special education and services for all individuals with exceptional needs residing in the geographic area served by the plan. The county office shall coordinate the implementation of the plan, unless otherwise specified in the plan. The plan shall include, through contractual agreements, all of the following:

- Join with County Office

(1) Establishment of a system for determining the responsibility of participating agencies for the education of

- Education Responsibilities

each individual with exceptional needs residing in the geographical area served by the plan.

(2) Designation of the county office, of a responsible local agency, or of any other administrative entity to perform functions such as the receipt and distribution of funds, provision of administrative support, and coordination of the implementation of the plan. Any participating agency may perform any of these services required by the plan.

    — RLA/Administrative Entity

(d) The service area covered by the local plan developed under subdivision (a), (b), or (c) shall be known as the special education local plan area.

    — SELPA Definition

(e) Nothing in this section shall be construed to limit the authority of a county office and a school district or group of school districts to enter into contractual agreements for services relating to the education of individuals with exceptional needs; provided that, except for instructional personnel service units serving infants, until a special education local plan area adopts a revised local plan approved pursuant to Section 56836.03, the county office of education or school district that reports a unit for funding shall be the agency that employs the personnel who staff the unit, unless the combined unit rate and support service ratio of the nonemploying agency is equal to or lower than that of the employing agency and both agencies agree that the nonemploying agency will report the unit for funding.

    — Contractual Agreements

(f) A charter school that is deemed a local educational agency for the purposes of special education pursuant to Article 4 (commencing with Section 47640) of Chapter 6 of Part 26.8 shall participate in an approved local plan pursuant to subdivision (a),(b), or (c). A charter school may submit written policies and procedures to the State Department of Education for approval by the State Board of Education, which establish compliance with the Individuals with Disabilities Education Act (20 U.S.C. Sec. 1400 et seq.), and implementing regulations, either individually, pursuant to subdivision (a) or with other charter schools pursuant to subdivision (b). The State Board of Educaiton shall review these policies and procedures, based on the criteria established pursuant to Section 56100. Upon approval by the State Board of Education, these written policies and procedures shall become the local plan

    — Charter School Participation in Local Plan; Policies and Procedures

56195.3. In developing a local plan under Section 56195.1, each district shall do the following:

    — Duties of District

(a) Involve special and general teachers selected by their peers and parents selected by their peers in an active role.

    — Involve Teacher/Parents

(b) Cooperate with the county office and other school districts in the geographic areas in planning its option under Section 56195.1 and each fiscal year, notify the department, impacted special education local plan areas, and participating county offices of its intent to elect an alternative option from those specified in Section 56195.1, at least one year prior to the proposed effective date of the implementation of the alternative plan.

- Cooperate in Planning Option; Intent to Elect Alternative Option

(c) Cooperate with the county office to assure that the plan is compatible with other local plans in the county and any county plan of a contiguous county.

- Compatible Plan

(d) Submit to the county office for review any plan developed under subdivision (a) or (b) of Section 56195.1.

- Submit Plan for Review

56195.5. (a) Each county office and district governing board shall have authority over the programs it directly maintains, consistent with the local plan submitted pursuant to Section 56195.1. In counties with more than one special education local plan area for which the county office provides services, relevant provisions of contracts between the county office and its employees governing wages, hours, and working conditions shall supersede like provisions contained in a plan submitted under Section 56195.1.

- County Office/District Governing Board Authority Over Programs

(b) Any county office or district governing board may provide for the education of individual pupils in special education programs maintained by other districts or counties, and may include within the special education programs pupils who reside in other districts or counties. Section 46600 shall apply to interdistrict attendance agreements for programs conducted pursuant to this part.

- Pupils Who Reside in Other Districts or Counties

Article 2. Local Requirements

56195.7. In addition to the provisions required to be included in the local plan pursuant to Chapter 3 (commencing with Section 56200), each special education local plan area that submits a local plan pursuant to subdivision (b) of Section 56195.1 and each county office that submits a local plan pursuant to subdivision (c) of Section 56195.1 shall develop written agreements to be entered into by entities participating in the plan. The agreements need not be submitted to the superintendent. These agreements shall include, but not be limited to, the following:

- Written Agreements

(a) A coordinated identification, referral, and placement system pursuant to Chapter 4 (commencing with Section 56300).

- Coordinate Identification, Referral and Placement System

(b) Procedural safeguards pursuant to Chapter 5 (commencing with Section 56500).

- Procedural Safeguards

(c) Regionalized services to local programs, including, but not limited to, all of the following:

- Regionalized Services

(1) Program specialist service pursuant to Section 56368.

(2) Personnel development, including training for staff, parents, and members of the community advisory committee pursuant to Article 3 (commencing with Section 56240).

(3) Evaluation pursuant to Chapter 6 (commencing with Section 56600).

(4) Data collection and development of management information systems.

(5) Curriculum development.

(6) Provision for ongoing review of programs conducted, and procedures utilized, under the local plan, and a mechanism for correcting any identified problem.

(d) A description of the process for coordinating services with other local public agencies that are funded to serve individuals with exceptional needs.

- Coordination with Local Public Agencies

(e) A description of the process for coordinating and providing services to individuals with exceptional needs placed in public hospitals, proprietary hospitals, and other residential medical facilities pursuant to Article 5.5 (commencing with Section 56167) of Chapter 2.

- Public/Proprietary Hospitals

(f) A description of the process for coordinating and providing services to individuals with exceptional needs placed in licensed children's institutions and foster family homes pursuant to Article 5 (commencing with Section 56155) of Chapter 2.

- Licensed Children's Institutions and Foster Family Homes

(g) A description of the process for coordinating and providing services to individuals with exceptional needs placed in juvenile court schools or county community schools pursuant to Section 56150.

- Juvenile Court Schools and County Community Schools

(h) A budget for special education and related services that shall be maintained by the special education local plan area and be open to the public covering the entities providing programs or services within the special education local plan area. The budget language shall be presented in a form that is understandable by the general public. For each local educational agency or other entity providing a program or service, the budget, at minimum, shall display the following:

- Budget for Special Education and Related Services

(1) Expenditures by object code and classification for the previous fiscal year and the budget by the same object code classification for the current fiscal year.

- Expenditures by Object Code and Classification

(2) The number and type of certificated instructional and support personnel, including the type of class setting to which they are assigned, if appropriate.

- Number and Type of Personnel/Class Setting

(3) The number of instructional aides and other qualified classified personnel.

- Number of Aides and Other Qualified Classified Personnel

(4) The number of enrolled individuals with exceptional needs receiving each type of service provided.

- Number of Enrolled Pupils Receiving Type of Service

(i) For multidistrict special education local plan areas, a description of the policymaking process that shall include a description of the local method used to distribute state and federal funds among the local education agencies in the special educational local plan area. The local method to distribute funds shall be approved according to the policymaking process established consistent with subdivision (f) of Section 56001 and pursuant to paragraph (3) of subdivision (b) of Section 56205 or subdivision (c) of Section 56200, whichever is appropriate.

- Description of Policymaking Process and Local Method Used to Distribute State/Federal Funds

56195.8. (a) Each entity providing special education under this part shall adopt policies for the programs and services it operates, consistent with agreements adopted pursuant to subdivision (b) or (c) of Section 56195.1 or Section 56195.7. The policies need not be submitted to the superintendent.

- Adopt Policies

(b) The policies shall include, but not be limited to, all of the following:

(1) Nonpublic, nonsectarian services, including those provided pursuant to Sections 56365 and 56366.

- Nonpublic, Nonsectarian Services

(2) Review, at a general education or special education teacher's request, of the assignment of an individual with exceptional needs to his or her class and a mandatory meeting of the individualized education program team if the review indicates a change in the pupil's placement, instruction, related services, or any combination thereof. The procedures shall indicate which personnel are responsible for the reviews and a timetable for completion of the review.

- Review of Class Assignment at Teacher's Request

(3) Procedural safeguards pursuant to Chapter 5 (commencing with Section 56500).

- Procedural Safeguards

(4) Resource specialists pursuant to Section 56362.

(5) Transportation, where appropriate, which describes how special education transportation is coordinated with regular home-to-school transportation. The policy shall set forth criteria for meeting the transportation needs of special education pupils. The policy shall include procedures to ensure compatibility between mobile seating devices, when used, and the securement systems required by Federal Motor

- Resource Specialists
- Transportation

Vehicle Safety Standard No. 222 (49 C.F.R. 571.222) and to ensure that schoolbus drivers are trained in the proper installation of mobile seating devices in the securement systems.

(6) Information on the number of individual with exceptional needs who are being provided special education and related services.

- Information on Number of Pupils Being Provided Special Education/Related Services

(7) Caseloads pursuant to Chapter 4.45 (commencing with Section 56440) of Part 30. The policies, with respect to caseloads, shall not be developed until guidelines or proposed regulations are issued pursuant to Section 56441.7. The guidelines or proposed regulations shall be considered when developing the caseload policy. A statement of justification shall be attached if the local caseload policy exceeds state guidelines or proposed regulations.

- Caseloads

(c) The policies may include, but are not limited to, provisions for involvement of district and county governing board members in any due process hearing procedure activities conducted pursuant to, and consistent with, state and federal law.

- Governing Board Members/Due Process Hearing Procedures

56195.9. The plan for special education shall be developed and updated cooperatively by a committee of representatives of special and regular teachers and administrators selected by the groups they represent and with participation by parent members of the community advisory committee, or parents selected by the community advisory committee, to ensure adequate and effective participation and communication.

- Local Plan Developed and Updated by Committee

56195.10. Unless the process described in subdivision (i) of Section 56195.7 specifies an alternative method of distribution of state and local funds among the participating local educational agencies, the funds shall be distributed by the special education local plan area as allocated instructional personnel service units and operated as computed in Chapter 7 (commencing with Section 56700) as that chapter existed on December 31, 1998, or Chapter 7.1 (commencing with Section 56835).

- Distribution of State and Local Funds

CHAPTER 3. ELEMENTS OF THE LOCAL PLAN

Article 1. State Requirements

56200. Each local plan submitted to the superintendent under this part shall contain all the following:

(a) Compliance assurances, including general compliance with the Individuals with Disabilities Education Act (20 U.S.C. Sec. 1400 et seq.), Section 504 of the Rehabilitation Act of 1973 (29 U.S.C. Sec. 794), and this part.

- Compliance Assurances (1)

(b) A description of services to be provided by each district and county office. This description shall demonstrate that all individuals with exceptional needs shall have access to services and instruction appropriate to meet their needs as specified in their individualized education programs.

- Description of Services

(c) (1) A description of the governance and administration of the plan, including the role of county office and district governing board members.

- Description of Governance Administration

(2) Multidistrict plans, submitted pursuant to subdivision (b) or (c) of Section 56195.1, shall specify the responsibilities of each participating county office and district governing board in the policymaking process, the responsibilities of the superintendents of each participating district and county in the implementation of the plan, and the responsibilities of district and county administrators of special education in coordinating the administration of the local plan.

- Policymaking Responsibilities

(d) Copies of joint powers agreements or contractual agreements, as appropriate, for districts and counties that elect to enter into those agreements pursuant to subdivision (b) or (c) of Section 56195.1.

- Joint Powers/Contractual Agreements

(e) An annual budget plan to allocate instructional personnel service units, support services, and transportation services directly to entities operating those services and to allocate regionalized services funds to the county office, responsible local agency, or other alternative administrative structure. The annual budget plan shall be adopted at a public hearing held by the district, special education local plan area, or county office, as appropriate. Notice of this hearing shall be posted in each school in the local plan area at least 15 days prior to the hearing. The annual budget plan may be revised during the fiscal year, and these revisions may be submitted to the superintendent as amendments to the allocations set forth in the plan. However, the revisions shall, prior to submission to the superintendent, be approved according to the policymaking process, established pursuant

- Annual Budget Plan

to paragraph (2) of subdivision (c).

(f) Verification that the plan has been reviewed by the community advisory committee and that the committee had at least 30 days to conduct this review prior to submission of the plan to the superintendent.

- CAC Review of Plan

(g) A description of the identification, referral, assessment, instructional planning, implementation, and review in compliance with Chapter 4 (commencing with Section 56300).

- Description of Program Requirements

(h) A description of the process being utilized to meet the requirements of Section 56303.

- Description of Process Utilized Considering Regular Education

(i) A description of the process being utilized to meet the requirements of the California Early Intervention Services Act, Title 14 (commencing with Section 95000) of the Government Code.

- Description of Process Utilized to Meet Early Intervention Services Act

(j) A description of the process being utilized to oversee and evaluate placements in nonpublic, nonsectarian schools and the method for ensuring that all requirements of each pupil's individualized education program are being met. This description shall include a method for evaluating whether the pupil is making appropriate educational progress.

- Description of Process Utilized to Oversee and Evaluate Placements in Nonpublic Schools

56201. As a part of the local plan submitted pursuant to Section 56200, each special education local plan area shall describe how specialized equipment and services will be distributed within the local plan area in a manner that minimizes the necessity to serve pupils in isolated sites and maximizes the opportunities to serve pupils in the least restrictive environments.

- Specialized Equipment and Services

56202. This article shall only apply to districts, county offices, and special education local plan areas that have not had a revised local plan approved pursuant to Section 56836.03.

- Application of Article

This article shall become inoperative on July 1, 2003, and, as of January 1, 2004, is repealed, unless a later enacted statute, that becomes operative on or before January 1, 2004, deletes or extends the dates on which it becomes inoperative and is repealed.

- Repeal Clause; Inoperative 7/1/03

56203. A request by a charter school to participate as a local educational agency in a special education local plan area may not be treated differently from a similar request made by a school district. In reviewing and approving a request by a charter school to participate as a local educational agency in a special education local plan area, the following requirements shall apply:

- Charter School Participation in a Special Education Local Plan

(a) The special education local plan area shall comply with Section 56140.

(b) The charter school shall participate in state and federal funding for special education and the allocation plan developed pursuant to subdivision (i) of Section 56195.7 or Section 56836.05 in the same manner as other local educational agencies of the special education local plan area.

(c) The charter school shall participate in governance of the special educaiton local plan area in the same manner as other local educational agencies of the special education local plan area.

Article 1.1. State Requirements

56205. (a) Each special education local plan area submitting a local plan to the superintendent under this part shall demonstrate, in conformity with subsection (a) of Section 1412 of, and paragraph (1) of subsection (a) of Section 1413 of, Title 20 of the United States Code, that it has in effect policies, procedures, and programs that are consistent with state laws, regulations, and policies governing the following:

(1) Free appropriate public education.

(2) Full educational opportunity.

(3) Child find and referral.

(4) Individualized education programs, including development, implementation, review, and revision.

(5) Least restrictive environment.

(6) Procedural safeguards.

(7) Annual and triennial assessments.

(8) Confidentiality.

(9) Transition from Subchapter III (commencing with Section 1431) of Title 20 of the United States Code to the preschool program.

(10) Children in private schools.

(11) Compliance assurances, including general compliance with the Individuals with Disabilities Education Act (20 U.S.C. Sec. 1400 et seq.), Section 504 of the Rehabilitation Act of 1973 (29 U.S.C. Sec. 794), the Americans with Disabilities Act of 1990 (42 U.S.C. Sec. 12101 et seq.), federal regulations relating thereto, and this part.

(12) (A) A description of the governance and administration of the plan, including identification of the governing body of a multidistrict plan or the individual responsible for administration in a single district plan, and of

Margin notes:

- SELPA Shall Comply with Section 56140

- Charter School Participation in State and Federal Funding

- Charter School Participation in Governance

- SELPA Submitting Local Plan Shall Demonstrate It Has in Effect Policies, Procedures, and Programs

the elected officials to whom the governing body or individual is responsible.

(B) A description of the regionalized operations and services listed in Section 56836.23 and the direct instructional support provided by program specialists in accordance with Section 56368 to be provided through the plan.

(C) Verification that a community advisory committee has been established pursuant to Section 56190.

(D) Multidistrict plans, submitted pursuant to subdivision (b) or (c) of Section 56195.1, shall do the following:

(i) Specify the responsibilities of each participating county office and district governing board in the policymaking process, the responsibilities of the superintendents of each participating district and county in the implementation of the plan, and the responsibilities of district and county administrators of special education in coordinating the administration of the local plan.

(ii) Identify the respective roles of the administrative unit and the administrator of the special education local plan area and the individual local education agencies within the special education local plan area in relation to the following:

(I) The hiring, supervision, evaluation, and discipline of the administrator of the special education local plan area and staff employed by the administrative unit in support of the local plan.

(II) The allocation from the state of federal and state funds to the special education local plan area administrative unit or to local education agencies within the special education local plan area.

(III) The operation of special education programs.

(IV) Monitoring the appropriate use of federal, state, and local funds allocated for special education programs.

(V) The preparation of program and fiscal reports required of the special education local plan area by the state.

(E) The description of the governance and administration of the plan, and the policymaking process, shall be consistent with subdivision (f) of Section 56001, subdivision (a) of Section 56195.3, and Section 56195.9, and shall reflect a schedule of regular consultations regarding policy and budget development with representatives of special education and regular education teachers and administrators selected by the groups they represent and parent members of the community advisory committee established pursuant to Article 7 (commencing with Section 56190) of Chapter 2.

(13) Copies of joint powers agreements or contractual

agreements, as appropriate, for districts and counties that elect to enter into those agreements pursuant to subdivision (b) or (c) of Section 56195.1.

(14) Comprehensive system of personnel development.

(15) Personnel standards, including standards for training and supervision of paraprofessionals.

(16) Performance goals and indicators.

(17) Participation in state and districtwide assessments, and reports relating to assessments.

(18) Supplementation of state, local, and other federal funds, including nonsupplantation of funds.

(19) Maintenance of financial effort.

(20) Opportunities for public participation prior to adoption of policies and procedures.

(21) Suspension and expulsion rates.

(b)   Each local plan submitted to the superintendent under this part shall also contain all the following:

- Additional Contents of Local Plan

(1) An annual budget plan that shall be adopted at a public hearing held by the special education local plan area. Notice of this hearing shall be posted in each school in the local plan area at least 15 days prior to the hearing. The annual budget plan may be revised during any fiscal year according to the policymaking process established pursuant to subparagraph (D) and (E) of paragraph (12) of subdivision (a) and consistent with subdivision (f) of Section 56001 and Section 56195.9. The annual budget plan shall identify expected expenditures for all items required by this part which shall include, but not be limited to, the following:

(A) Funds received in accordance with Chapter 7.2 (commencing with Section 56836).

(B) Administrative costs of the plan.

(C) Special education services to pupils with severe disabilities and low incidence disabilities.

(D) Special education services to pupils with nonsevere disabilities.

(E) Supplemental aids and services to meet the individual needs of pupils placed in regular education classrooms and environments.

(F) Regionalized operations and services, and direct instructional support by program specialists in accordance with Article 6 (commencing with Section 56836.23) of Chapter 7.2.

(G) The use of property taxes allocated to the special education local plan area pursuant to Section 2572.

(2) An annual service plan shall be adopted at a public

hearing held by the special education local plan area. Notice of this hearing shall be posted in each school district in the special education local plan area at least 15 days prior to the hearing. The annual service plan may be revised during any fiscal year according to the policymaking process established pursuant to subparagraphs (D) and (E) of paragraph (12) of subdivision (a) and consistent with subdivision (f) of Section 56001 and with Section 56195.9. The annual service plan shall include a description of services to be provided by each district and county office, including the nature of the services and the physical location at which the services will be provided, including alternative schools, charter schools, opportunity schools and classes, community day schools operated by school districts, community schools operated by county offices of education, and juvenile court schools, regardless of whether the district or county office of education is participating in the local plan. This description shall demonstrate that all individuals with exceptional needs shall have access to services and instruction appropriate to meet their needs as specified in their individualized education programs.

(3) A description of programs for early childhood special education from birth through five years of age.

(4) A description of the method by which members of the public, including parents or guardians of individuals with exceptional needs who are receiving services under the plan, may address questions or concerns to the governing body or individual identified in subparagraph (A) of paragraph (12) of subdivision (a).

(5) A description of a dispute resolution process, including mediation and final and binding arbitration to resolve disputes over the distribution of funding, the responsibility for service provision, and the other governance activities specified within the plan.

(6) Verification that the plan has been reviewed by the community advisory committee and that the committee had at least 30 days to conduct this review prior to submission of the plan to the superintendent.

(7) A description of the process being utilized to meet the requirements of Section 56303.

(c) A description of the process being utilized to oversee and evaluate placements in nonpublic, nonsectarian schools and the method of ensuring that all requirements of each pupil's individualized education program are being met. The description shall include a method for evaluating whether the

- Description of Process Utilized to Oversee and Evaluate Placements in Nonpublic Schools

pupil is making appropriate educational progress.

(d)   The local plan, budget plan, and annual service plan shall be written in language that is understandable to the general public.

- All Plans Shall Be Written for General Public Understanding

56206.   As a part of the local plan submitted pursuant to Section 56205, each special education local plan area shall describe how specialized equipment and services will be distributed within the local plan area in a manner that minimizes the necessity to serve pupils in isolated sites and maximizes the opportunities to serve pupils in the least restrictive environments.

- Specialized Equipment and Services

56207.   (a) No educational programs and services already in operation in school districts or a county office of education pursuant to Part 30 (commencing with Section 56000) shall be transferred to another school district or a county office of education or from a county office of education to a school district unless the special education local plan area has developed a plan for the transfer which addresses, at a minimum, all of the following:

- Transfer of Programs (2)

(1)   Pupil needs.

(2)   The availability of the full continuum of services to affected pupils.

(3)   The functional continuation of the current individualized education programs of all affected pupils.

(4)   The provision of services in the least restrictive environment from which affected pupils can benefit.

(5)   The maintenance of all appropriate support services.

(6)   The assurance that there will be compliance with all federal and state laws and regulations and special education local plan area policies.

(7)   The means through which parents and staff were represented in the planning process.

(b)   The date on which the transfer will take effect may be no earlier than the first day of the second fiscal year beginning after the date on which the sending or receiving agency has informed the other agency and the governing body or individual identified in subparagraph (A) of paragraph (12) of subdivision (a) of Section 56205, unless the governing body or individual identified in subparagraph (A) of paragraph (12) of subdivision (a) of Section 56205 unanimously approves the transfer taking effect on the first day of the first fiscal year following that date.

- Date Transfer Takes Effect

(c)   If either the sending or receiving agency disagree with the proposed transfer, the matter shall be resolved by the alternative resolution process established pursuant to

- Resolving Disagreements

paragraph (5) of subdivision (b) of Section 56205.

(d) Notwithstanding Section 56208, this section shall apply to all special education local plan areas commencing on July 1, 1998, whether or not a special education local plan area has submitted a revised local plan for approval or has an approved revised local plan pursuant to Section 56836.03.

56207.5. A request by a charter school to participate as a local educational agency in a special education local plan area may not be treated differently from a similar request made by a school district. In reviewing and approving a request by a charter school to participate as a local educational agency in a special education local plan area, the following requirements shall apply:

(a) The special education local plan area shall comply with Section 56140.

(b) The charter school shall participate in state and federal funding for special education and the allocation plan developed pursuant to subdivision (i) of Section 56195.7 or Section 56836.05 in the same manner as other local educational agencies of the special education local plan area.

(c) The charter school shall participate in governance of the special educaiton local plan area in the same manner as other local educational agencies of the special education local plan area.

56208. This article shall apply to special education local plan areas that are submitting a revised local plan for approval pursuant to Section 56836.03 or that have an approved revised local plan pursuant to Section 56836.03.

Article 1.5. Special Education Local Plan Areas with Small or Sparse Populations

56211. A special education local plan area submitting a local plan, pursuant to subdivision (c) of Section 56195.1, which includes all of the school districts located in the county or counties submitting the plan, except those participating in a countywide special education local plan area located in an adjacent county, and which meets the criteria for special education local plan areas with small populations set forth in Section 56212, is eligible to request that designation in its local plan application.

This section shall become operative on July 1, 1998.

56212. An eligible special education local plan area, which submits a local plan under the provisions of Section 56211, may request designation as a necessary small special

- Application of Section

- Charter School Participation in a Special Education Local Plan

- SELPA Shall Comply with Section 5614

- Charter School Participation in State and Federal Funding

- Charter School Participation in Governance of the Special Education Local Plan Area

- Application of Article

- Request Designation

- Operative Date

- Designation Criteria

3-8

education local plan area if its total reported units of average daily attendance in kindergarten and grades 1 to 12, inclusive, is less than 15,000, and if it includes all of the school districts located in the county or counties participating in the local plan, except those districts participating in a countywide special education local plan area located in an adjacent county that also meets the criteria of this section.

This section shall become operative on July 1, 1998. — Operative Date

56213. If the computation made pursuant to Section 56836.15 results in a reduction in the funding of a necessary small special education local plan area pursuant to Section 56212, compared to that local plan area's funding in the prior year, the local plan area may claim, in addition to the current year funding, an amount equal to 40 percent of the reduction. — Reduction in Funding and Claiming Additional Funds (3)

Article 3. Staff Development

56240. Staff development programs shall be provided for regular and special education teachers, administrators, certificated and classified employees, volunteers, community advisory committee members and, as appropriate, members of the district and county governing boards. The programs shall be coordinated with other staff development programs in the district, special education local plan area, or county office, including school level staff development programs authorized by state and federal law. — Participants

56241. Staff development programs shall include, but not be limited to, all the following:

(a) Provision of opportunities for all school personnel, paraprofessionals, and volunteers to participate in ongoing development activities pursuant to a systematic identification of pupil and personnel needs. — Opportunities

(b) Be designed and implemented by classroom teachers and other participating school personnel, including the school principal. Teachers shall comprise the majority of any group designated to design local staff development programs for instructional personnel to be established pursuant to this part. Positive efforts shall be made to ensure the individuals with exceptional needs and parents of such individuals are involved in the design and implementation of staff development programs. — Design and Implementation

(c) Allowance for diversity in development activities, including, but not limited to, small groups, self-directed learning, and systematic observation during visits to other classrooms or schools. — Diversity in Development

(d) Scheduling of time which is set aside for such purpose throughout the school year, including, but not limited to, time when participating school personnel are released from their regular duties.

(e) Evaluation and modification on a continuing basis by participating school personnel with the aid of outside personnel, as necessary.

(f) Inclusion of the school principal and other administrative personnel as active participants in one or more staff development activities implemented pursuant to this chapter.

(g) Provision of a budget for reasonable and necessary expenses, relating to staff development programs.

56243. It is the intent of the Legislature, pursuant to this article, that each district, special education local plan area, and county office provide regular classroom teachers serving individuals with exceptional needs appropriate training each year relating to the needs of those individuals.

56244. The superintendent shall, to the extent possible using federal and state funds appropriated for this purpose, provide staff development to child care center staff and family day care providers to improve child care services to individuals with exceptional needs.

56245. The Legislature encourages the inclusion, in local in-service training programs for regular education teachers and special education teachers in school districts, special education local plan areas, and county offices of education, of a component on the recognition of, and teaching strategies for, specific learning disabilities, including dyslexia and related disorders.

- Scheduling

- Evaluation/Modification

- Administrators

- Expense Budget

- Regular Classroom Teachers

- Staff Development to Improve Child Care Services

- In-Service Training Regarding Specific Learning Disabilities Including Dyslexia

NOTE

(1) Education Code Section 56200 was amended by Assembly Bill 804, Chapter 734, Statutes of 2001.

(2) Education Code Section 56207 was amended by Assembly Bill 804, Chapter 734, Statutes of 2001.

(3) Education Code Section 56213 was added by Assembly Bill 303, Chapterr 551, Statutes of 2001.

CHAPTER 4. IDENTIFICATION AND REFERRAL, ASSESSMENT, INSTRUCTIONAL PLANNING, IMPLEMENTATION, AND REVIEW

Article 1. Identification and Referral

56300. Each district, special education local plan area, or county office shall actively and systematically seek out all individuals with exceptional needs, ages 0 through 21 years, including children not enrolled in public school programs, who reside in the district or are under the jurisdiction of a special education local plan area or a county office.

- Systematically Seek Out

56301. All individuals with disabilities residing in the state, including pupils with disabilities who are enrolled in elementary and secondary schools and private schools, including parochial schools, regardless of the severity of their disabilities, and who are in need of special education and related services, shall be identified, located, and assessed as required by paragraph (3) and clause (ii) of paragraph (10) of subsection (a) of Section 1412 of Title 20 of the United States Code. Each district, special education local plan area, or county office shall establish written policies and procedures for a continuous child-find system which addresses the relationships among identification, screening, referral, assessment, planning, implementation, review, and the triennial assessment. The policies and procedures shall include, but need not be limited to, written notification of all parents of their rights under this chapter, and the procedure for initiating a referral for assessment to identify individuals with exceptional needs. Parents shall be given a copy of their rights and procedural safeguards upon initial referral for assessment, upon notice of an individualized education program meeting or reassessment, upon filing a complaint, and upon filing for a prehearing mediation conference pursuant to Section 56500.3 or a due process hearing request pursuant to Section 56502.

- Continuous Child-Find System

56302. Each district, special education local plan area, or county office shall provide for the identification and assessment of an individual's exceptional needs, and the planning of an instructional program to meet the assessed needs. Identification procedures shall include systematic methods of utilizing referrals of pupils from teachers, parents, agencies, appropriate professional persons, and from

- Identification Procedures

other members of the public. Identification procedures shall be coordinated with school site procedures for referral of pupils with needs that cannot be met with modification of the regular instructional program.

56302.5. The term "assessment," as used in this chapter, shall have the same meaning as the term "evaluation" in the Individuals with Disabilities Education Act, as provided in Section 1414 of Title 20 of the United States Code.

- Definition of Assessment

56303. A pupil shall be referred for special educational instruction and services only after the resources of the regular education program have been considered and, where appropriate, utilized.

- Consider Regular Education Program Resources

Article 2. Assessment

56320. Before any action is taken with respect to the initial placement of an individual with exceptional needs in special education instruction, an individual assessment of the pupil's educational needs shall be conducted, by qualified persons, in accordance with requirements including, but not limited to, all the following:

- Individual Assessment Conducted by Qualified Persons

(a) Testing and assessment materials and procedures used for the purposes of assessment and placement of individuals with exceptional needs are selected and administered so as not to be racially, culturally, or sexually discriminatory.

- Testing and Assessment Materials

(b) Tests and other assessment materials meet all the following requirements:

- Meet Requirements

(1) Are provided and administered in the pupil's primary language or other mode of communication, unless the assessment plan indicates reasons why this provision and administration are not clearly feasible.

- Provided in Primary Language

(2) Have been validated for the specific purpose for which they are used.

- Validated for Specific Purposes

(3) Are administered by trained personnel in conformance with the instructions provided by the producer of the tests and other assessment materials, except that individually administered tests of intellectual or emotional functioning shall be administered by a credentialed school psychologist.

- Administered by Trained Personnel

(c) Tests and other assessment materials include those tailored to assess specific areas of educational need and not merely those which are designed to provide a single general intelligence quotient.

- Assess Specific Areas of Need

(d) Tests are selected and administered to best ensure that when a test administered to a pupil with impaired sensory, manual, or speaking skills produces test results that

- Accurate Test Results

accurately reflect the pupil's aptitude, achievement level, or any other factors the test purports to measure and not the pupil's impaired sensory, manual, or speaking skills unless those skills are the factors the test purports to measure.

(e) No single procedure is used as the sole criterion for determining an appropriate educational program for an individual with exceptional needs.

- No Single Procedure Used

(f) The pupil is assessed in all areas related to the suspected disability including, where appropriate, health and development, vision, including low vision, hearing, motor abilities, language function, general ability, academic performance, self-help, orientation and mobility skills, career and vocational abilities and interests, and social and emotional status. A developmental history is obtained, when appropriate. For pupils with residual vision, a low vision assessment shall be provided in accordance with guidelines established pursuant to Section 56136.

- Assessed in All Areas

(g) The assessment of a pupil, including the assessment of a pupil with a suspected low incidence disability, shall be conducted by persons knowledgeable of that disability. Special attention shall be given to the unique educational needs, including, but not limited to, skills and the need for specialized services, materials, and equipment consistent with guidelines established pursuant to Section 56136.

- Assessment Conducted by Persons Knowledgeable of Disability

56320.1. All identification, evaluation, and assessment procedures for individuals with exceptional needs who are younger than three years of age shall be provided pursuant to Chapter 4.4 (commencing with Section 56425) and the California Early Intervention Services Act, Title 14 (commencing with Section 95000) of the Government Code.

- Identification, Evaluation, and Assessment Procedures for Infants

56321. (a) Whenever an assessment for the development or revision of the individualized education program is to be conducted, the parent of the pupil shall be given, in writing, a proposed assessment plan within 15 days of the referral for assessment not counting days between the pupil's regular school sessions or terms or days of school vacation in excess of five schooldays from the date of receipt of the referral, unless the parent agrees, in writing, to an extension. However, in any event, the assessment plan shall be developed within 10 days after the commencement of the subsequent regular school year or the pupil's regular school term as determined by each district's school calendar for each pupil for whom a referral has been made 10 days or less prior to the end of the regular school year. In the case of pupil school vacations, the 15-day time shall recommence on the

- Proposed Assessment Plan

date that the pupil's regular schooldays reconvene. A copy of the notice of parent rights shall be attached to the assessment plan. A written explanation of all the procedural safeguards under the Individuals with Disabilities Education Act (20 U.S.C. Sec. 1400 and following), and the rights and procedures contained in Chapter 5 (commencing with Section 56500), shall be included in the notice of parent rights, including information on the procedures for requesting an informal meeting, prehearing mediation conference, mediation conference, or due process hearing; the timelines for completing each process; whether the process is optional; and the type of representative who may be invited to participate. - Notice of Parent Rights

(b) The proposed assessment plan given to parents shall meet all the following requirements: - Requirements

(1) Be in language easily understood by the general public.

(2) Be provided in the primary language of the parent or other mode of communication used by the parent, unless to do so is clearly not feasible.

(3) Explain the types of assessments to be conducted.

(4) State that no individualized education program will result from the assessment without the consent of the parent.

(c) No assessment shall be conducted unless the written consent of the parent is obtained prior to the assessment except pursuant to subdivision (e) of Section 56506. The parent shall have at least 15 days from the receipt of the proposed assessment plan to arrive at a decision. Assessment may begin immediately upon receipt of the consent. - Written Consent of Parent

56321.5. The copy of the notice of parent rights shall include the right to electronically record the proceedings of individualized education program meetings as specified in Section 56341. - Right to Electronically Record IEP Proceedings

56322. The assessment shall be conducted by persons competent to perform the assessment, as determined by the school district, county office, or special education local plan area. - Assessment Conducted by Competent Persons

56323. Admission of a pupil to special education instruction shall be made only in accordance with this article, Article 2.5 (commencing with Section 56333) and standards established by the board and upon a recommendation by the individualized education program team. - Admission to Special Education

56324. (a) Any psychological assessment of pupils shall be made in accordance with Section 56320 and shall be conducted by a credentialed school psychologist who is trained and prepared to assess cultural and ethnic factors - Psychological Assessment appropriate to the pupil being assessed.

(b) Any health assessment of pupils shall be made in accordance with Section 56320 and shall be conducted by a credentialed school nurse or physician who is trained and prepared to assess cultural and ethnic factors appropriate to the pupil being assessed.

- Health Assessment

56325. (a) Whenever a pupil transfers into a school district from a school district not operating programs under the same local plan in which he or she was last enrolled in a special education program, the administrator of a local program under this part shall ensure that the pupil is immediately provided an interim placement for a period not to exceed 30 days. The interim placement must be in conformity with an individualized education program, unless the parent or guardian agrees otherwise. The individualized education program implemented during the interim placement may be either the pupil's existing individualized education program, implemented to the extent possible within existing resources, which may be implemented without complying with subdivision (a) of Section 56321, or a new individualized education program, developed pursuant to Section 56321.

- Pupil Transfers

- Interim Placement Not to Exceed 30 Days and Must Be in Conformity with an IEP, as Specified

(b) Before the expiration of the 30-day period, the interim placement shall be reviewed by the individualized education program team and a final recommendation shall be made by the team in accordance with the requirements of this chapter. The team may utilize information, records, and reports from the school district or county program from which the pupil transferred.

- IEP Team Review and Final Recommendation

(c) Commencing on July 1, 1998, whenever a pupil described in subdivision (a) was placed and residing in a residential nonpublic, nonsectarian school, prior to transferring to a school district in another special education local plan area, and this placement is not eligible for funding pursuant to Section 56836.16, the special education local plan area that contains the district that made the residential nonpublic, nonsectarian school placement shall continue to be responsible for the funding of the placement, including related services, for the remainder of the school year. An extended year session is included in the school year in which the session ends.

- SELPA Responsible for Funding Residential Nonpublic, Nonsectarian School Placement

56326. A pupil may be referred, as appropriate, for further assessment and recommendations to the California Schools for the Deaf or Blind or the Diagnostic Centers.

- Assessment Referral to State Schools

56327. The personnel who assess the pupil shall prepare a

- Written Assessment Report

written report, or reports, as appropriate, of the results of each assessment. The report shall include, but not be limited to, all the following:

(a) Whether the pupil may need special education and related services.

(b) The basis for making the determination.

(c) The relevant behavior noted during the observation of the pupil in an appropriate setting.

(d) The relationship of that behavior to the pupil's academic and social functioning.

(e) The educationally relevant health and development, and medical findings, if any.

(f) For pupils with learning disabilities, whether there is such a discrepancy between achievement and ability that it cannot be corrected without special education and related services.

(g) A determination concerning the effects of environmental, cultural, or economic disadvantage, where appropriate.

(h) The need for specialized services, materials, and equipment for pupils with low incidence disabilities, consistent with guidelines established pursuant to Section 56136.

56328. Notwithstanding the provisions of this chapter, a district, special education local plan area, or county office may utilize a school site level and a regional level service, as provided for under Section 56336.2 as it read immediately prior to the operative date of this section, to provide the services required by this chapter.

- School Site/Regional Level Assessment Options

56329. As part of the assessment plan given to parents pursuant to Section 56321, the parent of the pupil shall be provided with a written notice that shall include all of the following information:

- Written Notice Provided to Parent

(a) Upon completion of the administration of tests and other assessment materials, an individualized education program team meeting, including the parent and his or her representatives, shall be scheduled, pursuant to Section 56341, to determine whether the pupil is an individual with exceptional needs as defined in Section 56026, and to discuss the assessment, the educational recommendations, and the reasons for these recommendations. A copy of the assessment report and the documentation of determination of eligibility shall be given to the parent.

- IEP Team Meeting

- Copy of Assessment Report Shall Be Given to Parent

(b) A parent has the right to obtain, at public expense, an independent educational assessment of the pupil from

- Independent Educational Assessment

qualified specialists, as defined by regulations of the board, if the parent disagrees with an assessment obtained by the public education agency.

However, the public education agency may initiate a due process hearing pursuant to Chapter 5 (commencing with Section 56500) to show that its assessment is appropriate. If the final decision resulting from the due process hearing is that the assessment is appropriate, the parent still has the right for an independent educational assessment, but not at public expense.

- Due Process Hearing on Assessment

If the parent obtains an independent educational assessment at private expense, the results of the assessment shall be considered by the public education agency with respect to the provision of free, appropriate public education to the child, and may be presented as evidence at a due process hearing pursuant to Chapter 5 (commencing with Section 56500) regarding the child.

- Results of Independent Assessment

Article 2.5. Eligibility Criteria for Special Education and Related Services on the Basis of Language and Speech Disorder or Specific Learning Disabilities

56333. A pupil shall be assessed as having a language or speech disorder which makes him or her eligible for special education and related services when he or she demonstrates difficulty understanding or using spoken language to such an extent that it adversely affects his or her educational performance and cannot be corrected without special education and related services. In order to be eligible for special education and related services, difficulty in understanding or using spoken language shall be assessed by a language, speech, and hearing specialist who determines that such difficulty results from any of the following disorders:

- Language/Speech Disorder Eligibility Criteria

(a) Articulation disorders, such that the pupil's production of speech significantly interferes with communication and attracts adverse attention.

(b) Abnormal voice, characterized by persistent, defective voice quality, pitch, or loudness. An appropriate medical examination shall be conducted, where appropriate.

(c) Fluency difficulties which result in an abnormal flow of verbal expression to such a degree that these difficulties adversely affect communication between the pupil and listener.

(d) Inappropriate or inadequate acquisition, comprehension, or expression of spoken language such that the pupil's language performance level is found to be significantly below the language performance level of his or her peers.

(e) Hearing loss which results in a language or speech disorder and significantly affects educational performance.

56337. A pupil shall be assessed as having a specific learning disability which makes him or her eligible for special education and related services when it is determined that all of the following exist:

- Specific Learning Disability Eligibility Criteria

(a) A severe discrepancy exists between the intellectual ability and achievements in one or more of the following academic areas:

(1) Oral expression.

(2) Listening comprehension.

(3) Written expression.

(4) Basic reading skills.

(5) Reading comprehension.

(6) Mathematics calculation.

(7) Mathematics reasoning.

(b) The discrepancy is due to a disorder in one or more of the basic psychological processes and is not the result of environmental, cultural, or economic disadvantages.

(c) The discrepancy cannot be corrected through other regular or categorical services offered within the regular instructional program.

56337.5. (a) A pupil who is assessed as being dyslexic and meets eligibility criteria specified in Section 56337 and subdivision (j) of Section 3030 of Title 5 of the California Code of Regulations for the federal Individuals with Disabilities Education Act (20 U.S.C. Sec. 1400 and following) category of specific learning disabilities is entitled to special education and related services.

- Assessed as Being Dyslexic

(b) If a pupil who exhibits the characteristics of dyslexia or another related reading dysfunction is not found to be eligible for special education and related services pursuant to subdivision (a), the pupil's instructional program shall be provided in the regular education program.

- Regular Education Responsibility

(c) It is the intent of the Legislature that the program guidelines developed pursuant to Section 2 of Chapter 1501 of the Statutes of 1990, for specific learning disabilities, including dyslexia and other related disorders, be available for use by teachers and parents in order for them to have knowledge of the strategies that can be utilized with pupils for the remediation of the various types of specific learning

- Program Guidelines

disabilities.

56338. As used in Section 56337, "specific learning disability" includes, but is not limited to, disability within the function of vision which results in visual perceptual or visual motor dysfunction.

- Visual Perception/Visual Motor Dysfunction

Article 2.6. Attention Deficit and Hyperactivity Disorders

56339. (a) A pupil whose educational performance is adversely affected by a suspected or diagnosed attention deficit disorder or attention deficit hyperactivity disorder and demonstrates a need for special education and related services by meeting eligibility criteria specified in subdivision (f) or (i) of Section 3030 of Title 5 of the California Code of Regulations or Section 56337 and subdivision (j) of Section 3030 of Title 5 of the California Code of Regulations for the federal Individuals with Disabilities Education Act (20 U.S.C. Sec. 1400 and following) categories of "other health impairments," "serious emotional disturbance," or "specific learning disabilities," is entitled to special education and related services.

- Eligibility Criteria

(b) If a pupil with an attention deficit disorder or attention deficit hyperactivity disorder is not found to be eligible for special education and related services pursuant to subdivision (a), the pupil's instructional program shall be provided in the regular education program.

- Regular Education Responsibility

(c) It is the intent of the Legislature that local educational agencies promote coordination between special education and regular education programs to ensure that all pupils, including those with attention deficit disorders or attention deficit hyperactivity disorders, receive appropriate instructional interventions.

- Coordination Between Special and Regular Education

(d) It is further the intent of the Legislature that regular education teachers and other personnel be trained to develop an awareness about attention deficit disorders and attention deficit hyperactivity disorders and the manifestations of those disorders, and the adaptations that can be implemented in regular education programs to address the instructional needs of pupils having these disorders.

- Awareness Training for Regular Education Teachers

Article 3. Instructional Planning and Individualized Education Program

56340. Each district, special education local plan area, or

- Initiate and Conduct Meetings

county office shall initiate and conduct meetings for the purposes of developing, reviewing, and revising the individualized education program of each individual with exceptional needs.

56340.1. All instructional planning procedures for individuals with exceptional needs who are younger than three years of age shall be provided pursuant to Chapter 4.4 (commencing with Section 56425) and the California Early Intervention Services Act, Title 14 (commencing with Section 95000) of the Government Code.

- Instructional Planning Procedures for Infants

56341. (a) Each meeting to develop, review, or revise the individualized education program of an individual with exceptional needs shall be conducted by an individualized education program team.

- IEP Team Meeting (1)

(b) The individualized education program team shall include all of the following:

- IEP Team Members

(1) One or both of the pupil's parents, a representative selected by a parent, or both, in accordance with the Individuals with Disabilities Education Act (20 U.S.C. Sec. 1400 et seq.).

- Pupil's Parents, Representative Selected by Parent, or Both

(2) At least one regular education teacher of the pupil, if the pupil is, or may be, participating in the regular education environment. If more than one regular education teacher is providing instructional services to the individual with exceptional needs, one regular education teacher may be designated by the district, special education local plan area, or county office to represent the others.

- Regular Education Teacher

The regular education teacher of an individual with exceptional needs shall, to the extent appropriate, participate in the development, review, and revision of the pupil's individualized education program, including assisting in the determination of appropriate positive behavioral interventions and strategies for the pupil and supplementary aids and services, and program modifications or supports for school personnel that will be provided for the pupil, consistent with paragraph (3) of subsection (a) of Section 300.347 of Title 34 of the Code of Federal Regulations.

(3) At least one special education teacher of the pupil, or if appropriate, at least one special education provider of the pupil.

- Special Education Teacher

(4) A representative of the district, special education local plan area, or county office who meets all of the following :

- Representative of Local Educational Agency

(A) Is qualified to provide, or supervise the provision of, specially designed instruction to meet the unique needs of individuals with exceptional needs.

(B) Is knowledgeable about the general curriculum.

(C) Is knowledgeable about the availability of resources of the local educational agency.

(5) An individual who conducted an assessment of the pupil or who is knowledgeable about the assessment procedures used to assess the pupil, and is familiar with the assessment results or recommendations. The individual shall be qualified to interpret the instructional implications of the assessment results. The individual may be a member of the team described in paragraphs (2) to (6), inclusive.

- Individual Who Conducted Assessment or Is Knowledgeable About Assessment Procedures

(6) At the discretion of the parent, guardian, or the district, special education local plan area, or county office, other individuals who have knowledge or special expertise regarding the pupil, including related services personnel, as appropriate. The determination of whether the individual has knowledge or special expertise regarding the pupil shall be made by the party who invites the individual to be a member of the individualized education program team.

- Individuals Who Have Knowledge or Special Expertise Regarding Pupil

(7) Whenever appropriate, the individual with exceptional needs.

- Individual with Exceptional Needs, Whenever Appropriate

(c) For a pupil suspected of having a specific learning disability, at least one member of the individualized education program team shall be qualified to conduct individual diagnostic examinations of children, such as a school psychologist, speech-language pathologist, or remedial reading teacher. At least one team member other than the pupil's regular teacher shall observe the pupil's academic performance in the regular classroom setting. In the case of a child who is less than schoolage or out of school, a team member shall observe the child in an environment appropriate for a child of that age.

- Observation of Educational Performance

(d) (1) In the case of transition services, the district, special education local plan area, or county office shall invite an individual with exceptional needs of any age to attend his or her individualized education program meeting if a purpose of the meeting will be the consideration of either, or both, of the following:

- Transition Services

(A) The individual's transition service needs under subdivision (a) of Section 56345.1.

(B) The needed transition services for the individual under subdivision (b) of Section 56345.1.

(2) If the individual with exceptional needs does not attend the individualized education program meeting, the district, special education local plan area, or county office shall take steps to ensure that the individual's preferences and interests

- Consider Individual's Preferences and Interests

are considered.

(3) When implementing the requirements of subdivision (b) of Section 56345.1, the district, special education local plan area, or county office also shall invite to the individualized education program team meetings a representative that is likely to be responsible for providing or paying for transition services. If an agency invited to send a representative to a meeting does not do so, the district, special education local plan area, or county office shall take other steps to obtain participation of the other agency in the planning of any transition services.

- Representative Likely to Be Responsible for Providing or Paying for Transition Services

(e) A district, special education local plan area, or county office may designate another local educational agency member of the individualized education program team to serve also as the representative required pursuant to paragraph (4) of subdivision (b) if the requirements of subparagraphs (A), (B), and (C) of paragraph (4) of subdivision (b) are met.

- Designating a Public Agency Representative

56341.1. (a) When developing each pupil's individualized education program, the individualized education program team shall consider the following:

- Development of IEP (2)

(1) The strengths of the pupil and the concerns of the parents or guardians for enhancing the education of the pupil.

- Strengths of the Pupil; Concerns of Parents

(2) The results of the initial assessment or most recent assessment of the pupil.

- Results of Assessment

(3) As appropriate, the results of the pupil's performance on any general state or districtwide assessment programs.

- Results of Pupil's Performance on Statewide or Districtwide Assessments

(b) The individualized education program team shall do the following:

- Consideration of Special Factors

(1) In the case of a pupil whose behavior impedes his or her learning or that of others, consider, when appropriate, strategies, including positive behavioral interventions, strategies, and supports to address that behavior.

- Behavior

(2) In the case of a pupil with limited English proficiency, consider the language needs of the pupil as those needs relate to the pupil's individualized education program.

- Language Needs

(3) In the case of a pupil who is blind or visually impaired, provide for instruction in braille and the use of braille unless the individualized education program team determines, after an assessment of the pupil's reading and writing skills, needs, and appropriate reading and writing media, including an assessment of the pupil's future needs, that instruction in braille is not appropriate for the pupil.

- Instruction in Braille

(4) Consider the communication needs of the pupil, and in the case of the pupil who is deaf or hard of hearing, consider

- Communication Needs

the pupil's language and communication needs, opportunities for direct communications with peers and professional personnel in the pupil's language and communication mode, academic level, and full range of needs, including opportunities for direct instruction in the pupil's language and communication mode.

(5) Consider whether the pupil requires assistive technology devices and services.

- Assistive Technology Devices and Services
- Statement in IEP

(c) If, in considering the special factors described in subdivisions (a) and (b), the individualized education program team determines that a pupil needs a particular device or service, including an intervention, accommodation, or other program modification, in order for the pupil to receive a free appropriate public education, the individualized education program team shall include a statement to that effect in the pupil's individualized education program.

(d) The individualized education program team shall revise the individualized education program, as appropriate, to address among other matters the following:

- Review and Revision of IEP

(1) Any lack of expected progress toward the annual goals and in the general curriculum, where appropriate.

- Lack of Expected Progress

(2) The results of any reassessment conducted pursuant to Section 56381.

- Results of Any Reassessment

(3) Information about the pupil provided to, or by, the parents or guardians, as described in subdivision (b) of Section 56381.

- Information About Pupil Provided to or by Parents or Guardians

(4) The pupil's anticipated needs.

- Pupil's Anticipated Needs

(5) The factors described in subdivision (a).

- Other Factors

(e) The parent or guardian shall have the right to present information to the individualized education program team in person or through a representative and the right to participate in meetings, relating to eligibility for special education and related services, recommendations, and program planning.

- Right of Parent to Present Information

(f) (1) Notwithstanding Section 632 of the Penal Code, the parent or guardian, district, special education local plan area, or county office shall have the right to record electronically the proceedings of individualized education program team meetings on an audiotape recorder. The parent or guardian, district, special education local plan area, or county office shall notify the members of the individualized education program team of their intent to record a meeting at least 24 hours prior to the meeting. If the district, special education local plan area, or county office initiates the notice of intent to audiotape record a meeting and the parent or guardian objects or refuses to attend the meeting because it will be tape

- Right to Electronically Record IEP Meetings on Audio Tape

recorded, then the meeting shall not be recorded on an audiotape recorder.

(2) The Legislature hereby finds as follows:

(A) Under federal law, audiotape recordings made by a district, special education local plan area, or county office are subject to the federal Family Educational Rights and Privacy Act (20 U.S.C. Sec. 1232g), and would, therefore, be subject to the confidentiality requirements of the regulations under Sections 300.560 to 300.575, inclusive, of Part 34 of the Code of Federal Regulations.

(B) Parents or guardians have the right, pursuant to Sections 99.10 to 99.22, inclusive, of Title 34 of the Code of Federal Regulations, to do all of the following:

(i) Inspect and review the tape recordings.

(ii) Request that the tape recordings be amended if the parent or guardian believes that they contain information that is inaccurate, misleading, or in violation of the rights of privacy or other rights of the individual with exceptional needs.

(iii) Challenge, in a hearing, information that the parent or guardian believes is inaccurate, misleading, or in violation of the individual's rights of privacy or other rights.

(g) It is the intent of the Legislature that the individualized education program team meetings be nonadversarial and convened solely for the purpose of making educational decisions for the good of the individual with exceptional needs.

- Nonadversarial IEP Meetings

56341.5. (a) Each district, special education local plan area, or county office convening a meeting of the individualized education program team shall take steps to ensure that one or both of the parents of the individual with exceptional needs are present at each individualized education program meeting or are afforded the opportunity to participate.

- Parent Participation in IEP

(b) Parents shall be notified of the individualized education program meeting early enough to ensure an opportunity to attend.

- Notification of Parent

(c) The individualized education program meeting shall be scheduled at a mutually agreed upon time and place. The notice of the meeting under subdivision (b) shall indicate the purpose, time, and location of the meeting and who shall be in attendance. Parents may also be informed in the notice of the right to bring other people to the meeting who have knowledge or special expertise regarding the individual with exceptional needs.

- IEP Meeting Scheduled at Mutually Agreed upon Time and Place

(d) For an individual with exceptional needs beginning at age 14, or younger, if appropriate, the meeting notice shall also indicate that a purpose of the meeting will be the development of a statement of the transition services needs of the individual required by Section 56345.1, and indicate that the individual with exceptional needs is also invited to attend.

(e) The meeting notice shall also identify any other local agency that shall be invited to send a representative.

(f) If neither parent can attend the meeting, the district, special education local plan area, or county office shall use other methods to ensure parent participation, including individual or conference telephone calls.

(g) A meeting may be conducted without a parent in attendance if the district, special education local plan area, or county office is unable to convince the parent that he or she should attend. In this event, the district, special education local plan area, or county office shall maintain a record of its attempts to arrange a mutually agreed-upon time and place, as follows:

(1) Detailed records of telephone calls made or attempted and the results of those calls.

(2) Copies of correspondence sent to the parents and any responses received.

(3) Detailed records of visits made to the home or place of employment of the parent and the results of those visits.

(h) The district, special education local plan area, or county office shall take whatever action is necessary to ensure that the parent understands the proceedings at a meeting, including arranging for an interpreter for parents with deafness or whose native language is other than English.

(i) The district, special education local plan area, or county office shall give the parent a copy of the individualized education program.

56342. The individualized education program team shall review the assessment results, determine eligibility, determine the content of the individualized education program, consider local transportation policies and criteria developed pursuant to paragraph (5) of subdivision (b) of Section 56195.8, and make program placement recommendations.

Prior to recommending a new placement in a nonpublic, nonsectarian school, the individualized education program team shall submit the proposed recommendation to the local governing board of the district and special education local plan area for review and recommendation regarding the cost of the placement.

The local governing board shall complete its review and make its recommendations, if any, at the next regular meeting of the board. A parent or representative shall have the right to appear before the board and submit written and oral evidence regarding the need for nonpublic school placement for his or her child. Any recommendations of the board shall be considered at an individualized education program team meeting, to be held within five days of the board's review.

- Right of Parent to Appear Before Board

Notwithstanding Section 56344, the time limit for the development of an individualized education program shall be waived for a period not to exceed 15 additional days to permit the local governing board to meet its review and recommendation requirements.

- IEP Development Time Waiver

56342.5. Each district, special education local plan area, or county office shall ensure that the parent of each individual with exceptional needs is a member of any group that makes decisions on the educational placement of the individual with exceptional needs.

- Parent Shall Be Member of Any Group Making Decisions on Educational Placement

56343. An individualized education program team shall meet whenever any of the following occurs:

- IEP Team Meetings Required

(a) A pupil has received an initial formal assessment. The team may meet when a pupil receives any subsequent formal assessment.

- Initial Formal Assessment

(b) The pupil demonstrates a lack of anticipated progress.

(c) The parent or teacher requests a meeting to develop, review, or revise the individualized education program.

- Lack of Anticipated Progress
- Parent or Teacher Requests a Meeting

(d) At least annually, to review the pupil's progress, the individualized education program, including whether the annual goals for the pupil are being achieved, and the appropriateness of placement, and to make any necessary revisions. The individualized education program team conducting the annual review shall consist of those persons specified in subdivision (b) of Section 56341. Other individuals may participate in the annual review if they possess expertise or knowledge essential for the review.

- Review At Least Annually

56343.5. A meeting of an individualized education program team requested by a parent to review an individualized education program pursuant to subdivision (c) of Section 56343 shall be held within 30 days, not counting days in July and August, from the date of receipt of the parent's written request. If a parent makes an oral request, the school district shall notify the parent of the need for a written request and the procedure for filing a written request.

- Parent Request for IEP Review

56344. An individualized education program required as a result of an assessment of a pupil shall be developed within a total time not to exceed 50 days, not counting days between the pupil's regular school sessions, terms, or days of school vacation in excess of five schooldays, from the date of receipt of the parent's written consent for assessment, unless the parent agrees, in writing, to an extension. However, such an individualized education program shall be developed within 30 days after the commencement of the subsequent regular school year as determined by each district's school calendar for each pupil for whom a referral has been made 20 days or less prior to the end of the regular school year. In the case of pupil school vacations, the 50-day time shall recommence on the date that pupil schooldays reconvene.

- IEP Development Timeline

56345. (a) The individualized education program is a written statement determined in a meeting of the individualized education program team and shall include, but not be limited to, all of the following:

- IEP Contents

(1) The present levels of the pupil's educational performance, including the following:

- Levels of Pupil's Educational Performance

(A) For a schoolage child, how the pupil's disability affects the pupil's involvement and progress in the general curriculum.

(B) For a preschoolage child, as appropriate, how the disability affects the child's participation in appropriate activities.

(2) The measurable annual goals, including benchmarks or short-term objectives related to the following:

- Measurable Annual Goals

(A) Meeting the pupil's needs that result from the pupil's disability to enable the pupil to be involved in and progress in the general curriculum.

(B) Meeting each of the pupil's other educational needs that result from the pupil's disability.

(3) The specific special educational instruction and related services and supplementary aids and services to be provided to the pupil, or on behalf of the pupil, and a statement of the program modifications or supports for school personnel that will be provided for the pupil in order to do the following:

- Specific Special Educational Instruction, Related Services, Supplementary Aids and Services

(A) To advance appropriately toward attaining the annual goals.

(B) To be involved and progress in the general curriculum in accordance with subparagraph (A) of paragraph (1) and to participate in extracurricular and other nonacademic activities.

(C) To be educated and participate with other pupils with disabilities and nondisabled pupils in the activities described in this section.

(4) An explanation of the extent, if any, to which the pupil will not participate with nondisabled pupils in regular classes and in the activities described in paragraph (3).

- Explanation of Extent Pupil Will Not Participate in Regular Classes

(5) The individual modifications in the administration of state or districtwide assessments of pupil achievement that are needed in order for the pupil to participate in the assessment. If the individualized education program team determines that the pupil will not participate in a particular state or districtwide assessment of pupil achievement (or part of an assessment), a statement of the following:

- Individual Modifications in the Administration of Statewide or Districtwide Assessments

(A) Why that assessment is not appropriate for the pupil.

(B) How the pupil will be assessed.

(6) The projected date for the beginning of the services and modifications described in paragraph (3), and the anticipated frequency, location, and duration of those services and modifications included in the individualized education program.

- Projected Date for Beginning of Services and Modification; Anticipated Frequency, Location, and Duration of Services

(7) Appropriate objective criteria, evaluation procedures, and schedules for determining, on at least an annual basis, whether the annual goals are being achieved.

- Determining Whether Annual Goals are Being Achieved

(8) Beginning at least one year before the pupil reaches the age of 18, a statement shall be included in the individualized education program that the pupil has been informed of his or her rights under this part, if any, that will transfer to the pupil upon reaching the age of 18 pursuant to Section 56041.5.

- Statement in IEP That Pupil Has Been Notified of the Upcoming Transfer of Rights

(9) A statement of how the pupil's progress toward the annual goals described in paragraph (2) will be measured.

- Statement of Pupil's Progress Toward Annual Goals

(10) A statement of how the pupil's parents will be regularly informed, at least as often as parents are informed of their nondisabled pupil's progress in the following:

-Statement of How Pupil's Parents Will Be Regularly Informed

(A) The pupil's progress toward the annual goals described in paragraph (2).

(B) The extent to which that progress is sufficient to enable the pupil to achieve the goals by the end of the year.

(b) When appropriate, the individualized education program shall also include, but not be limited to, all of the following:

- Appropriate Additional IEP Content

(1) For pupils in grades 7 to 12, inclusive, any alternative means and modes necessary for the pupil to complete the district's prescribed course of study and to meet or exceed proficiency standards for graduation in accordance with

- Prescribed Course of Study

Section 51215.

(2) For individuals whose primary language is other than English, linguistically appropriate goals, objectives, programs and services.

- Linguistic Goals

(3) Extended school year services when needed, as determined by the individualized education program team.

- Extended School Year Services

(4) Provision for the transition into the regular class program if the pupil is to be transferred from a special class or center, or nonpublic, nonsectarian school into a regular class in a public school for any part of the schoolday, including the following:

- Transition Into Regular Program

(A) A description of activities provided to integrate the pupil into the regular education program. The description shall indicate the nature of each activity, and the time spent on the activity each day or week.

(B) A description of the activities provided to support the transition of pupils from the special education program into the regular education program.

(5) For pupils with low-incidence disabilities, specialized services, materials, and equipment, consistent with guidelines established pursuant to Section 56136.

- Specialized Services, Materials, and Equipment

(c) It is the intent of the Legislature in requiring individualized education programs that the district, special education local plan area, or county office is responsible for providing the services delineated in the individualized education program. However, the Legislature recognizes that some pupils may not meet or exceed the growth projected in the annual goals and objectives of the pupil's individualized education program.

- Responsibility for Providing Services

(d) Pursuant to subdivision (d) of Section 51215, a pupil's individualized education program shall also include the determination of the individualized education program team as to whether differential proficiency standards shall be developed for the pupil. If differential proficiency standards are to be developed, the individualized education program shall include these standards.

- Differential Proficiency Standards

(e) Consistent with Section 56000.5 and clause (iv) of subparagraph (B) of paragraph (3) of subsection (d) of Section 1414 of Title 20 of the United States Code, it is the intent of the Legislature that, in making a determination of what constitutes an appropriate education to meet the unique needs of a deaf or hard-of-hearing pupil in the least restrictive environment, the individualized education program team shall consider the related services and program options that provide the pupil with an equal opportunity for communication

- Communication Access for Deaf and Hard-of-Hearing Pupils

access. The individualized education program team shall specifically discuss the communication needs of the pupil, consistent with the guidelines adopted pursuant to Section 56136 and Page 49274 of Volume 57 of the Federal Register, including all of the following:

(1) The pupil's primary language mode and language, which may include the use of spoken language with or without visual cues, or the use of sign language, or a combination of both.

(2) The availability of a sufficient number of age, cognitive, and language peers of similar abilities which may be met by consolidating services into a local plan areawide program or providing placement pursuant to Section 56361.

(3) Appropriate, direct, and ongoing language access to special education teachers and other specialists who are proficient in the pupil's primary language mode and language consistent with existing law regarding teacher training requirements.

(4) Services necessary to ensure communication-accessible academic instructions, school services, and extracurricular activities consistent with the Vocational Rehabilitation Act of 1973 as set forth in Section 794 of Title 29 of the United States Code and the Americans with Disabilities Act of 1990 as set forth in Section 12000, and following, of Title 42 of the United States Code.

(f) No General Fund money made available to school districts or local agencies may be used for any additional responsibilities and services associated with paragraphs (1) and (2) of subdivision (e), including the training of special education teachers and other specialists, even if those additional responsibilities or services are required pursuant to a judicial or state agency determination. Those responsibilities and services shall only be funded by a local educational agency as follows:

- Restriction on the Use of Funds

(1) The costs of those activities shall be funded from existing programs and funding sources.

(2) Those activities shall be supported by the resources otherwise made available to those programs.

(3) Those activities shall be consistent with the provisions of Sections 56240 to 56243, inclusive.

(g) It is the intent of the Legislatur that the communication skills of teachers who work with hard-of-hearing and deaf children be improved; however, nothing in this section shall be construed to remove the local educational agency's discretionary authority in regard to in-service

- Communication Skills of Teachers of Hearing Impaired

activities.

56345.1. (a) Beginning at age 14, and updated annually, a statement of the transition service needs of the pupil shall be included in the pupil's individualized education program. The statement shall be included under applicable components of the pupil's individualized education program that focuses on the pupil's courses of study, such as participation in advanced-placement courses or a vocational education program.

(b) Beginning at age 16 or younger and annually thereafter, in accordance with Section 56462 and paragraph (30) of Section 1401 of Title 20 of the United States Code, a statement of needed transition services shall be included in the pupil's individualized education program, including whenever appropriate, a statement of interagency responsibilities or any needed linkages.

(c) The term "transition services" means a coordinated set of activities for an individual with exceptional needs that does the following:

(1) Is designed within an outcome-oriented process, that promotes movement from school to postschool activities, including postsecondary education, vocational training, integrated employment, including supported employment, continuing and adult education, adult services, independent living, or community participation.

(2) Is based upon the individual pupil's needs, taking into account the pupil's preferences and interests.

(3) Includes instruction, related services, community experiences, the development of employment and other postschool adult living objectives, and, when appropriate, acquisition of daily living skills and functional vocational evaluation.

(d) If a participating agency, other than the local educational agency, fails to provide the transition services described in the pupil's individualized education program in accordance with this section, the local educational agency shall reconvene the individualized education program team to identify alternative strategies to meet the transition service needs for the pupil set out in the program.

56345.5. Except as prescribed in subdivision (b) of Section 56324, nothing in this part shall be construed to authorize districts, special education local plan areas, or county offices to prescribe health care services.

56346. (a) No pupil shall be required to participate in all or part of any special education program unless the parent is first informed, in writing, of the facts that make participation in the program necessary or desirable, and of the contents of the individualized education program, and after this notice, consents, in writing, to all or part of the individualized education program. If the parent does not consent to all the components of the individualized education program, then those components of the program to which the parent has consented shall be implemented so as not to delay providing instruction and services to the pupil.

(b) If the district, special education local plan area, or county office determines that the part of the proposed special education program to which the parent does not consent is necessary to provide a free and appropriate public education to the pupil, a due process hearing shall be initiated pursuant to Chapter 5 (commencing with Section 56500), unless a prehearing mediation conference is held. During the pendency of the due process hearing, the district, special education local plan area, or county office may reconsider the proposed individualized education program, may choose to meet informally with the parent pursuant to subdivision (b) of Section 56502, or may hold a mediation conference pursuant to Section 56503. As an alternative to holding a due process hearing, the parties may hold a prehearing mediation conference pursuant to Section 56500.3 to resolve any issue or dispute. If a due process hearing is held, the hearing decision shall be the final administrative determination and shall be binding upon the parties. While a prehearing mediation conference or due process hearing is pending, the pupil shall remain in his or her then-current placement unless the parent and the district, special education local plan area, or county office agree otherwise.

- If Parent Does Not Consent

56347. Each district, special education local plan area, or county office shall, prior to the placement of the individual with exceptional needs, ensure that the regular teacher or teachers, the special education teacher or teachers, and other persons who provide special education, related services, or both to the individual with exceptional needs shall be knowledgeable of the content of the individualized education program. A copy of each individualized education program shall be maintained at each school site where the pupil is enrolled. Service providers from other agencies who provide instruction or a related service to the individual off the school site shall be provided a copy of the individualized education program. All individualized education programs shall be maintained in accordance with state and federal pupil record

- Be Knowledgeable of Content

confidentiality laws.

Article 3.5. Individualized Education Program for Visually Impaired Pupils

56350. Unless the context otherwise requires, the definitions set forth in this section shall govern the construction of this article.

- Definitions

(a) A "functionally blind pupil" means a pupil who relies basically on senses other than vision as major channels for learning.

- Functionally Blind

(b) A "pupil with low vision" means a pupil who uses vision as a channel for learning, but who may also benefit from instruction in braille.

- Pupil with Low Vision

(c) A "visually impaired pupil" means a pupil who is functionally blind or a pupil with low vision. For purposes of this article, a "visually impaired pupil" does not include a pupil who is eligible for special education and related services based on a specific learning disability identified pursuant to Section 56338.

- Visually Impaired Pupil

(d) "Braille" means the system of reading and writing through touch commonly known as "Standard English Braille, American Edition."

- Braille

56351. School districts, special education local plan areas, or county offices of education shall provide opportunities for braille instruction for pupils who, due to a prognosis of visual deterioration, may be expected to have a need for braille as a reading medium.

- Provide Opportunities for Braille Instruction

56351.5. (a) (1) A school district, special education local plan area, or county office of education may reinforce braille instruction using a braille instructional aide who meets the criteria set forth in paragraph (2) under the supervision of a teacher who holds an appropriate credential, as determined by the Commission on Teacher Credentialing, to teach pupils who are functionally blind or visually impaired. This instruction shall be in accordance with the pupil's individualized education program.

- Braille Instructional Aide (3)

(2) For purposes of this section, a braille instructional aide shall demonstrate to the supervising teacher that he or she is fluent in reading and writing grade 2 braille and possesses basic knowledge of the rules of braille construction.

(b) Any school district, special education local plan area, or county office of education that employs a braille instructional aide shall provide the aide with information regarding teaching credential programs, including the Pre-

- Provide Aide with Information Regarding Teaching Credential Programs

Internship Teaching Program (Article 5.6 (commencing with Section 44305) of Chapter 2 of Part 25), the Wildman-Keeley-Solis Exemplary Teacher Training Act of 1997 (Article 12 (commencing with Section 44390) of Chapter 2 of Part 25), and the Teacher Education Internship Act of 1967 (Article 3 (commencing with Section 44450) of Chapter 3 of Part 25).

56352. (a) A functional vision assessment conducted pursuant to Section 56320 shall be used as one criterion in determining the appropriate reading medium or media for the pupil.

- Functional Vision Assessment (4)

(b) An assessment of braille skills shall be required for functionally blind pupils who have the ability to read in accordance with guidelines established pursuant to Section 56136. A school district, special education local plan area, or county office of education may provide pupils with low vision with the opportunity to receive assessments to determine the appropriate reading medium or media, including braille instruction, for the pupils.

- Assessment of Braille Skills

(c) The determination, by a pupil's individualized education program team, of the most appropriate medium or media, including braille, for functionally blind pupils who have the ability to read shall use as one criterion the assessment provided for pursuant to subdivision (b) and shall be in accordance with guidelines established pursuant to Section 56136.

- Braille Instruction

(d) Except as provided in subdivision (b) of Section 56351.5, braille instruction shall be provided by a teacher who holds an appropriate credential, as determined by the Commission on Teacher Credentialing, to teach pupils who are functionally blind or visually impaired.

- Determining Appropriate Medium or Media

(e) Each visually impaired pupil shall be provided with the opportunity to receive an assessment to determine the appropriate reading medium or media, including braille instruction, if appropriate, for that pupil.

- Opportunity for Assessment

Article 4. Implementation

56360. Each special education local plan area shall ensure that a continuum of program options is available to meet the needs of individuals with exceptional needs for special education and related services, as required by the Individuals with Disabilities Education Act (20 U.S.C. Sec. 1400 et seq.) and federal regulations relating thereto.

- Ensure Continuum of Program Options

56361. The continuum of program options shall include, but not necessarily be limited to, all of the following or any combination of the following:

(a) Regular education programs consistent with subparagraph (A) of paragraph (5) of subsection (a) of Section 1412 of Title 20 of the United States Code and implementing regulations.

(b) A resource specialist program pursuant to Section 56362.

(c) Designated instruction and services pursuant to Section 56363.

(d) Special classes and centers pursuant to Section 56364 or Section 56364.2, as applicable.

(e) Nonpublic, nonsectarian school services pursuant to Section 56365.

(f) State special schools pursuant to Section 56367.

(g) Instruction in settings other than classrooms where specially designed instruction may occur.

(h) Itinerant instruction in classrooms, resource rooms, and settings other than classrooms where specially designed instruction may occur to the extent required by federal law or regulation.

(i) Instruction using telecommunication, and instruction in the home, in hospitals, and in other institutions to the extent required by federal law or regulation.

56361.2. All special education and related services for any individual with exceptional needs who is younger than three years of age shall be provided pursuant to Chapter 4.4 (commencing with Section 56425).

56361.5. (a) In addition to the continuum of program options listed in Section 56361, a district, special education local plan area, or county office may contract with a hospital to provide designated instruction and services, as defined in subdivision (b) of Section 56363, required by the individual with exceptional needs, as specified in the individualized education program. However, a district, special education local plan area, or county office of education may not contract with a sectarian hospital for instructional services. A district, special education local plan area, or county office shall contract with a hospital for designated instruction and services required by the individual with exceptional needs only when no appropriate public education program is available.

For the purposes of this section "hospital" means a health care facility licensed by the State Department of Health

Margin notes:
- List of Program Options
- Regular Education Programs
- Resource Specialist Program
- Designated Instruction and Services
- Special Classes
- Nonpublic, Nonsectarian School Services
- State Special Schools
- Instruction in Other Settings
- Itinerant Instruction
- Instruction Using Telecommunication; Home and Hospital; Other Institutions
- Infant Programs
- Contracting with Hospitals for DIS
- Sectarian Limitations
- No Public Program Available
- Definition of Hospital

Services.

(b)   Contracts with hospitals pursuant to subdivision (a) shall be subject to the procedures prescribed in Sections 56365, 56366, and 56366.5.

- Contract Procedures

56362.   (a)   The resource specialist program shall provide, but not be limited to, all of the following:

- Resource Specialist Duties

(1)   Provision for a resource specialist or specialists who shall provide instruction and services for those pupils whose needs have been identified in an individualized education program developed by the individualized education program team and who are assigned to regular classroom teachers for a majority of a schoolday.

(2)   Provision of information and assistance to individuals with exceptional needs and their parent.

(3)   Provision of consultation, resource information, and material regarding individuals with exceptional needs to their parents and to regular staff members.

(4)   Coordination of special education services with the regular school programs for each individual with exceptional needs enrolled in the resource specialist program.

(5)   Monitoring of pupil progress on a regular basis, participation in the review and revision of individualized education programs, as appropriate, and referral of pupils who do not demonstrate appropriate progress to the individualized education program team.

(6)   Emphasis at the secondary school level on academic achievement, career and vocational development, and preparation for adult life.

(b)   The resource specialist program shall be under the direction of a resource specialist who is a credentialed special education teacher, or who has a clinical services credential with a special class authorization, who has had three or more years of teaching experience, including both regular and special education teaching experience, as defined by rules and regulations of the Commission on Teacher Credentialing and who has demonstrated the competencies for a resource specialist, as established by the Commission on Teacher Credentialing.

- Resource Specialist Qualifications

(c)   Caseloads for resource specialists shall be stated in the local policies developed pursuant to Section 56195.8 and in accordance with regulations established by the board.   No resource specialist shall have a caseload which exceeds 28 pupils.

- Caseloads

(d)   Resource specialists shall not simultaneously be assigned to serve as resource specialists and to teach regular

- Resource Specialists Shall Not Teach Regular Classes

classes.

(e) Resource specialists shall not enroll a pupil for a majority of a schoolday without prior approval by the superintendent.

(f) At least 80 percent of the resource specialists within a local plan shall be provided with an instructional aide.

56362.1. For the purposes of Section 56362, "caseload" shall include, but not be limited to, all pupils for whom the resource specialist performs any of the services described in subdivision (a) of Section 56362.

56362.5. By July 1982, the Commission on Teacher Credentialing shall adopt rules and regulations for a resource specialist certificate of competence. The certificate shall provide all the following:

(a) Definition of the competencies required of a resource specialist.

(b) Provision for a system of direct application to the commission for a certificate of competence for each teacher who holds a valid special education credential, other than an emergency credential, and who satisfies any one of the following criteria:

(1) Provided instruction and services as specified in subdivision (a) of Section 80070.1 of Title 5 of the California Administrative Code as it read immediately prior to July 28, 1980, for two years prior to September 1, 1981.

(2) Provided instruction and services as specified in subdivision (b) of Section 80070.2 of Title 5 of the California Administrative Code as it read immediately prior to July 28, 1980, for two years prior to June 30, 1983.

(c) Provision for the issuance, for up to three years, of a preliminary nonrenewable certificate of competence for the resource specialist, and adoption of the standards for the issuance and continuing validity of such a certificate.

(d) Establishment of a system for verification of competencies through both of the following:

(1) Commission on Teacher Credentialing approved institution of higher education resource specialist certificate program.

(2) Commission on Teacher Credentialing approved competency assessment panels for resource specialist certification.

(e) Cooperation with the department in implementing these provisions.

Notwithstanding any other provision of law, any person who held a preliminary resource specialist certificate of competence on January 28, 1982, and who met the requirements for a clear resource specialist certificate of competence as specified in paragraph (1) of subdivision (b) may be issued a clear resource specialist certificate of competence upon submission of a completed application, but without any additional fee.

- Issuance of Certificate Without Additional Fee

56362.7. (a) The Legislature recognizes the need for specially trained professionals to assess and serve pupils of limited-English proficiency. This is particularly true of pupils with exceptional needs or pupils with suspected handicaps.

- Bilingual-Crosscultural Certificate of Assessment Competence

(b) The commission shall develop a bilingual-crosscultural certificate of assessment competence for those professionals who may participate in assessments for placements in special education programs. The certificate shall be issued to holders of appropriate credentials, certificates, or authorizations who demonstrate, by written and oral examination, all of the following:

- Written and Oral Exam

(1) That the person is competent in both the oral and written skills of a language other than English.

(2) That the person has both the knowledge and understanding of the cultural and historical heritage of the limited-English-proficient individuals to be served.

(3) That the person has the ability to perform the assessment functions the candidate is certified or authorized to perform in English and in a language other than English.

(4) That the person has knowledge of the use of instruments and other assessment techniques appropriate to evaluate limited-English--proficient individuals with exceptional needs and ability to develop appropriate data, instructional strategies, individual educational plans, and evaluations.

(c) Certificates of bilingual-crosscultural competence for special education professionals who implement individual education plans requiring bilingual services shall be granted by the commission pursuant to Section 44253.7.

- Certificates for Implementers

(d) It is not the intent of the Legislature in enacting this section that possession of any certificate established by this section be a state-mandated requirement for employment or continued employment. It is the intent that this is a matter for local educational agencies to determine.

- Not State-Mandated for Employment

56363. (a) Designated instruction and services as specified in the individualized education program shall be available when the instruction and services are necessary for the pupil to benefit educationally from his or her instructional program.

- Designated Instruction and Services

The instruction and services shall be provided by the regular class teacher, the special class teacher, or the resource specialist if the teacher or specialist is competent to provide the instruction and services and if the provision of such instruction and services by the teacher or specialist is feasible. If not, the appropriate designated instruction and services specialist shall provide the instruction and services. Designated instruction and services shall meet standards adopted by the board. - Providers

(b) These services may include, but are not limited to, the following: - DIS Services

(1) Language and speech development and remediation. The language and speech development and remediation services may be provided by a speech-language pathology assistant as defined in subdivision (f) of Section 2530.2 of the Business and Professions Code.

(2) Audiological services.

(3) Orientation and mobility instruction.

(4) Instruction in the home or hospital.

(5) Adapted physical education.

(6) Physical and occupational therapy.

(7) Vision services.

(8) Specialized driver training instruction.

(9) Counseling and guidance.

(10) Psychological services other than assessment and development of the individualized education program.

(11) Parent counseling and training.

(12) Health and nursing services.

(13) Social worker services.

(14) Specially designed vocational education and career development.

(15) Recreation services.

(16) Specialized services for low-incidence disabilities, such as readers, transcribers, and vision and hearing services.

56363.1. A district, special education local plan area, or county office is not required to purchase medical equipment for an individual pupil. However, the school district, special education local plan area, or county office is responsible for providing other specialized equipment for use at school that is needed to implement the individualized education program. For purposes of this section, "medical equipment" does not include an assistive technology device, as defined in paragraph (1) of Section 1401 of Title 20 of the United States Code. - Medical Equipment

56363.3. The average caseload for language, speech, and hearing specialists in districts, county offices, or special education local plan areas shall not exceed 55 cases, unless the local comprehensive plan specifies a higher average caseload and the reasons for the greater average caseload.

- Caseload for Language, Speech, and Hearing Specialist

56363.5. School districts, county offices of education, and special education local plan areas may seek, either directly or through the pupil's parents, reimbursement from insurance companies to cover the costs of related services to the extent permitted by federal law or regulation.

- Reimbursement from Insurance Companies

56364. (a) Special classes that serve pupils with similar and more intensive educational needs shall be available. The special classes may enroll the pupils only when the nature or severity of the disability of the individual with exceptional needs is such that education in the regular classes with the use of supplementary aids and services, including curriculum modification and behavioral support, cannot be achieved satisfactorily. These requirements also apply to separate schooling, or other removal of individuals with exceptional needs from the regular educational environment.

- Special Classes

(b) In providing or arranging for the provision of activities, each public agency shall ensure that each individual with exceptional needs participates in those activities with nondisabled pupils to the maximum extent appropriate to the needs of the individual with exceptional needs, including nonacademic and extracurricular services and activities. Special classes shall meet standards adopted by the board.

- Participate with Nondisabled Pupils

(c) This section shall not apply to any special education local plan area that has a revised local plan approved pursuant to Section 56836.03. This section shall apply to special education local plan areas that have not had a revised local plan approved pursuant to that section.

- Application of Section

(d) This section shall become inoperative on July 1, 2003, and, as of January 1, 2004, is repealed, unless a later enacted statute, that becomes operative on or before January 1, 2004, deletes or extends the dates on which it becomes inoperative and is repealed.

- Repeal Clause; Inoperative 7/1/03

56364.1. Notwithstanding the provisions of Section 56364 or 56346.2, as applicable, pupils with low incidence disabilities may receive all or a portion of their instruction in the regular classroom and may also be enrolled in special classes taught by appropriately credentialed teachers who serve these pupils at one or more schoolsites. The instruction shall be provided in a manner which is consistent with the guidelines adopted pursuant to Section 56136 and in

- Special Classes for Pupils with Low-Incidence Disabilities

accordance with the individualized education program.

56364.2. (a) Special classes that serve pupils with similar and more intensive educational needs shall be available. The special classes may enroll pupils only when the nature or severity of the disability of the individual with exceptional needs is such that education in the regular classes with the use of supplementary aids and services, including curriculum modification and behavioral support, cannot be achieved satisfactorily. These requirements also apply to separate schooling, or other removal of individuals with exceptional needs from the regular educational environment.

- Special Classes

(b) In providing or arranging for the provision of activities, each public agency shall ensure that each individual with exceptional needs participates in those activities with nondisabled pupils to the maximum extent appropriate to the needs of the individual with exceptional needs, including nonacademic and extracurricular services and activities. Special classes shall meet standards adopted by the board.

- Participate with Nondisabled Pupils

(c) This section shall only apply to special education local plan areas that have had a revised local plan approved pursuant to Section 56836.03.

- Application of Section

56364.5. The Commission on Teacher Credentialing shall establish standards for the issuance of credentials or permits for persons employed in special centers pursuant to Section 56364.

- Credentials/Permits for Special Center Personnel

56365. (a) Nonpublic, nonsectarian school services, including services by nonpublic, nonsectarian agencies shall be available. These services shall be provided pursuant to Section 56366 under contract with the district, special education local plan area, or county office to provide the appropriate special educational facilities, special education, or designated instruction and services required by the individual with exceptional needs when no appropriate public education program is available.

- Nonpublic, Nonsectarian Schools/Agencies

- No Public Program Available

(b) Pupils enrolled in nonpublic, nonsectarian schools and agencies under this section shall be deemed to be enrolled in public schools for all purposes of Chapter 4 (commencing with Section 41600) of Part 24 and Section 42238. The district, special education local plan area, or county office shall be eligible to receive allowances under Chapter 7.2 (commencing with Section 56836) for services that are provided to individuals with exceptional needs pursuant to the contract.

- Deemed to Be Enrolled in Public Schools

- Funding Eligibility

(c) If the state participates in the federal program of assistance for state-operated or state-supported programs for

- Public Law 89-313 Funding

children with disabilities (P.L. 89-313, Sec. 6), pupils enrolled in nonpublic, nonsectarian schools shall be deemed to be enrolled in state-supported institutions for all purposes of that program and shall be eligible to receive allowances under Chapter 7.2 (commencing with Section 56836) for supplemental services provided to individuals with exceptional needs pursuant to a contract with a district, special education local plan area, or county office of education. In order to participate in the federal program, the state must find that participation will not result in any additional expenditures from the General Fund.

(d)   The district, special education local plan area, or county office shall pay to the nonpublic, nonsectarian school or agency the full amount of the tuition for individuals with exceptional needs that are enrolled in programs provided by the nonpublic, nonsectarian school pursuant to the contract.

- Full Amount of Tuition

(e)   Before contracting with a nonpublic, nonsectarian school or agency outside of this state, the district, special education local plan area, or county office shall document its efforts to utilize public schools or to locate an appropriate nonpublic, nonsectarian school or agency program, or both, within the state.

- Before Contracting Outside of State

(f)   If a district, special education local plan area, or county office places a pupil with a nonpublic, nonsectarian school or agency outside of this state, the pupil's individualized education program team shall submit a report to the superintendent within 15 days of the placement decision.   The report shall include information about the special education and related services provided by the out-of-state program placement and the costs of the special education and related services provided, and shall indicate the efforts of the local educational agency to locate an appropriate public school or nonpublic, nonsectarian school or agency, or a combination thereof, within the state.   The superintendent shall submit a report to the State Board of Education on all placements made outside of this state.

- Reporting Out-of-State Placements

(g)   If a school district, special education local plan area, or county office of education decides to place a pupil with a nonpublic, nonsectarian school or agency outside of this state, that local education agency shall indicate the anticipated date for the return of the pupil to a public or nonpublic, nonsectarian school or agency placement, or a combination thereof, located in the state and shall document efforts during the previous placement year to return the pupil.

- Indicate Anticipated Date for Return of the Pupil

(h)   In addition to meeting the requirements of Section 56366.1, a nonpublic, nonsectarian school or agency that operates a program outside of this state shall be certified or licensed by that state to provide, respectively, special education and related services and designated instruction and related services to pupils under the Individuals with Disabilities Education Act (20 U.S.C. Sec. 1400 et seq.).

- Out-of-State School/Agency Shall Be Certified or Licensed

(i)   A nonpublic, nonsectarian school or agency that is located outside of this state is eligible for certification pursuant to Section 56366.1 only if a pupil is enrolled in a program operated by that school or agency pursuant to the recommendation of an individualized education program team in California, and if that pupil's parents or guardians reside in California.

- Requirements for Out-of-State Certification

56366. It is the intent of the Legislature that the role of the nonpublic, nonsectarian school or agency shall be maintained and continued as an alternative special education service available to districts, special education local plan areas, county offices, and parents.

- Role of Nonpublic School/Agency

(a)   The master contract for nonpublic, nonsectarian school or agency services shall be developed in accordance with the following provisions:

(1)   The master contract shall specify the general administrative and financial agreements between the nonpublic, nonsectarian school or agency and the district, special education local plan area, or county office to provide the special education and designated instruction and services, as well as transportation specified in the pupil's individualized education program.   The administrative provisions of the contract also shall include procedures for recordkeeping and documentation, and the maintenance of school records by the contracting district, special education local plan area, or county office to ensure that appropriate high school graduation credit is received by the pupil.   The contract may allow for partial or full-time attendance at the nonpublic, nonsectarian school.

- Master Contract Provisions

- Administrative/Financial Agreements

(2)   (A)   The master contract shall include an individual services agreement for each pupil placed by a district, special education local plan area, or county office that will be negotiated for the length of time for which nonpublic, nonsectarian school or agency special education and designated instruction services are specified in the pupil's individualized education program.

- Individual Services Agreement

(B)   The master contract shall include a description of the process being utilized by the school district, county office of education, or special education local plan area to oversee and evaluate placements in nonpublic, nonsectarian schools. This description shall include a method for evaluating whether the pupil is making appropriate educational progress.

(3) Changes in educational instruction, services, or placement provided under contract may only be made on the basis of revisions to the pupil's individualized education program.

- Changes in Instruction, Services, or Placement

At any time during the term of the contract or individual services agreement, the parent; nonpublic, nonsectarian school or agency; or district, special education local plan area, or county office may request a review of the pupil's individualized education program by the individualized education program team. Changes in the administrative or financial agreements of the master contract that do not alter the individual services agreement that outlines each pupil's educational instruction, services, or placement may be made at any time during the term of the contract as mutually agreed by the nonpublic, nonsectarian school or agency and the district, special education local plan area, or county office.

(4) The master contract or individual services agreement may be terminated for cause. The cause shall not be the availability of a public class initiated during the period of the contract unless the parent agrees to the transfer of the pupil to a public school program. To terminate the contract either party shall give 20 days' notice.

- May Be Terminated for Cause

(5) The nonpublic, nonsectarian school or agency shall provide all services specified in the individualized education program, unless the nonpublic, nonsectarian school or agency and the district, special education local plan area, or county office agree otherwise in the contract or individualized services agreement.

- Provide Specified Services

(6) Related services provided pursuant to a nonpublic, nonsectarian agency master contract shall only be provided during the period of the child's regular or extended school year program, or both, unless otherwise specified by the pupil's individualized education program.

- Related Services

(7) The nonpublic, nonsectarian school or agency shall report attendance of pupils receiving special education and designated instruction and services as defined by Section 46307 for purposes of submitting a warrant for tuition to each contracting district, special education local plan area, or county office.

- Report Attendance of Pupils

(b) The master contract or individual services agreement shall not include special education transportation provided

- Transportation Restrictions

through the use of services or equipment owned, leased, or contracted by a district, special education local plan area, or county office for pupils enrolled in the nonpublic, nonsectarian school or agency unless provided directly or subcontracted by that nonpublic, nonsectarian school or agency.

The superintendent shall withhold 20 percent of the amount apportioned to a school district or county office for costs related to the provision of nonpublic, nonsectarian school or agency placements if the superintendent finds that the local education agency is in noncompliance with this subdivision. This amount shall be withheld from the apportionments in the fiscal year following the superintendent's finding of noncompliance. The superintendent shall take other appropriate actions to prevent noncompliant practices from occurring and report to the Legislature on those actions.

- Penalty for Noncompliance

(c) (1) If the pupil is enrolled in the nonpublic, nonsectarian school or agency with the approval of the district, special education local plan area, or county office prior to agreement to a contract or individual services agreement, the district, special education local plan area, or county office shall issue a warrant, upon submission of an attendance report and claim, for an amount equal to the number of creditable days of attendance at the per diem tuition rate agreed upon prior to the enrollment of the pupil. This provision shall be allowed for 90 days during which time the contract shall be consummated.

- Issuance of Warrant

(2) If after 60 days the master contract or individual services agreement has not been finalized as prescribed in paragraph (1) of subdivision (a), either party may appeal to the county superintendent of schools, if the county superintendent is not participating in the local plan involved in the nonpublic, nonsectarian school or agency contract, or the superintendent, if the county superintendent is participating in the local plan involved in the contract, to negotiate the contract. Within 30 days of receipt of this appeal, the county superintendent or the superintendent, or his or her designee, shall mediate the formulation of a contract which shall be binding upon both parties.

- Appeal

- Mediate Formulation of Contract

(d) No master contract for special education and related services provided by a nonpublic, nonsectarian school or agency shall be authorized under this part unless the school or agency has been certified as meeting those standards relating to the required special education and specified related services and facilities for individuals with exceptional needs.

- Certification Standards

The certification shall result in the school's or agency's receiving approval to educate pupils under this part for a period no longer than four years from the date of the approval.

(e) By September 30, 1998, the procedures, methods, and regulations for the purposes of contracting for nonpublic, nonsectarian school and agency services pursuant to this section and for reimbursement pursuant to Sections 56836.16 and 56836.20 shall be developed by the superintendent in consultation with statewide organizations representing providers of special education and designated instruction and services. The regulations shall be established by rules and regulations issued by the board.

— Procedures, Methods, and Regulations for Contracting

56366.1. (a) A nonpublic, nonsectarian school or agency that seeks certification shall file an application with the superintendent on forms provided by the department and include the following information on the application:

— Application for Certification (5)

(1) A description of the special education and designated instruction and services provided to individuals with exceptional needs if the application is for nonpublic, nonsectarian school certification.

(2) A description of the designated instruction and services provided to individuals with exceptional needs if the application is for nonpublic, nonsectarian agency certification.

(3) A list of appropriately qualified staff, a description of the credential, license, or registration that qualifies each staff member to render special education or designated instruction and services, and copies of their credentials, licenses, or certificates of registration with the appropriate state or national organization that has established standards for the service rendered.

(4) An annual operating budget.

(5) Affidavits and assurances necessary to comply with all applicable federal, state, and local laws and regulations which include criminal record summaries required of all nonpublic school or agency personnel having contact with minor children under Section 44237.

(b) If the applicant operates a facility or program on more than one site, each site shall be certified.

— Each Site Shall Be Certified

(c) If the applicant is part of a larger program or facility on the same site, the superintendent shall consider the effect of the total program on the applicant. A copy of the policies and standards for the nonpublic, nonsectarian school or agency and the larger program shall be available to the

— Effect of Total Program

superintendent.

(d) Prior to certification, the superintendent shall conduct an onsite review of the facility and program for which the applicant seeks certification. The superintendent may be assisted by representatives of the special education local plan area in which the applicant is located and a nonpublic, nonsectarian school or agency representative who does not have a conflict of interest with the applicant. The superintendent shall conduct an additional onsite review of the facility and program within four years of the certification effective date, unless the superintendent conditionally certifies the school or agency or unless the superintendent receives a formal complaint against the school or agency. In the latter two cases, the superintendent shall conduct an onsite review at least annually.

- Onsite Review

(e) The superintendent shall make a determination on an application within 120 days of receipt of the application and shall certify, conditionally certify, or deny certification to the applicant. If the superintendent fails to take one of these actions within 120 days, the applicant is automatically granted conditional certification for a period terminating on August 31, of the current school year. If certification is denied, the superintendent shall provide reasons for the denial. The superintendent may certify the school or agency for a period of not longer than four years.

- Action on Application Within 120 Days of Receipt

(f) Certification becomes effective on the date the nonpublic, nonsectarian school or agency meets all the application requirements and is approved by the superintendent. Certification may be retroactive if the school or agency met all the requirements of this section on the date the retroactive certification is effective. Certification expires on December 31 of the terminating year.

- Effective Date of Certification

(g) The superintendent shall annually review the certification of each nonpublic, nonsectarian school and agency. For this purpose, a certified school or agency shall annually update its application between August 1 and October 31, unless the board grants a waiver pursuant to Section 56101. The superintendent may conduct an onsite review as part of the annual review.

- Annual Review of Certification

(h) The superintendent may monitor a nonpublic, nonsectarian school or agency onsite at any time without prior notice when there is substantial reason to believe that there is an immediate danger to the health, safety, or welfare of a child. The superintendent shall document the concern and submit it to the nonpublic, nonsectarian school or agency at

- Monitor Nonpublic School/Agency Onsite at Any Time Without Notice

the time of the onsite monitoring. The superintendent shall require a written response to any noncompliance or deficiency found.

(i) (1) Notwithstanding any other provision of law, the superintendent may not certify a nonpublic, nonsectarian school or agency that proposes to initiate or expand services to pupils currently educated in the immediate prior fiscal year in a juvenile court program, community school pursuant to Section 56150, or other nonspecial education program, including independent study or adult school, or both, unless the nonpublic, nonsectarian school or agency notifies the county superintendent of schools and the special education local plan area in which the proposed new or expanded nonpublic, nonsectarian school or agency is located of its intent to seek certification.

- Certification Exceptions and Notice to Initiate or Expand Services

(2) The notification shall occur no later than the December 1 prior to the new fiscal year in which the proposed or expanding school or agency intends to initiate services. The notice shall include the following:

- Notification No Later Than December 1

(A) The specific date upon which the proposed nonpublic, nonsectarian school or agency is to be established.

(B) The location of the proposed program or facility.

(C) The number of pupils proposed for services, the number of pupils currently served in the juvenile court, community school, or other nonspecial education program, the current school services including special education and related services provided for these pupils, and the specific program of special education and related services to be provided under the proposed program.

(D) The reason for the proposed change in services.

(E) The number of staff that will provide special education and designated instruction and services and hold a current valid California credential or license in the service rendered or certificate of registration to provide occupational therapy.

(3) In addition to the requirements in subdivisions (a) through (e), inclusive, the superintendent shall require and consider the following in determining whether to certify a nonpublic, nonsectarian school or agency as described in this subdivision:

- Items Superintendent Shall Consider

(A) A complete statement of the information required as part of the notice under paragraph (1).

(B) Documentation of the steps taken in preparation for the conversion to a nonpublic, nonsectarian school or agency, including information related to changes in the population to be served and the services to be provided pursuant to each pupil's individualized education program.

(4) Notwithstanding any other provision of law, the certification becomes effective no earlier than July 1, if the school or agency provided the notification required pursuant to paragraph (1).

- Certification Effective Date

(j) The school or agency shall be charged a reasonable fee for certification. The superintendent may adjust the fee annually commensurate with the statewide average percentage inflation adjustment computed for revenue limits of unified school districts with greater than 1,500 units of average daily attendance if the percentage increase is reflected in the district revenue limit for inflation purposes. For purposes of this section, the base fee shall be the following:

- Certification Fees

(1) 1-5 pupils .... $ 150
(2) 6-10 pupils 250
(3) 11-24 pupils 500
(4) 25-75 pupils 750
(5) 76 pupils and over 1,000

The school or agency shall pay this fee when it applies for certification and when it updates its application for annual review by the superintendent. The superintendent shall use these fees to conduct onsite reviews, which may include field experts. No fee shall be refunded if the application is withdrawn or is denied by the superintendent.

(k) (1) Notwithstanding any other provision of law, only those nonpublic, nonsectarian schools and agencies that provide special education and designated instruction and services utilizing staff who hold, or are receiving training under the supervision of staff who hold, a current valid California credential or license in the service rendered shall be eligible to receive certification. Only those nonpublic, nonsectarian schools or agencies located outside of California that employ staff who hold a current valid credential or license to render special education and related services as required by that state shall be eligible to be certified.

-Staff Qualifications

(2) Nothing in this subdivision restricts student teachers, interns, or other staff who are enrolled in training programs that lead to a license or credential that authorize the holder to render services to special education pupils and who are under the direct supervision of a staff member who holds a current valid California credential, license, or certificate of registration document.

- Student Teachers

(3) A nonpublic, nonsectarian school or agency that

- Restrictions on Staffing

employs only persons who hold a valid California credential authorizing substitute teaching pursuant to Section 56060 shall not be certified. At least one full-time person with a current valid California credential, license, or certificate of registration in the area of service to be rendered, or a current valid credential, license, or certificate of registration for appropriate special education and related services rendered that is required in another state, shall be required for purposes of certification under subdivision (d) of Section 56366.

(4) A nonpublic, nonsectarian school or agency that employs persons holding a valid emergency credential shall document efforts of recruiting appropriately credentialed, licensed, or registered personnel for the special education and related services rendered as a condition of renewing certification.

- Document Efforts

(5) Not later than August 1, 1997, the State Board of Education shall issue emergency regulations to implement the subdivision. The emergency regulations shall be developed by the Superintendent of Public Instruction, in collaboration with the Commission on Teacher Credentialing and other public agencies responsible for issuing licenses or certificates of registration to individuals providing designated instruction and services to individuals with exceptional needs. The regulations also shall be developed in consultation with statewide organizations representing public and nonpublic, nonsectarian schools or agencies that provide special education and designated instruction and services. The emergency regulations shall include, but shall not be necessarily limited to, all of the following:

- Emergency Regulations

(A) Requirements for minimum personnel qualifications for credentials to provide special education to individuals with exceptional needs issued by the Commission on Teacher Credentialing pursuant to this code and applicable federal laws.

(B) Requirements for minimum personnel qualifications for licenses or certifications of registration to provide designated instruction and services to individuals with exceptional needs issued by the California Board of Medical Quality Assurance, the Board of Behavioral Science Examiners, the Board of Consumer Affairs, and other state licensure agencies that are authorized under the Business and Professions Code to grant licenses or certificates of registration that may be applicable to the provision of designated instruction and services to individuals with exceptional needs.

(C) Requirements for personnel who are not licensed or credentialed to provide special education or designated instruction and services to pupils under the supervision of a credentialed or licensed professional in the service rendered, including direct and nondirect supervision requirements established by this code and the Business and Professions Code, and related regulations.

(D) Requirements for the certification of nonpublic, nonsectarian schools and agencies to provide individual and group designated instruction and services to individuals with exceptional needs.

(6) For purposes of the Administrative Procedure Act, the Legislature declares that the regulations issued pursuant to paragraph (5) shall be deemed to be in response to an emergency and necessary for the immediate preservation of the public peace, health and safety, or general welfare by ensuring that all personnel providing special education and designated instruction and services to individuals with exceptional needs are appropriately qualified to provide the services specified by a pupil's individualized education program.

- Necessity for Emergency Regulations

(l) The superintendent shall establish guidelines for the implementation of subdivision (a) in consultation with statewide organizations representing providers of special education and designated instruction and services. The State Board of Education shall approve the standards not later than August 1, 1997.

- Guidelines and Standards

(m) (1) By September 30, 1998, the superintendent shall, in consultation with statewide organizations representing providers of special education and designated instruction and services, develop the procedures, methods, and areas of certification, including, but not limited to, the following:

- Procedures, Methods, and Areas of Certification

(A) Information required for purposes of the application specified in subdivision (a).

(B) Procedures for conducting onsite reviews of the nonpublic, nonsectarian school or agency program.

(C) Provisions specific to minimum staff qualifications to provide special education and designated instruction and services that are required for certification.

(D) Provisions specific to the provision of special education and related services to individuals with exceptional needs from birth to preschool.

(2) The board shall issue as rules and regulations the procedures, methods, and areas of certification developed

pursuant to paragraph (1).

(n) In addition to meeting the standards adopted by the board, a nonpublic, nonsectarian school or agency shall provide written assurances that it meets all applicable standards relating to fire, health, sanitation, and building safety.

- Written Assurance

56366.2. (a) A district, special education local plan area, county office, nonpublic, nonsectarian school, or nonpublic, nonsectarian agency may petition the superintendent to waive one or more of the requirements under Sections 56365, 56366, 56366.3, 56366.6, and 56366.7. The petition shall state the reasons for the waiver request, and shall include the following:

- Petition to Waive Requirements

(1) Sufficient documentation to demonstrate that the waiver is necessary to the content and implementation of a specific pupil's individualized education program and the pupil's current placement.

(2) The period of time that the waiver will be effective during any one school year.

(3) Documentation and assurance that the waiver does not abrogate any right provided individuals with exceptional needs and their parents or guardians under state or federal law, and does not hinder the compliance of a district, special education local plan area, or county office with the Individuals with Disabilities Education Act (20 U.S.C. Sec. 1400 and following), Section 504 of the Rehabilitation Act of 1973 (29 U.S.C. Sec. 794), the Americans with Disabilities Act of 1990 (42 U.S.C. 12101 et seq.), and federal regulations relating thereto.

(b) No waiver shall be granted for reimbursement of those costs prohibited under Article 4 (commencing with Section 56836.20) of Chapter 7.2 of Part 30 or for the certification requirements pursuant to Section 56366.1 unless approved by the board pursuant to Section 56101.

- Approval by State Board of Education

(c) In submitting the annual report on waivers granted under Section 56101 and this section to the State Board of Education, the superintendent shall specify information related to the provision of special education and related services to individuals with exceptional needs through contracts with nonpublic, nonsectarian schools and agencies located in the state, nonpublic, nonsectarian school and agency placements in facilities located out of state, and the specific section waived pursuant to this section.

- Annual Report on Waivers

56366.3. (a) No contract for special education and related services provided by a nonpublic, nonsectarian agency shall be reimbursed by the state pursuant to Article 4 (commencing with Section 56836.20) of Chapter 7.2 and Section 56836.16 if the contract covers special education and related services, administration, or supervision by an individual who is or was an employee of a contracting district, special education local plan area, or county office within the last 365 days. Former contracting agency personnel may be employed by a nonpublic, nonsectarian agency if the personnel were involuntarily terminated or laid off as part of necessary staff reductions from the district, special education local plan area, or county office.

- Nonpublic, Nonsectarian Agency Contract Prohibitions for Former Employees of Local Educational Agency (6)

(b) This section does not apply to any person who is able to provide designated instruction and services during the extended school year because he or she is otherwise employed for up to 10 months of the school year by the district, special education local plan area, or county office.

- Exception for Providing DIS

56366.4. (a) The superintendent may revoke or suspend the certification of a nonpublic, nonsectarian school or agency for any of the following reasons:

- Revocation or Suspension of Certification

(1) Violation of any applicable state or federal rule or regulation, or aiding, abetting, or permitting the violation of any applicable state or federal rule or regulation.

(2) Falsification or intentional misrepresentation of any element of the application, pupil records, or program presented for certification purposes.

(3) Conduct in the operation or maintenance of the nonpublic, nonsectarian school or agency that is harmful to the health, welfare, or safety of an individual with exceptional needs.

(4) Failure to comply with any provision in the contract with the local education entity.

(5) Failure to notify the department in writing of any of the following within 45 days of the occurrence:

(A) Changes in credentialed, licensed, or registered staff who render special education and related services, ownership, management, or control of the nonpublic, nonsectarian school or agency.

(B) Major modification or relocation of facilities.

(C) Significant modification of the nonpublic, nonsectarian school or agency program.

(6) Failure to implement recommendations and compliance requirements following an onsite review of the school or agency.

(7) Failure to provide appropriate services, supplies, equipment, or facilities for a pupil as required in his or her individualized education program.

(8) Failure to notify the superintendent in writing within 10 days of the revocation or suspension of any license or permit including, but not limited to, any residential care license, business license, or other required license or permit.

(9) Failure to implement a pupil's individualized education program.

(10) Failure to notify the superintendent in writing within 10 days of the death of a pupil or any other individual of unnatural causes within the school or agency, including the circumstances surrounding the death and any appropriate preventative measures being taken or recommended.

(b) The superintendent shall notify contracting local education agencies and the special education local plan area in which the nonpublic, nonsectarian school or agency is located of the determination to suspend or revoke state certification.

- Notification to Suspend or Revoke State Certification

56366.5. (a) Upon receipt of a request from a nonpublic, nonsectarian school for payment for services provided under a contract entered into pursuant to Sections 56365 and 56366, the district, special education local plan area, or county office shall either (1) send a warrant for the amount requested within 45 days, or (2) notify the nonpublic, nonsectarian school within 10 working days of any reason why the requested payment shall not be paid.

- Payment for Services

(b) If the district, special education local plan area, or county office fails to comply with subdivision (a), the nonpublic, nonsectarian school may require the district, special education local plan area, or county office to pay an additional amount of 1½ percent of the unpaid balance per month until full payment is made. The district, special education local plan area, or county office may not claim reimbursement from the state for such additional amount pursuant to any provision of law, including any provision contained in Chapter 3 (commencing with Section 2201) of Part 4 of Division 1 of the Revenue and Taxation Code.

- Penalty for Late Payment

56366.6. (a) Within 20 working days following the nonpublic, nonsectarian school's or agency's receipt of the notice of denial, revocation, or suspension of certification, the nonpublic, nonsectarian school or agency may file a written petition to request a review of the decision by the superintendent. The petition may include written arguments or a request to present an oral argument.

- Request Review of Notice of Denial, Revocation, or Suspension of Certification

(b) Within 30 working days after the receipt of the written

- Final Administrative Decision

petition, the superintendent or a designee shall review the decision and the applicant's petition and render` a written, reasoned decision that shall be the final administrative decision. The designee of the superintendent shall be impartial, unbiased, and shall not have participated in the department decision to deny, revoke, or suspend the nonpublic, nonsectarian school or agency certification.

(c) Any public education agency that contracts with a certified nonpublic, nonsectarian school or agency may request the superintendent to review the status of the nonpublic school or agency. The request shall be in writing and a copy sent to the nonpublic school or agency.

56366.8. The State Department of Education, as a part of its certification process and complaint investigation process for nonpublic, nonsectarian schools or agencies shall do all of the following:

(a) Provide advance notice of certification reviews to the contracting district, special education local plan area, or county office, and to the nonpublic, nonsectarian school or agency under certification review.

(b) Provide advance notice of complaint investigations to the contracting district, special education local plan area, or county office of education.

(c) Include the contracting district, special education local plan area, or county office in certification reviews and complaint investigations.

(d) Transmit final reports of certification reviews and complaint investigations to districts, special education local plan areas, and county offices, placement agencies, and educational agencies that contract with the nonpublic, nonsectarian school or agency.

56366.9. A licensed children's institution at which individuals with exceptional needs reside shall not require as a condition of residential placement that it provide the appropriate educational programs to those individuals through a nonpublic, nonsectarian school or agency owned or operated by a licensed children's institution. Those services may only be provided if the special education local plan area determines that alternative educational programs are not available.

56367. (a) Placements in state special schools pursuant to Sections 59020, 59120, and 59220 shall be made only as a result of recommendations from the individualized education program team, upon a finding that no appropriate placement is available in the local plan area.

- Request to Superintendent to Review Status of NPS/A

- Department Responsibilities as Part of Certification and Complaint Investigation Processes

- Residential Licensed Children's Institutions; Placement Conditions

- State Special Schools Placement

(b) Notwithstanding the provisions of subdivision (a), referrals for further assessment and recommendations to the California Schools for the Deaf and Blind or the Diagnostic Centers, pursuant to Section 56326, shall not constitute placements in state special schools.

- Referrals for Further Assessment

56368. (a) A program specialist is a specialist who holds a valid special education credential, clinical services credential, health services credential, or a school psychologist authorization and has advanced training and related experience in the education of individuals with exceptional needs and a specialized in-depth knowledge in preschool disabilities, career vocational development, or one or more areas of major disabling conditions.

- Program Specialist Qualifications

(b) A program specialist may do all the following:

- Program Specialist Activities

(1) Observe, consult with, and assist resource specialists, designated instruction and services instructors, and special class teachers.

(2) Plan programs, coordinate curricular resources, and evaluate effectiveness of programs for individuals with exceptional needs.

(3) Participate in each school's staff development, program development, and innovation of special methods and approaches.

(4) Provide coordination, consultation and program development primarily in one specialized area or areas of his or her expertise.

(5) Be responsible for assuring that pupils have full educational opportunity regardless of the district of residence.

(c) For purposes of Section 41403, a program specialist shall be considered a pupil services employee, as defined in subdivision (c) of Section 41401.

- Program Specialists Considered as Pupil Services Employees

56369. A district, special education local plan area, or county office, may contract with another public agency to provide special education or related services to an individual with exceptional needs.

- Contracting with Another Public Agency

56370. A transfer of special education programs from a school district to the county superintendent of schools or to other school districts, or from the county superintendent of schools to school districts, shall not be approved by the Superintendent of Public Instruction if the transfer would result in diminishing the level of services or the opportunity of the affected pupils to interact with the general school population, as required in the individualized education programs of the affected pupils.

- Transfer of Special Education Programs

This section shall not apply to any special education local

plan approved pursuant to Section 56836.03. This section shall apply to special education local plan areas that have not had a revised local plan approved pursuant to this section.

This section shall become inoperative on July 1, 2003, and, as of January 1, 2004, is repealed, unless a later enacted statute, that becomes operative on or before January 1, 2004, deletes or extends the dates on which it becomes inoperative and is repealed.

- Repeal Clause; Inoperative 7/01/03

Article 5. Review

56380. (a) The district, special education local plan area, or county office shall maintain procedures for conducting, on at least an annual basis, reviews of all individualized education programs. The procedures shall provide for the review of the pupil's progress and the appropriateness of placement, and the making of any necessary revisions.

- At Least Annual Basis

(b) The district, special education local plan area, or county office shall notify, in writing, parents of their right to request a review by the individualized education program team. The notice may be part of the individualized education program.

- Parent Notification

(c) Each individualized education program review shall be conducted in accordance with the notice and scheduling requirements for the initial assessment.

- Conducting IEP Review

56381. (a) A reassessment of the pupil, based upon procedures specified in Article 2 (commencing with Section 56320) shall be conducted at least once every three years or more frequently, if conditions warrant a reassessment, or if the pupil's parent or teacher requests a reassessment and a new individualized education program to be developed.

- Reassessment

If the reassessment so indicates, a new individualized education program shall be developed.

(b) As part of any reassessment, the individualized education program team and other qualified professionals, as appropriate, shall do the following:

- Duties of the IEP Team and Other Qualified Professionals

(1) Review existing assessment data on the pupil, current classroom-based assessments and observations, and teacher and related services providers' observations.

(2) On the basis of the review conducted pursuant to paragraph (1), and input from the pupil's parents, identify what additional data, if any, is needed to determine:

(A) Whether the pupil continues to have a disability described in paragraph (3) of Section 1401 of Title 20 of the United States Code.

(B) The present levels of performance and educational needs of the pupil.

(C) Whether the pupil continues to need special education and related services.

(D) Whether any additions or modifications to the special education and related services are needed to enable the pupil to meet the measurable annual goals set out in the individualized education program of the pupil and to participate, as appropriate, in the general curriculum.

(c) The district, special education local plan area, or county office shall administer tests and other assessment materials as may be needed to produce the data identified by the individualized education program team.

- Administer Tests and Other Assessment Materials As Needed

(d) If the individualized education program team and other qualified professionals, as appropriate, determine that no additional data is needed to determine whether the pupil continues to be an individual with exceptional needs, the district, special education local plan area, or county office shall notify the pupil's parents of that determination and the reasons for it, and the right of the parents to request an assessment to determine whether the pupil continues to be an individual with exceptional needs; however, the district, special education local plan area, or county office shall not be required to conduct an assessment unless requested to by the pupil's parents.

- Notification of Pupil's Parents

(e) A district, special education local plan area, or county office shall assess an individual with exceptional needs in accordance with this section and procedures specified in Article 2 (commencing with Section 56320) before determining that the pupil is no longer an individual with exceptional needs.

- Assessment Procedures to Be Followed

(f) No reassessment shall be conducted unless the written consent of the parent is obtained prior to reassessment except pursuant to subdivision (e) of Section 56506.

- Need for Written Consent of Parent

56382. All review and reassessment procedures for individuals with exceptional needs who are younger than three years of age shall be provided pursuant to Chapter 4.4 (commencing with Section 56425) and the California Early Intervention Services Act, Title 14 (commencing with Section 95000) of the Government Code.

- Review and Reassessment Procedures for Infants

NOTE

(1) Education Code Section 56341 was repealed and added by Senate Bill 1105, Chapter 405, Statutes of 2001.

(2) Education Code Section 56341.1 was added by Senate Bill 1105, Chapter 405, Statutes of 2001.

(3) Education Code Section 56351.5 was added by Assembly Bill 306, Chapter 736, Statutes of 2001.

(4) Education Code Section 56352 was amended by Assembly Bill 306, Chapter 736, Statutes of 2001.

(5) Education Code Section 56366.1 was amended by Assembly Bill 804, Chapter 734, Statutes of 2001.

(6) Education Code Section 56366.3 was amended by Assembly Bill 992, Chapter 215, Statutes of 2001.

(7) Note: Education Code Section 56366.7 contained an automatic-repeal clause and became inoperative on June 30, 2001, and was repealed on January 1, 2002

CHAPTER 4.1. RECOGNITION FOR EDUCATIONAL ACHIEVEMENT OR COMPLETION OF PROGRAM

56390. Notwithstanding Section 51412 or any other provision of law, a local educational agency may award an individual with exceptional needs a certificate or document of educational achievement or completion if the requirements of subdivision (a), (b), or (c) are met.

- Certificate or Document May Be Awarded

(a) The individual has satisfactorily completed a prescribed alternative course of study approved by the governing board of the school district in which the individual attended school or the school district with jurisdiction over the individual and identified in his or her individualized education program.

- Individual Has Completed a Prescribed Alternative Course of Study

(b) The individual has satisfactorily met his or her individualized education program goals and objectives during high school as determined by the individualized education program team.

- Individual Has Met IEP Goals and Objectives

(c) The individual has satisfactorily attended high school, participated in the instruction as prescribed in his or her individualized education program, and has met the objectives of the statement of transition services.

- Individual Has Attended High School; Participated in IEP Prescribed Instruction; Met Objectives of Transition Services Statement

56391 An individual with exceptional needs who meets the criteria for a certificate or document described in Section 56390 shall be eligible to participate in any graduation ceremony and any school activity related to graduation in which a pupil of similar age without disabilities would be eligible to participate. The right to participate in graduation ceremonies does not equate a certificate or document described in Section 56390 with a regular high school diploma.

- Participation in Graduation Ceremony and Related Activities (1)

56392. It is not the intent of the Legislature by enacting this chapter to eliminate the opportunity for an individual with exceptional needs to earn a standard diploma issued by a local or state educational agency when the pupil has completed the prescribed course of study and has passed the proficiency requirements with or without differential standards pursuant to Section 51215.

- Legislative Intent

56393. On or before July 1, 2000, the Advisory Commission on Special Education shall, pursuant to Section 33595, study and report to the State Board of Education, the Superintendent of Public Instruction, the Legislature, and the Governor on the practice of awarding certificates or documents of educational achievement or completion and diplomas, as appropriate, to individuals with exceptional needs. The report shall contain recommendations for

- Advisory Commission Study and Report

improving the system of recognition for educational achievement or completion of studies to individuals with exceptional needs.

NOTE

(1) Education Code Section 56391 was amended by Assembly Bill 804, Chapter 734, Statutes of 2001.

CHAPTER 4.3. FAMILY EMPOWERMENT CENTERS ON DISABILITY

56400. It is the intent of the Legislature, through enactment of this chapter, to the extent feasible, to do all of the following:

- Legislative Intent (1)

(a) Ensure that children and young adults with disabilities are provided a free and appropriate public education in accordance with applicable federal and state law and regulations.

(b) Ensure that children and young adults with disabilities receive the necessary educational support and services they need to complete their education.

(c) Offer parents and guardians of children and young adults with disabilities access to accurate information, specialized training, and peer-to-peer support in their communities.

(d) Ensure that parents, guardians, and families of children and young adults with disabilities are full participants in their child's education, school reform, and comprehensive systems change efforts.

(e) Build upon existing local and regional service delivery systems to improve, expand, and offer coordinated technical assistance to the network of existing resources available for parents, guardians, and families of children and young adults with disabilities.

56402. (a) The State Department of Education shall award grants to establish Family Empowerment Centers on Disability in each of the 32 regions in the state established under the Early Start Family Resource Centers. In the first year of operation, the State Department of Education shall award these grants no later than February 15, 2002. In subsequent years, to the extent funding is available, the State Department of Education shall award these grants no later than February 15 of that year.

- Grant Awards to Establish Family Empowerment Centers on Disability

(b) Once funding is secured, and annually until all centers are established, the State Department of Education shall submit a report to the appropriate policy committees of the Legislature documenting progress in establishing the centers.

- Department Shall Submit Report to Legislative Policy Committees

(c) The department shall develop the grant application, with advice from stakeholders, including parents, guardians, and family members of children with disabilities, as well as adults with disabilities and representatives of community agencies serving children and adults with disabilities.

- Development of Grant Application

(d) The sum of twenty-five thousand dollars ($25,000) shall be made available to the department, from the funds appropriated for the purposes of this chapter, for the purpose of securing an outside contractor to develop a request for proposal, disseminate the proposal, empanel readers to evaluate the proposals, and cover other costs related to this process.

- Funding for Developing Request for Proposal

56404. To be eligible to receive funding to establish Family Empowerment Centers on Disability pursuant to this chapter, applicants shall meet the following organizational requirements:

- Eligibility Requirements of Applicants

(a) Be a nonprofit charitable organization organized under the Internal Revenue Code pursuant to paragraph (3) of subdivision (c) of Section 503 of Title 26 of the United States Code.

- Nonprofit Charitable Organization

(b) Be staffed primarily by parents, guardians, and family members of children and young adults with disabilities and by adults with disabilities.

- Staffing

(c) Have as a majority of board members of each center, parents, guardians, and family members of children and young adults with disabilities who have experience with local or regional disability systems and educational resources. Additional members shall include, but not be limited to, persons with disabilities and representatives of community agencies serving adults with disabilities, and other community agencies.

- Board Members

(d) Demonstrate the capacity to provide services in accordance with the family support guidelines developed by the Early Start Family Resource Centers pursuant to Section 95004 of the Government Code and administered by the State Department of Developmental Services, and Parent Training Information Centers established pursuant to Sections 1482 and 1483 of Title 20 of the United States Code.

- Capacity to Provide Services

56406. (a) The State Department of Education shall issue requests for proposals, select grantees, and award grants pursuant to this chapter by not later than February 15, 2002. Grants awarded to Family Empowerment Centers on Disability by the State Department of Education shall be based upon a formula that does the following:

- Issue Requests for Proposals; Select Grantees; Award Grants Based on Formula

(1) Establishes a minimum base rate of one hundred fifty thousand dollars ($150,000) for each center to provide the basic services pursuant to this chapter and serve parents and guardians of children and young adults from age three years to age 18 years, inclusive, and to those young adults from age 19 years to age 22 years who had an individualized education

plan prior to their 18th birthday.

(2) Establishes an allocation mechanism that is determined according to school enrollment of the region served.

(b) Each grant applicant shall demonstrate all of the following:

- Requirements of Grant Applicants

(1) That the need for training and information for underserved parents and guardians of children and young adults with disabilities in the area to be served will be effectively met.

(2) That services will be delivered in a manner that accomplishes all of the following:

(A) All families have access to services regardless of cultural, linguistic, geographical, socioeconomic, or other similar barriers.

(B) Services are provided in accordance with families' linguistic and cultural preferences and needs.

(C) Services are coordinated with the existing family support organizations within the region.

(D) Promotes positive parent and professional collaboration with local educational agencies, special education local plan areas, and other community agencies.

56408. As a condition of receipt of funds, each Family Empowerment Center on Disability that receives assistance under this chapter and serves the parents and guardians of children and young adults from age three years to age 18 years, inclusive, and those young adults from age 19 years to age 22 years, who had an individualized education plan prior to their 18th birthday shall do all of the following:

- Conditions for Receipt of Funds and Functions of Centers

(a) Provide training and information that meets the training and information needs of parents and guardians of children and young adults with disabilities living in the area served by the center, particularly those families and individuals who have been underserved .

(b) Work with community-based organizations and state and local agencies serving children with disabilities.

(c) Train and support parents and guardians of children and young adults with disabilities to do the following:

(1) Better understand the nature of their children's disabilities and their children's educational and developmental needs.

(2) Communicate effectively with personnel responsible for providing special education, early intervention, and related services.

(3) Participate in decisionmaking processes and the development of individualized education programs.

(4) Obtain appropriate information regarding the range of options, programs, services, and resources available to assist children and young adults with disabilities and their families.

(5) Participate in school improvement and reform activities.

(6) Advocate for the child's needs in a manner that promotes alternative forms of dispute resolution and positive relationships between parents and professionals .

56410. A statewide Family Empowerment and Disability Council composed of the executive directors for the Family Empowerment Centers on Disability shall be established. Membership on the Family Empowerment and Disability Council may also include the Executive Director or representative from the Family Resource Centers, funded by the Department of Developmental Services, and from the parent centers funded by the Individuals with Disabilities Education Act (20 U.S.C. Sec. 1400 et seq.).   The department shall contract with an outside entity experienced with developing a statewide technical assistance disability network.   A base amount of one hundred fifty thousand dollars ($150,000) shall be made available, from the annual appropriation made for the Family Empowerment Centers, to support the work of the council. The Family Empowerment and Disability Council shall, at a minimum, do all of the following:

-Statewide Council

(a) Provide central coordination of training and information dissemination, content, and materials for Family Empowerment Centers on Disability.

(b) Develop a technical assistance system and activities in accordance with a plan developed in conjunction with the directors of the Family Empowerment Centers on Disability.

(c) Ensure that a periodic assessment and evaluation of the service delivery and management of each Family Empowerment Center on Disability conducted by Family Empowerment Center on Disability directors and includes on the assessment and evaluation team at least one parent advocate from another region. The goal shall be to improve center management and the quality and efficiency of services delivered.

(d) Assist each center to build its capacity to serve its geographic region.

(e) Develop uniform tracking and data collection systems, which are not duplicative and interface with existing special education data systems, to be utilized by each Family Empowerment Center on Disability.

(f) Establish outcome-based evaluation procedures and processes to be used by the State Department of Education.

(g) Conduct media outreach and other public education efforts to promote the goals of the Family Empowerment Centers on Disability.

(h) Support and coordinate system change advocacy efforts at the local, state, and national level.

56412. When at least four Family Empowerment Centers on Disability have been in operation for two years, the State Department of Education shall contract, pursuant to funding made available in that fiscal year's Budget Act, with an outside entity to conduct an evaluation of the effectiveness of the services provided by the centers, including, but not limited to, the number of parents who have been trained, the number of cases handled by the centers, an estimate of the number of lawsuits avoided, and the overall effectiveness of the centers.

- Evaluation of the Effectiveness of Services Provided by Centers

56414. The State Department of Education is required to implement this chapter only if an appropriation is made for this purpose in the Budget Act.

- Implementation Based on Funds Appropriated

NOTE

(1) Chapter 4.3 (commencing with Section 56400) was added to Part 30 of the Education Code by Senate Bill 511, Chapter 690, Statutes of 2001.

CHAPTER 4.4. EARLY EDUCATION FOR INDIVIDUALS WITH EXCEPTIONAL NEEDS

56425. As a condition of receiving state aid pursuant to this part, each district, special education local plan area, or county office that operated early education programs for individuals with exceptional needs younger than three years of age, as defined in Section 56026, and that received state or federal aid for special education for those programs in the 1980-81 fiscal year, shall continue to operate early education programs in the 1981-82 fiscal year and each fiscal year thereafter.

- Infant Program Mandate

If a district or county office offered those programs in the 1980-81 fiscal year but in a subsequent year transfers the programs to another district or county office in the special education local plan area, the district or county office shall be exempt from the provisions of this section in any year when the programs are offered by the district or county office to which they were transferred.

- Program Transfer

A district, special education local plan area, or county office that is required to offer a program pursuant to this section shall be eligible for funding pursuant to Section 56432.

- Funding

This section shall become operative on July 1, 1998.

- Operative Date

56425.5. The Legislature hereby finds and declares that early education programs for infants identified as individuals with exceptional needs that provide educational services with active parent involvement, can significantly reduce the potential impact of many disabling conditions, and positively influence later development when the child reaches schoolage.

- Legislative Findings, Declarations and Intent

Early education programs funded pursuant to Sections 56427, 56428, and 56432 shall provide a continuum of program options provided by a transdiciplinary team to meet the multiple and varied needs of infants and their families. Recognizing the parent as the infant's primary teacher, it is the Legislature's intent that early education programs shall include opportunities for the family to receive home visits and to participate in family involvement activities pursuant to Sections 56426.1 and 56426.4. It is the intent of the Legislature that, as an infant grows older, program emphasis would shift from home-based services to a combination of home-based and group services.

It is further the intent of the Legislature that services

rendered by state and local agencies serving infants with exceptional needs and their families be coordinated and maximized.

This section shall become operative on July 1, 1998.

- Operative Date

56426. An early education program shall include services specially designed to meet the unique needs of infants, from birth to three years of age, and their families. The primary purpose of an early education program is to enhance development of the infant. To meet this purpose, the program shall focus upon the infant and his or her family, and shall include home visits, group services, and family involvement activities. Early education programs funded pursuant to Sections 56427, 56428, and 56432 shall include, as program options, home-based services pursuant to Section 56426.1 and home-based and group services pursuant to Section 56426.2, and shall be provided in accordance with the Individuals with Disabilities Education Act (20 U.S.C. Secs. 1431 to 1445, incl.), and the California Early Intervention Services Act, Title 14 (commencing with Section 95000) of the Government Code.

- Purpose and Focus

- Program Options

This section shall become operative on July 1, 1998.

- Operative Date
- Home-Based Services

56426.1. (a) Home-based early education services funded pursuant to Sections 56427, 56428, and 56432 shall include, but not be limited to, all of the following:

(1) Observing the infant's behavior and development in his or her natural environment.

(2) Presenting activities that are developmentally appropriate for the infant and are specially designed, based on the infant's exceptional needs, to enhance the infant's development. Those activities shall be developed to conform with the infant's individualized family service plan and to ensure that they do not conflict with his or her medical needs.

(3) Modeling and demonstrating developmentally appropriate activities for the infant to the parents, siblings, and other caregivers, as designated by the parent.

(4) Interacting with the family members and other caregivers, as designated by the parent, to enhance and reinforce their development of skills necessary to promote the infant's development.

(5) Discussing parental concerns related to the infant and the family, and supporting parents in coping with their infant's needs.

(6) Assisting parents to solve problems, to seek other services in their community, and to coordinate the services provided by various agencies.

(b) The frequency of home-based services shall be once or twice a week, depending on the needs of the infant and the family.

- Frequency of Home-Based Services

(c) This section shall become operative on July 1, 1998.

- Operative Date

56426.2. (a) Early education services funded pursuant to Sections 56427, 56428, and 56432 shall be provided through both home visits and group settings with other infants, with or without the parent. Home-based and group services shall include, but not be limited to, all of the following:

- Home Visits and Group Services

(1) All services identified in subdivision (a) of Section 56426.1.

(2) Group and individual activities that are developmentally appropriate and specially designed, based on the infant's exceptional needs, to enhance the infant's development. Those activities shall be developed to conform with the infant's individualized family service plan and to ensure that they do not conflict with his or her medical needs.

(3) Opportunities for infants to socialize and participate in play and exploration activities.

(4) Transdisciplinary services by therapists, psychologists, and other specialists as appropriate.

(5) Access to various developmentally appropriate equipment and specialized materials.

(6) Opportunities for family involvement activities, including parent education and parent support groups.

(b) Services provided in a center under this chapter shall not include child care or respite care.

- Services Shall Not Include Child Care or Respite Care

(c) The frequency of group services shall not exceed three hours a day for up to, and including, three days a week, and shall be determined on the basis of the needs of the infant and the family.

- Frequency of Group Services

(d) The frequency of home visits provided in conjunction with group services shall range from one to eight visits per month, depending on the needs of the infant and the family.

- Frequency of Home Visits

(e) Group services shall be provided on a ratio of no more than four infants to one adult.

- Group Services Ratio

(f) Parent participation in group services shall be encouraged.

- Parent Participation

(g) This section shall become operative on July 1, 1998.

- Operative Date

56426.25. The maximum service levels set forth in Sections 56426.1 and 56426.2 apply only for purposes of the allocation of funds for early education programs pursuant to Sections 56427, 56428, and 56432, and may be exceeded by a district, special education local plan area, or county office, in accordance with the infants' individualized family

- Maximum Service Levels

service plan, provided that no change in the level of entitlement to state funding under this part thereby results.

This section shall become operative on July 1, 1998.

- Operative Date

56426.3. In addition to home-based or home-based and group early education services, related services as defined in Section 300.13 of Title 34 of the Code of Federal Regulations, as that section read on April 1, 1986, shall be available to infants and their families. Related services may be provided in the home or at the center according to needs of the infant and the family.

- Related Services

56426.4. (a) Family involvement activities funded pursuant to Sections 56427, 56428, and 56432 shall support family members in meeting the practical and emotional issues and needs of raising their infant. These activities may include, but are not limited to, the following:

- Family Involvement Activities

(1) Educational programs that present information or demonstrate techniques to assist the family to promote their infant's development.

(2) Parent education and training to assist families in understanding, planning for, and meeting the unique needs of their infant.

(3) Parent support groups to share similar experiences and possible solutions.

(4) Instruction in making toys and other materials appropriate to their infant's exceptional needs and development.

(b) The frequency of family involvement activities shall be at least once a month.

- Frequency – At Least Once a Month

(c) Participation by families in family involvement activities shall be voluntary.

- Participation by Families Shall Be Voluntary

(d) This section shall become operative on July 1, 1998.

- Operative Date

56426.5. If the transdisciplinary team determines home-based and group early education services to be appropriate, but the parent chooses not to receive home-based services, group services shall be made available to the infant. Similarly, the choice not to participate in family involvement activities shall not limit the availability to the infant and his or her family of home-based services or home-based and group services as determined appropriate by the individualized education program team.

- Parental Choice

56426.6. (a) Early education services shall be provided by the district, special education local plan area, or county office through a transdisciplinary team consisting of a group of professionals from various disciplines, agencies, and parents who shall share their expertise and services to provide

- Services Provided Through Transdisciplinary Team

appropriate services for infants and their families. Each team member shall be responsible for providing and coordinating early education services for one or more infants and their families, and shall serve as a consultant to other team members and as a provider of appropriate related services to other infants in the program.

(b) Credentialed personnel with expertise in vision or hearing impairments shall be made available by the district, special education local plan area, or county office to early education programs serving infants identified in accordance with subdivision (a), (b), or (d) of Section 3030 of Title 5 of the California Code of Regulations, and shall be the primary providers of services under those programs whenever possible.

- Provision of Services for Vision and Hearing Impairments

(c) Transdisciplinary teams may include, but need not be limited to, qualified persons from the following disciplines:

- Composition of Transdisciplinary Team

(1) Early childhood special education.

(2) Speech and language therapy.

(3) Nursing, with a skill level not less than that of a registered nurse.

(4) Social work, psychology, or mental health.

(5) Occupational therapy.

(6) Physical therapy.

(7) Audiology.

(8) Parcnt to parent support.

(d) Any person who is authorized by the district, special education local plan area, or county office to provide early education or related services to infants shall have appropriate experience in normal and atypical infant development and an understanding of the unique needs of families of infants with exceptional needs, or, absent that experience and understanding, shall undergo a comprehensive training plan for that purpose, which plan shall be developed and implemented as part of the staff development component of the local plan for early education services.

- Personnel Experience

56426.7. Medically necessary occupational therapy and physical therapy shall be provided to the infant when warranted by medical diagnosis and contained in the individualized family service plan, as specified under Chapter 26.5 (commencing with Section 7570) of Division 7 of Title 1 of the Government Code.

- Medically Necessary OT/PT

56426.8. (a) Early education and related services shall be based on the needs of the infant and the family as determined by the individualized family service plan team, and shall be specified in the individualized family service plan, including

- Education and Services Based on Needs of Infant and Family

the frequency and duration of each type of service. Any early education or related service may be provided only upon written parental consent.

(b) The individualized family service plan for any infant shall be developed in consultation with the infant's physician in order to ensure that the services specified in the plan do not conflict with the infant's medical needs.

56426.9. Any child who becomes three years of age while participating in an early education program under this chapter may continue in the program until June 30 of the current program year, if the individualized education program team determines that the preschooler is eligible pursuant to Section 56441.11, develops an individualized education program, and determines that the early education program remains appropriate. No later than June 30 of that year, the individualized education program team shall meet to review the preschooler's progress and revise the individualized education program accordingly. The individualized education program team meeting shall be conducted by the local educational agency responsible for the provision of preschool special education services. Representatives of the early education program shall be invited to that meeting.

56427. (a) Not less than two million three hundred twenty-four thousand dollars ($2,324,000) of the federal discretionary funds appropriated to the State Department of Education under the Individuals with Disabilities Education Act (20 U.S.C. Sec. 1400 et seq.) in any fiscal year shall be expended for early education programs for infants with exceptional needs and their families, until the department determines, and the Legislature concurs, that the funds are no longer needed for that purpose.

(b) Programs ineligible to receive funding pursuant to Section 56425 or 56432 may receive funding pursuant to subdivision (a).

(c) This section shall become operative on July 1, 1998.

56428. (a) For the 1985-86 fiscal year, and each fiscal year thereafter, any instructional personnel service unit that was used in the prior fiscal year to provide services to children younger than three years of age shall continue to be used for that purpose. If a special education local plan area becomes ineligible for all or any portion of those instructional personnel service units operated and fundable in the prior fiscal year, the Superintendent of Public Instruction shall allocate those units to another local plan area for the purpose of providing services to children younger than three years of

- Infant's Physician

- Services Beyond Age Three

- Federal Funds for Infant Programs

- Funding Options

- Operative Date

- Maintenance of Infant Services

age.

(b) In the 1998-99 fiscal year, the instructional personnel service unit rates used to compute state funding under this chapter shall be adjusted to represent the actual, historic inflation adjustment amount funded for each provider of early education services under this chapter. To make this adjustment, the superintendent shall make the following calculation:

- Inflation Adjustment

(1) Divide the amount of funding received by the special education local plan area in the 1997-98 fiscal year from property taxes and state aid, after applying the deficit, for early education for individuals with exceptional needs by the amount the special education local plan area was entitled to receive for the 1997-98 fiscal year for that program.

(2) Multiply the amount determined in paragraph (1) by the instructional personnel service unit rates for the 1997-98 fiscal year used to compute state funding for early education for individuals with exceptional needs prior to the application of the inflation adjustment for the 1998-99 fiscal year.

(c) For the 1998-99 fiscal year, the department shall transfer an amount from schedule (a) to schedule (b) of Item 6110-161-0001 of Section 2.00 of the Budget Act of 1998, equal to the amount determined by the department, with the approval of the Department of Finance, to be the amount of funding received by the special education local plan area from property taxes in the 1997-98 fiscal year for early education programs for individuals with exceptional needs, multiplied by the inflation factor computed pursuant to Section 42238.1 for the 1998-99 fiscal year and adjusted for the estimated growth in average daily attendance for kindergarten and grades 1 to 12, inclusive, pursuant to the May Revision of the Governor's Budget for the 1998-99 fiscal year.

- Transfer of Funds

56429. In order to assure the maximum utilization and coordination of local early education services, eligibility for the receipt of funds pursuant to Section 56425, 56427, 56428, or 56432 is conditioned upon the approval by the superintendent of a local plan for early education services, which approval shall apply for not less than one, nor more than four, years. The local plan shall identify existing public and private early education services, and shall include an interagency plan for the delivery of early education services in accordance with the California Early Intervention Services Act, Title 14 (commencing with Section 95000) of the Government Code.

- Local Plan for Early Education Services

This section shall become operative on July 1, 1998.

- Operative Date

56430. (a) Early education services may be provided by any of the following methods:

- Methods of Providing Services

(1) Directly by a local educational agency.

(2) Through an interagency agreement between a local educational agency and another public agency.

(3) Through a contract with another public agency pursuant to Section 56369.

(4) Through a contract with a certified nonpublic, nonsectarian school, or nonpublic, nonsectarian agency pursuant to Section 56366.

(5) Through a contract with a nonsectarian hospital in accordance with Section 56361.5.

(b) Contracts or agreements with agencies identified in subdivision (a) for early education services are strongly encouraged when early education services are currently provided by another agency, and when found to be a cost-effective means of providing the services. The placement of individual infants under the contract shall not require specific approval by the governing board of the district or the county office.

- Contracts or Agreements

(c) Early education services provided under this chapter shall be funded pursuant to Sections 56427, 56428, and 56432.

- Funding

(d) This section shall become operative on July 1, 1998.

- Operative Date

56431. The superintendent shall develop procedures and criteria to enable a district, special education local plan area, or county office to contract with private nonprofit preschools or child development centers to provide special education and related services to infant and preschool age individuals with exceptional needs. The criteria shall include minimum standards that the private, nonprofit preschool or center shall be required to meet.

- Criteria for Private Preschool Contracting

56432. (a) For the 1998-99 fiscal year and each fiscal year thereafter, a special education local plan area shall be eligible for state funding of those instructional personnel service units operated and fundable for services to individuals with exceptional needs younger than three years of age at the second principal apportionment of the prior fiscal year, as long as the pupil count of these pupils divided by the number of instructional personnel service units is not less than the following:

- SELPA Funding for 1998-99 and Each Subsequent Fiscal Year

(1) For special classes and centers--12, based on the unduplicated pupil count.

(2) For resource specialist programs--24, based on the unduplicated pupil count.

(3) For designated instruction and services--12, based on the unduplicated pupil count, or 39, based on the duplicated pupil count.

(b) A special education local plan area shall be eligible for state funding of instructional personnel service units for services to individuals with exceptional needs younger than three years of age in excess of the number of instructional personnel service units operated and fundable at the second principal apportionment of the prior fiscal year only with the authorization of the superintendent.

- Funding for Excess Number of Units

(c) The superintendent shall base the authorization of funding for special education local plan areas pursuant to this section, including the reallocation of instructional personnel service units, upon criteria that shall include, but not be limited to, the following:

- Criteria for Funding

(1) Changes in the total number of pupils younger than three years of age enrolled in special education programs.

(2) High- and low-average caseloads per instructional personnel service unit for each instructional setting.

(d) Infant programs in special classes and centers funded pursuant to this item shall be supported by two aides, unless otherwise required by the superintendent.

- Infant Programs in Special Classes and Centers

(e) Infant services in resource specialist programs funded pursuant to this item shall be supported by one aide.

- Infant Services in Resource Specialist Programs

(f) When units are allocated pursuant to this subdivision, the superintendent shall allocate only the least expensive unit appropriate.

- Superintendent Shall Allocate Only Least Expensive Unit Appropriate

(g) Notwithstanding Sections 56211 and 56212, a special education local plan area may apply for, and the superintendent may grant, a waiver of any of the standards and criteria specified in this section if compliance would prevent the provision of a free, appropriate public education or would create undue hardship. In granting the waivers, the superintendent shall give priority to the following factors:

- Superintendent Waivers of Standards and Criteria

(1) Applications from special education local plan areas for waivers for a period not to exceed three years to specifically maintain or increase the level of special education services necessary to address the special education service requirements of individuals with exceptional needs residing in sparsely populated districts or attending isolated schools designated in the application.

(A) Sparsely populated districts are school districts that meet one of the following conditions:

(i) A school district or combination of contiguous school districts in which the total enrollment is less than 600 pupils, kindergarten and grades 1 to 12, inclusive, and in which one or more of the school facilities is an isolated school.

(ii) A school district or combination of contiguous school districts in which the total pupil density ratio is less than 15 pupils, kindergarten and grades 1 to 12, inclusive, per square mile and in which one or more of the school facilities is an isolated school.

(B) Isolated schools are schools with enrollments of less than 600 pupils, kindergarten and grades 1 to 12, inclusive, that meet one or more of the following conditions:

(i) The school is located more than 45 minutes average driving time over commonly used and well-traveled roads from the nearest school, including schools in adjacent special education local plan areas, with an enrollment greater than 600 pupils, kindergarten and grades 1 to 12, inclusive.

(ii) The school is separated, by roads that are impassable for extended periods of time due to inclement weather, from the nearest school, including schools in adjacent special education local plan areas, with an enrollment greater than 600 pupils, kindergarten and grades 1 to 12, inclusive.

(iii) The school is of a size and location that, when its enrollment is combined with the enrollments of the two largest schools within an average driving time of not more than 30 minutes over commonly used and well-traveled roads, including schools in adjacent special education local plan areas, the combined enrollment is less than 600 pupils, kindergarten and grades 1 to 12, inclusive.

(iv) The school is the one of normal attendance for a severely disabled individual, as defined in Section 56030.5, or an individual with a low-incidence disability, as defined in Section 56026.5, who otherwise would be required to be transported more than 75 minutes, average one-way driving time over commonly used and well-traveled roads, to the nearest appropriate program.

(2) The location of licensed children's institutions, foster family homes, residential medical facilities, or similar facilities that serve children younger than three years of age and are within the boundaries of a local plan if 3 percent or more of the local plan's unduplicated pupil count resides in those facilities.

(h) By authorizing units pursuant to this section, the superintendent shall not increase the statewide total number of instructional personnel service units for purposes of state apportionments unless an appropriation specifically for growth in the number instructional personnel service units is

- Restriction on Increasing
Statewide Total Number of IPSUs

made in the annual Budget Act or other legislation. If that growth appropriation is made, units authorized by the superintendent pursuant to this section are subject to the restrictions that the units shall be funded only by that growth appropriation and no other funds may be apportioned for the units.

(i) The superintendent shall monitor the use of instructional personnel service units retained or authorized by the granting of waivers pursuant to subdivision (h) to ensure that the instructional personnel service units are used in a manner wholly consistent with the basis for the waiver request.

- Superintendent Shall Monitor Use of IPSUs Retained or Authorized by Waivers

(j) This section shall become operative July 1, 1998.

- Operative Date

56435. When a child with exceptional needs will be transferring to a local public school, the program may choose, with the permission of the parent or guardian, to transfer information from the previous year deemed beneficial to the pupil and the teacher, including, but not limited to, development issues, social interaction abilities, health background, and diagnostic assessments, if any, to the public school.

- Transfer of Information (1)

NOTE

(1) Education Code Section 56435 was added by Assembly Bill 1539, Chapter 629, Statutes of 2001.

CHAPTER 4.45. SPECIAL EDUCATION PROGRAMS FOR INDIVIDUALS WITH EXCEPTIONAL NEEDS BETWEEN THE AGES OF THREE AND FIVE YEARS, INCLUSIVE

56440. (a) Each special education local plan area shall submit a plan to the superintendent by September 1, 1987, for providing special education and services to individuals with exceptional needs, as defined by the State Board of Education, who are between the ages of three and five years, inclusive, who do not require intensive special education and services under Title II of the Education of the Handicapped Act Amendments of 1986, Public Law 99-457 (20 U.S.C. Secs. 1411, 1412, 1413, and 1419). — Local Plan

(b) The superintendent shall provide for a five-year phase-in of the individuals with exceptional needs qualifying for special education and services under Public Law 99-457 who do not require intensive special education and services, through an application process to be developed by the superintendent. — Five-Year Phase-In

(c) All individuals with exceptional needs between the ages of three and five years, inclusive, identified in subdivision (a) shall be served by the districts and county offices within each special education local plan area by June 30, 1992, to the extent required under federal law and pursuant to the local plan and application approved by the superintendent. — Serve All by June 30, 1992

(d) Individuals with exceptional needs between the ages of three and five years, inclusive, who are identified by the district, special education local plan area, or county office as requiring special education and services, as defined by the State Board of Education, shall be eligible for special education and services pursuant to this part and shall not be subject to any phase-in plan. — Eligibility

(e) In special education local plan areas where individuals with exceptional needs between the ages of three and five, inclusive, who do not require intensive special education and services, are expected to have an increased demand on school facilities as a result of projected growth, pursuant to this chapter, the special education local plan area director shall submit a written report on the impacted local educational agencies to the State Allocation Board by December 1, 1987. The State Allocation Board shall assess the situation and explore ways of resolving the school facilities impaction situation. — School Facilities Impaction

(f) The superintendent shall provide technical assistance to — Alternative Instructional Settings

local educational agencies in order to help identify suitable alternative instructional settings to alleviate the school facilities impaction situation. Alternative instructional settings may include, but are not limited to, state preschool programs, or the child's home. Nothing in this chapter shall cause the displacement of children currently enrolled in these settings.

(g) Special education facilities operated by local educational agencies serving children under this chapter and Chapter 4.4 (commencing with Section 56425) shall meet all applicable standards relating to fire, health, sanitation, and building safety, but are not subject to Chapter 3.4 (commencing with Section 1596.70), Chapter 3.5 (commencing with Section 1596.90), and Chapter 3.6 (commencing with Section 1597.30) of Division 2 of the Health and Safety Code.

— Special Education Facilities

(h) This chapter applies to all individuals with exceptional needs between the ages of three and five years, inclusive.

— Application of Chapter

56441. The Legislature hereby finds and declares that early education programs for individuals with exceptional needs between the ages of three and five years, inclusive, that provide special education and related services within the typical environment appropriate for young children, and include active parent involvement, may do the following:

— Legislative Findings and Declarations

(a) Significantly reduce the potential impact of any disabling conditions.

(b) Produce substantial gains in physical development, cognitive development, language and speech development, psychosocial development, and self-help skills development.

(c) Help prevent the development of secondary disabling conditions.

(d) Reduce family stresses.

(e) Reduce societal dependency and institutionalization.

(f) Reduce the need for special class placement in special education programs once the children reach schoolage.

(g) Save substantial costs to society and our schools.

56441.1. (a) Services rendered by state and local agencies serving preschool children with exceptional needs and their families shall be provided in coordination with other state and local agencies. Educational agencies offering similar educational services shall coordinate and not duplicate these services. The Superintendent of Public Instruction shall identify similar services by other state and local agencies. Any child identified as currently being served and qualified as an individual with exceptional needs as defined in Section 56026, and who meets the eligibility criteria of Section

— Services Provided in Coordination with Other Agencies

56441.11 shall be counted as an individual under the funding cap prescribed by Section 56447.

(b) As the preschool child approaches the age to enter an elementary school environment, the child's preparation shall be geared toward a readiness for kindergarten and later school success.

56441.2. An early education program for individuals with exceptional needs between the ages of three and five, inclusive, shall include specially designed services to meet the unique needs of preschool children and their families. To meet this purpose, the program focus is on the young child and his or her family and shall include both individual and small group services which shall be available in a variety of typical age-appropriate environments for young children, including the home, and shall include opportunities for active parent involvement. — Early Education Program

56441.3. (a) Early education services for preschool children may be provided to individuals or small groups and shall include: — Services to Individuals or Small Groups

(1) Observing and monitoring the child's behavior and development in his or her environment.

(2) Presenting activities that are developmentally appropriate for the preschool child and are specially designed, based on the child's exceptional needs, to enhance the child's development. Those activities shall be developed to conform with the child's individualized education program and shall be developed so that they do not conflict with his or her medical needs.

(3) Interacting and consulting with the family members, regular preschool teachers, and other service providers, as needed, to demonstrate developmentally appropriate activities necessary to implement the child's individualized education program in the appropriate setting pursuant to Section 56441.4 and necessary to reinforce the expansion of his or her skills in order to promote the child's educational development. These interactions and consultations may include family involvement activities.

(4) Assisting parents to seek and coordinate other services in their community that may be provided to their child by various agencies.

(5) Providing opportunities for young children to participate in play and exploration activities, to develop self-esteem, and to develop preacademic skills.

(6) Providing access to various developmentally appropriate equipment and specialized materials.

(7) Providing related services as defined in Section 300.13 of Title 34 of the Code of Federal Regulations, that include parent counseling and training to help parents understand the special needs of their children and their children's development, as that section read on May 1, 1987.

(b) The duration of group services shall not exceed four hours per day unless determined otherwise by the individualized education program team.

56441.4. Appropriate settings for these services include any of the following:

- Appropriate Setting

(a) The regular public or private nonsectarian preschool program.

(b) The child development center or family day care home.

(c) The child's regular environment that may include the home.

(d) A special site where preschool programs for both children with disabilities and children who are not disabled are located close to each other and have an opportunity to share resources and programming.

(e) A special education preschool program with children who are not disabled attending and participating for all or part of the program.

(f) A public school setting which provides an age-appropriate environment, materials, and services, as defined by the superintendent.

56441.5. Appropriate instructional adult-to-child ratios for group services shall be dependent on the needs of the child. However, because of the unique needs of individuals with exceptional needs between the ages of three and five years, inclusive, who require special education and related services, the number of children per instructional adult shall be less than ratios set forth in subsection (b) of Section 18204 of Title 5 of the California Code of Regulations, as it read on May 1, 1987, for young children in a regular preschool program. Group services provided to individuals with exceptional needs between the ages of three and five years, inclusive, identified as severely disabled pursuant to Section 56030.5 shall not exceed an instructional adult-to-child ratio of one to five.

- Instructional Adult-to-Child Ratios

56441.6. Early education services for preschool children shall be provided through a transdisciplinary team approach of professionals as described in Section 56426.6. Responsibilities of early education program staff shall include consultation with regular preschool program providers, consultation with other specialists, assessment services, and

- Transdisciplinary Team Approach

direct services.

56441.7. (a) The maximum caseload for a speech and language specialist providing services exclusively to individuals with exceptional needs, between the ages of three and five years, inclusive, as defined in Section 56441.11 or 56026, shall not exceed a count of 40.

(b) The superintendent shall issue caseload guidelines or proposed regulations to local educational agencies for individuals with exceptional needs between the ages of three and five years, inclusive, by January 1, 1988.

56441.8. Early education services for preschoolers may be provided by any of the following methods:

(a) Directly by a local educational agency.

(b) Through an interagency agreement between a local educational agency and another public agency.

(c) Through a contract with another public agency pursuant to Section 56369.

(d) Through a contract with a certified nonpublic, nonsectarian school; or nonpublic, nonsectarian agency pursuant to Section 56366.

(e) Through a contract with a nonsectarian hospital in accordance with Section 56361.5.

56441.9. Contracts or agreements with agencies identified in Section 56441.8 are strongly encouraged when these services are currently provided by another agency, and when found to be a cost-effective means of providing the services. The placement of an individual preschool child under any of these contracts shall not require specific approval by the governing board of the school district or the county superintendent of schools.

56441.11. (a) Notwithstanding any other provision of law or regulation, the special education eligibility criteria in subdivision (b) shall apply to preschool children, between the ages of three and five years.

(b) A preschool child, between the ages of three and five years, qualifies as a child who needs early childhood special education services if the child meets the following criteria:

(1) Is identified as having one of the following disabling conditions, as defined in Section 300.7 of Title 34 of the Code of Federal Regulations, or an established medical disability, as defined in subdivision (d):

(A) Autism.

(B) Deaf-blindness.

(C) Deafness.

(D) Hearing impairment.

- Maximum Caseload for Speech and Language Specialist

- Caseload Guidelines/Proposed Regulations

- Methods of Providing Early Education Services

- Contracts/Agreements

- Eligibility Requirements for Preschool Children

- Disabling Conditions

(E) Mental retardation.

(F) Multiple disabilities.

(G) Orthopedic impairment.

(H) Other health impairment.

(I) Serious emotional disturbance.

(J) Specific learning disability.

(K) Speech or language impairment in one or more of voice, fluency, language and articulation.

(L) Traumatic brain injury.

(M) Visual impairment.

(N) Established medical disability.

(2) Needs specially designed instruction or services as defined in Sections 56441.2 and 56441.3.

- Needs Specially Designed Instruction or Service

(3) Has needs that cannot be met with modification of a regular environment in the home or school, or both, without ongoing monitoring or support as determined by an individualized education program team pursuant to Section 56431.

- Needs Cannot Be Met with Modifications of Regular Environment

(4) Meets eligibility criteria specified in Section 3030 of Title 5 of the California Code of Regulations.

- Meets Specified Eligibility Criteria

(c) A child is not eligible for special education and services if the child does not otherwise meet the eligibility criteria and his or her educational needs are due primarily to:

- Not Individual with Exceptional Needs

(A) Unfamiliarity with the English language.

(B) Temporary physical disabilities.

(C) Social maladjustment.

(D) Environmental, cultural, or economic factors.

(d) For purposes of this section, "established medical disability" is defined as a disabling medical condition or congenital syndrome that the individualized education program team determines has a high predictability of requiring special education and services.

- Definition of Established Medical Disability

(e) When standardized tests are considered invalid for children between the ages of three and five years, alternative means, for example, scales, instruments, observations, and interviews shall be used as specified in the assessment plan.

- Alternative Means to Standardized Tests

(f) In order to implement the eligibility criteria in subdivision (b), the superintendent shall:

- Implementing the Eligibility Criteria

(1) Provide for training in developmentally appropriate practices, alternative assessment and placement options.

(2) Provide a research-based review for developmentally appropriate application criteria for young children.

(3) Provide program monitoring for appropriate use of the eligibility criteria.

(g) If legislation is enacted mandating early intervention

- Reconsider Eligibility Criteria

services to infants and toddlers with disabilities pursuant to the Individuals with Disabilities Education Act (20 U.S.C. Sec. 1400 et seq.), the superintendent shall reconsider the eligibility criteria for preschool children, between the ages of three and five years, and recommend appropriate changes to the Legislature.

56441.13. The superintendent shall provide training and technical assistance for the implementation of early education programs for preschool children with exceptional needs, and shall develop:

- Training and Technical Assistance

(a) Methods and models for modifications to the regular program prior to referral.

(b) Guidelines for program providers.

(c) Curriculum and content for programs.

(d) Personnel standards for program providers.

(e) A plan to meet the unique needs of preschool children who require special education services and who are limited-English proficient and of diverse cultural backgrounds.

56441.14. Criteria and options for meeting the special education transportation needs of individuals with exceptional needs between the ages of three and five, inclusive, shall be included in the local transportation policy required pursuant to paragraph (5) of subdivision (b) of Section 56195.8.

- Transportation Criteria and Options

56442. The superintendent shall ensure that state preschool programs and programs for individuals with exceptional needs between the ages of three and five years, inclusive, provided pursuant to this part, are coordinated at the state and local levels.

- Coordination of Preschool Programs

56443. (a) The State Department of Education shall amend its interagency agreement with the Administration for Children, Youth, and Families, Region IX, Head Start, United States Department of Health and Human Services, to permit a district, special education local plan area, or county office to contract with a Head Start program for special education and services for individuals with exceptional needs between the ages of three and five years pursuant to this part.

- Head Start Interagency Agreement

(b) Apportionments allocated to Head Start programs for special education and services to individuals with exceptional needs between the ages of three and five years shall supplement and not supplant funds for which the Head Start programs are eligible, or are already receiving, from other funding sources.

- Supplement - Not Supplant - Head Start Funds

56445. (a) Prior to transitioning an individual with exceptional needs from a preschool program to kindergarten, or first grade as the case may be, an appropriate reassessment

- Reassessment Prior to Transitioning to Kindergarten or First Grade

of the individual shall be conducted pursuant to Article 2 (commencing with Section 56320) of Chapter 4 to determine if the individual is still in need of special education and services.

(b) It is the intent of the Legislature that gains made in the special education program for individuals who received special education and services, in accordance with this chapter, are not lost by too rapid a removal of individualized programs and supports for these individuals.

- Gains Made in Program

(c) As part of the transitioning process, a means of monitoring continued success of the child shall be identified by the individualized education program team for those children of kindergarten or first grade equivalency who are determined to be eligible for less intensive special education programs.

- Monitoring Continued Success

(d) As part of the exit process from special education, the present performance levels and learning style shall be noted by the individualized education program team. This information shall be made available to the assigned regular education teacher upon the child's enrollment in kindergarten or first grade as the case may be.

- Exit Process from Special Education

56446. Public special education funding shall not be used to purchase regular preschool services or to purchase any instructional service other than special education and services permitted by this chapter.

- Prohibition on Purchasing Regular Preschool Services

56447.1. (a) Nothing in this chapter shall be construed to limit the responsibility of noneducational public agencies in the State of California from providing or paying for some or all of the costs of a free appropriate public education for individuals with exceptional needs between the ages of three and five years, inclusive.

- Funding Responsibilities of Other Public Agencies

(b) Nothing in this chapter shall be construed to permit a noneducational public agency to reduce medical and other assistance available or to alter eligibility under Titles V and XIX of the Social Security Act (Subchapter V (commencing with Section 701) and Subchapter XIX (commencing with Section 1396) of Chapter 7 of Title 42 of the United States Code) with respect to the provision of a free appropriate public education for individuals with exceptional needs between the ages of three and five years, inclusive, within the State of California.

- Chapter Does Not Permit a Noneducational Public Agency to Reduce Medical/Other Assistance

56449. When a child between the ages of three and five years with special education needs will be transferring to a local public school, the program may choose, with the permission of the parent or guardian, to transfer information

- Transfer of Information (1)

from the previous year deemed beneficial to the pupil and the teacher, including, but not limited to, development issues, social interaction abilities, health background, and diagnostic assessments, if any, to the public school.

NOTE

(1) Education Code Section 56449 was added by Assembly Bill 1539, Chapter 629, Statutes of 2001.

CHAPTER 4.5. CAREER AND VOCATIONAL EDUCATION PROGRAMS, TRANSITION SERVICES, AND PROJECT WORKABILITY

Article 1. Career and Vocational Education Programs

56452. The superintendent shall ensure that the state annually secures all federal funds available for career and vocational education of individuals with exceptional needs.

- Secure Federal Funds

56453. The superintendent and the Department of Rehabilitation shall enter into an interagency agreement to ensure that the state annually secures all federal funds available under the Rehabilitation Act of 1973, as amended, and that coordination in applying for, distributing, and using funds available under the Vocational Education Act, as amended, the Rehabilitation Act of 1973, as amended, and the Education For All Handicapped Children Act of 1975, (P.L. 94-142), as amended, including, but not limited to, application for, and use thereof, be provided.

- Interagency Agreement with Department of Rehabilitation

56454. In order to provide districts, special education local plan areas, and county offices with maximum flexibility to secure and utilize all federal funds available to enable those entities to meet the career and vocational needs of individuals with exceptional needs more effectively and efficiently, and to provide maximum federal funding to those agencies for the provision of that education, the superintendent shall do all the following:

- State Superintendent's Responsibilities

(a) Provide necessary technical assistance to districts, special education local plan areas, and county offices.

(b) Establish procedures for these entities to obtain available federal funds.

(c) Apply for necessary waivers of federal statutes and regulations including, but not limited to, those governing federal career and vocational education programs.

56456. It is the intent of the Legislature that districts, special education local plan areas, and county offices may use any state or local special education funds for approved vocational programs, services, and activities to satisfy the excess cost matching requirements for receipt of federal vocational education funds for individuals with exceptional needs.

- Excess Cost Matching Requirements

Article 2. Transition Services

56460. The Legislature finds and declares all of the following:

- Legislative Findings and Declarations

(a) That while the passage of the Education for All Handicapped Children Act of 1975 (Public Law 94-142) and the California Master Plan for Special Education have resulted in improved educational services for individuals with exceptional needs; this has not translated into paid employment opportunities or maximum integration into our heterogeneous communities for individuals with exceptional needs.

(b) That there is no formalized process that bridges the gap between the security and structure of school and the complexity of service options and resources available for individuals with exceptional needs in the adult community.

(c) That there is insufficient coordination between educators, adult service providers, potential employers, and families and students in order to effectively plan and implement a successful transition for students to the adult world of paid employment and social independence.

(d) That because of insufficient vocational training throughout the middle and secondary school years, and effective interagency coordination and involvement of potential employers in a planning process, the majority of options available for individuals with exceptional needs in the adult community are programs that support dependence rather than independence.

(e) The goal of transition services is planned movement from secondary education to adult life that provides opportunities which maximize economic and social independence in the least restrictive environment for individuals with exceptional needs. Planning for transition from school to postsecondary environments should begin in the school system well before the student leaves the system.

56461. The superintendent shall establish the capacity to provide transition services for a broad range of individuals with exceptional needs such as employment and academic training, strategic planning, interagency coordination, and parent training.

- Services Cover a Broad Range of Individuals

56462. The transition services shall include, but not be limited to, the following:

- Components of Transition Services

(a) In-service training programs, resource materials, and handbooks that identify the following:

- In-service Training

(1) The definition of "transition," including the major

components of an effective school-based transition program.

(2) Relevant laws and regulations.

(3) The roles of other agencies in the transition process including, but not limited to, the scope of their services, eligibility criteria, and funding.

(4) The components of effective transition planning.

(5) The role of families in the individualized transition process.

(6) Resources and model programs currently available in this state.

(b) Development of the role and responsibilities of special education in the transition process, including the following:

- Role of Special Education in Transition Process

(1) The provision of work skills training, including those skills that are necessary in order to exhibit competence on the job.

(2) The provision of multiple employment options and facilitating job or career choice by providing a variety of vocational experiences.

(3) The collection and analysis of data on what happens to pupils once they leave the school system and enter the adult world.

(4) The coordination of the transition planning process, including development of necessary interagency agreements and procedures at both state and local levels.

(5) The provision of instructional learning strategies that will assist pupils who find learning difficult in acquiring skills that will enable them to obtain diplomas, promote a positive attitude toward secondary and postsecondary education and training, and make a successful transition to postsecondary life.

(c) The development and implementation of systematic and longitudinal vocational education curriculum including the following:

- Systematic and Longitudinal Vocational Education Curriculum

(1) Instructional strategies that will prepare pupils with severe disabilities to make a successful transition to supported employment and the community.

(2) The introduction of vocational and career education curriculum in the elementary grades for those pupils who can benefit from it.

(d) Materials, resource manuals, and in-service training programs to support the active participation of families in the planning and implementation of transition-related goals and activities.

- Support Active Participation of Families

(e) The development of resources and in-service training that will support the implementation of individualized

- Resources and In-service Training

transition planning for all pupils with exceptional needs.

(f) The development of a network of model demonstration sites that illustrate a wide variety of transition models and implementation strategies.

- Demonstration Sites

(g) Coordination with other specialized programs that serve students who face barriers to successful transition.

- Coordination with Other Programs

(h) A research, evaluation, and dissemination program that will support the major programmatic aspects of transition services. Through a variety of competitive grants, bids, contracts, and other awards specific content areas will be developed in cooperation with a variety of field-based agencies, including local education agencies, special education local plan areas, county offices, institutions of higher education, and in-service training agencies.

- Research, Evaluation, and Dissemination

56463. Transition services shall be funded pursuant to the Budget Act.

- Services Funded Pursuant to Budget Act

Article 3. Project Workability

56470. The Legislature finds and declares all of the following:

- Legislative Findings and Declarations

(a) That an essential component of transition services developed and supported by the State Department of Education is project workability.

(b) That the workability program provides instruction and experiences that reinforce core curriculum concepts and skills leading to gainful employment.

(c) That since project workability was established by the State Department of Education in 1981, substantial numbers of individuals with exceptional needs have obtained full- or part-time employment.

(d) That project workability is a true partnership established at the state level through nonfinancial interagency agreements between the State Department of Education, the Department of Employment Development, and the Department of Rehabilitation, and has elevated awareness in the private sector of the employment potential of individuals with exceptional needs, and focuses its efforts in developing careers for these youth, and preventing needless economic and social dependency on state and community agencies and resources.

(e) That local education agencies in California establish linkage between agencies, eliminate duplication of effort, and develop precedent-setting employment training practices which should be preserved and advanced to better assure future productive employable citizens.

56471. (a) The program shall be administered by the State Department of Education.

- Administration of Workability Program

(b) The department shall establish an advisory committee. This committee will include representatives from local workability projects to ensure ongoing communications.

- Advisory Committee

(c) The superintendent shall develop criteria for awarding grants, funding, and evaluating workability projects.

- Grants, Funding, and Evaluation

(d) Workability project applications shall include, but are not limited to, the following elements: (1) recruitment, (2) assessment, (3) counseling, (4) preemployment skills training, (5) vocational training, (6) student wages for try-out employment, (7) placement in unsubsidized employment, (8) other assistance with transition to a quality adult life, and (9) utilization of an interdisciplinary advisory committee to enhance project goals.

- Project Applications

56472. The population served by workability projects may include secondary students with disabilities, adults with disabilities and other individuals who experience barriers to successful completion of school.

- Population Served

56473. Project workability shall be funded pursuant to Item 6100-161-001 and Item 6100-161-890 of the Budget Act.

- Funded Pursuant to Budget Act

56474. The superintendent shall continue to seek additional state and federal funding for project workability.

- Seek Additional Funding

CHAPTER 4.7. INTERAGENCY AGREEMENTS

56475. (a) The superintendent and the directors of the State Department of Health Services, the State Department of Mental Health, the State Department of Developmental Services, the State Department of Social Services, the Department of Rehabilitation, the Department of the Youth Authority, and the Employment Development Department shall develop written interagency agreements or adopt joint regulations that include fiscal responsibilities for the provision of special education and related services to individuals with exceptional needs in the State of California.

(b) The superintendent shall develop interagency agreements with other state and local public agencies, as deemed necessary by the superintendent, to carry out the provisions of state and federal law.

(c) (1) Each interagency agreement shall be submitted by the superintendent to each legislative fiscal committee, education committee, and policy committee, responsible for legislation relating to those individuals with exceptional needs that will be affected by the agreement if it is effective.

(2) An interagency agreement shall not be effective sooner than 30 days after it has been submitted to each of the legislative committees specified in paragraph (1).

- Written Agreement

- Fiscal Responsibilities

- Other Agreements

- Submit to Legislature

- Effective Date of Agreements

CHAPTER 4.9. ALTERNATIVE HEARING PROCESS PILOT PROJECT

56490. (a) Subject to an appropriation in the annual Budget Act or any other measures for these purposes, the State Department of Education shall select and allocate funds to three special education local plan areas to implement a three-year pilot project for alternative due process hearing procedures.

    - Three-Year Pilot Project

(b) To be eligible for selection for participation, a special education local plan area shall submit an application to the department based on criteria developed by the department.

    - Application Process

(c) The department shall select special education local plan areas that reflect the diversity of special education local plan areas in the state and ensure representation of urban, suburban, and small or rural special education local plan areas and northern, southern, and central regions of the state.

    - Reflect SELPA Diversity

(d) If funds are appropriated for the purposes of this chapter, the total sum of expenditures shall not exceed seven hundred thousand dollars ($700,000), pursuant to the following schedule:

    - Funding Limitations

(1) Five hundred thousand dollars ($500,000) for the purposes of implementing Section 56493.

(2) One hundred thousand dollars ($100,000) for the purposes of implementing Section 56492.

(3) One hundred thousand dollars ($100,000) for the purposes of implementing Section 56494.

56491. A special education local plan area selected pursuant to Section 56490 shall be subject to Chapter 5 (commencing with Section 56500).

    - Subject to Chapter 5

56492. A hearing officer employed pursuant to Section 56504.5 shall implement, in a special education local plan area selected pursuant to Section 56490, a voluntary, simplified nonattorney alternative process based on settlement and alternative dispute resolution models that would include, but not be limited to, all of the following:

    - Description of Alternative Process

(a) No rules of evidence, except for rules regarding privileged communications and hearsay.

(b) Presentation of evidence could be sharply curtailed.

(c) Parents shall represent themselves.

(d) Schoolsite staff, not central office staff, shall represent the district.

(e) The hearing should last no more than one day.

(f) Participation in the process established by this section does not waive a person's ability to exercise his or her rights to the due process procedure available pursuant to Chapter 5 (commencing with Section 56500). The decision issued pursuant to the process established by this section is not binding in any subsequent exercise of the person's right to due process proceedings pursuant to Chapter 5 (commencing with Section 56500). If a person elects to exercise his or her right to due process proceedings pursuant to Chapter 5 (commencing with Section 56500) after participating in the process established by this section, the subsequent proceeding shall be conducted by a different hearing officer who shall not communicate, and shall not have communicated, directly or indirectly, with the hearing officer who conducted the proceeding prescribed by this section regarding the nature or facts of the parties' dispute or the legal conclusions drawn or to be drawn thereon.

56493. (a) A special education local plan area selected pursuant to Section 56490 shall establish public advocacy services using an independent contractor to provide free advocacy and legal services to parents of pupils with disabilities. Services shall include all of the following:

— Public Advocacy Services

(1) Information about special education services, how to obtain services, including the individualized education program process, and the right to services under federal and state law.

(2) Representation in mediation and due process hearings at no charge.

(b) To be eligible for selection as an independent contractor to provide services pursuant to this chapter, the contractor shall demonstrate all of the following:

(1) Knowledge of the special education system and rights of pupils with disabilities.

(2) The ability to work effectively with pupils with disabilities, families of pupils with disabilities, school personnel, community groups, and other advocacy organizations.

(3) Skills in interviewing pupils with disabilities and their families, counseling individuals about their rights, and representation of pupils with disabilities in mediation and due process hearings.

(c) Compliance by the contractor with the terms of the contract shall be evaluated by the participating special education local plan area using objective performance measures that shall be specified in the contract.

(d) In order to be eligible under this section, the contractor shall not have represented a school district within the special education local plan area or any other education agency in any legal matter at any time prior to entering into the contract to provide advocacy services pursuant to this section.

56494. (a) On or before January 1, 2003, each special local plan area participating in the pilot project established pursuant to this chapter, shall submit a report to the Legislative Analyst, including, but not limited to, all of the following:

- Submit Report to Legislative Analyst

(1) The amount of funds used and the proportion used for small claims and legal services.

(2) The participation rate of pupils with special needs and their families in the programs offered pursuant to this chapter.

(3) The outcomes of participation in the small claims program, including how many cases were successfully dispensed with and how many cases continued through the existing due process hearing procedure available pursuant to Chapter 5 (commencing with Section 56500) of Part 30.

(4) The outcomes of the use of free legal services.

(5) Input from participating pupils and parents.

(b) On or before March 1, 2003, the Legislative Analyst shall coordinate the reports submitted pursuant to subdivision (a), analyze the data, compile one comprehensive evaluation, and submit the evaluation to the State Department of Education, the Legislature, and the Governor.

(c) Any funds appropriated for the evaluation shall be provided to the Legislative Analyst. No funds appropriated for the evaluation shall be provided to any participating special education local plan area.

56495. This chapter shall remain in effect only until January 1, 2004, and as of that date is repealed, unless a later enacted statute, that is enacted before January 1, 2004, deletes or extends that date.

- Repeal Clause; Inoperative 1-1-04

CHAPTER 5. PROCEDURAL SAFEGUARDS

56500. As used in this chapter, "public education agency" means a district, special education local plan area, or county office, depending on the category of local plan elected by the governing board of a school district pursuant to Section 56195.1, or any other public agency providing special education or related services.

- Definition of Public Education Agency

56500.1. (a) All procedural safeguards under the Individuals with Disabilities Education Act (20 U.S.C. Sec. 1400 and following) shall be established and maintained by each noneducational and educational agency that provides education, related services, or both, to children who are individuals with exceptional needs.

- Federal Procedural Safeguards

(b) At each individualized education program meeting, the public education agency responsible for convening the meeting shall inform the parent and pupil of the federal and state procedural safeguards that were provided in the notice of parent rights pursuant to Section 56321.

- Inform Parent/Pupil of Procedural Safeguards

56500.2. An expeditious and effective process shall be implemented for the resolution of complaints regarding any alleged violations of the Individuals with Disabilities Education Act (20 U.S.C. Sec. 1400 and following).

- Resolution of Complaints

56500.3 (a) It is the intent of the Legislature that parties to special education disputes be encouraged to seek resolution through mediation prior to filing a request for a due process hearing. It is also the intent of the Legislature that these voluntary prehearing request mediation conferences be an informal process conducted in a nonadversarial atmosphere to resolve issues relating to the identification, assessment, or educational placement of the child, or the provision of a free, appropriate public education to the child, to the satisfaction of both parties. Therefore, attorneys or other independent contractors used to provide legal advocacy services shall not attend or otherwise participate in the prehearing request mediation conferences.

- Prehearing Mediation Conference

- Mediation Conference Conducted in Nonadversarial Atmosphere

(b) Nothing in this part shall preclude the parent or the public education agency from being accompanied and advised by nonattorney representatives in the mediation conferences and consulting with an attorney prior to or following a mediation conference. For purposes of this section, "attorney" means an active, practicing member of the State Bar of California or another independent contractor used to provide legal advocacy services, but does not mean a parent of the pupil who is also an attorney.

- Nonattorney Representative

(c) Requesting or participating in a mediation conference is not a prerequisite to requesting a due process hearing.

(d) All requests for a mediation conference shall be filed with the superintendent. The party initiating a mediation conference by filing a written request with the superintendent shall provide the other party to the mediation with a copy of the request at the same time the request is filed with the superintendent. The mediation conference shall be conducted by a person knowledgeable in the process of reconciling differences in a nonadversarial manner and under contract with the department pursuant to Section 56504.5. The mediator shall be knowledgeable in the laws and regulations governing special education.

(e) The prehearing mediation conference shall be scheduled within 15 days of receipt by the superintendent of the request for mediation. The mediation conference shall be completed within 30 days after receipt of the request for mediation unless both parties to the prehearing mediation conference agree to extend the time for completing the mediation.

(f) Based upon the mediation conference, the district superintendent, the county superintendent, or the director of the public education agency, or his or her designee, may resolve the issue or issues. However, this resolution shall not conflict with state or federal law and shall be to the satisfaction of both parties. A copy of the written resolution shall be mailed to each party within 10 days following the mediation conference.

(g) If the mediation conference fails to resolve the issues to the satisfaction of all parties, the party who requested the mediation conference has the option of filing for a state-level hearing pursuant to Section 56505. The mediator may assist the parties in specifying any unresolved issues to be included in the hearing request.

(h) Any mediation conference held pursuant to this section shall be held at a time and place reasonably convenient to the parent and pupil.

(i) The mediation conference shall be conducted in accordance with regulations adopted by the board.

(j) Notwithstanding any procedure set forth in this chapter, a public education agency and a parent may, if the party initiating the mediation conference so chooses, meet informally to resolve any issue or issues to the satisfaction of both parties prior to the mediation conference.

(k) The procedures and rights contained in this section

- Not a Prerequisite to Hearing

- Requests for Mediation Conference

- Mediator

- Scheduled Within 15 Days

- Resolution of Issues

- Failure to Resolve Issues

- Time and Place

- State Board of Education Regulations

- Meeting Informally to Resolve Issues

- Notice of Parent Rights

shall be included in the notice of parent rights attached to the pupil's assessment plan pursuant to Section 56321.

56501. (a) The due process hearing procedures prescribed by this chapter extend to the parent, as defined in Section 56028, a pupil who has been emancipated, and a pupil who is a ward or dependent of the court or for whom no parent can be identified or located when the hearing officer determines that either the local educational agency has failed to appoint a surrogate parent as required by Section 7579.5 of the Government Code or the surrogate parent appointed by the local educational agency does not meet the criteria set forth in subdivision (f) of Section 7579.5 of the Government Code, and the public education agency involved in any decisions regarding a pupil. The appointment of a surrogate parent after a hearing has been requested by the pupil shall not be cause for dismissal of the hearing request. The parent and the public education agency involved may initiate the due process hearing procedures prescribed by this chapter under any of the following circumstances:

(1) There is a proposal to initiate or change the identification, assessment, or educational placement of the child or the provision of a free, appropriate public education to the child.

(2) There is a refusal to initiate or change the identification, assessment, or educational placement of the child or the provision of a free, appropriate public education to the child.

(3) The parent refuses to consent to an assessment of the child.

(b) The due process hearing rights prescribed by this chapter include, but are not limited to, all the following:

(1) The right to a mediation conference pursuant to Section 56500.3.

(2) The right to request a mediation conference at any point during the hearing process. A mediation conference shall be scheduled if both parties to the hearing agree to mediate and are willing to extend the 45-day limit for issuing a hearing decision for a period equal to the length of the mediation process. This limitation on the period of extension is not applicable if the parties agree to take the hearing off calendar. Notwithstanding subdivision (a) of Section 56500.3, attorneys and advocates are permitted to participate in mediation conferences scheduled after the filing of a request for due process hearing.

(3) The right to examine pupil records pursuant to Section

- Due Process Hearing Procedures

- Due Process Hearing Circumstances

- Hearing Rights

56504. This provision shall not be construed to abrogate the rights prescribed by Chapter 6.5 (commencing with Section 49060) of Part 27.

(4) The right to a fair and impartial administrative hearing at the state level, before a person knowledgeable in the laws governing special education and administrative hearings, under contract with the department, pursuant to Section 56505.

(c) In addition to the rights prescribed by subdivision (b), the parent has the following rights:

- Additional Parent Rights

(1) The right to have the pupil who is the subject of the state hearing present at the hearing.

(2) The right to open the state hearing to the public.

56502. (a) All requests for a due process hearing shall be filed with the superintendent. The party initiating a due process hearing by filing a written request with the superintendent shall provide the other party to the hearing with a copy of the request at the same time as the request is filed with the superintendent. The superintendent shall take steps to ensure that within 45 days after receipt of the written hearing request the hearing is immediately commenced and completed, including, any mediation requested at any point during the hearing process pursuant to paragraph (2) of subdivision (b) of Section 56501, and a final administrative decision is rendered, unless a continuance has been granted pursuant to Section 56505.

- Written Request for Hearing

- Forty-five Days to Complete Hearing

(b) Notwithstanding any procedure set forth in this chapter, a public education agency and a parent may, if the party initiating the hearing so chooses, meet informally to resolve any issue or issues relating to the identification, assessment, or education and placement of the child, or the provision of a free, appropriate public education to the child, to the satisfaction of both parties prior to the hearing. The informal meeting shall be conducted by the district superintendent, county superintendent, or director of the public education agency or his or her designee. Any designee appointed pursuant to this subdivision shall have the authority to resolve the issue or issues.

- Informal Meeting to Resolve Issues

(c) Upon receipt by the superintendent of a written request by the parent or public education agency, the superintendent or his or her designee or designees shall immediately notify, in writing, all parties of the request for the hearing and the scheduled date for the hearing. The notice shall advise all parties of all their rights relating to procedural safeguards. The superintendent or his or her designee shall provide both

- Notification of All Parties

parties with a list of persons and organizations within the geographical area that can provide free or reduced cost representation or other assistance in preparing for the due process hearing. This list shall include a brief description of the requirement to qualify for the services. The superintendent or his or her designee shall have complete discretion in determining which individuals or groups shall be included on the list.

56503. Nothing in this chapter shall preclude the parties to a hearing from agreeing to use a mediation conference or resolving their dispute in an informal, nonadversarial manner, even though a request for a state level hearing has been filed or even if the hearing has commenced.

- Mediation Conference or Informal Meeting Are Options to Hearing

56504. The parent shall have the right and opportunity to examine all school records of the child and to receive copies pursuant to this section and to Section 49065 within five days after such request is made by the parent, either orally or in writing. A public educational agency may charge no more than the actual cost of reproducing such records, but if this cost effectively prevents the parent from exercising the right to receive such copy or copies the copy or copies shall be reproduced at no cost.

- Parent Right to Examine School Records/Receive Copies

56504.5. The department shall contract with a single, nonprofit organization or entity to conduct mediation conferences and due process hearings that does the following:

- Contract for Mediators and Hearing Officers

(a) Employs persons knowledgeable in administrative hearings and laws and regulations governing special education.

(b) Does not have a conflict of interest under state and federal laws and regulations governing special education and related services in conducting mediation conferences and due process hearings.

(c) Is not in the business of providing, or supervising, special education, related services, or care to children and youth.

56505. (a) The state hearing shall be conducted in accordance with regulations adopted by the board.

- State Hearing

(b) The hearing shall be held at a time and place reasonably convenient to the parent and the pupil.

- Time and Place

(c) The hearing shall be conducted by a person knowledgeable in the laws governing special education and administrative hearings pursuant to Section 56504.5. The hearing officer shall encourage the parties to a hearing to consider the option of mediation as an alternative to a hearing.

- Conducted by Knowledgeable Person

- Consider Option of Mediation

(d) During the pendency of the hearing proceedings, including the actual state level hearing, the pupil shall remain in his or her present placement, except as provided in Section 48915.5, unless the public agency and the parent agree otherwise. A pupil applying for initial admission to a public school shall, with the consent of his or her parent, be placed in the public school program until all proceedings have been completed.

- Pupil Placement During Hearing

(e) Any party to the hearing held pursuant to this section shall be afforded the following rights consistent with state and federal statutes and regulations:

- Additional Hearing Rights

(1) The right to be accompanied and advised by counsel and by individuals with special knowledge or training relating to the problems of children and youth with disabilities.

(2) The right to present evidence, written arguments, and oral arguments.

(3) The right to confront, cross-examine, and compel the attendance of witnesses.

(4) The right to a written or electronic verbatim record of the hearing.

(5) The right to written findings of fact and decisions. The findings and decisions shall be made available to the public consistent with the requirements of subsection (c) of Section 1417 of Title 20 of the United States Code and shall also be transmitted to the Advisory Commission on Special Education pursuant to paragraph (4) of subsection (h) of Section 1415 of Title 20 of the United States Code.

(6) The right to be informed by the other parties to the hearing, at least 10 days prior to the hearing, as to what those parties believe are the issues to be decided at the hearing and their proposed resolution of those issues. Upon the request of a parent who is not represented by an attorney, the agency responsible for conducting hearings shall provide a mediator to assist the parent in identifying the issues and the proposed resolution of the issues.

(7) The right to receive from other parties to the hearing, at least five business days prior to the hearing, a copy of all documents and a list of all witnesses and their general area of testimony that the parties intend to present at the hearing. Included in the material to be disclosed to all parties at least five business days prior to a hearing shall be all assessments completed by that date and recommendations based on the assessments that the parties intend to use at the hearing.

(f) The hearing conducted pursuant to this section shall be completed and a written, reasoned decision mailed to all

- Written Decision Within 45 Days

parties to the hearing within 45 days from the receipt by the superintendent of the request for a hearing. Either party to the hearing may request the hearing officer to grant an extension. The extension shall be granted upon a showing of good cause. Any extension shall extend the time for rendering a final administrative decision for a period only equal to the length of the extension.

- Extension

(g) The hearing conducted pursuant to this section shall be the final administrative determination and binding on all parties.

- Final Administrative Determination

(h) In decisions relating to the placement of individuals with exceptional needs, the person conducting the state hearing shall consider cost, in addition to all other factors that are considered.

- Hearing Officer Considers Cost

(i) Nothing in this chapter shall preclude a party from exercising the right to appeal the decision to a court of competent jurisdiction. An appeal shall be made within 90 days of receipt of the hearing decision. During the pendency of any administrative or judicial proceeding conducted pursuant to Chapter 5 (commencing with Section 56500), unless the public education agency and the parents of the child agree otherwise, the child involved in the hearing shall remain in his or her present educational placement.

- Right to Appeal to Court

(j) Any request for a due process hearing arising under subdivision (a) of Section 56501 shall be filed within three years from the date the party initiating the request knew or had reason to know of the facts underlying the basis for the request.

- Time Limitation for Requesting a Due Process Hearing

56505.1. The hearing officer may do any of the following during the hearing:

- Hearing Officer Rights

(a) Question a witness on the record prior to any of the parties doing so.

- Question Witness

(b) With the consent of both parties to the hearing, request that conflicting experts discuss an issue or issues with each other while on the record.

- Request That Conflicting Experts Discuss Issues

(c) Visit the proposed placement site or sites when the physical attributes of the site or sites are at issue.

- Visit Proposed Placement Sites

(d) Call a witness to testify at the hearing if all parties to the hearing consent to the witness giving testimony or the hearing is continued for at least five days after the witness is identified and before the witness testifies.

- Call a Witness

(e) Order that an impartial assessment of the pupil be conducted for purposes of the hearing and continue the hearing until the assessment has been completed. The cost of any assessment ordered under this subdivision shall be

- Order an Impartial Assessment

included in the contract between the department and the organization or entity conducting the hearing.

(f) Bar introduction of any documents or the testimony of any witnesses not disclosed to the hearing officer at least five business days prior to the hearing and bar introduction of any documents or the testimony of any witnesses not disclosed to the parties at least five business days prior to the hearing pursuant to paragraph (7) of subdivision (e) of Section 56505.

- Barring Introduction of Documents or Testimony

(g) In decisions relating to the provision of related services by other public agencies, the hearing officer may call as witnesses independent medical specialists qualified to present evidence in the area of the pupil's medical disability. The cost for any witness called to testify under this subdivision shall be included in the contract between the department and the organization or entity conducting the hearing.

- Call as Witnesses Independent Medical Specialists

56505.2. (a) A hearing officer may not render a decision that results in the placement of an individual with exceptional needs in a nonpublic, nonsectarian school, or that results in a service for an individual with exceptional needs provided by a nonpublic agency, if the school or agency has not been certified pursuant to Section 56366.1.

- Nonpublic School/Agency Placement and Service Restrictions

(b) A hearing officer shall consider Sections 56365, 56365.5, 56366, and 56366.1 during a due process hearing concerning an issue of placement of an individual with exceptional needs in a nonpublic, nonsectarian school, or services for an individual with exceptional needs provided by a nonpublic, nonsectarian agency.

56506. In addition to the due process hearing rights enumerated in subdivision (b) of 56501, the following due process rights extend to the pupil and the parent:

- Additional Due Process Rights

(a) Written notice to the parent of his or her rights in language easily understood by the general public and in the primary language of the parent or other mode of communication used by the parent, unless to do so is clearly not feasible. The written notice of rights shall include, but not be limited to, those prescribed by Section 56341.

(b) The right to initiate a referral of a child for special education services pursuant to Section 56303.

(c) The right to obtain an independent educational assessment pursuant to subdivision (b) of Section 56329.

(d) The right to participate in the development of the individualized education program and to be informed of the availability under state and federal law of free appropriate public education and of all available alternative programs, both public and nonpublic.

(e) Written parental consent pursuant to Section 56321 shall be obtained before any assessment of the pupil is conducted unless the public education agency prevails in a due process hearing relating to the assessment. Informed parental consent need not be obtained in the case of a reassessment of the pupil if the local educational agency can demonstrate that it has taken reasonable measures to obtain consent and the pupil's parent has failed to respond.

(f) Written parental consent pursuant to Section 56321 shall be obtained before the pupil is placed in a special education program.

56507. (a) If either party to a due process hearing intends to be represented by an attorney in the state hearing, notice of that intent shall be given to the other party at least 10 days prior to the hearing. The failure to provide that notice shall constitute good cause for a continuance.

- Use of Attorney

(b) An award of reasonable attorneys' fees to the prevailing parent, guardian, or pupil, as the case may be, may only be made either with the agreement of the parties following the conclusion of the administrative hearing process or by a court of competent jurisdiction pursuant to paragraph (3) of subsection (i) of Section 1415 of Title 20 of the United States Code.

- Award of Attorneys' Fees

(c) Public education agencies shall not use federal funds distributed under Part B of the Individuals with Disabilities Education Act (20 U.S.C. Sec. 1400 et seq.), or other federal special education funds, for the agency's own legal counsel or other advocacy costs, that may include, but are not limited to, a private attorney or employee of an attorney, legal paraprofessional, or other paid advocate, related to a due process hearing or the appeal of a hearing decision to the courts. Nor shall the funds be used to reimburse parents who prevail and are awarded attorneys' fees, pursuant to subdivision (b), as part of the judgment. Nothing in this subdivision shall preclude public agencies from using these funds for attorney services related to the establishment of policy and programs, or responsibilities, under Part B of the Individuals with Disabilities Education Act (20 U.S.C. Sec. 1400 et seq.) and the program administration of these programs. This subdivision does not apply to attorneys and others hired under contract to conduct administrative hearings pursuant to subdivision (a) of Section 56505.

- Use of Federal Funds

(d) The hearing decision shall indicate the extent to which each party has prevailed on each issue heard and decided, including issues involving other public agencies named as

- Extent Each Party Prevailed

parties to the hearing.

56508. It is the intent of the Legislature that the department develop training materials that can be used locally by parents, public education agencies, and others and conduct workshops on alternative resolutions for resolving differences in a nonadversarial atmosphere with the mutual goal of providing a free and appropriate public education for children and youth with disabilities.

- Training Materials for Alternative Resolutions of Differences

CHAPTER 5.5. BEHAVIORAL INTERVENTIONS

56520. (a) The Legislature finds and declares all of the following:

- Legislative Findings and Declarations

(1) That the state has continually sought to provide an appropriate and meaningful educational program in a safe and healthy environment for all children regardless of possible physical, mental, or emotionally disabling conditions.

(2) That teachers of children with special needs require training and guidance that provides positive ways for working successfully with children who have difficulties conforming to acceptable behavioral patterns in order to provide an environment in which learning can occur.

(3) That procedures for the elimination of maladaptive behaviors shall not include those deemed unacceptable under Section 49001 or those that cause pain or trauma.

(b) It is the intent of the Legislature:

- Legislative Intent

(1) That when behavioral interventions are used, they be used in consideration of the pupil's physical freedom and social interaction, be administered in a manner that respects human dignity and personal privacy, and that ensure a pupil's right to placement in the least restrictive educational environment.

(2) That behavioral management plans be developed and used, to the extent possible, in a consistent manner when the pupil is also the responsibility of another agency for residential care or related services.

(3) That a statewide study be conducted of the use of behavioral interventions with California individuals with exceptional needs receiving special education and related services.

(4) That training programs be developed and implemented in institutions of higher education that train teachers and that in-service training programs be made available as necessary in school districts and county offices of education to assure that adequately trained staff are available to work effectively with the behavioral intervention needs of individuals with exceptional needs.

56521. (a) This chapter applies to any individual with exceptional needs who is in a public school program, including a state school for the disabled pursuant to Part 32 (commencing with Section 59000), or who is placed in a nonpublic school program pursuant to Sections 56365 to 56366.5, inclusive.

- Application of Chapter

(b)   The Superintendent of Public Instruction shall monitor and supervise the implementation of this chapter.

- Monitor and Supervise

56523. (a) On or before September 1, 1992, the Superintendent of Public Instruction shall develop and the State Board of Education shall adopt regulations governing the use of behavioral interventions with individuals with exceptional needs receiving special education and related services.

- Regulations

(b)   The regulations shall do all of the following:

- Scope of Regulations

(1) Specify the types of positive behavioral interventions which may be utilized and specify that interventions which cause pain or trauma are prohibited.

(2) Require that, if appropriate, the pupil's individual education plan includes a description of the positive behavioral interventions to be utilized which accomplishes the following:

(A)   Assesses the appropriateness of positive interventions.

(B)   Assures   the   pupil's   physical   freedom,   social interaction, and individual choices.

(C)   Respects the pupil's human dignity and personal privacy.

(D)   Assures the pupil's placement in the least restrictive environment.

(E)   Includes the method of measuring the effectiveness of the interventions.

(F)   Includes a timeline for the regular and frequent review of the pupil's progress.

(3) Specify   standards   governing   the   application   of restrictive   behavioral   interventions   in   the   case   of emergencies.   These emergencies must pose a clear and present danger of serious physical harm to the pupil or others. These standards shall include:

(A)   The definition of an emergency.

(B)   The types   of behavioral interventions that may be utilized in an emergency.

(C)   The duration of the intervention which shall not be longer than is necessary to contain the dangerous behavior.

(D)   A process and timeline for the convening of an individual education plan meeting to evaluate the application of the emergency intervention and adjust the pupil's individual education plan in a manner designed to reduce or eliminate   the   negative   behavior   through   positive programming.

(E)   A   process   for   reporting   annually   to   the   State

Department of Education and the Advisory Commission on Special Education the number of emergency interventions applied under this chapter.

56524. The superintendent shall explore with representatives of institutions of higher education and the Commission on Teacher Credentialing, the current training requirements for teachers to ensure that sufficient training is available in appropriate behavioral interventions for people entering the field of education.

- Explore Current Training Requirements

CHAPTER 6. EVALUATION, AUDITS, AND INFORMATION

56600. It is the intent of the Legislature to provide for ongoing comprehensive evaluation of special education programs authorized by this part. The Legislature finds and declares that the evaluation of these programs shall be designed to provide the Legislature, the State Board of Education, the State Department of Education, and program administrators at special education local plan area, county, district, and school levels with the information necessary to refine and improve programs, policies, regulations, guidelines, and procedures on a continuing basis, and to assess the overall merits of these efforts.

- Legislative Intent on Program Evaluation

56600.5. (a) The superintendent shall submit to the board, not later than July 1, 1989, an evaluation plan for special education. This plan shall outline a procedure to identify statewide evaluation priorities in special education and strategies to involve the special education local plan areas for their cooperation in conducting the studies.

- Evaluation Plan

(b) The plan developed pursuant to subdivision (a) shall be developed in consultation with the Advisory Commission on Special Education and with other groups or individuals the superintendent deems appropriate.

- Plan Development

(c) The plan developed pursuant to subdivision (a) shall include, but not be limited to, all of the following:

- Plan Components

(1) The identification of outcomes and goals against which programs can be judged.

(2) Questions requiring further research and how they are addressed in the evaluation plan.

(3) Research that has been conducted in these questions to date, including a brief summary of findings.

(4) Potential evaluation methodologies.

(5) The scope and probable duration of the evaluations.

(6) Organizations that could conduct these evaluations.

(7) Funding requirements for the evaluations.

(8) The potential policy implications of the proposed studies.

(d) The evaluation plan developed pursuant to subdivision (a) shall also include provisions for both of the following:

- Eligibility and Exit Criteria

(1) Analyzing the existing eligibility criteria for special education programs and services.

(2) The appropriateness of establishing specific, exit criteria for special education programs, and strengthening the exit process.

56601. (a) Each special education local plan area shall submit to the superintendent at least annually information, in a form and manner prescribed by the superintendent and developed in consultation with the special education local plan areas, in order for the superintendent to carry out the evaluation responsibilities pursuant to Section 56602. This information shall include other statistical data, program information, and fiscal information that the superintendent may require. The superintendent shall use this information to answer questions from the Legislature and other state and federal agencies on program, policy, and fiscal issues of statewide interest.

- Submit Annual Information

(b) In order to assist the state in evaluating the effectiveness of special education programs, including transition and work experience programs, the superintendent is authorized to collect and utilize social security numbers of individuals with exceptional needs as pupil identification numbers beginning in the 1993-94 fiscal year and phased in over a two-year period. In a situation where a social security number is not available, the superintendent shall assign another student identification number for purposes of evaluating special education programs and related services. The superintendent shall not disclose personally identifiable, individual pupil records to any person, institution, agency, or organization except as authorized by Section 1232g of Title 20 of the United States Code and Part 99 of Title 34 of the Code of Federal Regulations.

- Utilize Social Security Numbers

56602. In accordance with a program evaluation plan adopted pursuant to subdivision (e) of Section 56100, the superintendent shall submit to the board, the Legislature, and the Governor, an annual evaluation of the special education programs implemented under this part. This evaluation shall do all of the following:

- Annual Special Education Evaluation

(a) Utilize existing information sources including fiscal records, enrollment data, and other descriptive data, and program reviews to gather ongoing information regarding implementation of programs authorized by this chapter.

- Existing Information Sources

(b) Utilize existing information sources to the maximum extent feasible to conduct special evaluation studies of issues of statewide concern. The studies may include, but not be limited to, all the following:

- Special Evaluation Studies

(1) Pupil performance. The State Department of Education shall assist special education local plan areas in the development of models of pupil performance in order to determine the success or failure of special education

programs and services. As appropriate, special education pupils and parents of special education pupils shall be involved in the development of these models.

(2) Placement of pupils in least restrictive environments.

(3) Degree to which services identified in individualized education programs are provided.

(4) Parent, pupil, teacher, program specialist, resource specialist, and administrator attitudes toward services and processes provided.

(5) Program costs, including, but not limited to:

(A) Expenditures for instructional personnel services, support services, special transportation services, and regionalized services.

(B) Capital outlay costs at the district and school levels, and for special education local plan areas, county offices, state special schools, and nonpublic, nonsectarian schools.

(C) Funding sources at the district, special education local plan area, county office, state special school, nonpublic, nonsectarian school, and agency levels, including funding provided by state and local noneducational public agencies.

(c) Identify the numbers of individuals with exceptional needs, their racial and ethnic data, their classification by designated instructional sevices, resource specialist, special day class or center, nonpublic, nonsectarian schools, and agencies, including pupils referred to and placed in those programs by state and local noneducational public agencies, in accordance with criteria established by the board and consistent with federal reporting requirements.

- Data on Individuals/Settings

(d) The State Department of Education shall, as part of the department's regular data collection process for special education programs, collect data on the types of agencies that provide designated instruction and services or related services that are contracted for by special education local plan areas or programs for the disabled operated by the state pursuant to Public Law 89-313, in order to determine the number of special education pupils who are enrolled in nonpublic, nonsectarian special education schools or who are receiving nonpublic, nonsectarian agency services.

- Data on Types of Agencies That Provide DIS

56603. The Department of Education shall, as part of the annual evaluation, report the information necessary to refine and improve statewide policies, regulations, guidelines, and procedures developed pursuant to this part.

- Report Information

56604. (a) The superintendent shall coordinate the design of evaluations to prevent duplication and to minimize data collection and reporting requirements at the school and

- Coordinate Design of Evaluations

district levels.

(b) The State Department of Education shall utilize sampling procedures whenever feasible.

56605. The superintendent shall periodically sponsor or conduct workshops and seminars for the education of local education agency personnel assigned to, and responsible for, the evaluation of local special education programs.

56606. The superintendent shall provide for onsite program and fiscal reviews of the implementation of plans approved under this part. In performing the reviews and audits, the superintendent may utilize the services of persons outside of the department chosen for their knowledge of special education programs. Each district, special education local plan area, or county office shall be reviewed at least once during the period of approval of its local plan.

- Utilize Sampling Procedures

- Workshops and Seminars

- Onsite Program/Fiscal Reviews

CHAPTER 7.2. SPECIAL EDUCATION FUNDING

Article 1. Administration

56836. Commencing with the 1998-99 fiscal year and for each fiscal year thereafter, apportionments to special education local plan areas for special education programs operated by, and services provided by, districts, county offices, and special education local plan areas shall be computed pursuant to this chapter.

56836.01. Commencing with the 1998-99 fiscal year and each fiscal year thereafter, the administrator of each special education local plan area, in accordance with the local plan approved by the board, shall be responsible for the following:

(a) The fiscal administration of the annual budget plan pursuant to subdivision (f) [sic] of Section 56205 and annual allocation plan for multidistrict special education local plan areas pursuant to Section 56836.05 for special education programs of school districts and county superintendents of schools composing the special education local plan area.

(b) The allocation of state and federal funds allocated to the special education local plan area for the provision of special education and related services by those entities.

(c) The reporting and accounting requirements prescribed by this part.

56836.02. (a) The superintendent shall apportion funds from Section A of the State School Fund to districts and county offices of education in accordance with the allocation plan adopted pursuant to Section 56836.05, unless the allocation plan specifies that funds be apportioned to the administrative unit of the special education local plan area. If the allocation plan specifies that funds be apportioned to the administrative unit of the special education local plan area, the administrator of the special education local plan area shall, upon receipt, distribute the funds in accordance with the method adopted pursuant to subdivision (i) of Section 56195.7. The allocation plan shall, prior to submission to the superintendent, be approved according to the local policymaking process established by the special education local plan area.

(b) The superintendent shall apportion funds for regionalized services and program specialists from Section A of the State School Fund to the administrative unit of each special education local plan area. Upon receipt, the administrator of a special education local plan area shall direct the administrative unit of the special education local plan area to distribute the funds in accordance with the budget plan adopted pursuant to paragraph (1) of subdivision (b) of Section 56205.

56836.03. (a) On or after January 1, 1998, each special education local plan area shall submit a revised local plan. Each special education local plan area shall submit its revised local plan not later than the time it is required to submit its local plan pursuant to subdivision (b) of Section 56100 and the revised local plan shall meet the requirements of Chapter 3 (commencing with Section 56200).

- Submission of Revised Local Plans

(b) Until the board has approved the revised local plan and the special education local plan area begins to operate under the revised local plan, each special education local plan area shall continue to operate under the programmatic, reporting, and accounting requirements prescribed by the State Department of Education for the purposes of Chapter 7 (commencing with Section 56700) as that chapter existed on December 31, 1998. The department shall develop transition guidelines, and, as necessary, transition forms, to facilitate a transition from the reporting and accounting methods required for Chapter 7 (commencing with Section 56700) as that chapter existed on December 31, 1998, and related provisions of this part, to the reporting and accounting methods required for this chapter. Under no circumstances shall the transition guidelines exceed the requirements of the provisions described in paragraphs (1) and (2). The transition guidelines shall, at a minimum, do the following:

- SELPA Operates Under Prior Law Until Revised Local Plan Is Approved by State Board

- Transition Guidelines

(1) Describe the method for accounting for the instructional service personnel units and caseloads, as required by Chapter 7 (commencing with Section 56700) as that chapter existed on December 31, 1998.

(2) Describe the accounting that is required to be made, if any, for the purposes of Sections 56030, 56140, 56156.4, 56156.5, 56361.5, 56362, 56363.3, 56366.2, 56366.3, 56370, 56441.5, and 56441.7.

(c) Commencing with the 1997-98 fiscal year, through and including the fiscal year in which equalization among special education local plan areas has been achieved, the board shall not approve any proposal to divide a special education local plan area into two or more units, unless the division has no net impact on state costs for special education; provided, however, that the board may approve a proposal that was initially submitted to the department prior to January 1, 1997.

- State Board Shall Not Approve Any Proposal to Divide a SELPA Unless There Is No Impact on State Costs

56836.04. (a) The superintendent shall continuously monitor and review all special education programs approved under this part to assure that all funds appropriated to special education local plan areas under this part are expended for the purposes intended.

(b) Funds apportioned to special education local plan areas pursuant to this chapter shall be expended exclusively for programs operated under this part.

56836.05. (a) Apportionments made under this part shall be made by the superintendent as early as practicable in the fiscal year. Upon order of the superintendent, the Controller shall draw warrants upon the money appropriated, in favor of the eligible special education local plan areas.

(b) If the special education local plan area is a multidistrict special education local plan area, and the approved allocation plan does not specify that funds will be apportioned to the special education local plan area administrative unit, the special education local plan area shall submit to the superintendent an annual allocation plan to allocate funds received in accordance with this chapter among the local educational agencies within the special education local plan area. The annual allocation plan may be revised during any fiscal year, and these revisions may be submitted to the superintendent as amendments. The amendments shall, prior to submission to the superintendent, be approved according to the policymaking process established by the special education local plan area.

(c) If funds are apportioned to a special education local plan area administrative unit in the 1998-99 fiscal year and the special education local plan area administrative unit is changed in the 1998-99 fiscal year or thereafter, monthly payments shall be made according to the schedule in paragraph (2) of subdivision (a) of Section 14041 unless all local educational agencies are on the same schedule. If all local educational agencies are on the same schedule, the appropriate schedule in paragraph (2), (7), or (8) of subdivision (a) of Section 14041 shall apply.

Article 2. Computation of Apportionments

56836.06. For the purposes of this article, the following terms or phrases shall have the following meanings, unless the context clearly requires otherwise:

(a) "Average daily attendance reported for the special education local plan area" means the total of the following:

- State Superintendent Shall Continuously Monitor/Review All Special Education Programs

- Funds Apportioned Shall Be Expended Exclusively for Special Education Programs

- Timing of Apportionments; Order to Draw Warrants

- Annual Allocation Plan

- Administrative Unit

- Definition of Terms

- Average Daily Attendance

(1) The total number of units of average daily attendance reported for the second principal apportionment pursuant to Section 41601 for all pupils enrolled in the district or districts that are a part of the special education local plan area.

(2) The total number of units of average daily attendance reported pursuant to subdivisions (a) and (b) of Section 41601 for all pupils enrolled in schools operated by the county office or offices that compose the special education local plan area, or for those county offices that are a part of more than one special education local plan area, that portion of the average daily attendance of pupils enrolled in the schools operated by the county office that are under the jurisdiction of the special education local plan area.

(b) For the purposes of computing apportionments pursuant to this chapter for the special education local plan area identified as the Los Angeles County Juvenile Court and Community School/Division of Alternative Education Special Education Local Plan Area, the term "average daily attendance" shall mean the total number of units of average daily attendance reported for the second principal apportionment pursuant to subdivisions (a) and (b) of Section 41601 for all pupils enrolled in districts within Los Angeles County and all schools operated by the Los Angeles County Office of Education and the districts within Los Angeles County.

- Application to Los Angeles County Juvenile Court School/Division of Alternative Education SELPA

(c) "Special education local plan area" includes the school district or districts and county office or offices of education composing the special education local plan area.

- Special Education Local Plan Area

(d) "The fiscal year in which equalization among special education local plan areas has been achieved" means the first fiscal year in which each special education local plan area is funded at or above the statewide target amount per unit of average daily attendance, as computed pursuant to Section 56836.11.

- Fiscal Year in Which Equalization Among SELPAs Has Been Achieved

(e) For a charter school deemed a local educational agency for the purposes of special education, an amount equal to the amount computed pursuant to Section 56836.08 for the special education local plan area in which the charter school is included shall be apportioned by the State Department of Education pursuant to the local allocation plan developed pursuant to subdivision (i) of Section 56195.7 or 56836.05, or both. If the charter school is a participant in a local plan which only includes other charter schools pursuant to subdivision (f) of Section 56195.1, the amount computed pursuant to Section 56836.11, as adjusted for any amount for

- Charter School Computation

which the special education local plan area is eligible pursuant to the incidence multiplier set forth in Section 56836.155, shall be apportioned by the department pursuant for each unit of average daily attendance reported pursuant to subdivision (a).

56836.08. (a) For the 1998-99 fiscal year, the superintendent shall make the following computations to determine the amount of funding for each special education local plan area:

- Computations for 1998-99 Fiscal Year

(1) Add the amount of funding per unit of average daily attendance computed for the special education local plan area pursuant to paragraph (1) of subdivision (a) of Section 56836.10 to the inflation adjustment computed pursuant to subdivision (d) for the 1998-99 fiscal year.

(2) Multiply the amount computed in paragraph (1) by the units of average daily attendance reported for the special education local plan area for the 1997-98 fiscal year, exclusive of average daily attendance for absences excused pursuant to subdivision (b) of Section 46010, as that subdivision read on July 1, 1996.

(3) Add the actual amount of the equalization adjustment, if any, computed for the 1998-99 fiscal year pursuant to Section 56836.14 to the amount computed in paragraph (2).

(4) Add or subtract, as appropriate, the adjustment for growth computed pursuant to Section 56836.15 from the amount computed in paragraph (3).

(b) For the 1999-2000 fiscal year and each fiscal year thereafter, the superintendent shall make the following computations to determine the amount of funding for each special education local plan area for the fiscal year in which the computation is made:

- Computations for 1999-2000 Fiscal Year and Each Fiscal Year Thereafter

(1) Add the amount of funding per unit of average daily attendance computed for the special education local plan area for the prior fiscal year pursuant to Section 56836.10 to the inflation adjustment computed pursuant to subdivision (d) for the fiscal year in which the computation is made.

(2) Multiply the amount computed in paragraph (1) by the units of average daily attendance reported for the special education local plan area for the prior fiscal year.

(3) Add the actual amount of the equalization adjustment, if any, computed for the special education local plan area for the fiscal year in which the computation is made pursuant to Section 56836.14 to the amount computed in paragraph (2).

(4) Add or subtract, as appropriate, the adjustment for growth or decline in enrollment, if any, computed for the

special education local plan area for the fiscal year in which the computation is made pursuant to Section 56836.15 from the amount computed in paragraph (3).

(c) For the 1998-99 fiscal year and each fiscal year thereafter, the superintendent shall make the following computations to determine the amount of General Fund moneys that the special education local plan area may claim:

- Computation to Determine Amount of General Fund Moneys SELPA May Claim

(1) Add the total of the amount of property taxes for the special education local plan area pursuant to Section 2572 for the fiscal year in which the computation is made to the amount of federal funds allocated for the purposes of paragraph (1) of subdivision (a) of Section 56836.09 for the fiscal year in which the computation is made.

(2) Add the amount of funding computed for the special education local plan area pursuant to subdivision (a) for the 1998-99 fiscal year, and commencing with the 1999-2000 fiscal year and each fiscal year thereafter, the amount computed for the fiscal year in which the computations were made pursuant to subdivision (b) to the amount of funding computed for the special education local plan area pursuant to Article 3 (commencing with Section 56836.16).

(3) Subtract the sum computed in paragraph (1) from the sum computed in paragraph (2)

(d) For the 1998-99 fiscal year and each fiscal year thereafter, the superintendent shall make the following computations to determine the inflation adjustment for the fiscal year in which the computation is made:

- Computations to Determine Inflation Adjustment

(1) For the 1998-99 fiscal year, multiply the sum of the statewide target amount per unit of average daily attendance for special education local plan areas for the 1997-98 fiscal year computed pursuant to paragraph (3) of subdivision (a) of Section 56836.11 and the amount determined pursuant to paragraph (e) of Section 56836.155 for the 1997-98 fiscal year that corresponds to the amount determined pursuant to paragraph (1) of subdivision (d) of Section 56836.155 by the inflation adjustment computed pursuant to Section 42238.1 for the 1998-99 fiscal year.

(2) For the 1999-2000 fiscal year and each fiscal year thereafter, multiply the sum of the statewide target amount per unit of average daily attendance for special education local plan areas for the prior fiscal year computed pursuant to Section 56836.11 and the amount determined pursuant to paragraph (1) of subdivision (d) of Section 56836.155 for the prior fiscal year by the inflation adjustment computed pursuant to Section 42238.1 for the fiscal year in which the

computation is made.

(3) For the purposes of computing the inflation adjustment for the special education local plan area identified as the Los Angeles County Juvenile Court and Community School/Division of Alternative Education Special Education Local Plan Area for the 1998-99 fiscal year and each fiscal year thereafter, the superintendent shall multiply the amount of funding per unit of average daily attendance computed for that special education local plan area for the prior fiscal year pursuant to Section 56836.10 by the inflation adjustment computed pursuant to Section 42238.1 for the fiscal year in which the computation is being made.

(e) For the 1998-99 fiscal year and each fiscal year thereafter to and including the 2002-03 fiscal year, the superintendent shall perform the calculation set forth in Section 56836.155 to determine the adjusted entitlement for the incidence of disabilities for each special education local plan area, but this amount shall not be used in the next fiscal year to determine the base amount of funding for each special education local plan area for the current fiscal year, except as specified in this article.

- Adjusted Entitlement for Incidence of Disabilities

56836.09.   For the purpose of computing the amount to apportion to each special education local plan area for the 1998-99 fiscal year, the superintendent shall compute the total amount of funding received by the special education local plan area for the 1997-98 fiscal year as follows:

- Computations to Determine 1998-99 SELPA Apportionments

(a) Add the following amounts that were received for the 1997-98 fiscal year:

(1) The total amount of federal funds apportioned to the special education local plan area pursuant to subdivisions (b) and (h) of the Schedule in Item 6110-161-0890 of Section 2.00 of the Budget Act of 1997 for the purposes of special education for individuals with exceptional needs enrolled in kindergarten and grades 1 to 12, inclusive.

(2) The total amount of property taxes allocated to the special education local plan area pursuant to Section 2572, excluding any property taxes used to fund a program for individuals with exceptional needs younger than three years of age in the special education local plan area for the 1997-98 fiscal year.

(3) The total amount of General Fund moneys allocated to the special education local plan area pursuant to Chapter 7 (commencing with Section 56700) plus the total amount received for equalization pursuant to Chapter 7.1 (commencing with Section 56835), as those chapters existed

on December 31, 1998.

(4) The total amount of General Fund moneys allocated to another special education local plan area for any pupils with exceptional needs who are served by the other special education local plan area but who are residents of the special education local plan area for which this computation is being made.

(b) Add the following amounts received in the 1997-98 fiscal year:

(1) The total amount determined for the special education local plan area for the purpose of providing nonpublic, nonsectarian school services to licensed children's institutions, foster family homes, residential medical facilities, and other similar facilities for the 1997-98 fiscal year pursuant to Article 3 (commencing with Section 56836.16).

(2) The total amount of General Fund moneys allocated for any pupils with exceptional needs who are served by the special education local plan area but who do not reside within the boundaries of the special education local plan area.

(3) The total amount of General Fund moneys allocated to the special education local plan area to perform the regionalized operations and services functions listed in Article 6 (commencing with Section 56836.23) and to provide the direct instructional support of program specialists in accordance with Section 56368.

(4) The total amount of General Fund moneys allocated to the special education local plan area for individuals with exceptional needs younger than three years of age pursuant to Chapter 7 (commencing with Section 56700), as that chapter existed on December 31, 1998.

(5) The total amount of General Fund moneys allocated to local educational agencies within the special education local plan area pursuant to Section 56771, as that section existed on December 31, 1998, for specialized books, materials, and equipment for pupils with low-incidence disabilities.

(c) Subtract the sum computed in subdivision (b) from the sum computed in subdivision (a).

56836.095. For the 2001-02 fiscal year, the superintendent shall make the following computations in the following order:

- Computations Order for 2000-01 Fiscal Year (2)

(a) Calculate and carry out the equalization adjustments authorized pursuant to Sections 56836.12 and 56836.14.

(b) Complete the calculations required to adjust the statewide total average daily attendance pursuant to Section 56836.156, and adjust the statewide target per unit of average daily attendance for the 2001-02 fiscal year in accordance with this calculation.

(c) Determine and provide the amount of funding required for the special disabilities adjustment pursuant to Section 56836.155.

(d) Compute and distribute the amount of funding appropriated for increasing the statewide target amount per unit of average daily attendance pursuant to Section 56836.158.

(e) Compute and provide a permanent adjustment for each special education local plan area pursuant to Section 56836.159.

56836.10. (a) The superintendent shall make the following computations to determine the amount of funding per unit of average daily attendance for each special education local plan area for the 1998-99 fiscal year:

- Computations to Determine Amount of Funding Per Unit of ADA for Each SELPA for 1998-99 Fiscal Year

(1) Divide the amount of funding for the special education local plan area computed for the 1997-98 fiscal year pursuant to Section 56836.09 by the number of units of average daily attendance, exclusive of average daily attendance for absences excused pursuant to subdivision (b) of Section 46010 as that subdivision read on July 1, 1997, reported for the special education local plan area for the 1997-98 fiscal year.

(2) Add the amount computed in paragraph (1) to the inflation adjustment computed pursuant to subdivision (d) of Section 56836.08 for the 1998-99 fiscal year.

(b) Commencing with the 1999-2000 fiscal year and each fiscal year thereafter, the superintendent shall make the following computations to determine the amount of funding per unit of average daily attendance for each special education local plan area for the fiscal year in which the computation is made:

- Computations to Determine Amount of Funding Per Unit of ADA for Each SELPA for 1999-2000 and Each Fiscal Year Thereafter

(1) For the 1999-2000 fiscal year, divide the amount of funding for the special education local plan area computed for the 1998-99 fiscal year pursuant to subdivision (a) of Section 56836.08 by the number of units of average daily attendance upon which funding is based pursuant to subdivision (a) of Section 56836.15 for the special education local plan area for the 1998-99 fiscal year.

(2) For the 2000-01 fiscal year, and each fiscal year thereafter, divide the amount of funding for the special education local plan area computed for the prior fiscal year pursuant to subdivision (b) of Section 56836.08 by the number of units of average daily attendance upon which

funding is based pursuant to subdivision (a) of Section 56836.15 for the special education local plan area for the prior fiscal year.

56836.11. (a) For the purpose of computing the equalization adjustment for special education local plan areas for the 1998-99 fiscal year, the superintendent shall make the following computations to determine the statewide target amount per unit of average daily attendance for special education local plan areas:

- Statewide Target Amount Per Unit of Average Daily Attendance; Computation of Equalization Adjustment for Fiscal Year

(1) Total the amount of funding computed for each special education local plan area exclusive of the amount of funding computed for the special education local plan area identified as the Los Angeles County Juvenile Court and Community School/Division of Alternative Education Special Education Local Plan Area, pursuant to Section 56836.09 for the 1997-98 fiscal year.

(2) Total the number of units of average daily attendance reported for each special education local plan area for the 1997-98 fiscal year, exclusive of average daily attendance for absences excused pursuant to subdivision (b) of Section 46010 as that section read on July 1, 1996, and exclusive of the units of average daily attendance computed for the special education local plan area identified as the Los Angeles County Juvenile Court and Community School/Division of Alternative Education Special Education Local Plan Area.

(3) Divide the sum computed in paragraph (1) by the sum computed in paragraph (2) to determine the statewide target amount for the 1997-98 fiscal year.

(4) Add the amount computed in paragraph (3) to the inflation adjustment computed pursuant to subdivision (d) of Section 56836.08 for the 1998-99 fiscal year to determine the statewide target amount for the 1998-99 fiscal year.

(b) Commencing with the 1999-2000 fiscal year and each fiscal year thereafter, to determine the statewide target amount per unit of average daily attendance for special education local plan areas, the superintendent shall multiply the statewide target amount per unit of average daily attendance computed for the prior fiscal year pursuant to this section by one plus the inflation factor computed pursuant to subdivision (b) of Section 42238.1 for the fiscal year in which the computation is made.

- Determining the Statewide Target Amount Per Unit of ADA for SELPAs for 1999-2000 Fiscal Year and Thereafter

56836.12. (a) For the purpose of computing the equalization adjustment for special education local plan areas for the 1998-99 fiscal year, the superintendent shall make the following computations to determine the amount that each

- Determine Which SELPA May Request Equalization Adjustment

special education local plan area that has an amount per unit of average daily attendance that is below the statewide target amount per unit of average daily attendance may request as an equalization adjustment:

(1) Subtract the amount per unit of average daily attendance computed for the special education local plan area pursuant to subdivision (a) of Section 56836.10 from the statewide target amount per unit of average daily attendance determined pursuant to subdivision (a) of Section 56836.11.

(2) If the remainder computed in paragraph (1) is greater than zero, multiply that remainder by the number of units of average daily attendance reported for the special education local plan area for the 1997-98 fiscal year, exclusive of average daily attendance for absences excused pursuant to subdivision (b) of Section 46010, as that section read on July 1, 1996.

(b) Commencing with the 1999-2000 fiscal year, through and including the fiscal year in which equalization among the special education local plan areas has been achieved, the superintendent shall make the following computations to determine the amount that each special education local plan area that has an amount per unit of average daily attendance that is below the statewide target amount per unit of average daily attendance may request as an equalization adjustment:

- Computations to Determine Amount That Each SELPA Below Statewide Target May Request an Equalization Adjustment, Starting with 1999-2000 Fiscal Year

(1) Add to the amount per unit of average daily attendance computed for the special education local plan area pursuant to subdivision (b) of Section 56836.10 for the fiscal year in which the computation is made the inflation adjustment computed pursuant to subdivision (d) of Section 56836.08 for the fiscal year in which the computation is made.

(2) Subtract the amount computed pursuant to paragraph (1) from the statewide target amount per unit of average daily attendance computed pursuant to subdivision (b) of Section 56836.11 for the fiscal year in which the computation is made.

(3) If the remainder computed in paragraph (2) is greater than zero, multiply that remainder by the number of units of average daily attendance reported for the special education local plan area for the prior fiscal year, exclusive of average daily attendance for absences excused pursuant to subdivision (b) of Section 46010, as that section read on July 1, 1996.

(c) This section shall not apply to the special education local plan area identified as the Los Angeles County Juvenile Court and Community School/Division of Alternative Education Special Education Local Plan Area.

56836.13. Commencing with the 1998-99 fiscal year, through and including the fiscal year in which equalization among the special education local plan areas has been achieved, the superintendent shall make the following computations to determine the amount available for making equalization adjustments for the fiscal year in which the computation is made:

- Computations of Amounts Available for Making Equalization Adjustments

(a) Subtract the prior fiscal year funds pursuant to paragraph (1) of subdivision (c) of Section 56836.08 from the current fiscal year funds pursuant to paragraph (1) of subdivision (c) of Section 56836.08.

(b) The amount of any increase in federal funds computed pursuant to subdivision (a) shall result in a reduction in state general funds computed pursuant to paragraph (3) of subdivision (c) of Section 56836.08. This is the amount of state general funds that shall be designated in the annual Budget Act for the purpose of Section 56836.12, as augmented by any deficiency appropriation, for the purposes of equalizing funding for special education local plan areas pursuant to this chapter.

(c) Until the actual amount of any increase in federal funds pursuant to subdivision (a) can be determined for the current fiscal year, equalization apportionments pursuant to Section 56836.12 shall be certified based on the authority available in Item 6110-161-0001 of the Budget Act of 1998, or its successor in the annual Budget Act.

56836.14. Commencing with the 1998-99 fiscal year, through and including the fiscal year in which equalization among the special education local plan areas has been achieved, the superintendent shall make the following computations to determine the actual amount of the equalization adjustment for each special education local plan area that has an amount per unit of average daily attendance that is below the statewide target amount per unit of average daily attendance.

- Computations to Determine Actual Amount of Equalization Adjustment for SELPAs Below Statewide Target

(a) Add the amount determined for each special education local plan area pursuant to Section 56836.12 for the fiscal year in which the computation is made to determine the total statewide aggregate amount necessary to fund each special education local plan area at the statewide target amount per unit of average daily attendance for special education local plan areas.

(b) Divide the amount computed in subdivision (a) by the amount computed pursuant to Section 56836.13 to determine the percentage of the total amount of funds necessary to fund each special education local plan area at the statewide target amount per unit of average daily attendance for special education local plan areas that are actually available for that purpose.

(c) To determine the amount to allocate to the special education local plan area for a special education local plan area equalization adjustment, multiply the amount computed for the special education local plan area pursuant to Section 56836.12, if any, by the percentage determined in subdivision (b).

56836.15. (a) In order to mitigate the effects of any declining enrollment, commencing in the 1998-99 fiscal year, and each fiscal year thereafter, the superintendent shall calculate allocations to special education local plan areas based on the average daily attendance reported for the special education local plan area for the fiscal year in which the computation is made or the prior fiscal year, whichever is greater. However, the prior fiscal year average daily attendance reported for the special education local plan area shall be adjusted for any loss or gain of average daily attendance reported for the special education local plan area due to a reorganization or transfer of territory in the special education local plan area.

- Mitigating Effects of Declining Enrollment

(b) For the 1998-99 fiscal year only, the prior year average daily attendance used in this section shall be the 1997-98 average daily attendance reported for the special education local plan area, exclusive of average daily attendance for absences excused pursuant to subdivision (b) of Section 46010, as that section read on July 1, 1996.

(c) If in the fiscal year for which the computation is made, the number of units of average daily attendance upon which allocations to the special education local plan area are based is greater than the number of units of average daily attendance upon which allocations to the special education local plan area were based in the prior fiscal year, the special education local plan area shall be allocated a growth adjustment equal to the product determined by multiplying the amounts determined under paragraphs (1) and (2).

(1) The statewide target amount per unit of average daily attendance for special education local plan areas determined pursuant to Section 56836.11, added to the amount determined in paragraph (1) of subdivision (d) of Section 56836.155.

(2) The difference between the number of units of average daily attendance upon which allocations to the special

education local plan area are based for the fiscal year in which the computation is made and the number of units of average daily attendance upon which allocations to the special education local plan area were based for the prior fiscal year.

(d) If in the fiscal year for which the computation is made, the number of units of average daily attendance upon which allocations to the special education local plan area are based is less than the number of units of average daily attendance upon which allocations to the special education local plan area were based in the prior fiscal year, the special education local plan area shall receive a funding reduction equal to the product determined by multiplying the amounts determined under paragraphs (1) and (2):

(1) The amount of funding per unit of average daily attendance computed for the special education local plan area for the prior fiscal year.

(2) The difference between the number of units of average daily attendance upon which allocations to the special education local plan area are based for the fiscal year in which the computation is made and the number of units of average daily attendance upon which allocations to the special education local plan area were based for the prior fiscal year.

(e) If, in the fiscal year for which the computation is made, the number of units of average daily attendance upon which the allocations to the special education local plan area identified as the Los Angeles County Juvenile Court and Community School/Division of Alternative Education Special Education Local Plan Area are based is greater than the number of units of average daily attendance upon which the allocations to that special education local plan area were based in the prior fiscal year, that special education local plan area shall be allocated a growth adjustment equal to the product determined by multiplying the amounts determined under paragraphs (1) and (2).

(1) The amount of funding per unit of average daily attendance computed for the special education local plan area for the prior fiscal year pursuant to Section 56836.10 multiplied by one plus the inflation adjustment computed pursuant to Section 42238.1 for the fiscal year in which the computation is being made.

(2) The difference between the number of units of average daily attendance upon which allocations to the special education local plan area are based for the fiscal year in which the computation is made and the number of units of average daily attendance upon which allocations to the special

education local plan area were based for the prior fiscal year.

Article 2.5. Computation of Adjustment

56836.155. (a) On or before November 2, 1998, the department, in conjunction with the Office of the Legislative Analyst, shall do the following:

- Calculation of the Incidence Multiplier for Each SELPA

(1) Calculate an "incidence multiplier" for each special education local plan area using the definition, methodology, and data provided in the final report submitted by the American Institutes for Research pursuant to Section 67 of Chapter 854 of the Statutes of 1997.

(2) Submit the incidence multiplier for each special education local plan area and supporting data to the Department of Finance.

(b) The Department of Finance shall review the incidence multiplier for each special education local plan area and the supporting data, and report any errors to the department and the Office of the Legislative Analyst for correction.

(c) The Department of Finance shall approve the final incidence multiplier for each special education local plan area by November 23, 1998.

(d) For the 1998-99 fiscal year and each fiscal year thereafter to and including the 2002-03 fiscal year, the superintendent shall perform the following calculation to determine each special education local plan area's adjusted entitlement for the incidence of disabilities:

(1) The incidence multiplier for the special education local plan area shall be multiplied by the statewide target amount per unit of average daily attendance for special education local plan areas determined pursuant to Section 56836.11 for the fiscal year in which the computation is made:

(2) The amount determined pursuant to paragraph (1) shall be added to the statewide target amount per unit of average daily attendance for special education local plan area determined pursuant to Section 56836.11 for the fiscal year in which the computation is made.

(3) Subtract the amount of funding for the special education local plan area determined pursuant to paragraph (1) of subdivision (a) or paragraph (1) of subdivision (b) of Section 56836.08, as appropriate for the fiscal year in which the computation is made, or the statewide target amount per unit of average daily attendance for special education local plan areas determined pursuant to Section 56836.11 for the fiscal year in which the computation is made, whichever is

greater, from the amount determined pursuant to paragraph (2). If the result is less than zero, then the special education local plan area shall not receive an adjusted entitlement for the incidence of disabilities.

(4) Multiply the amount determined in paragraph (3) by either the average daily attendance reported for the special education local plan area for the fiscal year in which the computation is made, as adjusted pursuant to subdivision (a) of Section 56836.15, or the average daily attendance reported for the special education local plan area for the prior fiscal year, as adjusted pursuant to subdivision (a) of Section 56826.15, whichever is less.

(5) If there are insufficient funds appropriated in the fiscal year for which the computation is made for the purposes of this section, the amount received by each special education local plan area shall be prorated.

(e) For the 1997-98 fiscal year, the superintendent shall perform the calculation in paragraphs (1) to (3), inclusive of paragraph (d) only for the purposes of making the computation in paragraph (1) of subdivision (d) of Section 56836.08, but the special education local plan area shall not receive an adjusted entitlement for the incidence of disabilities pursuant to this section for the 1997-98 fiscal year.

(f) On or before March 1, 2003, the Office of the Legislative Analyst, in conjunction with the Department of Finance and the department, shall submit to the Legislature a new study of the incidence multiplier, with recommendations as the necessity of continuing to adjust the funding formula contained in this chapter for the purposes of this section to the extent that funding is provided for this purpose. The Office of the Legislative Analyst may contract for this study. It is the intent of the Legislature to provide funding for this study in the Budget Act of 2002.

56836.156. (a) The Superintendent of Public Instruction shall determine the statewide total average daily attendance used for the purposes of Section 56836.08 for the 2001-02 fiscal year. For the purposes of this calculation, the 2000-01 second principal average daily attendance for the court, community school, and special education programs served by the Los Angeles County Juvenile Court and Community School/Division of Alternative Education Special Education Local Plan Area shall be used in lieu of the average daily attendance used for that agency for the purposes of Section 56836.08.

- Computations to Permanently Increase Amount Per Unit of ADA (Mandated Cost Claims Settlement) (3)

(b) The superintendent shall divide one hundred million dollars ($100,000,000) by the amount determined pursuant to subdivision (a).

(c) For each special education local plan area, the superintendent shall permanently increase the amount per unit of average daily attendance determined pursuant to subdivision (b) of Section 56836.08 for the 2001-02 fiscal year by the quotient determined pursuant to subdivision (b). This increase shall be effective beginning in the 2001-02 fiscal year.

(d) Notwithstanding subdivision (c), for the Los Angeles County Juvenile Court and Community School/Division of Alternative Education Special Education Local Plan Area, the superintendent shall permanently increase the amount per unit of average daily attendance determined pursuant to subdivision (b) of Section 56836.08 by the ratio of the amount determined pursuant to subdivision (b) to the statewide target per unit of average daily attendance determined pursuant to Section 56836.11 for the 2000-01 fiscal year. This increase shall be effective beginning in the 2001-02 fiscal year.

(e) The superintendent shall increase the statewide target per unit of average daily attendance determined pursuant to Section 56836.11 for the 2001-02 fiscal year by the amount determined pursuant to subdivision (b).

(f) The funds provided in subdivisions (a) to (e), inclusive, shall be used for the costs of any state-mandated special education programs and services established pursuant to Sections 56000 to 56885, inclusive, and Sections 3000 to 4671, inclusive, of Title 5 of the California Code of Regulations, as those sections read on or before July 1, 2000. These funds shall be considered in full satisfaction of, and are in lieu of, any reimbursable mandate claims relating to special education programs and services, with the exception of the programs and services delineated in subdivision (g). By providing this funding, the state in no way concedes the existence of any unfunded special education reimbursable mandate. These funds shall be used exclusively for programs operated under this part and, as a first priority, for the following programs, which shall be deemed to be fully funded within the meaning of subdivision (e) of Section 17556 of the Government Code:

(1) Community advisory committees established pursuant to Sections 56190 to 56192, inclusive, and Section 56194, as these sections read on July 1, 2000.

(2) Governance structure established pursuant to subdivision (a) of Section 56195.3, as this section read on July 1, 2000.

(3) Enrollment caseloads established pursuant to subdivision (c) of Section 56362, and Section 56363.3, as these sections read on July 1, 2000.

(4) Extended school year established pursuant to subdivision (d) of Section 3043 of Title 5 of the California Code of Regulations, as this section read on July 1, 2000.

(5) Resource specialist program established pursuant to subdivisions (d), (e), and (f) of Section 56362, as this section read on July 1, 2000.

(6) Maximum age limit established pursuant to paragraph (4) of subdivision (c) of Section 56026, as this section read on July 1, 2000.

(7) Interim placements established pursuant to subdivision (b) of Section 56325, as this section read on July 1, 2000, and Section 3067 of Title 5 of the California Code of Regulations, as this section read on December 31, 1994.

(8) Written consent established pursuant to Sections 56321 and 56346, as these sections read on July 1, 2000.

(9) Preschool transportation programs for ages 3 to 5, inclusive, not requiring intensive services (Not-RIS) established pursuant to Section 56441.14, as this section read on July 1, 2000.

(10) Special education for pupils ages 3 to 5, inclusive, and 18 to 21, inclusive, established pursuant to Section 56026, as this section read on July 1, 2000.

(11) With the exception of the programs delineated in subdivision (g), any other state-mandated special education programs and services established by Sections 56000 to 56885, inclusive, and Sections 3000 to 4671, inclusive, of Title 5 of the California Code of Regulations, as those sections read on or before July 1, 2000, whether or not such a mandate has been found by the Commission on State Mandates. Pursuant to subdivision (e) of Section 17556 of the Government Code, these funds shall be deemed to be additional revenue specifically intended to fund the costs of any such state-mandated special education programs and services.

(g) Notwithstanding subdivision (f), the following existing mandate test claim remains subject to the normal mandate procedure, including judicial review, if any: behavioral interventions established pursuant to Section 56523 and Sections 3001 and 3052 of Title 5 of the California Code of

Regulations, as those sections read on July 1, 2000 (CSM-4464 filed by the San Diego Unified School District, the San Joaquin County Office of Education, and the Butte County Office of Education). The exclusion of this claim from subdivision (f) in no way constitutes a concession by the state that any unfunded special education mandate exists.

(h) Within the meaning of subdivision (e) of Section 17556 of the Government Code, the funds appropriated for purposes of this section are not specifically intended to fund any state-mandated special education programs and services resulting from amendments enacted after July 1, 2000, to any of the following statutes and regulations:

(1) The Individuals with Disabilities Education Act (20 U.S.C. Sec. 1400 et seq.), if the amendments result in circumstances where state law exceeds federal law.

(2) Federal regulations implementing the Individuals with Disabilities Education Act (34 C.F.R. 300 and 303), if the amendments result in circumstances where state law exceeds federal law.

(3) Part 30 (commencing with Section 56000).

(4) Sections 3000 to 4671, inclusive, of Title 5 of the California Code of Regulations.

(i) State funds otherwise allocated to each special education local plan area pursuant to Chapter 7.2 (commencing with Section 56836) of Part 30 and appropriated through the annual Budget Act shall supplement and not supplant these funds.

56836.157. (a) Commencing with the 2001-02 fiscal year to the 2010-11 fiscal year, inclusive, the amount of twenty-five million dollars ($25,000,000) shall be appropriated, on a one-time basis each fiscal year, from the General Fund for allocation to school districts on a per pupil basis. The Superintendent of Public Instruction shall compute the amount per pupil by dividing twenty-five million dollars ($25,000,000) by the total average daily attendance, excluding attendance for regional occupational centers and programs, adult education, and programs operated by the county superintendents of schools, for all pupils in kindergarten through grade 12 in all school districts as used by the Superintendent of Public Instruction for the second principal apportionment for the 1999-2000 fiscal year. Each school district's allocation shall equal the per pupil amount times the district's average daily attendance as reported to the Superintendent of Public Instruction for the second principal

- Calculation for Appropriating $25 Million Each Fiscal Year from 2001-02 to the 2010-11 Fiscal Year (Mandated Cost Claims Settlement) (4)

apportionment for the 1999-2000 fiscal year. The amount allocated to each school district shall be the same in all subsequent fiscal years as it is in the first fiscal year.

(1) In any fiscal year in which the provisions of paragraph (3) of subdivision (b) of Section 8 of Article XVI of the California Constitution are operative, the annual appropriation shall not be required to be made.

(2) The Director of Finance shall notify, in writing, the fiscal committees of both houses of the Legislature, the Controller, and the Superintendent of Public Instruction no later than May 14 that the appropriation for the following fiscal year is not required, pursuant to paragraph (1). If an appropriation is not made for a specific fiscal year, or years, it shall instead be made in the fiscal year, or years, immediately succeeding the final payment pursuant to subdivision (a).

(b) (1) From the funds appropriated for purposes of this section in subdivision (b) of Section 4 of the act adding this section, the Superintendent of Public Instruction shall allocate the following:

(A) From the appropriation provided by subdivision (b) of Section 4 of the act adding this section, the amount of ten million eight hundred thousand dollars ($10,800,000) shall be allocated by the superintendent to county offices of education on an equal per pupil amount. The superintendent shall determine the per pupil amount by dividing ten million eight hundred thousand dollars ($10,800,000) by the total statewide county special education pupil count only, reported by county offices of education as of December 1999. The allotment for each county office of education shall be the per pupil amount times the county's special education pupil count reported as of December 1999.

(B) From the appropriation provided by subdivision (b) of Section 4 of the act adding this section, the amount of two million seven hundred thousand dollars ($2,700,000) shall be allocated by the superintendent to SELPAs that existed for the 1999-2000 fiscal year. The superintendent shall determine the amount of each agency's allotment by dividing the two million seven hundred thousand dollars ($2,700,000) by the total statewide special education pupil count as of December 1999. The allotment for each agency shall be the statewide per pupil amount times the SELPA's special education pupil count reported as of December 1999. The superintendent shall adjust the computations in such a manner as to ensure that the minimum allotment to each SELPA is at least ten thousand dollars ($10,000).

(C) From the appropriation provided by subdivision (b) of Section 4 of the act adding this section, the amount of six million dollars ($6,000,000) shall be allocated by the superintendent to the Riverside County Office of Education.

(2) The superintendent shall compute a per pupil amount from the balance of the appropriation provided by subdivision (b) of Section 4 of the act adding this section, after the appropriation has been reduced by the amounts in paragraph (1), by dividing the remaining portion of the appropriation by the total average daily attendance, excluding attendance for regional occupational centers and programs, adult education, and programs operated by the county superintendents of schools, for all pupils in kindergarten through grade 12 in all school districts as used by the Superintendent of Public Instruction for the second principal apportionment for the 1999-2000 fiscal year.

The superintendent shall apportion to each school district an amount equal to the per pupil amount times the district's reported average daily attendance for the second principal apportionment for the 1999-2000 fiscal year, excluding attendance for regional occupational centers and programs, adult education, and programs operated by the county superintendent of schools.

(c) The amounts appropriated by subdivisions (a) and (b) of Section 4 of the act adding this section are in full satisfaction and in lieu of mandate claims resulting from the Commission on State Mandates cases identified as (1) Riverside County Superintendent of Schools, et al., CSM-3986 on remand from the Superior Court of Sacramento County, No. 352795, and (2) Long Beach Unified School District, CSM-3986A (consolidated with the Santa Barbara County Superintendent of Schools, SB 90-3453).

56836.158. (a) The superintendent shall determine the statewide total average daily attendance used for the purposes of Section 56836.08 for the 2000-01 fiscal year. For the purposes of this calculation, the 2000-01 second principal average daily attendance for the court, community school, and special education programs served by the Los Angeles County Juvenile Court and Community School/Division of Alternative Education special education local plan area shall be used in lieu of the average daily attendance used for that agency for the purposes of Section 56836.08.

(b) The Superintendent of Public Instruction shall distribute the amount appropriated for purposes of this section

- Computation for Increasing Statewide Target Amount Per Unit of ADA (5)

from the 2001-02 Budget Act. The Superintendent of Public Instruction shall divide that amount of funding by the amount calculated in subdivision (a).

(c) For each special education local plan area, the superintendent shall permanently increase the amount per unit of average daily attendance determined pursuant to subdivision (b) of Section 56836.10 for the 2001-02 fiscal year by the quotient determined pursuant to subdivision (b) of this section. This increase shall be effective beginning in the 2001-02 fiscal year.

(d) Notwithstanding subdivision (c), for the Los Angeles County Juvenile Court and Community School/Division of Alternative Education special education local plan area, the superintendent shall permanently increase the amount per unit of average daily attendance determined pursuant to subdivision (b) of Section 56836.10 by the ratio of the amount determined pursuant to subdivision (b) to the statewide target per unit of average daily attendance determined pursuant to Section 56836.11 for the 2000-01 fiscal year. This increase shall be effective beginning in the 2001-02 fiscal year.

(e) The superintendent shall increase the statewide target per unit of average daily attendance determined pursuant to Section 56836.11 for the 2001-02 fiscal year by the amount determined pursuant to subdivision (b).

56836.159. (a) For the 2001-02 fiscal year, the superintendent shall compute a permanent adjustment for each special education local plan area as determined by this section.

- Computation for Providing a Permanent Adjustment for Each SELPA (6)

(b) The superintendent shall rank each special education local plan area by its funding level per unit of average daily attendance as determined by dividing the amount calculated for each special education local plan area for the 2001-02 fiscal year pursuant to Section 56836.08 plus the amount provided to each special education local plan area pursuant to subdivision (c) of Section 56836.158 by each special education local plan area's average daily attendance upon which funding is based for the 2001-02 fiscal year pursuant to Section 56836.15.

(c) The superintendent shall increase the special education local plan areas with the lowest level of funding per unit of average daily attendance as determined in subdivision (b) to that of the special education local plan area with the next highest level of funding per unit of average daily attendance by allocating an amount from that available for this purpose from the Budget Act to the lowest level special education local plan areas. The amount to be allocated shall equal the difference between the funding level per unit of average daily attendance of the lowest level special education local plan areas and the next highest level special education local plan area multiplied by the average daily attendance upon which funding is based for the 2001-02 fiscal year pursuant to Section 56836.15 of the lowest level special education local plan areas.

(d) If there is additional funding available after the allocation pursuant to subdivision (c), the allocation pursuant to subdivision (c) shall be repeated until all the funds appropriated for this purpose in the Budget Act have been used. If the amount appropriated for the purposes of this section from the 2001-02 Budget Act is not sufficient to fully fund the allocation pursuant to subdivision (c), then the funding provided to each special education local plan area in the last iteration pursuant to subdivision (c) shall be prorated.

(e) The amount, if any, computed pursuant to subdivision (c) and subdivision (d) for each special education local plan area shall be a permanent increase and shall, commencing in the 2002-03 fiscal year, be included in the prior year amount determined pursuant to paragraph (2) of subdivision (b) of Section 56836.10.

Article 3. Licensed Children's Institutions

56836.16. (a) For the 1998-99 fiscal year and each fiscal year thereafter, the superintendent shall apportion to each district and county superintendent providing programs pursuant to Article 5 (commencing with Section 56155) of Chapter 2 an amount equal to the difference, if any, between (1) the costs of master contracts with nonpublic, nonsectarian schools and agencies to provide special education instruction, designated instruction and services, or both, to pupils in licensed children's institutions, foster family homes, residential medical facilities, and other similar facilities funded under this chapter, and (2) the state income received by the district or county superintendent for providing these programs. The sum of the excess cost, plus any state or federal income for these programs, shall not exceed the cost of master contracts with nonpublic, nonsectarian schools and agencies to provide special education and designated instruction and services for these pupils, as determined by the superintendent.

- Apportionments

(b) The cost of master contracts with nonpublic, nonsectarian schools and agencies that a district or county office of education reports under this section shall not include any of the following costs that a district, county office, or special education local plan area may incur:

(1) Administrative or indirect costs for the local education agency.

(2) Direct support costs for the local education agency.

(3) Transportation costs provided either directly, or through a nonpublic, nonsectarian school or agency master contract or individual services agreement for use of services or equipment owned, leased, or contracted, by a district, special education local plan area, or county office for any pupils enrolled in nonpublic, nonsectarian schools or agencies, unless provided directly or subcontracted by that nonpublic, nonsectarian school or agency pursuant to subdivisions (a) and (b) of Section 56366.

(4) Costs for services routinely provided by the district or county office including the following, unless the board grants a waiver under 56101:

(A) School psychologist services other than those described in Sections 56324 and 56363 and included in a master contract and individual services agreement under subdivision (a) of Section 56366.

(B) School nurse services other than those described in Sections 49423.5, 56324, and 56363 and included in a master contract and individual services agreement under subdivision (a) of Section 56366.

(C) Language, speech, and hearing services other than those included in a master contract and individual services agreement under subdivision (a) of Section 56366.

(D) Modified, specialized, or adapted physical education services other than those included in a master contract and individual services agreement under subdivision (a) of Section 56366.

(E) Other services not specified by a pupil's individualized education program or funded by the state on a caseload basis.

(5) Costs for nonspecial education programs or settings, including those provided for individuals with exceptional needs between the ages of birth and five years, inclusive, pursuant to Sections 56431 and 56441.8

(6) Costs for nonpublic, nonsectarian school or agency placements outside of the state unless the board has granted a waiver pursuant to subdivisions (e) and (f) of Section 56365.

(7) Costs for related nonpublic, nonsectarian school pupil

assessments by a school psychologist or school nurse pursuant to Sections 56320 and 56324.

(8) Costs for services that the nonpublic, nonsectarian school or agency is not certified to provide.

(9) Costs for services provided by personnel who do not meet the requirements specified in subdivision (l) of Section 56366.1.

(10) Costs for services provided by public school employees.

(c) A nonpublic, nonsectarian school or agency shall not claim and is not entitled to receive reimbursement for attendance unless the site where the pupil is receiving special education or designated instruction and services is certified.

- No Reimbursement for Attendance Unless Site Is Certified

56836.17. (a) The superintendent may reimburse each district and county office of education providing programs pursuant to Article 5 (commencing with Section 56155) of Chapter 2 for assessment and identification costs for pupils in licensed children's institutions, foster family homes, residential medical facilities, and other similar facilities who are placed in state-certified nonpublic, nonsectarian schools.

- Reimbursement for Assessment, Identification Costs; Nonpublic School Placements

(b) Actual costs under this section shall not include either administrative or indirect costs, or any proration of support costs.

(c) The total amount reimbursed statewide under this section shall not exceed the amount appropriated for these purposes in any fiscal year. If the superintendent determines that this amount is insufficient to reimburse all claims, the superintendent shall prorate the deficiency among all districts or county offices submitting claims.

56836.18. (a) The superintendent shall establish and maintain an emergency fund for the purpose of providing relief to special education local plan areas when a licensed children's institution, foster family home, residential medical facility, or other similar facility serving individuals with exceptional needs opens or expands in a special education local plan area during the course of the school year which impacts the special education local plan area, or when a pupil is placed in a facility for which no public or state-certified nonpublic program exists within the special education local plan area in which the pupil's individualized education program can be implemented during the course of the school year and impacts the educational program.

- Emergency Fund

(b) The special education local plan area in which the impaction occurs shall be responsible for submitting a written request to the superintendent for emergency funding. The

- Written Request for Emergency Funding

written request shall contain, at a minimum, all of the following:

(1) Specific information on the new or expanded licensed children's institution, foster family home, residential medical facility, or other similar facility described in subdivision (a), including information on the new unserved or underserved pupils residing in the facility, or specific information relating to the new unserved or underserved pupils residing in those facilities.

(2) The identification of the steps undertaken demonstrating that no public special education program exists within the special education local plan area capable of programmatically meeting the needs of the identified pupils.

(3) A plan from the special education local plan area describing the services to be provided.

(c) The superintendent shall approve, modify, or disapprove the written request for emergency funding within 30 days of the receipt of the written request and shall notify the special education local plan area administrator, in writing, of the final decision.

- Superintendent Shall Act Within 30 Days

(d) It is the intent of the Legislature that appropriations necessary to fund these emergency situations shall be included in the Budget Act for each fiscal year.

- Legislative Intent

Article 4. Nonpublic, Nonsectarian School Contracts

56836.20. (a) The cost of master contracts with nonpublic, nonsectarian schools and agencies that a special education local plan area enters into shall not include any of the following costs that a special education local plan area may incur:

- Limitations on Cost of Master Contracts

(1) Administrative or indirect costs of the special education local plan area.

(2) Direct support costs for the special education local plan area.

(3) Transportation costs provided either directly, or through a nonpublic, nonsectarian school or agency contract for use of services or equipment owned, leased, or contracted, by a special education local plan area for any pupils enrolled in nonpublic, nonsectarian schools or agencies, unless provided directly or subcontracted by that nonpublic, nonsectarian school or agency pursuant to subdivisions (a) and (b) of Section 56366.

(4) Costs for services routinely provided by the special education local plan area including the following, unless the

board grants a waiver under Section 56101:

(A) School psychologist services other than those described in Sections 56324 and 56363 and included in a master contract and individual services agreement under subdivision (a) of Section 56366.

(B) School nurse services other than those described in Sections 49423.5, 56324, and 56363 and included in a master contract and individual services agreement under subdivision (a) of Section 56366.

(C) Language, speech, and hearing services other than those included in a master contract and individual services agreement under subdivision (a) of Section 56366.

(D) Modified, specialized, or adapted physical education services other than those included in a master contract and individual services agreement under subdivision (a) of Section 56366.

(E) Other services not specified by a pupil's individualized education program or funded by the state on a caseload basis.

(5) Costs for nonspecial education programs or settings, including those provided for individuals with exceptional needs between the ages of birth and five years, inclusive, pursuant to Sections 56431 and 56441.8.

(6) Costs for nonpublic, nonsectarian school or agency placements outside of the state unless the board has granted a waiver pursuant to subdivisions (e) and (f) of Section 56365.

(7) Costs for related nonpublic, nonsectarian school pupil assessments by a school psychologist or school nurse pursuant to Sections 56320 and 56324.

(8) Costs for services that the nonpublic, nonsectarian school or agency is not certified to provide.

(9) Costs for services provided by personnel who do not meet the requirements specified in subdivision (l) of Section 56366.1.

(10) Costs for services provided by public school employees.

(b) A nonpublic, nonsectarian school or agency shall not claim and is not entitled to receive reimbursement for attendance unless the site where the pupil is receiving special education or designated instruction and services is certified.

- No Reimbursement for Attendance Unless Site Is Certified

56836.21. (a) The State Department of Education shall administer an extraordinary cost pool to protect special education local plan areas from extraordinary costs associated with single placements in nonpublic, nonsectarian schools, excluding placements reimbursed pursuant to Article 3

- Extraordinary Cost Pool to Protect SELPAs from Extraordinary Single NPS Placement Costs (commencing with Section 56836.16). Funds shall be appropriated for this purpose in the annual Budget Act. Special education local plan areas shall be eligible for reimbursement from this pool in accordance with this section.

(b) The threshold amount for claims under this section shall be the lesser of the following:

- Threshold Amount for Claims

(1) One percent of the allocation calculated pursuant to Section 56836.08 for the special education local plan area for the current fiscal year for any special education local plan area that meets the criteria in Section 56212.

(2) The State Department of Education shall calculate the average cost of a nonpublic, nonsectarian school placement in the 1997-98 fiscal year. This amount shall be multiplied by 2.5, then by one plus the inflation factor computed pursuant to Section 42238.1, to obtain the alternative threshold amount for claims in the 1998-99 fiscal year. In subsequent fiscal years, the alternative threshold amount shall be the alternative threshold amount for the prior fiscal year multiplied by one plus the inflation factor computed pursuant to Section 42238.1.

(c) Special education local plan areas shall be eligible to submit claims for costs of any nonpublic, nonsectarian school placements in excess of those in existence in the 1997-98 fiscal year and exceeding the threshold amount on forms developed by the State Department of Education. All claims for a fiscal year shall be submitted by November 30 following the close of the fiscal year. If the total amount claimed by special education local plan areas exceeds the amount appropriated, the claims shall be prorated.

- Submitting Claims Exceeding the Threshold Amount

Article 5. Low Incidence Funding

56836.22. (a) Commencing with the 1985-86 fiscal year, and for each fiscal year thereafter, funds to support specialized books, materials, and equipment as required under the individualized education program for each pupil with low incidence disabilities, as defined in Section 56026.5, shall be determined by dividing the total number of pupils with low incidence disabilities in the state, as reported on December 1 of the prior fiscal year, into the annual appropriation provided for this purpose in the Budget Act.

- Funding Formula

(b) The per-pupil entitlement determined pursuant to subdivision (a) shall be multiplied by the number of pupils with low incidence disabilities in each special education local plan area to determine the total funds available for each local

- Per-Pupil Entitlement

plan.

(c) The superintendent shall apportion the amount determined pursuant to subdivision (b) to the special education local plan area for purposes of purchasing and coordinating the use of specialized books, materials, and equipment.

- Apportion Funds to SELPA

(d) As a condition of receiving these funds, the special education local plan area shall ensure that the appropriate books, materials, and equipment are purchased, that the use of the equipment is coordinated as necessary, and that the books, materials, and equipment are reassigned to local educational agencies within the special education local plan area once the agency that originally received the books, materials, and equipment no longer needs them.

- Funding Condition

(e) It is the intent of the Legislature that special education local plan areas share unused specialized books, materials, and equipment with neighboring special education local plan areas.

- SELPAs Share Unused Books, Materials, and Equipment

Article 6. Program Specialists and Administration of Regionalized Operations and Services

56836.23. Funds for regionalized operations and services and the direct instructional support or program specialists shall be apportioned to the special education local plan areas. As a condition to receiving those funds, the special education local plan area shall assure that all functions listed below are performed in accordance with the description set forth in its local plan adopted pursuant to subdivision (c) of Section 56205:

- Program Specialists and Regionalized Services Funds

- Functions Performed in Accordance with Local Plan

(a) Coordination of the special education local plan area and the implementation of the local plan.

(b) Coordinated system of identification and assessment.

(c) Coordinated system of procedural safeguards.

(d) Coordinated system of staff development and parent education.

(e) Coordinated system of curriculum development and alignment with the core curriculum.

(f) Coordinated system of internal program review, evaluation of the effectiveness of the local plan, and implementation of a local plan accountability mechanism.

(g) Coordinated system of data collection and management.

(h) Coordination of interagency agreements.

(i) Coordination of services to medical facilities.

(j) Coordination of services to licensed children's institutions and foster family homes.

(k) Preparation and transmission of required special education local plan area reports.

(l) Fiscal and logistical support of the community advisory committee.

(m) Coordination of transportation services for individuals with exceptional needs.

(n) Coordination of career and vocational education and transition services.

(o) Assurance of full educational opportunity.

(p) Fiscal administration and the allocation of state and federal funds pursuant to Section 56836.01.

(q) Direct instructional program support that may be provided by program specialists in accordance with Section 56368.

56836.24. Commencing with the 1998-99 fiscal year and each year thereafter, the superintendent shall make the following computations to determine the amount of funding for the purposes specified in Section 56836.23 to apportion to each special education local plan area for the fiscal year in which the computation is made:

- Computations to Determine Amount of Funding

(a) For the 1998-99 fiscal year the superintendent shall make the following computations:

- Computations for 1998-99 Fiscal Year

(1) Multiply the total amount of state General Fund money allocated to the special education local plan areas in the 1997-98 fiscal year, for the purposes of Article 9 (commencing with Section 56780) of Chapter 7, as that chapter existed on December 31, 1998, by one plus the inflation factor computed pursuant to subdivision (b) of Section 42238.1 for the 1998-99 fiscal year.

(2) Divide the amount calculated in paragraph (1) by the units of average daily attendance, exclusive of average daily attendance for absences excused pursuant to subdivision (b) of Section 46010 as that subdivision read on July 1, 1997, reported for the special education local plan area for the 1997-98 fiscal year.

(3) To determine the amount to be allocated to each special education local plan area in the 1998-99 fiscal year, the superintendent shall multiply the amount computed in paragraph (2) by the number of units of average daily attendance reported for the special education local plan area for the 1998-99 fiscal year, except that a special education local plan area designated as a necessary small special education local plan area in accordance with Section 56212

and reporting fewer than 15,000 units of average daily attendance for the 1998-99 fiscal year shall be deemed to have 15,000 units of average daily attendance, and no special education local plan area shall receive less than it received in the 1997-98 fiscal year.

(b) For the 1999-2000 fiscal year and each fiscal year thereafter, the superintendent shall make the following calculations:

- Calculations for 1999-2000 Fiscal Year and Each Fiscal Year Thereafter

(1) Multiply the amount determined in paragraph (2) of subdivision (a) by one plus the inflation factor computed pursuant to subdivision (b) of Section 42238.1 for the current fiscal year.

(2) Multiply the amount determined in paragraph (1) by the number of units of average daily attendance reported for the special education local plan area for the current fiscal year, except that a special education local plan area designated as a necessary small special education local plan area in accordance with Section 56212 and reporting fewer than 15,000 units of average daily attendance for the current fiscal year shall be deemed to have 15,000 units of average daily attendance.

56836.25. Funds received pursuant to this article shall be expended for the purposes specified in Section 56836.23.

- Use of Funds for Specified Purposes

Article 7. Federal Funding Allocations

56837. In each fiscal year for which the amounts appropriated by the federal government for Part B of the Individuals with Disabilities Education Act (20 U.S.C. Sec. 1400 et seq.), other than for preschool grants under Section 1419 of Title 20 of the United States Code, reaches four billion nine hundred twenty-four million six hundred seventy-two thousand two hundred dollars ($4,924,672,200) for the various states, the federal funding for local entitlements shall be allocated through the annual Budget Act in the following manner:

- Formula Changes When Federal Appropriations for Part B Grant Reaches $4,924,672,200

(a) The base year amount shall be allocated in a per pupil amount based on the number of pupils that have an individualized education program on December 1 of the fiscal year preceding the fiscal year for which the determination is made. The term "base year" me ans the federal fiscal year preceding the first fiscal year in which this section applies.

- Base Year

(b) Of the remaining federal funds for local entitlements exceeding the amount calculated for the base year, 85 percent shall be allocated to districts, special education local plan

- 85 Percent of Relative Number of Pupils; 15 Percent of Relative Number of Children Living in Poverty

areas, and county offices on the basis of the relative number of pupils enrolled in public and private elementary and secondary schools within the districts', special education local plan areas', and county offices' jurisdiction; and 15 percent shall be allocated to districts, special education local plan areas, and county offices in accordance with the relative number of children living in poverty in the jurisdiction, as determined by the superintendent.

(c) At least 75 percent of the federal grant funds under Part B of the Individuals with Disabilities Education Act (20 U.S.C. Sec. 1400 et seq.) shall be allocated to districts, special education local plan areas, and county offices.

- At Least 75 Percent of Federal Grant Funds Allocated as Local Entitlements

(d) Until the federal appropriation for Part B of the Individuals with Disabilities Education Act (20 U.S.C. Sec. 1400 et seq.) reaches four billion nine hundred twenty-four million six hundred seventy-two thousand two hundred dollars ($4,924,672,200), the federal funding for local entitlements shall be allocated on a per pupil amount based on the number of pupils having an individualized education program on December 1 of the fiscal year preceding the fiscal year for which the appropriation is made.

- Federal Funding for Local Entitlements Until Federal Formula Changes

56838. In each fiscal year for which federal funds are received by the state pursuant to Section 1419 of Title 20 of the United States Code for individuals with exceptional needs between the ages of 3 and 5, inclusive, the portion of funds available for local entitlements shall be allocated through the annual Budget Act in the following manner:

- Formula for Preschool Programs

(a) The district, special education local plan area, or county office shall receive a base entitlement calculated pursuant to its share of the federal fiscal year 1997 state grant for this program.

- Base Entitlement

(b) Of the remaining federal funds for local entitlements beyond the amount received for the federal fiscal year 1997, 85 percent shall be allocated to districts, special education local plan areas, and county offices on the basis of the relative number of pupils enrolled in public and private elementary and secondary schools within the jurisdiction of the district, special education local plan area, or county office; and 15 percent shall be allocated to districts, special education local plan areas, and county offices in accordance with the relative number of children in the jurisdiction living in poverty, as determined by the superintendent.

- 85 Percent of Relative Number of Pupils; 15 Percent of Relative Number of Children Living in Poverty

56839. For purposes of Sections 56837 and 56838, the superintendent shall use the most recent population data, including data on children living in poverty, that are available

- Most Recent Population Data

and are satisfactory to the United States Secretary of Education.

56840. The federal funding allocations for local entitlements in Sections 56837 and 56838 shall also apply to state agencies that were eligible to receive federal Part B funds pursuant to subsection (a) of Section 1414 of Title 20 of the United States Code as that provision read prior to the enactment of Public Law 105-17, the Individuals with Disabilities Education Act Amendments of 1997.

- Eligible State Agencies

56841. (a) Federal funds available through Part B of the Individuals with Disabilities Education Act (20 U.S.C. Sec. 1400 et seq.) and appropriated through the annual Budget Act shall only be used as follows:

- How Federal Funds May Be Used

(1) For the excess costs of special education.

(2) To supplement state, local, and other federal funds and not supplant those funds.

(b) Except as provided in subdivisions (c) and (d), the funds shall not be used to reduce the level of expenditures for the education of individuals with exceptional needs made by districts, special education local plan areas, and county offices from local funds below the level of those expenditures in the preceding fiscal year.

- Local Expenditures

(c) Notwithstanding subdivision (b), a district, special education local plan area, or county office may reduce the level of expenditures from local funds where the reduction is attributable to the following:

- Exceptions

(1) The voluntary departure, by retirement or otherwise, or departure for just cause, of special education personnel.

(2) A decrease in the enrollment of individuals with exceptional needs.

(3) The termination of the obligation of the district, special education local plan area, and county office, consistent with this part, to provide a program of special education to an individual or individuals with exceptional needs.

(4) The termination of costly expenditures for long-term purchases, such as the acquisition of equipment or the construction of facilities.

(d) Notwithstanding the provisions of subdivisions (a) and (b), for any fiscal year in which the amounts appropriated by Congress for the purposes of Section 1411 of Title 20 of the United States Code exceed four billion one hundred million dollars ($4,100,000,000), a district, special education local plan area, or county office, may reduce expenditures from local funds for the education of individuals with exceptional needs by an amount that shall not exceed 20 percent of the

- Reducing Expenditures from Local Funds

amount of federal funds available under Part B of the Individuals with Disabilities Education Act (20 U.S.C. Sec. 1400 et seq.) and allocated to the district, special education local plan area, and county office which exceeds the amount of these funds received by the district, special education local plan area, or county office in the preceding fiscal year.

(e) A district, special education local plan area, or county office may reduce expenditures from local funds for the education of individuals with exceptional needs pursuant to subdivision (d) only if the superintendent determines that the district, special education local plan area, or county office is meeting the requirements of this part and the requirements of the Individuals with Disabilities Education Act (20 U.S.C. Sec. 1400 et seq.) regarding the education of individuals with exceptional needs.

- State Superintendent Determines If Local Funds May Be Reduced

56842. The superintendent shall annually identify and submit to the Director of Finance recommendations for capacity-building and improvement grants for districts, special education local plan areas, or county offices for appropriation through the annual Budget Act. The capacity-building and improvement grants, if approved by the Legislature and the Governor, would be available to districts, special education local plan areas, and county offices pursuant to paragraph (4) of subsection (f) of Section 1411 of Title 20 of the United States Code. The capacity-building and improvement grant recommendations shall be submitted to meet the annual deadline of the Director of Finance for the development of the annual Budget Act.

- Recommendations for Capacity-Building and Improvement Grants

Article 8. Withholding of Payments

56845. (a) The superintendent may withhold, in whole or in part, state funds or federal funds allocated under the Individuals with Disabilities Education Act (20 U.S.C. Sec. 1400 et seq.) from a district, special education local plan area, or county office after reasonable notice and opportunity for a hearing if the superintendent finds either of the following:

- Superintendent May Withhold State or Federal Funds (7)

(1) The district, special education local plan area, or county office failed to comply substantially with a provision of state law, federal law, or regulations governing the provision of special education and related services to individuals with exceptional needs which results in the failure to comply substantially with corrective action orders issued by the department resulting from monitoring findings or

complaint investigations.

(2) The district, special education local plan area, or county office failed to implement the decision of a due process hearing officer based on noncompliance with provisions of this part, the implementing regulations, provisions of the Individuals with Disabilities Education Act (20 U.S.C. Sec. 1400 et seq.), or the implementing regulations, which noncompliance results in the denial of, or impedes the delivery of, a free and appropriate public education for an individual with exceptional needs.

(b) When the superintendent determines that a district, special education local plan area, or county office made substantial progress toward compliance with state law, federal law, or regulations governing the provision of special education and related services to individuals with exceptional needs, the superintendent may apportion the state or federal funds withheld from the district, special education local plan area, or county office.

- Substantial Progress Toward Compliance

(c) Notwithstanding any other provision of law, state funds may not be allocated to offset any federal funding intended for individuals with exceptional needs, as defined in Section 56026, and withheld from a local educational agency due to the agency's noncompliance with state or federal law.

- Noncompliance: State Funds May Not Offset Federal Funding

(d) For purposes of this section, in order to enter into contracts with one or more local education agencies to serve individuals with exceptional needs who are not being served as required under this part, the department is exempt from the requirements of Part 2 (commencing with Section 10100) of Division 2 of the Public Contract Code and from the requirements of Article 6 (commencing with Section 999) of Chapter 6 of Division 4 of the Military and Veterans Code.

- Contract Exemptions

NOTE

(1) Education Code Section 56836.02 was amended by Assembly Bill 804, Chapter 734, Statutes of 2001.
(2) Education Code Section 56836.095 was added by Senate Bill 735, Chapter 891, Statutes of 2001.
(3) Education Code Section 56836.156 was added by Senate Bill 982, Chapter 203, Statutes of 2001.
(4) Education Code Section 56836.157 was added by Senate Bill 982, Chapter 203, Statutes of 2001.
(5) Education Code Section 56836.158 was added by Senate Bill 735, Chapter 891, Statutes of 2001.
(6) Education Code Section 56836.159 was added by Senate Bill 735, Chapter 891, Statutes of 2001.
(7) Education Code Section 56845 was amended by Senate Bill 662, Chapter 159, Statutes of 2001.

CHAPTER 8. SPECIAL EDUCATION PROGRAMS FOR INDIVIDUALS WITH EXCEPTIONAL NEEDS RESIDING IN STATE HOSPITALS

56850. The purpose of the Legislature, in enacting this chapter, is to recognize that individuals with exceptional needs of mandated schoolage, residing in California's state hospitals for the developmentally disabled and mentally disordered, are entitled to, under the Individuals with Disabilities Education Act (20 U.S.C. Sec. 1400 et seq.), and the Rehabilitation Act of 1973 (29 U.S.C. Sec. 701 et seq.), the same access to educational programs as is provided for individuals with exceptional needs residing in our communities.

It is the intent of the Legislature to ensure that services shall be provided in the community near the individual state hospitals to the maximum extent appropriate, and in the least restrictive environment.

It is the further intent of the Legislature to ensure equal access to the educational process and to a full continuum of educational services for all individuals, regardless of their physical residence.

It is the further intent of the Legislature that educational services designated for state hospital residents not eligible for services mandated by the Individuals with Disabilities Education Act (20 U.S.C. Sec. 1400 et seq.) shall not be reduced or limited in any manner as a result of the enactment of this chapter.

It is the further intent of the Legislature that any cooperative agreements to provide educational services for state hospitals shall seek to maximize federal financial participation in funding these services.

56851. (a) In developing the individualized educational program for an individual residing in a state hospital who is eligible for services under the Individuals with Disabilities Education Act (20 U.S.C. Sec. 1400 et seq.), a state hospital shall include on its interdisciplinary team a representative of the district, or special education local plan area, or county office in which the state hospital is located, and the individual's state hospital teacher, depending on whether the state hospital is otherwise working with the district, special education local plan area, or county office for the provision of special education programs and related services to individuals with exceptional needs residing in state hospitals. However, if a district or special education local plan area that

- Legislative Intent

- Equal Access to Educational Services

- Ensure Services in Community

- Full Continuum of Educational Services

- No Reduction in Services to Others

- Maximize Federal Funding

- Representative on Hospital's Interdisciplinary Team

is required by this section to provide a representative from the district or special education local plan area does not do so, the county office shall provide a representative.

(b) The state hospital shall reimburse the district, special education local plan area, or the county office, as the case may be, for the costs, including salary, of providing the representative.

- State Hospital Reimburses

(c) Once the individual is enrolled in the community program, the educational agency providing special education shall be responsible for reviewing and revising the individualized education program with the participation of a representative of the state hospital and the parent. The agency responsible for the individualized education program shall be responsible for all individual protections, including notification and due process.

- Reviewing and Revising IEP

56852. In developing the individualized educational program and providing all special education programs and related services to individuals with exceptional needs residing in the state hospitals, the state hospitals shall comply with the requirements of the Individuals with Disabilities Education Act (20 U.S.C. Sec. 1400 et seq.), the Rehabilitation Act of 1973 (29 U.S.C. Sec. 701 et seq.), and special education provisions of this part and implementing regulations. Special education and related services shall be provided to each individual residing in a state hospital pursuant to the individualized education program for that individual.

- State Hospital Shall Comply with Federal and State Laws and Regulations

56852.5. The State Department of Education, within its existing program review process, shall specifically review the appropriateness of pupil placement for educational services as designated in the pupil's individualized education program and the criteria used in determining such placement.

- Department of Education Reviews Appropriations

56853. Nothing contained in this chapter shall affect the continued authority of the State Departments of Developmental Services and Mental Health over educational programs for individuals not eligible for services under the Individuals with Disabilities Education Act (20 U.S.C. Sec. 1400 et seq.) nor shall it affect the overall responsibility of the state hospitals for the care, treatment, and safety of individuals with exceptional needs under their control. The state hospitals shall continue to render appropriate and necessary developmental services, health related services, psychiatric services, and related services assigned to the state hospitals in the local written agreements, as part of their responsibilities for the care and treatment of state hospital residents.

- Department of Developmental Services and Mental Health Authority and Responsibility

- State Hospital Services

Health related services shall include services provided by physicians, psychiatrists, psychologists, audiologists, registered nurses, social workers, physical therapists, occupational therapists, psychiatric technicians, and developmental specialists, and shall be the responsibility of the state hospital if the individual with exceptional needs requires these services while in the community program.

56854. (a) The Superintendent of Public Instruction and the Directors of the State Departments of Developmental Services and Mental Health shall develop written interagency agreements to carry out the purposes of this chapter.

(b) For each county in which a state hospital is located, the county superintendent of schools, with the approval of the county board of education and the administrator of the state hospital, shall develop a local written agreement to carry out the purposes of this chapter. Such agreements shall be reviewed and updated annually and may be modified at any time with the concurrence of both parties to the agreements.

56855. For each county in which a state hospital is located the county superintendent of schools shall ensure that appropriate special education and related services are available in the community for which the state hospitals can contract. Such contract shall provide for any eligible individual with exceptional needs residing in the state hospitals whose individualized education program specifies that educational services for that individual should be most appropriately provided, in whole or in part, in a program other than on the hospital grounds. The county board of education shall approve any programs operated by the county superintendent pursuant to this chapter.

56856. In order to provide appropriate special education and related services to an individual residing in a state hospital, the State Departments of Developmental Services and Mental Health shall contract with a county superintendent of schools, nonpublic, nonsectarian school, or other agency to provide all or part of the services that the individual's individualized education program indicates should be provided in a program other than on state hospital grounds. A contract between a state hospital and a nonpublic, nonsectarian school shall only be entered into when no appropriate public education program is available.

56857. Nothing in this chapter shall preclude the State Departments of Developmental Services and Mental Health from contracting with a local public education agency, a nonpublic, nonsectarian school, or another agency to provide

- Health-Related Services

- State Interagency Agreements

- Duty of County Superintendent

- Contracts by Departments of Developmental Services and Mental Health

- Contracting for Services on State Hospital Grounds

special education and related services on the state hospital grounds for those pupils whose individualized education programs do not indicate that such education and services should be provided in a program other than on state hospital grounds. These contracts shall not involve funds appropriated for purposes of community-based special education programs provided for state hospital pupils pursuant to this chapter.

56857.5. (a) Commencing with the 1982-83 fiscal year, community school agencies providing school programs on state hospital grounds shall begin the orderly transfer of all state hospital pupils whose individualized education programs indicate that a community school program is appropriate, to schools located in the community.

- Orderly Transfer of Pupils to Community Schools

(b) Commencing with the 1983-84 fiscal year, all pupils covered by subdivision (a) shall be served in community schools other than on state hospital grounds, and the contracting provisions of this chapter shall apply only to pupils in community school programs other than on state hospital grounds.

- Contracting Provisions

(c) Waivers to subdivisions (a) and (b) may be granted only when approved by both the State Superintendent of Public Instruction and the Director of the State Department of Developmental Services.

- Waiver Provision

56858. (a) The State Department of Developmental Services shall, commencing August 1, 1985, and on the first day of each month thereafter, upon submission of an invoice by the county superintendent of schools, pay to the county superintendent of schools 8 percent of the amount projected to cover the cost of hospital pupils education in community school programs.

- Contract Payments

(b) The amount projected to cover the cost of hospital pupils educated in community school programs shall be determined according to procedures agreed by the State Department of Developmental Services and the State Department of Education.

(c) Upon completion of the fiscal year, the county superintendent of schools shall calculate the actual cost of hospital pupils educated in community schools according to procedures in subdivision (b) approved by the State Department of Developmental Services and the State Department of Education.

(d) If the calculated actual cost of educating these pupils is more or less than the total amount the county superintendent of schools has received for the fiscal year pursuant to subdivision (a), the following year's distribution shall be adjusted accordingly.

(e)   The county superintendent of schools shall distribute funds to participating districts on a pro rata basis.

56858.5.   (a)   Any contract prescribed by this chapter shall become effective unless disapproved by the State Department of Finance or State Department of General Services within 20 working days of receipt of the contract. Each department shall have 10 working days to consider the contract.

- Contract Review by Departments of Finance and General Services

(b)   Contracts shall be submitted to the State Department of Developmental Services for approval before May 15.

- Contract Submittal

(c)   No payments shall be processed in advance of contract approval, and no educational services shall be provided in the community school programs in advance of contract approval.

- Conditions for Payment

56858.7.   (a)   Nothing in this chapter shall prohibit the inclusion of in-kind services or the assignment of state hospital personnel in a contract for services pursuant to this chapter.

- In-Kind Services

(b)   Ten percent of the contract costs shall be attributed to in-kind services.   In-kind services above 10 percent of the contract costs shall be mutually agreed upon by both parties to the contract. Any disagreement over in-kind services above 10 percent shall not be cause for delaying approval of the contract.

- Ten Percent of Contract Costs

(c)   A 60 day prior written notice shall be given by the state hospital to the county superintendent of schools for the initiation or removal of in-kind state hospital classified personnel.

- Initiation or Removal of In-Kind Personnel

56859.   All certificated state hospital employees hired to provide educational services to individuals of mandated school age after September 29, 1980, shall possess an appropriate California credential in special education. Current certificated state hospital employees who do not possess appropriate California credentials in special education shall be given a period of not more than five years from September 29, 1980, to obtain such appropriate credentials. Certificated state hospital employees who do not possess appropriate California credentials in special education at the end of the five-year period shall be reassigned to provide educational services to individuals residing in state hospitals who are not eligible for services under the Individuals with Disabilities Education Act (20 U.S.C. Sec. 1400 et seq.).

- Employees Shall Possess Appropriate Credential

56860.   Special transportation shall be the responsibility of the state hospital.

- Transportation Responsibility

56862. It is not the intent of this chapter to displace educational and related services personnel already employed by the state hospitals under the administration of the State Department of Developmental Services or the State Department of Mental Health, or to reduce their salaries or other employee benefits.

The State Department of Developmental Services and the State Department of Mental Health shall complete an annual review of the impact that implementation of this act will have in reducing the need for positions in state hospitals due to time spent by residents in community education programs and shall submit a report on its findings to the Department of Finance for approval.

56863. The state hospitals, as part of the notification to parents of pupils of their rights pursuant to the Individuals with Disabilities Education Act (20 U.S.C. Sec. 1400 et seq.), the Rehabilitation Act of 1973 (29 U.S.C. Sec. 701 et seq.), and this part and implementing regulations, shall notify parents of the right that their child can be considered for education programs other than on state hospital grounds.

For the purposes of this section, the term "parent of pupil" shall mean a parent, a legal guardian, a conservator, a person acting as a parent of a child, or a surrogate parent appointed pursuant to Public Law 94-142.

Information and records concerning state hospital patients in the possession of the Superintendent of Public Instruction shall be treated as confidential under Section 5328 of the Welfare and Institutions Code and the Federal Privacy Act of 1974, Public Law 93-579.

56864. Individuals with exceptional needs residing in state hospitals shall not be included within the funding calculation made pursuant to Chapter 7.2 (commencing with Section 56836).

56865. Funds appropriated by Section 11 of Chapter 1191 of the Statutes of 1980 may be used for remodeling classrooms located in a community school, in addition to the purposes of Chapter 25 (commencing with Section 17785) of Part 10, in order to serve state hospital pupils whose individualized education programs require a community school program.

- Impact on State Hospital Personnel

- Notification of Parent of Pupil

- Definition of Parent of Pupil

- Confidentiality of Records

- Individuals Not Subject to Service Proportions

- Remodeling Classrooms

CHAPTER 8.5. SPECIAL EDUCATION AT THE YOUTH AUTHORITY

56867. (a) The State Department of Education is responsible for monitoring the Department of the Youth Authority for compliance with state and federal laws and regulations regarding special education.

- Department of Education Responsible for Monitoring (1)

(b) Notwithstanding any other provision of law, the State Department of Education and the California State University shall enter into an interagency agreement under which the Center for the Study of Correctional Education, located on the California State University, San Bernardino campus, shall provide technical assistance to the State Department of Education regarding compliance with state and federal laws and regulations regarding special education at the Department of the Youth Authority.

- Interagency Agreement Between Department of Education and California State University

(c) The State Department of Education shall prepare the interagency agreement in consultation with the California State University, San Bernardino, and the superintendent of education for the Department of the Youth Authority. The interagency agreement shall require the center to provide all of the following services to the Special Education Division of the State Department of Education:

- Requirements of Interagency Agreement

(1) Assistance in providing reviews and assessments of special education at each schoolsite in the Department of the Youth Authority.

(2) Assistance in drafting reports of findings for each review.

(3) Assistance in drafting corrective action plans, based on preliminary findings of noncompliance that include specific suggested outcomes to achieve compliance, and other instruments conveying recommendations and suggestions resulting from reviews and assessments.

(4) Onsite technical assistance and support to the Department of the Youth Authority, as authorized by the Special Education Division of the State Department of Education.

(5) Identifying and developing suggested draft protocols and best practices for providing special education services in correctional settings.

(6) Developing suggested draft protocols and a suggested draft best practices model for providing monitoring and technical assistance services for special education in youthful correctional settings.

(7) Evaluating the training needs and priorities of educational personnel serving wards with exceptional needs at the Department of the Youth Authority.

(8) Reviewing the Department of the Youth Authority's current special education local plan, policies, procedures, and forms, for compliance with state and federal special education law and, with the approval of the State Department of Education, providing suggested revisions as necessary to provide better compliance and to better reflect the best practices in a correctional setting.

(d) Technical assistance provided pursuant to this section shall reflect existing or subsequently adopted standards for state and federal compliance. Reviews conducted pursuant to this section shall include, but not be limited to, assessments of the following special education services for wards at the Department of the Youth authority with exceptional needs:

- Technical Assistance and Reviews

(1) Identification and assessment of wards with exceptional needs.

(2) Parent notification, consent, and participation.

(3) Individual education plan development and content, including behavior intervention and transition plans.

(4) Assessment of ward progress.

(5) Provision of services in the least restrictive environment maximizing inclusion.

(6) Services to pupils who are not proficient in English.

(7) Observance of procedural safeguards and compliance with state and federal law.

(e) Commencing no later than one year after entering into the interagency agreement specified in this section and annually thereafter until termination of the agreement, with the assistance of the center, the State Department of Education shall provide interim status reports of the services received from the center pursuant to this section to the Department of Finance and the Legislature.

- Interim Status Reports

(f) No later than December 1, 2006, the State Department of Education shall submit a report to the Legislature on the usefulness of the services received from the center pursuant to the interagency agreement required by this section.

- Report to the Legislature

(g) The interagency agreement required by this section shall be funded through an appropriation made in the annual Budget Act with federal funds made available for state agencies under Part B of the federal Individuals with Disabilities Education Act (20 U.S.C. Sec. 1400 and following).

- Funding for Interagency Agreement

(h) This section shall remain in effect only until January 1, 2007, and as of that date is repealed, unless a later enacted statute, that is enacted before January 1, 2007, deletes or extends that date.

- Repeal Clause; Inoperative 1/1/07

NOTE

(1) Chapter 8.5 (commencing with Section 56867) was added to Part 30 of the Education Code by Senate Bill 505, Chapter 536, Statutes of 2001.

CHAPTER 9. JOINT FUNDING FOR EDUCATION OF HANDICAPPED CHILDREN ACT OF 1980

56875. (a) The Legislature hereby finds and declares that numerous federal and state programs make funds available for the provision of education and related services to individuals with exceptional needs. The Legislature further finds and declares that the state has not maximized the use of available federal funds for provision of such services to these children. The Legislature further recognizes the need to simplify procedures for securing all available funds for services to individuals with exceptional needs and for utilizing federal financial resources to the greatest possible extent.

- Legislative Findings, Declarations and Intent

(b) It is the intent of the Legislature to provide local educational agencies with maximum flexibility to secure and utilize all available state and federal funds so as to enable such agencies to meet the needs of individuals with exceptional needs more effectively and efficiently. Furthermore, it is the intent of the Legislature to provide maximum federal funding to local educational agencies for the provision of education and related services to individuals with exceptional needs.

56876. On or before April 1, 1981, the Department of Education, the State Department of Health Services, the State Department of Mental Health, the State Department of Developmental Services, the State Department of Social Services, the Department of Rehabilitation, the Employment Development Department, the Department of the Youth Authority, and the State Council on Developmental Disabilities shall, in conformance with procedures established by the Office of Planning and Research, submit a plan to both the Senate Finance Committee and the Assembly Ways and Means Committee that shall include a timetable for implementation of this chapter, including, but not limited to the following:

- Timetable for Implementation of Chapter

(a) A list of provisions of state regulations and laws for which waivers may be granted in order that local educational agencies may maximize available federal funds to provide education and related services to individuals with exceptional needs without decreasing funds available to other state and local agencies.

(b) A list of provisions of federal law, federal regulations, or both, for which it is recommended that the state seek waiver.

(c) A list of specific related services which shall be provided by the respective departments and their political subdivisions to carry out the mandate of the Individuals with Disabilities Education Act (20 U.S.C. Sec. 1400 et seq.) and its implementing regulations.

56877. (a) Implementation of the funding procedures established pursuant to this chapter shall commence on July 1, 1981.

- Implementation of Funding

(b) The State Department of Education shall, in order to implement the provisions of this chapter, do all of the following:

(1) Provide necessary technical assistance to local educational agencies.

(2) Establish procedures for such agencies to obtain available federal funds.

(3) Apply for necessary waivers of federal statutes and regulations governing federal education programs that provide education and related services to individuals with exceptional needs.

(c) The State Board of Education shall grant necessary waivers of applicable state laws and administrative regulations relating to special education programs to participating local educational agencies.

56878. If necessary to simplify procedures for securing all available funds for services to individuals with exceptional needs and for utilizing federal financial resources to the greatest possible extent, the Health and Welfare Agency, at the request of the State Department of Health Services, the State Department of Mental Health, the State Department of Developmental Services, the State Department of Social Services, the Department of Rehabilitation, or the Employment Development Department; and the Youth and Adult Corrections Agency, at the request of the Department of the Youth Authority, may grant waivers of state laws and regulations for which they have administrative responsibility. Waivers granted pursuant to this section may be only for those laws and regulations identified in the plan submitted to the Legislature pursuant to Section 56876, and only when necessary to implement this part.

- Waivers of State Laws and Regulations

56879. Based upon the plan submitted pursuant to Section 56876, the State Department of Health Services, the State Department of Mental Health, the State Department of Developmental Services, the State Department of Social Services, the Department of Rehabilitation, the Employment Development Department, and the Department of the Youth

- Duties of State Agencies

Authority shall, in order to implement the provisions of this chapter, do the following:

(1) Grant necessary waivers of applicable state laws and administrative regulations under their respective jurisdictions to local educational agencies and other agencies, and issue such other administrative regulations as are necessary.

(2) Apply for necessary waivers of federal statutes and regulations governing federal programs which provide services to individuals with exceptional needs and which are under their respective jurisdictions.

56881. (a) The Office of Planning and Research shall establish procedures for development and review of state agency plans for funds available under all federal programs which may provide services to individuals with exceptional needs and which are within the jurisdictions of the Department of Education, the State Department of Health Services, the State Department of Mental Health, the State Department of Developmental Services, the State Department of Social Services, the Department of Rehabilitation, the Employment Development Department, the Department of the Youth Authority, and the State Council on Developmental Disabilities. Results of the review shall be transmitted to the state agency preparing the plan and to the responsible cabinet level agency to make a determination if the plan shall be changed. Such planning procedures and review shall assure coordination between state agencies and shall assure that applicable plans enable local education agencies to secure maximum available federal funding, without decreasing funds available to other state and local agencies, under each of the following federal programs:

- Governor's Office of Planning and Research Responsibilities

(1) Education for All Handicapped Children as provided under P.L. 91-230, Education of the Handicapped Act, Title VI, Part B, as amended by P.L. 93-380 and by P.L. 94-142.

(2) Medical Assistance (Medicaid), as provided under the Social Security Act of 1935, Title XIX, as amended.

(3) Early and Periodic Screening, Diagnosis and Treatment as provided under P.L. 74-271, Social Security Act of 1935, Title XIX as amended, Section 1905 (a)(4)(B).

(4) Developmental Disabilities Services as provided under P.L. 91-517, the Developmental Disabilities Services and Construction Act of 1970, as amended by P.L. 94-103 and the Developmental Disabilities Assistance and Bill of Rights Act, as amended by P.L. 95-602, Amendments to the Rehabilitation Act of 1973.

(5) Social Services as provided under P.L 74-271, Social Security Act of 1935, Title XX, as amended by P.L. 93-647, P.L. 94-401, P.L. 94-566, and P.L. 95-171.

(6) Crippled Children's Services as provided under P.L. 74-271, Social Security Act of 1935, Title V, Section 504, as amended.

(7) Vocational Training and Counseling Services as provided under P.L. 94-482, Vocational Educational Act; P.L. 93-112, as amended by P.L. 93-516, the Rehabilitation Act of 1973; and P.L. 93-203, the Comprehensive Employment and Training Act, as amended.

(8) Maternal and Child Health Services, as provided under P.L. 74-271, Social Security Act of 1935, Title V, Section 503, as amended.

(9) Supplementary Security Income, Disabled Children's Program, as provided under P.L. 74-271, Social Security Act of 1935, Title XVI, Section 1615(b) as amended by P.L. 94-566.

(b) In addition to the programs enumerated in subdivision (a), any other programs under which the following services may be provided to individuals with exceptional needs shall be subject to the review procedure specified in subdivision (a) as conducted by the Office of Planning and Research.

(1) Screening and identification.

(2) Assessment and diagnosis.

(3) Health related services, including, but not limited to, speech pathology and audiological services, physical therapy, occupational therapy, and vision services and therapy.

(4) Psychological counseling.

(5) Mental health services.

(6) Vocational related services.

(7) Social services.

(8) Transportation services.

(9) Other services necessary to assist individuals with exceptional needs in benefiting from their education.

56882. On or before May 1, 1981, the State Board of Education shall, after consultation with the Office of Planning and Research and all state agencies listed in Section 56876, issue regulations for implementation of the provisions of this chapter, to be used by local educational agencies, in implementing the provisions of this chapter. Such regulations shall identify all other administrative regulations relating to education and related services which shall be waived for local educational agencies. Such regulations shall include, but not be limited to regulations relating to application, accounting,

- State Board of Education Issues Regulations for Local Educational Agencies and reporting procedures for programs which may provide education and related services for individuals with exceptional needs.

56883. (a) On or before July 1, 1981, the Department of Education shall, after consultation with the Office of Planning and Research and the agencies listed in Section 56876, and based upon the plan required in Section 56876, issue guidelines to local educational agencies, for implementation of the provisions of this chapter.

- Department of Education Issues Guidelines to Local Educational Agencies

(b) Such guidelines shall include, but not be limited to, the following:

(1) Identification of sources of funds available under all state and federal programs which may provide education and related services to individuals with exceptional needs and for which local educational agencies and other applicable agencies are eligible.

(2) Identification of all statutes and regulations applicable to programs for individuals with exceptional needs under the jurisdictions of the Department of Education, the State Department of Health Services, the State Department of Mental Health, the State Department of Developmental Services, the State Department of Social Services, the Department of Rehabilitation, the Employment Development Department, and the Department of the Youth Authority, which may be waived pursuant to subdivisions (b), (c), and (d) of Section 56877.

56884. To assist in implementation of the provisions of this chapter, the Department of Education and state agencies listed in Section 56876 shall, by April 1, 1981, after consultation with representatives of their respective local administering agencies, negotiate and enter into interagency agreements to help promote coordination of services for individuals with exceptional needs. The interagency agreements shall include, but not be limited to, the definition of each agency's roles and responsibilities for serving individuals with exceptional needs.

- State Interagency Agreements

- Definition of Each Agency's Roles and Responsibilities

56885. The Department of Finance shall, after consultation with appropriate state agencies, ascertain the amounts of funds, if any, that should be transferred between state agencies in order to achieve the purposes of the bill.

- Amounts of Funds for Transfer Between State Agencies (1)

Any savings that may occur to any program due to maximized use of federal funds or services to individuals with exceptional needs as provided in this article shall be utilized to defer projected increased costs to meet full mandates of the Individuals with Disabilities Education Act (20 U.S.C. Sec. 1400 et seq.).

NOTE

(1) Section 56885 was amended by Senate Bill 1191, Chapter 745, Statutes of 2001.

CALIFORNIA CODE OF REGULATIONS
TITLE 5. EDUCATION
DIVISION 1. STATE DEPARTMENT OF EDUCATION
CHAPTER 3. HANDICAPPED CHILDREN

Subchapter 1. Special Education

Article 1. General Provisions

3000. Scope.

- Scope of Regulations

(a) This chapter applies to those special education programs which are administered under a local plan as defined in Section 56027 and Part 30 of the Education Code. Provisions of this chapter shall be construed as supplemental to, and in the context of, Federal laws and regulations relating to individuals with exceptional needs in effect on January 1, 1981, and state laws and regulations relating to individuals with exceptional needs. The intent of this chapter is to assure conformity with the Education for All Handicapped Children Act, Public Law 94-142 (20 USC 1401, et seq.) and Section 504 of the Rehabilitation Act of 1973, Public Law 93-112 (29 USC 794), and their implementing regulations including Title 34, Code of Federal Regulations, Sections 300.1 et seq.; Sections 104.1 et seq.; and Sections 76.1 et seq.

(b) A school district, special education local plan area, or county office shall use federal, state, local, and private sources of support which are available to provide services as specified in an individualized education program.

(c) Nothing in this chapter relieves any other agency from an otherwise valid obligation to provide or pay for services for individuals with exceptional needs. Clarification and specificity of responsibilities shall be included in but not limited to interagency agreements.

[Authority cited: Section 56100(a), (i), and (j), Education Code] [Reference: Sections 56000-56001, Education Code; and 34 CFR 300.301]

3001. Definitions.

- Definitions

In addition to those found in Education Code sections 56020-56033, Public Law 94-142 as amended (20 U.S.C. 1401 et seq.), and Title 34, Code of Federal Regulations,

Part 300 and 301, the following definitions are provided:

(a) "Applicant" means an individual, firm, partnership, association, or corporation who has made application for certification as a nonpublic, nonsectarian school, or agency.

- Applicant

(b) "Assessment and development of the individualized education program" (IEP) means services described in Education Code sections 56320 et seq. and 56340 et seq.

- Assessment and Development of the Individualized Education Program

(c) "Behavioral emergency" is the demonstration of a serious behavior problem: (1) which has not previously been observed and for which a behavioral intervention plan has not been developed; or (2) for which a previously designed behavioral intervention is not effective. Approved behavioral emergency procedures must be outlined in the special education local planning area (SELPA) local plan.

- Behavioral Emergency

(d) "Behavioral intervention" means the systematic implementation of procedures that result in lasting positive changes in the individual's behavior. "Behavioral intervention" means the design, implementation, and evaluation of individual or group instructional and environmental modifications, including programs of behavioral instruction, to produce significant improvements in human behavior through skill acquisition and the reduction of problematic behavior. "Behavioral interventions" are designed to provide the individual with greater access to a variety of community settings, social contacts and public events; and ensure the individual's right to placement in the least restrictive educational environment as outlined in the individual's IEP. "Behavioral interventions" do not include procedures which cause pain or trauma. "Behavioral interventions" respect the individual's human dignity and personal privacy. Such interventions shall assure the individual's physical freedom, social interaction, and individual choice.

- Behavioral Intervention

(e) "Behavioral intervention case manager" means a designated certificated school/district/county/nonpublic school or agency staff member(s) or other qualified personnel pursuant to subsection (ac) contracted by the school district or county office or nonpublic school or agency who has been trained in behavior analysis with an emphasis on positive behavioral interventions. The "behavioral intervention case manager" is not intended to be a new staffing requirement and does not create any new credentialing or degree requirements. The duties of the "behavioral intervention case manager" may be performed by any existing staff member trained in behavior analysis with an emphasis on positive

- Behavioral Intervention Case Manager

behavioral interventions, including, but not limited to, a teacher, resource specialist, school psychologist, or program specialist.

(f) "Behavioral intervention plan" is a written document which is developed when the individual exhibits a serious behavior problem that significantly interferes with the implementation of the goals and objectives of the individual's IEP. The "behavioral intervention plan" shall become part of the IEP. The plan shall describe the frequency of the consultation to be provided by the behavioral intervention case manager to the staff members and parents who are responsible for implementing the plan. A copy of the plan shall be provided to the person or agency responsible for implementation in noneducational settings. The plan shall include the following:

- Behavioral Intervention Plan

(1) a summary of relevant and determinative information gathered from a functional analysis assessment;

(2) an objective and measurable description of the targeted maladaptive behavior(s) and replacement positive behavior(s);

(3) the individual's goals and objectives specific to the behavioral intervention plan;

(4) a detailed description of the behavioral interventions to be used and the circumstances for their use;

(5) specific schedules for recording the frequency of the use of the interventions and the frequency of the targeted and replacement behaviors; including specific criteria for discontinuing the use of the intervention for lack of effectiveness or replacing it with an identified and specified alternative;

(6) criteria by which the procedure will be faded or phased-out, or less intense/frequent restrictive behavioral intervention schedules or techniques will be used;

(7) those behavioral interventions which will be used in the home, residential facility, work site or other noneducational settings; and

(8) specific dates for periodic review by the IEP team of the efficacy of the program.

(g) "Board" means the State Board of Education.

(h) "Certification" means authorization by the State Superintendent of Public Instruction (Superintendent) for a nonpublic school or nonpublic agency to service individuals with exceptional needs under a contract pursuant to the provisions of Education Code section 56366(c).

- Board
- Certification

(i) "Contracting education agency," means school district, special education local plan area, or county office of

- Contracting Education Agency

A-3

education.

(j) "Credential" means a valid credential, life diploma, permit, or document in special education or pupil personnel services issued by, or under the jurisdiction of, the State Board of Education prior to 1970 or the California Commission on Teacher Credential, which entitles the holder thereof to perform services for which certification qualifications are required.

- Credential

(k) "Department" means the California Department of Education.

- Department

(l) "Department of Consumer Affairs" means the California Department of Consumer Affairs.

- Department of Consumer Affairs

(m) "Dual enrollment" means the concurrent attendance of the individual in a public education agency and a nonpublic school and/or a nonpublic agency.

- Dual Enrollment

(n) "Feasible" as used in Education Code Section 56363(a) means the individualized education program team:

- Feasible

(1) has determined the regular class teacher, special class teacher, and/or resource specialist possesses the necessary competencies and credentials/certificates to provide the designated instruction and service specified in the individualized education program, and

(2) has considered the time and activities required to prepare for and provide the designated instruction and service by the regular class teacher, special class teacher, and/or resource specialist.

(o) "Free appropriate public education" means special education and related services that:

- Free Appropriate Public Education

(1) have been provided at public expense, under public supervision and direction and without charge;

(2) meets any of the standards established by state or federal law;

(3) include an appropriate preschool, elementary, or secondary school education in California; and

(4) are provided in conformity with the individualized education program required under state and federal law.

(p) "Individual Services Agreement" means a document, prepared by the local education agency, that specifies the length of time for which special education and designated instruction and services are to be provided, by nonpublic schools and/or nonpublic agencies, to individuals with exceptional needs.

- Individual Services Agreement

(q) "Instructional day" shall be the same period of time as regular school day for that chronological peer group unless otherwise specified in the individualized education program.

- Instructional Day

(r) "License" means a valid nonexpired document issued by a licensing agency within the Department of Consumer Affairs or other state licensing office authorized to grant licenses and authorizing the bearer of the document to provide certain professional services or refer to themselves using a specified professional title. If a license is not available through an appropriate state licensing agency, a certificate of registration with the appropriate professional organization at the national or state level which has standards established for the certificate that are equivalent to a license shall be deemed to be a license.

- License

(s) "Linguistically appropriate goals, objectives, and programs" means:

- Linguistically Appropriate Goals

(1)(A) Those activities which lead to the development of English language proficiency; and

(B) Those instructional systems either at the elementary or secondary level which meet the language development needs of the limited English language learner.

(2) For individuals whose primary language is other than English, and whose potential for learning a second language, as determined by the individualized education program team, is severely limited, nothing in this section shall preclude the individualized education program team from determining that instruction may be provided through an alternative program pursuant to a waiver under Education Code section 311(c), including a program provided in the individual's primary language, provided that the IEP team periodically, but not less than annually, reconsiders the individual's ability to receive instruction in the English language.

(t) "Local education agency" means a public board of education or other public authority legally constituted in California for either administrative control or direction of, or to perform a service function for, public elementary or secondary schools in a city, county, township, school district, or other political subdivision of California, or such combination of school districts or counties as are recognized in California as an administrative agency for its public elementary or secondary schools.

- Local Education Agency

(u) "Local governing board," means either district or county board of education.

- Local Governing Board

(v) "Master contract" means the legal document that binds the public education agency and the nonpublic school or nonpublic agency.

- Master Contract

(w) "Nonsectarian" means a private, nonpublic school or agency that is not owned, operated, controlled by, or

- Nonsectarian

formally affiliated with a religious group or sect, whatever might be the actual character of the education program or the primary purpose of the facility and whose articles of incorporation and/or by-laws stipulate that the assets of such agency or corporation will not inure to the benefit of a religious group.

(x) "Primary language" means the language other than English, or other mode of communication, the person first learned, or the language which is spoken in the person's home.

- Primary Language

(y) "Qualified" means that a person has met federal and state certification, licensing, registration, or other comparable requirements which apply to the area in which he or she is providing special education or related services, or, in the absence of such requirements, the state-education-agency-approved or recognized requirements, and adheres to the standards of professional practice established in federal and state law or regulation, including the standards contained in the California Business and Professions Code. Nothing in this definition shall be construed as restricting the activities in services of a graduate needing direct hours leading to licensure, or of a student teacher or intern leading to a graduate degree at an accredited or approved college or university, as authorized by state laws or regulations.

- Qualified

(z) "Related services" means transportation, and such developmental, corrective, and other supportive services (including speech pathology and audiology, psychological services, physical and occupational therapy, recreation, including therapeutic recreation, social work services, counseling services, including rehabilitation counseling, and medical services, except that such medical services shall be for diagnostic and evaluation purposes only) as required to assist an individual with exceptional needs to benefit from special education, and includes the early identification and assessment of disabling conditions in children. Related services include, but are not limited to, Designated Instruction and Services. The list of related services is not exhaustive and may include other developmental, corrective, or supportive services if they are required to assist a child with a disability to benefit from special education. Each related service defined under this part may include appropriate administrative and supervisory activities that are necessary for program planning, management, and evaluation.

- Related Services

(aa) "Serious behavior problems" means the individual's

- Serious Behavior Problems

behaviors which are self-injurious, assaultive, or cause serious property damage and other severe behavior problems that are pervasive and maladaptive for which instructional/behavioral approaches specified in the student's IEP are found to be ineffective.

(ab) "Specified education placement" means that unique combination of facilities, personnel, location or equipment necessary to provide instructional services to an individual with exceptional needs, as specified in the IEP, in any one or a combination of public, private, home and hospital, or residential setting. The IEP team shall document its rationale for placement in other than the pupil's school and classroom in which the pupil would otherwise attend if the pupil were not disabled. The documentation shall indicate why the pupil's disability prevents his or her needs from being met in a less restrictive environment even with the use of supplementary aids and services.

- Specified Education Placement

(ac) "Special education" means specially designed instruction, at no cost to the parents, to meet the unique needs of individuals with exceptional needs whose educational needs cannot be met with modification of the regular instruction program, and related services, at no cost to the parent, that may be needed to assist these individuals to benefit from specially designed instruction.

- Special Education

(ad) "Specialized physical health care services" means those health services prescribed by the individual's licensed physician and surgeon requiring medically related training for the individual who performs the services and which are necessary during the school day to enable the individual to attend school.

- Specialized Physical Health Care Services

(ae) "Superintendent" means the State Superintendent of Public Instruction.

- Superintendent

(af) "Temporary physical disability" means a disability incurred while an individual was in a regular education class and which at the termination of the temporary physical disability, the individual can, without special intervention, reasonably be expected to return to his or her regular education class.

- Temporary Physical Disability

[Authority cited: Sections 56100 and 56523(a), Education Code.] [Reference: Sections 33000, 33300, 49423.5, 56026, 56034, 56320, 56361, 56366, 56520 and 56523, Education Code; Section 2, Article IX, Constitution of the State of California; Sections 1401(8) and (17), United States Code, Title 20; and Sections 300.4 and 300.12, Code of Federal

Article 2. Administration

3010. Other Public Agencies.

Educational programs and services administered by other public agencies which provide educational programs and services to individuals with exceptional needs shall adhere to the provisions of federal and state laws and regulations relating to individuals with exceptional needs.

- Other Public Agencies

[Authority cited: Education Code Section 56100(a) and (i); 20 USC 1414(c)(2)(B); and 34 CFR 300.600] [Reference: Sections 56000, 56100(i), and 56500, Education Code; and 34 CFR 300.2, 300.11, 300.60]

Article 3. Identification, Referral, and Assessment

3021. Referral.

(a) All referrals for special education and related services shall initiate the assessment process and shall be documented. When a verbal referral is made, staff of the school district, special education local plan area, or county office shall offer assistance to the individual in making a request in writing, and shall assist the individual if the individual requests such assistance.

(b) All school staff referrals shall be written and include:

(1) A brief reason for the referral.

(2) Documentation of the resources of the regular education program that have been considered, modified, and when appropriate, the results of intervention.   This documentation shall not delay the time lines for completing the assessment plan or assessment.

- Referrals

[Authority cited: Section 56100(a), (i), and (j), Education Code] [Reference: Sections 56300-56303, Education Code; 34 CFR 300.128, 300.220]

3021.1. Referral of Pupils Having a Diagnosed Chronic Illness.

(a) When a pupil has been medically diagnosed as having a chronic illness or acute health problem, the pupil may be referred to the school district or county office for an assessment to determine the need for special education.

- Referral of Pupils Who Have a Diagnosed Chronic Illness

(b) The following information shall be reviewed by the individualized education program team:

(1) The type of chronic illness;

(2) The possible medical side effects and complications of treatment that could affect school functioning;

(3) The educational and social implications of the disease and treatment to include but not limited to the likelihood of fatigue, absences, changes in physical appearance, amputations, or problems with fine and gross motor control, and

(4) Special considerations necessitated by outbreaks of infectious diseases, if applicable.

(c) The individualized education program team shall designate the school's liaison with the pupil's primary health provider.

[Authority cited: Section 56100(a), (i), and (j), Education Code] [Reference: Sections 56300-56303, Education Code; 34 CFR 300.128, 300.220]

3022. Assessment Plan.

In addition to the assessment plan requirements of Education Code Section 56321, the proposed written assessment plan shall include a description of any recent assessment conducted, including any available independent assessments and any assessment information the parent requests to be considered, and information indicating the pupil's primary language and the pupil's language proficiency in the primary language as determined by Education Code Section 52164.1.

- Assessment Plan

[Authority cited: Section 56100(a), (i), (j), Education Code; and 20 USC 1414(c)(2)(B)] [Reference: Sections 56321, 56329, Education Code; and 34 CFR 300.500-502, and 300.515-541]

3023. Assessment.

(a) In addition to provisions of Section 56320 of the Education Code, assessments shall be administered by qualified personnel who are competent in both the oral or sign language skills and written skills of the individual's primary language or mode of communication and have a knowledge and understanding of the cultural and ethnic background of the pupil. If it clearly is not feasible to do so, an interpreter must be used, and the assessment report shall

- Assessment Administered by Qualified Personnel

document this condition and note that the validity may have been affected.

(b) The normal process of second-language acquisition, as well as manifestations of dialect and sociolinguistic variance shall not be diagnosed as a handicapping condition.

[Authority cited: Section 56100(a), (i), and (j), Education Code] [Reference: Sections 56001, 56320, 56324, and 56327, Education Code; and 34 CFR 300.530, 300.532 and 300.543]

3024. Transfer.

In addition to the requirements specified in Education Code Section 56325 and all applicable sections in this chapter, the following shall apply:

(a) Transfer of Records. Upon receipt of a request from an educational agency where an individual with exceptional needs has enrolled, a former educational agency shall send the pupil's special education records, or a copy thereof, within five working days.

(b) Transition from Elementary School District to High School District.

When a pupil is to enroll in a high school district from an elementary district, the elementary district shall invite the high school district to the individualized education program team meeting prior to the last scheduled review. If the authorized high school personnel participate with the elementary district personnel in the individualized education program team meeting, the individualized education program shall specify the appropriate high school placement.

If the authorized representative of the high school district has not participated in the individualized education program development prior to transfer from the elementary program, the elementary school district shall notify the high school district of those individuals with exceptional needs who require special education and related services. For each pupil listed who enrolls in the high school district, the administrator shall make an interim placement in accordance with Education Code 56325 or shall immediately convene an individualized education program team meeting.

[Authority cited: Sections 49068 and 56100(a), Education Code] [Reference: Section 49068 and 56325, Education Code]

3025. Assessment Option: Referral to State Schools for Further Assessment.

(a) Prior to referring a pupil for further assessment to California Schools for the Deaf or Blind or the Diagnostic Schools, districts, special education local plan areas, counties, or other agencies providing education services, shall first conduct assessments at the local level within the capabilities of that agency. Results of local assessments shall be provided to parent(s) and shall state the reasons for referral to the State School. Results of local assessments shall accompany the referral request.

(b) The Schools for the Deaf and Blind and the Diagnostic Schools shall conduct assessments pursuant to the provisions of Education Code Section 56320 et seq..

(c) A representative of the district, special education local plan area, or county individualized education program team shall participate in the staffing meeting and shall receive the final report and recommendations. Conference calls are acceptable forms of participation, provided that written reports and recommendations have been received by the representative prior to the meeting.

[Authority cited: Section 56100(a), Education Code] [Reference: Section 56326, Education Code]

3027. Hearing and Vision Screening.

All pupils being assessed for initial and three-year review for special education services shall have had a hearing and vision screening, unless parental permission was denied.

[Authority cited: Section 56100(a), Education Code] [Reference: Sections 56320, 56321 and 56327, Education Code; and 34 CFR 300.532]

3028. Audiological Assessment.

All pupils continuing to fail a threshold hearing test shall be assessed by a licensed or credentialed audiologist and such assessment shall be a part of the assessment plan.

[Authority cited: Section 56100(a), Education Code] [Reference: Sections 56320 and 56327, Education Code; and 34 CFR 300.532]

- Assessment Option: Referral to State Schools for Further Assessment

- Results of Local Assessments

- Assessments Conducted Pursuant to EC Section 56320

- Local Participation

- Hearing and Vision Screening

- Audiological Assessment

3029. Contracting for Individually Administered Tests of Psychological Functioning Due to the Unavailability of School Psychologists.

(a) School districts, county offices, and special education local plan areas shall ensure that credentialed school psychologists are available to perform individually administered tests of intellectual or emotional functioning pursuant to Section 56320(b)(3) of the Education Code.

(b) Due to the temporary unavailability of a credentialed school psychologist, a school district or county office may contract with qualified personnel to perform individually administered tests of intellectual or emotional functioning including necessary reports pursuant to Section 56327 of the Education Code.

(c) The district or county office shall seek appropriately credentialed school psychologists for employment. These efforts, which include but are not limited to contacting institutions of higher education having approved school psychology programs and utilizing established personnel recruitment practices, shall be documented and available for review.

(d) The only persons qualified to provide assessment services under this section shall be educational psychologists licensed by the Board of Behavioral Science Examiners.

[Authority cited: Sections 56100(a), 56320(f), Education Code] [Reference: Sections 56320(b)(3), and 56327, Education Code]

Article 3.1. Individuals with Exceptional Needs

3030. Eligibility Criteria.

A pupil shall qualify as an individual with exceptional needs, pursuant to Section 56026 of the Education Code, if the results of the assessment as required by Section 56320 demonstrate that the degree of the pupil's impairment as described in Section 3030 (a through j) requires special education in one or more of the program options authorized by Section 56361 of the Education Code. The decision as to whether or not the assessment results demonstrate that the degree of the pupil's impairment requires special education shall be made by the individualized education program team, including assessment personnel in accordance with Section 56341(d) of the Education Code. The individualized education program team shall take into account all the relevant material which is available on the pupil. No single score or product of scores shall be used as the sole criterion for the decision of the individualized education program team as to the pupil's eligibility for special education. The specific processes and procedures for implementation of these criteria shall be developed by each special education local plan area and be included in the local plan pursuant to Section 56220(a) of the Education Code.

(a) A pupil has a hearing impairment, whether permanent or fluctuating, which impairs the processing of linguistic information through hearing, even with amplification, and which adversely affects educational performance. Processing linguistic information includes speech and language reception and speech and language discrimination.

- Hearing Impairment

(b) A pupil has concomitant hearing and visual impairments, the combination of which causes severe communication, developmental, and educational problems.

- Hearing and Visual Impairments

(c) A pupil has a language or speech disorder as defined in Section 56333 of the Education Code, and it is determined that the pupil's disorder meets one or more of the following criteria:

- Language or Speech Disorder

(1) Articulation disorder.

(A) The pupil displays reduced intelligibility or an inability to use the speech mechanism which significantly interferes with communication and attracts adverse attention. Significant interference in communication occurs when the pupil's production of single or multiple speech sounds on a developmental scale of articulation competency is below that expected for his or her chronological age or developmental level, and which adversely affects educational performance.

(B) A pupil does not meet the criteria for an articulation disorder if the sole assessed disability is an abnormal swallowing pattern.

(2) Abnormal Voice. A pupil has an abnormal voice which is characterized by persistent, defective voice quality, pitch, or loudness.

(3) Fluency Disorders. A pupil has a fluency disorder when the flow of verbal expression including rate and rhythm adversely affects communication between the pupil and listener.

(4) Language Disorder. The pupil has an expressive or receptive language disorder when he or she meets one of the following criteria:

(A) The pupil scores at least 1.5 standard deviations below the mean, or below the 7th percentile, for his or her chronological age or developmental level on two or more standardized tests in one or more of the following areas of language development: morphology, syntax, semantics, or pragmatics. When standardized tests are considered to be invalid for the specific pupil, the expected language performance level shall be determined by alternative means as specified on the assessment plan, or

(B) The pupil scores at least 1.5 standard deviations below the mean or the score is below the 7th percentile for his or her chronological age or developmental level on one or more standardized tests in one of the areas listed in subsection (A) and displays inappropriate or inadequate usage of expressive or receptive language as measured by a representative spontaneous or elicited language sample of a minimum of fifty utterances. The language sample must be recorded or transcribed and analyzed, and the results included in the assessment report. If the pupil is unable to produce this sample, the language, speech, and hearing specialist shall document why a fifty utterance sample was not obtainable and the contexts in which attempts were made to elicit the sample. When standardized tests are considered to be invalid for the specific pupil, the expected language performance level shall be determined by alternative means as specified in the assessment plan.

(d) A pupil has a visual impairment which, even with correction, adversely affects a pupil's educational performance. — Visual Impairment

(e) A pupil has a severe orthopedic impairment which adversely affects the pupil's educational performance. Such orthopedic impairments include impairments caused by congenital anomaly, impairments caused by disease, and impairments from other causes. — Severe Orthopedic Impairment

(f) A pupil has limited strength, vitality or alertness, due to chronic or acute health problems, including but not limited to a heart condition, cancer, leukemia, rheumatic fever, chronic kidney disease, cystic fibrosis, severe asthma, epilepsy, lead poisoning, diabetes, tuberculosis and other communicable infectious diseases, and hematological disorders such as sickle cell anemia and hemophilia which adversely affects a pupil's educational performance. In accordance with Section 56026(e) of the Education Code, such physical disabilities shall not be temporary in nature as defined by Section 3001(v). — Other Health Impairments

(g) A pupil exhibits any combination of the following autistic-like behaviors, to include but not limited to: — Autistic-Like Behaviors

(1) An inability to use oral language for appropriate communication.

(2) A history of extreme withdrawal or relating to people inappropriately and continued impairment in social interaction from infancy through early childhood.

(3) An obsession to maintain sameness.

(4) Extreme preoccupation with objects or inappropriate use of objects or both.

(5) Extreme resistance to controls.

(6) Displays peculiar motoric mannerisms and motility patterns.

(7) Self-stimulating, ritualistic behavior.

(h) A pupil has significantly below average general intellectual functioning existing concurrently with deficits in adaptive behavior and manifested during the developmental period, which adversely affect a pupil's educational performance. — Mental Retardation

(i) Because of a serious emotional disturbance, a pupil exhibits one or more of the following characteristics over a long period of time and to a marked degree, which adversely affect educational performance: — Serious Emotional Disturbance

(1) An inability to learn which cannot be explained by intellectual, sensory, or health factors.

(2) An inability to build or maintain satisfactory interpersonal relationships with peers and teachers.

(3) Inappropriate types of behavior or feelings under normal circumstances exhibited in several situations.

(4) A general pervasive mood of unhappiness or depression.

(5) A tendency to develop physical symptoms or fears associated with personal or school problems.

(j) A pupil has a disorder in one or more of the basic psychological processes involved in understanding or in using language, spoken or written, which may manifest itself in an impaired ability to listen, think, speak, read, write, spell, or do mathematical calculations, and has a severe discrepancy between intellectual ability and achievement in one or more of the academic areas specified in Section 56337(a) of the Education Code. For the purpose of Section 3030(j): — Specific Learning Disabilities

(1) Basic psychological processes include attention, visual processing, auditory processing, sensory-motor skills, cognitive abilities including association, conceptualization and expression.

(2) Intellectual ability includes both acquired learning and learning potential and shall be determined by a systematic

assessment of intellectual functioning.

(3) The level of achievement includes the pupil's level of competence in materials and subject matter explicitly taught in school and shall be measured by standardized achievement tests.

(4) The decision as to whether or not a severe discrepancy exists shall be made by the individualized education program team, including assessment personnel in accordance with Section 56341(d), which takes into account all relevant material which is available on the pupil. No single score or product of scores, test or procedure shall be used as the sole criterion for the decisions of the individualized education program team as to the pupil's eligibility for special education. In determining the existence of a severe discrepancy, the individualized education program team shall use the following procedures:

(A) When standardized tests are considered to be valid for a specific pupil, a severe discrepancy is demonstrated by: first, converting into common standard scores, using a mean of 100 and standard deviation of 15, the achievement test score and the ability test score to be compared; second, computing the difference between these common standard scores; and third, comparing this computed difference to the standard criterion which is the product of 1.5 multiplied by the standard deviation of the distribution of computed differences of students taking these achievement and ability tests. A computed difference which equals or exceeds this standard criterion, adjusted by one standard error of measurement, the adjustment not to exceed 4 common standard score points, indicates a severe discrepancy when such discrepancy is corroborated by other assessment data which may include other tests, scales, instruments, observations and work samples, as appropriate.

(B) When standardized tests are considered to be invalid for a specific pupil, the discrepancy shall be measured by alternative means as specified on the assessment plan.

(C) If the standardized tests do not reveal a severe discrepancy as defined in subparagraphs (A) or (B) above, the individualized education program team may find that a severe discrepancy does exist, provided that the team documents in a written report that the severe discrepancy between ability and achievement exists as a result of a disorder in one or more basic psychological processes. The report shall include a statement of the area, the degree, and the basis and method used in determining the discrepancy. The report shall contain information considered by the team which shall include, but not be limited to:

1. Data obtained from standardized assessment instruments;

2. Information provided by the parent;

3. Information provided by the pupil's present teacher;

4. Evidence of the pupil's performance in the regular and/or special education classroom obtained from observations, work samples, and group test scores;

5. Consideration of the pupil's age, particularly for young children; and

6. Any additional relevant information.

(5) The discrepancy shall not be primarily the result of limited school experience or poor school attendance.

[Authority cited: Statutes of 1981, Chapter 1094, Section 25(a); and Section 56100(a), (g), (i), Education Code] [Reference: 20 U.S.C. 1401(a)(15) and 1412(5); 34 CFR 300.5(b)(7) and (9), 300.532(a) (2), (d) and (e), 300.533, 300.540, 300.541-43; and Sections 56026, 56320, 56333, and 56337, Education Code]

3031. Additional Eligibility Criteria for Individuals with Exceptional Needs – Age Birth to Four Years and Nine Months.

- Note: Subdivision (a) Has Been Superseded by EC Section 56441.11. Subdivision (b) Has Been Superseded by Title 14 of the Government Code

(a) A child, age birth to four years and nine months, shall qualify as an individual with exceptional needs pursuant to Education Code Section 56026(c)(1) and (2) if the Individualized Education Program Team determines that the child meets the following criteria:

(1) Is identified as an individual with exceptional needs pursuant to Section 3030, and

(2) Is identified as requiring intensive special education and services by meeting one of the following:

(A) The child is functioning at or below 50% of his or her chronological age level in any one of the following skill areas:

1. gross or fine motor development;

2. receptive or expressive language development;

3. social or emotional development;

4. cognitive development; and

5. visual development.

(B) The child is functioning between 51% and 75% of his or her chronological age level in any two of the skill areas identified in Section 3031(2)(A).

(C) The child has a disabling medical condition or

congenital syndrome which the Individualized Education Program Team determines has a high predictability of requiring intensive special education and services.

(b) Programs for individuals with exceptional needs younger than three years of age are permissive in accordance with Section 56001(c) of the Education Code except for those programs mandated pursuant to Section 56425 of the Education Code.

[Authority cited: Statutes of 1981, Chapter 1094, Section 25(a); and Section 56100(a), (g), (i), Education Code] [Reference: 20 USC 1401(a)(15); 34 CFR 300.5; Statutes of 1981, Chapter 1094, Section 25 (a); and Sections 56026, 56030.5, 56333 and 56337, Education Code]

Article 4. Instructional Planning and Individualized Education Program

3040. Individualized Education Program Implementation.

- Individualized Education Program Implementation

(a) Upon completion of the individualized education program, that individualized education program shall be implemented as soon as possible following the individualized education program team meeting.

(b) A copy of the individualized education program shall be provided to the parents at no cost, and a copy of the individualized education program shall be provided in the primary language at the request of the parent.

(c) The individualized education program shall show a direct relationship between the present levels of performance, the goals and objectives, and the specific educational services to be provided.

[Authority cited: Section 56100(a), (i), and (j), Education Code] [Reference: Section 56341, Education Code; 34 CFR 300.342-300.345]

3042. Placement.

- Placement

(a) Specific educational placement means that unique combination of facilities, personnel, location or equipment necessary to provide instructional services to an individual with exceptional needs, as specified in the individualized education program, in any one or a combination of public, private, home and hospital, or residential settings.

(b) The individualized education program team shall document its rationale for placement in other than the pupil's school and classroom in which the pupil would otherwise attend if the pupil were not handicapped. The documentation shall indicate why the pupil's handicap prevents his or her needs from being met in a less restrictive environment even with the use of supplementary aids and services.

[Authority cited: Section 56100(a), Education Code] [Reference: Sections 56001(g), 56031, 56341 and 56343, Education Code]

3043. Extended School Year.

- Extended School Year Services

Extended school year services shall be provided for each individual with exceptional needs who has unique needs and requires special education and related services in excess of the regular academic year. Such individuals shall have handicaps which are likely to continue indefinitely or for a prolonged period, and interruption of the pupil's educational programming may cause regression, when coupled with limited recoupment capacity, rendering it impossible or unlikely that the pupil will attain the level of self-sufficiency and independence that would otherwise be expected in view of his or her handicapping condition. The lack of clear evidence of such factors may not be used to deny an individual an extended school year program if the individualized education program team determines the need for such a program and includes extended school year in the individualized education program pursuant to subsection (f).

(a) Extended year special education and related services shall be provided by a school district, special education local plan area, or county office offering programs during the regular academic year.

- Services Provided During Regular Academic Year

(b) Individuals with exceptional needs who may require an extended school year are those who:

- Individuals Who May Require Extended Year

(1) Are placed in special classes or centers; or

(2) Are individuals with exceptional needs whose individualized education programs specify an extended year program as determined by the individualized education program team.

(c) The term "extended year" as used in this section means the period of time between the close of one academic year and the beginning of the succeeding academic year. The term "academic year" as used in this section means that portion of the school year during which the regular day school is maintained, which period must include not less than the number of days required to entitle the district, special

- Definition of Extended Year

education services region, or county office to apportionments of state funds.

(d) An extended year program shall be provided for a minimum of 20 instructional days, including holidays. For reimbursement purposes:

(1) A maximum of 55 instructional days excluding holidays, shall be allowed for individuals in special classes or centers for the severely handicapped; and

(2) A maximum of 30 instructional days excluding holidays, shall be allowed for all other eligible pupils needing extended year.

(e) A local governing board may increase the number of instructional days during the extended year period, but shall not claim revenue for average daily attendance generated beyond the maximum instructional days allowed in subsection (d)(1) and (2).

(f) An extended year program, when needed, as determined by the individualized education program team, shall be included in the pupil's individualized education program.

(g) In order to qualify for average daily attendance revenue for extended year pupils, all of the following conditions must be met:

(1) Extended year special education shall be the same length of time as the school day for pupils of the same age level attending summer school in the district in which the extended year program is provided, but not less than the minimum school day for that age unless otherwise specified in the individualized education program to meet a pupil's unique needs.

(2) The special education and related services offered during the extended year period are comparable in standards, scope and quality to the special education program offered during the regular academic year.

(h) If during the regular academic year an individual's individualized education program specifies integration in the regular classroom, a public education agency is not required to meet that component of the individualized education program if no regular summer school programs are being offered by that agency.

(i) This section shall not apply to schools which are operating a continuous school program pursuant to Chapter 5 (commencing with Section 37600) of Part 22, Division 3, Title 2, of the Education Code.

- Minimum Instructional Days

- Increase in Instructional Days

- Extended Year Program

- Conditions to Qualify for Average Daily Attendance

- Integration in the Regular Education Program

- Continuous School Program

[Authority cited: Section 56100(a) and (j), Education Code]
[Reference: Sections 37600, 41976.5 and 56345, Education Code; and 34 CFR 300.346]

Article 5. Implementation (Program Components)

3051. Standards for Designated Instruction and Services (DIS).

- Standards for Designated Instruction and Services

(a) General Provisions.

(1) Designated instruction and services may be provided to individuals or to small groups in a specialized area of educational need, and throughout the full continuum of educational settings.

(2) Designated instruction and services, when needed as determined by the individualized education program, shall include frequency and duration of services.

(3) All entities and individuals providing designated instruction and services shall be qualified.

(4) All entities and individuals providing designated instruction and services shall be:

(A) Employees of the school district or county office, or

(B) Employed under contract pursuant to Education Code sections 56365-56366.7. Such persons shall be certified by the Department pursuant to Sections 3060-3064 of this Title, or

(C) Employees, vendors or contractors of the State Departments of Health Services or Mental Health, or any designated local public health or mental health agency.

[Authority cited: Sections 33031, 56100(a) and (i) and 56366.1(l)(5), Education Code.] [Reference: Sections 56363 and 56365-56366.7, Education Code; and Section 300.12, Code of Federal Regulations, Title 34.]

3051.1. Language, Speech and Hearing Development and Remediation.

- Appropriate Credential Required for Language, Speech, and Hearing Development and Remediation

(a) An individual holding an appropriate credential with specialization in language, speech, and hearing may provide services which include:

(1) Referral and assessment of individuals suspected of having a disorder of language, speech, or hearing. Such individuals are not considered as part of the caseload pursuant to Section 56363.3 of the Education Code unless an individualized education program is developed and services are provided pursuant to Section 3051.1(a)(2) and (3).

(2) Specialized instruction and services for individuals with disorders of language, speech, and hearing, including monitoring of pupil progress on a regular basis, providing information for the review, and when necessary participating in the review and revision of individualized educational programs of pupils.

(3) Consultative services to pupils, parents, teachers, or other school personnel.

(4) Coordination of speech and language services with an individual's regular and special education program.

(b) Caseloads of full-time equivalent language, speech, and hearing specialists providing instruction and services within the district, special education local plan area, or county office shall not exceed a district-wide, special education local plan area-wide, or county-wide average of fifty-five (55) individuals unless prior written approval has been granted by the State Superintendent of Public Instruction. — Caseloads

(c) Services may be provided by an aide working under the direct supervision of a credentialed language, speech, and hearing specialist if specified in the individualized education program. No more than two aides may be supervised by one credentialed language, speech, and hearing specialist. The caseloads of persons in subsection (b) shall not be increased by the use of noncertificated personnel. — Services by an Aide

[Authority cited: Section 56100(a) and (i), Education Code] [Reference: Section 56363(b)(1), 56363.3, Education Code; and 34 CFR 300.13(b)(12)]

3051.2. Audiological Services. — Audiological Services
(a) In addition to provisions of Title 34, Code of Federal Regulations, Section 300.13(b)(1), designated audiological instruction and services may include:

(1) Aural rehabilitation (auditory training, speech reading, language habilitation, and speech conservation) and habilitation with individual pupils or groups and support for the hearing-impaired pupils in the regular classroom.

(2) Monitoring hearing levels, auditory behavior, and amplification for all pupils requiring personal or group amplification in the instructional setting.

(3) Planning, organizing, and implementing an audiology program for individuals with auditory dysfunctions, as specified in the individualized education program.

(4) Consultative services regarding test findings, amplification needs and equipment, otological referrals, home

training programs, acoustic treatment of rooms, and coordination of educational services to hearing-impaired individuals.

(b) The person providing audiological services shall hold a valid credential with a specialization in clinical or rehabilitative services in audiology.

- Valid Credential

[Authority cited: Section 56100(a) and (i), Education Code; 20 USC 1414(c)(2)(B); and 34 CFR 300.600] [Reference: Section 56363(b)(2), Education Code; and 34 CFR 300.13(b)(1)]

3051.3. Mobility Instruction.

- Mobility Instruction

(a) Mobility instruction may include:

(1) Specialized instruction for individuals in orientation and mobility techniques.

(2) Consultative services to other educators and parents regarding instructional planning and implementation of the individualized education program relative to the development of orientation and mobility skills and independent living skills.

(b) The person providing mobility instruction and services shall hold a credential as an orientation and mobility specialist.

- Credential Requirement

[Authority cited: Section 56100(a) and (i), Education Code; 20 USC 1414(c)(2)(B); and 34 CFR 300.600] [Reference: Section 56363, Education Code]

3051.4. Instruction in the Home and Hospital.

- Instruction in the Home or Hospital

(a) Special education and related services provided in the home or hospital for school age pupils is limited to those pupils who have been identified as individuals with exceptional needs in accordance with Section 3030 and for whom the individualized education program team recommends such instruction or services.

(b) Instruction may be delivered individually, in small groups or by teleclass.

- Instruction Options

(c) For those individuals with exceptional needs with a medical condition such as those related to surgery, accidents, short-term illness or medical treatment for a chronic illness, the individualized education program team shall review, and revise, if appropriate, the individualized education program whenever there is a significant change in the pupil's current medical condition.

- Change in Medical Condition

(d) When recommending placement for home instruction, the individualized education program team shall have in the assessment information a medical report from the attending physician and surgeon or the report of the psychologist, as appropriate, stating the diagnosed condition and certifying that the severity of the condition prevents the pupil from attending a less restrictive placement. The report shall include a projected calendar date for the pupil's return to school. The individualized education program team shall meet to reconsider the individualized education program prior to the projected calendar date for the pupil's return to school.

(e) Instruction in the home or hospital shall be provided by a regular class teacher, the special class teacher or the resource specialist teacher, if the teacher or specialist is competent to provide such instruction and services and if the provision of such instruction and services by the teacher or specialist is feasible. If not, the appropriate designated instruction and services specialist shall provide such instruction.

(f) The teacher providing the home instruction shall contact the pupil's previous school and teacher to determine:

(1) The course work to be covered;

(2) The books and materials to be used;

(3) Who is responsible for issuing grades and promoting the pupil when appropriate;

(4) For pupils in grades 7 to 12, the teacher shall confer with the school guidance counselor to determine:

(A) The hours the pupil has earned toward semester course credit in each subject included in the individualized education program and the grade as of the last day of attendance;

(B) Who is responsible for issuing credits when the course work is completed;

(C) Who will issue the diploma if the pupil is to graduate.

[Authority cited: Section 56100(a) and (i), Education Code]
[Reference: Section 56001, 56363(b)(4), Education Code]

3051.5. Adapted Physical Education for Individuals with Exceptional Needs.

(a) Adapted physical education is for individuals with exceptional needs who require developmental or corrective instruction and who are precluded from participation in the activities of the general physical education program, modified general physical education program, or in a specially designed physical education program in a special class.

Consultative services may be provided to pupils, parents, teachers, or other school personnel for the purpose of identifying supplementary aids and services or modifications necessary for successful participation in the regular physical education program or specially designed physical education programs.

- Credential Requirement

(b) The person providing instruction and services shall have a credential authorizing the teaching of adapted physical education as established by the Commission on Teacher Credentialing.

[Authority cited: Section 56100(a) and (i), Education Code]
[Reference: 34 CFR 300.307]

3051.6. Physical and Occupational Therapy.

- Physical and Occupational Therapy

(a) When the district, special education local plan area, or county office contracts for the services of a physical therapist or an occupational therapist, the following standards shall apply:

(1) Occupational or physical therapists shall provide services based upon recommendation of the individual education program team. Physical therapy and occupational therapy services for infants are limited by Education Code 56426.6. Physical therapy services may not exceed the services specified in the Business and Professions Code at Section 2620.

(2) The district, special education services region, or county office shall assure that the therapist has available safe and appropriate equipment.

(b) Qualifications of therapists:

- Qualifications of Therapists

(1) The therapists shall have graduated from an accredited school.

(2) A physical therapist shall be currently licensed by the Board of Medical Quality Assurance of the State of California and meet the educational standards of the Physical Therapy Examining Committee.

(3) An occupational therapist shall be currently registered with the American Occupational Therapy Association.

[Authority cited: Section 56100(a) and (i), Education Code]
[Reference: Section 56363(b)(6), Education Code; and 34 CFR 300.13(b)(5) and (7), 300.600]

3051.7. Vision Services.

- Vision Services

(a) Vision services shall be provided by a credentialed

teacher of the visually handicapped and may include:

(1) Adaptations in curriculum, media, and the environment, as well as instruction in special skills.

(2) Consultative services to pupils, parents, teachers, and other school personnel.

(b) An assessment of and provision for services to visually impaired pupils may be conducted by an eye specialist who has training and expertise in low vision disabilities and has available the appropriate low vision aids for the purposes of assessment. The eye specialist may provide consultation to the pupil, parents, teacher and other school personnel as may be requested by the individualized education program team.

- Assessment of and Provision for Services

(c) Procedures which may be utilized by qualified personnel are those procedures authorized by federal and state laws and regulations and performed in accordance with these laws and regulations and standards of the profession.

- Procedures Utilized by Qualified Personnel

(d) For the purposes of this section, an eye specialist shall mean a licensed optometrist, ophthalmologist, or other licensed physician and surgeon who has training and expertise in low vision disabilities.

- Eye Specialist

[Authority cited: Section 56100(a) and (i), Education Code] [Reference: Sections 44265.5 and 56363(b)(7), Education Code]

3051.75. Vision Therapy.

(a) Vision therapy may include: Remedial and/or developmental instruction provided directly by or in consultation with the optometrist, ophthalmologist, or other qualified licensed physician and surgeon providing ongoing care to the individual.

- Vision Therapy

(b) Vision therapy shall be provided by an optometrist, ophthalmologist, or by appropriate qualified school personnel when prescribed by a licensed optometrist, ophthalmologist, or other qualified licensed physician and surgeon.

- Providers of Vision Therapy

(c) Procedures which may be utilized by qualified personnel are those procedures authorized by federal and state laws and regulations and performed in accordance with these laws and regulations and standards of the profession.

- Procedures Utilized by Qualified Personnel

[Authority cited: Section 56100(a) and (i), Education Code; 20 USC 1414 (c) (2) (B); and 34 CFR 300.600] [Reference: Section 56363(b)(7), Education Code]

3051.8. Specialized Driver Training Inistruction.

(a) Specialized driver training instruction may include instruction to an individual with exceptional needs to supplement the regular driver training program. The individualized education program shall determine the need for supplementary specialized driver training team instruction. The need to supplement the regular program shall be based on an assessment of the pupil's health, physical, and/or educational needs which require modifications which cannot be met through a regular driver training program.

- Specialized Driver Training Instruction

(b) Driver training for individuals herein described must be provided by qualified teachers, as defined by Education Code Sections 41906 and 41907.

- Training Provided by Qualified Teachers

[Authority cited: Section 56100(a) and (i), Education Code; 20 USC 1414(c)(2)(B); and 34 CFR 300.600] [Reference: Sections 41305-41306; 41906-41907 and 56363(b)(8), Education Code]

3051.9. Counseling and Guidance Services.

(a) Counseling and guidance services may be provided to an individual with exceptional needs who requires additional counseling and guidance services to supplement the regular guidance and counseling program.   The individualized education program team shall determine the need for additional guidance and counseling services.

- Counseling and Guidance Services

(b) Counseling and guidance services necessary to implement the individualized education program may include:

- Types of Services

(1) Educational counseling in which the pupil is assisted in planning and implementing his or her immediate and long-range educational program.

(2) Career counseling in which the pupil is assisted in assessing his or her aptitudes, abilities, and interests in order to make realistic career decisions.

(3) Personal counseling in which the pupil is helped to develop his or her ability to function with social and personal responsibility.

(4) Counseling and consultation with parents and staff members on learning problems and guidance programs for pupils.

(c) The individual performing counseling services to pupils shall be qualified.

- Qualified Individual

[Authority cited: Section 56100(a) and (i), Education Code; 20 USC 1414(c)(2)(B); and 34 CFR 300.600] [Reference:

Sections 35300 and 56363(b)(11), Education Code, and 34 CFR 300.13(b)(2), (b)(6), and (b)(8)]

3051.10. Psychological Services Other Than Assessment and Development of the Individualized Education Program.

- Psychological Services Other Than Assessment and Development of the IEP

Psychological services may include:

(a) Counseling provided to an individual with exceptional needs by a credentialed or licensed psychologist or other qualified personnel.

(b) Consultative services to parents, pupils, teachers, and other school personnel.

(c) Planning and implementing a program of psychological counseling for individuals with exceptional needs and parents.

[Authority cited: Section 56100(a) and (i), Education Code; 20 USC 1414(c)(2)(B); and 34 CFR 300.600] [Reference: Section 56363(b)(10), Education Code; and 34 CFR 300.13(b)(8)]

3051.11. Parent Counseling and Training.

- Parent Counseling and Training

Parent counseling and training may include:

(a) Assisting parents in understanding the special needs of their child, and

(b) Providing parents with information about child development.

[Authority cited: Education Code Section 56100(a) and (i); 20 USC 1414(c)(2)(B); and 34 CFR 300.600] [Reference: Section 56363(b)(11), Education Code; and 34 CFR 300.13(b)(6)]

3051.12. Health and Nursing Services.

- Health and Nursing Services

(a) Health and nursing services may include:

(1) Providing services by qualified personnel.

(2) Managing the individual's health problems on the school site.

(3) Consulting with pupils, parents, teachers, and other personnel.

(4) Group and individual counseling with parents and pupils regarding health problems.

(5) Maintaining communication with health agencies providing care to individuals.

(b) Specialized physical health care may be provided as described in Education Code Section 49423.5.

- Care Provided as Described in EC Section 49423.5

(1) Definitions.

(A) "Specialized physical health care services" means those health services prescribed by the child's licensed physician and surgeon requiring medically related training for the individual who performs the services and which are necessary during the school day to enable the child to attend school.

(B) "Standardized procedures" means protocols and procedures developed through collaboration among school or hospital administrators and health professionals, including licensed physicians and surgeons and nurses, to be utilized in the provision of the specialized physical health care services.

(C) "Qualified" means ability to demonstrate competence in Cardio-Pulmonary Resuscitation, current knowledge of community emergency medical resources, and skill in the use of equipment and performance of techniques necessary to provide specialized physical health care services for individuals with exceptional needs. In addition:

1. "Qualified" for the professional school or public health nurse or licensed physician and surgeon shall mean trained in the procedures to a level of competence and safety which meets the objectives of the training.

2. "Qualified" for the designated school personnel shall mean trained in the procedures to a level of competence and safety which meets the objectives of the training as provided by the school nurse, public health nurse, licensed physician and surgeon, or other programs which provide the training.

(D) "Supervision" means review, observation, and/or instruction of a designated school person's performance and of physical health care services, but does not necessarily require the immediate presence of the supervisor at all times.

1. "Immediate supervision" means that the supervisor shall be physically present while a procedure is being administered.

2. "Direct supervision" means that the supervisor shall be present in the same building as the person being supervised and available for consultation and/or assistance.

3. "Indirect supervision" means that the supervisor shall be available to the qualified designated school person either in person or through electronic means to provide necessary instruction, consultation, and referral to appropriate care and services as needed. Supervision of designated school persons shall include review on-site by a qualified school nurse, qualified public health nurse, or qualified licensed physician and surgeon. Supervision shall also include review of the

competence of that individual in performing the specialized health care service, maintenance of appropriate records, physical environment, and equipment.

(E) "Training" means preparation in the appropriate delivery and skillful performance of specialized physical health care services. In addition:

- Training

1. Medically related training of credentialed school nurses or public health nurses shall be that training in an approved program which may be necessary to update or make current the nurse's professional skills and knowledge related to meeting pupils' needs for specialized physical health care services.

2. Medically related training of employed designated school personnel is that training in an approved program in standardized procedures provided by a qualified school nurse, qualified public health nurse, qualified licensed physician and surgeon, or other approved programs to enable the person to provide the specialized physical health care services necessary to enable the child to attend school.

(F) "Competence in Cardio-Pulmonary Resuscitation" means possession of a current valid certificate from an approved program.

- CPR Competence

(2) Standards and Staffing.

- Standards and Staffing
- Allocation of Personnel

(A) Allocation of qualified designated school personnel shall be determined by the amount and type of supervision necessary to this regulation, and also the type and frequency of services needed by students in special classes and centers, and regular instructional settings.

(B) Approved training for qualified personnel shall be provided in one or more of the following ways:

- Approved Training

1. By a qualified school nurse, qualified public health nurse, or qualified licensed physician and surgeon, as defined in these regulations.

2. By career and continuing education programs, approved by the appropriate licensing board.

3. By training programs through public or private medical institutions, i.e., hospitals, public health agencies, Visiting Nurses Associations, and Red Cross.

(3) Organization and Administration.

- Organization and Administration
- Continuing Services

(A) Specific continuing specialized physical health care services required in order for the individual to benefit from special education will be included in the individualized education program. If the parent elects to perform the service during the school day, a waiver shall be signed relieving the school of the responsibility.

(B) Appropriate accommodations for safety and necessary physical care services for the individual with exceptional needs in the school setting shall be provided by the school. Personal privacy and dignity of an individual with exceptional needs shall be assured.

- Appropriate Accommodations

(C) The school district shall not be required to purchase medical equipment for an individual pupil. However, the school district, special education local plan area, or county office is responsible for providing other specialized equipment for use at school that is needed to implement the individualized education program.

- Medical Equipment

(D) In accordance with Education Code Section 49423.5(a)(2), a qualified school nurse, qualified public health nurse, or qualified licensed physician and surgeon responsible for supervising the physical health care of an individual with exceptional needs in the school setting shall:

- Duties of Medical Professional

1. Coordinate the health care services to the individuals with exceptional needs on the school site.

2. Consult with appropriate personnel regarding management of health care services for individuals with exceptional needs.

3. Make appropriate referrals and maintain communication with health agencies providing care to individuals with exceptional needs.

4. Maintain or review licensed physician and surgeon and parent requests and daily documentation records.

(E) Written licensed physician and surgeon and parent requests, as well as the specific standardized procedures to be used if physical health care services are provided, shall be maintained for each individual with exceptional needs. Daily documentation of specific services which are provided shall be maintained on a district-approved form which shall include the signatures of the qualified designated school person(s) who performs the procedure.

- Written Procedures and Documentation

1. Any pupil who is required to have specialized physical health care services during the school day, prescribed for him or her by a licensed physician and surgeon, may be assisted by a qualified school nurse, qualified public health nurse, or other qualified school personnel, if the school district receives:

a. A written statement from the licensed physician and surgeon stating the procedure and time schedules by which such procedures are to be given; and

b. A written statement from the parent or guardian of the pupil, indicating the desire that the school district assist the pupil in the matters set forth in the licensed physician and surgeon's statement, and granting consent for the delivery of such services.

2. This written statement of a licensed physician and surgeon and parent requests and daily documentation shall be maintained in accordance with the requirements of confidentiality of pupil records, and are considered mandatory interim pupil records.

[Authority cited: Sections 49423.5(c) and 56100(a) and (i), Education Code; 20 USC 1414(c)(2)(B); and 34 CFR 300.600] [Reference: Sections 49423.5 and 56363(b)(12), Education Code; and 34 CFR 300.13(b)(10)]

3051.13. Social Worker Services.

- Social Worker Services

(a) Personnel providing social worker services shall be qualified.

(b) Social work services may include:

(1) Individual and group counseling with the individual and his or her immediate family.

(2) Consultation with pupils, parents, teachers, and other personnel regarding the effects of family and other social factors on the learning and developmental requirements of individual pupils with exceptional needs.

(3) Developing a network of community resources, making appropriate referral and maintaining liaison relationships among the school, the pupil with exceptional needs, the family, and the various agencies providing social, income maintenance, employment development, mental health, or other developmental services.

[Authority cited: Section 56100(a) and (i), Education Code; 20 USC 1414(c)(2)(B); and 34 CFR 300.600] [References: Section 56363(b)(13), Education Code; and 34 CFR 300.13(b)(11)]

3051.14. Specially Designed Vocational Education and Career Development.

- Specially Designed Vocational Education and Career Development

Specially designed vocational education and career development for individuals with exceptional needs regardless of severity of disability may include:

(a) Providing prevocational programs and assessing work-related skills, interests, aptitudes, and attitudes.

(b) Coordinating and modifying the regular vocational education program.

(c) Assisting individuals in developing attitudes, self-confidence, and vocational competencies to locate, secure, and retain employment in the community or sheltered environment, and to enable such individuals to become participating members of the community.

(d) Establishing work training programs within the school and community.

(e) Assisting in job placement.

(f) Instructing job trainers and employers as to the unique needs of the individuals.

(g) Maintaining regularly scheduled contact with all work stations and job-site trainers.

(h) Coordinating services with the Department of Rehabilitation, the Department of Employment Development and other agencies as designated in the individualized education program.

[Authority cited: Section 56100(a) and (i), Education Code]
[Reference: Section 56363(b)(14), Education Code; 34 CFR 300.14 (b)(3)]

3051.15. Recreation Services.

- Recreation Services

Recreation services include but are not limited to:

(a) Therapeutic recreation services which are those specialized instructional programs designed to assist pupils in becoming as independent as possible in leisure activities, and when possible and appropriate, facilitate the pupil's integration into regular recreation programs.

(b) Recreation programs in schools and the community which are those programs that emphasize the use of leisure activity in the teaching of academic, social, and daily living skills; and, the provision of nonacademic and extracurricular leisure activities and the utilization of community recreation programs and facilities.

(c) Leisure education programs which are those specific programs designed to prepare the pupil for optimum independent participation in appropriate leisure activities, including teaching social skills necessary to engage in leisure activities, and developing awareness of personal and community leisure resources.

[Authority cited: Section 56100(a) and (l), Education Code]
[Reference: Section 56363(b)(15), Education Code; 34 CFR 300.13 (b)(9)]

3051.16. Specialized Services for Low-Incidence
Disabilities.

- Specialized Services for Low-Incidence Disabilities

Specialized Services for low-incidence disabilities may include:

(a) Specially designed instruction related to the unique needs of pupils with low-incidence disabilities provided by teachers credentialed pursuant to Education Code 44265;

(b) Specialized services related to the unique needs of pupils with low-incidence disabilities provided by qualified individuals such as interpreters, notetakers, readers, transcribers, and other individuals who provide specialized materials and equipment.

[Authority cited: Section 56100(a) and (i), Education Code]
[Reference: Section 56363(b)(16), Education Code]

3051.17. Services for Pupils with Chronic Illnesses or
Acute Health Problems.

- Services for Pupils with Chronic Illnesses or Acute Health Problems

(a) Specialized services may be provided to pupils determined eligible pursuant to Section 3030(f).   Such services include but are not limited to:

(1) Individual consultation;

(2) Home or hospital instruction; and

(3) Other instructional methods using advanced communication technology.

(b) For pupils whose medical condition is in remission or in a passive state, the individualized education program team shall specify the frequency for monitoring the pupil's educational progress to assure that the illness does not interfere with the pupil's educational progress.

- Monitoring Educational Progress

(c) When a pupil identified pursuant to Section 3030(f) experiences an acute health problem which results in his or her non-attendance at school for more than five consecutive days, upon notification of the classroom teacher or the parent, the school principal or designee shall assure that an individualized education program team is convened to determine the appropriate educational services.

- Acute Health Problem

(d) If there is a pattern of sporadic illnesses, the individualized education program team shall convene to consider alternative means for the pupil to demonstrate competencies in the required course of study so that the cumulative number of absences do not prevent educational progress.

- Alternative Means to Demonstrate Competencies

[Authority cited: Section 56100(a), (i), Education Code]

[Reference: Section 56363(a), Education Code; 34 CFR 300.14(a) (1)]

3051.18. Designated Instruction and Services for the Deaf and Hard of Hearing.

- Designated Instruction and Services for Deaf and Hard of Hearing Pupils

(a) Instruction and services for deaf and hard of hearing pupils shall be provided by an individual holding an appropriate credential, who has competencies to provide services to the hearing impaired and who has training, experience and proficient communication skills for educating pupils with hearing impairments. Such services may include but need not be limited to:

(1) Speech, speech reading and auditory training.

(2) Instruction in oral, sign, and written language development.

(3) Rehabilitative and educational services for hearing impaired individuals to include monitoring amplification, coordinating information for the annual review, and recommending additional services.

(4) Adapting curricula, methods, media, and the environment to facilitate the learning process.

(5) Consultation to pupils, parents, teachers, and other school personnel as necessary to maximize the pupil's experiences in the regular education program.

(b) A specially trained instructional aide, working with and under the direct supervision of the credentialed teacher of the deaf and hard-of-hearing, may assist in the implementation of the pupil's educational program.

[Authority cited: Section 56100(a) and (i), Education Code]
[Reference: Section 56363(b)(16), Education Code; and 34 CFR 300.13(a)]

3052. Designated Positive Behavioral Interventions.

- Behavioral Intervention Plans

(a) General Provisions.

(1) An IEP team shall facilitate and supervise all assessment, intervention, and evaluation activities related to a individual's behavioral intervention plan. When the behavioral intervention plan is being developed, the IEP team shall be expanded to include the behavioral intervention case manager with documented training in behavior analysis including positive behavioral intervention(s), qualified personnel knowledgeable of the student's health needs, and others as described in Education Code Section 56341(c)(2). The behavioral intervention case manager is not intended to

be a new staff person and may be an existing staff member trained in behavior analysis with an emphasis on positive behavioral interventions.

(2) Behavioral intervention plans shall only be implemented by, or be under the supervision of, staff with documented training in behavior analysis, including the use of positive behavioral interventions. Such interventions shall only be used to replace specified maladaptive behavior(s) with alternative acceptable behavior(s) and shall never be used solely to eliminate maladaptive behavior(s).

(3) Behavioral intervention plans shall be based upon a functional analysis assessment, shall be specified in the individualized education program, and shall be used only in a systematic manner in accordance with the provisions of this section.

(4) Behavioral emergency interventions shall not be used as a substitute for behavioral intervention plans.

(5) The elimination of any maladaptive behavior does not require the use of intrusive behavioral interventions that cause pain or trauma.

(6) To the extent possible, behavioral intervention plans shall be developed and implemented in a consistent manner appropriate to each of the individual's life settings.

(b) Functional Analysis Assessments. A functional analysis assessment must be conducted by, or be under the supervision of a person who has documented training in behavior analysis with an emphasis on positive behavioral interventions. A functional analysis assessment shall occur after the individualized education program team finds that instructional/behavioral approaches specified in the student's IEP have been ineffective. Nothing in this section shall preclude a parent or legal guardian from requesting a functional analysis assessment pursuant to the provisions of Education Code sections 56320 et seq.

- Functional Analysis Assessments

Functional analysis assessment personnel shall gather information from three sources: direct observation, interviews with significant others, and review of available data such as assessment reports prepared by other professionals and other individual records. Prior to conducting the assessment, parent notice and consent shall be given and obtained pursuant to Education Code Section 56321.

(1) A functional analysis assessment procedure shall include all of the following:

(A) Systematic observation of the occurrence of the

targeted behavior for an accurate definition and description of the frequency, duration, and intensity;

(B) Systematic observation of the immediate antecedent events associated with each instance of the display of the targeted inappropriate behavior;

(C) Systematic observation and analysis of the consequences following the display of the behavior to determine the function the behavior serves for the individual, i.e., to identify the specific environmental or physiological outcomes produced by the behavior. The communicative intent of the behavior is identified in terms of what the individual is either requesting or protesting through the display of the behavior;

(D) Ecological analysis of the settings in which the behavior occurs most frequently. Factors to consider should include the physical setting, the social setting, the activities and the nature of instruction, scheduling, the quality of communication between the individual and staff and other students, the degree of independence, the degree of participation, the amount and quality of social interaction, the degree of choice, and the variety of activities;

(E) Review of records for health and medical factors which may influence behaviors (e.g. medication levels, sleep cycles, health, diet); and

(F) Review of the history of the behavior to include the effectiveness of previously used behavioral interventions.

(2) Functional Analysis Assessment Reports. Following the assessment, a written report of the assessment results shall be prepared and a copy shall be provided to the parent. The report shall include all of the following:

(A) A description of the nature and severity of the targeted behavior(s) in objective and measurable terms;

(B) A description of the targeted behavior(s) that includes baseline data and an analysis of the antecedents and consequences that maintain the targeted behavior, and a functional analysis of the behavior across all appropriate settings in which it occurs;

(C) A description of the rate of alternative behaviors, their antecedents and consequences; and

(D) Recommendations for consideration by the IEP team which may include a proposed plan as specified in Section 3001(f).

(c) IEP Team Meeting. Upon completion of the functional analysis assessment, an IEP team meeting shall be held to review results and, if necessary, to develop a behavioral

- IEP Team Meeting to Develop a Behavioral Intervention Plan

intervention plan, as defined in Article 1, Section 3001(f) of these regulations. The IEP team shall include the behavioral intervention case manager. The behavioral intervention plan shall become a part of the IEP and shall be written with sufficient detail so as to direct the implementation of the plan.

(d) Intervention. Based upon the results of the functional analysis assessment, positive programming for behavioral intervention may include the following:

(1) Altering the identified antecedent event to prevent the occurrence of the behavior (e.g., providing choice, changing the setting, offering variety and a meaningful curriculum, removing environmental pollutants such as excessive noise or crowding, establishing a predictable routine for the individual);

(2) Teaching the individual alternative behaviors that produce the same consequences as the inappropriate behavior (e.g., teaching the individual to make requests or protests using socially acceptable behaviors, teaching the individual to participate with alternative communication modes as a substitute for socially unacceptable attention-getting behaviors, providing the individual with activities that are physically stimulating as alternatives for stereotypic, self-stimulatory behaviors);

(3) Teaching the individual adaptive behaviors (e.g., choice-making, self-management, relaxation techniques, and general skill development) which ameliorate negative conditions that promote the display of inappropriate behaviors; and

(4) Manipulating the consequences for the display of targeted inappropriate behaviors and alternative, acceptable behaviors so that it is the alternative behaviors that more effectively produce desired outcomes (i.e., positively reinforcing alternative and other acceptable behaviors and ignoring or redirecting unacceptable behaviors).

(e) Acceptable Responses. When the targeted behavior(s) occurs, positive response options shall include, but are not limited to one or more of the following:

- Acceptable Responses

(1) the behavior is ignored, but not the individual;

(2) the individual is verbally or verbally and physically redirected to an activity;

(3) the individual is provided with feedback (e.g., "You are talking too loudly");

(4) the message of the behavior is acknowledged (e.g., "You are having a hard time with your work"); or

(5) a brief, physical prompt is provided to interrupt or

prevent aggression, self-abuse, or property destruction.

(f) Evaluation of the Behavioral Intervention Plan Effectiveness. Evaluation of the effectiveness of the behavioral intervention plan shall be determined through the following procedures:

(1) Baseline measure of the frequency, duration, and intensity of the targeted behavior, taken during the functional analysis assessment. Baseline data shall be taken across activities, settings, people, and times of the day. The baseline data shall be used as a standard against which to evaluate intervention effectiveness;

(2) Measures of the frequency, duration, and intensity of the targeted behavior shall be taken after the behavioral intervention plan is implemented at scheduled intervals determined by the IEP team. These measures shall also be taken across activities, settings, people, and times of the day, and may record the data in terms of time spent acting appropriately rather than time spent engaging in the inappropriate behavior;

(3) Documentation of program implementation as specified in the behavioral intervention plan (e.g., written instructional programs and data, descriptions of environmental changes); and

(4) Measures of program effectiveness will be reviewed by the teacher, the behavioral intervention case manager, parent or care provider, and others as appropriate at scheduled intervals determined by the IEP team. This review may be conducted in meetings, by telephone conference, or by other means, as agreed upon by the IEP team.

(5) If the IEP team determines that changes are necessary to increase program effectiveness, the teacher and behavioral intervention case manager shall conduct additional functional analysis assessments and, based on the outcomes, shall propose changes to the behavioral intervention plan.

(g) Modifications Without IEP Team Meeting. Minor modifications to the behavioral intervention plan can be made by the behavioral intervention case manager and the parent or parent representative. If the case manager is unavailable, a qualified designee who meets the training requirements of subsection (a)(1) shall participate in such modifications. Each modification or change shall be addressed in the behavioral intervention plan provided that the parent, or parent representative, is notified of the need and is able to review the existing program evaluation data prior to implementing the modification or change. Parents shall be informed of

- Evaluation of Plan Effectiveness

- Modifications to Plan IEP Team Meeting

their right to question any modification to the plan through the IEP procedures.

(h) Contingency Behavioral Intervention Plans. Nothing in this section is intended to preclude the IEP team from initially developing the behavioral intervention plan in sufficient detail to include schedules for altering specified procedures, or the frequency or duration of the procedures, without the necessity for reconvening the IEP team. Where the intervention is to be used in multiple settings, such as the classroom, home and job sites, those personnel responsible for implementation in the other sites must also be notified and consulted prior to the change.

- Contingency Behavioral Intervention Plans

(i) Emergency Interventions. Emergency interventions may only be used to control unpredictable, spontaneous behavior which poses clear and present danger of serious physical harm to the individual or others and which cannot be immediately prevented by a response less restrictive than the temporary application of a technique used to contain the behavior.

- Emergency Interventions

(1) Emergency interventions shall not be used as a substitute for the systematic behavioral intervention plan that is designed to change, replace, modify, or eliminate a targeted behavior.

(2) Whenever a behavioral emergency occurs, only behavioral emergency interventions approved by the special education local planning area (SELPA) may be used.

(3) No emergency intervention shall be employed for longer than is necessary to contain the behavior. Any situation which requires prolonged use of an emergency intervention shall require staff to seek assistance of the school site administrator or law enforcement agency, as applicable to the situation.

(4) Emergency interventions may not include:

(A) Locked seclusion, unless it is in a facility otherwise licensed or permitted by state law to use a locked room;

(B) Employment of a device or material or objects which simultaneously immobilize all four extremities, except that techniques such as prone containment may be used as an emergency intervention by staff trained in such procedures; and

(C) An amount of force that exceeds that which is reasonable and necessary under the circumstances.

(5) To prevent emergency interventions from being used in lieu of planned, systematic behavioral interventions, the parent and residential care provider, if appropriate, shall be

notified within one school day whenever an emergency intervention is used or serious property damage occurs. A "Behavioral Emergency Report" shall immediately be completed and maintained in the individual's file. The report shall include all of the following:

(A) The name and age of the individual;

(B) The setting and location of the incident;

(C) The name of the staff or other persons involved;

(D) A description of the incident and the emergency intervention used, and whether the individual is currently engaged in any systematic behavioral intervention plan; and

(E) Details of any injuries sustained by the individual or others, including staff, as a result of the incident.

(6) All "Behavioral Emergency Reports" shall immediately be forwarded to, and reviewed by, a designated responsible administrator.

(7) Anytime a "Behavioral Emergency Report" is written regarding an individual who does not have a behavioral intervention plan, the designated responsible administrator shall, within two days, schedule an IEP team meeting to review the emergency report, to determine the necessity for a functional analysis assessment, and to determine the necessity for an interim behavioral intervention plan. The IEP team shall document the reasons for not conducting the assessment and/or not developing an interim plan.

(8) Anytime a "Behavioral Emergency Report" is written regarding an individual who has a behavioral intervention plan, any incident involving a previously unseen serious behavior problem or where a previously designed intervention is not effective should be referred to the IEP team to review and determine if the incident constitutes a need to modify the plan.

(9) "Behavioral Emergency Report" data shall be collected by SELPAs which shall report annually the number of Behavioral Emergency Reports to the California Department of Education and the Advisory Commission on Special Education.

(j) SELPA Plan. The local plan of each SELPA shall include procedures governing the systematic use of behavioral interventions and emergency interventions. These procedures shall be part of the SELPA local plan.

- SELPA Plan

(1) Upon adoption, these procedures shall be available to all staff members and parents whenever a behavioral intervention plan is proposed.

(2) At a minimum, the plan shall include:

(A) The qualifications and training of personnel to be designated as behavioral intervention case managers, which shall include training in behavior analysis with an emphasis on positive behavioral interventions, who will coordinate and assist in conducting the functional analysis assessments and the development of the behavioral intervention plans;

(B) The qualifications and training required of personnel who will participate in the implementation of the behavioral intervention plans; which shall include training in positive behavioral interventions;

(C) Special training that will be required for the use of emergency behavioral interventions and the types of interventions requiring such training; and

(D) Approved behavioral emergency procedures.

(k) Nonpublic School Policy. Nonpublic schools and agencies, serving individuals pursuant to Education Code Section 56365 et seq., shall develop policies consistent with those specified in subsection (i) of this section.

- Nonpublic School Policy

(l) Prohibitions. No public education agency, or nonpublic school or agency serving individuals pursuant to Education Code Section 56365 et seq., may authorize, order, consent to, or pay for any of the following interventions, or any other interventions similar to or like the following:

- Prohibitions

(1) Any intervention that is designed to, or likely to, cause physical pain;

(2) Releasing noxious, toxic or otherwise unpleasant sprays, mists, or substances in proximity to the individual's face;

(3) Any intervention which denies adequate sleep, food, water, shelter, bedding, physical comfort, or access to bathroom facilities;

(4) Any intervention which is designed to subject, used to subject, or likely to subject the individual to verbal abuse, ridicule or humiliation, or which can be expected to cause excessive emotional trauma;

(5) Restrictive interventions which employ a device or material or objects that simultaneously immobilize all four extremities, including the procedure known as prone containment, except that prone containment or similar techniques may be used by trained personnel as a limited emergency intervention pursuant to subsection (i);

(6) Locked seclusion, except pursuant to subsection (i)(4)(A);

(7) Any intervention that precludes adequate supervision of the individual; and

(8) Any intervention which deprives the individual of one or more of his or her senses.

(m) Due Process Hearings. The provisions of this chapter related to functional analysis assessments and the development and implementation of behavioral intervention plans are subject to the due process hearing procedures specified in Education Code Section 56501 et seq. No hearing officer may order the implementation of a behavioral intervention that is otherwise prohibited by this section, by SELPA policy, or by any other applicable statute or regulation.

- Due Process Hearings

[Authority cited: Section 56523(a), Education Code. Reference: Sections 56520 and 56523, Education Code.]

3053. Special Classes.

- Special Day Classes

(a) Placement in a special day class shall not limit or restrict the consideration of other options, including services provided in a vocational education program or any combination of programs and placements as may be required to provide the services specified in a pupil's individualized education program.

(b) The following standards for special classes shall be met:

- Standards

(1) A special class shall be composed of individuals whose needs as specified in the individualized education programs can be appropriately met within the class.

(2) Pupils in a special class shall be provided with an educational program in accordance with their individualized education programs for at least the same length of time as the regular school day for that chronological peer group:

(A) When an individual can benefit by attending a regular program for part of the day, the amount of time shall be written in the individualized education program.

(B) When the individualized education program team determines that an individual cannot function for the period of time of a regular school day, and when it is so specified in the individualized education program, an individual may be permitted to attend a special class for less time than the regular school day for that chronological peer group.

(3) The procedure for allocation of aides for special classes shall be specified in the local plan. Additional aide time may be provided when the severity of the handicapping conditions of the pupils or the age of the pupils justifies it, based on the individualized education programs.

(4) Special class(es) shall be located to promote maximum appropriate interaction with regular educational programs.

(c) The special class shall be taught by a full-time-equivalent teacher whose responsibility is the instruction, supervision, and coordination of the educational program for those individuals enrolled in the special class.

- Special Class Teacher

The special class shall be taught by a teacher who holds an appropriate special education credential authorized by the Commission on Teacher Credentialing and who possesses the necessary competencies to teach individuals assigned to the class. Special class teachers with a Special Education Credential employed as of September 1, 1975, as teachers in special classes for pupils in severe language disorder aphasia programs and who possess the necessary competencies to teach individuals assigned to the class, shall be authorized to continue to teach.

[Authority cited: Section 56100(a), (i), Education Code] [Reference: Sections 56001 and 56364, Education Code; and 34 CFR 300.550-554]

3054. Special Center.

- Special Center

(a) Standards. Special centers operating under this section shall:

- Standards

(1) Provide pupils in a special center with an educational program in accordance with their individualized education programs for at least the same length of time as the regular school day for that chronological peer group:

(A) When an individual can benefit by attending a regular class(es) or other program part of the day, the amount of time shall be written in the individualized education program.

(B) When the individualized education program team determines that an individual cannot function for the period of time of a regular school day, and when it is so specified in the individualized education program, an individual may be permitted to attend a special center for less time than the regular school day for that chronological peer group.

(2) Be staffed by qualified personnel at a pupil/adult ratio to enable implementation of the pupils' individualized education programs.

(3) Provide an emergency communication system for the health and safety of individuals with exceptional needs, such as fire, earthquake, and smog alerts.

(4) Have specialized equipment and facilities to meet the needs of individuals served in the special centers.

(b) Special centers should be located to promote maximum, appropriate interaction with regular educational programs.

- Interaction with Regular Educational Programs

[Authority cited: Section 56100(a) and (i), Education Code; 20 USC 1414(c)(2)(B); and 34 CFR 300.600] [References: Sections 56001 and 56364, Education Code; and 34 CFR 300.550-554]

Article 6. Nonpublic, Nonsectarian School and Agency Services

3060. Application for Certification.

- Application for Certification

(a) Any school, person or agency desiring to obtain certification as a nonpublic school or nonpublic agency shall file an application with the Superintendent on forms developed and provided by the Department.

(b) Applications to be certified as a nonpublic school or a nonpublic agency shall be filed at the time allowed by Education Code section 56366.1(b) and (h);

(c) Each nonpublic school or nonpublic agency application shall include information pursuant to Education Code section 56366.1(a) and:

(1) the name and address of the nonpublic school or nonpublic agency;

(2) the name of the administrator and contact person;

(3) the telephone and FAX numbers;

(4) for nonpublic schools, the name of the teacher(s) with a credential authorizing service in special education;

(5) the types of disabling conditions served;

(6) the age, gender and grade levels served;

(7) the total capacity of the program;

(8) a brief description of the program;

(9) per hour, per day or monthly fees for services provided;

(10) written directions and a street map describing the location of the nonpublic school from the major freeways, roads, streets, thoroughfares and closet major airport;

(11) tuberculosis expiration dates for all staff;

(12) criminal record summary or criminal history clearance dates for all staff who may have contact with pupils;

(13) a list of school districts, county offices of education and special education local plan areas for whom the applicant has a contract to provide school and/or related services;

(14)   for out-of-state applicants, a copy of the current certification or license by the state education agency to provide education services to individuals with exceptional needs under the Individuals with Disabilities Education Act;

(15)   for in-state private schools currently providing educational services to six (6) or more students, a copy of the Private School Affidavit which has been filed with their county superintendent of schools;

(16)   a copy of the current school year calendar; and

(17)   a fire inspection clearance completed within the past twelve months.

(d)   In addition to the requirements set forth in section 3060.2, each nonpublic school with a residential component shall include, as part of the application for certification:

(1)   the name of the residential program attached to the nonpublic school;

(2)   a copy of the current residential care license;

(3)   the proprietary status of the residential program;

(4)   a list of all residential facilities affiliated with the nonpublic school;

(5)   the total capacity of all the residential facilities affiliated with the nonpublic school;

(6)   the per day or monthly fee for the residential component; and

(7)   the rate of care level for each residential facility affiliated with the nonpublic school.

(e)   The applicant shall file affidavits, assurances and clearances that verify compliance with:

(1)   Fair Employment Act;

(2)   Drug Free Workplace Act of 1988;

(3)   Section 504 of the Rehabilitation Act of 1973;

(4)   Individuals with Disabilities Education Act;

(5)   Civil Rights Act of 1964, as amended;

(6)   Education Code Section 33190 (Private School Affidavit);

(7)   Nonsectarian status;

(8)   OSHA Bloodborne Pathogens Standards;

(9)   all local, county, or state ordinances and/or statutes relating to fire, health, sanitation, and building safety;

(10)   use permit, conditional permit or zoning; and

(11)   other assurances as required by state or federal law set forth in the Assurance Statement in the nonpublic school or nonpublic agency application for certification.

(f)   The applicant shall submit, with the application, a fee in accordance with Education Code Section 56366.1(k).

(g) No fee shall be refunded to the applicant if the application is withdrawn or if the Superintendent denies the application.

(h) Applicants shall submit a separate application for each nonpublic school or nonpublic agency site.

(i) A nonpublic school or agency shall be certified for a period of two years, terminating on December 31 of the second year. An annual renewal application shall be required. The renewal application shall require the nonpublic school or agency to update information that has changed since the submission of its previous application including, but not limited to, a copy of the current school year calendar and if the nonpublic school has a residential component, a copy of the current residential care license.

(j) To allow transition of separate cycles between nonpublic schools and nonpublic agencies, beginning January 2000, nonpublic schools shall receive a one-time three-year certification that requires annual updates. Beginning January 2000, nonpublic agencies shall begin a two-year period of certification that requires annual updates. When nonpublic school certifications expire on December 31, 2003, the two-year period of certification shall become effective thereafter.

[Authority cited: Sections 33031, 56100 and 56366(e), Education Code.] [Reference: Section 56366.1, Education Code.]

3061. Service Fees, Finance and Maintenance of Records. All certified nonpublic schools and agencies shall:

- Service Fees, Finance, and Maintenance of Records

(a) provide the Superintendent with specified cost data, pursuant to Education Code Section 56366.7 for providing education and designated instruction and services to individuals with exceptional needs;

(b) maintain cost data in sufficient detail to verify the annual operating budget in providing education and designated instruction and services to individuals with disabilities. Fiscal records shall be maintained for a minimum of five years from the date or origination or until audit findings have been resolved, which is longer;

(c) make available any books and records associated with the delivery of education and designated instruction and services to individuals with exceptional needs for audit inspection or reproduction by the Superintendent or the Superintendent's authorized representatives. These records shall include those management records associated with the delivery of education and designated instruction and services, costs of providing services and personnel records necessary to ensure that staff qualifications comply with the requirements contained in Article 6 of these regulations; and

(d) not charge parents for services covered in the master contract with the public education agency.

[Authority cited: Sections 33031, 56100 and 56366(e), Education Code.] [Reference: Section 56366.7, Education Code.]

3062. Contracts and Agreements.

- Contracts and Agreements

(a) A master contract shall be used by a local education agency for entering into formal agreements with certified nonpublic schools or nonpublic agencies. The term of contract shall not exceed one year. The contract shall specify the administrative and financial agreements between the local education agency and the nonpublic school or nonpublic agency.

(b) No master contract with the local education agency shall be contingent upon nonpublic school or nonpublic agency individual contracts or agreements with parents.

(c) The master contract shall, at a minimum, include:

(1) General provisions relating to modifications and amendments, notices, waivers, disputes, contractor's status, conflicts of interest, termination, inspection and audits, complaince with applicable state and federal laws and regulations, attendance, record-keeping, and reporting requirements;

(2) Payment schedules to include, but not limited to payment amounts, payment demand, right to withhold and audit exceptions;

(3) Indemnification and reasonable insurance requirements; and

(4) Procedures and responsibilities for attendance and unexcused absences.

(d) All master contracts shall be re-negotiated prior to June 30.

(e) Services may be provided through dual enrollment in public and nonpublic school or nonpublic agency programs to meet the educational requirements specified in the individualized education program. The master contract or individual service agreement shall specify the provider of each service. The individual with exceptional needs shall be formally enrolled in both nonpublic and public school programs. The nonpublic school or noonpublic agency shall be reimbursed by the local education agency for services as agreed upon in the contract.

(f) Substitute teachers shall be used consistent with the provisions of Education Code Section 56061.

(g) Nonpublic schools and nonpublic agencies shall provide contracting local education agencies with copies of current valid California credentials and licenses for staff providing services to individuals with exceptional needs.

(h) Nonpublic schools and agencies shall notify the Superintendnet and contracting local education agencies in writing within forty-five (45) days of any credential or licensed personnel changes. Failure to provide properly qualified personnel to provide services as specified in the individualized education progarm shall be cause for the termination of all contracts between the local education agency and the nonpublic school or nonpublic agency.

[Note: Authority cited: Sections 33031, 56100 and 56366(e), Education Code.] [Reference: Sections 56366 and 56366.1, Education Code.]

3063. Program Reviews.

(a) The Superintendent shall conduct a validation review of the nonpublic school prior to an initial conditional certification. An on-site review shall be conducted within 90 days of the initial conditional certification and student enrollment. On-site reviews shall be scheduled at least once every four years thereafter.

(b) The nonpublic school, the contracting education agency and the special education local plan area shall be given a minimum thirty (30) days prior notice before an on-site review.

(c) The person serving the lead of the review team shall confer with the school administrator at least 48 hours prior to the on-site review to discuss the procedures and the number of days required for the review. The lead of the review team shall identify those persons who are to participate in the on-site review.

(d) Nonpublic schools and nonpublic agencies may be visited at any time without prior notice when there is substantial reason to believe that there is an immediate danger to the health, safety, or welfare of a child or group of children. The Superintendent shall document the concern and submit it to the nonpublic school or nonpublic agency at the

- Program Reviews

time of the on-site monitoring.

(e) On-site reviews shall include the following procedures:

(1) an entrance meeting to acquaint the on-site review team with the nonpublic school or nonpublic agency staff and site to discuss the purpose and objectives of the review;

(2) a review and examination of files and documents, classroom observations and interviews with the site administrator, teachers, students, volunteers and parents to determine compliance with all applicable state and federal laws and regulations; and

(3) an exit meeting to provide the nonpublic school or nonpublic agency with a preliminary preview of the on-site review findings, verify compliance and offer technical assistance including how to resolve issues of noncompliance.

(f) The Superintendent shall provide the nonpublic school or nonpublic agency, the contracting educational agency and the special education local plan area with a written report within 60 days of the on-site review.

(g) The Superintendent shall request a written response, within a timeframe to be determined by the Superintendent, but in no case to exceed 180 days, to any noncompliance finding that resulted from the on-site review.

(h) The Superintendent shall provide a written notification, within 30 days of receipt, to the nonpublic school or nonpublic agency regarding their response to each noncompliance finding.

(i) On-site reviews shall be conducted only by personnel who have been trained by Department staff to perform such administrative and program examinations.

[Authority cited: Sections 33031, 56100 and 56366(e), Education Code.] [Reference: Sections 56366.1 and 56366.8, Education Code.]

3064. Staff Qualifications - Special Education Instruction.

- Staff Qualifications – Special Education Instruction

(a) The nonpublic school or nonpublic agency shall deliver instruction utilizing personnel who possess a credential authorizing the holder to deliver special education instruction according to the age range and disabling conditions of individuals with exceptional needs enrolled in the nonpublic school.

(b) Instruction shall be directed and delivered pursuant to the master contract and the individual service agreement.

(c) To provide special education instruction for individuals with exceptional needs younger than three years of age, as described in Education Code, Part 30, Chapter 4.4, the nonpublic school shall comply with the provisions of Education Code Section 56425 et seq., and Education Code Section 56426.2(e) regarding adult to child ratios.

(d) To provide special education instruction for individuals with exceptional needs between the ages of three and five years, inclusive, as described in Education Code, Part 30, Chapter 4.45, the nonpublic school shall comply with the provisions of Education Code Section 56440 et seq., and Education Code Section 56441.5 regarding appropriate instructional adult to child ratios.

(e) Nonpublic schools and nonpublic agencies shall comply with the personnel standards and qualifications pursuant to Education Code Section 45340 et seq., and Education Code Section 45350 et seq., regarding instructional aids and teacher assistants, respectively.

(f) Nonpublic schools and nonpublic agencies shall comply with all of the laws and regulations governing the licensed professions, in particular the provisions with respect to supervision. Nonpublic schools and nonpublic agencies may use assistants to the extent authorized by state and federal law.

[Authority cited: Sections 33031, 56100 and 56366(e), Education Code.] [Reference: Sections 45340, 45350, 56366.1 and 56425, Education Code.]

3065. Staff Qualifications - Related Services including Designated Instruction and Services.

- Staff Qualifications – Related Services Including Designated Instruction and Services

To be eligible for certification to provide designated instruction and services for individuals with exceptional needs, nonpublic schools and agencies shall meet the following requirements:

(a)(1) "Adapted physical education" means:

- Adapted Physical Education

(A) a modified general physical education program, or a specially designed physical education program in a special class; or

(B) consultative services provided to pupils, parents, teachers, or other school personnel for the purpose of identifying supplementary aids and services or modifications necessary for successful participation in the general physical education program or specially designed physical education programs.

(2) Adapted physical education shall be provided only by personnel who possess a credential that authorizes service in

adapted physical education.

(b)(1) "Assistive technology service" means any service
that directly assists an individual with exceptional needs in the
selection or use of an assistive technology device that is
educationally necessary. The term includes the evaluation of
the needs of an individual with exceptional needs including a
functional evaluation of the individual in the individual's
customary environment; coordinating and using other
therapies, interventions, or services with assistive technology
devices, such as those associated with existing education
programs and rehabilitation plans and programs; training or
technical assistance for an individual with exceptional needs
or, where appropriate, teh family of an individual with
exceptional needs or,if appropriate, that indivdiual's family;
and training or technical assistance for professionals
(including individuals providing education and rehabilitation
services), employers or other individuals who provide
services to, employ, or are otherwise substantially involved in
the major life functions of individuals with exceptional needs.

(2) Assistive technology services shall be provided only by
personnel who possess a:

(A) license in Physical Therapy issued by a licensing
agency within the Department of Consumer Affairs, where
the utilization of assistive technology services falls within the
scope of practice of physical therapy as defined in Business
and Professions Code section 2620 and implementing
regulations; or

(B) certificate of registration as an Occupational Therapist
pursuant to Business and Professions Code section 2570 et
seq., where the utilization of assistive technology services
falls within the scope of practice of occupational therapy; or

(C) license in Speech-Language Pathology issued by a
licensing agency within the Department of Consumer Affairs
or a valid document, issued by the Commission on Teacher
Credentialing, where the function of the assistive technology
service is augmentative communication; or

(D) baccalaureate degree in engineering, with emphasis in
assistive technology; or

(E) baccalaureate degree in a related field of engineering
with a graduate certificate in rehabilitation technlogy or
assistive technology; or

(F) certification from the Rehabilitation Engineering and
Assistive Technology Society of North America and Assistive
Technology Provider (RESNA/ATP); or

(G) a certificate in assistive technology applications issued by a regionally accredited post-secondary institution; or

(H) a credential that authorizes special education of physically handicapped, orthopedically handicapped, or severely handicapped pupils.

(c)(1) "Audiological services" means aural rehabilitation (auditory training, speech reading, language habilitation, and speech conservation) and habilitation with individual pupils in the general classroom; monitoring hearing levels, auditory behavior, and amplification for all pupils requiring personal or group amplification in the instructional setting; planning, organizing, and implementing an audiology program for individuals with auditory dysfunctions, as specified in the individualized education program; or consultative services regarding test finding, amplification needs and equipment, otological referrals, home training programs, acoustic treatment of rooms, and coordination of educational services to hearing-impaired individuals.

- Audiological Services

(2) Audiological services shall be provided only by personnel who possess:

(A) a license in Audiology issued by a licensing agency within the Department of Consumer Affairs, or

(B) a credential authorizing audiology services.

(d) Behavior intervention shall be designed or planned only by personnel who have:

- Behavior Intervention

(1) pupil personnel services credential that authorizes school counseling or school psychology; or

(2) credential authorizing the holder to deliver special education instruction; or

(3) license as a Marriage, Family, and Child Counselor issued by a licensing agency within the Department of Consumer Affairs; or

(4) license as a Clinical Social Worker issued by a licensing agency within the Department of Consumer Affairs; or

(5) license as an Educational Psychologist issued by a licensing agency within the Department of Consumer Affairs;

(6) license as Psychologist issued by a licensing agency within the Department of Consumer Affairs; or

(7) master's degree issued by a regionally accredited post-secondary institution in education, psychology, counseling, behavior analysis, behavior science, human development, social work, rehabilitation, or in a related field.

(e) To be eligible for certification to provide behavior intervention, including implementation of behavior modification plans, but not including development or

- Certification to Provide Behavior Intervention

modification of behavior intervention plans, a nonpublic school or agency shall deliver those services utilizing personnel who:

(1) possess the qualifications under subdivision (d); or

(2)(A) are under the supervision of personnel qualified under subdivision (d);

(B) possess a high school diploma or its equivalent; and

(C) receive the specific level of supervision required in the pupil's IEP.

(f)(1) "Counseling and guidance" means educational counseling in which the pupil is assisted in planning and implementing his or her immediate and long-range educational program; career counseling in which the pupil is assisted in assessing his or her aptitudes, abilities, and interests in order to make realistic career decisions; personal counseling in which the pupil is helped to develop his or her ability to function with social and personal responsibility; or counseling with parents and staff members on learning problems and guidance programs for pupils.

- Counseling and Guidance

(2) Counseling and guidance shall be provided only by personnel who possess a:

(A) license as a Marriage, Family, and Child Counselor issued by a licensing agency within the Department of Consumer Affairs; or

(B) license in Clinical Social Work issued by a licensing agency within the Department of Consumer Affairs; or

(C) license as an Educational Psychologist issued by a licensing agency within the Department of Consumer Affairs; or

(D) license as a Psychologist issued by a licensing agency within the Department of Consumer Affairs; or

(E) pupil personnel services credential, which authorizes school counseling or school psychology.

(g)(1) "Early education programs for children with disabilities" means the program and services specified by Education Code Part 30 Section 56425 et seq.

- Early Education Programs for Children with Disabilities

(2) Early education programs for children with disabilities shall be provided only by personnel who meet the appropriate personnel qualifications set forth in this Article and comply with all other requirements of Education Code Chapter 4.4 commencing with Section 56425.

(h)(1) "Health and nursing services" means:

- Health and Nursing Services

(A) managing the child's health problems on the school site;

(B) consulting with pupils, parents, teachers, and other

personnel;

(C) group and individual counseling with parents and pupils regarding health problems;

(D) maintaining communication with health agencies providing care to individuals with disabilities; or

(E) providing services by qualified personnel.

(2) Health and nursing services shall be provided only by personnel who possess:

(A) a license as a Registered Nurse, issued by a licensing agency within the Department of Consumer Affairs; or

(B) a license as a Vocational Nurse, issued by a licensing agency within the Department of Consumer Affairs, under the supervision of a licensed registered nurse; or

(C) a school nurse credential; or

(D) demonstrated competence in cardio-pulmonary resuscitation, current knowledge of community emergency medical resources, and skill in the use of equipment and performance of techniques necessary to provide specialized physical health care services for individuals with exceptional needs. In addition, possession of training in these procedures to a level of competence and safety that meet the objectives of the training as provided by the school nurse, public health nurse, licensed physician and surgeon, or other training programs. "Demonstrated competence in cardio-pulmonary resuscitation" means possession of a current valid certificate from an approved program; or

(E) a valid license, certificate, or registration appropriate to the health service to be designated, issued by the California agency authorized by law to license, certificate, or register persons to practice health service in California.

(i)(1) "Home and hospital services" means instruction delivered to children with disabilities, individually, in small groups, or by teleclass, whose medical condition such as those related to surgery, accidents, short-term illness or medical treatment for a chronic illness prevents the individual from attending school.

- Home and Hospital Services

(2) Home or hospital instruction shall be provided only by personnel who possess a valid teaching credential.

(j)(1) "Language and speech development and remediation" means screening, assessment, individualized education program development and direct speech and language services delivered to children with disabilities who demonstrate difficulty understanding or using spoken language to such an extent that it adversely affects their educational performance and cannot be corrected without

- Language and Speech Development and Remediation

special education and related services.

(2) Language and speech development and remediation shall be provided only by personnel who possess:

(A) a license in Speech-Language Pathology issued by a licensing agency within the Department of Consumer Affairs; or

(B) a credential authorizing language or speech services.

(k)(1) "Occupational therapy" means the use of various treatment modalities including self-help skills, language and educational techniques as well as sensory motor integration, physical restoration methods, and prevocation exploration to facilitate physical and psychosocial growth and development.

- Occupational Therapy

(2) Occupational therapy shall be provided only by personnel who have certification in good standing with the National Board for Certification in Occupational Therapy, Inc. as a registered occupational therapist (OTR) or certified occupational therapy assistant (COTA). Services provided by a COTA shall be supervised by an OTR in accordance with professional standards outlined by the American Occupational Therapy Association.

(l)(1) "Orientation and mobility instruction" means specialized instruction for individuals in orientation and mobility techniques or consultative services to other educators and parents regarding instructional planning and implementation of the individualized education program relative to the development of orientation and mobility skills and independent living skills.

- Orientation and Mobility Instruction

(2) Orientation and mobility instruction shall be provided only by personnel who possess a credential that authorizes services in orientation and mobility instruction.

(m)(1) "Parent counseling and training" means assisting parents in understanding the special needs of their child and providing parents with information about child development.

- Parent Counseling and Training

(2) Parent counseling and training shall be provided only by personnel who possess a:

(A) credential that authorizes special education instruction; or

(B) credential that authorizes health and nursing services; or

(C) license as a Marriage, Family, and Child Counselor, issued by a licensing agency within the Department of Consumer Affairs; or

(D) license as a Clinical Social Worker, issued by a licensing agency within the Department of Consumer Affairs; or

(E) license as an Educational Psychologist, issued by a licensing agency within the Department of Consumer Affairs; or

(F) license as a Psychologist, issued by a licensing agency within the Department of Consumer Affairs; or

(G) pupil personnel services credential that authorizes school counseling or school psychology or school social work.

(n)(1) "Physical therapy" means the:

- Physical Therapy

(A) administration of active, passive, and resistive therapeutic exercises and local or general massage, muscle training and corrective exercises and coordination work;

(B) administration of hydrotherapy treatments;

(C) assistance in administering various types of electrotherapy including ultraviolet, infrared, diathermy and inductothermy;

(D) teaching parents of hospitalized pupils exercises which are to be continued at home and interpret to them the significance of physical therapy services; and

(E) instruction in walking, standing, balance, use of crutches, cane, or walker and in the care of braces and artificial limbs.

(2) Physical therapy shall be provided only by personnel who possess a valid license in Physical Therapy issued by a licensing agency within the Department of Consumer Affairs.

(o)(1) "Psychological services" means:

- Psychological Services

(A) psychological counseling provided to children with disabilities;

(B) consultative services to parents, pupils, teachers, and other school personnel; or

(C) planning and implementing a program of psychological counseling for children with disabilities and parent by a credentialed or licensed psychologist or other qualified personnel.

(D) This term does not include assessment services and the development of an individualized education program.

(2) Psychological services, other than assessment and development of the individualized education program, shall be provided only by personnel who possess a:

(A) license as a Marriage, Family, and Child Counselor, issued by a licensing agency within the Department of Consumer Affairs; or

(B) license as a Clinical Social Worker, issued by a licensing agency within the Department of Consumer Affairs; or

(C)   license as an Educational Psychologist, issued by a licensing agency within the Department of Consumer Affairs; or

(D)   license in Psychology, issued by a licensing agency within the Department of Consumer Affairs; or

(E)   pupil personnel services credential that authorizes school psychology.

(p)(1)   "Recreation services" means:

- Recreation Services

(A)   therapeutic recreation and specialized instructional programs designed to assist pupils to become as independent as possible in leisure activities, and when possible and appropriate, facilitate the pupil's integration into general recreation programs;

(B)   recreation programs in schools and the community which are those programs that emphasize the use of leisure activity in the teaching of academic, social, and daily living skills and the provision of nonacademic and extracurricular leisure activities and the utilization of community recreation programs and facilities; or

(C)   leisure education programs which are those specific programs designed to prepare the pupil for optimum independent participation in appropriate leisure activities, and developing awareness of personal and community leisure resources.

(2)   Recreation services shall be provided only by personnel who possess a:

(A)   certificate, issued by the California Board of Recreation and Park Certification; or

(B)   certificate issued by the National Council for Therapeutic Recreation; or

(C)   the National Recreation and Park Association, authorizing services in recreation or therapeutic recreation.

(q)(1)   "Social worker services" means:

- Social Worker Services

(A)   individual and group counseling with the individual and his or her immediate family;

(B)   consultation with pupils, parents, teachers, and other personnel regarding the effects of family and other social factors on the learning and developmental requirements of children with disabilities; or

(C)   developing a network of community resources, making appropriate referral and maintaining liaison relationships among the school, the pupil, the family, and the various agencies providing social income maintenance, employment development, mental health, or other developmental services.

(2)   Social worker services shall be provided only by

personnel who possess a:

(A) license in Clinical Social Work issued by a licensing agency within the Department of Consumer Affairs; or

(B) license as a Marriage, Family, and Child Counselor, issued by a licensing agency within the Department of Consumer Affairs; or

(C) credential authorizing school social work.

(r)(1) "Specialized driver training instruction" means instruction to children with disabilities to supplement the general driver-training program.

- Specialized Driver Training Instruction

(2) Specialized driver education and driver training shall be provided only by personnel who possess a credential that authorizes service in driver education and driver training.

(s)(1) "Specially designed vocational education and career development" means"

- Specially Designed Vocational Education and Career Development

(A) providing prevocational programs and assessing work-related skills, interests, aptitudes, and attitudes;

(B) coordinating and modifying the general vocational education program;

(C) assisting pupils in developing attitudes, self-confidence, and vocational competencies to locate, secure, and retain employment in the community or shelter environment, and to enable such individuals to become participating members of the community;

(D) establishing work training programs within the school and community;

(E) assisting in job placement;

(F) instructing job trainers and employers as to the unique needs of the individuals;

(G) maintaining regularly scheduled contract with all work stations and job-site trainers; or

(H) coordinating services with the Department of Rehabilitation, the Employment Development Department and other agencies as designated in the individualized education program.

(2) Specially designed vocation education and career development shall be provided only by personnel who possess a:

(A) adult education credential with a career development authorization; or

(B) credential that authorizes instruction in special education or vocational education; or

(C) pupil personnel services credential that authorizes school counseling.

(t) Specialized interpreting or transcribing services for pupils with low incidence disabilities shall be provided only by personnel who possess a:

(1) certification issued by the Registry of Interpreters for the Deaf or the national Association for the Deaf or any of its affiliated state organizations; or

(2) certificate issued by the Library of Congress as a Braille Transcriber; or

(3) credential authorizing services for deaf and hard of hearing; or

(4) certificate or degree from a regionally accredited post-secondary institution affirming that the bearer has successfully completed a prescribed course of study in sign language interpreting.

(u)(1) "Specialized services for low-incidence disabilities" means:

(A) specially designed instruction related to the unique needs of pupils with low-incidence disabilities; or

(B) specialized services related to the unique needs of individuals with low-incidence.

(2) Specialized services for pupils with low-incidence disabilities shall be provided only be personnel who possess a credential that authorizes services in special education or clinical or rehabilitation scrvices in the appropriate area of disability.

(v)(1) "Vision services" means:

(A) adaptations in curriculum, media, and the environment, as well as instruction in special skills; or

(B) consultative services to pupils, parents, teachers, and other school personnel.

(2) Vision services shall be provided only by personnel who possess;

(A) a license as an Optometrist, Ophthalmologist, Physician or Surgeon, issued by a licensing agency with the Department of Consumer Affairs and authorizing the licensee to provide the services rendered; or

(B) a valid credential authorizing vision instruction or services.

(w) Other designated instruction and services not identified in this section shall only be provided by staff who possess a license issued by a licensing agency with the Department of Consumer Affairs authorizing the licensee to provide the specific service or possess a credential authorizing the service or is qualified to provide the service.

- Specialized Interpreting and Transcribing Services

- Specialized Services for Low-Incidence Disabilities

- Vision Services

- Other Designated Instruction and Services

[Authority cited: Sections 33031, 56100 and 56366(e), Education Code.] [Reference: Sections 2620 and 17505.2, Business and Professions Code; Section 56366.1, Education Code; Section 1401(1), Title 20, U.S. Code; and Sections 3051.2, 3051.4, 3051.5, 3051.7-3051.12, and 3051.14-3051.16.]

3066. Out-of-State Nonpublic Schools/Agencies.

- Out-of-State Nonpublic Schools/Agencies

For purposes of determining eligibility for certification for a nonpublic school or nonpublic agency located in a state other than California, the Department may accept a valid certificate, credential, license, or registration issued by another state for the requirements set forth in Sections 3064 and 3065.

[Authority: Sections 33031, 56100 and 56366(e), Education Code.] [Reference: Section 56366.1, Education Code.]

3067. Certification Status.

- Certification Status

(a) Certification shall become effective on the date when the nonpublic school or nonpublic agency meets all the application requirements and is approved by the Superintendent except as specified in Subdivision 3067(d)(1).

(b) Certification may be retroactive, provided the nonpublic agency met all the requirements for certification on the date the retroactive certification is effective.

(c) The certification status of a nonpublic school or nonpublic agency shall be one of the following:

(1) approved certification with no conditions or limitations;

(2) conditional certification for a limited period of time. A conditional certification indicates that the nonpublic school or nonpublic agency has not met all the certification requirements;

(3) suspended certification for a defined period of time pursuant to the provisions of Education Code Section 56366.4. Nonpublic schools or nonpublic agencies with a suspended certification cannot accept new pupils.

(d) Any local education agency that contracts with a certified nonpublic school or nonpublic agency may request the Superintendent to review the status of the nonpublic school or nonpublic agency. Such requests shall be in writing and a copy shall be sent to the nonpublic school or nonpublic agency.

[Authority cited: Sections 33031, 56100 and 56366(e), Education Code.] [Reference: Sections 56366.1 and 56366.4, Education Code.]

3068. Appeals and Waivers.

(a) Within twenty (20) working days of receipt of notice, nonpublic schools or nonpublic agencies (appellant) may file a written petition (appeal), on forms provided by the Superintendent, to request a review of the decision to deny, suspend or revoke certification pursuant to Education Code Section 56366.6.

(b) All appeals shall be mailed to the Office of Administrative Hearings, Department of General Services.

(c) There shall be three options for appealing the denial, suspension or revocation of certification. The nonpublic school or nonpublic agency may request:

(1) a written review of the decision to deny, suspend or revoke certification. The Office of Administrative Hearings shall analyze the documentation provided by the appellant and materials provided by the Department and render a decision;

(2) a written review with an oral argument. The Office of Administrative Hearings shall analyze the documentation provided by the appellant and materials provided by the Department. The appellant shall also appear before a hearing officer, on a date scheduled by the Office of Administrative Hearings, to provide oral testimony in support of the appeal. The Department shall also attend the hearing and present testimony to support the decision to deny, suspend or revoke certification. The hearing officer may ask questions of either party. All testimony shall be tape-recorded; or

(3) an oral hearing. The appellant shall appear before a hearing officer, on a date scheduled by the Office of Administrative Hearings, to provide oral testimony in support of the appeal. The Department shall also attend the hearing and present testimony to support the decision to deny, suspend or revoke certification. The hearing officer shall provide the opportunity for both parties to review evidence, call witnesses and cross-examine witnesses. If the appellant fails to appear at the hearing, the petitioner waives the right to a future hearing, unless the hearing officer agrees to reschedule the hearing because of extenuating circumstances.

(d) The Office of Administrative Hearings shall issue the decision, in writing, simultaneously to the appellant and to the Department within thirty (30) working days after receipt of all materials and evidence. This shall be the final administrative decision.

(e) Local education agencies and nonpublic schools and agencies may request the Superintendent to waive Education Code sections 56365, 56366, 56366.3, 56366.6 and 56366.7. Such petitions shall be made in accordance with the provisions of Education Code section 56366.2 and shall be necessary in order to provide services to individuals with exceptional needs consistent with their individualized education program.

[Authority cited: Sections 33031, 56100 and 56366(e), Education Code.] [Reference: Sections 56101, 56366.2 and 56366.6.]

3069. Annual Review of Individualized Education
Program.

- Annual Review of IEP

Review of the pupil's individualized education program shall be conducted at least annually by the public education agency. The public education agency shall ensure that review schedules are specified in the individualized education program and contract for the pupil. An elementary school district shall notify a high school district of all pupils placed in nonpublic school or agency programs prior to the annual review of the individualized education program for each pupil who may transfer to the high school district.

[Authority cited: Sections 56100(a), (i), (j), Education Code; 20 U.S.C. 1414(c)(2)(B); and 34 CFR 300.600.] [Reference: Sections 56345, 56365-56366.5, Education Code and 34 CFR 300.4, 300.302, 300.317, 300.343-348 and 300.400-403.]

3070. Graduation.

- Graduation

When an individual with exceptional needs meets public education agency requirements for completion of prescribed course of study and adopted differential proficiency standards as designated in the pupil's individualized education program, the public education agency which developed the individualized education program shall award the diploma.

[Authority cited: Sections 56100(a),(i), (j), Education Code; 20 U.S.C. 1414(c)(2)(B); and 34 C.F.R. 300.600.] [Reference: Sections 56345, 56365-56366.5, Education Code; and 34 C.F.R. 300.4, 300.302, 300.317, 300.343-348 and 300.400.403.]

Article 7. Procedural Safeguards

3080. General Provisions.

- General Provisions

(a)   Sections 4600 through 4671 apply to the filing of a complaint, in accordance with provisions of Title 34, Code of Federal Regulations, Section 76.780-783, regarding a public agency's alleged violation of federal or state law or regulation relating to the provision of a free appropriate public education.

(b) Section 3082 applies to due process hearing procedures which the resolution of disagreements between a parent and a public agency regarding the proposal, or refusal of a public agency to initiate or change the identification, assessment, or educational placement of the pupil or the provision of a free appropriate public education to the pupil.

[Authority cited: Section 56100(a) and (j), Education Code] [Reference: Sections 56500.1 and 56500.2, Education Code; and 34 CFR 76.780-783]

3082. Due Process Hearing Procedures.

- Due Process Hearing Procedures

(a)   A parent or public education agency may initiate a hearing pursuant to Education Code Sections 56500 through 56507 and Title 34, Code of Federal Regulations, Sections 300.506 through 300.514 on any of the matters described in Education Code Section 56501. The hearing shall be conducted by a hearing officer knowledgeable in administrative hearings and under contract with the State Department of Education.

(b) The hearings conducted pursuant to this section shall not be conducted according to the technical rules of evidence and those related to witnesses. Any relevant evidence shall be admitted if it is the sort of evidence on which responsible persons are accustomed to rely in the conduct of serious affairs, regardless of the existence of any common law or statutory rule which might make improper the admission of such evidence over objection in civil actions. Hearsay evidence may be used for the purpose of supplementing or explaining other evidence but shall not be sufficient in itself to support a finding unless it would be admissible over objection in civil actions. All testimony shall be under oath or affirmation which the hearing officer is empowered to administer.

(c) In addition to the rights afforded both parties to the hearing pursuant to Education Code Sections 56500-56507 and Title 34, Code of Federal Regulations, Section 300.514, the parties shall also have the following rights:

(1) To call witnesses, including adverse witnesses, and to cross examine witnesses for the other party.

(2) To compel the attendance of witnesses. The hearing officer shall have the right to issue Subpoenas (order to appear and give testimony) and Subpoenas Duces Tecum (order to produce document(s) or paper(s) upon a showing of reasonable necessity by a party).

(3) Absent compelling circumstances to the contrary, and upon motion to the hearing officer to have witnesses excluded from the hearing.

(d) Hearings shall be conducted in the English language; when the primary language of a party to a hearing is other than English, or other mode of communication, an interpreter shall be provided who is competent as determined by the hearing officer. Cost for an interpreter shall be borne by the State Department of Education. Interpreters shall take an oath to interpret fully and accurately.

(e) If either the school district or the parents have an attorney present as an observer, the attorney may watch the proceedings to advise his party at a later date, but the attorney may not present oral argument, written argument or evidence, or consult in any manner in or out of the room, during the due process hearing.

(f) Notwithstanding Government Code section 11425.10(a)(3) of the Administrative Procedure Act, special education due process hearings are open/closed to the public at the discretion of the parent.

(g) Notwithstanding Government Code section 11440.30 of the Administrative Procedure Act, the hearing officer may conduct all or part of a hearing by telephone, television, or other electronic means if each participant in the hearing has an opportunity to participate in and to hear the entire proceeding while it is taking place and to observe exhibits.

[Authority cited: Section 56100(a) and (j) and 56505, Education Code.] [Reference: Sections 56500-56507, Education Code; Sections 11425.10 and 11440.30, Government Code; Sections 1415(b)(2) and (c), U.S. Code,

Title 20; and Sections 300.506-300.513, Code of Federal Regulations, Title 34.]

3083. Service Notice.

Notwithstanding Government Code section 11440.20 of the Administrative Procedures Act, service of notice, motions, or other writings pertaining to special education due process hearing procedures to the California Special Education Hearing Office and any other person or entity are subject to the following provisions:

(a) The notice, motion, or writing shall be delivered personally or sent by mail or other means to the Hearing Office, person, or entity at their last known address and, if the person or entity is a party with an attorney or other authorized representative of record in the proceeding, to the party's attorney or other authorized representative.

(b) Unless a provision specifies the form of mail, service or notice by mail may be by first-class mail, registered mail, or certified mail, by mail delivery service, by facsimile transmission if complete and without error, or by other electronic means as provided by regulation, in the discretion of the sender.

(c) Service must be made by a method that ensures receipt by all parties and the Hearing Office in a comparable and timely manner.

[Authority: Sections 56100(a) and (j) and 56505, Education Code.] [Reference: Sections 56500-56507, Education Code; Section 11440.20, Government Code; Sections 1415(b)(2) and (c), U.S. Code, Title 20; and Sections 300.506-300.513, Code of Federal Regulations, Title 34.]

3084. Ex Parte Communications.

(a) Notwithstanding Government Code sections 11425.10(a)(8), 11430.20, and 11430.30 of the California Administrative Procedure Act, while special education due process hearing proceedings are pending, there shall be no communication, direct or indirect, regarding any issue in the proceeding, to a hearing officer from an employee or representative of a party or from an interested person unless the communication is made on the record at the hearing.

(b) A proceeding is pending from the date of receipt by the California Special Education Hearing Office of the request for hearing.

(c) If a hearing officer receives a communication in

violation of this section, the hearing officer shall disclose the content of the communication on the record and give the parties an opportunity to address the matter if so requested within 10 days of receipt of notification of the communication.

(1) The hearing officer has discretion to allow the party to present evidence concerning the subject of the communication.

(2) The hearing officer has discretion to reopen a hearing that has been concluded.

(d) If a hearing officer receives a communication in violation of this section, the hearing officer shall make all of the following a part of the record in the proceeding:

(1) If the communication is written, the writing and any written response of the hearing officer.

(2) If the communication is oral, a memorandum stating the substance of the communication, any response made by the hearing officer, and the identity of each person from whom the hearing officer received the communication.

(e) The hearing officer shall notify all parties that the communication has been made a part of the record.

(f) Receipt by the hearing officer of a communication in violation of this section may be grounds for disqualification of the hearing officer. If the hearing officer is disqualified, the portion of the record pertaining to the ex parte communication may be sealed by order of the disqualified hearing officer.

[Authority cited: Sections 56100(a) and (j) and 56505, Education Code.] [Reference: Sections 56500-56507, Education Code; Sections 11425.10, 11430.10-11430.30, 11430.50, and 11430.60, Government Code; Sections 1415(b)(2) and (c), U.S. Code, Title 20; and Sections 300.506-300.513, Code of Federal Regulations, Title 34.]

3085. Precedent Decisions.   - Precedent Decisions

Notwithstanding Government Code section 11425.10(a)(7) of the Administrative Procedure Act, orders and decisions rendered in special education due process hearing proceedings may be cited as persuasive but not binding authority by parties and hearing officers in subsequent proceedings.

[Authority cited: Sections 56100(a) and (j) and 56505, Education Code.] [Reference: Sections 56500-56507, Education Code; Section 11425.10, Government Code;

Sections 1415(b)(2) and (c), U.S. Code, Title 20; and Sections 300.506-300.513, Code of Federal Regulations, Title 34.]

3086. Mediation.

(a) Government Code section 11420.10 of the Administrative Procedure Act does not apply to special education due process hearing procedures because Education Code sections 56500-56507 provide for mediation.

(b) Notwithstanding any other provision of law, a communication made in mediation is protected to the following extent:

(1) Anything said, any admission made, and any document prepared in the course of, or pursuant to, mediation under this article is a confidential communication, and a party to the mediation has a privilege to refuse to disclose and to prevent another from disclosing the communication, whether in an adjudicative proceeding, civil action, or other proceeding. This subsection does not limit the admissibility of evidence if all parties to the proceedings consent.

(2) No reference to mediation proceedings, the evidence produced, or any other aspect of the mediation may be made in adjudicative proceeding or civil action, whether as affirmative evidence, by way of impeachment, or for any other purpose.

(3) No mediator or interpreter or other participants are competent to testify in a subsequent administrative or civil proceeding as to any statement, conduct, decision, or order occurring at, or in conjunction with, the mediation.

(c) Evidence otherwise admissible outside of mediation under this section is not inadmissible or protected from disclosure solely by reason of its introduction or use in mediation under this section.

(d) Interim and final agreements in writing that result from mediation are admissible for purposes of enforcement unless the written agreement specifies otherwise.

[Authority cited: Sections 56100(a) and (j) and 56505, Education Code.] [Reference: Sections 56500-56507, Education Code; Section 11420.10, Government Code; Sections 1415(b)(2) and (c), U.S. Code, Title 20; and Sections 300.506-300.513, Code of Federal Regulations, Title 34.]

3087. Decision by Settlement.

Notwithstanding Government Code section 11415.60 of the Administrative Procedure Act, a decision by settlement may be issued on terms the parties determine are appropriate so long as the agreed-upon terms are not contrary to the law.

[Authority cited: Sections 56100(a) and (j) and 56505, Education Code.] [Reference: Sections 56500-5607, Education Code; Section 11415.60, Government Code; Sections 1415(b)(2) and (c), U.S. Code, Title 20; and Sections 300.506-300.513, Code of Federal Regulations, Title 34.]

3088. Sanctions.

(a) Provisions for contempt sanctions, order to show cause, and expenses contained in Government Code sections 11455.10-11455.30 of the Administrative Procedure Act apply to special education due process hearing procedures except as modified by (b) through (e) of this section.

(b) Only the presiding hearing officers may initiate contempt sanctions and/or place expenses at issue.

(c) Prior to initiating contempt sanctions with the court, the presiding hearing officer shall obtain approval from the General Counsel of the California Department of Education.

(d) The failure to initiate contempt sanctions and/or impose expenses is not appealable.

(e) The presiding hearing officer may, with approval from the General Counsel of the California Department of Education, order a party, the party's attorney or other authorized representative, or both, to pay reasonable expenses, including costs of personnel, to the California Special Education Hearing Office for the reasons set forth in Government Code section 11455.30(a).

[Authority cited: Sections 56100(a) and (j) and 56505, Education Code.] [Reference: Sections 56500-56507, Education Code; Sections 11455.10-11455.30, Government Code; Sections 1415(b)(2) and (c), U.S. Code, Title 20; and Sections 300.506-300.513, Code of Federal Regulations, Title 34.]

3089. Partial Non-Applicability of Certain Sections of the Administrative Procedure Act to Special Education Due Process Hearing Procedures.

Special education due process hearing procedures shall not

be subject to the following provisions of the Administrative Procedure Act; Government Code sections 11415.60 (Decision by settlement); 11420.10 and 11420.30 (Referral of proceedings); 11425.10 (Governing procedures); 11440.10 (Authority of agency head following decision); 11440.20 (Service notice); 11440.30 (b) (Conduct of hearing by electronic means); 11445.10-11445.60 (Informal hearing); 11450.05-11450-30 (Subpoenas); 11460.10-11460.70 (Emergency decision); 11465.10-11465.60 (Declaratory decisions); and 11470.10-11470.50 (Conversion of proceeding).

[Authority cited: Sections 56100(a) and (j) and 56505, Education Code.] [Reference: Sections 56500-56507, Education Code; Sections 11415.60, 11420.10, 11420.30, 11425.10, 11440.10-11440.30, 11445.10-11445.60, 11450.05-11450.30, 11460.10-11460.70, 11465.10-11465.60, and 11470.10-11470.50, Government Code; Sections 1415(b)(2) and (c), U.S. Code, Title 20; and Sections 300.506-300.513, Code of Federal Regulations, Title 34.]

Article 8. State Board of Education Waivers

3100. Resource Specialist Caseload Waivers.

(a) A school district, special education local plan area, county office of education, or any other public agency providing special education or related services may request the State Board of Education to grant a waiver of the maximum resource specialist caseload, as set forth in Education Code 56362(c), only if the waiver is necessary or beneficial either (1) to the content and implementation of a pupil's individualized education program and does not abrogate any right provided individuals with exceptional needs by specified federal law or (2) to the agency's compliance with specified federal law.

(b) The State Board of Education shall grant any waiver request submitted in accordance with subdivision (a) only:

(1) When the facts indicate that failure to do so would hinder either

(A) Implementation of a pupil's individualized education program or

(B) Compliance by the requesting agency with specified federal law; and

(2) When the waiver request meets all of the conditions set

- Resource Specialist Caseload Waivers

forth in subdivisions (c) and (d).

(c) A request to waive the maximum resource specialist caseload shall be "necessary or beneficial" within the meaning of subdivision (a) and Education Code Section 56101 only if all of the following conditions are met.

(1) The waiver's effective period does not exceed one past school year and/or the school year in which it is submitted.

(2) The number of students to be served by an affected resource specialist under the waiver does not exceed the maximum statutory caseload of 28 students by more than four students.

(3) The waiver does not result in the same resource specialist having a caseload in excess of the statutory maximum for more than two school years.

(d) For the purposes of subdivision (b), a request to waive the maximum resource specialist caseload shall not "hinder" either (1) implementation of a pupil's individualized education program or (2) compliance by the requesting agency with specified federal law if all of the following conditions are met:

(1) The requesting agency demonstrates to the satisfaction of the State Board of Education (A) that the excess resource specialist caseload results from extraordinary fiscal and/or programmatic conditions and (B) that the extraordinary conditions have been resolved or will be resolved by the time the waiver expires.

(2) The waiver stipulates that an affected resource specialist will have the assistance of an instructional aide at least five hours daily whenever that resource specialist's caseload exceeds the statutory maximum during the waiver's effective period.

(3) The waiver confirms that the students served by an affected resource specialist will receive all the services called for in their individualized education programs.

(4) The waiver was agreed to by any affected resource specialist, and the bargaining unit, if any, to which the resource specialist belongs participated in the waiver's development.

(5) The waiver demonstrates to the satisfaction of the State Board of Education that the excess caseload can be reasonably managed by an affected resource specialist in particular relation to (A) the resource specialist's pupil contact time and other assigned duties and (B) the programmatic conditions faced by the resource specialist, including, but not limited to, student age level, age span, and

behavioral characteristics; number of curriculum levels taught at any one time or any given session; and intensity of student instructional needs.

[Authority cited: Sections 33031 and 56100(a), Education Code.][Reference: Sections 56101 and 56362(c), Education Code]

NOTE

Reference citations to Title 34 of the Code of Federal Regulations may not match the regulations issued on March 12, 1999, implementing Public Law 105-17, the Individuals with Disabilities Education Act Amendments of 1997.

CALIFORNIA CODE OF REGULATIONS
TITLE 5. EDUCATION
DIVISION 1. STATE DEPARTMENT OF EDUCATION
CHAPTER 5.1. UNIFORM COMPLAINT PROCEDURES

Subchapter 1. Complaint Procedures

Article 1. Definitions

4600. General Definitions.

As used in this Chapter, the term:

— Definitions

(a) "Appeal" means a request made in writing to a level higher than the original reviewing level by an aggrieved party requesting reconsideration or a reinvestigation of the lower adjudicating body's decision.

— Appeal

(b) "Complainant" means any individual , including a person's duly authorized representative or an interested third party, public agency, or organization who files a written complaint alleging violation of federal or state laws or regulations, including allegations of unlawful discrimination in programs and activities funded directly by the state or receiving any financial assistance from the state.

— Complainant

(c) "Complaint" means a written and signed statement alleging a violation of a federal or state law or regulation, which may include an allegation of unlawful discrimination. If the complainant is unable to put the complaint in writing, due to conditions such as illiteracy or other handicaps, the public agency shall assist the complainant in the filing of the complaint.

— Complaint

(d) "Complaint Investigation" means an administrative process used by the Department or local agency for the purpose of gathering data regarding the complaint.

— Complaint Investigation

(e) "Complaint Procedure" means an internal process used by the Department or local agency to process and resolve complaints.

— Complaint Procedure

(f) "Compliance Agreement" means an agreement between the Department and a local agency, following a finding of noncompliance by the Department, developed by the local agency and approved by Department to resolve the noncompliance.

— Compliance Agreement

(g) "Days" means calendar days unless designated otherwise.

— Days

(h) "Department" means the California Department of Education.

- Department

(i) "Direct State Intervention" means the steps taken by the Department to initially investigate complaints or effect compliance.

- Direct State Intervention

(j) "Local Agency" means a school district governing board or a local public or private agency which receives direct or indirect funding or any other financial assistance from the state to provide any school programs or activities or special education or related services. "Local educational agency" includes any public school district and county office of education.

- Local Agency

(k) "Mediation" means a problem-solving activity whereby a third party assists the parties to a dispute in resolving the problem.

- Mediation

(l) "State Mediation Agreement" means a written, voluntary agreement, approved by the Department, which is developed by the local agency and complainant with assistance from the Department to resolve an allegation of noncompliance.

- State Mediation Agreement

(m) "State Agency" means the State Departments of Mental Health or Health Services or any other state administrative unit that is or may be required to provide special education or related services to handicapped pupils pursuant to Government Code Section 7570 et seq.

- State Agency

(n) "Superintendent" means the Superintendent of Public Instruction or his or her designee.

- Superintendent

[Authority cited: Sections 232 and 33031, Education Code; Section 11138, Government Code] [Reference: Sections 210, 220, and 260, Education Code; Sections 11135 and 11138, Government Code]

Article 2. Purpose and Scope

4610. Purpose and Scope.

- Purpose and Scope

(a) This Chapter applies to the filing, investigation and resolution of a complaint regarding an alleged violation by a local agency of federal or state law or regulations governing educational programs, including allegations of unlawful discrimination, in accordance with the provisions of Title 34, CFR, Sections 76.780-783 and 106.8; Title 22, CCR, Sections 98300-98382; and California Education Code Sections 49556 and 8257. The purpose of this Chapter is to establish a uniform system of complaint processing for specified programs or activities which receive state or federal funding.

(b) This Chapter applies to the following programs administered by the Department:

(i) Adult Basic Education established pursuant to Education Code Sections 8500 through 8538 and 52500 through 52616.5;

(ii) Consolidated Categorical Aid Programs as listed in Education Code Section 64000(a);

(iii) Migrant Education established pursuant to Education Code Sections 54440 through 54445;

(iv) Vocational Education established pursuant to Education Code Sections 52300 through 52480;

(v) Child Care and Development programs established pursuant to Education Code Sections 8200 through 8493;

(vi) Child Nutrition programs established pursuant to Education Code Sections 49490 through 49560; and

(vii) Special Education programs established pursuant to Education Code Sections 56000 through 56885 and 59000 through 59300.

(c) This Chapter also applies to the filing of complaints which allege unlawful discrimination on the basis of ethnic group identification, religion, age, sex, color, or physical or mental disability, in any program or activity conducted by a local agency, which is funded directly by, or that receives or benefits from any state financial assistance.

[Authority cited: Sections 232, 8261, 33031, 49531, 49551, 54445, 52355, 52451, and 56100(a) and (j), Education Code; Section 11138 Government Code] [Reference: Sections 210, 220, 260, and 49556, Education Code; Sections 11135 and 11138, Government Code]

4611. Referring Complaint Issues to Other Appropriate State or Federal Agencies.

- Referring Complaint Issues to Other Appropriate State or Federal Agencies

The following complaints shall be referred to the specified agencies for appropriate resolution and are not subject to the local and Department complaint procedures set forth in this Chapter unless these procedures are made applicable by separate interagency agreements:

(a) Allegations of child abuse shall be referred to the applicable County Department of Social Services (DSS), Protective Services Division or appropriate law enforcement agency. However, nothing in this section relieves the Department from investigating complaints pursuant to section

4650(a) (viii) (C).

(b) Health and safety complaints regarding a Child Development Program shall be referred to Department of Social Services for licensed facilities, and to the appropriate Child Development regional administrator for licensing-exempt facilities.

(c) Discrimination issues involving Title IX of the Educational Amendments of 1972 shall be referred to the U.S. Office of Civil Rights (OCR). Title IX complainants will only be referred to the OCR if there is no state discrimination law or regulation at issue. Unless otherwise negotiated through a memorandum of understanding/agreement, a preliminary inquiry and/or investigation concerning these complaints will be conducted by OCR. The complainant shall be notified by certified mail if his or her complaint is transferred to OCR by the Superintendent.

(d) Complaints of discrimination involving Child Nutrition Programs administered by the Department from program participants or applicants shall be referred to either Administrator, U.S. Department of Agriculture, Food and Nutrition Service, 3101 Park Center Drive, Alexandria, VA 22302 or Secretary of Agriculture, Washington, D.C. 20250. Discrimination complaints received by a local agency or the Department shall be immediately directed to U.S. Department of Agriculture, Food and Nutrition Service, Western Regional Office.

(e) Employment discrimination complaints shall be sent to the State Department of Fair Employment and Housing (DFEH) pursuant to Title 22, CCR, Section 98410. The complainant shall be notified by certified mail of any DFEH transferral.

(f) Allegations of fraud shall be referred to the responsible Department Division Director and the Department's Legal Office.

[Authority cited: Sections 33031, 71020 and 71025, Education Code; Section 11138, Government Code. [Reference: Sections 11135, 11136, and 11138, Government Code; 34 CFR 76.780-76.783.]

Article 3. Local Agency Compliance

4620. Local Educational Agency Responsibilities.
Each local education agency shall have the primary

- Local Educational Agency Responsibilities

responsibility to insure compliance with applicable state and federal laws and regulations. Each local educational agency shall investigate complaints alleging failure to comply, and seek to resolve those complaints in accordance with the procedures set out in this Chapter.

[Authority cited: Sections 232 and 33031, Education Code; Section 11138, Government Code] [Reference: Section 260, Education Code; Sections 11135, Government Code; and 34 CFR 76.780 - 76.783 and 106.8]

4621. District Policies and Procedures.

- District and County Office Policies and Procedures

(a) Each local educational agency shall adopt policies and procedures consistent with this Chapter for the investigation and resolution of complaints. Local policies shall ensure that complainants are protected from retaliation and that the identity of the complainant alleging discrimination remain confidential as appropriate. School Districts and County Offices of Education shall submit their policies and procedures to the local governing board for adoption within one year from the effective date of this chapter. Upon adoption, the district may forward a copy to the Superintendent.

(b) Each local educational agency shall include in its policies and procedures the person(s), employee(s) or agency position(s) or unit(s) responsible for receiving complaints, investigating complaints and ensuring local educational agency compliance. The local educational agency's policies shall ensure that the person(s), employee(s), position(s) or unit(s) responsible for compliance and/or investigations shall be knowledgeable about the laws/programs that he/she is assigned to investigate.

[Authority cited: Sections 232 and 33031, Education Code; Section 11138, Government Code] [Reference: Section 260, Education Code; Sections 11135, Government Code; and 34 CFR 76.780 - 76.783 and 106.8]

4622. Notice; Notice Recipients; Notice Requirements.

- Notice

Each local educational agency shall annually notify in writing, as applicable, its students, employees, parents or guardians of its students, the district advisory committee, school advisory committees, and other interested parties of their local educational agency complaint procedures, including the opportunity to appeal to the Department and the provisions of this Chapter. The notice shall include the identity (identities) of the person(s) responsible for processing complaints. The notice shall also advise the recipient of the notice of any civil law remedies that may be available, and of the appeal and review procedures contained in Sections 4650, 4652, and 4671 of this Chapter. This notice shall be in English, and when necessary, in the primary language, pursuant to Section 48985 of the Education Code, or mode of communication of the recipient of the notice.

[Authority cited: Sections 232 and 33031, Education Code; Section 11138, Government Code] [Reference: Sections 11135 and 11138, Government Code; 34 CFR 76.780-76.783 and 106.8]

Article 4. Local Complaint Procedures

4630. Filing A Local Complaint; Procedures; Time Lines.

- Filing a Local Complaint

(a) For other than discrimination complaints, any individual, public agency or organization may file a written complaint with the administrator/superintendent of the local educational agency, alleging a matter which, if true, would constitute a violation by that local educational agency of federal or state law or regulation governing the programs listed in Section 4610(b) of this Chapter.

(b) An investigation of alleged unlawful discrimination shall be initiated by filing a complaint not later than six months from the date the alleged discrimination occurred, or the date the complainant first obtained knowledge of the facts of the alleged discrimination unless the time for filing is extended by the Superintendent, upon written request by the complainant setting forth the reasons for the extension. Such extension by the Superintendent shall be made in writing. The period for filing may be extended by the Superintendent for good cause for a period not to exceed 90 days following the expiration of the time allowed. The Superintendent shall respond immediately upon receipt of requests for extensions.

(1) The complaint shall be filed by one who alleges that he or she has personally suffered unlawful discrimination, or by one who believes an individual or any specific class of individuals has been subjected to discrimination prohibited by this part.

(2) The complaint shall be filed with the local educational agency director/district superintendent or his or her designee, unless the complainant requests direct intervention by the

Department pursuant to Article 6 of this Chapter.

(3) An investigation of a discrimination complaint shall be conducted in a manner that protects confidentiality of the parties and the facts.

[Authority cited: Sections 232 and 33031, Education Code; Section 11138, Government Code] [Reference: Sections 11135, 11136, and 11138, Government Code; 34 CFR 76.780-76.783 and 106.8]

4631. Responsibilities of the Local Agency.
- Local Agency Responsibilities

(a) Within 60 days from receipt of the complaint, the local educational agency superintendent or his or her designee shall complete the investigation of the complaint in accordance with the local procedures developed pursuant to Section 4621 and prepare a written Local Educational Agency Decision. This time period may be extended by written agreement of the complainant.

(b) The investigation shall provide an opportunity for the complainant, or the complainant's representative, or both, and local educational agency representatives to present information relevant to the complaint. The investigation may include an opportunity for the parties to the dispute to meet to discuss the complaint or to question each other or each other's witnesses.

(c) The Local Educational Agency Decision (the Decision), shall be in writing and sent to the complainant within sixty (60) days from receipt of the complaint by the local agency. The Decision shall contain the findings and disposition of the complaint, including corrective actions if any, the rationale for such disposition, notice of the complainant's right to appeal the local educational agency decision to the Department, and the procedures to be followed for initiating an appeal to the Department.

(d) Local Educational Agencies may establish procedures for attempting to resolve complaints through mediation prior to the initiation of a formal compliance investigation. Conducting local mediation shall not extend the local time lines for investigating and resolving complaints at the local level unless the complainant agrees, in writing, to the extension of the time line. In no event shall mediation be mandatory in resolving complaints.

[Authority cited: Sections 232 and 33031, Education Code; Section 11138, Government Code] [Reference: Sections

11135, 11136, and 11138, Government Code; 34 CFR 76.780-76.783 and 106.8]

4632. Forward to Superintendent.

- Forward to Superintendent

Upon notification by the Superintendent that the Local Educational Agency Decision has been appealed to the state level pursuant to Section 4652, the local educational agency shall forward the following to the Superintendent:

(a) The original complaint;

(b) A copy of the Local Educational Agency Decision;

(c) A summary of the nature and extent of the investigation conducted by the local agency, if not covered in the Local Educational Agency Decision;

(d) A report of any action taken to resolve the complaint;

(e) A copy of the local educational agency complaint procedures; and

(f) Such other relevant information as the Superintendent may require.

[Authority cited: Section 232 and 33031, Education Code; Section 11138, Government Code] [Reference: Sections 11135, 11136, and 11138, Government Code; 34 CFR 76.780-76.783 and 106.8]

Article 5. State Complaint Procedures

4640. Filing a State Complaint That Has Not First Been Filed at the Local Agency; Time Lines, Notice, Appeal Rights.

- Filing a State Complaint

(a) Referral to the Local Educational Agency for Local Resolution.

(1) If a complaint is erroneously first sent to the Superintendent without local educational agency investigation, the Superintendent shall immediately forward the complaint to the local educational agency for processing in accordance with Article 4 of this Chapter, unless circumstances necessitating Department intervention as described at Section 4650 exist.

(2) The complainant(s) shall be sent a letter to notify him, her, or them of 1) the transferred complaint, 2) the State request for local educational agency resolution, and 3) to advise of Department appeal procedures.

[Authority cited: Sections 232 and 33031, Education Code; Section 11138, Government Code] [Reference: Sections

11135, 11136, and 11138, Government Code; 34 CFR 76.780-76.783 and 106.8]

Article 6. Direct State Intervention

4650. Basis of Direct State Intervention.

- Basis of Direct State Intervention

(a) The Superintendent shall directly intervene without waiting for local agency action if one or more of the following conditions exists.

(i) The complaint includes an allegation, and the Department verifies, that a local educational agency failed to comply with the complaint procedures required by this Chapter;

(ii) Discrimination is alleged by the complainant and the facts alleged indicate that the complainant will suffer an immediate loss of some benefit such as employment or education if the Department does not intervene. However, nothing in this section gives the Department jurisdiction over employment discrimination claims.

(iii) The complaint relates to agencies other than local educational agencies funded through the Child Development and Child Nutrition Programs;

(iv) The complaint requests anonymity and presents clear and convincing evidence and the Department verifies that he or she would be in danger of retaliation if a complaint were filed locally, or has been retaliated against because of past or present complaints;

(v) The complainant alleges that the local educational agency failed or refused to implement the final decision resulting from its local investigation or local Mediation Agreement;

(vi) The local agency refuses to respond to the Superintendent's request for information regarding a complaint;

(vii) The complainant alleges and the Department verifies, or the Department has information that no action has been taken by the local educational agency within 60 calendar days of the date the complaint was filed locally.

(viii) For complaints relating to special education the following shall also be conditions for direct state intervention:

(A) The complainant alleges that a public agency, other than a local educational agency, as specified in Government Code Section 7570 et seq., fails or refuses to comply with an applicable law or regulation relating to the provision of free appropriate public education to handicapped individuals;

(B) The complainant alleges that the local educational agency or public agency fails or refuses to comply with the due process procedures established pursuant to federal and state law and regulation; or has failed or refused to implement a due process hearing order;

(C) The complainant alleges facts that indicate that the child or group of children may be in immediate physical danger or that the health, safety or welfare of a child or group of children is threatened;

(D) The complainant alleges that a handicapped pupil is not receiving the special education or related services specified in his or her Individualized Education Program (IEP);

(E) The complaint involves a violation of federal law governing special education, 20 U.S.C. Section 1400 et seq., or its implementing regulations.

(b) The complaint shall identify upon which basis, as described in paragraph (a) of this section, that direct filing to the State is being made.

[Authority cited: Section 232 and 33031, Education Code; Section 11138, Government Code] [Reference: Sections 11135, 11136, and 11138, Government Code; 34 CFR 76.780-76.783 and 106.8]

4651. Direct State Intervention Time Line.

- Direct State Intervention Time Line

When the Superintendent receives a complaint requesting direct State intervention, the Superintendent shall determine whether the complaint meets one or more of the criterion specified in Section 4650 for direct State intervention and shall immediately notify the complainant by mail of his or her determination. If the complaint is not accepted, it shall be referred for local investigation pursuant to Section 4631, or referred to another agency pursuant to Section 4611.

[Authority cited: Sections 232 and 33031, Education Code; Section 11138, Government Code] [Reference: Sections 11135, 11136, and 11138, Government Code; 34 CFR 76.780-76.783 and 106.8]

4652. Appealing Local Agency Decisions.

- Appealing Local Agency Decisions

(a) Any complainant(s) may appeal a Local Educational Agency Decision to the Superintendent by filing a written appeal with the Superintendent within (15) days of receiving the Local Educational Agency Decision. Extensions for filing appeals may be granted, in writing, for good cause.

(b) The complainant shall specify the reason(s) for appealing the local educational agency decision.

(c) The appeal shall include:

(1) a copy of the locally filed complaint; and

(2) a copy of the Local Educational Agency Decision.

[Authority cited: Sections 232 and 33031, Education Code; Section 11138, Government Code] [Reference: Sections 11135, 11136, and 11138, Government Code; 34 CFR 76.780-76.783 and 106.8]

Article 7. State Resolution Procedures

4660. Department Resolution Procedures.

- Department Resolution Procedures

(a) When direct State intervention is warranted pursuant to any provision of Section 4650, or when an appeal has been filed of a local agency decision pursuant to Section 4652, the following procedures shall be used to resolve the issues of the complaint:

(1) The Department shall offer to mediate the dispute which may lead to a state mediation agreement; and

(2) The Department shall conduct an on-site investigation if either the district or the complainant waives the mediation process or the mediation fails to resolve the issues.

(b) If the complaint involves several issues, nothing shall prohibit the parties from agreeing to mediate some of the issues while submitting the remainder for Department investigation. Mediation shall be conducted within the 60 day time line specified in Section 4662(d), and

(c) Mediation shall not exceed thirty (30) days unless the local or public agency and the complainant agree to an extension.

[Authority cited: Sections 232 and 33031, Education Code; Section 11138, Government Code] [Reference: Sections 11135, 11136, and 11138, Government Code; 34 CFR 76.780-76.783 and 106.8]

4661. Mediation Procedures; State Mediation Agreements; Notice.

- Mediation Procedures

(a) Initial process.

(1) Agency and Complainant(s) Notification. Each party in the dispute shall be contacted by the Department and offered the mediation process as a possible means of

resolving the complaint. Should the parties agree to enter into mediation, written confirmation shall be sent indicating the time and place of the mediation conference, and the allegations to be addressed.

(2) Upon local agency and complainant acceptance of the Department's offer to mediate, the allegations to be addressed shall be sent by certified mail to each party.

(3) The Superintendent shall appoint a trained mediator or mediation team to assist the parties in reaching a voluntary agreement.

(b) Mediation Results - State Mediation Agreement.

(1) The mediation results will be documented in a state mediation agreement and signed by the involved parties to the dispute using the following forms as appropriate (Stipulation to Initiate Mediation, Form CS-19; Signed Mediation Agreement Letter to District, Form CS-24; and Mediation Process Agreement, Form CS-25).

(2) The mediator or mediation team shall confirm that the agreement is consistent with all applicable state and federal laws and regulations.

(3) A copy of the written state mediation agreement shall be sent to each party.

(4) The compliance status of a local agency will revert to noncompliance if the local agency does not perform the provisions of the mediation agreement within the time specified in the mediation agreement.

[Authority cited: Section 232 and 33031, Education Code; Section 11138, Government Code] [Reference: Sections 11135, 11136, and 11138, Government Code; 34 CFR 76.780-76.783 and 106.8]

4662. On-Site Investigation Process; Appointment, Notification, Time Line; Extending Investigation Time Lines.

- On-Site Investigation Process

(a) If either party waives mediation or the mediation fails, in part or in whole, those remaining unresolved issues shall be addressed through the investigation process.

(b) Appointment.

If an on-site investigation is necessary, an investigator(s) shall be appointed by the Superintendent.

(c) Agency and Complainant(s) Notification.

At least two weeks prior to the date of an investigation, each party in the dispute shall be sent written notification by the Department of the name(s) of the investigation(s) and the investigation date(s). The notice shall explain the investigation process.

(d) Time line.

An investigation shall be completed within sixty (60) days after receiving a request for direct intervention or an appeal request, unless the parties have agreed to mediate and agree to extend the time lines. The Superintendent or his or her designee may grant extensions for the investigation only if exceptional circumstances exist with respect to the particular complaint, and provided that the complainant is informed of the extension and the reasons therefore and provided that the facts supporting the extension are documented and maintained in the complaint file.

[Authority cited: Sections 232 and 33031, Education Code; Section 11138, Government Code] [Reference: Sections 11135, 11136, and 11138, Government Code; 34 CFR 76.780-76.783 and 106.8]

4663. Department Investigation Procedures.

(a) The investigator(s) shall request all documentation regarding the allegations. The investigator(s) shall interview the complainant(s), agency administrators, staff, related committees/groups, and any other involved persons, as appropriate, to determine the facts in the case. An opportunity shall be provided for the complainant(s), or the complainant's(s') representative, or both, and the agency involved to present information.

(b) Refusal by the local agency or complainant to provide the investigator with access to records and other information relating to the complaint which the investigator is privileged to review, or any other obstruction of the investigative process shall result in either a dismissal of the complaint or imposition of official applicable sanctions against the local agency.

[Authority cited: Sections 232 and 33031, Education Code; Section 11138, Government Code] [Reference: Sections 11135, 11136, and 11138, Government Code; 34 CFR 76.780-76.783 and 106.8]

4664. Department Investigation Report.

An investigation report shall be submitted to the Superintendent for review and approval. The investigation report shall include the following information:

- Department Investigation Procedures

- Department Investigation Report

(1) A transmittal letter that includes information about how the agency or the complainants may appeal the decision to the Office of the State Superintendent;

(2) General procedures of the investigation;

(3) Citations of applicable law and regulations;

(4) Department findings of facts;

(5) Department conclusions;

(6) Department required actions, if applicable;

(7) Department recommended actions, if applicable; and

(8) Time line for corrective actions, if applicable.

(c) Report time line.

An investigation report shall be mailed to the parties within sixty (60) days from the date of receipt of the request for direct state intervention or an appeal, unless the parties have participated in mediation and agreed to an extension of the mediation time lines or the Superintendent has granted an extension pursuant to Section 4662(d).

[Authority cited: Sections 232 and 33031, Education Code; Section 11138, Government Code] [Reference: Sections 11135, 11136, and 11138, Government Code; 34 CFR 76.780-76.783 and 106.8]

4665. Discretionary Reconsideration Or Appeal Of CDE Investigation Report.

- Discretionary Reconsideration or Appeal of CDE Investigation Report

(a) Within 35 days of receipt of the Department investigation report, either party may request reconsideration by the Superintendent.   The Superintendent may, within fifteen (15) days of receipt of the request, respond in writing to the parties either modifying the conclusions or required corrective actions of the Department report or denying the request outright. During the pending of the Superintendent's reconsideration, the Department report remains in effect and enforceable.

(b) Appeals by private agencies regarding Child Care Food Programs shall be made to the State Office of Administrative Hearings in accordance with applicable laws rather than the Superintendent.   Appeals from investigations of complaints involving Child Development contractors, whether public or private, shall be made to the Superintendent of Public Instruction as provided in subsection (a) except as otherwise provided in Division 19 of Title 5 of the Code of California Regulations.

(c) For those programs governed by Part 76 of Title 34 of the Code of Federal Regulations, the parties shall be notified of the right to appeal to the United States Secretary of Education.

[Authority cited: Sections 232 and 33031, Education Code; Section 11138, Government Code] [Reference: Sections 11135, 11136, and 11138, Government Code; 34 CFR 76.1 and 76.780-76.783 and 106.8]

Article 8. Enforcement -- State Procedures to Effect Compliance

4670. Enforcement.

(a) Upon determination that a local agency violated the provisions of this chapter, the Superintendent shall notify the local agency of the action he or she will take to effect compliance. The Superintendent may use any means authorized by law to effect compliance, including:

(1) The withholding of all or part of the local agency's relevant state or federal fiscal support;

(2) Probationary eligibility for future state or federal support, conditional or compliance with specified conditions;

(3) Proceeding in a court of competent jurisdiction for an appropriate order compelling compliance.

(b) No decision to curtail state or federal funding to a local agency under this chapter shall be made until the Superintendent has determined that compliance cannot be secured by voluntary means.

(c) If the Superintendent determines that a Child Development Contractor's Agreement shall be terminated, the procedures set forth in Sections 8257(d) or 8400 et seq. of the Education Code and the regulations promulgated pursuant thereto (Chapter 19 of Title 5, CCR, commencing with Section 17906), shall be followed.

(d) If the Superintendent determines that a school district or county office has failed to comply with any provision of Sections 49550 through 49554 of the Education Code, the Superintendent shall certify such noncompliance to the Attorney General for investigation pursuant to Section 49556 of the Education Code.

[Authority cited: Sections 232 and 33031, Education Code; Section 11138, Government Code] [Reference: Sections 11135, 11136, and 11138, Government Code; 34 CFR 76.780-76.783 and 106.8]

4671. Federal Review Rights.

If the Superintendent elects to withhold funds from a local agency that refuses or fails to comply in a program governed by 34 CFR Part 76, the Superintendent shall notify the local agency of the decision to withhold funding and of the local agency's rights of appeal pursuant to 34 CFR Section 76.401.

[Authority cited: Sections 232 and 33031, Education Code; Section 11138, Government Code] [Reference: 34 CFR 76.780-76.783]

NEW BUILDING AREA ALLOWANCES FOR SPECIAL EDUCATION PROGRAMS

(Education Code – Part 10)

(SB 1686, Chapter 691, Statutes of 1998)
(Formerly Education Code Section 17747)

17047. (a) The allowable new building area for the purpose of providing special day class and Resource Specialist Program facilities for special education pupils shall be negotiated and approved by the State Allocation Board, with any necessary assistance to be provided by the Special Education Division of the State Department of Education. The square footage allowances shall be computed within the maximum square footage set forth in the following schedule:

- Allowable New Building Area for Special Education Programs

- Maximum Square Footage Schedule

Special Day Class Basic Needs	Grade Levels	Loading*	Square Footage
Nonsevere Disability			
--Specific Learning Disability	All	12	1080
--Mildly Mentally Retarded	All	12	1080
--Severe Disorder of Language	All	10	1080
Severe Disability			
--Deaf and Hard of Hearing	All	10	1080
--Visually Impaired	All	10	1330 (1080 + 250 storage)
--Orthopedically and Other Health Impaired	All	12	2000 (1080+400 toilets + 250 storage + 270 daily living skills + 3000 therapy + 750 therapy per additional classroom)
--Autistic	All	6	1160 (1080 + 80 toilets)
--Severely Emotionally Disturbed	All	6	1160 (1080 + 80 toilets)

--Severely Mentally Retarded	Elem.	12	1750 (1080 + 400 toilets + 270 daily living skills)
	Secon.		2150 (1080 + 400 toilets + 270 daily living skills + 400 vocational)
--Developmentally Disabled	All	10	2000 1080 + 400 toilets + 250 storage + 270 daily living skills + 3000 therapy** + 750 therapy per additional CR)
--Deaf-Blind/Multi	All	5	1400 (1080 + 200 storage + 150 toilets)

		Pupils	Square Feet
Resource Specialist Program for those pupils with disabling conditions whose needs have been identified by the Individualized Education Program (IEP) Team, who require special education for a portion of the day, and who are assigned to a regular classroom for a majority of the schoolday.***	All Maximum caseload for RS is 28, not all served at same time.	1-8	240
		9-28	480
		29-37	720
		38-56	960
		57-65	1200
		66-85	1440
		86-94	1680
		95-112	1920

* Special pupils may usually be grouped without accordance to type, especially in smaller districts or where attendance zones may indicate, to maximize loadings per classroom where there are children with similar educational need (Sec. 56364 or 56364.2, as applicable).

** Therapy add-ons not to be provided if one same site as orthopedically impaired.

*** To a maximum of 4 percent of the unhoused average daily attendance of the district, per new school or addition, to a maximum of 1920 square feet.

(b) The allowable new building area shall be computed by dividing the number of eligible pupils by the minimum required loading per classroom for special day classes for the type of pupils to be enrolled. No new or additional facility shall be provided for special day classes unless the number of additional eligible pupils equals one-third or more of the minimum required loading.

NEW SCHOOL FACILITIES - MAXIMIZING INTERACTION

(Education Code – Part 10)

(SB 50, Chapter 407, Statutes of 1998)
(Formerly Education Code Section 17047.5)

17070.80. (a) All school facilities purchased or newly constructed pursuant to this chapter for use, in whole or in part, by pupils who are individuals with exceptional needs, as defined in Section 56026, shall be designed and located on the schoolsite so as to maximize interaction between those individuals with exceptional needs and other pupils as appropriate to the needs of both.

- Maximize Interaction

(b) The governing board of each applicant school district and the county office of education shall ensure that school facilities for pupils who are individuals with exceptional needs are integrated with other school facilities.

- District and County Responsibilities

(c) The State Allocation Board, after consultation with the State Department of Education and representatives from county offices of education, special education services regions, and school districts, shall develop and adopt any regulations necessary to implement this section.

- Regulations

(d) Notwithstanding any other provision of law, the requirement set forth in subdivision (a) may be waived, by the Superintendent of Public Instruction, only upon compliance with the following procedure:

- Superintendent's Waiver Procedure

(1) The applicant school district or county superintendent of schools shall file a written request for waiver that documents the reasons for its inability to comply with the requirement.

(2) The State Department of Education shall verify the reasons set forth pursuant to paragraph (1), including the documentation submitted, which verification shall be completed no later than 30 days after the filing of the request for waiver with the Superintendent of Public Instruction.

(3) The Advisory Commission on Special Education, as established under Section 33590, at its first scheduled meeting following the verification conducted pursuant to paragraph (2), shall review the request for waiver, accompanying documentation, and the verification findings of the State Department of Education. No later than 15 days following the date of that meeting, the commission shall submit its written comments and recommendations regarding the request for waiver to the Superintendent of Public Instruction.

(4) The Superintendent of Public Instruction shall review the comments and recommendations submitted by the Advisory Commission on Special Education prior to approving or rejecting the request for waiver.

(5) Any request for waiver, submitted in accordance with this section, that is not rejected within 60 days of its receipt by the State Department of Education, shall be deemed approved.

PORTABLE CLASSROOMS FOR INFANT – PRESCHOOL CHILDREN

(Education Code – Part 10)

(SB 1562, Chapter 277, Statutes of 1996)
(Formerly Education Code Section 17789.5)

17089.5. The board may lease portable classrooms to any school district or county superintendent of schools which serves infant or preschool individuals with exceptional needs, as defined in Section 56026, and which operates programs pursuant to Part 30 (commencing with Section 56000). These portable classrooms shall be adequately equipped to meet the educational needs of these students, including, but not limited to, sinks and restroom facilities.

- Portable Classrooms for Infant and Preschool Programs

COMMISSION ON SPECIAL EDUCATION

(Education Code – Part 20)

(As Amended by SB 1686, Chapter 691, Statutes of 1998)

CHAPTER 4. STATE EDUCATIONAL COMMISSIONS AND COMMITTEES

ARTICLE 6. ADVISORY COMMISSION ON SPECIAL EDUCATION

33590. (a) There is in the state government the Advisory Commission on Special Education consisting of the following persons:

- Commission Membership; Composition; Terms

(1) A Member of the Assembly appointed by the Speaker of the Assembly.

(2) A Member of the Senate appointed by the Senate Committee on Rules.

(3) Three public members appointed by the Speaker of the Assembly, two of whom shall be individuals with a disability or parents of pupils in either a public or private school who have received or are currently receiving special education services due to a disabling condition.

(4) Three public members appointed by the Senate Committee on Rules, two of whom shall be individuals with a disability or parents of pupils in either a public or private school who have received or are currently receiving special education services due to a disabling condition.

(5) Four public members appointed by the Governor, two of whom shall be parents of pupils in either a public or private school who have received or are currently receiving special education services due to a disabling condition.

(6) Five public members appointed by the State Board of Education, upon the recommendation of the Superintendent of Public Instruction or the members of the State Board of Education, three of whom shall be parents of pupils in either a public or private school who have received or are currently receiving special education services due to a disabling condition.

(b) (1) The commission membership shall be selected to ensure that it is a representative group of the state population and shall be composed of individuals involved in, or

- Representative Group

concerned with, the education of children with disabilities, including parents of children with disabilities; individuals with disabilities; teachers; representatives of higher education that prepare special education and related services personnel; state and local education officials; administrators of programs for children with disabilities; representatives of other state agencies involved in the financing or delivery of related services to children with disabilities; representatives of private school and public charter schools; at least one representative of a vocational community or business organization concerned with the provision of transition services to children with disabilities; and representatives from the juvenile and adult corrections agencies.

(2) The individuals shall be knowledgeable about the wide variety of disabling conditions that require special programs in order to achieve the goal of providing an appropriate education to all eligible pupils.

(3) A majority of the members of the commission shall be individuals with disabilities or parents of children with disabilities.

(c) The commission shall select one of its members to be chairperson of the commission. In addition to other duties, the chairperson shall be responsible for notifying the appointing bodies when a vacancy occurs on the commission, including the type of representative listed in subdivision (b) who is required to be appointed to fill the vacancy.

- Commission Chairperson

(d) The term of each public member shall be for four years.

- Four-Year Term

(e) In no event shall any public member serve more than two terms.

- Term Limits

33591. The Member of the Legislature appointed to the commission pursuant to Section 33590 shall have the powers and duties of a joint legislative committee on the subject of special education and shall meet with, and participate in, the work of the commission to the extent that such participation is not incompatible with their positions as Members of the Legislature.

- Members of the Legislature

The Members of the Legislature appointed to the commission shall serve at the pleasure of the appointing power.

33592. The members of the commission shall serve without compensation, except they shall receive their actual and necessary expenses incurred in the performance of their duties and responsibilities, including traveling expenses.

- Commission Member Expenses

Reimbursement of other expenses, which are determined to be necessary for the commission to function, but do not exceed the commission's budget, may be approved by the commission and the executive secretary to the commission.

33593. The Superintendent of Public Instruction or the superintendent's designee shall serve as executive secretary to the commission.

- Executive Secretary

33595. (a) The commission shall study and provide assistance and advice to the State Board of Education, the Superintendent of Public Instruction, the Legislature, and the Governor in new or continuing areas of research, program development, and evaluation in special education. The commission shall also do the following:

- Study, Assist, and Advise

(1) Comment publicly on any rules or regulations proposed by the state regarding the education of individuals with exceptional needs, as defined in Section 56026.

- Comment Publicly on Proposed Rules and Regulations

(2) Advise the Superintendent of Public Instruction in developing evaluations and reporting on data to the Secretary of Education in the United States Department of Education under Section 1418 of Title 20 of the United States Code.

- Advise Superintendent in Developing Evaluations and Reporting on Data

(3) Advise the Superintendent of Public Instruction in developing corrective action plans to address findings identified in federal monitoring reports under the Individuals with Disabilities Education Act (20 U.S.C. 1400 et seq.)

- Advise Superintendent in Developing Corrective Action Plans Relating to Federal Monitoring

(4) Advise the Superintendent of Public Instruction and the State Board of Education in developing and implementing policies relating to the coordination of services for individuals with exceptional needs.

- Advise Superintendent and Board in Developing and Implementing Policies Regarding Services

(b) The commission shall report to the State Board of Education, the Superintendent of Public Instruction, the Legislature, and the Governor not less than once a year on the following with respect to special education:

- Reporting Responsibilities

(1) Activities enumerated in Section 56100 that are necessary to be undertaken regarding special education for individuals with exceptional needs.

(2) The priorities and procedures utilized in the distribution of federal and state funds.

(3) The unmet educational needs of individuals with exceptional needs within the state.

(4) Recommendations relating to providing better education services to individuals with exceptional needs, including, but not limited to, the development, review, and revision, of the definition of "appropriate" as that term is used in the phrase "free and appropriate public education" for the purposes of the federal Individuals with Disabilities

Education Act (20 U.S.C. Sec. 1400 et seq.).

(c) Commission recommendations or requests shall be transmitted by letter from the commission chairperson to the president of the State Board of Education. Each communication shall be placed on the agenda of the next forthcoming state board meeting in accordance with the announced annual state board agenda cutoff dates. Following the state board meeting, the commission shall be notified by the state board as to what action has been taken on each request. Commission requests shall also be transmitted by letter from the commission chairperson to the Superintendent of Public Instruction, the Governor, and to appropriate Members of the Legislature.

- Recommendations and Requests

33596. As used in this article, "commission" means the Advisory Commission on Special Education. The commission shall also serve as the State Advisory Panel required by paragraph (21) of subdivision (a) of Section 1412 of Title 20 of the United States Code.

- Definition of Commission

- Commission Serves as State and Federal Advisory Panel

TRANSPORTATION FEES

(Education Code – Part 23.5)

(Added by Chapter 646, Statutes of 1999)
(Formerly Education Code Section 38028)

39807.5. (a) When the governing board of any school district provides for the transportation of pupils to and from schools in accordance with Section 39800, or between the regular full-time occupational training classes attended by them as provided by a regional occupation center or program, the governing board of the district may require the parents and guardians of all or some of the pupils transported, to pay a portion of the cost of this transportation in an amount determined by the governing board.

- Payment of Transportation Costs

(b) The amount determined by the board shall be no greater than the statewide average nonsubsidized cost of providing this transportation to a pupil on publicly owned or operated transit system as determined by the Superintendent of Public Instruction, in cooperation with the Department of Transportation.

(c) For the purposes of this section, "nonsubsidized cost" means actual operating costs less federal subventions.

(d) The governing board shall exempt from these charges

pupils of parents and guardians who are indigent as set forth in rules and regulations adopted by the board.

(e) A charge under this section may not be made for the transportation of handicapped children.

- No Charge for Disabled Children

(f) Nothing in this section shall be construed to sanction, perpetuate, or promote the racial or ethnic segregation of pupils in the schools.

TRANSPORTATION ALLOWANCES

(Education Code – Part 24)

(As Amended by SB 86, Chapter 536, Statutes of 1998 and SB 1640, Chapter 202, Statutes of 1998)

Article 10. Allowances for Transportation

41850. (a) Apportionments made pursuant to this article shall only be made for home-to-school transportation and special education transportation, as defined in this section.

- Apportionments

(b) As used in this article, "home-to-school transportation" includes all of the following:

- Definition of Home-to-School Transportation

(1) The transportation of pupils between their homes and the regular full-time day school they attend, as provided by a school district or county superintendent of schools.

(2) The payment of moneys by a school district or county superintendent of schools to parents or guardians of pupils made in lieu of providing for the transportation of pupils between their homes and the regular full-time day schools they attend.

(3) Providing board and lodging to pupils by a school district or county superintendent of schools made in lieu of providing for the transportation of pupils between their homes and the regular full-time day schools they attend.

(4) The transportation of pupils between the regular full-time day schools they would attend and the regular full-time occupational training classes they attend, as provided by a regional occupational center or program.

(5) The transportation of individuals with exceptional needs as specified in their individualized education programs, who do not receive special education transportation as defined in subdivision (d).

- Individuals with Exceptional Needs

(6) The payment of moneys by a school district or county superintendent of schools for the replacement or acquisition of schoolbuses.

(c) For purposes of this article, the computation of the allowances provided to a regional occupational center or program shall be subject to all of the following:

- ROC/P Computation

(1) A regional occupational center or program shall receive no allowance for 50 percent of the total transportation costs.

(2) A regional occupational center or program shall be eligible for a transportation allowance only if the total transportation costs exceed 10 percent of the total operational budget of the regional occupational center or program.

(3) A regional occupational center or program eligible for a transportation allowance pursuant to paragraph (2) shall receive an amount equal to one-third of the transportation costs subject to reimbursement.

(d) As used in this article, "special education transportation" means either of the following:

- Definition of Special Education Transportation

(1) The transportation of severely disabled special day class pupils, and orthopedically impaired pupils who require a vehicle with a wheelchair lift, who received transportation in the prior fiscal year, as specified in their individualized education program.

(2) A vehicle that was used to transport special education pupils.

41851. (a) For the 1992-93 fiscal year, from Section A of the State School Fund, the Superintendent of Public Instruction shall apportion to each school district or county superintendent of schools, as appropriate, an amount computed pursuant to this section. School districts and county superintendents of schools that provide transportation services by means of a joint powers agreement, a cooperative pupil transportation program, or a consortium shall receive transportation allowances pursuant to this section.

- Apportionment Computation for Regular Education Transportation

(b) For the 1992-93 fiscal year, each school district or county office of education shall receive a home-to-school transportation apportionment equal to the transportation allowance received in the prior fiscal year reduced by the amount of the special education transportation allowance identified pursuant to Section 41851.5.

(c) For the 1993-94 fiscal year and each fiscal year thereafter, each school district or county office of education shall receive the same home-to-school transportation allowance received in the prior fiscal year, but in no event shall that home-to-school transportation allowance exceed the prior year's approved home-to-school transportation costs, increased by the amount provided in the Budget Act.

(d) For the 1993-94 and 1994-95 fiscal years, and each fiscal year thereafter, each county unified school district for which the county board of education serves as the governing board that meets all of the following criteria shall receive an additional apportionment of three hundred fifty thousand dollars ($350,000):

(1) Over 50 percent of the pupils enrolled in the school district require home-to-school transportation services.

(2) Total enrollment of the school district is less than 3,500.

(3) Total miles driven each fiscal year for home-to-school transportation exceeds 500,000.

(e) If, in any fiscal year, a county unified school district operates one or more necessary small schools pursuant to Article 4 (commencing with Section 42280) of Chapter 7 that the district did not operate in the 1994-95 fiscal year, that district shall not be eligible to receive an apportionment pursuant to subdivision (d) in that fiscal year or in any subsequent fiscal year.

(f) If a later enacted statute amends subdivision (b) of Section 42280 or amends or adds any other provision of law authorizing a county unified school district that has 3,001 or more units of average daily attendance to be designated as a small school district for the purposes of Article 4 (commencing with Section 42280) of Chapter 7, subdivision (d) shall become inoperative on the date that the later enacted statute becomes operative.

(g) Each county unified school district that receives an additional apportionment pursuant to subdivision (d) shall report, by September 1 of each year, commencing with September 1, 1995, on the amount of revenues received and the funds expended for the home-to-school transportation program in the prior fiscal year. The report shall be submitted to the fiscal committees and education policy committees of the Legislature and to the Legislative Analyst.

41851.1. (a) For the 1989-90 fiscal year, from Section A of the State School Fund, the Superintendent of Public Instruction shall apportion to each school district or county superintendent of schools, as appropriate, an amount computed pursuant to this section. School districts and county superintendents of schools that provide transportation services by means of a joint powers agreement, a cooperative pupil transportation program, or a consortium shall receive transportation allowances pursuant to this section.

- Fiscal Year 1989-90
Transportation Apportionment
Joint Powers, Cooperative
Program, Consortium

(b) For the 1989-90 fiscal year, each school district, joint powers agency, cooperative pupil transportation program, or consortium shall receive a transportation apportionment equal to the greater of the following:

(1) Sixty-five percent of the prior year's approved transportation costs.

(2) The prior year's transportation allowance.

(c) For the 1989-90 fiscal year, each county office of education shall receive a transportation apportionment equal to the greater of the following:

(1) Eighty percent of the prior year's approved transportation costs.

(2) The prior year's transportation allowance.

(d) In the event that funds appropriated for the purposes of this section are not sufficient to fully fund the formula established by that section, the amounts apportioned shall be reduced on a proportionate basis.

41851.2. No later than December 31, 1992, the Superintendent of Public Instruction shall develop guidelines for use by individualized education program teams during their annual reviews pursuant to Section 56343. The guidelines shall clarify when special education transportation services, as defined in Section 41850, are required. The guidelines shall be developed in accordance with Section 33308.5 and shall be exemplary in nature.

- Guidelines for Use by IEP Teams

41851.5. (a) For the 1992-93 fiscal year and each fiscal year thereafter, from Section A of the State School Fund, the Superintendent of Public Instruction shall apportion to each school district or county superintendent of schools, as appropriate, an amount computed pursuant to this section. School districts and county superintendents of schools that provide special education transportation services by means of a joint powers agreement, a cooperative pupil transportation program, or a consortium shall receive special education transportation allowances pursuant to this section.

- Special Education Transportation Allowance and Computation

(b) For the 1992-93 fiscal year, each school district or county office of education shall receive a special education transportation allowance equal to the lesser of the following:

(1) The prior year's approved special education transportation costs identified pursuant to Section 41850.

(2) That portion of the prior year's transportation allowance that the school district or county superintendent of schools designates as a special education transportation allowance.

- 1992-93 Fiscal Year School District or County Office of Education Special Education Transportation Allowance

(c) For the 1993-94 fiscal year and each fiscal year thereafter, each school district or county office of education shall receive a special education transportation allowance received in the prior fiscal year, but in no event shall that special education transportation allowance exceed the prior year's approved special education transportation costs, increased by the amount provided in the annual Budget Act.

41851.7. For the purpose of receiving an allowance pursuant to this section, a school district, county superintendent, or joint powers agency which transfers any part of its pupil transportation service to another entity shall report to the Superintendent of Public Instruction the proportion of the costs in the fiscal year prior to the transfer that are attributable to the part of the service transferred. In determining the allowance for the fiscal years subsequent to the transfer, the Superintendent of Public Instruction, prior to the application of any cost-of-living adjustment, shall reduce the allowance of the entity transferring the service in proportion to the costs reported, and, if appropriate, increase or establish the allowance of the entity assuming the transferred service by that amount.

41851.12. For purposes of this article:

(a) "Approved costs of home-to-school transportation" means the approved home-to-school transportation expense determined pursuant to the Annual Report of Pupil Transportation as utilized by the State Department of Education.

(b) "Approved costs of special education transportation" means the approved special education transportation expense determined pursuant to the Annual Report of Pupil Transportation as utilized by the State Department of Education.

41852. (a) Any school district or county superintendent of schools that receives a transportation apportionment in the 1984-85 fiscal year, or any fiscal year thereafter, shall establish a restricted pupil transportation account within its general fund. The district or county superintendent shall deposit in the restricted pupil transportation account all transportation apportionments received pursuant to this article in any fiscal year and any other funds at the option of the district or county superintendent. Any funds remaining in the restricted home-to-school transportation account at the end of the fiscal year may remain in the restricted pupil transportation account for expenditure in subsequent fiscal years or may be transferred to the pupil transportation equipment fund.

(b) Any school district or county superintendent of schools may establish a pupil transportation equipment fund. The fund shall receive all state and local funds designated for acquisition, rehabilitation, or replacement of pupil transportation equipment. Funds deposited in the pupil transportation equipment fund shall be used exclusively for acquisition, rehabilitation and replacement of pupil transportation equipment, except as provided in Section 41853.

41853. If a school district or county superintendent of schools decides to discontinue its transportation services, any unencumbered funds remaining in the restricted home-to-school transportation account after transportation services are discontinued shall be transferred to the general fund of the district or county superintendent.

In the fiscal year in which the funds are transferred, the Superintendent of Public Instruction shall reduce the state apportionment pursuant to Section 2558 or 42238 to the district or county superintendent by the amount of the funds transferred from the restricted home-to-school transportation account to the general fund of the district or county superintendent, exclusive of reimbursements for prior year expenditures to Section 41851.5.

41854. This article shall become operative July 1, 1984.

41855. (a) For the 1996-97 fiscal year, the Superintendent of Public Instruction shall provide a home-to-school transportation allowance of three million twelve thousand dollars ($3,012,000) to school districts and county superintendents of schools that provide transportation services by means of a joint powers authority in lieu of the amount that would otherwise have been provided pursuant to the provisions of this article and Article 10.5 (commencing with Section 41860), if the joint powers authority meets the following conditions as of June 30, 1996:

(1) The joint powers authority provides pupils of member school districts with home-to-school transportation on school buses that are operated by the joint powers authority.

(2) The joint powers authority provides school transportation services to at least six other school districts in the area who are not members of the joint powers authority.

(3) The joint powers authority provides maintenance services for vehicles owned and operated by the member school districts, other school districts in the area, fire districts, and vehicles owned by cities or counties.

- Equipment Fund

- Discontinuing Services

- Operative Date

- Joint Powers Authority

(4) The cost per mile of home-to-school transportation services provided by the joint powers authority to member districts for the 1994-95 school year did not exceed the statewide average cost per mile for home-to-school transportation for all school districts in the state for the 1994-95 school year.

(b) For the 1997-98 fiscal year and each fiscal year thereafter, the home-to-school transportation allowance shall revert to 1995-96 level.

41856. For purposes of this article and Article 10.5 (commencing with Section 41860), the home-to-school transportation allowance received by the Oakland Unified School District in the 1996-97 fiscal year and each fiscal year thereafter shall be computed as if the home-to-school transportation aid received by the school district in the 1995-96 fiscal year was two million five hundred thousand dollars ($2,500,000). The amounts allocated to the Oakland Unified School District pursuant to this section shall be contingent upon approval of the district's home-to-school transportation costs and shall not exceed those costs.

- Oakland Unified School District

41857. A charter school is eligible for funding pursuant to, and shall comply with all requirements of, this article. For purposes of this article, a reference to a school district shall be deemed to be also a reference to a charter school.

- Charter Schools

Article 10.5. Supplemental Allowances for Transportation

41860. (a) Sections 41850, 41851.12, 41852, and 41853 shall apply to this article.

- Application Sections

(b) As used in this article, "average daily attendance" means the average daily attendance used to compute a school district's second principal apportionment.

- Definition of Average Daily Attendance

41861. For any fiscal year in which funds are specifically appropriated for home-to-school transportation apportionments pursuant to this article, the Superintendent of Public Instruction shall apportion to each school district that is eligible under this article, in addition to any apportionments pursuant to Sections 41851 and 41851.11, the amount calculated pursuant to Section 41863.

- Apportionments

41862. School districts that meet all of the following criteria are eligible to receive an apportionment pursuant to this article:

- Criteria for School Districts

(a) The number of pupils who received home-to-school transportation services in the prior fiscal year was equivalent to at least 33 percent of the total number of units of average daily attendance in the prior fiscal year.

(b) The total cost per mile for the prior fiscal year for home-to-school transportation does not exceed the statewide average cost per mile, or if the total cost per mile for the prior fiscal year for home-to-school transportation exceeds the statewide average cost per mile, the school district demonstrates to the satisfaction of the Superintendent of Public Instruction that the increased cost per mile is due either weather-related or terrain-related conditions. The Superintendent of Public Instruction should determine that the increased cost per mile is due to weather-related or terrain-related conditionsif those conditions meet any of the following criteria:

(1) Snow and ice create roadway and safety problems.

(2) Fifty percent or more of publicly maintained roads in the school district are considered to be curves.

(3) There are changes in elevation of 2,000 feet or more on publicly maintained roads in the school district.

(c) In the prior fiscal year, the amount of the school district's approved cost of home-to-school transportation per unit of average daily attendance exceeded one hundred thirty dollars ($130).

41863. (a) The Superintendent of Public Instruction shall determine for each school district meeting the standards of Section 41862 the apportionment for that school district's unreimbursed costs of home-to-school transportation in the prior fiscal year as follows:

- Formula for Supplemental Allowances

(1) Add the following amounts:

(A) The home-to-school transportation allowance for the school district received pursuant to Sections 41851 and 41851.11 for the prior fiscal year.

(B) The amount of funding received for the costs of transportation associated with court-ordered or voluntary desegregation programs.

(2) Subtract from the sum computed pursuant to paragraph (1) all supplemental grant funding received in the prior fiscal year by the school district for home-to-school transportation or court-ordered or voluntary desegregation.

(3) Subtract from the school district's prior year's approved costs of home-to-school transportation the amount computed pursuant to paragraph (2).

(b) The Superintendent of Public Instruction shall calculate data for school districts within a joint powers authority as separate entities, but apportionments shall be the same as under existing law, provided that the joint powers authority submits in a timely fashion the data required by the superintendent to make the calculation.

(c) In the event the funds appropriated for the purposes of this article are not sufficient to fully fund the formula established by this section, the amounts apportioned shall be reduced on a proportionate basis.

REVENUE LIMITS FOR PUPILS IN SPECIAL CLASSES AND CENTERS

(Education Code – Part 24)

(As Amended by SB 1468, Chapter 846, Statutes of 1998)

42238.9. The amount per unit of average daily attendance subtracted pursuant to Section 56712 for revenue limits for pupils in special classes and centers shall be the district's total revenue limit for the current fiscal year computed pursuant to Section 42238, including funds received pursuant to Article 4 (commencing with Section 42280), but excluding the total amount of funds received pursuant to Sections 46200 to 46206, inclusive, and Section 45023.4, as that section read on July 1, 1986, divided by the district's current year average daily attendance pursuant to Section 42238.5. The amount per unit of average daily attendance that is excluded in this calculation for each school district shall be increased for the 1998-99 fiscal year by the quotient for that district of the amount determined pursuant to subparagraph (B) of paragraph (3) of subdivision (a) of Section 42238.8 divided by the amount determined pursuant to subparagraph (C) of paragraph (3) of subdivision (a) Section 42238.8.

- Revenue Limits

42238.95. (a) The amount per unit of average daily attendance for pupils in special classes and centers that shall be apportioned to each county office of education shall be equal to the amount determined for the district of residence pursuant to Section 42238.9, increased by the quotient equal to the amount determined pursuant to paragraph (1) divided by the amount determined pursuant to paragraph (2). This subdivision only applies to average daily attendance served by employees of the county office of education.

- Amount Per Unit of ADA for Pupils in Special Classes/Centers

(1) Determine the second principal apportionment average daily attendance for special education for the county office of education for the 1996-97 fiscal year, including attendance for excused absences, divided by the corresponding average daily attendance excluding attendance for excused absences pursuant to subdivision (b) of Section 46010 as it read on July 1, 1996, reported pursuant to Section 41601 for the 1996-97

fiscal year.

(2) Determine the second principal apportionment average daily attendance for the 1996-97 fiscal year, including attendance for excused absences, for all of the school districts within the county, excluding average daily attendance for county office special education and county community school programs and nonpublic nonsectarian schools, divided by the corresponding average daily attendance, excluding attendance for excused absences determined pursuant to subdivision (b) of Section 46010 as it read on July 1, 1996, and reported pursuant to Section 41601 for the 1996-97 fiscal year.

(b) A county office of education shall provide the data required to perform the calculation specified in paragraph (1) of subdivision (a) to the Superintendent of Public Instruction in order to be eligible for the adjustment pursuant to subdivision (a).

REAPPROPRIATION OF FEDERAL FUNDS

(Education Code – Part 24)

(AB 369 - Chapter 1296, Statutes of 1993)

42242. The Superintendent of Public Instruction shall determine at the time of each apportionment the proposed receipts and expenditures of funds under the provisions of the Individuals with Disabilities Education Act (20 U.S.C. Sec. 1400 et seq.). In the event that the proposed distribution of funds results in funds not being expended, those funds are hereby reappropriated for reallocation for local entitlements for special education.

- Unexpended Federal Funds

This section shall become operative July 1, 1984.

RECOGNIZING LEARNING DISABILITIES

(Education Code – Part 25)

(AB 3040 - Chapter 1501, Statutes of 1990)

44227.7. The Legislature encourages institutions of higher education to provide, in teacher training programs, increased emphasis on the recognition of, and teaching strategies for, specific learning disabilities, including dyslexia and related disorders. Experts in the field of these disabilities should be utilized for that purpose.

- Teacher Training Programs

TEACHER QUALIFICATIONS – PUPILS WITH LOW-INCIDENCE DISABILITIES

(Education Code – Part 25)

(AB 3235 - Chapter 1288, Statutes of 1994)

44265.5. (a) Pupils who are visually impaired shall be taught by teachers whose professional preparation and credential authorization are specific to that impairment.

    - Visually Impaired

    (b) Pupils who are deaf or hard of hearing shall be taught by teachers whose professional preparation and credential authorization are specific to that impairment.

    - Deaf or Hard of Hearing

    (c) Pupils who are orthopedically impaired shall be taught by teachers whose professional preparation and credential authorization are specific to that impairment.

    - Orthopedically Impaired

CERTIFICATED EMPLOYEE EMPLOYMENT RIGHTS

(Education Code – Part 25)

(AB 602 - Chapter 854, Statutes of 1997)

44903.7. When a local plan for the education of individuals with exceptional needs is developed pursuant to Chapter 2.5 (commencing with Section 56195) of Part 30, the following provisions shall apply:

    - When Local Plan Is Developed

    (a) Whenever any certificated employee, who is performing service for one employer, is terminated, reassigned, or transferred, or becomes an employee of another employer because of the reorganization of special education programs pursuant to Chapter 797 of the Statutes of 1980, the employee shall be entitled to the following:

    - Employee Entitlements

    (1) The employee shall retain the seniority date of his or her employment with the district or county office from which he or she was terminated, reassigned, or transferred, in accordance with Section 44847. In the case of termination, permanent employees shall retain the rights specified in Section 44956 or, in the case of probationary employees,

    - Employees Retain Seniority Rights

Section 44957 and 44958, with the district or county office initiating the termination pursuant to Section 44955.

(2) The reassignment, transfer, or new employment caused by the reorganization of special education programs pursuant to Chapter 797 of the Statutes of 1980, shall not affect the seniority or classification of certificated employees already attained in any school district that undergoes the reorganization. These employees shall have the same status with respect to their seniority or classification, with the new employer, including time served as probationary employees. The total number of years served as a certificated employee with the former district or county office shall be credited, year for year, for placement on the salary schedule of the new district or county office.

- Seniority of Classification Not Affected

(b) All certificated employees providing service to individuals with exceptional needs shall be employed by a county office of education or an individual school district. Special education local plan areas or responsible local agencies resulting from local plans for the education of individuals with exceptional needs formulated in accordance with Part 30 (commencing with Section 56000) shall not be considered employers of certificated personnel for purposes of this section.

- Employers

(c) Subsequent to the reassignment or transfer of any certificated employee as a result of the reorganization of special education programs, pursuant to Chapter 797 of the Statutes of 1980, that employee shall have priority, except as provided in subdivision (d), in being informed of and in filling certificated positions in special education in the areas in which the employee is certificated within the district or county office by which the certificated employee is then currently employed. This priority shall expire 24 months after the date of reassignment or transfer, and may be waived by the employee during that time period.

- Priority on Being Informed of and in Filling Positions

(d) A certificated employee who has served as a special education teacher in a district or county office and has been terminated from his or her employment by that district or county office pursuant to Section 44955, shall have first priority in being informed of and in filling vacant certificated positions in special education, for which the employee is certificated and was employed, in any other county office or school district that provides the same type of special education programs and services for the pupils previously served by the terminated employee. For a period of 39 months for permanent employees and 24 months for

- Other County Office or School District

probationary employees from the date of termination, the employee shall have the first priority right to reappointment as provided in this section, if the employee has not attained the age of 65 years before reappointment.

LONGER DAY AND YEAR FOR COUNTY-OPERATED
SPECIAL EDUCATION PROGRAMS

(Education Code – Part 26)

(As Amended by Senate Bill 178, Chapter 573, Statutes of 2001)

46200.5. (a) In the 1985-86 fiscal year, for each county office of education that certifies to the Superintendent of Public Instruction that it offers 180 days or more of instruction per school year of special day classes pursuant to Section 56364 or Section 56364.2, as applicable, the Superintendent of Public Instruction shall determine an amount equal to seventy dollars ($70) per unit of current year second principal apportionment average daily attendance for special day classes. This computation shall be included in computations made by the superintendent pursuant to Chapter 7.2 (commencing with Section 56836) of Part 30.

- 180 Days or More (1)

(b) For any county office of education that received an apportionment pursuant to subdivision (a) and that offered less than 180 days of instruction in the 1986-87 fiscal year, to the 2000-01 fiscal year, inclusive, and that does not provide the minimum number of instructional minutes specified in subdivision (a) of Section 46201 for that fiscal year, the Superintendent of Public Instruction shall reduce the special education apportionment per unit of average daily attendance for that fiscal year by an amount attributable to the increase received pursuant to subdivision (a), as adjusted in fiscal years subsequent to the 1985-86 fiscal year.

- Less Than 180 Days

(c) For any county office of education that receives an apportionment pursuant to subdivision (a) and that offers less than 180 days of instruction in the 2001-02 fiscal year, or any fiscal year thereafter, the Superintendent of Public Instruction shall withhold from the county office of education's revenue limit apportionment for the average daily attendance of each affected grade level the sum of 0.0056 multiplied by that apportionment, for each day less than 180 that the county office of education offered.

- Withholding Factor

46201.5. (a) In each of the 1985-86 and 1986-87 fiscal years, for each county office of education that certifies to the Superintendent of Public Instruction that, for special day classes pursuant to Section 56364 or Section 56364.2, as applicable, it offers at least the amount of instructional time specified in this subdivision, the Superintendent of Public Instruction shall determine an amount equal to eighty dollars ($80) in the 1985-86 fiscal year and forty dollars ($40) in the 1986-87 fiscal year per unit of current year second principal apportionment average daily attendance for special day classes in kindergarten and grades 1 to 8, inclusive, and one hundred sixty dollars ($160) in the 1985-86 fiscal year and eighty dollars ($80) in the 1986-87 fiscal year per unit of current year second principal apportionment average daily attendance for special day classes in grades 9 to 12, inclusive.

- Computation for Special Classes (2)

This computation shall be included in computations made by the superintendent pursuant to Article 2 (commencing with Section 56836.06) of Chapter 7.2 of Part 30.

(1) In the 1985-86 fiscal year:

(A) 34,500 minutes in kindergarten.

(B) 47,016 minutes in grades 1 to 3, inclusive.

(C) 50,000 minutes in grades 4 to 8, inclusive.

(D) 57,200 minutes in grades 9 to 12, inclusive.

(2) In the 1986-87 fiscal year:

(A) 36,000 minutes in kindergarten.

(B) 50,400 minutes in grades 1 to 3, inclusive.

(C) 54,000 minutes in grades 4 to 8, inclusive.

(D) 64,800 minutes in grades 9 to 12, inclusive.

(b) Each county office of education that receives an apportionment pursuant to subdivision (a) in a fiscal year shall, in the subsequent fiscal year, add the amount received per pupil to the county office's base special education apportionment.

- Add to Base Apportionment

(c) For each county office of education that receives an apportionment pursuant to subdivision (a) in the 1985-86 fiscal year, and that reduces the amount of instructional time offered below the minimum amounts specified in paragraph (1) of subdivision (a) in the 1986-87 fiscal year, or any fiscal year thereafter, up to and including the 2000-01 fiscal year, the Superintendent of Public Instruction shall reduce the special education apportionment for the fiscal year in which the reduction occurs by an amount attributable to the increase in the 1986-87 fiscal year special education apportionment pursuant to subdivision (b), as adjusted in the 1986-87 fiscal

- Reduction of Apportionment When Instructional Time Is Reduced

year and fiscal years thereafter.

(d) For each county office of education that receives an apportionment pursuant to subdivision (a) in the 1986-87 fiscal year and that reduces the amount of instructional time offered below the minimum amounts specified in paragraph (2) of subdivision (a) in the 1987-88 fiscal year, or any fiscal year thereafter, up to and including the 2000-01 fiscal year, the superintendent shall reduce the special education apportionment for the fiscal year in which the reduction occurs by an amount attributable to the increase in the 1987-88 fiscal year special education apportionment pursuant to subdivision (b), as adjusted in the 1987-88 fiscal year and fiscal years thereafter.

(e) For each county office of education that receives an apportionment pursuant to subdivision (a) in the 1986-87 fiscal year and that reduces the amount of instructional time offered below the minimum amounts specified in paragraph (2) of subdivision (a) in the 2001 02 fiscal year, or any fiscal year thereafter, the Superintendent of Public Instruction shall withhold from the special education apportionment for the average daily attendance of each affected grade level, the sum of that apportionment multiplied by the percentage of the minimum offered minutes at that grade level that the county office of education failed to offer.

DAY OF ATTENDANCE

(Education Code – Part 26)

46307. Attendance of individuals with exceptional needs, identified pursuant to Chapter 4 (commencing with Section 56300) of Part 30, enrolled in a special day class or given instruction individually or in a home, hospital, or licensed children's institution who attend school for either the same number of minutes that constitutes a minimum schoolday pursuant to Chapter 2 (commencing with Section 46100), or for the number of minutes of attendance specified in that pupil's individualized education program developed pursuant to Article 3 (commencing with Section 56340) of Chapter 4 of Part 30, whichever is less, shall constitute a day of attendance.

- Average Daily Attendance for Individuals with Exceptional Needs

46307.1. The computation of average daily attendance pursuant to this chapter shall not include the attendance of minors between the ages of 18 months and three years, inclusive, enrolled in programs operated by a county superintendent of schools who are physically handicapped,

- Exclusion of Minors Between the Ages of 18 Months and Three Years

deaf or hard of hearing, or have speech disorders or speech defects.

COUNTY SCHOOL SERVICE FUND

(Education Code – Part 26)

46360. The average daily attendance of individuals with exceptional needs given instruction by a county superintendent of schools and whose attendance is credited to the county school service fund, shall be computed by dividing the total days of attendance of such pupils during the fiscal year by 175.

- Average Daily Attendance Credited to County School Service Fund

CHARTER SCHOOLS

(Education Code – Part 26.8)

(AB 1115 - Chapter 78, Statutes of 1999)

Article 4. Special Education Funding

47640. For the purposes of this article, "local educational agency" means a school district as defined in Section 41302.5 or a charter school that is deemed a local educational agency pursuant to Section 47641. As used in this article, "local educational agency" also means a charter school that is responsible for complying with all provisions of the Individuals with Disabilities Education Act (20 U.S.C. Sec. 1400 et seq.) and implmenting regulations as they relate to local educational agencies.

- Definition of Local Educational Agency

47641. (a) A charter school that includes in its petition for establishment or renewal, or that otherwise provides, verifiable, written assurances that the charter school will participate as a local educational agency in a special education plan approved by the State Board of Education shall be deemed a local educational agency for the purposes of compliance with federal law (Individuals with Disabilities Education Act; 20 U.S.C. Sec. 1400 et seq.) and for eligibility for federal and state special education funds. A charter school that is deemed a local educational agency for the purposes of special education pursuant to this article shall be permitted to participate in an approved special education local plan that is consistent with subdivision (a), (b), or (c) of Section 56195.1.

- Deemed a Local Educational Agency for Purposes of Compliance and Funding

(b) A charter school that was granted a charter by a local educational agency that does not comply with subdivision (a) may not be deemed a local educational agency pursuant to this article, but shall be deemed a public school of the local educational agency that granted the charter.

(c) A charter school that has been granted a charter by the State Board of Education, and for which the board has delegated its supervisorial and oversight responsibilities pursuant to paragraph (1) of subdivision (k) of Section 47605, and does not comply with subdivision (a), shall be deemed a public school of the local educational agency to which the board has delegated its supervisorial and oversight responsibilities.

(d) A charter school that has been granted a charter by the State Board of Education, and for which the board has not delegated its supervisorial and oversight responsibilities pursuant to paragraph (1) of subdivision (k) of Section 47605, may not be deemed a local educational agnecy unless the charter school complies with subdivision (a).

47642. Notwithstanding Section 47651, all state and federal funding for special education apportioned on behalf of pupils enrolled in a charter school shall be included in the allocation plan adopted pursuant to subdivision (i) of Section 56195.7 or Section 56836.05, or both, by the special education local plan area that includes the charter school.

- Funding Shall Be Included in Allocation Plan

47643. If the approval of a petition for a charter school requires a change to the allocation plan developed pursuant to subdivision (i) of Section 56195.7 or Section 56836.05, the change shall be adopted pursuant to the policymaking process of the special education local plan area.

- Change in Allocation Plan

47644. For each charter school deemed a local educational agency for the purposes of special education, an amount equal to the amount computed pursuant to Section 56836.08 for the special education local plan area in which the charter school is included shall be apportioned by the Superintendent of Public Instruction pursuant to the local allocation plan developed pursuant to subdivision (i) of Section 56195.7 or Section 56836.05, or both. If the charter school is a participant in a local plan that only includes other charter schools pursuant to subdivision (f) of Section 56195.1, the amount computed pursuant to Section 56836.11, as adjusted pursuant to the incidence multiplier set forth in Section 56836.155, shall be apportioned by the superintendent for

- Apportionment by Superintendent of Public Instruction

each unit of average daily attendance reported purusant to subdivision (a) of Section 56836.06.

47645. An agency reviewing a request by a charter school to participate as a local educational agency in a special education local plan area may not treat the charter school differently from the manner in which it treats a similar request made by a school district. In reviewing and approving a request by a charter school to participate as a local educational agency in a special educaiton local plan area, a local or state agency shall ensure all of the following:

- Reviewing a Request to Participate as a Local Educational Agency

(a) The special education local plan area complies with Section 56140.

(b) The charter school participates in state and federal funding for special education and the allocation plan developed pursuant to subdivision (i) of Section 56195.7 or Section 56836.05 in the same manner as other local educational agencies of the special education local plan area.

(c) The charter school participates in governance of the special educaiton local plan area and benefits from services provided throughout the special education local plan area, in the same manner as other local educational agencies of the special education local plan area.

47646. (a) A charter school that is deemed to be a public school of the local educational agency that granted the charter for purposes of special education shall participate in the state and fedeal funding for special education in the same manner as any other public school of that local educational agency. A child with disabilities attending the charter school shall receive special education instruction or designated instruciton and services, or both, in the same manner as a child with disabilities who attends another public school of that local educational agnecy. The agency that granted the charter shall ensure that all children with disabilities enrolled in the charter school receive special education and designated instruction and services in a manner that is consistent with their individualized education program and is in compliance with the Individuals with Disabilities Education Act (20 U.S.C. Sec. 1400 et seq.) and implementing regulations.

- Child with a Disability Shall Receive Instruction in Same Manner

(b) In administering the local operation of special education pursuant to the local plan established pursuant to Chapter 3 (commencing with Section 56200) of Part 30, in which the local educational agency that granted the charter participates, the local educational agency that granted the charter shall ensure that each charter school that is deemed a public school for purposes of special education receives an equitable share of special education funding and services consisting of either, or both, of the following:

(1) State and federal funding provided to support special education instruction or designated instruction and services, or both, provided or procured by the charter school that serve pupils enrolled in and attending the charter school.

(2) Any necessary special education services, including administrative and support services and itinerant services, that is provided by the local educational agency on behalf of pupils with disabilities enrolled in the charter school.

(c) In administering the local operation of special education pursuant to the local plan established pursuant to Chapter 3 (commencing with Section 56200) of Part 30, in which the local educational agency that granted the charter participates, the local educational agency that granted the charter shall ensure that each charter school that is deemed a public school for purposes of special education also contributes an equitable share of its charter school block grant funding to support districtwide special education instruction and services, including, but not limited to, special education instruction and services for pupils with disabilities enrolled in the charter school.

47647. A local educational agency reviewing a petition for the establishment or renewal of a charter school may not refuse to grant the petition solely because the charter might enroll pupils with disbilities who reside in a special education local plan area other than the special education local plan area that includes the local educational agency reviewing the petition.

- LEA Reviewing Petition May Not Refuse Granting Petition Based on Residence Factor

EDUCATIONAL PLACEMENT OF PUPILS RESIDING IN LICENSED CHILDREN'S INSTITUTIONS

(Education Code – Part 27)

(SB 933 - Chapter 311, Statutes of 1998)

48850. (a) Every county office of education shall make available to agencies that place children in licensed children's institutions information on educational options for children residing in license children's institutions within the jurisdiction of the county office of education for use by the placing agencies in assisting parents and foster children to choose educational placements.

- Information on Educational Options

(b) For purposes of individuals with exceptional needs residing in licensed children's institutions, making a copy of the annual service plan, prepared pursuant to subdivision (g) of Section 56205, available to those special education local plan areas that have revised their local plans pursuant to Section 56836.03 shall meet the requirements of subdivision (a).

- Annual Service Plan

48852. Every agency that places a chld in a licensed children's institution shall notify the local educational agency at the time a pupil is placed in a licensed children's institution. As part of that notification, the placing agency shall provide any available information on immediate past educational placements to facilitate prompt transfer of records and appropriate educational placement. Nothing in this section shall be construed to prohibit prompt educational placement prior to notification.

- Notification of Local Educational Agency

48854. A licensed children's institution or nonpublic, nonsectarian school, or agency may not require as a condition of placement that educational authority for a child, as defined in Section 48859 be designated to that institution, school, or agency.

- Designation of Educational Authority

48856. A local educational agency shall invite at least one noneducational agency representative that has placement responsibility for a pupil residing in a licensed children's institution to collaborate with the local educational agency in the monitoring of a placement in a nonpublic, nonsectarian school or agency.

- Collaborative Monitoring of Placement

48859. For purposes of this chapter, "educational authority" means an entity designated to represent the interests of a child for educational and related services.

- Definition of Educational Authority

SUSPENSION OR EXPULSION OF PUPILS

(Education Code – Part 27)

(As Amended AB 653, Chapter 484, and SB 166, Chapter 116, Statutes of 2001)

48900. A pupil may not be suspended from school or recommended for expulsion unless the superintendent or the principal of the school in which the pupil is enrolled determines that the pupil has committed an act as defined pursuant to one or more of subdivisions (a) to (q), inclusive:

(a) (1) Caused, attempted to cause, or threatened to cause physical injury to another person.

(2) Willfully used force or violence upon the person of another, except in self-defense.

(b) Possessed, sold, or otherwise furnished any firearm, knife, explosive, or other dangerous object, unless, in the case of possession of any object of this type, the pupil had obtained written permission to possess the item from a certificated school employee, which is concurred in by the principal or the designee of the principal.

(c) Unlawfully possessed, used, sold, or otherwise furnished, or been under the influence of, any controlled substance listed in Chapter 2 (commencing with Section 11053) of Division 10 of the Health and Safety Code, an alcoholic beverage, or an intoxicant of any kind.

(d) Unlawfully offered, arranged, or negotiated to sell any controlled substance listed in Chapter 2 (commencing with Section 11053) of Division 10 of the Health and Safety Code, an alcoholic beverage, or an intoxicant of any kind, and then either sold, delivered, or otherwise furnished to any person another liquid, substance, or material and represented the liquid, substance, or material as a controlled substance, alcoholic beverage, or intoxicant.

(e) Committed or attempted to commit robbery or extortion.

(f) Caused or attempted to cause damage to school property or private property.

(g) Stolen or attempted to steal school property or private property.

(h) Possessed or used tobacco, or any products containing tobacco or nicotine products, including, but not limited to, cigarettes, cigars, miniature cigars, clove cigarettes, smokeless tobacco, snuff, chew packets, and betel.

- Grounds for Suspension or Expulsion (3)

However, this section does not prohibit use or possession by a pupil of his or her own prescription products.

(i) Committed an obscene act or engaged in habitual profanity or vulgarity.

(j) Unlawfully possessed or unlawfully offered, arranged, or negotiated to sell any drug paraphernalia, as defined in Section 11014.5 of the Health and Safety Code.

(k) Disrupted school activities or otherwise willfully defied the valid authority of supervisors, teachers, administrators, school officials, or other school personnel engaged in the performance of their duties.

(l) Knowingly received stolen school property or private property.

(m) Possessed an imitation firearm. As used in this section, "imitation firearm" means a replica of a firearm that is so substantially similar in physical properties to an existing firearm as to lead a reasonable person to conclude that the replica is a firearm.

(n) Committed or attempted to commit a sexual assault as defined in Section 261, 266c, 286, 288, 288a, or 289 of the Penal Code or committed a sexual battery as defined in Section 243.4 of the Penal Code.

(o) Harassed, threatened, or intimidated a pupil who is a complaining witness or witness in a school disciplinary proceeding for the purpose of either preventing that pupil from being a witness or retaliating against that pupil for being a witness, or both.

(p) A pupil may not be suspended or expelled for any of the acts enumerated unless that act is related to school activity or school attendance occurring within a school under the jurisdiction of the superintendent or principal or occurring within any other school district. A pupil may be suspended or expelled for acts that are enumerated in this section and related to school activity or attendance that occur at any time, including, but not limited to, any of the following:

(1) While on school grounds.

(2) While going to or coming from school.

(3) During the lunch period whether on or off the campus.

(4) During, or while going to or coming from, a school sponsored activity.

(q) A pupil who aids or abets, as defined in Section 31 of the Penal Code, the infliction or attempted infliction of physical injury to another person may suffer suspension, but not expulsion, pursuant to the provisions of this section.

Except that a pupil who has been adjudged by a juvenile court to have committed, as an aider and abettor, a crime of physical violence in which the victim suffered great bodily injury or serious bodily injury shall be subject to discipline pursuant to subdivision (a).

(r) A superintendent or principal may use their discretion to provide alternatives to suspension or expulsion, including, but not limited to, counseling and an anger management program, for a pupil subject to discipline under this section.

(s) It is the intent of the Legislature that alternatives to suspensions or expulsion be imposed against any pupil who is truant, tardy, or otherwise absent from school activities.

48900.1. (a) The governing board of each school district shall adopt a policy authorizing teachers to provide that the parent or guardian of a pupil who has been suspended by a teacher pursuant to Section 48910 for reasons specified in subdivision (i) or (k) of Section 48900, attend a portion of a schoolday in his or her child's or ward's classroom. The policy shall take into account reasonable factors that may prevent compliance with a notice to attend. The attendance of the parent or guardian shall be limited to the class from which the pupil was suspended.

- Attendance of Suspended Child's Parent or Guardian for Portion of Day; Policy and Procedures

(b) The policy shall be adopted pursuant to the procedures set forth in Sections 35291 and 35291.5. Parents and guardians shall be notified of this policy prior to its implementation. A teacher shall apply any policy adopted pursuant to this section uniformly to all pupils within the classroom.

The adopted policy shall include the procedures that the district will follow to accomplish the following:

(1) Ensure that parents or guardians who attend school for the purposes of this section meet with the school administrator or his or her designee after completing the classroom visitation and before leaving the schoolsite.

(2) Contact parents or guardians who do not respond to the request to attend school pursuant to this section.

(c) If a teacher imposes the procedure pursuant to subdivision (a), the principal shall send a written notice to the parent or guardian stating that attendance by the parent or guardian is pursuant to law. This section shall apply only to a parent or guardian who is actually living with the pupil.

(d) A parent or guardian who has received a written notice pursuant to subdivision (c) shall attend class as specified in the written notice. The notice may specify that the parent's or guardian's attendance be on the day in which the pupil is scheduled to return to class, or within a reasonable period of time thereafter, as established by the policy of the board adopted pursuant to subdivision (a).

48900.2. In addition to the reasons specified in Section 48900, a pupil may be suspended from school or recommended for expulsion if the superintendent or the principal of the school in which the pupil is enrolled determines that the pupil has committed sexual harassment as defined in Section 212.5.

- Additional Grounds for Suspension and Expulsion; Sexual Harassment

For the purposes of this chapter, the conduct described in Section 212.5 must be considered by a reasonable person of the same gender as the victim to be sufficiently severe or pervasive to have a negative impact upon the individual's academic performance or to create an intimidating, hostile, or offensive educational environment. This section shall not apply to pupils enrolled in kindergarten and grades 1 to 3, inclusive.

48900.3. In addition to the reasons set forth in Sections 48900 and 48900.2, a pupil in any of grades 4 to 12, inclusive, may be suspended from school or recommended for expulsion if the superintendent or the principal of the school in which the pupil is enrolled determines that the pupil has caused, attempted to cause, threatened to cause, or participated in an act of, hate violence, as defined in subdivision (e) of Section 233.

- Hate Violence

48900.4. In addition to the grounds specified in Sections 48900 and 48900.2, a pupil enrolled in any of grades 4 to 12, inclusive, may be suspended from school or recommended for expulsion if the superintendent or the principal of the school in which the pupil is enrolled determines that the pupil has intentionally engaged in harassment, threats, or intimidation, directed against a pupil or group of pupils, that is sufficiently severe or pervasive to have the actual and reasonably expected effect of materially disrupting classwork, creating substantial disorder, and invading the rights of that pupil or group of pupils by creating an intimidating or hostile educational environment.

- Additional Grounds for Suspension or Expulsion; Harassment, Threats, or Intimidation

48900.5. Suspension shall be imposed only when other means of correction fail to bring about proper conduct. However, a pupil, including an individual with exceptional needs, as defined in Section 56026, may be suspended for any of the reasons enumerated in Section 48900 upon a first offense, if the principal or superintendent of schools determines that the pupil violated subdivision (a), (b), (c), (d), or (e) of Section 48900 or that the pupil's presence

- Suspension: Equal Treatment of Disabled and Nondisabled Pupils

causes a danger to persons or property or threatens to disrupt the instructional process.

48900.6. As part of or instead of disciplinary action prescribed by this article, the principal of a school, the principal's designee, the superintendent of schools, or the governing board may require a pupil to perform community service on school grounds or, with written permission of the parent or guardian of the pupil, off school grounds, during the pupil's nonschool hours. For the purposes of this section, "community service" may include, but is not limited to, work performed in the community or on school grounds in the areas of outdoor beautification, community or campus betterment, and teacher, peer, or youth assistance programs. This section does not apply if a pupil has been suspended, pending expulsion, pursuant to Section 48915. However, this section applies if the recommended expulsion is not implemented or is, itself, suspended by stipulation or other administrative action.

- Community Service, Alternative Disciplinary Action

48900.7. (a) In addition to the reasons specified in Sections 48900, 48900.2, 48900.3, and 48900.4, a pupil may be suspended from school or recommended for expulsion if the superintendent or the principal of the school in which the pupil is enrolled determines that the pupil has made terroristic threats against school officials or school property, or both.

- Terroristic Threats

(b) For the purposes of this section, "terroristic threat" shall include any statement, whether written or oral, by a person who willfully threatens to commit a crime which will result in death, great bodily injury to another person, or property damage in excess of one thousand dollars ($1,000), with the specific intent that the statement is to be taken as a threat, even if there is no intent of actually carrying it out, which, on its face and under the circumstances in which it is made, is so unequivocal, unconditional, immediate, and specific as to convey to the person threatened, a gravity of purpose and an immediate prospect of execution of the threat, and thereby causes that person reasonably to be in sustained fear for his or her own safety or for his or her immediate family's safety, or for the protection of school district property, or the personal property of the person threatened or his or her immediate family.

48900.8. For purposes of notification to parents, and for the reporting of expulsion or suspension offenses to the State Department of Education, each school district shall specifically identify, by offense committed, in all appropriate official records of a pupil each suspension or expulsion of

- Identify Offenses in All Appropriate Official School Records

that pupil for the commission of any of the offenses set forth in subdivisions (a) to (o), inclusive, of Section 48900, in Section 48900.2, in Section 48900.3, in Section 48900.4, or in paragraphs (1) to (5), inclusive, of subdivision (a) of, or paragraphs (1) to (4), inclusive, of subdivision (c), Section 48915.

48901. (a) No school shall permit the smoking or use of tobacco, or any product containing tobacco or nicotine products, by pupils of the school while the pupils are on campus, or while attending school-sponsored activities or while under the supervision and control of school district employees.

- Prohibition on Smoking or Use of Tobacco or Nicotine Products

(b) The governing board of any school district maintaining a high school shall take all steps it deems practical to discourage high school students from smoking.

48901.5. (a) No school shall permit the possession or use of any electronic signaling device that operates through the transmission or receipt of radio waves, including, but not limited to, paging and signaling equipment, by pupils of the school while the pupils are on campus, while attending school-sponsored activities, or while under the supervision and control of school district employees, without the prior consent of the principal or his or her designee. No pupil shall be prohibited from possessing or using an electronic signaling device that is determined by a licensed physician and surgeon to be essential for the health of a pupil and use of which is limited for purposes related to the health of the pupil.

- Prohibition on Use of Electronic Signaling Device

(b) The governing board of each school district shall take all steps it deems practical within existing resources to discourage pupils from possessing or using electronic signaling devices, except where the use of an electronic signaling device is essential for the health of a pupil.

48902. (a) The principal of a school or the principal's designee shall, prior to the suspension or expulsion of any pupil, notify the appropriate law enforcement authorities of the county or city in which the school is situated, of any acts of the student which may violate Section 245 of the Penal Code.

- Notification of Law Enforcement Authorities

(b) The principal of a school or the principal's designee shall, within one schoolday after suspension or expulsion of any pupil, notify, by telephone or any other appropriate method chosen by the school, the appropriate law enforcement authority of the county or the school district in which the school is situated of any acts of the students which may violate subdivision (c) or (d) of Section 48900 of the Education Code.

(c) Notwithstanding subdivision (b), the principal of a school or the principal's designee shall notify the appropriate law enforcement authorities of the county or city in which the school is located of any acts of a student that may involve the possession or sale of narcotics or of a controlled substance or a violation of Section 626.9 or 626.10 of the Penal Code.

(d) A principal, the principal's designee, or any other person reporting a known or suspected act described in subdivision (a) or (b) is not civilly or criminally liable as a result of making any report authorized by this article unless it can be proven that a false report was made and that the person knew the report was false or the report was made with reckless disregard for the truth or falsity of the report.

(e) The willful failure to make any report required by this section is an infraction punishable by a fine to be paid by the principal or principal's designee who is responsible for the failure of not more than five hundred dollars ($500).

48903. (a) Except as provided in subdivision (g) of Section 48911 and in Section 48912, the total number of days for which a pupil may be suspended from school shall not exceed 20 schooldays in any school year, unless for purposes of adjustment, a pupil enrolls in or is transferred to another regular school, an opportunity school or class, or a continuation education school or class, in which case the total number of school days for which the pupil may be suspended shall not exceed 30 days in any school year.

- Restrictions on Days of Suspension

(b) For the purposes of this section, a school district may count suspensions that occur while a pupil is enrolled in another school district toward the maximum number of days for which a pupil may be suspended in any school year.

48904. (a) (1) Notwithstanding Section 1714.1 of the Civil Code, the parent or guardian of any minor whose willful misconduct results in injury or death to any pupil or any person employed by, or performing volunteer services for, a school district or private school or who willfully cuts, defaces, or otherwise injures in any way any property, real or personal, belonging to a school district or private school, or personal property of any school employee, shall be liable for all damages so caused by the minor. The liability of the parent or guardian shall not exceed ten thousand dollars ($10,000). The parent or guardian shall also be liable for the amount of any reward not exceeding ten thousand dollars ($10,000) paid pursuant to Section 53069.5 of the

- Liability of Parent or Guardian for Willful Pupil Misconduct

Government Code. The parent or guardian of a minor shall be liable to a school district or private school loaned to the minor and not returned upon demand of an employee of the district or private school authorized to make the demand.

(2) The Superintendent of Public Instruction shall compute an adjustment of the liability limits prescribed by this subdivision at a rate equivalent to the percentage change in the Implicit Price Deflator for State and Local Government Purchases of Goods and Services for the United States, as published by the United States Department of Commerce for the 12-month period ending in the third quarter of the prior fiscal year.

(b) (1) Any school district or private school whose real or personal property has been willfully cut, defaced, or otherwise injured, or whose property is loaned to a pupil and willfully not returned upon demand of an employee of the district or private school authorized to make the demand may, after affording the pupil his or her due process rights, withhold the grades, diploma, and transcripts of the pupil responsible for the damage until the pupil or the pupil's parent or guardian has paid for the damages thereto, as provided in subdivision (a).

(2) The school district or private school shall notify the parent or guardian of the pupil in writing of the pupil's alleged misconduct before withholding the pupil's grades, diploma, or transcripts pursuant to this subdivision. When the minor and parent are unable to pay for the damages, or to return the property, the school district or private school shall provide a program of voluntary work for the minor in lieu of the payment of monetary damages. Upon completion of the voluntary work, the grades, diploma, and transcripts of the pupil shall be released.

(3) The governing board of each school district or governing body of each private school shall establish rules and regulations governing procedures for the implementation of this subdivision. The procedures shall conform to, but are not necessarily limited to, those procedures established in this code for the expulsion of pupils.

48904.3. (a) Upon receiving notice that a school district has withheld the grades, diploma, or transcripts of any pupil pursuant to Section 48904, any school district to which the pupil has transferred shall likewise withhold the grades, diploma, or transcripts of the pupil as authorized by that section, until such time as it receives notice, from the district that initiated the decision to withhold, that the decision has

- Withholding Grades, Diplomas, or Transcripts of Pupils Causing Property Damage or Injury

been rescinded under the terms of that section.

(b) Any school district that has decided to withhold a pupil's grades, diploma, or transcripts pursuant to Section 48904 shall, upon receiving notice that the pupil has transferred to any school district in this state, notify the parent or guardian of pupil in writing that the decision to withhold will be enforced as specified in subdivision (a)

(c) For purposes of this section and Section 48904, "school district" is defined to include any county superintendent of schools.

48905. An employee of a school district whose person or property is injured or damaged by the willful misconduct of a pupil who attends school in such district, when the employee or the employee's property is (1) located on property owned by the district, (2) being transported to or from an activity sponsored by the district or a school within the district, (3) present at an activity sponsored by such district or school, or (4) otherwise injured or damaged in retaliation for acts lawfully undertaken by the employee in execution of the employee's duties, may request the school district to pursue legal action against the pupil who caused the injury or damage, or the pupil's parent or guardian pursuant to Section 48904.

- Injury or Damage to Person or Property of School District Employee

48906. When a principal or other school official releases a minor pupil to a peace officer for the purpose of removing the minor from the school premises, the school official shall take immediate steps to notify the parent, guardian, or responsible relative of the minor regarding the release of the minor to the officer, and regarding the place to which the minor is reportedly being taken, except when a minor has been taken into custody as a victim of suspected child abuse, as defined in Section 11165 of the Penal Code, or pursuant to Section 305 of the Welfare and Institutions Code. In those cases, the school official shall provide the peace officer with the address and telephone number of the minor's parent or guardian. The peace officer shall take immediate steps to notify the parent, guardian, or responsible relative of the minor that the minor is in custody and the place where he or she is being held. If the officer has a reasonable belief that the minor would be endangered by a disclosure of the place where the minor is being held, or that the disclosure would cause the custody of the minor to be disturbed, the officer may refuse to disclose the place where the minor is being held for a period not to exceed 24 hours. The officer shall, however, inform the parent, guardian, or responsible relative

- Notification of Parent, Guardian, or Relative of Release of Pupil to Peace Officer

whether the child requires and is receiving medical or other treatment. The juvenile court shall review any decision not to disclose the place where the minor is being held at a subsequent detention hearing.

48907. Students of the public schools shall have the right to exercise freedom of speech and the press including, but not limited to, the use of bulletin boards, the distribution of printed materials or petitions, the wearing of buttons, badges, and other insignia, and the right of expression in official publications, whether or not such publications or other means of expression are supported financially by the school or by use of school facilities, except that expression shall be prohibited which is obscene, libelous, or slanderous. Also prohibited shall be material which so incites students as to create a clear and present danger of the commission of unlawful acts on school premises or the violation of lawful school regulations, or the substantial disruption of orderly operation of the school.

- Student Exercise of Free Expression

Each governing board of a school district and each county board of education shall adopt rules and regulations in the form of a written publications code, which shall include reasonable provisions for the time, place, and manner of conducting such activities within its respective jurisdiction.

Student editors of official school publications shall be responsible for assigning and editing the news, editorial, and feature content of their publications subject to the limitations of this section. However, it shall be the responsibility of a journalism adviser or advisers of student publications within each school to supervise the production of the student staff, to maintain professional standards of English and journalism, and to maintain the provisions of this section.

There shall be no prior restraint of material prepared for official school publications except insofar as it violates this section. School officials shall have the burden of showing justification without undue delay prior to any limitation of student expression under this section.

"Official school publications" refers to material produced by students in the journalism, newspaper, yearbook, or writing class and distributed to the student body either free or for a fee.

Nothing in this section shall prohibit or prevent any governing board of a school district from adopting otherwise valid rules and regulations relating to oral communication by students upon the premises of each school.

48908. All pupils shall comply with the regulations, pursue the required course of study, and submit to the authority of the teachers of the schools.

- Duties of Pupil

48909. When a petition is requested in juvenile court or a complaint is filed in any court alleging that a minor of compulsory school attendance age or any pupil currently enrolled in a public school in a grade to and including grade 12 is a person who (a) has used, sold, or possessed narcotics or other hallucinogenic drugs or substances; (b) has inhaled or breathed the fumes of, or ingested any poison classified as such in Section 4160 of the Business and Professions Code; or (c) has committed felonious assault, homicide, or rape the district attorney may, within 48 hours, provide written notice to the superintendent of the school district of attendance, notwithstanding the provisions of Section 827 of the Welfare and Institutions Code, and to the pupil's parent or guardian.

- Drug or Poison Use, Assault, Homicide, or Rape

48910. (a) A teacher may suspend any pupil from the teacher's class, for any of the acts enumerated in Section 48900, for the day of the suspension and the day following. The teacher shall immediately report the suspension to the principal of the school and send the pupil to the principal or the principal's designee for appropriate action. If that action requires the continued presence of the pupil at the school site, the pupil shall be under appropriate supervision, as defined in policies and related regulations adopted by the governing board of the school district. As soon as possible, the teacher shall ask the parent or guardian of the pupil to attend a parent-teacher conference regarding the suspension. Whenever practicable, a school counselor or a school psychologist shall attend the conference. A school administrator shall attend the conference if the teacher or the parent or guardian so requests. The pupil shall not be returned to the class from which he or she was suspended, during the period of the suspension, without the concurrence of the teacher of the class and the principal.

- Suspension of Teacher

(b) A pupil suspended from a class shall not be place in another regular class during the period of suspension. However, if the pupil is assigned to more than one class per day this subdivision shall apply only to other regular classes scheduled at the same time as the class from which the pupil was suspended.

(c) A teacher may also refer a pupil, for any of the acts enumerated in Section 48900, to the principal or the principal's designee for consideration of a suspension from the school.

48911. (a) The principal of the school, the principal's designee, or the superintendent of schools may suspend a pupil from the school for any of the reasons enumerated in Section 48900, and pursuant to Section 48900.5, for no more than five consecutive schooldays.

(b) Suspension by the principal, the principal's designee, or the superintendent shall be preceded by an informal conference conducted by the principal or the principal's designee, or the superintendent of schools between the pupil and, whenever practicable, the teacher or supervisor or school employee who referred the pupil to the principal or the principal's designee, or the superintendent of schools. At the conference, the pupil shall be informed of the reason for the disciplinary action and the evidence against him or her and shall be given the opportunity to present his or her version and evidence in his or her defense.

(c) A principal, or the principal's designee, or the superintendent of schools may suspend a pupil without affording the pupil an opportunity for a conference only if the principal, or the principal's designee, or the superintendent of schools determines that an emergency situation exists. "Emergency situation," as used in this article, means a situation determined by the principal, the principal's designee, or the superintendent to constitute a clear and present danger to the lives, safety, or health of pupils or school personnel. If a pupil is suspended without a conference prior to suspension, both the parent and the pupil shall be notified of the pupil's right to a conference and the pupil's right to return to school for the purpose of a conference. The conference shall be held within two schooldays, unless the pupil waives this right or is physically unable to attend for any reason, including, but not limited to, incarceration or hospitalization. The conference shall then be held as soon as the pupil is physically able to return to school for the conference.

(d) At the time of suspension, a school employee shall make reasonable effort to contact the pupil's parent or guardian in person or by telephone. Whenever a pupil is suspended from school, the parent or guardian shall be notified in writing of the suspension.

(e) A school employee shall report the suspension of the pupil, including the cause therefor, to the governing board of the school district or to the district superintendent in accordance with the regulations of the governing board.

(f) The parent or guardian of any pupil shall respond without delay to any request from school officials to attend a conference regarding his or her child's behavior.

No penalties may be imposed on a pupil for failure of the pupil's parent or guardian to attend a conference with school officials. Reinstatement of the suspended pupil shall not be contingent upon attendance by the pupil's parent or guardian at the conference.

(g) In a case where expulsion from any school or suspension for the balance of the semester from continuation school is being processed by the governing board, the school district superintendent or other person designated by the superintendent in writing may extend the suspension until the governing board has rendered a decision in the action. However, an extension may be granted only if the superintendent or the superintendent's designee has determined, following a meeting in which the pupil and the pupil's parent or guardian are invited to participate, that the presence of the pupil at the school or in an alternative school placement would cause a danger to persons or property or a threat of disrupting the instructional process. If the pupil or the pupil's parent or guardian has requested a meeting to challenge the original suspension pursuant to Section 48914, the purpose of the meeting shall be to decide upon the extension of the suspension order under this section and may be held in conjunction with the initial meeting on the merits of the suspension.

(h) Notwithstanding subdivisions (a) and (g), an individual with exceptional needs may be suspended for up to, but not more than, 10 consecutive schooldays if he or she poses an immediate threat to the safety of himself or herself or others. In the case of a truly dangerous child, a suspension may exceed 10 consecutive schooldays, or the pupil's placement may be changed, or both, if either of the following occurs:

- Suspension for Up to 10 Consecutive Schooldays

(1) The pupil's parent or guardian agrees.

(2) A court order so provides.

(i) For the purposes of this section, a "principal's designee" is any one or more administrators at the schoolsite specifically designated by the principal, in writing, to assist with disciplinary procedures.

In the event that there is not an administrator in addition to the principal at the schoolsite, a certificated person at the schoolsite may be specifically designated by the principal, in writing, as a "principal's designee," to assist with disciplinary procedures. The principal may designate only one such person at a time as the principal's primary designee for the school year.

An additional person meeting the requirements of this subdivision may be designated by the principal, in writing, to act for the purposes of this article when both the principal and the principal's primary designee are absent from the schoolsite. The name of the person, and the names of any person or persons designated as "principal's designee," shall be on file in the principal's office.

This section is not an exception to, nor does it place any limitation on, Section 48903.

48911.1. (a) A pupil suspended from a school for any of the reasons enumerated in Sections 48900 and 48900.2 may be assigned, by the principal or the principal's designee, to a supervised suspension classroom for the entire period of suspension if the pupil poses no imminent danger or threat to the campus, pupils, or staff, or if an action to expel the pupil has not been initiated.

- Supervised Suspension Classroom

(b) Pupils assigned to a supervised suspension classroom shall be separated from other pupils at the schoolsite for the period of suspension in a separate classroom, building, or site for pupils under suspension.

(c) School districts may continue to claim apportionments for each pupil assigned to and attending a supervised suspension classroom provided as follows:

(1) The supervised suspension classroom is staffed as otherwise provided by law.

(2) Each pupil has access to appropriate counseling services.

(3) The supervised suspension classroom promotes completion of schoolwork and tests missed by the pupil during the suspension.

(4) Each pupil is responsible for contracting his or her teacher or teachers to receive assignments to be completed while the pupil is assigned to the supervised suspension classroom. The teacher shall provide all assignments and tests that the pupil will miss while suspended. If no classroom work is assigned, the person supervising the suspension classroom shall assign schoolwork.

(d) At the time a pupil is assigned to a supervised suspension classroom, a school employee shall notify, in person or by telephone, the pupil's parent or guardian. Whenever a pupil is assigned to a supervised suspension classroom for longer than one class period, a school employee shall notify, in writing, the pupil's parent or guardian.

(e) This section does not place any limitation on a school district's ability to transfer a pupil to an opportunity school or class or a continuation education school or class.

(f) Apportionments claimed by a school district for pupils assigned to supervised suspension shall be used specifically to mitigate the cost of implementing this section.

48911.2. (a) If the number of pupils suspended from school during the prior school year exceeded 30 percent of the school's enrollment, the school should consider doing at least one of the following:

- Consideration by School When Suspensions Exceed 30 Percent of School's Enrollment

(1) Implement the supervised suspension program described in Section 48911.1.

(2) Implement an alternative to the school's off-campus suspension program, which involves a progressive discipline approach that occurs during the schoolday on campus, using any of the following activities:

(A) Conferences between the school staff, parents, and pupils.

(B) Referral to the school counselor, psychologist, child welfare attendance personnel, or other school support service staff.

(C) Detention.

(D) Study teams, guidance teams, resource panel teams, or other assessment-related teams.

(b) At the end of the academic year, the school may report to the district superintendent in charge of school support services, or other comparable administrator if that position does not exist, on the rate of reduction in the school's off-campus suspensions and the plan or activities used to comply with subdivision (a).

(c) It is the intent of the Legislature to encourage schools that choose to implement this section to examine alternatives to off-campus suspensions that lead to resolution of pupil misconduct without sending pupils off campus. Schools that use this section should not be precluded from suspending pupils to an off-campus site.

48911.5. The site principal of a contracting nonpublic, nonsectarian school providing services to individuals with exceptional needs under Section 56365 and 56366, shall have the same duties and responsibilities with respect to the suspension of pupils with previously identified exceptional needs prescribed for the suspension of pupils under Section 48911.

- Nonpublic School Principal

48912. (a) The governing board may suspend a pupil from school for any of the acts enumerated in Section 48900

- Consideration of Suspension or Other Disciplinary Action

for any number of schooldays within the limits prescribed by Section 48903.

(b) Notwithstanding the provisions of Section 35145 of this code and Section 54950 of the Government Code, the governing board of a school district shall, unless a request has been made to the contrary, hold closed sessions if the board is considering the suspension of, disciplinary action against, or any other action against, except expulsion, any pupil, if a public hearing upon that question would lead to the giving out of information concerning a school pupil which would be in violation of Article 5 (commencing with Section 49073) of Chapter 6.5.

(c) Before calling a closed session to consider these matters, the governing board shall, in writing, by registered or certified mail or by personal service, notify the pupil and the pupil's parent or guardian, or the pupil if the pupil is an adult, of the intent of the governing board to call and hold a closed session. Unless the pupil or the pupil's parent or guardian shall, in writing, within 48 hours after receipt of the written notice of the board's intention, request that the hearing be held as a public meeting, the hearing to consider these matters shall be conducted by the governing board in closed session. In the event that a written request is served upon the clerk or secretary of the governing board, the meeting shall be public, except that any discussion at that meeting which may be in conflict with the right to privacy of any pupil other than the pupil requesting the public meeting, shall be in closed session.

48912.5. The governing board of a school district may suspend a pupil enrolled in a continuation school or class for a period not longer than the remainder of the semester if any of the acts enumerated in Section 48900 occurred. The suspension shall meet the requirements of Section 48915.

- Continuation School Suspension

48913. The teacher of any class from which a pupil is suspended may require the suspended pupil to complete any assignments and tests missed during the suspension.

- Completion of Work Missed by Suspended Pupil

48914. Each school district is authorized to establish a policy that permits school officials to conduct a meeting with the parent or guardian of a suspended pupil to discuss the causes, the duration, the school policy involved, and other matters pertinent to the suspension.

- Policy on Meeting with Parent or Guardian

48915. (a) Except as provided in subdivisions (c) and (e), the principal or the superintendent of schools shall recommend the expulsion of a pupil for any of the following

- Expulsion: Particular Circumstances (4)

acts committed at school or at a school activity off school grounds, unless the principal or superintendent finds that expulsion is inappropriate, due to the particular circumstance:

(1) Causing serious physical injury to another person, except in self-defense.

(2) Possession of any knife or other dangerous object of no reasonable use to the pupil.

(3) Unlawful possession of any controlled substance listed in Chapter 2 (commencing with Section 11053) of Division 10 of the Health and Safety Code, except for the first offense for the possession of not more than one avoirdupois ounce of marijuana, other than concentrated cannabis.

(4) Robbery or extortion.

(5) Assault or battery, as defined in Sections 240 and 242 of the Penal Code, upon any school employee.

(b) Upon recommendation by the principal, superintendent of schools, or by a hearing officer or administrative panel appointed pursuant to subdivision (d) of Section 48918, the governing board may order a pupil expelled upon finding that the pupil committed an act listed in subdivision (a) or in subdivision (a), (b), (c), (d), or (e) of Section 48900. A decision to expel shall be based on a finding of one or both of the following:

(1) Other means of correction are not feasible or have repeatedly failed to bring about proper conduct.

(2) Due to the nature of the act, the presence of the pupil causes a continuing danger to the physical safety of the pupil or others.

(c) The principal or superintendent of schools shall immediately suspend, pursuant to Section 48911, and shall recommend expulsion of a pupil that he or she determines has committed any of the following acts at school or at a school activity off school grounds:

(1) Possessing, selling, or otherwise furnishing a firearm. This subdivision does not apply to an act of possessing a firearm if the pupil had obtained prior written permission to possess the firearm from a certificated school employee, which is concurred in by the principal or the designee of the principal. This subdivision applies to an act of possessing a firearm only if the possession is verified by an employee of a school district.

(2) Brandishing a knife at another person.

(3) Unlawfully selling a controlled substance listed in Chapter 2 (commencing with Section 11053) of Division 10 of the Health and Safety Code.

(4) Committing or attempting to commit a sexual assault as defined in subdivision (n) of Section 48900 or committing a sexual battery as defined in subdivision (n) of Section 48900.

(5) Possession of an explosive.

(d) The governing board shall order a pupil expelled upon finding that the pupil committed an act listed in subdivision (c), and shall refer that pupil to a program of study that meets all of the following conditions:

(1) Is appropriately prepared to accommodate pupils who exhibit discipline problems.

(2) Is not provided at a comprehensive middle, junior, or senior high school, or at any elementary school.

(3) Is not housed at the schoolsite attended by the pupil at the time of suspension.

(e) Upon recommendation by the principal, superintendent of schools, or by a hearing officer or administrative panel appointed pursuant to subdivision (d) of Section 48918, the governing board may order a pupil expelled upon finding that the pupil, at school or at a school activity off of school grounds violated subdivision (f), (g), (h), (i), (j), (k), (l), or (m) of Section 48900, or Section 48900.2, 48900.3, or 48900.4, and either of the following:

(1) That other means of correction are not feasible or have repeatedly failed to bring about proper conduct.

(2) That due to the nature of the violation, the presence of the pupil causes a continuing danger to the physical safety of the pupil or others.

(f) The governing board shall refer a pupil who has been expelled pursuant to subdivision (b) or (e) to a program of study which meets all of the conditions specified in subdivision (d). Notwithstanding this subdivision, with respect to a pupil expelled pursuant to subdivision (e), if the county superintendent of schools certifies that an alternative program of study is not available at a site away from a comprehensive middle, junior, or senior high school, or an elementary school, and that the only option for placement is at another comprehensive middle, junior, or senior high school, or another elementary school, the pupil may be referred to a program of study that is provided at a comprehensive middle, junior, or senior high school, or at an elementary school.

(g) As used in this section, "knife" means any dirk, dagger, or other weapon with a fixed, sharpened blade fitted primarily for stabbing, a weapon with a blade fitted primarily for stabbing, a weapon with a blade longer than 3 ½ inches, a folding knife with a blade that locks into place, or a razor with an unguarded blade.

(h)   As used in this section, the term "explosive" means "destructive device" as described in Section 921 of Title 18 of the United States Code.

48915.01.   If the governing board of a school district has established a community day school pursuant to Section 48661 on the same site as a comprehensive middle, junior, or senior high school, or at any elementary school, the governing board does not have to meet the condition in paragraph (2) of subdivision (d) of Section 48915 when the board, pursuant to subdivision (f) of Section 48915, refers a pupil to a program of study and that program of study is at the community day school.   All the other conditions of subdivision (d) of Section 48915 are applicable to the referral as required by subdivision (f) of Section 48915.

- Location of Community School

48915.1.   (a)   If the governing board of a school district receives a request from an individual who has been expelled from another school district for an act other than those described in subdivision (a) or (c) of Section 48915, for enrollment in a school maintained by the school district, the board shall hold a hearing to determine whether that individual poses a continuing danger either to the pupils or employees of the school district.   The hearing and notice shall be conducted in accordance with the rules and regulations governing procedures for the expulsion of pupils as described in Section 48918.   A school district may request information from another school district regarding a recommendation for expulsion or the expulsion of an applicant for enrollment. The school district receiving the request shall respond to the request with all deliberate speed but shall respond no later than five working days from the date of the receipt of the request.

- Expelled Individuals, Enrollment in Another School

(b)   If a pupil has been expelled from his or her previous school for an act other than those listed in subdivision (a) or (c) of Section 48915, the parent, guardian, or pupil, if the pupil is emancipated or otherwise legally of age, shall upon enrollment, inform the receiving school district of his or her status with the previous school district.   If this information is not provided to the school district and the school district later determines the pupil was expelled from the previous school, the lack of compliance shall be recorded and discussed in the hearing required pursuant to subdivision (a).

(c)   The governing board of a school district may make a determination to deny enrollment to an individual who has been expelled from another school district for an act other than those described in subdivision (a) or (c) of Section 48915, for the remainder of the expulsion period after a determination has been made, pursuant to a hearing, that the individual poses a potential danger to either the pupils or employees of the school district.

(d) The governing board of a school district, when making its determination whether to enroll an individual who has been expelled from another school district for these acts, may consider the following options:

(1) Deny enrollment.

(2) Permit enrollment.

(3) Permit conditional enrollment in a regular school program or another educational program.

(e) Notwithstanding any other provision of law, the governing board of a school district, after a determination has been made, pursuant to a hearing, that an individual expelled from another school district for an act other than those described in subdivision (a) or (c) of Section 48915 does not pose a danger to either the pupils or employees of the school district, shall permit the individual to enroll in a school in the school district during the term of the expulsion, provided that he or she, subsequent to the expulsion, either has established legal residence in the school district, pursuant to Section 48200, or has enrolled in the school pursuant to an interdistrict agreement executed between the affected school districts pursuant to Chapter 5 (commencing with Section 46600).

48915.2. (a) A pupil expelled from school for any of the offenses listed in subdivision (a) or (c) of Section 48915, shall not be permitted to enroll in any other school or school district during the period of expulsion unless it is a county community school pursuant to subdivision (c) of Section 1981, or a juvenile court school, as described in Section 48645.1, or a community day school pursuant to Article 3 (commencing with Section 48660) of Chapter 4 of Part 27.

- Enrollment During and After Period of Expulsion

(b) After a determination has been made, pursuant to a hearing under Section 48918, that an individual expelled from another school district for any act described in subdivision (a) or (c) of Section 48915 does not pose a danger to either the pupils or employees of the school district, the governing board of a school district may permit the individual to enroll in the school district after the term of expulsion, subject to one of the following conditions:

(1) He or she has established legal residence in the school

district, pursuant to Section 48200.

(2) He or she is enrolled in the school pursuant to an interdistrict agreement executed between the affected school districts pursuant to Chapter 5 (commencing with Section 46600) of Part 26.

48915.5. (a) In a matter involving a pupil with previously identified exceptional needs who is currently enrolled in a special education program, the governing board may order the pupil expelled pursuant to subdivision (b) or (d) of Section 48915 only if all of the following conditions are met:

- Expulsion Conditions for Disabled Pupils Enrolled in a Special Education Program

(1) An individualized education program team meeting is held and conducted pursuant to Article 3 (commencing with Section 56340) of Chapter 2 of Part 30.

(2) The team determines that the misconduct was not caused by, or was not a direct manifestation of, the pupil's identified disability.

(3) The team determines that the pupil had been appropriately placed at the time the misconduct occurred.

The term "pupil with previously identified exceptional needs," as used in this section, means a pupil who meets the requirements of Section 56026 and who, at the time the alleged misconduct occurred, was enrolled in a special education program, including enrollment in nonpublic schools pursuant to Section 56365 and state special schools.

(b) For purposes of this section, all applicable procedural safeguards prescribed by federal and state law and regulations apply to proceedings to expel pupils with previously identified exceptional needs, except that, notwithstanding Section 56321, subdivision (e) of Section 56506, or any other provision of law, parental consent is not required prior to conducting a preexpulsion educational assessment pursuant to subdivision (e), or as a condition of the final decision of the local board to expel.

- Procedural Safeguards

(c) Each local educational agency, pursuant to the requirements of Section 56195.8, shall develop procedures and timelines governing expulsion procedures for individuals with exceptional needs.

- Expulsion Procedures and Timelines

(d) The parent of each pupil with previously identified exceptional needs has the right to participate in the individualized education program team meeting conducted pursuant to subdivision (a) preceding the commencement of expulsion proceedings, following the completion of a preexpulsion assessment pursuant to subdivision (e), through actual participation, representation, or a telephone conference call. The meeting shall be held at a time and place mutually

- Parent Rights

convenient to the parent and local educational agency within the period, if any, of the pupil's preexpulsion suspension. A telephone conference call may be substituted for the meeting. Each parent shall be notified of his or her right to participate in the meeting at least 48 hours prior to the meeting. Unless a parent has requested a postponement, the meeting may be conducted without the parent's participation, if the notice required by this subdivision has been provided. The notice shall specify that the meeting may be held without the parent's participation, unless the parent requests a postponement for up to three additional schooldays pursuant to this subdivision. Each parent may request that the meeting be postponed for up to three additional schooldays. If a postponement has been granted, the local educational agency may extend any suspension of a pupil for the period of postponement if the pupil continues to pose an immediate threat to the safety of himself, herself, or others and the local educational agency notifies the parent that the suspension will be continued during the postponement. However, the suspension shall not be extended beyond 10 consecutive schooldays unless agreed to by the parent, or by a court order. If a parent who has received proper notice of the meeting refuses to consent to an extension beyond 10 consecutive schooldays and chooses not to participate, the meeting may be conducted without the parent's participation.

(e) In determining whether a pupil should be expelled, the individualized education program team shall base its decision on the results of a preexpulsion educational assessment conducted in accordance with the guidelines of Section 104.35 of Title 34 of the Code of Federal Regulation, which shall include a review of the appropriateness of the pupil's placement at the time of the alleged misconduct, and a determination of the relationship, if any, between the pupil's behavior and his or her disability.

- Expulsion Decision Based on Results of Preexpulsion Educational Assessment

In addition to the preexpulsion educational assessment results, the individualized education program team shall also review and consider the pupil's health records and school discipline records. The parent, pursuant to Section 300.504 of Title 34 of the Code of Federal Regulations, is entitled to written notice of the local educational agency's intent to conduct a preexpulsion assessment. The parent shall make the pupil available for the assessment at a site designated by the local educational agency without delay. The parent's right to an independent assessment under Section 56329 applies despite the fact that the pupil has been referred for expulsion.

(f) If the individualized education program team determines that the alleged misconduct was not caused by, or a direct manifestation of, the pupil's disability, and if it is determined that the pupil was appropriately placed, the pupil shall be subject to the applicable disciplinary actions and procedures prescribed under this article.

(g) The parent of each pupil with previously identified exceptional needs has the right to a due process hearing conducted pursuant to Section 1415 of Title 20 of the United States Code if the parent disagrees with the decision of the individualized education program team made pursuant to subdivision (f), or if the parent disagrees with the decision to rely upon information obtained, or proposed to be obtained, pursuant to subdivision (e).

(h) No expulsion hearing shall be conducted for an individual with exceptional needs until all of the following have occurred:

(1) A preexpulsion assessment is conducted.

(2) The individualized education program team meets pursuant to subdivision (a).

(3) Due process hearings and appeals, if initiated pursuant to Section 1415 of Title 20 of the United States Code, are completed.

(i) Pursuant to subdivision (a) of Section 48918, the statutory times prescribed for expulsion proceedings for individuals with exceptional needs shall commence after the completion of paragraphs (1), (2), and (3) in subdivision (h).

(j) If an individual with exceptional needs is excluded from schoolbus transportation, the pupil is entitled to be provided with an alternative form of transportation at no cost to the pupil or parent.

48915.6. The restrictions and special procedures provided in Section 48915.5 for the expulsion of a pupil with exceptional needs shall not apply when the pupil possessed a firearm, knife, explosive, or other dangerous object of no reasonable use to the pupil, or the pupil committed or attempted to commit a sexual assault or committed sexual battery, at school or at a school activity off school grounds, unless for these acts the restrictions and special procedures in Section 48915.5 are mandated under federal law, including Section 1415 of Title 20 of the United States Code.

48916. (a) An expulsion order shall remain in effect until the governing board, in the manner prescribed in this article, orders the readmission of a pupil. At the time an expulsion of a pupil is ordered for an act other than those described in subdivision (c) of Section 48915, the governing board shall set a date, not later than the last day of the semester following the semester in which the expulsion occurred, when the pupil shall be reviewed for readmission to a school maintained by the district or to the school the pupil last attended. For a pupil who has been expelled pursuant to subdivision (c) of Section 48915, the governing board shall set a date of one year from the date the expulsion occurred, when the pupil shall be reviewed for readmission to a school maintained by the district, except that the governing board may set an earlier date for readmission on a case-by-case basis.

(b) The governing board shall recommend a plan of rehabilitation for the pupil at the time of the expulsion order, which may include, but not be limited to, periodic review as well as assessment at the time of review for readmission. The plan may also include recommendations for improved academic performance, tutoring, special education assessments, job training, counseling, employment, community services, or other rehabilitative programs.

(c) The governing board of each school district shall adopt rules and regulations establishing a procedure for the filing and processing of requests for readmission and the process for the required review of all expelled pupils for readmission. Upon completion of the readmission process, the governing board shall readmit the pupil, unless the governing board makes a finding that the pupil has not met the conditions of the rehabilitation plan or continues to pose a danger to campus safety or to other pupils or employees of the school district. A description of the procedure shall be made available to the pupil and the pupil's parent or guardian at the time the expulsion order is entered.

(d) If the governing board denies the readmission of an expelled pupil pursuant to subdivision (c), the governing board shall make a determination either to continue the placement of the pupil in the alternative educational program initially selected for the pupil during the period of the expulsion order or to place the pupil in another program that may include, but need not be limited to, serving expelled pupils, including placement in a county community school.

(e) The governing board shall provide written notice to the expelled pupil and the pupil's parent or guardian describing the reasons for denying the pupil readmittance into the regular school district program. The written notice shall also include the determination of the educational program for the expelled pupil pursuant to subdivision (d). The expelled pupil shall enroll in that educational program unless the parent or guardian of the pupil elects to enroll the pupil in another school district.

48916.1. (a) At the time an expulsion of a pupil is ordered, the governing board of the school district shall ensure that an education program is provided to the pupil who is subject to the expulsion order for the period of the expulsion. Except for pupils expelled pursuant to subdivision (d) of Section 48915, the governing board of a school district is required to implement the provisions of this section only to the extent funds are appropriated for this purpose in the annual Budget Act or other legislation, or both.

- Post-Expulsion Educational Program

(b) Notwithstanding any other provision of law, any educational program provided pursuant to subdivision (a) may be operated by the school district, the county superintendent of schools, or a consortium of districts or in joint agreement with the county superintendent of schools.

(c) Any educational program provided pursuant to subdivision (b) shall not be situated within or on the grounds of the school from which the pupil was expelled.

(d) If the pupil who is subject to the expulsion order was expelled from any of kindergarten or grades 1 to 6, inclusive, the educational program provided pursuant to subdivision (b) may not be combined or merged with educational programs offered to pupils in any of grades 7 to 12, inclusive. The district or county program is the only program required to be provided to expelled pupils as determined by the governing board of the school district. This subdivision, as it relates to the separation of pupils by grade levels, does not apply to community day schools offering instruction in any of kindergarten and grades 1 to 8, inclusive, and established in accordance with Section 48660.

(e) (1) Each school district shall maintain data as specified in this subdivision and report the data annually to the State Department of Education, commencing June 1, 1997, on forms provided by the State Department of Education. The school district shall maintain the following data:

(A) The number of pupils recommended for expulsion.

(B) The grounds for each recommended expulsion.

(C) Whether the pupil was subsequently expelled.

(D) Whether the expulsion order was suspended.

(E) The type of referral made after the expulsion.

(F) The disposition of the pupil after the end of the period of expulsion.

(2) When a school district does not report outcome data as required by this subdivision, the Superintendent of Public Instruction may not apportion any further money to the school district pursuant to Section 48664 until the school district is in compliance with the provisions of this subdivision. Before withholding the apportionment of funds to a school pursuant to this subdivision, the Superintendent of Public Instruction shall give written notice to the governing board of the school district that the school district has failed to report the data required by paragraph (1) and that the school district has 30 calendar days from the date of the written notice of noncompliance to report the requested data and thereby avoid the withholding of the apportionment of funds.

(f) If the county superintendent of schools is unable for any reason to serve the expelled pupils of a school district within the county, the governing board of that school district may enter into an agreement with a county superintendent of schools in another county to provide education services for the district's expelled pupils.

48916.5. The governing board may require a pupil who is expelled from school for reasons relating to controlled substances, as defined in Sections 11054 to 11058, inclusive, of the Health and Safety Code, or alcohol, prior to returning to school to enroll in a county-supported drug rehabilitation program. No pupil shall be required to enroll in a rehabilitation program pursuant to this section without the consent of his or her parent or guardian.

- Expulsion Relating to Controlled Substances or Alcohol

48917. (a) The governing board, upon voting to expel a pupil, may suspend the enforcement of the expulsion order for a period of not more than one calendar year and may, as a condition of the suspension of enforcement, assign the pupil to a school, class, or program that is deemed appropriate for the rehabilitation the pupil. The rehabilitation program to which the pupil is assigned may provide for the involvement of the pupil's parent or guardian in his or her child's education in ways that are specified in the rehabilitation program. A parent or guardian's refusal to participate in the rehabilitation program shall not be considered in the governing board's determination as to whether the pupil has satisfactorily completed the rehabilitation program.

- Suspension of Order to Expel, Rehabilitation Program, Expungement of Records

(b) The governing board shall apply the criteria for suspending the enforcement of the expulsion order equally to all pupils, including individuals with exceptional needs as defined in Section 56026.

(c) During the period of the suspension of the expulsion

order, the pupil is deemed to be on probationary status.

(d) The governing board may revoke the suspension of an expulsion order under this section if the pupil commits any of the acts enumerated in Section 48900 or violates any of the district's rules and regulations governing pupil conduct. When the governing board revokes the suspension of an expulsion order, a pupil may be expelled under the terms of the original expulsion order.

(e) Upon satisfactory completion of the rehabilitation assignment of a pupil, the governing board shall reinstate the pupil in a school of the district and may also order the expungement of any or all records of the expulsion proceedings.

(f) A decision of the governing board to suspend an expulsion order does not affect the time period and requirements for the filing of an appeal of the expulsion order with the county board of education required under Section 48919. Any appeal shall be filed within 30 days of the original vote of the governing board.

48918. The governing board of each school district shall establish rules and regulations governing procedures for the expulsion of pupils. These procedures shall include, but are not necessarily limited to, all of the following:

- Rules Governing Expulsion Procedures, Hearings, Notice

(a) The pupil shall be entitled to a hearing to determine whether the pupil should be expelled. An expulsion hearing shall be held within 30 schooldays after the date the principal or the superintendent of schools determines that the pupil has committed any of the acts enumerated in Section 48900, unless the pupil requests, in writing, that the hearing be postponed. The adopted rules and regulations shall specify that the pupil is entitled to at least one postponement of an expulsion hearing, for a period of not more than 30 calendar days. Any additional postponement may be granted at the discretion of the governing board.

Within 10 schooldays after the conclusion of the hearing, the governing board shall decide whether to expel the pupil, unless the pupil requests in writing that the decision be postponed. If the hearing is held by a hearing officer or an administrative panel, or if the district governing board does not meet on a weekly basis, the governing board shall decide whether to expel the pupil within 40 schooldays after the date of the pupil's removal from his or her school of attendance for the incident for which the recommendation for expulsion is made by the principal or the superintendent, unless the pupil requests in writing that the decision be postponed.

If compliance by the governing board with the time requirements for the conducting of an expulsion hearing under this subdivision is impracticable during the regular school year, the superintendent of schools or the superintendent's designee may, for good cause, extend the time period for the holding of the expulsion hearing for an additional five schooldays. If compliance by the governing board with the time requirements for the conducting of an expulsion hearing under this subdivision is impractical due to a summer recess of governing board meetings of more than two weeks, the days during the recess period shall not be counted as schooldays in meeting the time requirements. The days not counted as schooldays in meeting the time requirements for an expulsion hearing because of a summer recess of governing board meetings shall not exceed 20 schooldays, as defined in subdivision (c) of Section 48925, and unless the pupil requests in writing that the expulsion hearing be postponed, the hearing shall be held not later than 20 calendar days prior to the first day of school for the school year. Reasons for the extension of the time for the hearing shall be included as a part of the record at the time the expulsion hearing is conducted. Upon the commencement of the hearing, all matters shall be pursued and conducted with reasonable diligence and shall be concluded without any unnecessary delay.

(b) Written notice of the hearing shall be forwarded to the pupil at least 10 calendar days prior to the date of the hearing. The notice shall include all of the following:

(1) The date and place of the hearing.

(2) A statement of the specific facts and charges upon which the proposed expulsion is based.

(3) A copy of the disciplinary rules of the district that relate to the alleged violation.

(4) A notice of the parent, guardian, or pupil's obligation pursuant to subdivision (b) of Section 48915.1.

(5) Notice of opportunity for the pupil or the pupil's parent or guardian to appear in person or to be represented by legal counsel or by a nonattorney adviser, to inspect and obtain copies of all documents to be used at the hearing, to confront and question all witnesses who testify at the hearing, to question all other evidence presented, and to present oral and documentary evidence on the pupil's behalf, including witnesses. In a hearing in which a pupil is alleged to have committed or attempted to commit a sexual assault as specified in subdivision (n) of Section 48900 or committing a

sexual battery as defined in subdivision (n) of Section 48900 or committing a sexual battery as defined in subdivision (n) of Section 48900, a complaining witness shall be given five days' notice before being called to testify, and shall be entitled to have up to two adult support persons, including, but not limited to, a parent, guardian, or legal counsel, present during their testimony. Before a complaining witness testifies, support persons shall be admonished that the hearing is confidential. Nothing in this subdivision shall preclude the person presiding over an expulsion hearing from removing a support person whom the presiding person finds is disrupting the hearing. If one or both of the support persons is also a witness, the provisions of Section 868.5 of the Penal Code shall be followed for the hearing. Nothing in this section is intended to require a pupil or the pupil's parent or guardian to be represented by legal counsel or by a nonattorney advisor at the hearing.

(A) For purposes of this section, "legal counsel" means an attorney or lawyer who is admitted to the practice of law in California, and is an active member of the State Bar of California.

(B) For purposes of this section, "nonattorney advisor" means an individual who is familiar with the facts of the case, and has been selected by the pupil or the pupil's parent or guardian to provide assistance at the hearing.

(c) Notwithstanding Section 54593 of the Government Code and Section 35145, the governing board shall conduct a hearing to consider the expulsion of a pupil in a session closed to the public, unless the pupil requests, in writing, at least five days before the date of the hearing, that the hearing be conducted at a public meeting. Regardless of whether the expulsion hearing is conducted in a closed or public session, the governing board may meet in closed session for the purpose of deliberating and determining whether the pupil should be expelled.

If the governing board or the hearing officer or administrative panel appointed under subdivision (d) to conduct the hearing admits any other person to a closed deliberation session, the parent or guardian of the pupil, the pupil, and the counsel of the pupil also shall be allowed to attend the closed deliberations.

If the hearing is to be conducted at a public meeting, and there is a charge of committing or attempting to commit a sexual assault as defined in subdivision (n) of Section 48900 or committing a sexual battery as defined in subdivision (n) of

Section 48900, a complaining witness shall have the right to have his or her testimony heard in a session closed to the public when testifying at a public meeting would threaten serious psychological harm to the complaining witness and there are no alternative procedures to avoid the threatened harm, including, but not limited to, videotaped deposition or contemporaneous examination in another place communicated to the hearing room by means of closed-circuit television.

(d) Instead of conducting an expulsion hearing itself, the governing board may contract with the county hearing officer, or with the Office of Administrative Hearings of the State of California pursuant to Chapter 14 (commencing with Section 27720) of Part 3 of Division 2 of Title 3 of the Government Code and Section 35207, for a hearing officer to conduct the hearing. The governing board may also appoint an impartial administrative panel of three or more certificated persons, none of whom is a member of the board or employed on the staff of the school in which the pupil is enrolled. The hearing shall be conducted in accordance with all of the procedures established under this section.

(e) Within three schooldays after the hearing, the hearing officer or administrative panel shall determine whether to recommend the expulsion of the pupil to the governing board. If the hearing officer or administrative panel decides not to recommend expulsion, the expulsion proceedings shall be terminated and the pupil immediately shall be reinstated and permitted to return to a classroom instructional program, any other instructional program, a rehabilitation program, or any combination of these programs. Placement in one or more of these programs shall be made by the superintendent of schools or the superintendent's designee after consultation with school district personnel, including the pupil's teachers, and the pupil's parent or guardian. The decision not to recommend expulsion shall be final.

(f) If the hearing officer or administrative panel recommends expulsion, findings of fact in support of the recommendation shall be prepared and submitted to the governing board. All findings of fact and recommendations shall be based solely on the evidence adduced at the hearing. If the governing board accepts the recommendation calling for expulsion, acceptance shall be based either upon a review of the findings of fact and recommendations submitted by the hearing officer or panel or upon the results of any supplementary hearing conducted pursuant to this section that the governing board may order.

The decision of the governing board to expel a pupil shall be based upon substantial evidence relevant to the charges adduced at the expulsion hearing or hearings. Except as provided in this section, no evidence to expel shall be based solely upon hearsay evidence. The governing board or the hearing officer or administrative panel may, upon a finding that good cause exists, determine that the disclosure of either the identity of a witness or the testimony of that witness at the hearing, or both, would subject the witness to an unreasonable risk of psychological or physical harm. Upon this determination, the testimony of the witness may be presented at the hearing in the form of sworn declarations which shall be examined only by the governing board or the hearing officer or administrative panel. Copies of these sworn declarations, edited to delete the name and identity of the witness, shall be made available to the pupil.

(g) A record of the hearing shall be made. The record may be maintained by any means, including electronic recording, so long as a reasonably accurate and complete written transcription of the proceedings can be made.

(h) Technical rules of evidence shall not apply to the hearing, but relevant evidence may be admitted and given probative effect only if it is the kind of evidence upon which reasonable persons are accustomed to rely in the conduct of serious affairs. A decision of the governing board to expel shall be supported by substantial evidence showing that the pupil committed any of the acts enumerated in Section 48900.

In hearings which include an allegation of committing or attempting to commit a sexual assault as defined in subdivision (n) of Section 48900 or committing a sexual battery as defined in subdivision (n) of Section 48900, evidence of specific instances, of a complaining witness' prior sexual conduct is to be presumed inadmissible and shall not be heard absent a determination by the person conducting the hearing that extraordinary circumstances exist requiring the evidence be heard. Before the person conducting the hearing makes the determination on whether extraordinary circumstances exist requiring that specific instances of a complaining witness' prior sexual conduct be heard, the complaining witness shall be provided notice and an opportunity to present opposition to the introduction of the evidence. In the hearing on the admissibility of the evidence, the complaining witness shall be entitled to be represented by a parent, guardian, legal counsel, or other support person. Reputation or opinion evidence regarding the sexual behavior of the complaining witness is not admissible for any purpose.

(i) (1) Before the hearing has commenced, the governing board may issue subpoenas at the request of either the superintendent of schools or the superintendent's designee or the pupil, for the personal appearance of percipient witnesses at the hearing. After the hearing has commenced, the governing board or the hearing officer or administrative panel may, upon request of either the county superintendent of schools or the superintendent's designee or the pupil, issue subpoenas. All subpoenas shall be issued in accordance with Sections 1985, 1985.1, and 1985.2 of the Code of Civil Procedure. Enforcement of subpoenas shall be done in accordance with Section 11525 of the Government Code.

(2) Any objection raised by the superintendent of schools or the superintendent's designee or the pupil to the issuance of subpoenas may be considered by the governing board in closed session, or in open session, if so requested by the pupil before the meeting. Any decision by the governing board in response to an objection to the issuance of subpoenas shall be final and binding.

(3) If the governing board, hearing officer, or administrative panel determines, in accordance with subdivision (f), that a percipient witness would be subject to an unreasonable risk of harm by testifying at the hearing, a subpoena shall not be issued to compel the personal attendance of that witness at the hearing. However, that witness may be compelled to testify by means of a sworn declaration as provided for in subdivision (f).

(4) Service of process shall be extended to all parts of the state and shall be served in accordance with Section 1987 of the Code of Civil Procedure. All witnesses appearing pursuant to subpoena, other than the parties or officers or employees of the state or any political subdivision thereof, shall receive fees, and all witnesses appearing pursuant to subpoena, except the parties, shall receive mileage in the same amount and under the same circumstances as prescribed for witnesses in civil actions in a superior court. Fees and mileage shall be paid by the party at whose request the witness is subpoenaed.

(j) Whether an expulsion hearing is conducted by the governing board or before a hearing officer or administrative panel, final action to expel a pupil shall be taken only by the governing board in a public session. Written notice of any decision to expel or to suspend the enforcement of an expulsion order during a period of probation shall be sent by the superintendent of schools or his or her designee to the pupil or the pupil's parent or guardian and shall be accompanied by all of the following:

(1) Notice of the right to appeal the expulsion to the county board of education.

(2) Notice of the education alternative placement to be provided to the pupil during the time of expulsion.

(3) Notice of the obligation of the parent, guardian, or pupil under subdivision (b) of Section 48915.1, upon the pupil's enrollment in a new school district, to inform that district of the pupil's expulsion.

(k) The governing board shall maintain a record of each expulsion, including the cause therefor. Records of expulsions shall be nonprivileged, disclosable public record.

The expulsion order and the causes therefor shall be recorded in the pupil's mandatory interim record and shall be forwarded to any school in which the pupil subsequently enrolls upon receipt of a request from the admitting school for the pupil's school records.

48918.5. In expulsion hearings involving allegations brought pursuant to subdivision (n) of Section 48900, the governing board of each school district shall establish rules and regulations governing procedures. The procedures shall include, but are not limited to, all of the following:

- Expulsion Hearing Procedures for Sexual Assault Allegations

(a) At the time that the expulsion hearing is recommended, the complaining witness shall be provided with a copy of the applicable disciplinary rules and advised of his or her right to: (1) receive five days' notice of the complaining witness's scheduled testimony at the hearing, (2) have up to two adult support persons of his or her choosing, present in the hearing at the time he or she testifies; and (3) to have the hearing closed during the time they testify pursuant to subdivision (c) of Section 48918.

(b) An expulsion hearing may be postponed for one schoolday in order to accommodate the special physical, mental, or emotional needs of a pupil who is the complaining witness where the allegations arise under subdivision (n) of Section 48900.

(c) The district shall provide a nonthreatening environment for a complaining witness in order to better enable them to speak freely and accurately of the experiences that are the subject of the expulsion hearing, and to prevent discouragement of complaints. Each school district shall provide a room separate from the hearing room for the use of the complaining witness prior to and during the breaks in testimony. In the discretion of the person conducting the hearing, the complaining witness shall be allowed reasonable periods of relief from examination and cross-examination during which he or she may leave the hearing room. The person conducting the hearing may arrange the seating within the hearing room of those present in order to facilitate a less intimidating environment for the complaining witness. The person conducting the hearing may limit the time for taking the testimony of a complaining witness to the hours he or she is normally in school, if there is no good cause to take the testimony during other hours. The person conducting the hearing may permit one of the complaining witness's support persons to accompany him or her to the witness stand.

(d) Whenever any allegation is made of conduct violative of subdivision (n) of Section 48900, complaining witnesses and accused pupils are to be advised immediately to refrain from personal or telephonic contact with each other during the pendency of any expulsion process.

48919. If a pupil is expelled from school, the pupil or the pupil's parent or guardian may, within 30 days following the decision of the governing board to expel, file an appeal to the county board of education which shall hold a hearing thereon and render its decision.

- Expulsion Appeals to County Board of Education

The county board of education, or in a class 1 or class 2 county a hearing officer or impartial administrative panel, shall hold the hearing within 20 schooldays following the filing of a formal request under this section. If the county board of education hears the appeal without a hearing conducted pursuant to Section 48919.5, then the board shall render a decision within three schooldays of the hearing conducted pursuant to Section 48920, unless the pupil requests a postponement.

The period within which an appeal is to be filed shall be determined from the date a governing board votes to expel even if enforcement of the expulsion action is suspended and the pupil is placed on probation pursuant to Section 48917. A pupil who fails to appeal the original action of the board within the prescribed time may not subsequently appeal a decision of the board to revoke probation and impose the original order of expulsion.

The county board of education shall adopt rules and regulations establishing procedures for expulsion appeals conducted under this section. If the county board of education in a class 1 or class 2 county elects to use the procedures in Section 48919.5, then the board shall adopt rules and regulations establishing procedures for expulsion appeals conducted under Section 48919.5. The adopted rules and regulations shall include, but need not be limited to, the requirements for filing a notice of appeal, the setting of a hearing date, the furnishing of notice to the pupil and the governing board regarding the appeal, the furnishing of a copy of the expulsion hearing record to the county board of education, procedures for the conduct of the hearing, and the preservation of the record of the appeal.

The pupil shall submit a written request for a copy of the written transcripts and supporting documents from the school district simultaneously with the filing of the notice of appeal with the county board of education. The school district shall provide the pupil with the transcriptions, supporting documents, and records within 10 schooldays following the pupil's written request. Upon receipt of the records, the pupil shall immediately file suitable copies of these records with the county board of education.

48919.5. (a) A county board of education in a class 1 or class 2 county may have a hearing officer pursuant to Chapter 14 (commencing with Section 27720) of Part 3 of Title 3 of the Government Code, or an impartial administrative panel of three or more certificated persons appointed by the county board of education, hear appeals filed pursuant to Section 48919. The members of the impartial administrative panel shall not be members of the governing board of the school district nor employees of the school district, from which the pupil filing the appeal was expelled. Neither the hearing officer, nor any member of the administrative panel, hearing a pupil's appeal shall have been the hearing officer or a member of the administrative panel that conducted the pupil's expulsion hearing.

(b) A hearing conducted pursuant to this section shall not issue a final order of the county board. The hearing officer or impartial administrative panel shall prepare a recommended decision, including any findings or conclusions required for that decision, and shall submit that recommendation and the record to the county board of education within three schooldays of hearing the appeal.

(c) Sections 48919, 48920, 48921, 48922, 48923, and 48925 are applicable to a hearing conducted pursuant to this section.

(d) Within 10 schooldays of receiving the recommended decision and record from the hearing officer or the impartial administrative panel, the county board of education shall

- Expulsion Appeals; Hearing Officer or Impartial Administrative Panel review the recommended decision and record and render a final order of the board.

(e) For purposes of this article, the following definitions shall apply:

(1) "Countywide ADA" means the aggregate number of annual units of regular average daily attendance for the fiscal year in all school districts within the county.

(2) "Class 1 county" means a county with 1994/95 countywide ADA of more than 500,000.

(3) "Class 2 county" means a county with 1994/95 countywide ADA of at least 180,000 but less than 500,000.

48920. Notwithstanding the provisions of Section 54950 of the Government Code and Section 35145 of this code, the county board of education shall hear an appeal of an expulsion order in closed session, unless the pupil requests, in writing, at least five days prior to the date of the hearing, that the hearing be conducted in a public meeting. Upon the timely submission of a request for a public meeting, the county board of education shall be required to honor the request. Whether the hearing is conducted in closed or public session, the county board may meet in closed session for the purpose of deliberations. If the county board admits any representative of the pupil or the school district, the board shall, at the same time, admit representatives from the opposing party.

- County Board; Hearing Expulsion Appeal

48921. The county board of education shall determine the appeal from a pupil expulsion upon the record of the hearing before the district governing board, together with such applicable documentation or regulations as may be ordered. No evidence other than that contained in the record of the proceedings of the school board may be heard unless a de novo proceeding is granted as provided in Section 48923.

- Expulsion Appeals to County Board; Transcripts

It shall be the responsibility of the pupil to submit a written transcription for review by the county board. The cost of the transcript shall be borne by the pupil except in either of the following situations:

(1) Where the pupil's parent or guardian certifies to the school district that he or she cannot reasonably afford the cost of the transcript because of limited income or exceptional necessary expenses, or both.

(2) In a case in which the county board reverses the decision of the local governing board, the county board shall require the local board reimburse the pupil for the cost of such transcription.

48922. (a) The review by the county board of education of the decision of the governing board shall be limited to the following questions:

(1) Whether the governing board acted without or in excess of it jurisdiction.

(2) Whether there was a fair hearing before the governing board.

(3) Whether there was a prejudicial abuse of discretion in the hearing.

(4) Whether there is relevant and material evidence which, in the exercise of reasonable diligence, could not have been produced or which was improperly excluded at the hearing before the governing board.

(b) As used in this section, a proceeding without or in excess of jurisdiction includes, but is not limited to, a situation where an expulsion hearing is not commenced within the time periods prescribed by this article, a situation where an expulsion order is not based upon the acts enumerated in Section 48900, or a situation involving acts not related to school activity or attendance.

(c) For purposes of this section, an abuse of discretion is established in any of the following situations:

(1) If school officials have not met the procedural requirements of this article.

(2) If the decision to expel a pupil is not supported by the findings prescribed by Section 48915.

(3) If the findings are not supported by the evidence.

A county board of education may not reverse the decision of a governing board to expel a pupil based upon a finding of an abuse of discretion unless the county board of education also determines that the abuse of discretion was prejudicial.

48923. The decision of the county board shall be limited as follows:

(a) If the county board finds that relevant and material evidence exists which, in the exercise of reasonable diligence, could not have been produced or which was improperly excluded at the hearing before the governing board, it may do either of the following:

(1) Remand the matter to the governing board for reconsideration and may in addition order the pupil reinstated pending the reconsideration.

(2) Grant a hearing de novo upon reasonable notice thereof to the pupil and to the governing board. The hearing shall be conducted in conformance with the rules and regulations adopted by the county board under Section 48919.

(b) If the county board determines that the decision of the governing board is not supported by the findings required to be made by Section 48915, but evidence supporting the required findings exists in the record of the proceedings, the county board shall remand the matter to the governing board for adoption of the required findings. This remand for the adoption and inclusion of the required findings shall not result in an additional hearing pursuant to Section 48918, except that final action to expel the pupil based on the revised findings of fact shall meet all requirements of subdivisions (j) and (k) of Section 48918.

(c) In all other cases, the county board shall enter an order either affirming or reversing the decision of the governing board. In any case in which the county board enters a decision reversing the local board, the county board may direct the local board to expunge the record of the pupil and the records of the district of any references to the expulsion action and the expulsion shall be deemed not to have occurred.

48924. The decision of the county board of education shall be final and binding upon the pupil and upon the governing board of the school district. The pupil and the governing board shall be notified of the final order of the county board, in writing, either by personal service or by certified mail. The order shall become final when rendered.

- Finality of County Board Decision

48925. As used in this article:

- Definitions
- Day

(a) "Day" means a calendar day unless otherwise specifically provided.

(b) "Expulsion" means a removal of a pupil from (1) the immediate supervision and control, or (2) the general supervision, of school personnel, as those terms are used in Section 46300.

-Expulsion

(c) "Schoolday" means a day upon which the schools of the district are in session or weekdays during the summer recess.

- Schoolday

(d) "Suspension" means removal of a pupil from ongoing instruction for adjustment purposes. However, "suspension" does not mean any of the following:

- Suspension

(1) Reassignment to another education program or class at the same school where the pupil will receive continuing instruction for the length of the day prescribed by the governing board for pupils of the same grade level.

(2) Referral to a certificated employee designated by the principal to advise pupils.

(3) Removal from the class, but without reassignment to

another class or program, for the remainder of the class period without sending the pupil to the principal or the principal's designee as provided in Section 48910. Removal from a particular class shall not occur more than once every five schooldays.

(e) "Pupil" includes a pupil's parent or guardian or legal counsel.

48926. Each county superintendent of schools in counties that operate community schools pursuant to Section 1980, in conjunction with superintendents of the school districts within the county, shall develop a plan for providing education services to all expelled pupils in that county. The plan shall be adopted by the governing board of each school district within the county and by the county board of education.

The plan shall enumerate existing educational alternatives for expelled pupils, identify gaps in educational services to expelled pupils, and strategies for filling those service gaps. The plan shall also identify alternative placements for pupils who are expelled and placed in district community day school programs, but who fail to meet the terms and conditions of their rehabilitation plan or who pose a danger to other district pupils, as determined by the governing board.

Each county superintendent of schools, in conjunction with the superintendents of the school districts, shall submit to the Superintendent of Public Instruction the county plan for providing educational services to all expelled pupils in the county no later than June 30, 1997, and shall submit a triennial update to the plan to the Superintendent of Public Instruction, including the outcome data pursuant to Section 48916.1, on June 30th thereafter.

CORPORAL PUNISHMENT PROHIBITION

(Education Code – Part 27)

49000. The Legislature finds and declares that the protection against corporal punishment, which extends to other citizens in other walks of like, should include children while they are under the control of the public schools. Children of school age are at the most vulnerable and impressionable period of their lives and it is wholly reasonable that the safeguards to the integrity and sanctity of their bodies should be, at this tender age, at least equal to that afforded to other citizens.

49001. (a) For the purposes of this section "corporal punishment" means the willful infliction of, or willfully causing the infliction of, physical pain on a pupil. An amount of force that is reasonable and necessary for a person employed by or engaged in a public school to quell a disturbance threatening physical injury to persons or damage to property, for purposes of self-defense, or to obtain possession of weapons or other dangerous objects within the control of the pupil, is not and shall not be construed to be corporal punishment within the meaning and intent of this section. Physical pain or discomfort caused by athletic competition or other such recreational activity, voluntarily engaged in by the pupil, is not and shall not be construed to be corporal punishment within the meaning and intent of this section.

- Definition of Corporal Punishment

(b) No person employed by or engaged in a public school shall inflict, or cause to be inflicted corporal punishment upon a pupil. Every resolution, bylaw, rule, ordinance, or other act or authority permitting or authorizing the infliction of corporal punishment upon a pupil attending a public school is void and unenforceable.

PUPIL RECORDS – PARENTAL ACCESS

(Education Code – Part 27)

(AB 3235 - Chapter 1288, Statutes of 1994)

49060. It is the intent of the Legislature to resolve potential conflicts between California law and the provisions of Public Law 93-380 regarding parental access to, and the confidentiality of, pupil records in order to insure the continuance of federal education funds to public educational institutions within the state, and to revise generally and update the law relating to such records.

- Legislative Intent; Effect of Law

This chapter applies to public agencies that provide educationally related services to pupils with disabilities pursuant to Chapter 26.5 (commencing with Section 7570) of Division 7 of Title 1 of the Government Code and to public agencies that educate pupils with disabilities in state hospitals or developmental centers and in youth and adult facilities.

This chapter shall have no effect regarding public community colleges, other public or private institutions of higher education, other governmental or private agencies which receive federal education funds unless described herein, or, except for Sections 49068 and 49069 and subdivision (b)(5) of Section 49076, private schools.

The provisions of this chapter shall prevail over the provisions of Section 12400 of this code and Chapter 3.5 (commencing with Section 6250) of Division 7 of Title 1 of the Government Code to the extent that they may pertain to access to pupil records.

CHALLENGING CONTENT OF RECORDS

(Education Code – Part 27)

(AB 3235 - Chapter 1288, Statutes of 1994)

49070. Following an inspection and review of a pupil's records, the parent of a pupil or former pupil of a school district may challenge the content of any pupil record.

- Procedures for Correcting or Removing Information

(a) The parent of a pupil may file a written request with the superintendent of the district to correct or remove any information recorded in the written records concerning his or her child which the parent alleges to be any of the following:

(1) Inaccurate.

(2) An unsubstantiated personal conclusion or inference.

(3) A conclusion or inference outside of the observer's area of competence.

(4) Not based on the personal observation of a named person with the time and place of the observation noted.

(5) Misleading.

(6) In violation of the privacy or other rights of the pupil.

(b) Within 30 days of receipt of a request pursuant to subdivision (a), the superintendent or the superintendent's designee shall meet with the parent and the certificated employee who recorded the information in question, if any, and if the employee is presently employed by the school district. The superintendent shall then sustain or deny the allegations.

If the superintendent sustains any or all of the allegations, he or she shall order the correction or the removal and destruction of the information. However, in accordance with Section 49066, the superintendent shall not order a pupil's grade to be changed unless the teacher who determined the grade is, to the extent practicable, given an opportunity to state orally, in writing, or both, the reasons for which the grade was given and is, to the extent practicable, included in all discussions relating to the changing of the grade.

If the superintendent denies any or all of the allegations and refuses to order the correction or the removal of the information, the parent may, within 30 days of the refusal, appeal the decision in writing to the governing board of the school district.

(c) Within 30 days of receipt of an appeal pursuant to subdivision (b), the governing board shall, in closed session with the parent and the certified employee who recorded the information in question, if any, and if the employee is presently employed by the school district, determine whether or not to sustain or deny the allegations.

If the governing board sustains any or all of the allegations, it shall order the superintendent to immediately correct or remove and destroy the information from the written records of the pupil. However, in accordance with Section 49066, the governing board shall not order a pupil's grade to be changed unless the teacher who determined the grade is, to the extent practicable, given an opportunity to state orally, in writing, or both, the reasons for which the grade was given and is, to the extent practicable included in all discussions relating to the changing of the grade.

The decision of the governing board shall be final.

Records of these administrative proceedings shall be maintained in a confidential manner and shall be destroyed one year after the decision of the governing board, unless the parent initiates legal proceedings relative to the disputed information within the prescribed period.

(d) If the final decision of the governing board is unfavorable to the parent, or if the parent accepts an unfavorable decision by the district superintendent, the parent shall have the right to submit a written statement of his or her objections to the information. This statement shall become a part of the pupil's school record until the information objected to is corrected or removed.

SPECIALIZED PHYSICAL HEALTH CARE SERVICES

(Education Code – Part 27)

(SB 1549 – Chapter 281, Statutes of 2000)

49423.5. (a) Notwithstanding the provisions of Section 49422, any individual with exceptional needs who requires specialized physical health care services, during the regular school day, may be assisted by the following individuals:

(1) Qualified persons who possess an appropriate credential issued pursuant to Section 44267, or hold a valid certificate of public health nursing issued by the State Department of Health Services; or

(2) Qualified designated school personnel trained in the administration of specialized physical health care provided they perform such services under the supervision of a school nurse, public health nurse, or licensed physician and surgeon.

(b) Specialized health care or other services that require medically related training shall be provided pursuant to the procedures prescribed by Section 49423.

(c) Persons providing specialized physical health care services shall also demonstrate competence in basic cardiopulmonary resuscitation and shall be knowledgeable of the emergency medical resources available in the community in which the services are performed.

(d) "Specialized physical health care services" as used in this section include catheterization, gavage feeding, suctioning, or other services that require medically related training.

(e) Regulations necessary to implement the provisions of this section shall be developed jointly by the State Department of Education and the State Department of Health Services, and adopted by the State Board of Education.

49423.5.1. On or before June 15, 2001, the State Department of Education shall review and make recommendations to the State Board of Education regarding any needed updates to the regulations adopted pursuant to subdivision (e) of Section 49423.5.

49423.6. (a) On or before June 15, 2001, the State Department of Education shall develop and recommend to the State Board of Education, and the board shall adopt regulations, regarding the administration of medication in the

- Qualifications of Service Providers

- Medically Related Training

- Providers Must Demonstrate CPR Competence

- Definition of Services

- Regulations

- Department of Education Reviews and Recommends Updates to Regulations

- Administration of Medication Regulations

public schools pursuant to Section 49423. These regulations shall be developed in consultation with parents, representatives of the medical and nursing professions, and other individuals jointly designated by the Superintendent of Public Instruction, the Advisory Commission on Special Education established pursuant to Section 33590, and the Department of Health Services. The Board of Registered Nursing may designate a liaison to consult with the Board of Education in the adoption of these regulations.

(b) Any regulations adopted pursuant to this section shall be limited to addressing a situation where a pupil's parent or legal guardian has initiated a request to have a local educational agency dispense medicine to a pupil, based on the written consent of the pupil's parent or legal guardian, for a specified medicine with a specified dosage, for a specified period of time, as prescribed by a physician or other authorized medical personnel.

- Limitation

EARLY DIAGNOSIS OF LEARNING DISABILITIES

(Education Code – Part 27)

(As Amended by AB 2587, Chapter 922, Statutes of 1994)

Article 1.3. Early Diagnosis of Learning Disabilities

49580. The State Department of Education shall develop a testing program to be utilized at the kindergarten grade level to determine which pupils have a potential for developing learning disability problems. The testing procedure shall include an overall screening test for learning disabilities and testing for dyslexia. To the extent feasible, the department shall use existing tests and screening instruments in developing the early diagnosis of the learning disabilities testing program. In developing the program, the department shall consult with experts in the areas of learning and reading difficulties, including, but not limited to, neurologists, psychologists, persons working in these areas in postsecondary educational institutions, teachers, school nurses, education consultants, school psychologists, and other persons with appropriate knowledge and experience in the detection and treatment of learning problems and reading difficulties in early grades.

- Testing Programs for Learning Disabilities

49582. The State Department of Education shall prescribe guidelines for the early diagnosis of the learning disabilities testing program and pilot project. The guidelines shall include but need not be limited to, all of the following:

(a) A definition of "pupils with the potential to develop learning disability problems," as used in this article.

(b) The methods and criteria for selecting one or more sites for the establishment of the pilot project.

(c) The number of sites to be selected for purposes of establishing the pilot project.

(d) Criteria for judging the results and effectiveness of the early diagnosis testing program, as well as criteria for determining the feasibility for implementing the program at the conclusion of the pilot project.

WITHHOLDING OF DIPLOMA OF GRADUATION

(Education Code – Part 28)

(AB 2907 - Chapter 1058, Statutes of 2000)

51412. No diploma, certificate or other document, except transcripts and letters of recommendation, shall be conferred on a pupil as evidence of completion of a prescribcd course of study or training, or of satisfactory attendance, unless the pupil has met the standards of proficiency in basic skills prescribed by the governing board of the high school district, or equivalent thereof.

WAGES TO INDIVIDUALS WITH EXCEPTIONAL NEEDS

(Education Code – Part 28)

(AB 369 - Chapter 1296, Statutes of 1993)

51768. The governing board of any school district providing work experience and work study education may provide for employment under the program of pupils in part-time jobs located in areas outside the district, either within this state or in a contiguous state, and the employment may be by any public or private employer. The districts may pay wages to persons receiving the training whether assigned within or without the district and may provide workers' compensation insurance as may be necessary, but no payments may be made to or for private employers. However, wages to individuals with exceptional needs, as defined in Section 56026, may be paid to or for private employers as part of work experience programs funded through the annual Budget Act for these individuals.

LOW INCIDENCE DISABILITIES AND VOCATIONAL EDUCATION OPPORTUNITIES

(Education Code – Part 28)

(As Amended by AB 3235, Chapter 1288, Statutes of 1994)

52315. Any visually impaired, orthopedically impaired, or deaf person who is not enrolled in a regular high school or community college program may attend a regional occupational center or regional occupational program on the same basis as a high school pupil. Additional special instruction and support services shall be provided to these persons.

- Admission of Certain Impaired Pupils

If the Superintendent of Public Instruction determines that there would be a duplication of effort to these impaired persons if a regional occupational center or regional occupational program provided services to them, in that other programs exist that are available to them, the superintendent may disapprove of the curriculum to provide programs to these impaired persons pursuant to Section 52309 and of any state funding made available pursuant to Section 41897 for these purposes.

SCHOOL-BASED PROGRAMS COORDINATION

(Education Code – Part 28)

(As Amended by AB 3235, Chapter 1288, Statutes of 1994)

52860. If a school district and school choose to include within the provisions of this article funds allocated pursuant to Part 30 (commencing with Section 56000), the school district shall comply with all requirements of that part, with

- Inclusion of Funds Allocated Pursuant to Special Education Programs

the following exceptions:

(a) Resource specialist program services, designated instruction and services, and team teaching for special day classes, except special day classes operating pursuant to Section 56364.1, may be provided to pupils who have not been identified as individuals with exceptional needs, provided that all identified individuals with exceptional needs are appropriately served and a description of the services is included in the schoolsite plan.

(b) Programs for individuals with exceptional needs shall be under the direction of credentialed special education personnel, but services may be provided entirely by personnel not funded by special education moneys, provided that all services specified in the individualized education program are received by the pupil.

52862. School districts and schools that choose to operate programs pursuant to Article 3 (commencing with Section 52850) shall insure compliance with all requirements of federal law.

- Compliance with Federal Law

52863. Any governing board, on behalf of a school site council, may request the State Board of Education to grant a waiver of this article. The State Board of Education may grant a request when it finds that the failure to do so would hinder the implementation or maintenance of a successful school-based coordinated program.

- Waiver of Provisions

If the State Board of Education approves a waiver request, the waiver shall apply only to the school or schools which requested the waiver and shall be effective for no more than two years. The State Board of Education may renew a waiver request.

(Persons interested in the School-Based Program Coordination Act should review all of Chapter 12 (commencing with Section 52800) of Part 28 of the Education Code.)

NOTE

(1) Education Code Section 46200.5 was amended by Senate Bill 178, Chapter 573, Statutes of 2001.

(2) Education Code Section 46201.5 was amended by Senate Bill 178, Chapter 573, Statutes of 2001.

(3) Education Code Section 48900 was amended by Assembly Bill 653, Chapter 484, Statutes of 2001.

(4) Education Code Section 48915 was amended by Senate Bill 166, Chapter 116, Statutes of 2001.

EDUCATION CODE – PART 32 – STATE SPECIAL SCHOOLS AND CENTERS

CHAPTER 1. CALIFORNIA SCHOOLS FOR THE DEAF

Article 1. Administration

59000. There are two state schools for the deaf, known and designated as the California School for the Deaf, Northern California, and the California School for the Deaf, Southern California. The term "California School for the Deaf" shall refer to both schools unless the context otherwise requires.

- Location and Designation of Schools

59001. The California School for the Deaf is part of the public school system of the state except that it derives no revenue from the State School Fund, and has for its object the education of the deaf who, because of their severe hearing loss and educational needs, cannot be provided an appropriate educational program and related services in the regular public schools.

- Purpose

59002. The California Schools for the Deaf are under the administration of the State Department of Education.

- Administration

The Superintendent of Public Instruction, in connection with the California Schools for the Deaf, shall do all of the following:

(a) Provide educational assessments and individual educational recommendations for individuals who are referred for those services pursuant to Section 56326.

(b) Maintain a comprehensive elementary educational program, including related services, for deaf individuals.

(c) Serve as a regional secondary educational program providing a comprehensive secondary education, including a full-range academic curriculum, appropriate prevocational and vocational preparation opportunities, and nonacademic and extracurricular activities.

59002.5. The Superintendent of Public Instruction, in connection with the California Schools for the Deaf and in cooperation with public and private agencies, may do one or more of the following:

- Duties of Superintendent of Public Instruction

(a) Serve as a demonstration school to promote personnel development through student teaching, in-service education, internships, professional observations for special education and related services personnel in cooperation with institutions of higher education and local education agencies.

of higher education and local education agencies.

(b) Serve as a resource center to develop and disseminate special curriculum, media teaching methods, and instructional materials adapted for deaf individuals, achievement tests and other assessment methods useful to the instruction of deaf individuals.

(c) Provide counseling and information services for parents, guardians, and families of deaf individuals, and public information about deafness to community groups and other agencies.

(d) Conduct experimental programs and projects to promote improvement in special education for deaf individuals.

(e) Promote and coordinate community and continuing education opportunities for deaf individuals utilizing existing community resources.

59003. The State Department of Education in relation to the California Schools for the Deaf shall:

— Duties of Department of Education

(a) Prescribe rules for the government of the schools.

(b) Appoint the superintendents and other officers and employees.

(c) Remove for cause any officer, teacher, or employee.

(d) Fix the compensation of officers, teachers, and employees.

59004. The superintendent of the school shall have had not less than three years' experience in the art of teaching the deaf and shall hold a credential issued by the State Board of Education authorizing him to teach in secondary schools of this state.

— Qualifications of School Superintendent

59005. The powers and duties of the superintendents of the schools are such as are assigned by the Superintendent of Public Instruction.

— Powers and Duties

59006. The Superintendent of Public Instruction may authorize the California Schools for the Deaf to establish and maintain teacher training courses designed to prepare teachers of the public schools and such other persons holding a credential issued by the State Board of Education as are recommended by the president of a campus of the California State University, to give instruction to the deaf and the hard of hearing. The Superintendent of Public Instruction shall prescribe standards for the admission of persons to the courses, and for the content of the courses.

— Teacher Training Courses

The California Schools for the Deaf may enter into agreements with the Trustees of the California State University, the University of California, or any other university or college accredited by the State Board of Education as a teacher training educational institution, to provide practice teaching required for issuance of the credential authorizing the holder to teach the deaf and severely hard of hearing. The agreement may provide a reasonable payment, for services rendered, to teachers of the California Schools for the Deaf who have practice teachers under their direction.

59007. The State Department of Education may employ any person, otherwise qualified, who has retired for service under either the Public Employees' Retirement System or the State Teachers' Retirement System as a substitute in a position requiring certification qualifications at the California Schools for the Deaf, except that the total of that service and any service rendered pursuant to Section 23919 shall not exceed 90 teaching days in any one fiscal year.

- Employment of Retired Teacher as Substitute

Article 2. Pupils

59020. Every deaf person between the ages of 3 and 21 years, who is a resident of the state and who meets the criteria set forth in this section, is entitled to an education in the California School for the Deaf free of charge.

- Eligibility and Priority for Admission

Priority in admission to the California School for the Deaf shall be given to elementary age deaf minors residing in sparsely populated regions and to secondary age deaf minors in need of a high school program, for whom appropriate comprehensive educational facilities and services are not available or cannot be reasonably provided by their local school districts or county educational agencies.

The criteria of admission to California Schools for the Deaf and Blind shall be administratively determined by the Superintendent of Public Instruction.

59023. If the parent or guardian of any pupil in the school is unable either himself or from the estate of the child to clothe the child, or pay for its transportation to and from school, or for necessary dental work, eye care, operations, and hospitalization of the child while at the school, or is unable either himself or from the estate of the child to reimburse the Department of Education for expenses incurred by it inn providing dental work, eye care, operations, or hospitalization for the child in an emergency, the parent or guardian may apply for a certificate to that effect to the superior court of the county of which the parent or guardian of the child is a resident. If the court is satisfied that the

- Inability to Pay Expenses

parent or guardian either himself or from the estate of the child is unable to pay for any such service, it shall issue a certificate to that effect. The application for the certificate may also be made to the court by the superintendent of the school.

59024. If it appears to the satisfaction of the court that the parent or guardian has sufficient pecuniary ability or that there are sufficient funds in the estate of the child to provide the service for the child or to reimburse the Department of Education for expenses incurred by it in providing the service for the child in an emergency, the court shall not issue the certificate, but shall, according to the nature of the application before it, either order the superintendent to provide the child with the service or order the parent or guardian either himself or from the estate of the child, as the court determines, to reimburse the Department of Education for expenses incurred by it in providing the service for the child in an emergency.

- Court Action Regarding Funds to Support the Child

59025. If the Department of Education is not reimbursed by the parent or guardian personally or from the estate of the child for expenditures made by the superintendent under the order of the court or if the parent or guardian does not comply with an order of the court to reimburse the Department of Education either personally or from the estate of the child for expenses incurred by it in providing the service for the child in an emergency, the superintendent may sue the parent or guardian, in the name of the state, to recover any money paid out by order of the court or due the Department of Education as reimbursement under an order of the court.

- Suit for Recovery

59026. All money expended under the authority of any such certificate for clothing and transportation, necessary dental work, eye care, operations, and hospitalization, and all money expended by the Department of Education for expenses incurred by it in providing dental work, eye care, operations, or hospitalization for the child in an emergency for which the Department of Education cannot be reimbursed by the parent or guardian of the child as shown by the certificate, constitutes a legal charge against the county from which the certificate is issued. Expenditures for clothing and transportation shall not exceed the sum of three hundred eight-five ($385) for the 1974-75 school year, and an amount thereafter which shall be adjusted annually in conformance with the Consumer Price Index, all items, of the Bureau of Labor Statistics of the United States Department of Labor,

- County Responsibility for Nonreimbursed Expenditures

measured for the calendar year next preceding the fiscal year to which it applies. The State Controller shall determine the amount authorized pursuant to this section for the 1975-76 school year and thereafter.

59027. The certificate shall be presented to the superintendent of the school. When the certificate shows that the parent or guardian of the child is unable either himself or from the estate of the child to clothe the child, or pay for his transportation to and from school, or for necessary dental work, eye care, operations, and hospitalization of the child while in school, the superintendent shall clothe the child and provide the transportation, necessary dental work, eye care, operations, and hospitalization. The expense of the services, or any of them, shall be advanced by the Department of Education out of money appropriated for the support of the school.

- Payment of Expenses

59028. Upon presentation to the county in which the certificate is issued, of an itemized claim, duly sworn to by the superintendent of the school before an officer authorized to administer oaths, for the expense for clothing, transportation, and other items provided and furnished under the authority of the certificate, or for the reimbursement of the Department of Education, the claim shall be processed and paid pursuant to the provisions of Chapter 4 (commencing with Section 29700) of Division 3 of Title 3 of the Government Code. The amount paid and all reimbursements of the Department of Education under this section shall be credited to the current appropriation for the support and maintenance of the school.

- Audit, Approval, and Credit of the Claim

59029. All pupils in the school shall be maintained at the expense of the state, except as provided in Sections 59021, 59023 to 59028, inclusive, 59030, and 59031.

- Maintenance of Pupils

59030. The governing board of each school district of residence shall, from the general fund of the school district, pay for the transportation cost of each pupil of the district in attendance at the California School for the Deaf as a day-class pupil.

- Payment of Transportation Cost for Day-Class Pupils by District of Residence

For determining the school district responsible under the provisions of this section for making the payment when the pupils reside in other than unified school district, pupils 15 years of age or older as of September 1 of each fiscal year shall be considered residents of the high school district, and pupils 14 years of age or under as of September 1 shall be considered residents of the elementary district.

59030.5. The Superintendent of Public Instruction shall allow to the California Schools for the Deaf, an amount not to exceed three hundred eighty-nine dollars ($389) per fiscal year per unit of average daily attendance of each deaf pupil attending one of the schools as a five-day residential pupil for the purpose of providing transportation to and from the pupil's home on weekends and school holiday periods. In no case shall the total apportionment made to the schools exceed the actual total transportation expenditures of the schools.

The administrators of such schools shall arrange for transportation of such pupils utilizing the most practical means including but not be limited to, commercial bus, rail, or air, charter bus or private passenger vehicle.

59031. Deaf persons not residents of this state may be admitted to the benefits of the school upon paying to the Department of Education the school year cost for the maintenance, care, and instruction of persons at the school, payable quarterly in advance. The cost of the care, maintenance, and instruction shall be determined by the Department of Education with the approval of the Department of Finance.

- Transportation of Pupils to and from Home on Weekends and School Holiday Periods

- Payment Required of Nonresidents

Article 3. Services

59040. The Department of Education, in connection with the California School for the Deaf, may establish and maintain a preschool and kindergarten service for the care and teaching of children under school age. The department shall prescribe the rules and regulations which shall govern the conduct of the preschool and kindergarten service, appoint such teachers as it determines necessary, and fix their salaries.

59041. The Department of Education, in connection with the California School for the Deaf, may offer courses of instruction to parents of a deaf child to assist and instruct the parents in the early care and training of such child, to train the child in play, and to do everything which will assure the child's physical, mental and social adjustment to its environment.

59042. The Superintendent of Public Instruction may authorize the California School for the Deaf to establish and maintain a testing center for deaf and hard-of-hearing minors. It shall be the purpose of this center to test hearing acuity and to give such other tests as may be necessary for advising parents and school authorities concerning an appropriate

- Authority to Establish Preschool and Kindergarten Service

- Courses of Instruction for Parents

- Testing Center

educational program for the child.

59043. Nothing in this article and no rule or regulation established thereunder shall authorize the compulsory physical examination or medical treatment of any child or minor if the parent or guardian objects on the ground that such examination or treatment is contrary to the religious beliefs of such parent or guardian.

- Prohibition of Compulsory Medical Treatment Over Objection of Parents

59044. The Department of Education, in connection with the California School for the Deaf which maintains automobile driver training courses, may purchase from available funds public liability, property damage, collision, fire, theft, and comprehensive automobile insurance for motor vehicles, whether owned by private parties or such school for the deaf, used in connection with such courses.

- Insurance for Automobile Driver Training Courses

59045. The Superintendent of Public Instruction, in conjunction with the California Schools for the Deaf, shall provide assessment and instructional planning services for individuals who are referred for those services pursuant to Section 56326.

- Educational Assessment Service

CHAPTER 2. CALIFORNIA SCHOOL FOR THE BLIND

Article 1. Administration

59100. There is one state school for the blind, known and designated as the California School for the Blind.

- Designation of School

59101. The California School for the Blind is a part of the public school system of the state except that it derives no revenue from the State School Fund, and has for its object the education of visually impaired, blind, and deaf-blind pupils who, because of their severe sensory loss and educational needs, cannot be provided an appropriate educational needs, cannot be provided an appropriate educational program and related services in the regular public schools.

- Purpose

59102. The California School for the Blind is under the administration of the State Department of Education.

- Administration

The Superintendent of Public Instruction, in connection with the California School for the Blind, shall do all of the following:

(a) Provide educational assessments and individual educational recommendations for individuals referred for those services pursuant to Section 56326.

(b) Maintain a comprehensive elementary and secondary educational program, including related services and nonacademic and extracurricular activities for visually impaired, blind, and deaf-blind individuals.

59102.5. The Superintendent of Public Instruction, in connection with the California School for the Blind and in cooperation with public and private agencies, may:

- Duties of Superintendent of Public Instruction

(a) Serve as a demonstration school to promote personnel development through student teaching, in-service education, internships, and professional observations for special education and related services personnel, in cooperation with institutions of higher education and local education agencies.

(b) Serve as a resource center to develop and disseminate special curriculum, media, teaching methods and instructional materials adapted for visually impaired, blind, and deaf-blind individuals, achievement tests, and other assessment methods useful to the instruction of visually impaired, blind, and deaf-blind individuals.

(c) Provide counseling and information services to parents, guardians, and families of visually impaired, blind, or deaf-blind individuals, and public information about sensory losses to community groups and other agencies.

(d) Conduct experimental programs and projects to

promote improvement in special education for visually impaired, blind, and deaf-blind individuals.

(e) Promote community and continuing education opportunities for visually impaired, blind, and deaf-blind individuals utilizing existing community resources.

59103. The Department of Education in relation to the California School for the Blind shall: — Duties of Department of Education

(a) Prescribe rules for the government of the school.

(b) Appoint the superintendent and other officers and employees.

(c) Remove for cause any officer, teacher, or employee.

(d) Fix the compensation of officers, teachers, and employees.

Article 2. Teaching Force

59110. The superintendent of the school shall have had not less than three years' experience in the art of teaching the blind and shall hold a credential issued by the State Board of Education authorizing him to teach in secondary schools of this state. — Qualifications of Superintendent

59111. The powers and duties of the superintendent of the school are such as are assigned by the Superintendent of Public Instruction. — Powers and Duties

59112. There is hereby created at the California School for the Blind the position of fieldworker to be appointed by the superintendent of the school with the approval of the Superintendent of Public Instruction. The fieldworker shall be a member of the teaching staff of the California School for the Blind and shall receive a salary fixed and payable in accordance with law. — Qualifications of Fieldworker

The fieldworker shall visit graduates and former pupils of the school in their homes to advise them regarding the extension and continuance of their education, to assist them in securing remunerative employment, to improve their economic condition in all possible ways, and to provide them with preparatory instruction found necessary for a selected occupation. The fieldworker shall be a person who has had special training for such work. Blindness shall not be grounds to disqualify a person for this position.

59113. The Department of Education may employ any person, otherwise qualified, who has retired for service under either the Public Employees' Retirement System or the State Teachers' Retirement System as a substitute in a position requiring certification qualifications at the California School — Employment of Retired Teacher as Substitute for the Blind; provided, that the total of such service and any service rendered pursuant to Section 23919 shall not exceed 90 teaching days in any one fiscal year.

Article 3. Pupils

59120. Every blind person resident of this state, of suitable age and capacity, is entitled to an education in the California School for the Blind free of charge.

- Entrance Qualifications

59123. All pupils in the school shall be maintained at the expense of the state, except as provided in Sections 59121, 59124 to 59128, inclusive, and 59131.

- Maintenance of Pupils

59124. The governing board of each school district of residence shall, from the general fund of the school district, pay for the transportation cost of each pupil of the district in attendance at the California School for the Blind as a day-class pupil.

- Payment of Transportation Cost by District of Residence for Day-Class Pupils

For determining the school district responsible under the provisions of this section for making the payment when the pupils reside in other than a unified school district, pupils 15 years of age or older as of September 1 of each fiscal year shall be considered residents of the high school district, and pupils 14 years of age or under as of September 1 shall be considered residents of the elementary district.

59124.5. The Superintendent of Public Instruction shall allow to the California School for the Blind, an amount not to exceed three hundred eighty-nine dollars ($389) per fiscal year per unit of average daily attendance of each blind pupil attending the school as a five-day residential pupil for the purpose of providing transportation to and from the pupil's home on weekends and school holiday periods. In no case shall the total apportionment made to the school exceed the actual total transportation expenditures of the school.

- Transportation of Pupils to and from Home on Weekends and School Holiday Periods

The administrators of such schools shall arrange for transportation of such pupils utilizing the most practical means including, but not limited to, commercial bus, rail, or air, charter bus or private passenger vehicle.

59125. If the parent or guardian of any pupil in the school is unable either himself or from the estate of the child to clothe the child, or pay for its transportation to and from school, or for necessary dental work, eye care, operations, and hospitalization of the child while at the school, or is unable either himself or from the estate of the child to reimburse the Department of Education for expenses incurred by it in providing dental work, eye care, operations, or

- Inability to Pay Expenses

hospitalization for the child in an emergency, the parent or guardian may apply for a certificate to that effect to the superior court of the county of which the parent or guardian of the child is resident. If the court is satisfied that the parent or guardian either himself or from the estate of the child is unable to pay for any such service, it shall issue a certificate to that effect. The application for the certificate may also be made to the court by the superintendent of the school.

59126. The certificate shall be presented to the superintendent of the school and the superintendent when the certificate shows the parent or guardian of the child is unable either himself or from the estate of the child to clothe the child, or pay for his transportation to and from school, or for necessary dental work, eye care, operations, and hospitalization of the child while in school, shall clothe the child and provide the transportation, dental work, eye care, operations, and hospitalization. The expense of the services, or any of them, shall be advanced by the Department of Education out of money appropriated for the support of the school.

- Payment of Expenses

59127. All money expended under the authority of any such certificate for clothing and transportation, necessary dental work, eye care, operations and hospitalization, and all money expended by the Department of Education for expenses incurred by it in providing dental work, eye care, operations, or hospitalization for the child in an emergency for which the Department of Education cannot be reimbursed by the parent or guardian of the child as shown by the certificate, constitutes a legal charge against the county from which the certificate is issued. Expenditures for clothing and transportation shall not exceed the sum of three hundred eighty-five dollars ($385) for the 1974-75 school year, and an amount thereafter which shall be adjusted annually in conformance with the Consumer Price Index, all items, of the Bureau of Labor Statistics of the United States Department of Labor, measured for the calendar year next preceding the fiscal year to which it applies. The State Controller shall determine the amount authorized pursuant to this section for the 1975-76 school year and thereafter.

- County Responsibility for Nonreimbursed Expenditures

59128. Upon presentation to the county in which the certificate is issued, of an itemized claim, duly sworn to by the superintendent of the school before an officer authorized to administer oaths, for the expense for clothing, transportation, and other items provided and furnished under the authority of the certificate, or for the reimbursement of

- Presentation, Audit, Approval of Claim Against County

the Department of Education, the claim shall be processed and paid pursuant to the provisions of Chapter 4 (commencing with Section 29700) of Division 3 of Title 3 of the Government Code. The amount paid and all reimbursements of the Department of Education under this section shall be credited to the current appropriation for the support and maintenance of the school.

59129. If it appears to the satisfaction of the court that the parent or guardian has sufficient pecuniary ability or that there are sufficient funds in the estate of the child to provide the service for the child or to reimburse the Department of Education for expenses incurred by it on providing the service for the child in an emergency, the court shall not issue the certification, but shall according to the nature of the application before it, either order the superintendent to provide the child with the service, or order the parent or guardian either himself or from the estate of the child, as the court determines, to reimburse the Department of Education for expenses incurred by it in providing the service for the child in an emergency.

- Court Powers

59130. If the Department of Education is not reimbursed by the parent or guardian personally or from the estate of the child for expenditures made by the superintendent under the order of the court or if the parent or guardian does not comply with an order of the court to reimburse the Department of Education either personally or from the estate of the child for expenses incurred by it in providing the service for the child in an emergency the superintendent may sue the parent or guardian, in the name of the state, to recover any money paid out by order of the court or due the Department of Education as reimbursement under an order of the court.

- Suit by Department to Recover Money Paid Out or Due a Reimbursement

59131. Blind persons not residents of this state may be admitted to the benefits of the school upon paying the Department of Education the sum of the school year for the maintenance, care, and instruction of persons at the school, payable in quarterly in advance. The cost of the care, maintenance, and instruction shall be determined by the Department of Education with the approval of the Department of Finance.

- Payment Required of Nonresidents

Article 4. Services and Courses

59140. The Department of Education, in connection with the California School for the Blind, shall establish and

- Kindergarten

maintain a kindergarten service for the care and teaching of children under school age. The department shall prescribe the rules and regulations which shall govern the conduct of the kindergarten service, appoint such teachers as it determines necessary, and fix their salaries.

59141. The Department of Education shall create the position of visiting teacher to blind children of preschool age. With the consent of the parents of any blind child of preschool age it shall be the duties of such visiting teacher to assist and instruct the parents in the early care and training of said child, to train the child in play, and to do everything which will assure the child's physical, mental and social adjustment to its environment. The Department of Education shall maintain a sufficient number of visiting teachers to adequately serve the need of parents of preschool blind children in accordance with the known number of such children. In any event the caseload of each visiting teacher shall not exceed a number of clients that can be adequately and fully served.

- Visiting Teachers

59142. The Department of Education, in addition to the teaching and education of the blind of suitable age, shall adopt measures and prescribe rules for the giving of vocational training to the pupils at the school, in order that they may be equipped upon their graduation to engage in occupations or industries by which they may become self-supporting. The board shall determine the nature and scope of the vocational training, with the view of best adapting the blind to follow useful and productive pursuits, after the completion of their education.

- Vocational Training

59143. The Superintendent of Public Instruction may authorize the California School for the Blind to establish and maintain, either independently or in cooperation with the University of California or Trustees of the California State University, teacher training courses for teachers of the blind. The Superintendent of Public Instruction shall establish standards for the admission of persons to the courses, and for the content of the courses.

- Teacher Training

The California School for the Blind may enter into one or more agreements with the Trustees of the California State University, the University of California, or any other university or college accredited by the State Board of Education as a teacher training educational institution, to provide practice teaching required for issuance of the credentials authorizing the holder to teach visually impaired, blind, or deaf-blind individuals, or provide orientation and mobility instruction. The agreement or agreements may provide for a reasonable payment, for services rendered, to teachers of the California School for the Blind who have practice teachers under their direction.

59144. The Superintendent of Public Instruction, in conjunction with the California School for the Blind, shall provide assessment and instructional planning services for individuals who are referred for those services pursuant to Section 56326.

- Instructional Planning Service for the Blind

CHAPTER 2.5. TUBERCULOSIS TESTING IN SPECIAL SCHOOLS

59150. Students attending the California School for the Deaf, Northern California, California School for the Deaf, Southern California, and California School for the Blind shall be tested for exposure to tuberculosis at least once every two years. The results of these tests shall be provided to the director of the appropriate special school. The parent or guardian of the student shall be responsible for the cost, if any, of the test.

- Testing at Least Once Every Two Years

CHAPTER 3. DIAGNOSTIC CENTERS

Article 1. Administration

59200. There are three diagnostic centers, to be known and designated as Diagnostic Center, Northern California, Diagnostic Center, Central California, and Diagnostic Center, Southern California.

- Designation of Centers

59201. The diagnostic centers are a part of the public school system of the state, except that they derive no revenue from the State School Fund, and have for their object the diagnosis of disabled children, and the determination of the treatment and educational program for those children. These centers provide temporary residence for children, who, by reason of their disabilities, need educational diagnostic services not available in regular public school classes.

- Status and Purpose

59202. The centers are under the administration of the Superintendent of Public Instruction.

- Administration

59203. The Superintendent of Public Instruction, in relation to the diagnostic centers, shall do all of the following:

- Duties of Superintendent of Public Instruction

(a) Prescribe rules for the government of the centers.

(b) Appoint the superintendents of the centers and

other officers and employees.

(c) Remove for cause any officer, teacher, or employee.

(d) Fix the compensation of teachers.

(e) Determine the length of, and the time for, vacations of teachers.

(f) Contract with the University of California, or with other public or private hospitals or schools of medicine, for the establishment and maintenance of diagnostic service and treatment centers for disabled children.

59204. The Superintendent of Public Instruction, in connection with the diagnostic centers, also shall do all of the following:

- Special Services and Assessments

(a) Make comprehensive diagnostic assessments of individuals referred for that service pursuant to Section 56326.

(b) Provide instructional planning services for individuals assessed under subdivision (a).

(c) Provide counseling services for parents, guardians, and families of disabled children.

(d) Maintain a model assessment service and demonstration classrooms to develop appropriate individual educational programs for pupils and to assist local school districts in providing appropriate programs and services for disabled children.

59204.5. The Superintendent of Public Instruction, in connection with the diagnostic centers and in cooperation with public and private agencies, may:

- Experimental Assessment Projects; Demonstration School

(a) Conduct experimental assessment projects designed to meet needs of those categories of disabled children selected by the Superintendent of Public Instruction.

(b) Serve as a demonstration program to promote personnel development through student teaching, in-service education, internships, and professional observations for special education and related services personnel, in cooperation with institutions of higher education and local education agencies.

Article 2. Teaching Force

59210. The powers and duties of the superintendents of the diagnostic centers are such as are assigned by the Superintendent of Public Instruction.

- Powers and Duties of Superintendent

59211. The Superintendent of Public Instruction may, in cooperation with an accredited college or university, authorize the diagnostic centers to establish and maintain

- Teacher Training Courses

teacher training courses designed to prepare teachers to
teacher training courses designed to prepare teachers to
instruct disabled children in special classes in the public
school system. The Superintendent of Public Instruction, in
cooperation with an accredited college or university, shall
prescribe standards for the admission of persons to the
courses, and for the contents of the courses. Courses
conducted in the diagnostic centers shall be counted toward
requirements of a credential in the area of the educationally
handicapped upon the establishment of the credential.

The diagnostic centers may enter into one or more
agreements with Trustees of the California State University,
the University of California, or any other university or
college accredited by the State Board of Education as a
teacher training educational institution, to provide practice
teaching required for issuance of the credential authorizing
the holder to teach the educationally handicapped. The
agreement or agreements may provide for a reasonable
payment, for services rendered, to teachers of the diagnostic
centers who have practice teachers under their direction.

Article 3. Pupils

59220. Every resident of California less than 21 years of
age, of suitable age and capacity, as determined by means of
diagnosis at the diagnostic centers, is entitled to services, free
of charge.

- Entrance Qualifications and Nonresident Charges

Disabled children who are not residents of California may
be admitted to a diagnostic center upon paying to the State
Department of Education, quarterly in advance, the actual
support cost at the average cost of maintaining pupils in the
center for the period in question. This cost shall be
determined by the State Department of Education with the
approval of the Department of Finance.

59223. The Superintendent of Public Instruction shall
allow to the diagnostic centers an amount not to exceed three
hundred eighty-nine dollars ($389) per fiscal year per unit of
average daily attendance of each pupil attending one of the
diagnostic centers as a five-day residential pupil for the
purpose of providing transportation to and from the pupil's
home on weekends and school holiday periods. In no case
shall the total apportionment made to the centers exceed the
actual total transportation expenditures of the centers.

- Transportation of Pupils to and from Home on Weekends and School Holiday Periods

The administrators of the centers shall arrange for
transportation of the pupils, utilizing the most practical

means, including, but not limited to, commercial bus, rail, or air, charter bus, or private passenger vehicle.

CHAPTER 4. FINANCE

Article 1. Local Contribution

59300. Notwithstanding any provision of this part to the contrary, the district of residence of the parent or guardian of any pupil attending a state-operated school pursuant to this part, excluding day pupils, shall pay the school of attendance for each pupil an amount equal to 10 percent of the excess annual cost of education of pupils attending a state-operated school pursuant to this part.

- Ten Percent Excess Cost

INSTRUCTIONAL MATERIALS
(Selected Sections)
(Education Code – Part 33)

REQUIREMENTS, PUBLISHERS
AND MANUFACTURERS

(As Amended by AB 306, Chapter 736, Statutes of 2001)

60061. (a) A publisher or manufacturer shall do all of the following:

(1) Furnish the instructional materials offered by the publisher at a price in this state that, including all costs of transportation to that place, does not exceed the lowest price at which the publisher offers those instructional materials for adoption or sale to any state or school district in the United States.

(2) Automatically reduce the price of those instructional materials to any governing board to the extent that reductions are made elsewhere in the United States.

(3) Provide any instructional materials free of charge in this state to the same extent as that received by any state or school district in the United States.

(4) Guarantee that all copies of any instructional materials sold in this state are at least equal in quality to the copies of those instructional materials that are sold elsewhere in the United States, and are kept revised, free from all errors, and up to date as may be required by the state board.

(5) Not in any way, directly or indirectly, become associated or connected with any combination in restraint of trade in instructional materials, or enter into any understanding, agreement, or combination to control prices or restrict competition in the sale of instructional materials for use in this state.

(6) Maintain a representative, office, or depository in the State of California or arrange with an independently owned and operated depository in the State of California to receive and fill orders for instructional materials.

(7) Provide to the state, at no cost, computer files or other electronic versions of each state-adopted literary title and the right to transcribe, reproduce, modify, and distribute the material in braille, large print if the publisher does not offer a large print edition, recordings, American Sign Language videos for the deaf, or other specialized accessible media exclusively for use by pupils with visual disabilities or other

- Publishers' and Manufacturers' Duties (1)

D-18

disabilities that prevent use of standard instructional materials. Computer files or other electronic versions of materials adopted shall be provided within 30 days of request by the state as needed for the purposes described in this subdivision as follows:

(A) Computer files or other electronic versions of literary titles shall maintain the structural integrity of the standard instructional materials, be compatible with commonly used braille translation and speech synthesis software, and include corrections and revisions as may be necessary.

(B) Computer files or other electronic versions of nonliterary titles, including science and mathematics, shall be provided when technology is available to convert those materials to a format that maintains the structural integrity of the standard instructional materials and is compatible with braille translation and speech synthesis software.

(b) Upon the willful failure of the publisher or manufacturer to comply with the requirements of this section, the publisher or manufacturer shall be liable to the governing board in the amount of three times the total sum that the publisher or manufacturer was paid in excess of the price required under paragraphs (1), (2), and (5) of subdivision (a), and in the amount of three times the total value of the instructional materials and services that the governing board is entitled to receive free of charge under subdivision (a).

STATE INSTRUCTIONAL MATERIALS FUND

(Education Code – Part 33)

(As Amended by AB 804, Chapter 734, Statutes of 2001)

60240. (a) The State Instructional Materials Fund is hereby continued in existence in the State Treasury. The fund shall be a means of annually funding the acquisition of instructional materials as required by the Constitution of the State of California. Notwithstanding Section 13340 of the Government Code, all money in the fund is continuously appropriated to the State Department of Education without regard to fiscal years for carrying out the purposes of this part. It is the intent of the Legislature that the fund shall provide for flexibility of instructional materials.

- Continued Existence of Fund; Continuous Appropriation; Administration; Encumbrance of Fund (2)

(b) The State Department of Education shall administer the fund under policies established by the state board.

(c) (1) The state board shall encumber part of the fund to pay for accessible instructional materials to accommodate pupils who are visually impaired pursuant to Sections 60312 and 60313 or have other disabilities and are unable to access the general curriculum.

(2) The state board may encumber funds, in an amount not to exceed two hundred thousand dollars ($200,000), for replacement of instructional materials, obtained by a school district with its allowance that are lost or destroyed by reason of fire, theft, natural disaster, or vandalism.

(3) The state board may encumber funds for the costs of warehousing and transporting instructional materials it has acquired.

MEDIA ACCESSIBLE TO PUPILS WITH VISUAL IMPAIRMENTS

(Education Code – Part 33)

(As Amended by SB 152, Chapter 413, Statutes of 1995)

60312. The state board shall make available copies of adopted textbooks and other state adopted print materials in large print and other accessible media for pupils enrolled in the elementary schools whose visual acuity is 10/70 or less or who have other visual impairments making the use of these textbooks and alternate formats necessary. The state board shall make available adopted textbooks in braille characters for pupils enrolled in elementary schools whose corrected visual acuity is 20/200 or less. The state board may purchase or contract for the development of those materials.

- Availability of Textbooks and Other Print Materials in Media Accessible to Pupils with Visual Impairments

CLEARINGHOUSE-DEPOSITORY

(Education Code – Part 33)

(As Amended by AB 804, Chapter 734, Statutes of 2001)

60313. (a) The Superintendent of Public Instruction shall maintain a central clearinghouse-depository and duplication center for the design, production, modification, and distribution of Braille, large print, special recordings, and other accessible versions of instructional materials for use by pupils with visual impairments or other disabilities who are enrolled in the public schools of California.

(b) Assistive devices placed in the depository shall consist

- Central Clearinghouse-Depository and Duplication Center for Specialized Items (3)

of items designed for use by pupils with visual impairments.

(c) The instructional materials in specialized media shall be available, in a manner determined by the State Board of Education, to other pupils with disabilities enrolled in the public schools of California who are unable to progress in the general curriculum using conventional print copies of textbooks and other study materials.

(d) The specialized textbooks, reference books, recordings, study materials, tangible apparatus, equipment, and other similar items shall be available for use by students with visual impairments enrolled in the public community colleges, the California State University, and the University of California.

NOTE

(1) Education Code Section 60061 was amended by Assembly Bill 306, Chapter 736, Statutes of 2001.
(2) Education Code Section 60240 was amended by Assembly Bill 804, Chapter 734, Statutes of 2001.
(3) Education Code Section 60313 was amended by Assembly Bill 804, Chapter 734, Statutes of 2001.

NONCODIFIED SECTIONS

Noncodified sections of statutes have the same force of law as codified sections but they do not appear in a specific code (e.g. Education Code or Government Code). If a noncodified section becomes law, it appears in the chaptered version of the legislative bill.

SPECIAL EDUCATION PROGRAMS FOR HARD-OF-HEARING OR DEAF PUPILS

(Noncodified Sections)

(AB 1836 - Chapter 1126, Statutes of 1994)

Section 5. By amending Sections 56000.5, 56001, and 56345 of the Education Code by Sections 1, 2, 2.5, and 4 of this act, and by adding Section 56026.2 to the Education Code by Section 3, it is the intent of the Legislature to ensure that state law complies with the requirements of federal law under the Individuals with Disabilities Education Act (20 U.S.C. Sec. 1400 et seq.)

- Legislative Intent

Section 6. The changes made to Section 56000.5, 56001, and 56345 of the Education Code by Sections 1, 2, 2.5, and 4 and the provisions of Section 56026.2, as added to the Education Code by Section 3, shall be implemented only to the extent that funds are specifically appropriated for that purpose in the annual Budget Act. Notwithstanding Section 17610 of the Government Code, if the Commission on State Mandates determines that this act contains costs mandated by the state, reimbursement to local agencies and school districts for those costs shall be made pursuant to Part 7 (commencing with Section 17500) of Division 4 of Title 2 of the Government Code. If the statewide cost of the claim for reimbursement does not exceed one million dollars ($1,000,000), reimbursement shall be made from the State Mandates Claims Fund. Notwithstanding Section 17580 of the Government Code, unless otherwise specified in this act, the provisions of this act shall become operative on the same date that the act takes effect pursuant to the California Constitution.

- Implemented to Extent Funds Are Appropriated

INDIVIDUALIZED EDUCATION PROGRAM FOR VISUALLY IMPAIRED PUPILS

(Noncodified Sections)

(AB 2445 - Chapter 998, Statutes of 1994)

Section 1. The Legislature hereby finds and declares the following:

    (a) Functionally blind pupils and some pupils with other severe visual impairments who have the ability to read require instruction in braille if they are to maximize their academic potential and have the greatest chances for success throughout their lives. There are pupils in California who are visually impaired for whom braille is the appropriate reading method but who are not receiving instruction in braille. In the development of the individualized education programs for pupils who are visually impaired, there is a presumption that proficiency in braille reading and writing is essential for the pupils' satisfactory education progress and independent functioning.

    (b) The most appropriate reading medium or media for an individual pupil is that which is most efficient in terms of comprehension, speed, and stamina, commensurate with the pupil's ability and grade level. It is not the intention of the Legislature to require the exclusive use of braille if other educational media are appropriate for the pupil's educational needs. It is the intent of the Legislature, however, that all pupils who are visually impaired be given the opportunity to be assessed to determine the appropriate reading medium or media of each pupil.

— Legislative Findings and Declarations

Section 4. It is the intent of the Legislature in enacting this act not to exceed any requirements mandated by federal law or its implementing regulations.

— Not to Exceed Federal Mandate

RESTRAINING DEVICES IN SCHOOLBUSES

(Noncodified Section)

(AB 2798 - Chapter 513, Statutes of 1994)

Section 1. The Legislature recognizes that disabled pupils are entitled to safe and secure transportation. It is the intent of the Legislature, therefore, that schoolbuses be properly

— Transporting Pupils Confined to Wheelchairs

of the Legislature, therefore, that schoolbuses be properly equipped with restraining devices to safely transport pupils who are confined to wheelchairs. It is also the intent of the Legislature that no school district deny transportation to any pupil due to the incompatibility of a wheelchair and bus securement systems.

COMMUNITY MENTAL HEALTH SERVICES; OUT-OF-STATE PLACEMENTS

(Noncodified Section)

(AB 2726 - Chapter 654, Statutes of 1996)

Section 1. (a) The fiscal and program responsibilities of community mental health services shall be the same regardless of the location of placement. Local education agencies and community mental health services shall make out-of-state placements under Chapter 26.5 (commencing with Section 7570 of Division 7 of Title 1 of the Government Code only if other options have been considered and are determined to be inappropriate. In making these placements, local education agencies and community mental health services shall comply with relevant sections of the Education Code, including Section 56365.

- Fiscal and Program Responsibilities

(b) This section shall become operative on July 1, 1997.

AB 602 LEGISLATIVE FINDINGS, DECLARATIONS, AND INTENT

(Noncodified Sections)

(AB 602 - Chapter 854, Statutes of 1997)

Section 1. (a) This act shall be known and may be cited as the Poochigian and Davis Special Education Reform Act.

- Poochigian and Davis Special Education Reform Act

(b) The Legislature hereby finds and declares the following:

- Legislative Findings and Declarations

(1) On December 1, 1995, approximately 9.4 percent of the 5,467,224 pupils enrolled in kindergarten and grades 1 to 12, inclusive, in California required some form of special education programming or service.

(2) Significant inequities in funding for special education exist in California. Special education funding derives from the value of a local education agency's various instructional

the value of a local education agency's various instructional personnel services unit rates plus the funds it generates from multiplying the total unit values by the agency's support services ratio. Since these values and ratios vary greatly among the local education agencies, widely disparate funding amounts are generated for the same type of program among local education agencies.

(3) In the 1994-95 fiscal year, the following range in funding amounts existed for each of the four types of instructional personnel services units providing services to the nonseverely disabled:

Unit Type	Lowest	Highest
Special classes and centers	$31,137	$80,044
Resource specialists	$26,064	$84,579
Designated instruction and services	$30,080	$91,760
Instructional aides	$ 9,601	$49,883

(4) The range in funding amounts in the 1994-95 fiscal year was even greater for instructional personnel services units for special education services for severely disabled pupils in special education classes, as follows:

Unit Type	Lowest	Highest
Special classes and centers	$31,137	$89,181
Instructional aides	$ 9,601	$55,577

(5) Equalization aid has not been provided to correct the disparities in special education funding since the Master Plan for Special Education was enacted for statewide implementation in 1980. Consequently, funding figures, based primarily on expenditures made in the base year 1979-80, are still being used.

(6) In recent years, some additional money has been provided to school districts to equalize revenue limit funding for regular education programs, and school districts with lower base revenue limits have had those revenue limits increased, resulting in those school districts attaining a base revenue limit that is closer to the statewide average.

(7) In February 1994, the Legislative Analyst, in the "Analysis of the 1994-95 Budget Bill," cited a number of major problems with the state's current special education funding formula. Among the shortfalls cited included:

(A) Unjustified funding variation among local education agencies.

(B)   Unnecessary complexity.

(C)   Constraint on local innovation and on responses to changing requirements.

(D)   Inappropriate fiscal incentives related to special education placements.

(8)   The current method of funding special education programs unduly influences the manner and methods through which special education services are provided and inhibits the ability of local education agencies to appropriately individualize the provision of special education services to individuals with exceptional needs.

(9)   Existing law provides for the annual calculation of additional instructional personnel services necessary to address the enrollment growth in special education programs. Over the last four years, the number of additional instructional personnel service units actually funded to address the enrollment growth has been well under one-half the number for which the calculation provides:

Fiscal Year	Calculated Need	Amount Funded	Percent Funded
1993-94	$ 87,259,893	$ 30, 376,332	34.8
1994-95	106,704,203	51,947,000	48.7
1995-96	99,634,692	31,589,000	31.7
1996-97	134,444,158	56,887,715	42.3

(10)   Individuals with exceptional needs and their families are protected by provisions of the Individuals with Disabilities Education Act (20 U.S.C. Sec. 1400 et seq.), Section 504 of the Rehabilitation Act of 1973 (29 U.S.C. Sec. 794), the Americans with Disabilities Act of 1990 (42 U.S.C. Sec. 12101 et seq.), and federal regulations relating thereto. These protections include, but are not limited to, the following:

(A)   Individuals with exceptional needs shall be identified, located, and appropriately evaluated in a nondiscriminatory manner.

(B)   Individuals with exceptional needs have the right to a free appropriate public education pursuant to an individualized education program developed by local education agency representatives in partnership with the individual's parents.

(C)   Individuals with exceptional needs and their families shall receive prior notification whenever a local educational agency intends or refuses to initiate the evaluation of the individual with exceptional needs.

(D) Whenever a local educational agency intends to change the educational placement of an individual with exceptional needs, the individual with exceptional needs and his or her family may review the contents of any records or other materials used to make educational decisions regarding the individual with exceptional needs.

(E) Due process protections, including the protection of seeking redress in the courts

(11) The protections set forth in paragraph (10) and other requirements of federal law and regulations shall not be adversely affected or negated by any changes to state law which may occur form this act.

Section 2. It is the intent of the Legislature, in enacting this act, to accomplish the following: - Legislative Intent

(a) To establish a funding mechanism that:

(1) Ensures greater equity in funding among special education local plan areas so that pupils with exceptional needs receive the necessary level of services regardless of their geographical location.

(2) Eliminates financial incentives to inappropriately place pupils in special education programs.

(3) Recognizes the interaction among funding for special education programs and services, revenue limits for school districts, and funding for categorical programs.

(4) Phases in the newly developed funding formula on a gradual basis so as not to disrupt educational services to pupils enrolled in general or special education programs.

(5) Requires fiscal and program accountability in a manner that ensures effective services are provided to pupils who require special education services in compliance with federal laws and regulations and ensures that federal and state funds are used for the intended special education purposes.

(6) Establishes a funding formula that is understandable and avoids unnecessary complexity.

(b) To recognize and establish the following principles to guide the new funding mechanism:

(1) Allocations to special education local plan areas encourage and support an areawide approach to service delivery that incorporates collaborative administration and coordination of special education services within an area, allows for the tailoring of the organizational structures to differing population densities and demographic attributes, and provides local flexibility for the planning and provision of special education services in an efficient and cost-effective

manner.

(2) Allocations to special education local plan areas are best based on a neutral factor such as total pupil population in the special education local plan area.

(3) Local education agencies need the flexibility to adopt innovative approaches to the delivery of special education services.

(c) It is also the intent of the Legislature that alternative delivery systems that include effective schoolwide and districtwide screening practices, the development of effective teaching and intervention strategies, and regular and special education program collaboration, including team teaching, consultation, and home-school partnerships, be fully utilized in the identification process so as to prevent pupils from needing special education services.

(d) It is further the intent of the Legislature that the new funding mechanism based on total pupil population, does not create, in any way, a disincentive to identify and serve pupils with exceptional needs or eliminate or reduce the continuum of placement options.

Section 3. The Legislature further finds and declares as follows:

- Further Legislative Findings and Declarations

(a) It is the intent of the Legislature to equalize special education program funding imbalances among local education agencies in the 1997-98 fiscal year, pursuant to Chapter 7.1 (commencing with Section 56835) of Part 30 of the Education Code, only to the extent that funds are provided for that purpose in the Budget Act of 1997 or in this act. It is further the intent of the Legislature to implement a population-based funding formula in the 1998-99 fiscal year, pursuant to Chapter 7.2 (commencing with Section 56836) of Part 30 of the Education Code, to allocate special education program funds instead of instructional personnel service units to the special education local plan areas, and to equalize per-pupil funding among the special education local plan areas over a multiyear period, only to the extent that funds are appropriated for those purposes in the annual Budget Act.

(b) As part of the new special education funding system, this act proposes to achieve local administrative savings by simplifying the administrative processes of the current funding system that govern the activities of special education local plan areas, school districts, and county offices of education. Specifically, this act eliminates the process-intensive J-50 claim system that drains local resources away from providing services to completing numerous, lengthy reports in order to secure state funding for special education. To ensure program accountability when the resource-based funding system is replaced by the population-based funding system, this act also provides for additional information to be included in each local plan that will provide the public and other units of government specific information on how services shall be provided and funded. The Legislature finds and declares that the administrative savings resulting from this act will more than offset any increased costs from any new administrative workload resulting from this act.

(c) It is further the intent of the Legislature that the funds provided for equalization entitlements pursuant to this act shall fully compensate any mandated costs associated with maintaining pupil caseload for the purpose of any cost claim filed with the Commission on State Mandates.

Section 66. (a) The Legislature finds and declares as follows:

(1) The Individuals with Disabilities Education Act (20 U.S.C. Sec. 1400 et seq.), as amended by the Individuals with Disabilities Education Act Amendments of 1997 (105 P.L. 17), effective in part upon enactment and in part as further specified in the act, provides as follows:

"Sec. 612. STATE ELIGIBILITY

(a) In general.--A State is eligible for assistance under this part for a fiscal year if the State demonstrates to the satisfaction of the Secretary that the State has in effect policies and procedures to ensure that it meets each of the following conditions:

[Language Omitted]

(5) LEAST RESTRICTIVE ENVIRONMENT-

(A) IN GENERAL-To the maximum extent appropriate, children with disabilities, including children in public or private institutions or other care facilities, are educated with children who are not disabled, and special classes, separate schooling, or other removal of children with disabilities from the regular educational environment occurs only when the nature or severity of the disability of a child is such that education in regular classes with the use of supplementary aids and services cannot be achieved satisfactorily.

(B) ADDITIONAL REQUIREMENT-

(i) IN GENERAL-If the State uses a funding mechanism by which the State distributes State funds on the basis of the type of setting in which a child is served, the funding

- Legislative Findings and Declarations Regarding the Federal Individuals with Disabilities Education Act

mechanism does not result in placements that violate the requirements of subparagraph (A).

(ii) ASSURANCE-If the State does not have policies and procedures to ensure compliance with clause (i), the State shall provide the Secretary an assurance that it will revise the funding mechanism as soon as feasible to ensure that such mechanism does not result in such placements.

[Language Omitted]"

(16) PERFORMANCE GOALS AND INDICATORS--The State--

(A) has established goals for the performance of children with disabilities in the State that--

(i) will promote the purposes of this Act, as stated in section 601 (d); and

(ii) are consistent, to the maximum extent appropriate, with other goals and standards for children established by the State;

(B) has established performance indicators the State will use to assess progress toward achieving those goals that, at a minimum, address the performance of children with disabilities on assessments, drop-out rates, and graduation rates;

(C) will, every two years, report to the Secretary and the public on the progress of the State, and of children with disabilities in the State, toward meeting the goals established under subparagraph (A); and

(D) based on its assessment of that progress, will revise its State improvement plan under subpart 1 of part D as may be needed to improve its performance, if the State receives assistance under that subpart.

(17) PARTICIPATION IN ASSESSMENTS--

(A) IN GENERAL-Children with disabilities are included in general State and district-wide assessment programs, with appropriate accommodations, where necessary. As appropriate, the State or local education agency--

(i) develops guidelines for the participation of children with disabilities in alternate assessments for those children who cannot participate in State and district-wide assessment programs; and

(ii) develops and, beginning not later than July 1, 2000, conducts those alternate assessments.

(B) REPORTS-The State educational agency makes available to the public, and reports to the public with the same frequency and in the same detail as it reports on the assessment of nondisabled children, the following:

(i) The number of children with disabilities participating in regular assessments.

(ii) The number of those children participating in alternate assessments.

(iii) (I) The performance of those children on regular assessments (beginning not later than July 1, 1998) and on alternate assessments (not later than July 1,2000), if doing so would be statistically sound and would not result in the disclosure of performance results identifiable to individual children.

(II) Data relating to the performance of children described under subclause (I) shall be disaggregated--

(aa) for assessments conducted after July 1, 1998; and

(bb) for assessments conducted before July 1, 1998, if the State is required to disaggregate such data prior to July 1, 1998.

[Language Omitted]"

"Sec. 616. WITHHOLDING AND JUDICIAL REVIEW

(a) WITHHOLDING OF PAYMENTS-

(1) IN GENERAL-Whenever the Secretary, after reasonable notice and opportunity for hearing to the State educational agency involved (and to any local educational agency or State agency affected by any failure described in subparagraph (B)), finds--

(A) that there has been a failure by the State to comply substantially with any provision of this part; or

(B) that there is failure to comply with any condition of a local educational agency's or State agency's eligibility under this part, including the terms of any agreement to achieve compliance with this part within the timelines specified in the agreement; the Secretary shall, after notifying the State educational agency, withhold, in whole or in part, any further payments to the State under this part, or refer the matter for appropriate enforcement action, which may include referral to the Department of Justice.

(2) NATURE OF WITHHOLDING-If the Secretary withholds further payments under paragraph (1), the Secretary may determine that such withholding will be limited to programs or projects, or portions thereof affected by the failure, or that the State educational agency shall not make further payments under this part to specified local educational agencies or State agencies affected by the failure. Until the Secretary is satisfied that there if (sic) no longer any failure to comply with the provisions of this part, as specified in subparagraph (A) or (B) of paragraph (1), payments to the

State under this part shall be withheld in whole or in part, or payments by the State educational agency under this part shall be limited to local educational agencies and State agencies whose actions did not cause or were not involved in the failure, as the case may be. Any State educational agency, State agency, or local educational agency that has received notice under paragraph (1) shall, by means of a public notice, take such measures as may be necessary to bring the pendency of an action pursuant to this subsection to the attention of the public within the jurisdiction of such agency."

[Language Omitted]"

(2) State and local education agencies are required to abide by federal laws that are in effect.

(b) This section shall remain in effect only if the Individuals with Disabilities Education Act (20 U.S.C. Sec. 1400 et seq.), as amended by the Individuals with Disabilities Education Act Amendments of 1997 (105 P.L.17), is not further amended or repealed, and this section is repealed upon any further amendment or repeal of the Individuals with Disabilities Education Act (20 U.S.C. Sec. 1400 et seq.), as amended by the Individuals with Disabilities Education Act Amendments of 1997 (105 P.L.17).

(c) It is the intent of the Legislature that this section be reenacted to incorporate any changes to the Individuals with Disabilities Education Act Amendments of 1997 (105 P.L.17), as soon as possible after the amendment of the Individuals with Disabilities Education Act (20 U.S.C. Sec. 1400 et seq.), as amended by the Individuals with Disabilities Education Act Amendments of 1997 (105 P.L.17).

STUDY ON INCIDENCE OF DISABILITIES
AND
DISTRIBUTION AMONG POPULATION

(Noncodified Section)

(AB 602 - Chapter 854, Statutes of 1997)

Section 67. (a) The Office of the Legislative Analyst, in conjunction with the Department of Finance and the State Department of Education, shall conduct a study to gather, analyze, and report on data that would indicate the extent to which the incidence of disabilities, that are medically defined or severe and significantly above-average in cost, or both, are evenly or unevenly distributed among the population of special education local plan areas. The Office of the Legislative Analyst shall contract for both the development of the request for proposal for the study and for the study itself. The Office of the Legislative Analyst, the Department of Finance, and the State Department of Education, shall submit a report of the contractor's findings and recommendations no later than June 1, 1998, to the Governor and the appropriate policy and fiscal committees of the California State Senate and the California State Assembly. The report shall include, if feasible and appropriate, a method to adjust the funding formula contained in Chapter 7.2 (commencing with Section 56836) of Part 30 of the Education Code in order to recognize the distribution of disabilities that are medically defined or severe and significantly above-average in cost, or both, among the special education local plan areas. The report shall use the definition of severe orthopedic impairment developed by the State Department of Education pursuant to Section 70.

(b) There is hereby appropriated to the State Department of Education for transfer to the Office of the Legislative Analyst for the 1997-98 fiscal year the sum of two hundred thousand dollars ($200,000) from supplemental federal special education grant funds for Part B of the Individuals with Disabilities Education Act. The funds are only to be used for the purpose of contracting for the request for proposal and study in subdivisions (a) and (b) and for the purpose of paying any necessary overhead associated with the supervision of the independent contracts. Provision 1 of Item 6110-161-0890 of the 1997-98 Budget Act on funds received over the amount of federal funds budgeted shall only apply to the balance of supplemental federal special education grant funds for Part B of the Individuals with Disabilities Education Act remaining after the appropriation made by this subdivision is deducted from that supplemental funding.

- Appropriation for Study

(c) Of the amount needed to fully fund the equalization formula in Article 2 (commencing with Section 56836.06) of Chapter 7.2 of Part 30 of the Education Code as it read on January 1, 1998, fifteen million dollars ($15,000,000) shall be available for an adjustment to that formula pursuant to the results of the study required pursuant to Section 67. The amount actually required to fully fund the adjustment enacted by an act of the Legislature subsequent to the results of the study shall be funded in whole in the 1998-99 fiscal year if eighty million dollars ($80,000,000), or more, in federal

- Funding Available for Adjustment Pursuant to Results of Study

funds becomes available, or proportionately less if less federal funds are available, during years of equalization carried out pursuant to Article 2 (commencing with Section 56836.06) of Chapter 7.2 of Part 30 of the Education Code. At the time an adjustment is enacted, the formula in Article 2 (commencing with Section 56836.06) of Chapter 7.2 of Part 30 of the Education Code shall also be amended in an act other than the Budget Act to reduce the full funding level by the total cost of the adjustment which may be more or less than fifteen million dollars ($15,000,000) such that the total cost of the formula in Article 2 (commencing with Section 56836.06) of Chapter 7.2 of Part 30 of the Education Code plus the adjustment shall equal the cost of the equalization formula as it existed before enacting the adjustment. The adjustment shall be enacted to amend or replace the formula established in Article 2.5 (commencing with Section 56836.155) of Chapter 7.2 of Part 30 of the Education Code and shall not be enacted in addition to the formula established in that article.

STUDY OF NONPUBLIC SCHOOL AND NONPUBLIC AGENCY COSTS

(Noncodified Section)

(AB 602 - Chapter 854, Statutes of 1997)

Section 68. (a) The Office of the Legislative Analyst, the Department of Finance, and the State Department of Education shall conduct a study, in consultation with the other interested parties, of nonpublic school and nonpublic agency costs as compared to the cost of public school placements, the cause of continuing increases in nonpublic school and agency costs, and recommendations for cost containment. In carrying out this study the Office of the Legislative Analyst shall examine the impact on nonpublic school and nonpublic agency costs of children residing in out-of-home placements, and of mediation and due process hearings. The Office of the Legislative Analyst may contract with an independent party to conduct this study on behalf of the Office of the Legislative Analyst. The Office of the Legislative Analyst shall submit a final report of its findings and recommendations on or before May 1, 1998, to the appropriate policy and fiscal committees of the Senate and the Assembly of the California Legislature.

- Study of Nonpublic School and Nonpublic Agency Costs

(b) There is hereby appropriated to the State Department of Education for transfer to the Office of the Legislative Analyst for the 1997-98 fiscal year the sum of one hundred thousand dollars ($100,000) from supplemental federal special education grant funds for Part B of the Individuals with Disabilities Education Act. The funds are only to be used for the purpose of conducting the study in subdivision (a). Provision 1 of Item 6110-161-0890 of the 1997-98 Budget Act on funds received over the amount of federal funds budgeted shall only apply to the balance of supplemental federal special education grant funds for Part B of the Individuals with Disabilities Education Act remaining after the appropriation made by this subdivision is deducted from that supplemental funding.

- Appropriation for Study

WORK GROUP ON COMPLIANCE

(Noncodified Section)

(AB 602 - Chapter 854, Statutes of 1997)

Section 69. (a) The State Department of Education shall convene a working group to develop recommendations for improving the compliance of state and local education agencies with state and federal special education laws and regulations. These recommendations shall define how the State Department of Education and local education agencies will assure and maintain compliance of special education laws and regulations in providing services to individuals with exceptional needs. Final recommendations shall include, but not be limited to, state compliance training and technical assistance, state review and monitoring of local compliance, the state complaint process and timetable, state corrective action and follow up, and local and state agency sanctions for noncompliance.

- Recommendation for Improving Compliance

(b) The working group shall include members representing the State Board of Education, the State Department of Education, county offices of education, school districts, special education local plan areas, the Special Education Advisory Commission, the State Department of Education administrative hearing office, the federal Office of Civil Rights or Office for Special Education Programs, organizations advocating for, or consisting of, individuals with exceptional needs and their families, parents of

- Members of Work Group

individuals with exceptional needs, and organizations serving individuals with exceptional needs. It is the intent of the Legislature that the working group convened by the State Department of Education shall include a balance of members representing state and local education agencies and employees, and members representing individuals with exceptional needs and their families.

(c) The State Department of Education shall submit a report of the working group's recommendations no later than September 1, 1998, to the Governor and the appropriate policy and fiscal committees of the Senate and the Assembly of the California Legislature.

- Required Report

DEFINITION OF SEVERE ORTHOPEDIC IMPAIRMENT

(Noncodified Section)

(AB 602 - Chapter 854, Statutes of 1997)

Section 70. On or before January 1, 1998, the State Department of Education shall develop a definition of severe orthopedic impairment for use in the application and distribution of low-incidence funding in the 1998-99 fiscal year.

- Definition of Severe Orthopedic Impairment for Use in Application and Distribution of Low-Incidence Funding

RECOGNITION FOR EDUCATIONAL ACHIEVEMENT OR COMPLETION OF PROGRAM

(Noncodified Section)

(AB 1062 - Chapter 392, Statutes of 1999)

Section 1. (a) The Legislature finds and declares that individuals with exceptional needs are not being appropriately recognized when they complete their schooling by means of an alternative course of study, or when they satisfactorily meet the goals and objectives in their individualized education program, or have satisfactorily attended high school, participated in the instruction prescribed in their individualized education program and have met their individualized education program transition plan.

- Legislative Findings and Declarations

(b) The Legislature further finds and declares that individuals with exceptional needs are often excluded from participation in graduation ceremonies and related activities even though they have achieved or completed what was prescribed in their individualized education program during their high school years. - Further Findings and Declarations

(c) It is, therefore, the intent of the Legislature that Chapter 4.1 (commencing with Section 56375) be added to Part 30 of the Education Code to recognize the educational achievement or completion of individuals with exceptional needs when they complete high school and allow these individuals to participate in graduation ceremonies and related activities along with their nondisabled peers. - Legislative Intent

IMPORTANCE FOR VISUALLY IMPAIRED INDIVIDUALS TO LEARN BRAILLE

(Noncodified Section)

AB 306 - Chapter 736, Statutes of 2001

Section 1. The Legislature finds and declares all of the following: - Legislative Findings and Declarations

(a) This state is in need of more credentialed teachers who are able to teach braille to visually impaired pupils.

(b) It is vitally important for visually impaired individuals to learn braille. There is a direct correlation between braille literacy and the level of employment and education attained by people who are visually impaired and blind.

(c) This state should ensure that visually impaired pupils are able to read at the same level as their peers.

INTERAGENCY RESPONSIBILITIES FOR RELATED SERVICES

(Government Code)
(Chapter 26.5, Division 7, Title 1)

(AB 3632 - Chapter 1747, Statutes of 1984, As Amended by
AB 882 - Chapter 1274, Statutes of 1985, As Amended by
AB 3012 - Chapter 1133, Statutes of 1986, As Amended by
AB 1744 - Chapter 677, Statutes of 1989, As Amended by
AB 1528 - Chapter 182, Statutes of 1990, As Amended by
AB 1060 - Chapter 223, Statutes of 1991, As Amended by
AB 1248 - Chapter 759, Statutes of 1992, As Amended by
AB 1399 - Chapter 489, Statutes of 1993, As Amended by
AB 1892 - Chapter 1128, Statutes of 1994, As Amended by
AB 2726 - Chapter 654, Statutes of 1996, And
SB 1497 - Chapter 1023, Statutes of 1996, As Amended by
SB 1686 - Chapter 691, Statutes of 1998, As Amended by
SB 1191 - Chapter 745, Statutes of 2001)

SECTION 1. The Legislature hereby finds and declares that a number of state and federal programs make funds available for the provision of education and related services to children with handicaps who are of school age. The Legislature further finds and declares that California has not maximized, or sufficiently coordinated existing state programs, in providing supportive services which are necessary to assist a handicapped child to benefit from special education.

It is the intent of the Legislature that existing services rendered by state and local government agencies serving handicapped children be maximized and coordinated. It is the further intent of the Legislature that specific state and local interagency responsibilities be clarified by this act in order to better serve the educational needs of the state's handicapped children.

- Legislative Findings and Intent

CHAPTER 26.5. INTERAGENCY RESPONSIBILITIES FOR PROVIDING SERVICES TO HANDICAPPED CHILDREN

7570. Ensuring maximum utilization of all state and federal resources available to provide a child with a disability, as defined in paragraph (3) of Section 1401 of Title

- Joint Responsibility

20 of the United States Code, with a free appropriate public education, the provision of related services, as defined in paragraph (22) of Section 1401 of Title 20 of the United States Code, and designated instruction and services, as defined in Section 56363 of the Education Code, to a child with a disability, shall be the joint responsibility of the Superintendent of Public Instruction and the Secretary of Health and Welfare. The Superintendent of Public Instruction shall ensure that this chapter is carried out through monitoring and supervision.

7571. The Secretary of Health and Welfare may designate a department of state government to assume he responsibilities described in Section 7570. The secretary, or his or her designee, shall also designate a single agency in each county to coordinate the service responsibilities described in Section 7572.

- Secretary May Designate Department to Assume Responsibilities

7572. (a) A child shall be assessed in all areas related to the suspected disability by those qualified to make a determination of the child's need for the service before any action is taken with respect to the provision of related services or designated instruction and services to a child, including, but not limited to, services in the areas of, occupational therapy, physical therapy, psychotherapy, and other mental health assessments. All assessments required or conducted pursuant to this section shall be governed by the assessment procedures contained in Article 2 (commencing with Section 56320) of Chapter 4 of Part 30 of the Education Code.

- Child Assessed in All Areas Related to Suspected Disability

(b) Occupational therapy and physical therapy assessments shall be conducted by qualified medical personnel as specified in regulations developed by the State Department of Health Services in consultation with the State Department of Education.

- OT/PT Assessments

(c) Psychotherapy and other mental health assessments shall be conducted by qualified mental health professionals as specified in regulations developed by the State Department of Mental Health, in consultation with the State Department of Education, pursuant to this chapter.

- Psychotherapy Assessment

(d) A related service or designated instruction and service shall only be added to the child's individualized education program by the individualized education program team, as described in Part 30 (commencing with Section 56000) of the Education Code, if a formal assessment has been conducted pursuant to this section, and a qualified person conducting the assessment recommended the service in order for the child to

- Adding to IEP

benefit from special education. In no case shall the inclusion of necessary related services in a pupil's individualized education plan be contingent upon identifying the funding source. Nothing in this section shall prevent a parent from obtaining an independent assessment in accordance with subdivision (b) of Section 56329 of the Education Code, which shall be considered by the individualized education program team.

(1) Whenever an assessment has been conducted pursuant to subdivision (b) or (c), the recommendation of the person who conducted the assessment shall be reviewed and discussed with the parent and with appropriate members of the individualized education program team prior to the meeting of the individualized education program team. When the proposed recommendation of the person has been discussed with the parent and there is disagreement on the recommendation pertaining to the related service, the parent shall be notified in writing and may require the person who conducted the assessment to attend the individualized education program team meeting to discuss the recommendation. The person who conducted the assessment shall attend the individualized education program team meeting if requested. Following this discussion and review, the recommendation of the person who conducted the assessment shall be the recommendation of the individualized education program team members who are attending on behalf of the local educational agency.

- Related Service Recommendation

(2) If an independent assessment for the provision of related services or designated instruction and services is submitted to the individualized education program team, review of that assessment shall be conducted by the person specified in subdivisions (b) and (c). The recommendation of the person who reviewed the independent assessment shall be reviewed and discussed with the parent and with appropriate members of the individualized education program team prior to the meeting of the individualized education program team. The parent shall be notified in writing and may request the person who reviewed the independent assessment to attend the individualized education program team meeting to discuss the recommendation. The person who reviewed the independent assessment shall attend the individualized education program team meeting if requested. Following this review and discussion, the recommendation of the person who reviewed the independent assessment shall be the recommendation of the individualized education program

- Independent Assessment

team members who are attending on behalf of the local agency.

(3) Any disputes between the parent and team members representing the public agencies regarding a recommendation made in accordance with paragraphs (1) and (2) shall be resolved pursuant to Chapter 5 (commencing with Section 56500) of Part 30 of the Education Code.

- Resolving Recommendation Disputes

(e) Whenever a related service or designated instruction and service specified in subdivision (b) or (c) is to be considered for inclusion in the child's individualized educational program, the local education agency shall invite the responsible public agency representative to meet with the individualized education program team to determine the need for the service and participate in developing the individualized education program. If the responsible public agency representative cannot meet with the individualized education program team, then the representative shall provide written information concerning the need for the service pursuant to subdivision (d). Conference calls, together with written recommendations, are acceptable forms of participation. If the responsible public agency representative will not be available to participate in the individualized education program meeting, the local educational agency shall ensure that a qualified substitute is available to explain and interpret the evaluation pursuant to subdivision (d) of Section 56341 of the Education Code. A copy of the information shall be provided by the responsible public agency to the parents or any adult pupil for whom no guardian or conservator has been appointed.

- Participation in Developing IEP

7572.5. (a) When an assessment is conducted pursuant to Article 2 (commencing with Section 56320) of Chapter 4 of Part 30 of Division 4 of the Education Code, which determines that a child is seriously emotionally disturbed, as defined in Section 300.5 of Title 34 of the Code of Federal Regulations, and any member of the individualized education program team recommends residential placement based on relevant assessment information, the individualized education program team shall be expanded to include a representative of the county mental health department.

- Expanded IEP Team and Residential Recommendations

(b) The expanded individualized education program team shall review the assessment and determine whether:

- Review Assessment

(1) The child's needs can reasonably be met through any combination of nonresidential services, preventing the need for out-of-home care.

(2) Residential care is necessary for the child to benefit

from educational services.

(3) Residential services are available which address the needs identified in the assessment and which will ameliorate the conditions leading to the seriously emotionally disturbed designation.

(c) If the review required in subdivision (b) results in an individualized education program which calls for residential placement, the individualized education program shall include all the items outlined in Section 56345 of the Education Code, and shall also include:

- IEP Content

(1) Designation of the county mental health department as lead case manager. Lead case management responsibility may be delegated to the county welfare department by agreement between the county welfare department and the designated mental health department. The mental health department shall retain financial responsibility for provision of case management services.

(2) Provision for a review of the case progress, the continuing need for out-of-home placement, the extent of compliance with the individualized education program, and progress toward alleviating the need for out-of-home care, by the full individualized education program team at least every six months.

(3) Identification of an appropriate residential facility for placement with the assistance of the county welfare department as necessary.

7572.55. (a) Residential placements for a child with a disability who is seriously emotionally disturbed may be made out-of-state only after in-state alternatives have been considered and are found not to meet the child's needs and only when the requirements of Section 7572.5, and subdivision (e) of Section 56365 of the Education Code have been met. The local education agency shall document the alternatives to out-of-state residential placement that were considered and the reasons why they were rejected.

- Restriction on Out-of-State Placements

(b) Out-of-state placements shall be made only in a privately operated school certified by the California Department of Education.

- School Certified by CDE

(c) A plan shall be developed for using less restrictive alternatives and in-state alternatives as soon as they become available, unless it is in the best educational interest of the child to remain in the out-of-state school. If the child is a ward or dependent of the court, this plan shall be documented in the record.

- Plan for In-State Alternatives

7573. The Superintendent of Public Instruction shall

- LEA Responsibility

ensure that local education agencies provide special education and those related services and designated instruction and services contained in a child's individualized education program that are necessary for the child to benefit educationally from his or her instructional program. Local education agencies shall be responsible only for the provision of those services which are provided by qualified personnel whose employment standards are covered by the Education Code and implementing regulations.

7575. (a) (1) Notwithstanding any other provision of law, the State Department of Health Services, or any designated local agency administering the California Children's Services, shall be responsible for the provision of medically necessary occupational therapy and physical therapy, as specified by Article 5 (commencing with Section 123800) of Chapter 3 of Part 2 of Division 106 of the Health and Safety Code, by reason of medical diagnosis and when contained in the child's individualized education program.

- Responsibility for Provision of OT/PT

(2) Related services or designated instruction and services not deemed to be medically necessary by the State Department of Health Services, that the individualized education program team determines are necessary in order to assist a child to benefit from special education, shall be provided by the local education agency by qualified personnel whose employment standards are covered by the Education Code and implementing regulations.

(b) The department shall determine whether a California Children's Services eligible pupil, or a pupil with a private medical referral needs medically necessary occupational therapy or physical therapy. A medical referral shall be based on a written report from a licensed physician and surgeon who has examined the pupil. The written report shall include the following:

- Determination for Medically Necessary Therapy

(1) The diagnosed neuromuscular, musculoskeletal, or physical disabling condition prompting the referral.

(2) The referring physician's treatment goals and objectives.

(3) The basis for determining the recommended treatment goals and objectives, including how these will ameliorate or improve the pupil's diagnosed condition.

(4) The relationship of the medical disability to the pupil's need for special education and related services.

(5) Relevant medical records.

(c) The department shall provide the service directly or by contracting with another public agency, qualified individual,

- Providing the Service

or a state-certified nonpublic nonsectarian school or agency.

(d) Local education agencies shall provide necessary space and equipment for the provision of occupational therapy and physical therapy in the most efficient and effective manner.

(e) The department shall also be responsible for providing the services of a home health aide when the local education agency considers a less restrictive placement from home to school for a pupil for whom both of the following conditions exist:

(1) The California Medical Assistance Program provides a life-supporting medical service via a home health agency during the time in which the pupil would be in school or traveling between school and home.

(2) The medical service provided requires that the pupil receive the personal assistance or attention of a nurse, home health aide, parent or guardian, or some other specially trained adult in order to be effectively delivered.

7576. (a) The State Department of Mental Health, or any community mental health service, as defined in Section 5602 of the Welfare and Institutions Code, designated by the State Department of Mental Health, shall be responsible for the provision of mental health services, as defined in regulations by the State Department of Mental Health, developed in consultation with the State Department of Education, when required in the pupil's individualized education program. A local education agency shall not be required to place a pupil in a more restrictive educational environment in order for the pupil to receive the mental health services specified in the pupil's individualized education program if the mental health services can be appropriately provided in a less restrictive setting. It is the intent of the Legislature that the local education agency and the community mental health service vigorously attempt to develop a mutually satisfactory placement that is acceptable to the parent and addresses the pupil's educational and mental health treatment needs in a manner that is cost-effective for both public agencies, subject to the requirements of state and federal special education law, including the requirement that the placement be appropriate and in the least restrictive environment. For purposes of this section, "parent" is as defined in Section 56028 of the Education Code.

(b) A local education agency, individualized education program team, or parent may initiate a referral for assessment of a pupil's social or emotional status, pursuant to Section 56320 of the Education Code. Based on the results of assessments completed pursuant to Section 56320 of the Education Code, an individualized education program team may refer a pupil who has been determined to be an individual with exceptional needs as defined in Section 56026 of the Education Code and who is suspected of needing mental health services to a community mental health service when a pupil meets all of the criteria in paragraphs (1) to (5), inclusive. Referral packages shall include all documentation required in subdivision (c), and shall be provided immediately to the community mental health service.

(1) The pupil has been assessed by school personnel in accordance with Article 2 (commencing with Section 56320) of Chapter 4 of Part 30 of the Education Code. Local education agencies and community mental health services shall work collaboratively to ensure that assessments performed prior to referral are as useful as possible to the community mental health service in determining the need for mental health services and the level of services needed.

(2) The local education agency has obtained written parental consent for the referral of the pupil to the community mental health service, for the release and exchange of all relevant information between the local education agency and the community mental health service, and for the observation of the pupil by mental health professionals in an educational setting.

(3) The pupil has emotional or behavioral characteristics that:

(A) Are observed by qualified educational staff in educational and other settings, as appropriate.

(B) Impede the pupil from benefiting from educational services.

(C) Are significant as indicated by their rate of occurrence and intensity.

(D) Are associated with a condition that cannot be described solely as a social maladjustment or a temporary adjustment problem, and cannot be resolved with short-term counseling.

(4) As determined using educational assessments, the pupil's functioning, including cognitive functioning, is at a level sufficient to enable the pupil to benefit from mental health services.

(5) The local education agency has provided counseling, psychological, or guidance services to the pupil pursuant to Section 56363 of the Education Code, and the individualized education program team has determined that the services do

not meet the pupil's educational needs, or, in cases where these services are clearly inappropriate, the individualized education program team has documented which of these services were considered and why they were determined to be inappropriate.

(c) When referring a pupil to a community mental health service in accordance with subdivision (b), the local education agency or the individualized education program team shall provide the following documentation:

(1) Copies of the current individualized education program, all current assessment reports completed by school personnel in all areas of suspected disabilities pursuant to Article 2 (commencing with Section 56320) of Chapter 4 of Part 30 of the Education Code, and other relevant information, including reports completed by other agencies.

(2) A copy of the parent's consent obtained as provided in paragraph (2) of subdivision (b).

(3) A summary of the emotional or behavioral characteristics of the pupil, including documentation that the pupil meets the criteria set forth in paragraphs (3) and (4) of subdivision (b).

(4) A description of the counseling, psychological, and guidance services, and other interventions that have been provided to the pupil, including the initiation, duration, and frequency of these services, or an explanation of why a service was considered for the pupil and determined to be inappropriate.

(d) Based on preliminary results of assessments performed pursuant to Section 56320 of the Education Code, a local education agency may refer a pupil who has been determined to be, or is suspected of being, an individual with exceptional needs, and is suspected of needing mental health services, to a community mental health service when a pupil meets the criteria in paragraphs (1) and (2). Referral packages shall include all documentation required in subdivision (e) and shall be provided immediately to the community mental health service.

(1) The pupil meets the criteria in paragraphs (2) to (4), inclusive, of subdivision (b).

(2) Counseling, psychological, and guidance services are clearly inappropriate in meeting the pupil's needs.

(e) When referring a pupil to a community mental health service in accordance with subdivision (d), the local education agency shall provide the following documentation:

(1) Results of preliminary assessments to the extent they

- Documentation

- Referral of Pupil to a Community Mental Health Service

- Documentation

are available and other relevant information including reports completed by other agencies.

(2) A copy of the parent's consent obtained as provided in paragraph (2) of subdivision (b).

(3) A summary of the emotional or behavioral characteristics of the pupil, including documentation that the pupil meets the criteria in paragraphs (3) and (4) of subdivision (b).

(4) An explanation as to why counseling, psychological, and guidance services are clearly inappropriate in meeting the pupil's needs.

(f) The procedures set forth in this chapter are not designed for use in responding to psychiatric emergencies or other situations requiring immediate response. In these situations, a parent may seek services from other public programs or private providers, as appropriate. This subdivision shall not change the identification and referral responsibilities imposed on local education agencies under Article 1 (commencing with Section 56300) of Chapter 4 of Part 30 of the Education Code.

- Procedures Not Designed for Use in Responding to Psychiatric Emergencies

(g) Referrals shall be made to the community mental health service in the county in which the pupil lives. If the pupil has been placed into residential care from another county, the community mental health service receiving the referral shall forward the referral immediately to the community mental health service of the county of origin, which shall have fiscal and programmatic responsibility for providing or arranging for provision of necessary services. In no event shall the procedures described in this subdivision delay or impede the referral and assessment process.

- County in Which Pupil Lives

7577. (a) The State Department of Rehabilitation and the State Department of Education shall jointly develop assessment procedures for determining client eligibility for State Department of Rehabilitation services for disabled pupils in secondary schools to help them make the transition from high school to work. The assessment procedures shall be distributed to local education agencies.

- Assessment Procedures for Rehabilitation Services

(b) The State Department of Rehabilitation shall maintain the current level of services to secondary school pupils in project work ability and shall seek ways to augment services with funds that may become available.

- Project Workability

7578. The provision of special education programs and related services for disabled children and youth residing in state hospitals shall be ensured by the State Department of Developmental Services, the State Department of Mental

- Programs for State Hospital Children

Health and the Superintendent of Public Instruction in accordance with Chapter 8 (commencing with Section 56850) of Part 30 of the Education Code.

7579. (a) Prior to placing a disabled child or a child suspected of being disabled in a residential facility, outside the child's home, a court, regional center for the developmentally disabled, or public agency other than an educational agency, shall notify the administrator of the special education local plan area in which the residential facility is located. The administrator of the special education local plan area shall provide the court or other placing agency with information about the availability of an appropriate public or nonpublic, nonsectarian special education program in a special education local plan area where the residential facility is located.

- Prior Notification of Residential Placements

(b) Notwithstanding Section 56159 of the Education Code, the involvement of the administrator of the special education local plan area in the placement discussion, pursuant to subdivision (a), shall in no way obligate a public education agency to pay for the residential costs and the cost of noneducational services for a child placed in a licensed children's institution or foster family home.

- Involvement of SELPA Administrator

(c) It is the intent of the Legislature that this section will encourage communication between the courts and other public agencies that engage in referring children to, or placing children in, residential facilities, and representatives of local education agencies. It is not the intent of this section to hinder the courts or public agencies in their responsibilities for placing disabled children in residential facilities when appropriate.

- Encourage Communication

- Do Not Hinder Placement

7579.1. (a) Prior to the discharge of any disabled child or youth who has an active individualized education program from a public hospital, proprietary hospital, or residential medical facility pursuant to Article 5.5 (commencing with Section 56167) of Chapter 2 of Part 30 of the Education Code, a licensed children's institution or foster family home pursuant to Article 5 (commencing with Section 56155) of Chapter 2 of Part 30 of the Education Code, or a state hospital for the developmentally disabled or mentally disordered, the following shall occur:

- Requirements Prior to Discharging Disabled Child

(1) The operator of the hospital or medical facility, or the agency that placed the child in the licensed children's institution or foster family home, shall, at least 10 days prior to the discharge of a disabled child or youth, notify in writing the local educational agency in which the special education

- Notification of Impending Discharge

program for the child is being provided, and the receiving special education local plan area where the child is being transferred, of the impending discharge.

(2) The operator or placing agency, as part of the written notification, shall provide the receiving special education local plan area with a copy of the child's individualized education program, the identity of the individual responsible for representing the interests of the child for educational and related services for the impending placement, and other relevant information about the child that will be useful in implementing the child's individualized education program in the receiving special education local plan area.

- Provide Receiving SELPA with a Copy of Child's IEP

(b) Once the disabled child or youth has been discharged, it shall be the responsibility of the receiving local educational agency to ensure that the disabled child or youth receives an appropriate educational placement that commences without delay upon his or her discharge from the hospital, institution, facility, or foster family home in accordance with Section 56325 of the Education Code. Responsibility for the provision of special education rests with the school district of residence of the parent or guardian of the child unless the child is placed in another hospital, institution, facility, or foster family home in which case the responsibility of special education rests with the school district in which the child resides pursuant to Sections 56156.5, 56156.6, and 56167 of the Education Code.

- Ensure that Child Receives an Appropriate Educational Placement Without Delay

(c) Special education local plan area directors shall document instances where the procedures in subdivision (a) are not being adhered to and report these instances to the Superintendent of Public Instruction.

- Document Instances Where Procedures Not Being Adhered To

7579.2. It is the intent of the Legislature that any disabled individual who has an active individualized education program and is being discharged from a state developmental center or state hospital be discharged to the community as close as possible to the home of the individual's parent, guardian, or conservator in keeping with the individual's right to receive special education and related services in the least restrictive environment.

- Individuals Discharged to the Community Close to Home

7579.5. (a) A surrogate parent shall not be appointed for a child who is a dependent or ward of the court unless the court specifically limits the right of the parent or guardian to make educational decisions for the child. A surrogate parent shall not be appointed for a child who has reached the age of majority unless the child has been declared incompetent by a court of law.

- Appointment of Surrogate Parent

(b) A local educational agency shall appoint a surrogate parent for a child under one or more of the following circumstances:

- Local Educational Agency Shall Appoint the Surrogate Parent

(1) The child is adjudicated a dependent or ward of the court pursuant to Section 300, 601, or 602 of the Welfare and Institutions Code upon referral of the child to a local educational agency for special education and related services, or in cases where the child already has a valid individualized education program.

(2) No parent for the child can be identified.

(3) The local educational agency, after reasonable efforts, cannot discover the location of a parent.

(c) When appointing a surrogate parent, the local educational agency shall, as a first preference, select a relative caretaker, foster parent, or court appointed special advocate, if any of these individuals exist and is willing and able to serve. If none of these individuals is willing or able to act as a surrogate parent, the local educational agency shall select the surrogate parent of its choice. If the child is moved from the home of the relative caretaker or foster parent who has been appointed as a surrogate parent, the local educational agency shall appoint another surrogate parent.

- Preferences: Relative Caretaker, Foster Parent, Court Appointed Special Advocate

(d) For the purposes of this section, the surrogate parent shall serve as the child's parent and shall have the rights relative to the child's education that a parent has under Title 20 (commencing with Section 1400) of the United States Code and pursuant to Part 300 of Title 34 (commencing with Section 300.1) of the Code of Federal Regulations. The surrogate parent may represent the child in matters relating to identification, assessment, instructional planning and development, educational placement, reviewing and revising the individualized education program, and in all other matters relating to the provision of a free appropriate public education of the child. Notwithstanding any other provision of law, this representation shall include the provision of written consent to the individualized education program including nonemergency medical services, mental health treatment services, and occupational or physical therapy services pursuant to this chapter. The surrogate parent may sign any consent relating to individualized education program purposes.

- Educational and Representational Responsibilities

(e) As far as practical, a surrogate parent should be culturally sensitive to his or her assigned child.

- Culturally Sensitive

(f) Individuals who would have a conflict of interest in representing the child, as specified under federal regulations,

- Conflict of Interest

shall not be appointed as a surrogate parent. "An individual who would have a conflict of interest," for purposes of this section, means a person having any interests that might restrict or bias his or her ability to advocate for all of the services required to ensure a free appropriate public education for an individual with exceptional needs, as defined in Section 56026 of the Education Code.

(g) Except for individuals who have a conflict of interest in representing the child, and notwithstanding any other law or regulation, individuals who may serve as surrogate parents include, but are not limited to, foster care providers, retired teachers, social workers, and probation officers who are not employees of a public agency involved in the education or care of the child. The surrogate parent shall not be an employee of a public or private agency that is involved in the education or care of the child. If a conflict of interest arises subsequent to the appointment of the surrogate parent, the local educational agency shall terminate the appointment and appoint another surrogate parent.

- Persons Who May Serve as Surrogate Parents

(h) The surrogate parent and the local educational agency appointing the surrogate parent shall be held harmless by the State of California when acting in their official capacity except for acts or omissions that are found to have been wanton, reckless, or malicious.

- Liability Protection

(i) Nothing in this section shall be interpreted to prevent a parent or guardian of an individual with exceptional needs from designating another adult individual to represent the interests of the child for educational and related services.

- Parent or Guardian May Designate Another Adult to Represent Child's Interests

(j) If funding for implementation of this section is provided, it may only be provided from Item 6110-161-890 of the annual Budget Act.

- Funding for Implementation

7580. Prior to licensing a community care facility, as defined in Section 1502 of the Health and Safety Code, in which a disabled child or youth may be placed, or prior to a modification of a community care facility's license to permit expansion of the facility, the State Department of Social Services shall consult with the administrator of the special education local plan area in order to consider the impact of licensure upon local education agencies.

- Community Care Facility's Impact on Education

7581. The residential and noneducational costs of a child placed in a medical or residential facility by a public agency, other than a local education agency, or independently placed in a facility by the parent of the child, shall not be the responsibility of the state or local education agency, but shall be the responsibility of the placing agency or parent.

- Responsibility for Residential and Noneducational Costs

7582. Assessments and therapy treatment services provided under programs of the State Department of Health Services or the State Department of Mental Health, or their designated local agencies, rendered to a child referred by a local education agency for an assessment or a disabled child or youth with an individualized education program, shall be exempt from financial eligibility standards and family repayment requirements for these services when rendered pursuant to this chapter.

7584. As used in this chapter, "disabled youth," "child," or "pupil" means individuals with exceptional needs as defined in Section 56026 of the Education Code.

7585. (a) Whenever any department or any local agency designated by that department fails to provide a related service or designated instruction and service required pursuant to Section 7575 or 7576, and specified in the child's individualized education program, the parent, adult pupil, or any local education agency referred to in this chapter, shall submit a written notification of the failure to provide the service to the Superintendent of Public Instruction or the Secretary of Health and Welfare.

(b) When either the Superintendent of Public Instruction or the Secretary of Health and Welfare receives a written notification of the failure to provide a service as specified in subdivision (a), a copy shall immediately be transmitted to the other party. The superintendent, or his or her designee, and the secretary, or his or her designee, shall meet to resolve the issue within 15 calendar days of receipt of the notification. A written copy of the meeting resolution shall be mailed to the parent, the local education agency, and affected departments, within 10 days of the meeting.

(c) If the issue cannot be resolved within 15 calendar days to the satisfaction of the superintendent and the secretary, they shall jointly submit the issue in writing to the Director of the Office of Administrative Hearings, or his or her designee, in the State Department of General Services.

(d) The Director of the Office of Administrative Hearings, or his or her designee, shall review the issue and submit his or her findings in the case to the superintendent and the secretary within 30 calendar days of receipt of the case. The decision of the Director of the Office of Administrative Hearings, or his or her designee, shall be binding on the departments and their designated agencies who are parties to the dispute.

(e) If the meeting, conducted pursuant to subdivision (b), fails to resolve the issue to the satisfaction of the parent or local education agency, either party may appeal to the Director of the Office of Administrative Hearings, whose decision shall be the final administrative determination and binding on all parties.

- Appeal

(f) Whenever notification is filed pursuant to subdivision (a), the pupil affected by the dispute shall be provided with the appropriate related service or designated instruction and service pending resolution of the dispute, if the pupil had been receiving the service. The Superintendent of Public Instruction and the Secretary of Health and Welfare shall ensure that funds are available for provision of the service pending resolution of the issue pursuant to subdivision (e).

- Services Pending Dispute Resolution

(g) Nothing in this section prevents a parent or adult pupil from filing for a due process hearing under Section 7586.

- Due Process Hearing

(h) The contract between the State Department of Education and the Office of Administrative Hearings for conducting due process hearings shall include payment for services rendered by the Office of Administrative Hearings which are required by this section.

- Contract for Hearings

7586. (a) All state departments, and their designated local agencies shall be governed by the procedural safeguards required in Section 1415 of Title 20 of the United States Code. A due process hearing arising over a related service or designated instruction and service shall be filed with the Superintendent of Public Instruction. Resolution of all issues shall be through the due process hearing process established in Chapter 5 (commencing with Section 56500) of Part 30 of Division 4 of the Education Code. The decision issued in the due process hearing shall be binding on the department having responsibility for the services in issue as prescribed by this chapter.

- Procedural Safeguards

(b) Upon receipt of a request for a due process hearing involving an agency other than an educational agency, the Superintendent of Public Instruction shall immediately notify the state and local agencies involved by sending a copy of the request to the agencies.

- Notification of Hearing Request

(c) All hearing requests that involve multiple services that are the responsibility of more than one state department shall give rise to one hearing with all responsible state or local agencies joined as parties.

- One Hearing

(d) No public agency, state or local, may request a due process hearing pursuant to Section 56501 of the Education Code against another public agency.

- Restriction on Public Agency Hearing Requests

7586.5. Not later than January 1, 1988, the Superintendent of Public Instruction and the Secretary of Health and Welfare shall jointly submit to the Legislature and the Governor a report on the implementation of this chapter. The report shall include, but not be limited to, information regarding the number of complaints and due process hearings resulting from this chapter.

- Report on Implementation of Law

7586.6. (a) The Superintendent of Public Instruction and the Secretary of Health and Welfare shall ensure that the State Department of Education and the State Department of Mental Health enter into an interagency agreement by January 1, 1998. It is the intent of the Legislature that the agreement include, but not be limited to, procedures for ongoing joint training, technical assistance for state and local personnel responsible for implementing this chapter, protocols for monitoring service delivery, and a system for compiling data on program operations.

- State Interagency Agreement

(b) It is the intent of the Legislature that the designated local agencies of the State Department of Education and the State Department of Mental Health update their interagency agreements for services specified in this chapter at the earliest possible time. It is the intent of the Legislature that the state and local interagency agreements be updated at least every three years or earlier as necessary.

- Local Interagency Agreements

7586.7. The Superintendent of Public Instruction and the Secretary of Health and Welfare shall jointly prepare and implement within existing resources a plan for in-service training of state and local personnel responsible for implementing the provisions of this chapter.

- In-Service Training

7587. By January 1, 1986, each state department named in this chapter shall develop regulations, as necessary, for the department or designated local agency to implement this act. All regulations shall be reviewed by the Superintendent of Public Instruction prior to filing with the Office of Administrative Law, in order to ensure consistency with federal and state laws and regulations governing the education of disabled children. The directors of each department shall adopt all regulations pursuant to this section as emergency regulations in accordance with Chapter 3.5 (commencing with Section 11340) of Part 1 of Division 3 of Title 2. For the purpose of the Administrative Procedure Act, the adoption of the regulations shall be deemed to be an emergency and necessary for the immediate preservation of the public peace, health and safety, or general welfare. These regulations shall not be subject to the review and approval of

- Regulations

the Office of Administrative Law and shall not be subject to automatic repeal until the final regulations take effect on or before June 30, 1997, and the final regulations shall become effective immediately upon filing with the Secretary of State. Regulations adopted pursuant to this section shall be developed with the maximum feasible opportunity for public participation and comments.

7588. This chapter shall become operative on July 1, 1986, except Section 7583 which shall become operative on January 1, 1985.

- Operative Date

NOTE

(1) Government Code Section 7585 was amended by Senate Bill 1191, Chapter 745, Statutes of 2001.

CALIFORNIA CODE OF REGULATIONS
TITLE 2. ADMINISTRATION
DIVISION 9. JOINT REGULATIONS FOR PUPILS WITH DISABILITIES
CHAPTER 1. INTERAGENCY RESPONSIBILITIES FOR PROVIDING SERVICES TO PUPILS WITH DISABILITIES

Article 1. General Provisions

60000. Scope.

The provisions of this chapter shall implement Chapter 26.5, commencing with Section 7570, of Division 7 of Title 1 of the Government Code relating to interagency responsibilities for providing services to pupils with disabilities. This chapter applies to the State Departments of Mental Health, Health Services, Social Services, and their designated local agencies, and the California Department of Education, school districts, county offices, and special education local plan areas.

The intent of this chapter is to assure conformity with the federal Individuals with Disabilities Education Act or IDEA, Sections 1400 et seq. of Title 20 of the United States Code, and its implementing regulations, including Sections 76.1 et seq. and 300.1 et seq. of Title 34 of the Code of Federal Regulations. Thus, provisions of this chapter shall be construed as supplemental to, and in the context of, federal and state laws and regulations relating to interagency responsibilities for providing services to pupils with disabilities.

[Authority cited: Section 7587, Government Code]
[Reference: Section 7570, Government Code]

60010. Education Definitions.

(a) Words shall have their usual meaning unless the context or a definition of a word or phrase indicates a different meaning. Words used in their present tense shall include the future tense; words in the singular form shall include the plural form; and the use of a masculine gender shall include the feminine gender.

(b) "Administrative designee" means the individual who fulfills the role as described in paragraph (1) of subsection (b) of Section 56341 of the Education Code and

- Scope (1)

- Education Definitions

- Administrative Designee

paragraph (1) of subsection (a) of Section 300.344 of Title 34 of the Code of Federal Regulations.

(c) "Assessment" means an individual evaluation of a pupil in all areas of suspected disability in accordance with Sections 56320 through 56329 of the Education Code and Sections 300.530 through 300.534 of Title 34 of the Code of Federal Regulations.

- Assessment

(d) "Assessment plan" means a written statement that delineates how a pupil will be evaluated and meets the requirements of Section 56321 of the Education Code.

- Assessment Plan

(e) "Confidentiality" means the restriction of access to verbal and written communications, including clinical, medical and educational records, to appropriate parties under Section 99.3 of Title 34 of the Code of Federal Regulations, Section 300.560 et seq. of Title 45 of the Code of Federal Regulations, Sections 827, 4514, 5328, and 10850 of the Welfare and Institutions Code, Section 2890 of Title 17 of the California Code of Regulations, and Sections 49060 through 49079 of the Education Code.

- Confidentiality

(f) "County superintendent of schools" means either an appointed or elected official who performs the duties specified in Chapter 2 (commencing with Section 1240) of Part 2 of Title 1 of the Education Code.

- County Superintendent of Schools

(g) "Day" means a calendar day pursuant to Section 56023 of the Education Code.

- Day

(h) "Designated instruction and services" means specially designed instruction and related services described in subsection (b) of Section 56361 and subsection (b) of Section 56363 of the Education Code, and Section 3051 of Title 5 of the California Code of Regulations, as may be required to assist a pupil with a disability to benefit educationally.

- Designated Instruction and Services

(i) "Individualized education program," hereinafter "IEP," means a written statement developed in accordance with Section 7575 of the Government Code, Sections 56341 and 56342 of the Education Code and Sections 300.340 through 300.350 of Title 34 of the Code of Federal Regulations, which contains the elements specified in Section 56345 of the Education Code and Section 300.347 of Title 34 of the Code of Federal Regulations.

- Individualized Education Program

(j) "Individualized education program team," hereinafter "IEP team," means a group which is constituted in accordance with Section 56341 of the Education Code and Title 20, United States Code Section 1414(d)(1)(B).

- Individualized Education Program Team

(k) "Local education agency," hereinafter "LEA," means a school district or county office of education which provides

- Local Education Agency

special education and related services.

(l) "Local interagency agreement" means a written document negotiated between two or more public agencies which defines each agency's role and responsibilities for providing services to pupils with disabilities and for facilitating the coordination of these services in accordance with provisions of Section 56220 of the Education Code.

- Local Interagency Agreement

(m) "Necessary to benefit from special education" means a service that assists the pupil with a disability in progressing toward the goals and objectives listed in the IEP in accordance with subsection (d) of Section 7572 and paragraph (2) of subsection (a) of Section 7575 of the Government Code.

- Necessary to Benefit from Special Education

(n) "Nonpublic, nonsectarian agency" means a private, nonsectarian establishment or individual that is certified by the California Department of Education and that provides related services and/or designated instruction and services necessary for a pupil with a disability to benefit educationally from the pupil's IEP. It does not include an organization or agency that operates as a public agency or offers public service, including but not limited to, a state or local agency, or an affiliate of a state or local agency, including a private, nonprofit corporation established or operated by a state or local agency, a public university or college, or a public hospital.

- Nonpublic, Nonsectarian Agency

(o) "Nonpublic, nonsectarian school" means a private, nonsectarian school that enrolls individuals with exceptional needs pursuant to an IEP, employs at least one full-time teacher who holds an appropriate credential authorizing special education services, and is certified by the California Department of Education. It does not include an organization or agency that operates as a public agency or offers public services, including but not limited to, a state or local agency, or an affiliate of a state or local agency, including a private, nonprofit corporation established or operated by a state or local agency or a public university or college.

- Nonpublic, Nonsectarian School

(p) "Parent" includes any person having legal custody of a child. "Parent," in addition, includes any adult pupil for whom no guardian or conservator has been appointed and the person having custody of a minor if neither the parent nor legal guardian can be notified of the educational action under consideration. "Parent" also includes a parent surrogate who has been appointed in accordance with Section 7579.5 of the Government Code and Section 56050 of the Education Code. The term "Parent" does not include the state or any political

- Parent

subdivision of government.

(q) "Pupil" or "Pupil with a disability" means those students, birth through 21 years of age, as defined in Section 300.7 of Title 34 of the Code of Federal Regulations, including those with mental retardation or autism, who meet the requirements of Sections 56026 of the Education Code and Sections 3030 and 3031 of Title 5 of the California Code of Regulations and who, because of their impairments, need special education and related services as defined in of subsections (22) and (25) of Section 1401 of Title 20 of the United States Code. This term includes handicapped children, children with disabilities and individuals with exceptional needs as defined in Section 56026 of the Education Code. The determination that an individual is a pupil with a disability is made only by an IEP team pursuant to Section 56342 of the Education Code.

- Pupil or Pupil with a Disability

(r) "Qualified" means that a person has met federal and state certification, licensing, registration, or other comparable requirements which apply to the area in which he or she is providing special education or related services, or, in the absence of such requirements, meets the state-education-agency-approved or recognized requirements and adheres to the standards of professional practice established in federal and state law or regulation, including the standards contained in the California Business and Professions Code.

- Qualified

(s) "Related services" means those services that are necessary for a pupil with a disability to benefit from his or her special education program in accordance with paragraph Title 20, United States Code Section 1401(22).

- Related Services

(t) "Special education" means specially designed instruction and related services to meet the unique needs of a pupil with a disability, as described in Section 56031 of the Education Code and Section 300.26 of Title 34 of the Code of Federal Regulations.

- Special Education

(u) "Special education local plan" means a plan developed in accordance with Sections 56200 through 56218 of the Education Code which identifies each participating LEA's roles and responsibilities for the provision of special education and related services within the service area.

- Special Education Local Plan

(v) "Special education local plan area," hereinafter "SELPA," means the service area covered by a special education local plan, and is the governance structure created under any of the planning options of Section 56200 of the Education Code.

- Special Education Local Plan Area

[Authority cited: Section 7587, Government Code.]
[Reference: Sections 7570 and 7579.5, Government Code. Section 5328, Welfare and Institutions Code. Sections 1240, 49060 through 49079, 56023, 56026, 56028, 56031, 56034, 56035, 56050, 56200-56220, 56320-56329, 56341 and 56325, Education Code; Clovis Unified School District (1990, Ninth Circuit) 903 F.2d 635. Section 1401, Title 20, United States Code. Sections 300.7, 300.326, 300.330, 300.340-300.350, 300.530-300.534 and 300.560, Title 34, Code of Federal Regulations.]

60020. Mental Health Definitions.   - Mental Health Definitions

(a) "Community mental health service" means a mental   - Community Mental Health Service
health program established by a county in accordance with
the Bronzan-McCorquodale Act, Part 2 (commencing with
Section 5600) of Division 5 of the Welfare and Institutions
Code.

(b) "County of origin" for mental health services is the   - County of Origin
county in which the parent of a pupil with a disability
resides. If the pupil is a ward or dependent of the court, an
adoptee receiving adoption assistance, or a conservatee, the
county of origin is the county where this status currently
exists. For the purposes of this program the county of origin
shall not change for pupils who are between the ages of 18
and 22.

(c) "Expanded IEP team" means an IEP team constituted   - Expanded IEP Team
in accordance with Section 7572.5 of the Government Code.
This team shall include a representative of the community
mental health service authorized to make placement
decisions.

(d) "Host county" means the county where the pupil with   - Host County
a disability is living when the pupil is not living in the county
of origin.

(e) "Local mental health director" means the officer   - Local Mental Health Director
appointed by the governing body of a county to manage a
community mental health service.

(f) "Medication monitoring" includes all medication   - Medication Monitoring
support services with the exception of the medications or
biologicals themselves and laboratory work. Medication
support services include prescribing, administering,
dispensing and monitoring of psychiatric medications or
biologicals necessary to alleviate the symptoms of mental
illness.

(g) "Mental health assessment" is a service designed to   - Mental Health Assessment
provide formal, documented evaluation or analysis of the

nature of the pupil's emotional or behavioral disorder. It is conducted in accordance with California Code of Regulations, Title 9, Section 543 (b), and Sections 56320 through 56329 of the Education Code by qualified mental health professionals employed by or under contract with the community mental health service.

(h) "Mental health assessment plan" means a written statement developed for the individual evaluation of a pupil with a disability who has been referred to a community mental health service to determine the need for mental health services in accordance with Section 56321 of the Education Code.

    - Mental Health Assessment Plan

(i) "Mental health services" means mental health assessments and the following services when delineated on an IEP in accordance with Section 7572 (d) of the Government Code: psychotherapy as defined in Section 2903 of the Business and Professions Code provided to the pupil individually or in a group, collateral services, medication monitoring, intensive day treatment, day rehabilitation, and case management. These services shall be provided directly or by contract at the discretion of the community mental health service of the county of origin.

    - Mental Health Services

(j) "Qualified mental health professional" includes the following licensed practitioners of the healing arts: a psychiatrist; psychologist; clinical social worker; marriage, family and child counselor; registered nurse, mental health rehabilitation specialist, and others who have been waivered under Section 5751.2 of the Welfare and Institutions Code. Such individuals may provide mental health services, consistent with their scope of practice.

    - Qualified Mental Health Professional

[Authority cited: Section 7587, Government Code]
[Reference: Section 56320, Education Code. Sections 542 and 543 of Title 9, California Code of Regulations]

60025. Social Services Definitions.

(a) "Care and supervision" as defined in Welfare and Institutions Code Section 11460, includes food, clothing, shelter, daily supervision, school supplies, a child's personal incidentals, liability insurance with respect to a child, and reasonable travel to the child's home for visitation.

    - Social Services Definitions
    - Care and Supervision

(b) "Certified family home" as defined in Welfare and Institutions Code Section 11400 (c), means a family residence certified by a foster family agency licensed by the California Department of Social Services and issued a

    - Certified Family Home

certificate of approval by that agency as meeting licensing standards, and is used only by that foster family agency for placements.

(c) "Certified, license-pending home" as described in Welfare and Institutions Code Section 361.2(h), 727(b), and 16507.5 (b), is a home that has a pending application for licensure as a foster family home, has been certified by the county as meeting the minimum standards for foster family homes, and is lacking any deficiencies which would threaten the physical health, mental health, safety or welfare of the pupil.

- Certified, License-Pending Home

(d) "Community care facility" is a facility licensed by the California Department of Social Services as defined in Health and Safety Code Section 1502(a). For the purposes of this chapter, a community care facility means those facilities listed and defined in this article that provide 24-hour residential care to children.

- Community Care Facility

(e) "Community treatment facility" as defined in Health and Safety Code Section 1502(a)(8), means any residential facility that provides mental health treatment services to children in a group setting which has the capacity to provide secure containment. The facility's program components shall be subject to program standards developed and enforced by the State Department of Mental Health pursuant to Section 4094 of the Welfare and Institutions Code.

- Community Treatment Facility

(f) "Foster family agency" as defined in Welfare and Institutions Code Section 11400 (g) and Health and Safety Code Section 1502(a)(4), means any individual or organization engaged in the recruiting, certifying, and training of, and providing professional support to, foster parents, or in finding homes or other places for placement of children for temporary or permanent care who require that level of care as an alternative to a group home. Private agencies shall be organized and operated on a nonprofit basis.

- Foster Family Agency

(g) "Foster family home" as defined in Health and Safety Code Section 1502(a)(5) means any residential facility providing 24-hour care for six or fewer foster children that is owned, leased, or rented and is the residence of the foster parent or parents, including their family, in whose care the foster children have been placed. It also means a foster family home described in Health and Safety Code Section 1505.2. For the purposes of this Chapter a foster family home includes a small family home pursuant to Education Code Section 56155.5 (b), or the approved home of a

- Foster Family Home

relative.

(h) "Group home" as defined in Title 22 of the California Code of Regulations, Section 80001(g)(1) means any facility of any capacity, that provides 24-hour care and supervision to children in a structured environment with such services provided at least in part by staff employed by the licensee. The care and supervision provided by a group home shall be nonmedical except as permitted by Welfare and Institutions Code, Section 17736(b). For the purposes of this Chapter, a group home is a nondetention facility that is organized and operated on a nonprofit basis in accordance with Welfare and Institutions Section 11400 (h).

- Group Home

(i) "Licensed children's institution" as defined in Education Code Section 56155.5(a), for the purposes of this Chapter, means the following community care facilities licensed by the California Department of Social Services: a group home, foster family agency, and community treatment facility.

- Licensed Children's Institution

(j) "Small family home" as defined in Health and Safety Code Section 1502(a)(6), means any residential facility, in the licensee's family residence, that provides 24-hour care for six or fewer foster children who have mental disorders or developmental or physical disabilities and who require special care and supervision as a result of their disabilities. A small family home may accept children with special health care needs, pursuant to subdivision (a) of Section 17710 of the Welfare and Institutions Code.

- Small Family Home

[Authority cited: Section 7587, Government Code. Sections 10553, 10554, 11462(i) and (j) and 11466.1, Welfare and Institutions Code] [Reference: Sections 361.2(h), 727(b), 4094, 11400(c), 11400(g), 11400(h), 11402(a), 16507.5(b), 17710, 17736(b), and 18350, Welfare and Institutions Code. Section 1502(a), Health and Safety Code. Section 56155.5, California Education Code; and Section 80001(g)(1), Title 22, California Code of Regulations]

Article 2. Mental Health Related Services

60030. Local Mental Health and Education Interagency Agreement.

- Local Mental Health and Education Interagency Agreement

(a) Each community mental health service and each SELPA within that county shall develop a written local interagency agreement in order to facilitate the provision of mental health services.

(b) The local mental health director, the county superintendent of schools and/or the local SELPA director, or their designees, shall review the local interagency agreement(s) according to a schedule developed at the local level between the agencies but not less frequently than every three years and ensure that the agreement or agreements are revised as appropriate, to assure compliance with this chapter. This provision does not preclude revision of the local interagency agreement at any time that they determine a revision is necessary. The content of the agreement will remain in effect until the agencies mutually agree upon any revisions.

(c) The local interagency agreement shall identify a contact person for each agency and include, but not be limited to, a delineation of the procedures for:

(1) Monitoring compliance with the time lines specified in paragraph (a) of Section 56321 and Section 56344 of the Education Code. This system shall designate each participating agency's responsibilities and identify who will be responsible for monitoring the system;

(2) Resolving interagency disputes at the local level, including procedures for the continued provision of appropriate services during the resolution of any interagency dispute, pursuant to Government Code Section 7585(f). For purposes of this subdivision only, the term "appropriate" means any service identified in a pupil's IEP, or any service the pupil actually was receiving at the time of the interagency dispute;

(3) Delivery of a completed referral package to the community mental health service pursuant to subsection (d) of Section 60040 as well as any other relevant pupil information in accordance with procedures ensuring confidentiality within five (5) business days;

(4) A host county to notify the community mental health service of the county of origin within two (2) working days when a pupil with a disability is placed within the host county by courts, regional centers or other agencies for other than educational reasons;

(5) Development of a mental health assessment plan and its implementation;

(6) The participation of qualified mental health professionals at the IEP team meetings pursuant to subsections (d) and (e) of Section 7572 and Section 7572.5 of the Government Code;

(7) At least ten (10) working days prior notice to the

community mental health service of all IEP team meetings, including annual IEP reviews, when the participation of its staff is required;

(8) The development, review or amendment of the portions of the IEP relating to mental health services, including the goals and objectives of mental health services in accordance with Title 20, United States Code Section 1414(d)(1)(A)(vi);

(9) The provision of mental health services as soon as possible following the development of the IEP pursuant to Section 300.342 of Title 34 of the Code of Federal Regulations;

(10) Description of the length and duration of mental health services and transportation beyond the traditional school year including the extended year program;

(11) The transportation of pupils with disabilities when necessary for the provision of mental health services pursuant to the IEP and Section 60200 (d)(1)(2);

(12) The provision of space, support staff and services at the school site, as appropriate, for the delivery of mental health services;

(13) The identification of a continuum of placement options. These options may include day, public, and state certified nonpublic, nonsectarian school programs, and residential facilities as listed in Section 60025. The community mental health service and the SELPA shall identify a list of mental health, education, and community services that may serve as alternatives to a residential placement for a pupil with a disability who is seriously emotionally disturbed;

(14) The provision of a system for monitoring contracts with nonpublic, nonsectarian schools to ensure that services on the IEP are provided;

(15) The development of a resource list composed of qualified mental health professionals who conduct mental health assessments and provide mental health services. The community mental health service shall provide the LEA with a copy of this list and monitor these contracts to assure that services as specified on the IEP are provided;

(16) The residential placement of a pupil pursuant to Section 60100;

(17) Mutual staff development for education and mental health staff pursuant to Section 7586.6 (a) of the Government Code.

[Authority cited: Section 7587, Government Code]
[Reference: Section 5608, Welfare and Institutions Code.
Sections 56140, 56321, and 56344, Education Code. Section
1414(d), Title 20, United States Code]

60040. Referral to Community Mental Health Services for
Related Services.

(a) A LEA, IEP team, or parent may initiate a referral for
assessment of a pupil's social and emotional status pursuant
to Section 56320 of the Education Code. Based on the
results of assessments completed pursuant to Section 56320,
an IEP team may refer a pupil who has been determined to
be an individual with exceptional needs or suspected of being
an individual with exceptional needs as defined in Section
56026 of the Education Code and who is suspected of
needing mental health services to a community mental health
service when a pupil meets all of the criteria in paragraphs
(1) through (5) below. Referral packages shall include all
documentation required in subsection (b) and shall be
provided within five (5) working days of the LEA's receipt
of parental consent for the referral of the pupil to the
community mental health service.

(1) The pupil has been assessed by school personnel in
accordance with Article 2, commencing with Section 56320,
of Chapter 4 of Part 30 of the Education Code.

(2) The LEA has obtained written parental consent for the
referral of the pupil to the community mental health service,
for the release and exchange of all relevant information
between the LEA and the community mental health service,
and for the observation of the pupil by qualified mental
health professionals in an educational setting.

(3) The pupil has emotional or behavioral characteristics
that:

(A) Are observed by qualified educational staff as defined
in subsection (x) of Section 3001 of Title 5 of the California
Code of Regulations in educational and other settings, as
appropriate.

(B) Impede the pupil from benefiting from educational
services.

(C) Are significant, as indicated by their rate of
occurrence and intensity.

(D) Are associated with a condition that cannot be
described solely as a social maladjustment as demonstrated
by deliberate noncompliance with accepted social rules, a
demonstrated ability to control unacceptable behavior and the

absence of a treatable mental disorder.

(E) Are associated with a condition that cannot be described solely as a temporary adjustment problem that can be resolved with less than three months of school counseling.

(4) As determined using educational assessments, the pupil's functioning, including cognitive functioning, is at a level sufficient to enable the pupil to benefit from mental health services.

(5) The LEA has provided counseling, psychological, or guidance services to the pupil pursuant to Section 56363 of the Education Code, and the IEP team has determined that the services do not meet the pupil's educational needs; or, in cases where these services are clearly inappropriate, the IEP team has documented which of these services were considered and why they were determined to be inappropriate.

(b) When referring a pupil to a community mental health service in accordance with subsection (a), the LEA or the IEP team shall provide the following documentation:

(1) Copies of the current IEP, all current assessment reports completed by school personnel in all areas of suspected disabilities pursuant to Article 2, commencing with Section 56320, of Chapter 4 of Part 30 of the Education Code, and other relevant information, including reports completed by other agencies.

(2) A copy of the parent's consent obtained as provided in subsection (a)(2).

(3) A summary of the emotional or behavioral characteristics of the pupil, including documentation that the pupil meets the criteria in paragraphs (3) and (4) of subsection (a).

(4) A description of the school counseling, psychological, and guidance services, and other interventions that have been provided to the pupil, including the initiation, duration and frequency of the services, or an explanation of why a service was considered for the pupil and determined to be inappropriate.

(c) Based on preliminary results of assessments performed pursuant to Section 56320 of the Education Code, a LEA may refer a pupil who has been determined to be or is suspected of being an individual with exceptional needs, and is suspected of needing mental health services, to a community mental health service when a pupil meets the criteria in paragraphs (1) and (2) below. Referral packages shall include all documentation required in subsection (d) and shall be provided within one (1) working day to the community mental health service.

(1) The pupil meets the criteria in paragraphs (2) through (4) of subsection (a).

(2) School counseling, psychological and guidance services are clearly inappropriate in meeting the pupil's needs.

(d) When referring a pupil to a community mental health service in accordance with subsection (c), the LEA shall provide the following documentation:

(1) Results of preliminary assessments, including those conducted by school personnel in accordance with Article 2, commencing with Section 56320, of Chapter 4 of Part 30 of the Education Code, to the extent they are available, and other relevant information, including reports completed by other agencies.

(2) A copy of the parent's consent obtained as provided in paragraph (2) of subsection (a).

(3) A summary of the emotional or behavioral characteristics of the pupil, including documentation that the pupil meets the criteria in paragraphs (3) and (4) of subsection (b).

(4) An explanation as to why school counseling, psychological and guidance services are clearly inappropriate in meeting the pupil's needs.

(e) The procedures set forth in this chapter are not designed for use in responding to psychiatric emergencies or other situations requiring immediate response. In these situations, a parent may seek services from other public programs or private providers, as appropriate. Nothing in this subsection changes the identification and referral responsibilities imposed on local education agencies under Article 1, commencing with Section 56300, of Chapter 4 of Part 30 of the Education Code.

(f) The community mental health service shall accept all referrals for mental health assessments made pursuant to subsections (a) and (c).

(g) If the community mental health service receives a referral for a pupil with a different county of origin, the community mental health service receiving the referral shall forward the referral within one (1) working day to the county of origin, which shall have programmatic and fiscal responsibility for providing or arranging for provision of necessary services. The procedures described in this subsection shall not delay or impede the referral and assessment process.

[Authority cited: Section 7587, Government Code]
[Reference: Sections 56026, 56300 et seq., 56320 et seq.,
and 56363, Education Code; Section 3001, Title 5,
California Code of Regulations]

60045. Assessment to Determine the Need for Mental
Health Services.

(a) Within five (5) days of receipt of a referral, pursuant
to subsections (a), (c) or (g) of Section 60040, the
community mental health service shall review the
recommendation for a mental health assessment and
determine if such an assessment is necessary.

(1) If no mental health assessment is determined to be
necessary, or the referral is inappropriate, the reasons shall
be documented by the community mental health service. The
community mental health service shall notify the parent and
the LEA of this determination within one (1) working day.

(2) If the referral is determined to be incomplete, the
reasons shall be documented by the community mental health
service. The community mental health service shall notify
the LEA within one (1) working day and return the referral.

(b) If a mental health assessment is determined to be
necessary, the community mental health service shall notify
the LEA, develop a mental health assessment plan, and
provide the plan and a consent form to the parent, within 15
days of receiving the referral from the LEA, pursuant to
Section 56321 of the Education Code. The assessment plan
shall include, but is not limited to, the review of the pupil's
school records and assessment reports and observation of the
pupil in the educational setting, when appropriate.

(c) The community mental health service shall report back
to the referring LEA or IEP team within 30 days from the
date of the receipt of the referral by the community mental
health service if no parental consent for a mental health
assessment has been obtained.

(d) Upon receipt of the parent's written consent for a
mental health assessment, the community mental health shall
contact the LEA within one (1) working day to establish the
date of the IEP meeting. The LEA shall schedule the IEP
meeting to be held within fifty (50) days from the receipt of
the written consent pursuant to Section 56344 of the
Education Code.

(e) The mental health assessment shall be completed in

sufficient time to ensure that an IEP meeting is held within fifty (50) days from the receipt of the written parental consent for the assessment. This time line may only be extended upon the written request of the parent.

(f) The community mental health service assessor shall review and discuss their mental health service recommendation with the parent and appropriate members of the IEP team. The assessor shall also make a copy of the mental health service assessment report available to the parent at least two days prior to the IEP team meeting.

(1) If the parent disagrees with the assessor's mental health service recommendation, the community mental health service shall provide the parent with written notification that they may require the assessor to attend the IEP team meeting to discuss the recommendation. The assessor shall attend the meeting if requested to do so by the parent.

(2) Following the discussion and review of the community mental health service assessor's recommendation, it shall be the recommendation of the IEP team members attending on behalf of the LEA.

(g) The community mental health service shall provide to the IEP team a written assessment report in accordance with Education Code Section 56327.

(h) For pupils with disabilities receiving services under this Chapter, the community mental health service of the county of origin shall be responsible for preparing statutorily required IEP reassessments in compliance with the requirements of this Section.

[Authority cited: Section 7587, Government Code] [Reference: Sections 56321, 56327 and 56344, Education Code]

60050. Individualized Education Program for Mental Health Services.

- Individualized Education Program for Mental Health Services

(a) When it is determined, in accordance with Section 7572 of the Government Code, that a mental health service is necessary for a pupil with a disability to benefit from special education, the following documentation shall be included in the mental health portion of the IEP:

(1) A description of the present levels of social and emotional performance;

(2) The goals and objectives of the mental health services with objective criteria and evaluation procedures to determine whether they are being achieved;

(3) A description of the types of mental health services to be provided; and

(4) The initiation, duration and frequency of the mental health services.

(5) Parental approval for the provision of mental health services. This signed consent for treatment is in addition to the signed IEP.

(b) When completion or termination of IEP specified health services is mutually agreed upon by the parent and the community mental health service, or when the pupil is no longer participating in treatment, the community mental health service shall notify the parent and the LEA which shall schedule the IEP team meeting to discuss and document this proposed change if it is acceptable to the IEP team.

[Authority cited: Section 7587, Government Code] [Reference: Section 300.347, Title 34, Code of Federal Regulations]

60055. Transfers and Interim Placements.

- Transfers and Interim Placements

(a) Whenever a pupil who has been receiving mental health services, pursuant to an IEP, transfers into a school district from a school district in another county, the responsible LEA administrator or IEP team shall refer the pupil to the local community mental health service to determine appropriate mental health services.

(b) The local mental health director or designee shall ensure that the pupil is provided interim mental health services, as specified in the existing IEP, pursuant to Section 56325 of the Education Code, for a period not to exceed thirty (30) days, unless the parent agrees otherwise.

(c) An IEP team, which shall include an authorized representative of the responsible community mental health service, shall be convened by the LEA to review the interim services and make a determination of services within thirty (30) days of the pupil's transfer.

[Authority cited: Section 7587, Government Code] [Reference: Section 56325, Education Code]

Article 3. Residential Placement

60100. LEA Identification and Placement of a Seriously
          Emotionally Disturbed Pupil.

- LEA Identification and Placement of a Seriously Emotionally Disturbed Pupil

(a) This article shall apply only to a pupil with a disability who is seriously emotionally disturbed pursuant to paragraph (i) of Section 3030 of Title 5 of the California Code of Regulations.

(b) When an IEP team member recommends a residential placement for a pupil who meets the educational eligibility criteria specified in paragraph (4) of subsection (c) of Section 300.7 of Title 34 of the Code of Federal Regulations, the IEP shall proceed in the following manner:

(1) Am expanded IEP team shall be convened within thirty (30) days with an authorized representative of the community mental health service.

(2) If any authorized representative is not present, the IEP team meeting shall be adjourned and be reconvened within fifteen (15) calendar days as an expanded IEP team with an authorized representative from the community mental health service participating as a member of the IEP team pursuant to Section 7572.5 of the Government Code.

(3) If the community mental health service or the LEA determines that additional mental health assessments are needed, the LEA and the community mental health service shall proceed in accordance with Sections 60040 and 60045.

(c) Prior to the determination that a residential placement is necessary for the pupil to receive special education and mental health services, the expanded IEP team shall consider less restrictive alternatives, such as providing a behavioral specialist and full-time behavioral aide in the classroom, home and other community environments, and/or parent training in the home and community environments. The IEP team shall document the alternatives to residential placement that were considered and the reasons why they were rejected. Such alternatives may include any combination of cooperatively developed educational and mental health services.

(d) When the expanded IEP team recommends a residential placement, it shall document the pupil's educational and mental health treatment needs that support the recommendation for residential placement. This documentation shall identify the special education and related mental health services to be provided by a residential facility listed in Section 60025 that cannot be provided in a less restrictive environment pursuant to Title 20, United States Code Section 1412(a)(5),

(e) The community mental health service case manager, in consultation with the IEP team's administrative designee, shall identify a mutually satisfactory placement that is acceptable to the parent and addresses the pupil's educational and mental health needs in a manner that is cost-effective for both public agencies, subject to the requirements of state and federal special education law, including the requirement that the placement be appropriate and in the least restrictive environment.

(f) The residential placement shall be in a facility listed in Section 60025 that is located within, or in the county adjacent to, the county of residence of the parents of the pupil with a disability, pursuant to paragraph (3) of subsection (a) of Section 300.552 of Title 34 of the Code of Federal Regulations. When no nearby placement alternative which is able to implement the IEP can be identified, this determination shall be documented, and the community mental health service case manager shall seek an appropriate placement which is as close to the parents' home as possible.

(g) Rates for care and supervision shall be established for a facility listed in Section 60025 in accordance with Section 18350 of the Welfare and Institutions Code.

(h) Residential placements for a pupil with a disability who is seriously emotionally disturbed may be made out of California only when no in-state facility can meet the pupil's needs and only when the requirements of subsections (d) and (e) have been met. Out-of-state placements shall be made only in residential programs that meet the requirements of Welfare and Institutions Code Sections 11460 (c)(2) through (c)(3). For educational purposes, the pupil shall receive services from a privately operated non-medical, non-detention school certified by the California Department of Education.

(i) When the expanded IEP team determines that it is necessary to place a pupil with a disability who is seriously emotionally disturbed in residential care, the community mental health service shall ensure that:

(1) The mental health services are specified in the IEP in accordance with Title 20, United States Code Section 1414(d)(1)(A)(vi).

(2) Mental health services are provided by qualified mental health professionals.

(j) When the expanded IEP team determines that it is necessary to place a pupil with a disability who is seriously emotionally disturbed in a facility listed in Section 60025, the expanded IEP team shall ensure that placement is in accordance with admission criteria of the facility.

[Authority cited: Section 7587, Government Code. Sections 10553, 10554, 11462(i) and (j) and 11466.1, Welfare and Institutions Code] [Reference: Sections 7576(a) and 7579, Government Code. Sections 11460(c)(2)-(c)(3), 18350, and 18356, Welfare and Institutions Code. Sections 1412 and 1414, Title 20, United States Code. Sections 300.7 and 300.552, Title 34, Code of Federal Regulations]

60110. Case Management for a Pupil With a Disability Who is Seriously Emotionally Disturbed and is in a Residential Placement.

- Case Management for a Pupil with a Disability Who Is Seriously Emotionally Disturbed and Is in a Residential Placement

(a) Upon notification of the expanded IEP team's decision to place a pupil with a disability who is seriously emotionally disturbed into residential care, the local mental health director or designee shall immediately designate a case manager who will perform case management services as described in subsections (b) and (c).

(b) The case manager shall coordinate the residential placement plan of a pupil with a disability who is seriously emotionally disturbed as soon as possible after the decision has been made to place the pupil in a residential placement, pursuant to Section 300.342 of Title 34 of the Code of Federal Regulations.

(1) The residential placement plan shall include provisions, as determined in the pupil's IEP, for the care, supervision, mental health treatment, psychotropic medication monitoring, if required, and education of a pupil with a disability who is seriously emotionally disturbed.

(2) The LEA shall be responsible for providing or arranging for the special education and non-mental health related services needed by the pupil.

(3) When the expanded IEP team determines that it is necessary to place a pupil with a disability who is seriously emotionally disturbed in a community treatment facility, the casemanager shall ensure that placement is in accordance with admission and, continuing stay, and discharge criteria of the community treatment facility.

(c) Case management shall include, but not be limited to, the following responsibilities:

(1) To convene a meeting with the parents and representatives of public and private agencies, including educational staff, and to identify an appropriate residential placement from those defined in Section 60025 and excluding local inpatient, private psychiatric, and state hospital facilities.

(2) To identify, in consultation with the IEP team's administrative designee, a mutually satisfactory placement that is acceptable to the parent and addresses the pupil's educational and mental health needs in a manner that is cost-effective for both public agencies, subject to the requirements of state and federal special education law, including the requirement that the placement be appropriate and in the least restrictive environment.

(3) To complete the payment authorization in order to initiate payments for residential placement in accordance with Section 18351 of the Welfare and Institutions Code.

(4) To assure the completion of the community mental health service and LEA financial paperwork or contracts for the residential placement of a pupil with a disability who is seriously emotionally disturbed.

(5) To develop the plan an assist the family with the pupil's social and emotional transition from home to the residential placement and the subsequent return to the home.

(6) To facilitate the enrollment in the residential placement of a pupil with a disability who is seriously emotionally disturbed.

(7) To notify the LEA that the placement has been arranged and to coordinate the transportation of the pupil to the facility if needed.

(8) To conduct quarterly face-to-face contacts at the residential facility with a pupil with a disability who is seriously emotionally disturbed to monitor the level of care and supervision and the provision of the mental services as required by the IEP. In addition, for children placed in a community treatment facility, an evaluation shall be made within every 90 days of the residential placement of the pupil to determine if the pupil meets the continuing stay criteria as defined in Welfare and Institutions Code Section 4094 and implementing mental health regulations.

(9) To notify the parent and the LEA or designee if there is a discrepancy between the level of care, supervision, or provision of mental health services and the requirements of the IEP.

(10) To schedule and attend the next expanded IEP team meeting with the expanded IEP team's administrative designee within six months of the residential placement of a pupil with a disability who is seriously emotionally disturbed and every six months thereafter as long as the pupil remains in residential placement.

(11) To facilitate placement authorization from the

county's interagency placement committee pursuant to Section 4094.5(e)(1) of the Welfare and Institutions Code, by presenting the case of a pupil with a disability who is seriously emotionally disturbed prior to placement in a community treatment facility.

[Authority cited: Section 7587, Government Code] [Reference: Section 4094, Welfare and Institutions Code, Section 300.342, Title 34, Code of Federal Regulations. Section 3061, Title 5, California Code of Regulations]

Article 4. Financial Provision for Mental Health Services, Special Education and Residential Placement

60200. Financial Responsibilities.

- Financial Responsibilities

(a) The purpose of this article is to establish conditions and limitations for reimbursement for the provision of special education instruction, designated instruction and services, related services, and residential placement described in Articles 2 and 3 of this chapter.

(b) Special education instruction, designated instruction and services, related services, and residential placements are to be provided at no cost to the parent.

(c) The community mental health service of the county of origin shall be responsible for the provision of assessments and mental health services included in an IEP in accordance with Sections 60045, 60050, and 60100. Mental health services shall be provided either directly by the community mental service or by contractors. All services shall be delivered in accordance with Section 523 of Title 9 of the California Code of Regulations.

(1) The host county shall be responsible for making its provider network available and shall provide the county of origin a list of appropriate providers used by the host county's managed care plan who are currently available to take new referrals. Counties of origin shall negotiate with host counties to obtain access to limited resources, such as intensive day treatment and day rehabilitation.

(2) The county of origin may also contract directly with providers at a negotiated rate.

(d) The LEA shall be financially responsible for:

(1) The transportation of a pupil with a disability to and from the mental health services specified on the pupil's IEP and in accordance with subsection (a) of Section 300.13 of Title 34 of the Code of Federal Regulations;

(2) The transportation of a pupil to and from the residential placement as specified on the IEP and in accordance with Section 56221 of the Education Code; and

(3) The special education instruction, non-mental health related services, and designated instruction and services agreed upon in the nonpublic, nonsectarian school services contract or a public program arranged with another SELPA or LEA.

(e) The community mental health service shall be responsible for authorizing payment to the facilities listed in Section 60025 based upon rates established by the Department of Social Services in accordance with Sections 18350 through 18356 of the Welfare and Institutions Code.

(f) Upon receipt of the authorization from the community mental health service, pursuant to subsection (e), including documentation that the pupil is eligible for residential placement as a seriously emotionally disturbed pupil, the county welfare department shall issue payments in accordance with Section 18351 of the Welfare and Institutions Code to providers of residential placement.

[Authority cited: Section 7587, Government Code] [Reference: Sections 18350-18356, Welfare and Institutions Code. Section 300.13, Title 34, Code of Federal Regulations]

Article 5. Occupational Therapy and Physical Therapy

60300. California Children's Services (CCS) Medical Therapy Program Definitions.

(a) "Assessment for medically necessary occupational therapy and physical therapy" means the comprehensive evaluation of the physical and functional status of a pupil who has a medical therapy program eligible condition.

(b) "Assessment plan" for the CCS Medical Therapy Program for pupils with a disability who have an IEP means a written statement describing proposed:

(1) Procedures necessary for determination of medical eligibility for the CCS medical therapy program; or

(2) Procedures necessary for the redetermination of need for medically necessary physical therapy or occupational therapy for a pupil known to be eligible for the CCS medical therapy program.

(c) "Assessment report for therapy" means a written document of the results of a pupil's assessment for medically

- CCS Medical Therapy Program Definitions

- Assessment for Medically Necessary Occupational Therapy and Physical Therapy

- Assessment Plan

- Assessment Report for Therapy

necessary occupational therapy or physical therapy.

(d) "CCS Panel" means that group of physicians and other medical providers of services who have applied to and been approved by CCS.

(e) "Dependent county agency" means the CCS administrative organization in a county that administers the CCS program jointly with the State pursuant to Sections 123850 and 123905 of the Health and Safety Code.

(f) "Documented physical deficit" refers to a pupil's motor dysfunction recorded on the referral for special education and related services by the Local Education Agency and documented in the pupil's CCS medical record.

(g) "Independent county agency" means the CCS administrative organization in a county that administers the CCS program independently pursuant to Section 123850 of the Health and Safety Code.

(h) "Medical therapy conference" means a team meeting held in the medical therapy unit where medical case management for the pupil's medical therapy program eligible condition is provided by the medical therapy conference team as described in (i).

(i) "Medical therapy conference team" means a team composed of the pupil, parent, physician and occupational therapist and/or physical therapist, or both. The team may include, with the consent of the pupil's parent(s), an education representative who is present for the purpose of coordination with medical services.

(j) "Medical therapy program eligible condition" are those diagnoses that make a pupil eligible for medical therapy services and include the following diagnosed neuromuscular, musculoskeletal, or muscular diseases:

(1) Cerebral palsy, a nonprogressive motor disorder with onset in early childhood resulting from a lesion in the brain and manifested by the presence of one or more of the following findings:

(A) Rigidity or spasticity;

(B) Hypotonia, with normal or increased deep tendon reflexes and exaggeration or persistence of primitive reflexes beyond the normal age;

(C) Involuntary movements, athetoid, choreoid, or dystonic; or

(D) Ataxia, incoordination of voluntary movement, dysdiadochokinesia, intention tremor, reeling or shaking of trunk and head, staggering or stumbling, and broad-based gait.

- CCS Panel

- Dependent County Agency

- Documented Physical Deficit

- Independent County Agency

- Medical Therapy Conference

- Medical Therapy Conference Team

- Medical Therapy Program Eligible Condition

(2)   Other neuromuscular diseases that produce muscle weakness and atrophy, such as poliomyelitis, myasthenias, muscular dystrophies;

(3) Chronic musculoskeletal diseases, deformities or injuries, such as osteogenesis imperfecta, arthrogryposis, rheumatoid arthritis, amputation, and contractures resulting from burns.

(k) "Medical therapy services" are occupational therapy or physical therapy services that require a medical prescription and are determined to be medically necessary by CCS. Medical therapy services include: — Medical Therapy Services

(1) "Treatment", an intervention to individuals or groups of pupils in which there are occupational therapy or physical therapy services as per California Business and Professions Code, Chapter 5.7, Article 2, Section 2620.

(2) "Consultation", an occupational therapy or physical therapy activity that provides information and instruction to parents, care givers or LEA staff, and other medical services providers;

(3) "Monitoring", a regularly scheduled therapy activity in which the therapist reevaluates the pupil's physical status, reviews those activities in the therapy plan which are provided by parents, care givers or LEA staff, and updates the therapy plan as necessary; and

(4)   Medical therapy conference as defined in (h).

(l) "Medical therapy unit" means a CCS and LEA approved public school location where medical therapy services, including comprehensive evaluations and medical therapy conferences, are provided by CCS. — Medical Therapy Unit

(m) "Medical therapy unit satellite" means a CCS and LEA approved extension of an established medical therapy unit where medical therapy services may be provided by CCS. Comprehensive evaluations and medical therapy conferences are not a part of medical therapy unit satellite services. — Medical Therapy Unit Satellite

(n) "Medically necessary occupational therapy or physical therapy services" are those services directed at achieving or preventing further loss of functional skills, or reducing the incidence and severity of physical disability. — Medically Necessary Occupational Therapy or Physical Therapy Services

(o) "Necessary equipment" means that equipment, provided by the LEA, which is required by the medical therapy unit staff to provide medically necessary occupational therapy and/or physical therapy services to a pupil with a medical therapy program eligible condition. — Necessary Equipment

(p)   "Necessary space" means the facilities, which are — Necessary Space provided by the LEA for a medical therapy unit or a medical therapy unit satellite, and enable the medical therapy unit staff to provide medically necessary therapy services to a pupil with a medical therapy program eligible condition.

(q) "Occupational therapy and physical therapy" mean services provided by or under the supervision of occupational therapists and physical therapists pursuant to California Code of Regulations, Title 5, Section 3051.6(b).

- Occupational Therapy and Physical Therapy

(r) "Therapy plan" means the written recommendations for medically necessary occupational therapy or physical therapy services based on the results of the therapy assessment and evaluation and is to be included in the individualized education program or individualized family service plan.

- Therapy Plan

[Authority cited: Section 7587, Government Code] [Reference: Section 7575, Government Code. Sections 123825, 123850, 123875, and 123905, Health and Safety Code. Sections 3001(x) and 3051.6(b) of Title 5, California Code of Regulations; and Section 2620 of Chapter 5.7, Article 2, California Business and Professions Code]

60310. Local Interagency Agreements Between CCS and Education Agencies.

- Local Interagency Agreements Between CCS and Education Agencies

(a) In order to facilitate the provision of services described in subdivisions (a), (b), (d), and (e) of Section 7572 of the Government Code and subdivisions (a), (b), and (d) of Section 7575 of the Government Code, each independent county agency and each authorized dependent county agency of CCS shall appoint a liaison for the county agency of CCS. The county Superintendent of Schools or SELPA director shall ensure the designation of a liaison for each SELPA in each local plan.

(b) In the event of multi-SELPA counties or multi-county SELPAs, the liaisons representing education and CCS shall develop a process for interagency decision making that results in a local interagency agreement.

(c) Each independent county agency and each dependent county agency of CCS and the county Superintendent of Schools or SELPA director shall ensure the development and implementation of a local interagency agreement in order to facilitate the provision of medically necessary occupational therapy and physical therapy which shall include at a minimum a delineation of the process for:

(1) Identifying a contact person within each LEA in the

SELPA and within each CCS county agency;

(2) Referring pupils, birth to twenty-one years of age, who may have or are suspected of having a neuromuscular, musculoskeletal, or other physical impairment who may require medically-necessary occupational therapy or physical therapy.

(3) Exchanging between the agencies the educational and medical information concerning the pupil with a disability upon receiving the parent's written, informed consent obtained in accordance with Section 300.500 of Title 34 of the Code of Federal Regulations.

(4) Giving 10 days notice to the county CCS agency of all IEP team meetings for pupils served by CCS medical therapy program;

(5) Giving 10 days notice to the LEA and the parent of an impending change in the CCS medical therapy program services which may necessitate a change in the IEP;

(6) Describing the methods of participation of CCS in the IEP team meetings pursuant to Government Code Section 7572(e);

(7) Developing or amending the therapy services indicated in the pupil's IEP in accordance with Section 56341 of the Education Code;

(8) Transporting pupils with disabilities to receive medically-necessary occupational therapy or physical therapy services at the medical therapy unit or medical therapy unit satellite;

(9) Determining the need for and location of medical therapy units or medical therapy unit satellites, or other off-site facilities authorized by state CCS and the California Department of Education;

(10) Approving the utilization of designated therapy space when not in use by CCS staff.

(11) Planning for joint staff development activities;

(12) Resolving conflicts between the county CCS agency and the LEA; and

(13) Annually reviewing the local interagency agreement and modifying it as necessary.

(d)   The local interagency agreement shall also include:

(1)   The name of the LEA responsible for the provision, maintenance, and operation of the facilities housing the medical therapy unit or medical therapy unit satellite during the CCS work day on a twelve-month basis;

(2)   The name of the LEA having the fiscal/administrative responsibility for the provision and maintenance of necessary

space, equipment, and supplies; and

(3) The process for change in fiscal/administrative responsibility for the provision and maintenance of necessary space, equipment, and supplies.

[Authority cited: Section 7587, Government Code] [Reference: Sections 7572 and 7575, Government Code; Section 123875, Health and Safety Code; Section 300.500 of Title 34, Code of Federal Regulations. Section 56341, Education Code]

60320. Referral and Assessment.

(a) Pupils referred to the LEA for assessment of fine and gross motor or physical skills shall be considered for assessment either by the LEA or by CCS depending on the information contained in the referral and the pupil's documented physical deficit pursuant to Section 7572 of the Government Code.

(b) If the LEA determines that a referral to CCS is not appropriate, the LEA shall propose an assessment plan to the parents.

(c) If the pupil is referred to CCS by the LEA, the referral must be accompanied by:

(1) The pupil's medical diagnosis;

(2) Current medical records;

(3) Parental permission for exchange of information between agencies; and

(4) Application for the CCS program if the pupil is unknown to CCS.

(d) If medical eligibility cannot be determined by medical records submitted, CCS shall:

(1) Notify the parent and LEA within 15 days of the receipt of the referral;

(2) Seek additional medical information; and

(3) If the additional medical information sought in subdivision (2) does not establish medical eligibility, and if the pupil's diagnosis is cerebral palsy, then refer the pupil to a CCS panel physician for a neurological examination.

(e) If CCS determines that the pupil is ineligible because the pupil's medical condition is not a medical therapy program eligible condition, CCS shall notify the parent and LEA within five days of the determination of eligibility status for the medical therapy program.

(f) If CCS determines the pupil has a medical therapy program eligible condition, CCS shall propose a therapy assessment to the parents and obtain written consent for the assessment of the need for medically-necessary occupational therapy or physical therapy. This assessment for therapy shall be implemented not more than 15 days following the determination of whether the pupil has a medical therapy program eligible condition.

(g) Upon receipt of the parent's written consent for an assessment, the CCS agency shall send a copy of the parent's consent to the LEA which shall establish the date of the IEP team meeting. The LEA shall schedule an IEP team meeting to be held within 50 days from the date parental consent is received by CCS.

(h) When CCS determines a pupil needs medically necessary occupational therapy or physical therapy, CCS shall provide the LEA and the parent a copy of the completed assessment report for therapy or a proposed therapy plan prior to the scheduled IEP meeting.

(i) When CCS determines a pupil does not need medically-necessary physical therapy or occupational therapy, the LEA and the parent shall be provided with the completed assessment report for therapy and a statement which delineates the basis for the determination.

[Authority cited: Section 7587, Government Code] [Reference: Sections 7572 and 7575(a), Government Code; Sections 123830, 123860 and 123875, Health and Safety Code. Section 300.532 of Title 34, Code of Federal Regulations. Sections 56320,56321,56329,and 56344, Education Code; and Section 3051.6 of Title 5, California Code of Regulations]

60323. Medical Therapy Program Responsibilities.   - Program Responsibilities

(a) The Medical Therapy Conference shall assess the pupil's need for occupational therapy and physical therapy. The determination of medical necessity shall be based on the pupil's physical and functional status.

(b) The Medical Therapy Conference shall review the therapy plan to ensure the inclusion of measurable functional goals and objectives for services to be performed by occupational therapists and physical therapists, as well as activities that support the goals and objectives to be performed by parents or LEA staff to maintain or prevent loss of function.

(c) The Medical Therapy Conference team shall be responsible for approval of therapy plans and either the

Medical Therapy Conference physician shall write the prescription for those services provided to pupils under his supervision or review those prescriptions submitted by the pupil's private physician for compliance with (a) and (b) of this section.

(d)   Medically necessary therapy services are provided at a level dependent on the pupil's physical and functional status as determined and prescribed by the CCS paneled physician of the specialty appropriate for treating the pupil's Medical Therapy Program eligible condition and who has been authorized by the program to supervise the pupil's Medical Therapy Program eligible condition.

(e)   The medical necessity of occupational therapy or physical therapy services delivered to pupils not participating in a Medical Therapy Conference because there is not a Medical Therapy Conference in their geographical area shall be determined by the state program medical consultant or CCS designee.

(f)   Medical therapy services must be provided by or under the supervision of a registered occupational therapist or licensed physical therapist in accordance with CCS regulations and requirements. This therapy does not include fine and gross motor activities which can be provided by qualified personnel, pursuant to California Code of Regulations, Title 5, Section 2620.

[Authority cited: Section 7587, Government Code] [Reference: Section 7575, Government Code. Sections 123825, 123850 and 123905, Health and Safety Code; Section 3001(x) of Title 5, California Code of Regulations]

60325. Individualized Education Program for Therapy
          Services.

- Individualized Education Program for Therapy Services

(a)   CCS shall provide a copy of the assessment and evaluation report and the proposed therapy plan to the IEP team which shall include:

(1) A statement of the pupil's present level of functional performance;

(2) The proposed functional goals to achieve a measurable change in function or recommendations for services to prevent loss of present function and documentation of progress to date;

(3) The specific related services required by the pupil, including the type of physical therapy or occupational therapy intervention, treatment, consultation, or monitoring;

(4) The proposed initiation, frequency, and duration of the services to be provided by the medical therapy program; and

(5) The proposed date of medical evaluation.

(b) CCS shall participate in the IEP team as set forth in Government Code Section 7572(e).

(c) CCS shall notify the IEP team and parent in writing within 5 days of a decision to increase, decrease, change the type of intervention, or discontinue services for a pupil receiving medical therapy services. If the parent is present at time the decision is made, he or she will also be verbally informed of the decision.

(d) The IEP team shall be convened by the LEA pursuant to subsection (c) of this section or when there is an annual or triennial review or a review requested by the parent or other authorized persons.

(e) The LEA shall convene the IEP team to review all assessments, request additional assessments if needed, determine whether fine or gross motor or physical needs exist, and consider designated instruction and services or related services that are necessary to enable the pupil to benefit from the special education program.

(f) When the IEP team determines that occupational therapy or physical therapy services are necessary for the pupil to benefit from the special education program, goals and objectives relating to the activities identified in the assessment reports shall be written into the IEP and provided by personnel qualified pursuant to the California Code of Regulations, Title 5, Section 3051.6.

[Authority cited: Section 7587, Government Code] [Reference: Sections 7572(e) and 7575, Government Code. Section 56345, Education Code. Section 3051.6 of Title 5, California Code of Regulations]

60330. Space and Equipment for Occupational Therapy and Physical Therapy.

- Space and Equipment for Occupational Therapy and Physical Therapy

(a) The medical therapy unit shall have necessary space and equipment to accommodate the following functions: administration, medical therapy conference, comprehensive evaluation, private treatment, activities of daily living, storage, and modification of equipment. The specific space and equipment requirements are dependent upon local needs as determined by joint agreement of state CCS, county CCS, and LEAs, and approved by both the California Department of Education and the State Department of Health Services.

(b) The space and equipment of the medical therapy unit and medical therapy unit satellites shall be for the exclusive use of the CCS' staff when they are on site. The special education administration of the LEA in which the units are located shall coordinate with the CCS' staff for other use of the space and equipment when the CCS' staff is not present.

(c) All new construction, relocation, remodeling or modification of medical therapy units and medical therapy unit satellites shall be mutually planned and approved by the California Department of Education and the State Department of Health Services.

[Authority cited: Section 7587, Government Code]
[Reference: Section 7575(d), Government Code]

Article 6. Home Health Aide

60400. Specialized Home Health Aide.

- Specialized Home Health Aide

(a) The Department of Health Services shall be responsible for providing the services of a home health aide when the local education agency (LEA) considers a less restrictive placement from home to school for a pupil for whom both of the following conditions exist:

(1) The California Medical Assistance Program (Medi-Cal) provides life-supporting m edical services via a home health agency during the time the pupil would be in school or traveling between school and home.

(2) The medical services provided require that the pupil receive the personal assistance or attention of a nurse, home health aide, parent or guardian, or some other specially trained adult in order to be effectively delivered.

(b) For purposes of this section, "life supporting medical services' means services to a pupil with a disability that is dependent on a medical technology or device that compensates for loss of the normal use of vital bodily function and who requires daily skilled nursing care to divert further disability or death.

(c) The department shall determine the appropriate level of care-giver, based on medical necessity, to provide the services.

[Authority cited: Section 7587, Government Code]
[Reference: Section 7575(e), Government Code; and Section 51337 of Title 22, California Code of Regulations]

Article 7. Exchange of Information Between Education and Social Services

60505. Community Care Facilities.

(a) The Department of Social Services shall biannually provide the Superintendent of Public Instruction a current rates list of group homes and foster family agencies.

(b) The Superintendent of Public Instruction shall biannually provide each county office of education a current list of licensed children's institutions pursuant to Section 56156 of the Education Code.

(c) The county superintendent of schools, in accordance with Section 56156(d) of the Education Code, shall biannually provide the SELPA director a current list of the licensed children's institutions within the county.

(d) The county office of education shall notify the director of each licensed children's institution of the appropriate person to contact regarding pupils with disabilities.

(e) The SELPA director and the administrator of the LEA in which a group home or small family home is located shall provide the facility licensee the following information:

(1) The types and locations of public and state certified nonpublic, nonsectarian special education programs available within the SELPA; and

(2) The ability of the LEAs within the SELPA to absorb, expand, or to open new programs to meet the needs of the pupil population given the limitations of instructional personnel service units, available school facilities, funds, and staff.

[Authority cited: Section 7587, Government Code] [Reference: Section 7580, Government Code. Section 56156, Education Code]

60510. Prior Notification.

(a) The court, regional center for the developmentally disabled, or public agency other than an educational agency shall notify the SELPA director, in writing or by telephone, prior to placing a pupil with a disability in a facility listed in Section 60025, and provide the following relevant information within ten days:

(1) The name of the last school attended, the contact person at that school, and the available educational records, including the current IEP.

(2) A copy or summary of the most recent psychological

and medical records relevant to educational planning which are maintained by the agency.

(3) The name, address and telephone number of the parent who has the responsibility to represent the pupil in educational matters and to sign the IEP for special education, designated instruction and services and related services.

(4) The name, address and telephone number of the individual with designated responsibility to sign for consent for non-emergency medical services.

(5) The name of the administrator/designee, address, telephone number, and licensing status of a home under consideration for the pupil.

(6) A description of any special considerations related to transporting the pupil.

(7) Signed consents by the parent to exchange information relevant to IEP planning and individual program planning.

(8) When an agency makes an emergency placement to protect the physical, mental health or safety of a pupil, the agency shall furnish the SELPA director the required information within three days after the placement.

(b) The SELPA director shall provide the placing agency with information about the availability of an appropriate special education program in the SELPA in which the home is located. This should occur within seven days of receipt of the notice of placement.

(1) If no appropriate special education placements exist within the SELPA, and the placement options are home instruction or in a public or nonpublic facility located in another SELPA, the placing agency should make every effort to place the pupil in another SELPA that has appropriate available residential and educational programs.

(2) When the agency places a pupil in a licensed children's institution, as defined in this Chapter which has an on-grounds, certified, nonpublic, nonsectarian school, the pupil may attend the education program only if the SELPA's IEP team has determined that there is no appropriate public education program in the community and that the on-grounds program is appropriate and can implement the pupil's IEP.

(3) When the IEP team makes the determination that the on-grounds program is appropriate, the LEA may then contract for educational services with the nonpublic school.

[Authority cited: Section 7587, Government Code]
[Reference: Sections 7579 and 7580, Government Code; and Section 56156, Education Code]

Article 8. Procedural Safeguards

60550. Due Process Hearings.

(a) Due process hearing procedures apply to the resolution of disagreements between a parent and a public agency regarding the proposal or refusal of a public agency to initiate or change the identification, assessment, educational placement, or the provision of special education and related services to the pupil.

(b) Upon receiving a request for a due process hearing regarding the services provided or refused by another agency, the Superintendent of Public Instruction or designee shall send the state and local agency involved a copy of the hearing request, the name of the assigned mediator, and the date of the mediation meeting in accordance with Section 56503 of the Education Code. Nothing in this section shall preclude any party form waiving mediation.

(c) If the mediator cannot resolve the issues, a state level hearing shall be conducted by a hearing officer in accordance with Section 56505 of the Education Code.

(d) Each agency which is identified by the State Superintendent of Public Instruction or designee as a potentially responsible party and which has been involved in a proposal or refusal to provide a service is responsible for preparing documentation and providing testimony for the hearing officer.

(e) The hearing officer shall be knowledgeable in the laws governing administrative hearings. In addition, the hearing officer shall be knowledgeable about the provisions of Chapter 26.5 of the Government Code and applicable laws relevant to special education, community mental health and the California Children's Services Program. For hearings related to the provision of occupational and/or physical therapy, the hearing officer shall rule according to Government Code Section 7575(a) which specifies:

(1) "Notwithstanding any other provision of law, the State Department of Health Services, or any designated local agency administering the California Children Services, shall be responsible for the provision of medically necessary occupational therapy and physical therapy, as specified by Article 2, commencing with Section 123825 et. seq. of the Health and Safety Code, by reason of medical diagnosis and when contained in the pupil's IEP.

(2) Related services or designated instruction and services

G-34

not deemed to be medically necessary by the State Department of Health Services, which the IEP team determines are necessary in order to assist a pupil to benefit from special education, shall be provided by the LEA by qualified personnel whose employment standards are covered by the Education Code and implementing regulations."

(f) The hearing decision shall be the final administrative determination regarding the provision of educational and related services, and is binding on all parties.

(g) Nothing in this article shall preclude the Department of Social Services from instituting, maintaining and concluding an administrative action to revoke or temporarily suspend a license pursuant to the Community Care Facilities Act, Health and Safety Code Section 1500 et. seq.

(h) Nothing in this article shall interfere with the discharge of a pupil placed in a community treatment facility who does not meet admission or continuing stay criteria and/or does meet discharge criteria as defined in Welfare and Institutions Code Section 4094 and implementing CCL regulations.

(i) The California Department of Education is fiscally responsible for services provided by the mediator and the hearing officer in response to a parent's request for a due process hearing.

[Authority cited: Section 7587, Government Code] [Reference: Section 7586, Government Code; Sections 56501-56507, Education Code; Section 3082 of Title 5, California Code of Regulations. Section 4094, Welfare and Institutions Code; Corbett v. Regional Center of the East Bay Inc. and Linda McMahon , Director of the Department of Social Services, (1988) 9th Cir. 699 F. Supp. 230; In re Roger S. (1977) 19 Cal. 3d. 921; and In re Michael E. (1975) 15 Cal. 3d. 183]

60560. Compliance Complaints.   - Compliance Complaints

Allegations of failure by an LEA, Community Mental Health Service, or CCS to comply with these regulations shall be resolved pursuant to Chapter 5.1, commencing with Section 4600, of Division 1 of Title 5 of the California Code of Regulations.

[Authority cited: Section 7587, Government Code] [Reference: Section 7585, Government Code; Section 4650, Title 5, California Code of Regulations]

Article 9. Interagency Dispute Resolution

60600. Application of Procedures.

- Application of Procedures

(a) The procedures of this article apply as specified in Government Code 7585, when there is a dispute between or among the California Department of Education or a LEA or both and any agency included in Sections 7575 and 7576 of the Government Code over the provision of related services, when such services are contained in the IEP of a pupil with a disability. This article also applies when the responsibility for providing services, ordered by a hearing officer or agreed to through mediation pursuant to Sections 56503 and 56505 of the Education Code, is in dispute among or between the public agencies.

(b) A dispute over the provision of services means a dispute over which agency is to deliver or to pay for the services when the service is contained in the IEP, mediation agreement, or due process hearing decision. The IEP of a pupil with a disability, and, when appropriate, a copy of the mediation agreement negotiated through the mediator or decision of the hearing officer shall accompany the request for a state interagency dispute resolution.

(c) As specified in Section 7585 of the Government Code, when a service has been included in an IEP by an IEP team without the recommendation of the qualified professional in accordance with Section 7572 of the Government Code, the LEA shall be solely responsible for the provision of the service. In such circumstances, the dispute, if any, is between the parent and the LEA and shall be resolved pursuant to Title 5 of the California Code of Regulations.

[Authority cited: Section 7587, Government Code] [Reference: Sections 7572 and 7585, Government Code; and Sections 56503 and 56505, Education Code]

60610. Resolution Procedure.

- Resolution Procedure

(a) Whenever notification is filed pursuant to subsection (a) of Section 7585 of the Government Code, the dispute procedures shall not interfere with a pupil with a disability's right to receive a free, appropriate public education.

(1) If one of the departments or local agencies specified in Sections 7575, 7576, 7577, and 7578 of the Government Code has been providing the service prior to notification of

the failure to provide a related service or designated instruction and service, that department or local agency shall pay for, or provide, at it's discretion, the service until the dispute resolution proceedings are completed.

(2) If no department or local agency specified in this section has provided the service prior to the notification of the dispute, the State Superintendent of Public Instruction shall ensure that the LEA provides the service in accordance with the IEP, until the dispute resolution proceedings are completed.

(3) Arrangements, other than those specified in paragraphs (1) and (2) of subsection (a), may be made by written agreement between the involved public agencies, provided the pupil with disabilities' IEP is not altered, except as to which agency delivers or pays for the service if such specification is included in the IEP.

(b) In resolving the dispute, the State Superintendent of Public Instruction and Secretary of the Health and Welfare Agency or their designees shall meet to resolve the issue within 15 days of receipt of the notice.

(c) Once the dispute resolution procedures have been completed, the department or local agency determined responsible for the service shall pay for, or provide the service, and shall reimburse the other agency which provided the service pursuant to subsection (a) of this section, if applicable.

(d) A written copy of the resolution shall be mailed to affected parties pursuant to Section 7585 of the Government Code.

(e) The resolution of the dispute shall be communicated to the originating party within 60 days from the receipt of the complaint by either agency.

[Authority cited: Section 7587, Government Code] [Reference: Sections 7575, 7576, 7577, 7578 and 7585, Government Code]

NOTE

(1) The regulations contained in Chapter 1 (commencing with Section 60000) of Division 9 of Title 2 of the California Code of Regulations were amended and approved as final regulations in 1999 – implementing the provisions of Chapter 26.5, Division 7, Title 1, of the Government Code.

CALIFORNIA CHILDREN'S SERVICE
MEDICAL THERAPY

(Health and Safety Code)

(Formerly Section 255.3)

123875. When the California Children's Service medical therapy unit conference team, based on a medical referral recommending medically necessary occupational or physical therapy in accordance with subdivision (b) of Section 7575 of the Government Code, finds that a handicapped child, as defined in Section 123830, needs medically necessary occupational or physical therapy, that child shall be determined to be eligible for therapy services. If the California Children's Services medical consultant disagrees with the determination of eligibility by the California Children's Services medical therapy unit conference team, the medical consultant shall communicate with the conference team to ask for further justification of its determination, and shall weigh the conference team's arguments in support of its decision in reaching his or her own determination.

This section shall not change eligibility criteria for the California Children's Services programs as described in Sections 123830 and 123860.

This section shall not apply to children diagnosed as specific learning disabled, unless they otherwise meet the eligibility criteria of the California Children's Services.

- Medically Necessary OT/PT

DEPENDENT CHILD OF THE COURT
AND EDUCATIONAL DECISIONS

(Welfare and Institutions Code)

(As Amended by AB 1544, Chapter 793, Statutes of 1997)

361. (a) In all cases in which a minor is adjudged a dependent child of the court on the ground that the minor is a person described by Section 300, the court may limit the control to be exercised over the dependent child by any parent or guardian and shall by its order clearly and specifically set forth all such limitations. Any limitation on the right of the parent or guardian to make educational decisions for the child shall be specifically addressed in the court order. The limitations shall not exceed those necessary

- Dependent Child of the Court Educational Decisions

to protect the child.

(b) Nothing in subdivision (a) shall be construed to limit the ability of a parent to voluntarily relinquish his or her child to the State Department of Social Services or to a licensed county adoption agency at any time while the child is a dependent child of the juvenile court if the department or agency is willing to accept the relinquishment.

- Parent Can Voluntarily Relinquish Child

(c) No dependent child shall be taken from the physical custody of his or her parents or guardian or guardians with whom the child resides at the time the petition was initiated unless the juvenile court finds clear and convincing evidence of any of the following:

- Physical Custody

(1) There is a substantial danger to the physical health, safety, protection, or physical or emotional well-being of the minor or would be if the minor were returned home, and there are no reasonable means by which the minor's physical health can be protected without removing the minor from the minor's parents' or guardians' physical custody. The fact that a minor has been adjudicated a dependent child of the court pursuant to subdivision (e) of Section 300 shall constitute prima facie evidence that the minor cannot be safely left in the custody of the parent or guardian with whom the minor resided at the time of injury. The court shall consider, as a reasonable means to protect the minor, the option of removing an offending parent or guardian from the home. The court shall also consider, as a reasonable means to protect the minor, allowing a nonoffending parent or guardian to retain custody as long as that parent or guardian presents a plan acceptable to the court demonstrating that he or she will be able to protect the child from future harm.

(2) The parent or guardian of the minor is unwilling to have physical custody of the minor, and the parent or guardian has been notified that if the minor remains out of their physical custody for the period specified in Section 366.25 or 366.26, the minor may be declared permanently free from their custody and control.

(3) The minor is suffering severe emotional damage, as indicated by extreme anxiety, depression, withdrawal, or untoward aggressive behavior toward self or others, and there are no reasonable means by which the minor's emotional health may be protected without removing the minor from the physical custody of his or her parent or guardian.

(4) The minor or sibling of the minor has been sexually abused, or is deemed to be at substantial risk of being

sexually abused, by a parent, guardian, or member of his or her household, or other person known to his or her parent, and there are no reasonable means by which the minor can be protected from further sexual abuse or substantial risk of sexual abuse without removing the minor from his or her parent or guardian, or the minor does not wish to return to his or her parent or guardian.

(5) The minor has been left without any provision for his or her support, or a parent who has been incarcerated or institutionalized cannot arrange for the care of the minor, or a relative or other adult custodian with whom the child has been left by the parent is unwilling or unable to provide care or support for the child and the whereabouts of the parent is unknown and reasonable efforts to located him or her have been unsuccessful.

(d) The court shall make a determination as to whether reasonable efforts were made to prevent or to eliminate the need for removal of the minor from his or her home or, if the minor is removed for one of the reasons stated in paragraph (5) of subdivision (c), whether it was reasonable under the circumstances not to make any of those efforts. The court shall state the facts on which the decision to remove the minor is based. — Court Determination

(e) The court shall make all of the findings required by subdivision (a) of Section 366 in either of the following circumstances: — Court Findings

(1) The minor has been taken from the custody of his or her parents or guardians and has been living in an out-of-home placement pursuant to Section 319.

(2) The minor has been living in a voluntary out-of-home placement pursuant to Section 16507.4.

MENTAL HEALTH SERVICES FOR DEPENDENT CHILD OF THE COURT

(Welfare and Institutions Code)

(As Amended by AB 686, Chapter 911, Statutes of 2000)

362. (a) When a child is adjudged a dependent child of the court on the ground that the child is a person described by Section 300, the court may make any and all reasonable orders for the care, supervision, custody, conduct, maintenance, and support of the child, including medical treatment, subject to further order of the court. To facilitate — Dependent Child of the Court coordination and cooperation among government agencies, the court may, after giving notice and an opportunity to be heard, join in the juvenile court proceedings any agency that the court determines has failed to meet a legal obligation to provide services to the child. In any proceedings in which an agency is joined, the court shall not impose duties upon the agency beyond those mandated by law. Nothing in this section shall prohibit agencies which have received notice of the hearing on joinder from meeting prior to the hearing to coordinate services for the child.

The court has no authority to order services unless it has been determined through the administrative process of an agency that has been joined as a party, that the child is eligible for those services. With respect to mental health assessment, treatment, and case management services pursuant to Chapter 26.5 (commencing with Section 7570) of Division 7 of Title 1 of the Government Code, the court's determination shall be limited to whether the agency has complied with that chapter.

(b) When a child is adjudged a dependent child of the court, on the ground that the child is a person described by Section 300 and the court orders that a parent or guardian shall retain custody of the child subject to the supervision of the social worker, the parents or guardians shall be required to participate in child welfare services or services provided by an appropriate agency designated by the court.

– Parents/Guardians Participate in Child Welfare Services

(c) The juvenile court may direct any and all reasonable orders to the parents or guardians of the child who is the subject of any proceedings under this chapter as the court deems necessary and proper to carry out the provisions of this section, including orders to appear before a county financial evaluation officer. That order may include a direction to participate in counseling or education program, including, but not limited to, a parent education and parenting program operated by a community college, school district, or other appropriate agency designated by the court. A foster parent or relative with whom the child is placed may be directed to participate in such a program in cases in which the court deems participation is appropriate and is in the child's best interest. The program in which a parent or guardian is required to participate shall be designed to eliminate those conditions that led to the court's finding that the child is a person described by Section 300.

– Court Orders

(d) When a child is adjuged a dependent child of the court, the juvenile court may direct any and all reasonable orders to

– Ensure Child's Regular School Attendance

the parents or guardians of the child who is the subject of any proceedings under this chapter, to ensure the child's regular school attendance and to make reasonable efforts to obtain educational services necessary to meet the specific needs of the child.

(e) "Private service provider" means any agency or individual that receives federal, state, or local government funding or reimbursement for providing services directly to foster children.

- Private Service Provider

[Similar language concerning mental health assessment, treatment, and case management services pursuant to Chapter 26.5 (commencing with Section 7570) of the Government Code is in Section 727 of the Welfare and Institutions Code covering Section 601 and Section 602 wards of the court.]

PLACEMENT OUT-OF-HOME TO BE AS NEAR THE CHILD'S HOME AS POSSIBLE

(Welfare and Institutions Code)

(AB 1892 - Chapter 1128, Statutes of 1994)

362.2. It is the intent of the Legislature that if a placement out-of-home is necessary pursuant to an individualized education program, that this placement be as near the child's home as possible, unless it is not in the best interest of the child. When the court determines that it is the best interest of the child to be placed out-of-state, the court shall read into the record that in-state alternatives have been explored and that they cannot meet the needs of the child, and the court shall state on the record the reasons for the out-of-state placement.

- Legislative Intent

INDIVIDUALS WITH EXCEPTIONAL NEEDS COMMITTED TO YOUTH AUTHORITY

(Welfare and Institutions Code)

(AB 820 - Chapter 175, Statutes of 1993)

1742. When the juvenile court commits to the Youth Authority a person identified as an individual with exceptional needs, as defined by Section 56026 of the Education Code, the juvenile court, subject to the

- IEP of Individual Committed to Youth Authority

requirements of subdivision (a) of Section 727 and subdivision (b) of Section 737, shall not order the juvenile conveyed to the physical custody of the Youth Authority until the juvenile's individualized education program previously developed pursuant to Article 3 (commencing with Section 56340) of Chapter 4 of Part 30 of Division 4 of Title 2 of the Education Code for the individual with exceptional needs, has been furnished to the Department of the Youth Authority.

To facilitate this process the juvenile court shall assure that the probation officer communicates with appropriate staff at the juvenile court school, county office of education, or special education local planning area.

LOCKED OR SECURED COMMUNITY TREATMENT FACILITY PROGRAMS

(Welfare and Institutions Code)

(As Amended by AB 430, Chapter 171, Statutes of 2001))

4094. (a) The State Department of Mental Health shall establish, by regulations adopted at the earliest possible date, but no later than December 31, 1994, program standards for any facility licensed as a community treatment facility. This section shall apply only to community treatment facilities described in this subdivision.

- Regulations for Community Treatment Facility Program Standards

(b) A certification of compliance issued by the State Department of Mental Health shall be a condition of licensure for the community treatment facility by the State Department of Social Services. The department may, upon the request of a county, delegate the certification and supervision of a community treatment facility to the county department of mental health.

- Certification of Compliance

(c) The State Department of Mental Health shall adopt regulations to include, but not be limited to, the following:

- Department of Mental Health Regulations

(1) Procedures by which the Director of Mental Health shall certify that a facility requesting licensure as a community treatment facility pursuant to Section 1502 of the Health and Safety Code is in compliance with program standards established pursuant to this section.

(2) Procedures by which the Director of Mental Health shall deny a certification to a facility or decertify a facility licensed as a community treatment facility pursuant to Section 1502 of the Health and Safety Code, but no longer complying with program standards established pursuant to this section,

in accordance with Chapter 5 (commencing with Section 11500) of Part 1 of Division 3 of Title 2 of the Government Code.

(3) Provisions for site visits by the State Department of Mental Health for the purpose of reviewing a facility's compliance with program standards established pursuant to this section.

(4) Provisions for the community care licensing staff of the State Department of Social Services to report to the State Department of Mental Health when there is reasonable cause to believe that a community treatment facility is not in compliance with program standards established pursuant to this section.

(5) Provisions for the State Department of Mental Health to provide consultation and documentation to the State Department of Social Services in any administrative proceeding regarding denial, suspension, or revocation of a community treatment facility license.

(d) The standards adopted by regulations pursuant to subdivision (a) shall include, but not be limited to, standards for treatment staffing and for the use of psychotropic medication, discipline, and restraint in the facilities. The standards shall also meet the requirements of Section 4094.5.

— Standards

(e) During the initial public comment period for the adoption of the regulations required by this section, the community care facility licensing regulations proposed by the State Department of Social Services and the program standards proposed by the State Department of Mental Health shall be presented simultaneously.

— Public Comment Period for Adoption of Regulations

(f) A minor shall be admitted to a community treatment facility only if the requirements of Section 4094.5 and either of the following conditions is met:

— Admittance to Community Treatment Facility

(1) The minor is within the jurisdiction of the juvenile court, and has made voluntary application for mental health services pursuant to Section 6552.

(2) Informed consent is given by a parent, guardian, conservator, or other person having custody of the minor.

(g) Any minor admitted to a community treatment facility shall have the same due process rights afforded to a minor who may be admitted to a state hospital, pursuant to the holding in In re Roger S. (1977) 19 Cal. 3d 921. Minors who are wards or dependents of the court and to whom this subdivision applies shall be afforded due process in accordance with Section 6552 and related case law, including In re Michael E. (1975) 15 Cal. 3d 183. Regulations adopted

— Due Process Rights

pursuant to Section 4094 shall specify the procedures for ensuring these rights, including provisions for notification of rights and the time and place of hearings.

(h) Notwithstanding Section 13340 of the Government Code, the sum of forty-five thousand dollars ($45,000) is hereby appropriated annually from the General Fund to the State Department of Mental Health for one personnel year to carry out the provisions of this section.

- Personnel Funding to Carry Out Provisions

4094.1. (a) (1) The department and the State Department of Social Services, in consultation with community treatment providers, local mental health departments, and county welfare departments, shall develop joint protocols for the oversight of community treatment facilities.

- Joint Protocols for Oversight of Treatment Facilities

(2) Subject to subdivision (b), until the protocols and regulatory changes required by paragraph (1) are implemented, entities operating community treatment facilities shall comply with the current reporting requirements and other procedural and administrative mandates established in State Department of Mental Health regulations governing community treatment facilities.

(b) In accordance with all of the following, the State Department of Social Services shall modify existing regulations governing reporting requirements and other procedural and administrative mandates, to take into account the seriousness and frequency of behaviors that are likely to be exhibited by children placed in community treatment facilities. The modifications required by this subdivision shall apply for the entire 2000-01 fiscal year.

- Secure Containment

(1) Notwithstanding existing regulations, the State Department of Social Services shall issue alternative training and education requirements for community treatment facility managers and staff, which shall be developed in consultation with the State Department of Mental Health, patients' rights advocates, local mental health departments, county welfare offices, and providers.

(2) The department and the State Department of Social Services shall conduct joint bimonthly visits to licensed community treatment facilities to monitor operational progress and to provide technical assistance.

(3) The appropriate department shall centrally review any certification or licensure deficiency before notice of the citation is issued to the community care facility.

(4) A community treatment facility shall be exempt from reporting any occurrence of the use of restraint to the State Department of Social Services, unless physical injury is

sustained or unconsciousness or other medical conditions arise from the restraint.

All other reporting requirements shall apply.

4094.2. (a) For the purpose of establishing payment rates for community treatment facility programs, the private nonprofit agencies selected to operate these programs shall prepare a budget that covers the total costs of providing residential care and supervision and mental health services for their proposed programs. These costs shall include categories that are allowable under California's Foster Care program and existing programs for mental health services. They shall not include educational, nonmental health medical and dental costs.

- Establishing Payment Rates for Community Treatment Facility Programs (1)

(b) Each agency operating a community treatment facility program shall negotiate a final budget with the local mental health department in the county in which its facility is located (the host county) and other local agencies as appropriate. This budget agreement shall specify the types and level of care and services to be provided by the community treatment facility program and a payment rate that fully covers the costs included in the negotiated budget. All counties that place children in a community treatment facility program shall make payments using the budget agreement negotiated by the community treatment facility provider and the host county.

- Budget Agreement with Local Mental Health Department

(c) A foster care rate shall be established for each community treatment facility program by the State Department of Social Services. These rates shall be established using the existing foster care ratesetting system for group homes, with modifications designed as necessary. It is anticipated that all community treatment facility programs will offer the level of care and services required to receive the highest foster care rate provided for under the current group home ratesetting system.

- Foster Care Rate

(d) For the 2001-02 fiscal year, community treatment facility programs shall also be paid a community treatment facility supplemental rate of up to two thousand five hundred dollars ($2,500) per child per month on behalf of children eligible under the foster care program and children placed out of home pursuant to an individualized education program developed under Section 7572.5 of the Government Code. Subject to the availability of funds, the supplemental rate shall be shared by the state and the counties. Counties shall be responsible for paying a county share of cost equal to 60 percent of the community treatment rate for children placed by counties in community treatment facilities and the state

- Payment of Supplemental Rate

shall be responsible for 40 percent of the community treatment facility supplemental rate. The community treatment facility supplemental rate is intended to supplement, and not to supplant, the payments for which children placed in community treatment facilities are eligible to receive under the foster care program and the existing programs for mental health services.

(e) For initial ratesetting purposes for community treatment facility funding, the cost of mental health services shall be determined by deducting the foster care rate and the community treatment facility supplemental rate from the total allowable cost of the community treatment facility program. Payments to certified providers for mental health services shall be based on eligible services provided to children who are Medi-Cal beneficiaries, up to the statewide maximum allowances for these services.

- Ratesetting and Cost of Mental Health Services

(f) Although there is statutory authorization for up to 400 community treatment facility beds statewide, it is anticipated that there will be a phased-in implementation of community treatment facilities, and that the average monthly community treatment facility caseload during the 2001-02 fiscal year will be approximately 100.

- Phased-in Implementation of Community Treatment Facilities

(g) The department shall provide the community treatment facility supplemental rates to the counties for advanced payment to the community treatment facility providers in the same manner as the regular foster care payment and within the same required payment time limits.

- Advanced Payment

(h) In order to facilitate a study of the costs of community treatment facilities, licensed community treatment facilities shall provide all documents regarding facility operations, treatment, and placements requested by the department.

- Joint Report to Legislature

(i) It is the intent of the Legislature that the department and the State Department of Social Services work to maximize federal financial participation in funding for children placed in community treatment facilities through funds available pursuant to Titles IV-E and XIX of the federal Social Security Act (Title 42 U.S.C. Sec. 670 and following and Sec. 1396 and following) and other appropriate federal programs.

- Maximize Federal Financial Participation

(j) The department and the State Department of Social Services may adopt emergency regulations necessary to implement joint protocols for the oversight of community treatment facilities, to modify existing licensing regulations governing reporting requirements and other procedural and administrative mandates to take into account the seriousness

- Emergency Regulations to Implement Joint Protocols

and frequency of behaviors that are likely to be exhibited by the seriously emotionally disturbed children placed in community treatment facility programs, to modify the existing foster care ratesetting regulations, and to pay the community treatment facility supplemental rate. The adoption of these regulations shall be deemed to be an emergency and necessary for the immediate preservation of the public peace, health and safety, and general welfare. The regulations shall become effective immediately upon filing with the Secretary of State. The regulations shall not remain in effect more than 180 days unless the adopting agency complies with all the provisions of Chapter 3.5 (commencing with Section 11340) of Part 1 of Division 3 of Title 2 of the Government Code, as required by subdivision (e) of Section 11346.1 of the Government Code.

4094.5. Regulations for community treatment facilities adopted pursuant to Section 4094 shall include, but not be limited to, the following:

- Scope of Regulations

(a) Only seriously emotionally disturbed children, as defined in Section 5699.2, for whom other less restrictive mental health interventions have been tried, as documented in the case plan, or who are currently placed in an acute psychiatric hospital or state hospital or in a facility outside the state for mental health treatment, and who may require periods of containment to participate in, and benefit from, mental health treatment, shall be placed in a community treatment facility. For purposes of this subdivision, lesser restrictive interventions shall include, but are not limited to, outpatient therapy, family counseling, case management, family preservation efforts, special education classes, or nonpublic schooling.

- Seriously Emotionally Disturbed Children

(b) A facility shall have the capacity to provide secure containment. For purposes of this section, a facility or an area of a facility shall be defined as secure if residents are not permitted to leave the premises of their own volition. All or part of a facility, including its perimeter, but not a room alone, may be locked or secure. If a facility uses perimeter fencing, all beds within the perimeter shall be considered secure beds. All beds outside of a locked or secure wing or facility shall be considered nonsecure beds.

- Secure Containment

(c) A locked or secure program in a facility shall not be used for disciplinary purposes, but shall be used for the protection of the minor. It may be used as a treatment modality for a child needing that level of care. The use of the secure facility program shall be for as short a period as

- Locked or Secure Program Used for Protection of Minor

possible, consistent with the child's case plan and safety. The department shall develop regulations governing the oversight, review, and duration of the use of secure beds.

(d) Fire clearance approval shall be obtained pursuant to Section 1531.2 of the Health and Safety Code.

- Fire Clearance

(e) (1) Prior to admission, any child admitted to a community treatment facility shall have been certified as seriously emotionally disturbed, as defined in Section 5699.2, by a licensed mental health professional. The child shall, prior to admission, have been determined to be in need of the level of care provided by a community treatment facility, by a county interagency placement committee, as prescribed by Section 4096.

- Requirements Prior to Admission

(2) Any county cost associated with the certification and the determination provided for in paragraph (1) may be billed as a utilization review expense.

4094.6. The patients' rights provisions contained in Sections 5325, 5325.1, 5325.2, and 5326 shall be available to any child admitted to, or eligible for admission to, a community treatment facility. Every child placed in a community treatment facility shall have a right to a hearing by writ of habeas corpus, within two judicial days of the filing of a petition for the writ of habeas corpus with the superior court of the county in which the facility is located, for his or her release. Regulations adopted pursuant to Section 4094 shall specify the procedures by which this right shall be ensured. These regulations shall generally be consistent with the procedures contained in Section 5275 et seq., concerning habeas corpus for individuals, including children, subject to various involuntary holds.

- Patients' Rights

4094.7. (a) A community treatment facility may have both secure and nonsecure beds. However, the State Department of Mental Health shall limit the total number of beds in community treatment facilities to not more than 400 statewide. The State Department of Mental Health shall certify community treatment facilities in such a manner as to ensure an adequate dispersal of these facilities within the state. The State Department of Mental Health shall ensure that there is at least one facility in each of the State Department of Social Services' four regional licensing divisions.

- Secure and Nonsecure Beds

- Not More Than 400 Beds Statewide

(b) The State Department of Mental Health shall notify the State Department of Social Services when a facility has been certified and has met the program standards pursuant to Section 4094. The State Department of Social Services shall

- Certification Notification

license a community treatment facility for a specified number of secure beds and a specified number of nonsecure beds. The number of secure and nonsecure beds in a facility shall be modified only with the approval of both the State Department of Social Services and the State Department of Mental Health.

(c) The State Department of Mental Health shall develop, with the advice of the State Department of Social Services, county representatives, providers, and interested parties, the criteria to be used to determine which programs among applicant providers shall be licensed. The State Department of Mental Health shall determine which agencies best meet the criteria, certify them in accordance with Section 4094, and refer them to the State Department of Social Services for licensure.

- Criteria for Determining Program Licensing

(d) Any community treatment facility proposing to serve seriously emotionally disturbed foster children shall be incorporated as a nonprofit organization.

- Nonprofit Organization

(e) No later than January 1, 1996, the State Department of Mental Health shall submit its recommendation to the appropriate policy committees of the Legislature relative to the limitation on the number of beds set forth in this section.

- Recommendation to Legislature

MEDI-CAL COVERED SERVICES

(Welfare and Institutions Code)

(As Amended by AB 549, Chapter 883, Statutes of 1997)

14132.06. (a) Services specified in this section that are provided by a local educational agency are covered Medi-Cal benefits, to the extent federal financial participation is available, and subject to utilization controls and standards adopted by the department, and consistent with Medi-Cal requirements for physician prescription, order, and supervision.

- Services Provided by a Local Educational Agency

(b) Any provider enrolled on or after January 1, 1993, to provide services pursuant to this section may bill for those services provided on or after January 1, 1993.

(c) Nothing in this section shall be interpreted to expand the current category of professional health care practitioners permitted to directly bill the Medi-Cal program.

(d) Nothing in this section is intended to increase the scope of practice of any health professional providing services under this section or Medi-Cal requirements for physician prescription, order, and supervision.

(e) (1) For the purposes of this section, the local educational agency, as a condition of enrollment to provide services under this section, shall be considered the provider of services. A local educational agency provider, as a condition of enrollment to provide services under this section, shall enter into, and maintain, a contract with the department in accordance with guidelines contained in regulations adopted by the director and published in Title 22 of the California Code of Regulations.

(2) Notwithstanding paragraph (1), a local educational agency providing services pursuant to this section shall utilize current safety net and traditional health care providers, when those providers are accessible to specific schoolsites identified by the local educational agency to participate in this program, rather than adding duplicate capacity.

(f) For the purposes of this section, covered services may include all of the following local educational services:
- Included Services

(1) Health and mental health evaluations and health and mental health education.

(2) Medical transportation.

(3) Nursing services.

(4) Occupational therapy.

(5) Physical therapy.

(6) Physician services.

(7) Mental health and counseling services.

(8) School health aide services.

(9) Speech pathology services and audiology services.

(10) Targeted case management services for children with an individualized education plan [sic] (IEP), and individualized family service plan (IFSP), or an individualized health and support plan (IHSP) provided on or after July 1, 1997.

(g) Local educational agencies may, but need not, provide any or all of the services specified in subdivision (f).

(h) For the purposes of this section, "local educational agency" means the governing body of any school district or community college district, the county office of education, a state special school, a California State University campus, or a University of California campus.

(i) Any local educational agency provider enrolled to provide service pursuant to this section on January 1, 1995, may bill for targeted case management services for children with an individualized education plan [sic] (IEP), an individualized family service plan (IFSP), provided on or after January 1, 1995, or an individualized health and support plan (IHSP), provided on or after July 1, 1997.

(j) Notwithstanding any other provision of law, a community college district, a California State University campus, or a University of California campus, consistent with the requirements of this section, may bill for services provided to any student, regardless of age, who is a Medi-Cal recipient.

SERIOUSLY EMOTIONALLY DISTURBED OUT-OF-HOME CARE

(Welfare and Institutions Code)

(AB 882- Chapter 1274, Statutes of 1985; As Amended by SB 370 – Chapter 1294 , Statutes of 1989; As Amended by SB 1176 – Chapter 46, Statutes of 1990, And AB 3596 – Chapter 737, Statutes of 1990)

CHAPTER 6. SERIOUSLY EMOTIONALLY DISTURBED CHILDREN: 24-HOUR OUT-OF-HOME CARE

18350. (a) Payments for 24-hour out-of-home care shall be provided under this chapter on behalf of any seriously emotionally disturbed child who has been placed out-of-home pursuant to an individualized education program developed under Section 7572.5 of the Government Code. These payments shall not constitute an aid payment or aid program.

- Payments

(b) Payments shall only be made to children placed in privately operated residential facilities licensed in accordance with the Community Care Facilities Act.

(c) Payments for care and supervision shall be based on rates established in accordance with Sections 11460 to 11467, inclusive.

(d) Payments for 24-hour out-of-home care under this section shall not result in any cost to the seriously emotionally disturbed child or his or her parent or parents.

18351. (a) Payments shall be issued by the county welfare department to residential care providers upon receipt of authorization documents from the State Department of Mental Health or a designated county mental health agency. The county welfare department located in the same county as the county mental health agency designated to case management services shall be responsible for payment under

- Payments Issued by County Welfare Department

this section. Authorization documents shall be submitted directly to the county welfare department clerical unit responsible for issuance of warrants and shall include information sufficient to demonstrate that the child meets all eligibility criteria established in regulations by the State Department of Mental Health, developed in consultation with the State Department of Education.

(b) The county welfare department shall submit reports to the State Department of Social Services for reimbursement of payments issued to seriously emotionally disturbed children for 24-hour out-of-home care.

18352. County welfare departments may, at their option and with approval of the State Department of Social Services and other appropriate agencies, enter into agreements with other local agencies for the delivery of a single payment for all related services for a seriously emotionally disturbed child to a residential care provider.

- Agreements for Single Payment

18353. When an individualized education program calls for 24-hour out-of-home care, the county welfare department shall provide assistance, as necessary, in identifying a facility suited to the child's needs and in placing the child in the facility.

- Counties Provide Assistance in Identifying Facility

18354. (a) If a provider of 24-hour out-of-home care to a child who has been placed pursuant to Section 7572.5 of the Government Code in a 24-hour out-of-home placement disputes an action of the designated county mental health agency regarding the providers eligibility for payment, the provider may request a review of the issue by the designated county mental health agency. Designated county mental health agencies may establish policies and procedures, as may be necessary, to implement this subdivision.

- Disputes Regarding the Provider's Eligibility for Payment

(b) If the issue remains unresolved after the review by the designated county mental health agency, then the provider may request a review of the issue by the State Department of Mental Health. The Director of Mental Health may establish policies and procedures, as may be necessary, to implement this subdivision. The review under this subdivision shall be limited to the issue of whether the eligibility for payment criteria established by the State Department of Mental Health was correctly applied.

18355. Notwithstanding any other provision of the law, 24-hour out-of-home care for seriously emotionally disturbed children who are placed in accordance with Section 7572.5 of the Government Code shall be funded from a separate appropriation in the budget of the State Department of Social

- Separate Appropriation

Services in order to fund both 24-hour out-of-home care payment and local administrative costs. Reimbursement for 24-hour out-of-home care payment costs shall be from that appropriation, subject to the same sharing ratio as prescribed in subdivision (c) of Section 15200, and available funds. Reimbursements for local administrative costs shall also be from that appropriation, subject to the same sharing ratio as prescribed in Section 15204.2 for the Aid to Families with Dependent Children program, and available funds.

18356. (a) When a local mental health department places a client out-of-state pursuant to Chapter 26.5 (commencing with Section 7570) of Division 7 of Title 1 of the Government Code, it shall prepare a report for the Director of Mental Health. The report shall be sent to the State Department of Mental Health within 15 days after the actual placement.

- Report of Out-of-State Placements

(b) The report shall summarize the local mental health department's efforts to locate, develop, or adapt an appropriate program for the client within the state. The report shall also identify the circumstances which led to the out-of-state placement, including the child's experience with California placements, distance from the child's family, child treatment needs which cannot be met in California placement, and any other factors leading to the placement.

(c) The report shall identify any special circumstances, such as legal interventions, including mediation hearings, fair hearings, compliance complaints, or any other legal procedure resulting in an order which mandates the child's placement out of state.

(d) The report shall identify provisions for case management, case supervision, and family visitation in the case of out-of-state placements.

NOTE

(1) Welfare and Institutions Code Section 4094.2 was amended by Assembly Bill 430, Chapter 171, Statutes of 2001.

CALIFORNIA EARLY INTERVENTION SERVICES ACT

(Government Code)

(SB 1085 - Chapter 945, Statutes of 1993, As Amended by
SB   391 - Chapter 294, Statutes of 1997, As Amended by
AB 2780 - Chapter 310, Statutes of 1998, And
AB 2803 - Chapter 485, Statutes of 1998, As Amended by
AB 1107 - Chapter 146, Statutes of 1999, As Amended by
AB   430 - Chapter 171, Statutes of 2001)

TITLE 14. CALIFORNIA EARLY INTERVENTION SERVICES ACT

CHAPTER 1. GENERAL PROVISIONS

95000.   This title may be cited as the California Early Intervention Services Act.

- Title of Act

95001.   (a) The Legislature hereby finds and declares all of the following:

- Legislative Findings

(1)   There is a need to provide appropriate early intervention services individually designed for infants and toddlers from birth through two years of age, who have disabilities or are at risk of having disabilities, to enhance their development and to minimize the potential for developmental delays.

(2) Early intervention services for infants and toddlers with disabilities or at risk represent an investment of resources, in that these services reduce the ultimate costs to our society, by minimizing the need for special education and related services in later school years and by minimizing the likelihood of institutionalization. These services also maximize the ability of families to better provide for the special needs of their child.   Early intervention services for infants and toddlers with disabilities maximize the potential to be effective in the context of daily life and activities, including the potential to live independently, and exercise the full rights of citizenship. The earlier intervention is started, the greater is the ultimate cost-effectiveness and the higher is the educational attainment and quality of life achieved by children with disabilities.

(3) The family is the constant in the child's life, while the service system and personnel within those systems fluctuate. Because the primary responsibility of an infant or toddler's

well-being rests with the family, services should support and enhance the family's capability to meet the special developmental needs of their infant or toddler with disabilities.

(4) Family to family support strengthens families' ability to fully participate in services planning and their capacity to care for their infant or toddler with disabilities.

(5) Meeting the complex needs of infants with disabilities and their families requires active state and local coordinated, collaborative and accessible service delivery systems that are flexible, culturally competent and responsive to family identified needs. When health, developmental, educational and social programs are coordinated, they are proven to be cost-effective, not only for systems, but for families as well.

(6) Family-professional collaboration contributes to changing the ways that early intervention services are provided and to enhancing their effectiveness.

(7) Infants and toddlers with disabilities are a part of their communities, and as citizens make valuable contributions to society as a whole.

(b) Therefore, it is the intent of the Legislature that: - Legislative Intent

(1) Funding provided under Part H of the Individuals with Disabilities Education Act (20 U.S.C. Sec. 1471 et seq.), be uscd to improve and enhance early intervention services as defined in this title by developing innovative ways of providing family focused, coordinated services, which are built upon existing systems.

(2) The State Department of Developmental Services, the California Department of Education, the State Department of Health Services, the State Department of Mental Health, the State Department of Social Services, and the State Department of Alcohol and Drug Programs coordinate services to infants and toddlers with disabilities and their families. These agencies need to collaborate with families and communities to provide family- centered, comprehensive, multidisciplinary, interagency community-based, early intervention system for infants and toddlers with disabilities.

(3) Families be well informed, supported, and respected as capable and collaborative decisionmakers regarding services for their child.

(4) Professionals be supported to enhance their training and maintain a high level of expertise in their field, as well as knowledge of what constitutes most effective early intervention practices.

(5) Families and professionals join in collaborative

partnerships to develop early intervention services which meet the needs of infants and toddlers with disabilities, and that such partnerships be the basis for the development of services which meet the needs of the culturally and linguistically diverse population of California.

(6) To the maximum extent possible, infants and toddlers with disabilities and their families be provided services in the most natural environment, and include the use of natural supports and existing community resources.

(7) The services delivery system be responsive to the families and children it serves within the context of cooperation and coordination among the various agencies.

(8) Early intervention program quality be assured and maintained through established early intervention program and personnel standards.

(9) The early intervention system be responsive to public input and participation in the development of implementation policies and procedures for early intervention services through the forum of an interagency coordinating council established pursuant to federal regulations under Part H of the Individuals with Disabilities Education Act.

(c) It is not the intent of the Legislature to require the State Department of Education to implement this title unless adequate reimbursement, as specified and agreed to by the department, is provided to the department from federal funds from Part H of the Individuals with Disabilities Education Act.

95001.5. In order to prevent any potential conflict of interest and pursuant to Section 303.604 of the Code of Federal Regulations, no member of the interagency coordinating council may cast a vote on any matter that would provide direct financial benefit to that member or otherwise give the appearance of a conflict of interest.

- Voting by Members of the Interagency Coordinating Council

95002. The purpose of this title is to provide a statewide system of coordinated, comprehensive, family-centered, multidisciplinary, interagency programs, responsible for providing appropriate early intervention services and support to all eligible infants and toddlers and their families.

- Purpose

95003. (a) The state's participation in Part H of the Individuals with Disabilities Education Act (20 U.S.C. Sec. 1471 et seq.) shall be contingent on the receipt of federal funds to cover the costs of complying with the federal statutes and regulations that impose new requirements on the state. The State Department of Developmental Services and the State Department of Education shall annually report to the

- State's Participation Contingent on Receipt of Federal Funds

Department of Finance during preparation of the Governor's Budget, and the May revision, the budget year costs and federal funds projected to be available.

- Termination Provision

(b) If the amount of funding provided by the federal government pursuant to Part H of the Individuals with Disabilities Education Act for the 1993-94 fiscal year, or any fiscal year thereafter, is not sufficient to fund the full increased costs of participation in this federal program by the local education agencies, as required pursuant to this title, for infants and toddlers from birth through two years of age identified pursuant to Section 95014, and that lack of federal funding would require an increased contribution from the General Fund or a contribution from a local educational agency in order to fund those required and supplemental costs, the state shall terminate its participation in the program. Termination of the program shall occur on July 1 if local education agencies have been notified of the termination prior to March 10 of that calendar year. If this notification is provided after March 10 of a calendar year, then termination shall not occur earlier than July 1 of the subsequent calendar year. The voluntary contribution by a state or local agency of funding for any of the programs or services required pursuant to this title shall not constitute grounds for terminating the state's participation in that federal program. It is the intent of the Legislature that if the program terminates, the termination shall be carried out in an orderly manner with notification of parents and certificated personnel.

(c) This title shall remain in effect only until the state terminates its participation in Part H of the Individuals with Disabilities Education Act (20 U.S.C. Sec. 1471 et seq.) for individuals from birth through two years of age and notifies the Secretary of the Senate of the termination, and as of that later date is repealed. As the lead agency, the State Department of Developmental Services shall, upon notification by the Department of Finance or the State Department of Education as to the insufficiency of federal funds and the termination of this program, be responsible for the payment of services pursuant to this title when no other agency or department is required to make these payments.

- Title Remains in Effect Only Until State Terminates Participation in Part H (Now Part C) of the IDEA

- Responsibility of DDS if Termination of Program Occurs

95004. The early intervention services specified in this title shall be provided as follows:

- Early Intervention Services Specified (1)

(a) Direct services for eligible infants and toddlers and their families shall be provided pursuant to the existing regional center system under the Lanterman Developmental

- Provision of Direct Services

Disabilities Services Act (Division 4.5 (commencing with Section 4500) of the Welfare and Institutions Code) and the existing local education agency system under appropriate sections of Part 30 (commencing with Section 56000) of the Education Code and regulations adopted pursuant thereto, and Part C of the Individuals with Disabilities Education Act (20 U.S.C. Sec. 1431 et seq.).

(b) (1) In providing services under this title, regional centers shall comply with the Lanterman Developmental Disabilities Services Act (Division 4.5 (commencing with Section 4500) of the Welfare and Institutions Code, and its implementing regulations (Division 2 (commencing with Section 50201) of Title 17 of the California Code of Regulations) including, but not limited to, those provisions relating to vendorization and ratesetting, except where compliance with those provisions would result in any delays in, or any cost to the families for, the provision of early intervention, or otherwise conflict with this title and the regulations implementing this title (Chapter 2 (commencing with Section 52000) of Division 2 of Title 17 of the California Code of Regulations), or Part C of the Individuals with Disabilities Education Act (20 U.S.C. Sec. 1431) et seq., and applicable federal regulations contained in Part 303 (commencing with Section 303.1) of Title 34 of the Code of Federal Regulations.

- Regional Centers Shall Comply with Lanterman Developmental Disabilities Services Act

(2) When compliance with this subdivision would result in any delays in the provision of early intervention services or costs to families for the provision of any of these services, the department may authorize a regional center to use a special service code that allows immediate procurement of the service.

(c) Services shall be provided by family resource centers that provide, but are not limited to, parent-to-parent support, information dissemination and referral, public awareness, family professional collaboration activities, and transition assistance for families.

- Services Provided by Family Resource Centers

(d) Existing obligations of the state to provide these services at state expense shall not be expanded.

- State Expense Shall Not Be Expanded

(e) It is the intent of the Legislature that services be provided in accordance with Sections 303.124, 303.126, and 303.527 of Title 34 of the Code of Federal Regulations.

- Services Provided in Accordance with Federal Regulations

CHAPTER 2. ADMINISTRATION

95006. This title shall be administered under the shared direction of the Secretary of Health and Welfare Agency

- Title Administered Under Shared Direction

and the Superintendent of Public Instruction. The planning, development, implementation, and monitoring of the statewide system of early intervention services shall be conducted by the State Department of Developmental Services in collaboration with the State Department of Education with the advice and assistance of an interagency coordinating council established pursuant to federal regulations.

95007. The State Department of Developmental Services shall serve as the lead agency responsible for administration and coordination of the statewide system. The specific duties and responsibilities of the State Department of Developmental Services shall include, but are not limited to, all of the following:

- DDS Serves as Lead Agency; Duties and Responsibilities

(a) Establishing a single point of contact with the federal Office of Special Education Programs for the administration of Part H of the Individuals with Disabilities Education Act.

- Single Point of Contact

(b) Administering the state early intervention system in accordance with Part H of the Individuals with Disabilities Education Act (20 U.S.C. Sec. 1471 et seq.), and applicable regulations and approved state application.

- Administer System

(c) Administering mandatory and discretionary components as specified in Sections 95022 and 95024.

- Administer Components

(d) Administering fiscal arrangements and interagency agreements with participating agencies and community-based organizations to implement this title.

- Administer Fiscal Arrangements and Interagency Agreements

(e) Establishing interagency procedures, including the designation of local coordinating structures, as are necessary to share agency information and to coordinate policymaking activities.

- Establish Interagency Procedures

(f) Adopting written procedures for receiving and resolving complaints regarding violations of Part H of the Individuals with Disabilities Education Act by public agencies covered under this title, as specified in Section 1476(b)(9) of Title 20 of the United States Code and appropriate federal regulations.

- Adopt Procedures for Receiving and Resolving Complaints

(g) Establishing, adopting, and implementing procedural safeguards that comply with the requirements of Part H of the Individuals with Disabilities Education Act, as specified in Section 1480 of Title 20 of the United States Code and appropriate federal regulations.

- Procedural Safeguards

(h) (1) Monitoring of agencies, institutions, and organizations receiving assistance under this title.

- Monitor Entities Receiving Assistance

(2) Monitoring shall be conducted by interagency teams that are sufficiently trained to ensure compliance. Interagency teams shall consist of, but not be limited to, representatives from the State Department of Developmental Services, the State Department of Education, the interagency coordinating council, or a local family resource center or network parent, direct service provider, or any other agency responsible for providing early intervention services.

(3) All members of an interagency team shall have access to all information that is subject to review. Members of each interagency team shall maintain the confidentiality of the information, and each member of the interagency team shall sign a written agreement of confidentiality.

(4) A summary of monitoring issues and findings shall be forwarded biannually to the interagency coordinating council for review.

(i) Establishing innovative approaches to information distribution, family support services, and interagency coordination at the local level.

- Establish Innovative Approaches

(j) Ensuring the provision of appropriate early intervention services to all infants eligible under Part H of the Individuals with Disabilities Education Act (20 U.S.C. Sec. 1471 et seq.) and under Section 95014, except for those infants who have solely a low incidence disability as defined in Section 56026.5 of the Education Code and who are not eligible for services under the Lanterman Development Disabilities Services Act (Division 4.5 (commencing with Section 4500) of the Welfare and Institutions Code).

- Ensure Provision of Appropriate Services Except for Infants Who Have Solely a Low Incidence Disability

The development and implementation of subdivisions (e) to (h), inclusive, shall be a collaborative effort between the State Department of Developmental Services and the State Department of Education. In establishing the written procedures for receiving and resolving complaints as specified in subdivision (f) and in establishing and implementing procedural safeguards as specified in subdivision (g), it is the intent of the Legislature that these procedures be identical for all infants served under this act and shall be in accordance with Section 303.400 and subdivision (b) of Section 303.420 of Title 34 of the Code of Federal Regulations. The procedural safeguards and due process requirements established under this title shall replace and be used in lieu of due process procedures contained in Chapter 1 (commencing with Section 4500) of Division 4.5 of the Welfare and Institutions Code and Part 30 (commencing with Section 56500) of the Education Code for infants and

- Collaborative Effort

- Procedural Safeguards Identical for All Infants

their families eligible under this title.

95008. The State Department of Education shall be responsible for administering services and programs for infants with solely visual, hearing, and severe orthopedic impairments, and any combination thereof, who meet the criteria in Sections 56026 and 56026.5 of the Education Code, and in subdivisions (a), (b), (d), or (e) of Section 3030 of, and Section 3031 of, Title 5 of the California Code of Regulations and Part H of the Individuals with Disabilities Education Act (20 U.S.C. Section 1471 et seq.) and who are not eligible for services under the Lanterman Developmental Disabilities Services Act (Division 4.5 (commencing with Section 4500) of the Welfare and Institutions Code).

- Department of Education Responsible for Administering Programs for Infants with Solely Visual, Hearing, and Severe Orthopedic Impairments

95009. The development of joint regulations for meeting the requirements of this title shall be the shared responsibility of the State Department of Developmental Services on behalf of the Secretary of the Health and Welfare Agency, and the State Department of Education on behalf of the Superintendent of Public Instruction. The joint regulations shall be agreed upon by both departments. These regulations shall be developed and approved by October 1, 1995. The Department of Finance shall review and comment upon the joint regulations prior to any public hearing on them.

- Development of Joint Regulations

CHAPTER 3. STATE INTERAGENCY COORDINATION

95012. (a) The following departments shall cooperate and coordinate their early intervention services for eligible infants and their families under this title, and need to collaborate with families and communities, to provide a family-centered, comprehensive, multidisciplinary, interagency, community-based early intervention system:

- Departments Shall Cooperate and Coordinate Services

(1) State Department of Developmental Services.

(2) State Department of Education.

(3) State Department of Health Services.

(4) State Department of Social Services.

(5) State Department of Mental Health.

(6) State Department of Alcohol and Drug Programs.

(b) Each participating department shall enter into an interagency agreement with the State Department of Developmental Services. Each interagency agreement shall specify, at a minimum, the agency's current and continuing level of financial participation in providing services to infants and toddlers with disabilities and their families. Each

- Interagency Agreement with DDS

interagency agreement shall also specify procedures for resolving disputes in a timely manner. Interagency agreements shall also contain provisions for ensuring effective cooperation and coordination among agencies concerning policymaking activities associated with the implementation of this title, including legislative proposals, regulation development, and fiscal planning. All interagency agreements shall be reviewed annually and revised as necessary.

CHAPTER 4. ELIGIBILITY

95014. (a) The term "eligible infant or toddler" for the purposes of this title means infants and toddlers from birth through two years of age, for whom a need for early intervention services, as specified in the Individuals with Disabilities Education Act (20 U.S.C. Sec. 1471 et seq.) and applicable regulations, is documented by means of assessment and evaluation as required in Sections 95016 and 95018 and who meet one of the following criteria:

- Definition of Eligible Infant or Toddler

(1) Infants and toddlers with a developmental delay in one or more of the following five areas: cognitive development; physical and motor development, including vision and hearing; communication development; social or emotional development; or adaptive development. Developmentally delayed infants and toddlers are those who are determined to have a significant difference between the expected level of development for their age and their current level of functioning. This determination shall be made by qualified personnel who are recognized by, or part of, a multidisciplinary team, including the parents.

(2) Infants and toddlers with established risk conditions, who are infants and toddlers with conditions of known etiology or conditions with established harmful developmental consequences. The conditions shall be diagnosed by a qualified personnel recognized by, or part of, a multidisciplinary team, including the parents The condition shall be certified as having a high probability of leading to developmental delay if the delay is not evident at the time of diagnosis.

(3) Infants and toddlers who are at high risk of having substantial developmental disability due to a combination of biomedical risk factors, the presence of which is diagnosed by qualified clinicians recognized by, or part of, a multidisciplinary team, including the parents.

(b) Regional centers and local education agencies shall be responsible for ensuring that eligible infants and toddlers are served as follows:

- Regional Centers and Local Education Agencies

(1) The State Department of Developmental Services and regional centers shall be responsible for the provision of appropriate early intervention services in accordance with Part H of the Individuals with Disabilities Education Act (20 U.S.C. Sec. 1471 et seq.) for all infants eligible under Section 95014, except for those infants with solely a visual, hearing, or severe orthopedic impairment, or any combination thereof, who meet the criteria in Sections 56026 and 56026.5 of the Education Code, and in subdivisions (a), (b), (d), or (e) of Section 3030 of, and Section 3031 of, Title 5 of the California Code of Regulations.

- Services Provided by DDS and Regional Centers

(2) The State Department of Education and local education agencies shall be responsible for the provision of appropriate early intervention services in accordance with Part H of the Individuals with Disabilities Education Act (20 U.S.C. Sec. 1471 et seq.) for infants with solely a visual, hearing, or severe orthopedic impairment, or any combination thereof who meet the criteria in Sections 56026 and 56026.5 of the Education Code, and in subdivisions (a), (b), (d), or (e) of Section 3030 of, and Section 3031 of, Title 5 of the California Code of Regulations, and who are not eligible for services under the Lanterman Developmental Services Disabilities Act (Division 4.5 (commencing with Section 4500) of the Welfare and Institutions Code).

- Services Provided by Education

(c) For infants and toddlers and their families who are eligible to receive services from both a regional center and a local education agency, the regional center shall be the agency responsible for providing or purchasing appropriate early intervention services that are beyond the mandated responsibilities of local education agencies. The local education agency shall provide special education services up to its funded program capacity as established annually by the State Department of Education in consultation with the State Department of Developmental Services and the Department of Finance.

- Infants/Toddlers Eligible to Receive Services from Both a Regional Center and a Local Education Agency

(d) No agency or multidisciplinary team, including any agency listed in Section 95012, shall presume or determine eligibility, including eligibility for medical services, for any other agency. However, regional centers and local education agencies shall coordinate intake, evaluation, assessment, and individualized family service plans for infants and toddlers and their families who are served by an agency.

- Agencies/Teams Shall Not Determine Eligibility for Any Other Agency

(e) Upon termination of the program pursuant to Section 95003, the State Department of Developmental Services shall be responsible for the payment of services pursuant to this title.

- DDS Responsible for Payment of Services Upon Termination

CHAPTER 5. SERVICES

95016. (a) Each infant or toddler referred for evaluation for early intervention services shall have a timely, comprehensive, multidisciplinary evaluation of his or her needs and level of functioning in order to determine eligibility. In the process of determining eligibility of an infant or toddler, an assessment shall be conducted by qualified personnel, and shall include a family interview, to identify the child's unique strengths and needs and the services appropriate to meet those needs; and the resources, priorities and concerns of the family and the supports and services necessary to enhance the family's capacity to meet the developmental needs of their infant or toddler. Evaluations and assessments shall be shared and utilized between the regional center and the local education agency, and any other agency providing services for the eligible infant or toddler, as appropriate Family assessments shall be family directed and voluntary on the part of the family. Families shall be afforded the opportunity to participate in all decisions regarding eligibility and services..

- Timely, Comprehensive, Multidisciplinary Evaluation

(b) Regional centers and local education agencies or their designees shall be responsible for ensuring that the requirements of this section are implemented. The procedures, requirements, and timelines for evaluation and assessment shall be consistent with the statutes and regulations under Part H of the Individuals with Disabilities Education Act (20 U.S.C. 1471 et seq.), applicable regulations, and this title, and shall be specified in regulations adopted pursuant to Section 95028.

- Responsibility for Ensuring Requirements Are Implemented

95018. Each eligible infant or toddler and family shall be provided a service coordinator who will be responsible for facilitating the implementation of the individualized family service plan and for coordinating with other agencies and persons providing services to the family. The qualifications, responsibilities, and functions of service coordinators shall be consistent with the statutes and regulations under Part H and this title, and shall be specified in regulations adopted pursuant to Section 95028. The State Department of Developmental Services shall ensure that service

- Service Coordinator

coordinators, as defined in federal law, meet federal and state regulation requirements, are trained to work with infants and their families, and meet competency requirements set forth in subsection (d) of Section 303.22 of Title 34 of the Code of Federal Regulations. Service coordinator caseloads shall be an overall average of 62 consumers to each staff member. Pursuant to Section 303.521 of Title 34 of the Code of Federal Regulations, service coordination is not subject to any fees that might be established for any other federal or state program.

95020. (a) Each eligible infant or toddler shall have an individualized family service plan. The individualized family service plan shall be used in place of an individualized program plan required pursuant to Sections 4646 and 4646.5 of the Welfare and Institutions Code, the individual education plan required pursuant to Section 56340 of the Education Code, or any other applicable service plan.

- Individualized Family Service Plan (IFSP)

(b) For an infant or toddler who has been evaluated for the first time, a meeting to share the results of the evaluation, to determine eligibility and, for children who are eligible, to develop the initial individualized family service plan shall be conducted within 45 calendar days of receipt of the written referral. Evaluation results and determination of eligibility may be shared in a meeting with the family prior to the individualized family service plan. Written parent consent to evaluate and assess shall be obtained within the 45-day timeline. A regional center, local education agency, or their designees shall initiate and conduct this meeting. Families shall be afforded the opportunity to participate in all decisions regarding eligibility and services.

- Meeting to Determine Eligibility and Develop Initial IFSP Conducted Within 45 Days of Receipt of Written Referral

(c) Parents shall be fully informed of their rights, including the right to invite any other person, including a family member or an advocate or peer parent, or any or all of them, to accompany them to any or all individualized family service plan meetings. With parental consent, a referral shall be made to the local family resource center or network.

- Parents Shall Be Fully Informed of Their Rights

(d) The individualized family service plan shall be in writing and shall address all of the following:

- Content of IFSP

(1) A statement of the infant or toddler's present levels of physical development including vision, hearing, and health status, cognitive development, communication development, social and emotional development, and adaptive developments.

(2) With the concurrence of the family, a statement of the family's concerns, priorities, and resources related to meeting

the special developmental needs of the eligible infant or toddler.

(3) A statement of the major outcomes expected to be achieved for the infant or toddler and family where services for the family are related to meeting the special developmental needs of the eligible infant or toddler.

(4) The criteria, procedures, and timelines used to determine the degree to which progress toward achieving the outcomes is being made and whether modifications or revisions are necessary.

(5) A statement of the specific early intervention services necessary to meet the unique needs of the infant or toddler as identified in paragraph (3), including, but not limited to, the frequency, intensity, location, duration, and method of delivering the services, and ways of providing services in natural environments.

(6) A statement of the agency responsible for providing the identified services.

(7) The name of the service coordinator who shall be responsible for facilitating implementation of the plan and coordinating with other agencies and persons.

(8) The steps to be taken to ensure transition of the infant or toddler upon reaching three years of age to other appropriate services. These may include, as appropriate, special education or other services offered in natural environments.

(9) The projected dates for the initiation of services in paragraph (5) and the anticipated duration of those services.

(e) Each service identified on the individualized family service plan shall be designated as one of three types:

- Types of Services Identified in IFSP

(1) An early intervention service, as defined in Part H (20 U.S.C. Section 1472 (2)), and applicable regulations, that is provided or purchased through the regional center, local education agency, or other participating agency. The State Department of Health Services, State Department of Social Services, State Department of Mental Health, and State Department of Alcohol and Drug Programs shall provide services in accordance with state and federal law and applicable regulations, and up to the level of funding as appropriated by the Legislature. Early intervention services identified on an individualized family service plan that exceed the funding, statutory, and regulatory requirements of these departments shall be provided or purchased by regional centers or local education agencies under subdivisions (b) and

(c) of Section 95014.   The State Department of Health Services, State Department of Social Services, State Department of Mental Health, and State Department of Alcohol and Drug Programs shall not be required to provide early intervention services over their existing funding, statutory, and regulatory requirements.

(2) Any other service, other than those specified in paragraph (1), which the eligible infant or toddler or his or her family may receive from other state programs, subject to the eligibility standards of those programs.

(3) A referral to a nonrequired service that may be provided to an eligible infant or toddler or his or her family. Nonrequired services are those services that are not defined as early intervention services or do not relate to meeting the special developmental needs of an eligible infant or toddler related to the disability, but which may be helpful t o the family.   The granting or denial of nonrequired services by any public or private agency is not subject to appeal under this title.

(f)   An annual review, and other periodic reviews of the individualized family service plan for an infant's or toddler and the infant or toddler's family shall be conducted to determine the degree of progress that is being made in achieving the outcomes specified in the plan and whether modification or revision of the outcomes or services is necessary.   The frequency, participants, purpose, and required processes for annual and periodic reviews shall be consistent with the statutes and regulations under Part H and this title, and shall be specified in regulations adopted pursuant to Section 95028.

95022. The statewide system of early intervention shall be administered by the State Department of Developmental Services in   collaboration with the State Department of Education and with the advice and assistance of an interagency coordinating council established pursuant to fcdcral regulations and shall include all of the following mandatory components:

(a) A central directory that includes information about early intervention services, resources, and experts available in the state, professionals and other groups providing services to eligible infants and toddlers, and research and demonstration projects being conducted in the state.   The central directory shall specify the nature and scope of the services available and the telephone number and address for each of the sources listed in the directory.

- Annual and Periodic Reviews

- Components of Statewide System of Early Intervention

- Central Directory

(b) A public awareness program focusing on early identification of eligible infants and toddlers and the dissemination of information about the purpose and scope of the system of early intervention services and how to access evaluation and other early intervention services.

- Public Awareness Program

(c) Personnel standards that ensure that personnel are appropriately and adequately prepared and trained.

- Personnel Standards

(d) A comprehensive system of personnel development that provides training for personnel including, but not limited to, public and private providers, primary referral sources, paraprofessionals, and persons who will serve as service coordinators. The training shall specifically address at least all of the following:

- Comprehensive System of Personnel Development – Training

(1) Understanding the early intervention services system, including the family service plan process.

(2) Meeting the interrelated social, emotional, and health needs of eligible infants and toddlers.

(3) Assisting families in meeting the special developmental needs of the infant or toddler, assisting professionals to utilize best practices in family focused early intervention services and promoting family professional collaboration.

(4) Reflecting the unique needs of local communities and promoting culturally competent service delivery.

(e) A comprehensive child-find system, including policies and procedures that ensure that all infants and toddlers who may be eligible for services under this title are identified, located, and evaluated, that services are coordinated between participating agencies, and that infants and toddlers are referred to the appropriate agency.

- Child-Find System

(f) A surrogate parent program established pursuant to Section 303.406 of Title 34 of the Code of Federal Regulations to be used by regional centers and local education agencies.

- Surrogate Parent Program

CHAPTER 6. FUNDING

95024. (a) Any increased cost to local educational agencies due to the implementation of this title shall be funded from the Part H federal funds provided for the purposes of this title.

- Increased Cost to Local Educational Agencies

(b) Any increased costs to regional centers due to the implementation of this title shall be funded from the Part H federal funds provided for the purposes of this title.

- Increased Cost to Regional Centers

(c) The annual Budget Act shall specify the amount of federal Part H funds allocated for local assistance and for

- Annual Budget Act

state operations individually, for the State Department of Developmental Services, and for the State Department of Education.

(d) If federal funds are available after mandatory components and increased costs in subdivisions (a) and (b), if any, are funded, the lead agency, in consultation with the State Department of Education, may do the following:

- Use of Federal Funds After Mandatory Components and Increased Costs Are Funded

(1) Designate local interagency coordination areas throughout the state and allocate available Part H funds to fund interagency coordination activities, including, but not limited to, outreach and public awareness, and interagency approaches to service planning and delivery. If the lead agency chooses to designate and fund local interagency coordination areas, the lead agency shall first offer to enter into a contract with the regional center or a local education agency. If the regional center or any of the local education agencies do not accept the offer, the lead agency, in consultation with the State Department of Education and the approval of the regional center and local education agencies in the area, may directly enter into a contract with a private, nonprofit organization. Nothing in this section shall preclude a regional center or local education agency that enters into a contract with the lead agency from subcontracting with a private, nonprofit organization.

(2) Allocate funds to support family resource services, including, but not limited to, parent-to-parent support, information dissemination and referral, public awareness, family-professional collaboration activities, and transition assistance for families.

(e) If an expenditure plan is developed under subdivision (d), the lead agency, in consultation with the State Department of Education, shall give high priority to funding family resource services.

- Funding Family Resource Services

(f) Nothing in this section shall be construed to limit the lead agency's authority, in consultation with the State Department of Education, to allocate discretionary Part H funds for any legitimate purpose consistent with the statutes and regulations under Part H (20 U.S.C. Secs. 1471 to 1485, inclusive) and this title.

- No Limitation on DDS to Allocate Discretionary Funds

CHAPTER 7. DATA COLLECTION

95026. The lead agency shall maintain a system for compiling data required by the federal Office of Special Education Programs, through Part H of the Individuals with

- DDS Shall Maintain System for Compiling Data

Disabilities Education Act, including the number of eligible infants and toddlers and their families in need of appropriate early intervention services, the number of eligible infants and toddlers and their families served, the types of services provided, and other information required by the federal Office of Special Education Programs. All participating agencies listed in Section 95012 shall assist in the development of the system and shall cooperate with the lead agency in meeting federal data requirements. The feasibility of using existing systems and including social security numbers shall be explored to facilitate data collection.

CHAPTER 8. REGULATIONS

95028. (a) On or before October 1, 1995, the State Department of Developmental Services, on behalf of the Secretary of the Health and Welfare Agency, and the State Department of Education, on behalf of the Superintendent of Public Instruction, shall jointly develop, approve, and implement regulations, as necessary, to comply with the requirements of this title and Part H, as specified in federal statutes and regulations.

- Timeline for Regulations

(b) The regulations developed pursuant to this section shall include, but are not limited to, the following requirements:

- Scope of Regulations

(1) The administrative structure for planning and implementation of the requirements of this title and Part H.

(2) Eligibility for Part H services.

(3) Evaluation and assessment.

(4) Individualized family service plans.

(5) Service coordination.

(6) The program and service components of the statewide system for early intervention services.

(7) The duties and responsibilities of the lead agency as specified in Section 95006, including procedural safeguards and the process for resolving complaints against a public agency for violation of the requirements of Part H.

(c) The State Department of Developmental Services shall adopt regulations to implement this title in accordance with Chapter 3.5 (commencing with Section 11340) of Part 1 of Division 3 of Title 2. Initial regulations to implement this title shall be adopted as emergency regulations. The adoption of these initial emergency regulations shall be considered by the Office of Administrative Law to be an emergency and necessary for the immediate preservation of the public peace, health and safety, or general welfare. The initial emergency

- DDS Shall Adopt Regulations

regulations shall remain in effect for no more than 180 days. These regulations shall be jointly developed by the State Department of Developmental Services and the State Department of Education by July 1, 1994. The Department of Finance shall review and comment upon the emergency regulations prior to their adoption.

CHAPTER 9. EVALUATION

95029. The State Department of Developmental Services and the State Department of Education shall ensure that an independent evaluation of the program and its structure is completed by October 1, 1996. The evaluation shall address the following issues:

- Scope of Evaluation

(a)   The efficiency and cost-effectiveness of the state administrative structure, the local interagency coordinating structure, and the mandatory program components.

(b)   The degree to which programs and services provided through regional centers and local education agencies fulfill the purpose of Part H of the Individuals with Disabilities Education Act.

(c)   The extent to which implementation of the program has resulted in improved services for infants and their families, and greater satisfaction with service delivery by families.

(d)   The outcomes and effectiveness of family resource centers.

(e)   The adequacy of the Part H funding models.   The evaluation shall be funded with federal funds.

NOTE

(1) Government Code Section 95004 was amended by Assembly Bill 430, Chapter 171, Statutes of 2001.

CALIFORNIA CODE OF REGULATIONS
TITLE 17. PUBLIC HEALTH
DIVISION 2. DEPARTMENT OF DEVELOPMENTAL SERVICES
CHAPTER 2. EARLY INTERVENTION SERVICES

Subchapter 1. General Provisions

Article 1. Definitions

52000. Meaning of Words.

(a) Words shall have their usual meaning unless the context of a definition clearly indicates a different meaning. Words used in their present tense include the future tense; words in the singular form include the plural form. Use of the word "shall" denotes mandatory conduct; "may" denotes permissive conduct.

(b) The following definitions shall apply to the words used in this subchapter:

(1) "Acidemia" means an excessive acidity of the blood wherein the acid-base balance of the body is disturbed.

(2) "Adaptive development" means the acquisition of skills that are required to meet environmental demands. Adaptive development includes, but is not limited to, activities of self-care, such as dressing, eating, toileting, self-direction, environmental problem-solving and attention/arousal.

(3) "Asphyxia neonatorum" means a condition caused by insufficient oxygen at or near the time of birth.

(4) "Assessment" means the ongoing procedures used by qualified personnel throughout the period of an infant's or toddler's eligibility for early intervention services to identify the infant's or toddler's unique strengths and needs and the services appropriate to meet those needs. Assessment also includes the identification of the family's resources, priorities, and concerns regarding the development of the infant or toddler and the supports and services necessary to enhance the family's capacity to meet the developmental needs of the eligible infant or toddler.

(5) "Authorized representative" means the parent or guardian of a minor, or person who is legally entitled to act on behalf of the infant, toddler or family.

— Meaning of Words

— Definitions

— Acidemia

— Adaptive Development

— Asphyxia Neonatorum

— Assessment

— Authorized Representative

(6) "Biomedical insult" is a general term referring to those biological or medical conditions such as infection or brain injury which may result in developmental delay or disability.

(7) "Cognitive development" means the acquisition of learning through ongoing interactions with the environment. Cognitive development involves perceiving, thinking, problem solving and remembering information.

(8) "Communication development" means the acquisition of expressive and/or receptive language skills which include understanding and/or using any of the following: gestures, facial expressions, speech reading, sign language, body postures and vocal and visual contacts with another person.

(9) "Complainant" means any individual or organization filing a written complaint pursuant to the provisions of Subchapter 5, Article 3.

(10) "Concerns" means areas that family members identify as needs, issues or problems they want to address as part of the individualized family service plan (IFSP) or the evaluation and assessment process which are related to meeting the developmental needs of the infant or toddler.

(11) "Day" means calendar day unless otherwise stated.

(12) "Early intervention services" means those services designed to meet the developmental needs of each eligible infant or toddler and the needs of the family related to the infant's or toddler's development. The services include but are not limited to assistive technology; audiology; family training, counseling and home visits; health services; medical services only for diagnostic or evaluation purposes; nursing services; nutrition services; occupational therapy; physical therapy; psychological services; service coordination; social work services; special instruction; speech and language services; transportation and related costs; and vision services. Early intervention services may include such services as respite and other family support services.

(13) "Evaluation" means procedures used by qualified personnel to determine an infant's or toddler's present level of development.

(14) "Exceptional circumstances" means events beyond the control of the regional center or local education agency (LEA). These include but are not limited to the infant's or toddler's or parent's illness, the infant's or toddler's and parent's absence from the geographical area, inability to locate the parent, or a natural disaster. Delays caused by the failure to obtain copies of existing records or other administrative events do not constitute exceptional

circumstances.

(15) "Family" means the primary caregivers and others who assume major long-term roles in an infant's or toddler's daily life.

- Family

(16) "Fine motor" means the use of muscles that control small and detailed movements of the body, as an example, in the hand related to manual dexterity and coordination.

- Fine Motor

(17) "Funded Capacity" means the number of eligible infants, between 12 and 16 students per instructional unit, that the California Department of Education requires LEAs to serve to maintain funding for their classes/programs/services in a given year pursuant to Education Code Section 56728.8 as it read on November 1, 1993.

- Funded Capacity

(18) "Gross motor" means the use of large muscle groups of the body, arms, or legs, as in sitting up, walking, or balancing.

- Gross Motor

(19) "Health status" means a description of the physical and mental condition of an infant or toddler. Health status may include current diagnoses, medications, required regular medical procedures, current medical supplies and technological devices, primary and specialty care providers, and immunization status, nutrition and oral health

- Health Status

(20) "Hearing impairment" means a condition, whether permanent or fluctuating, which impairs the processing of linguistic information through hearing, even with amplification, and which adversely affects an infant's or toddler's development. Processing linguistic information includes speech and language reception and speech and language discrimination.

- Hearing Impairment

(21) "Hyperbilirubinemia" means a condition in which an excessive amount of bilirubin, a bile pigment released from the breakdown of red blood cells, is in the blood.

- Hyperbilirubinemia

(22) "Hypertonia" means a condition of excessive tone or tension in the skeletal muscles.

- Hypertonia

(23) "Hypotonia" means a condition of diminished tone of the skeletal muscles.

- Hypotonia

(24) "Hypoglycemia" means a condition in which the blood sugar is abnormally low.

- Hypoglycemia

(25) "Immediate need" means a situation in which an infant or toddler requires early intervention services without delay pursuant to a physician's order or written determination by the multidisciplinary team specifying consequences of a delay in the provision of services.

- Immediate Need

(26) "Individual program plan (IPP)" means a plan developed for persons with developmental disabilities to

- Individual Program Plan

describe the provision of services and supports to meet the written goals and objectives pursuant to Welfare and Institutions Code Sections 4646-4648.

(27) "Individualized education program (IEP)" means a written statement that is developed and implemented pursuant to Title 20 United States Code Section 1401(b)(20).

- Individualized Education Program

(28) "Individualized family service plan (IFSP)" means a written plan for providing early intervention services to infants or toddlers and their families who have been determined eligible for early intervention services. The plan must: (1) Be developed in accordance with Sections 52100 through 52110; and, (2) Be based on the evaluation and assessment processes described in Sections 52082 through 52086 of these regulations.

- Individualized Family Service Plan

(29) "Informed clinical opinion" means the judgment of a qualified professional who is a member of the multidisciplinary team. Informed clinical opinion is based on but is not limited to opinions derived from: a review of records, parental and professional observation of the infant or toddler, and professional knowledge.

- Informed Clinical Opinion

(30) "Language of the parent's choice" means a primary written or oral language or mode of communication that the family chooses as a means of communication. Language of the parent's choice may be the native language. If the parent is deaf or blind or has no written language, the mode of communication shall be that normally used by the parent such as sign language, braille, or oral communication.

- Language of the Parent's Choice

(31) "Local education agency (LEA)" means the school district in which the infant or toddler resides or the county office of education or the special education local plan area (SELPA) that is responsible for providing early intervention services to infants and toddlers with disabilities.

- Local Education Agency

(32) "Low incidence disability" means a severe disabling condition with an expected incidence rate of less than one percent of the total statewide enrollment in kindergarten through grade 12. For purposes of this definition, severe disabling conditions are hearing impairments, vision impairments, and severe orthopedic impairments, or any combination thereof.

- Low Incidence Disability

(33) "Mediation" means a voluntary resolution process in which an impartial third party may assist the disagreeing parties to resolve issues prior to a due process hearing.

- Mediation

(34) "Multidisciplinary team" means two or more individuals of various disciplines or professions, and the parent, who participate in the provision of integrated and

- Multidisciplinary Team

coordinated services, including evaluation, assessment, and IFSP development.

(35) "Natural environments" means settings that are natural or typical for the infant or toddler's age peers who have no disability including the home and community settings in which children without disabilities participate.

- Natural Environments

(36) "Parent" means a parent, guardian or a person acting as a parent of an infant or toddler such as a grandparent or stepparent with whom an infant or toddler lives. Parent also means a person who is legally responsible for the infant's or toddler's welfare or a surrogate parent who has been appointed in accordance with 34 CFR 303.406. The term does not include the State if an infant or toddler is a ward of the State.

- Parent

(37) "Payor of last resort" means the regional center or LEA that is required to pay for early intervention services listed on the IFSP when third party payers or other agencies do not have an obligation to pay as required by 34 CFR 303.527.

- Payor of Last Resort

(38) "Personally identifiable" means information that includes:

- Personally Identifiable

(A) The full name of the infant or toddler, infant's or toddler's parent, or other family member;

(B) The address of the infant or toddler;

(C) A personal identifier, such as the infant's, toddler's or parent's social security number; or

(D) A list of personal characteristics or other information that would make it possible to identify the infant or toddler with reasonable certainty.

(39) "Physical development" means the acquisition of fine and gross motor skills involved in functional movement. Physical development includes vision, hearing and health status.

- Physical Development

(40) "Priorities" means a family's choices for the focus of early intervention services as well as for the ways in which early intervention services will be incorporated into the family's day-to-day organization, routine and planning.

- Priorities

(41) "Qualified" means that a person meets state certification, licensing, credentialing, registration, or other comparable requirements for the area in which he or she is providing early intervention services, or, in the absence of such approved or recognized requirements, meets the Department of Developmental Services or California Department of Education requirements.

- Qualified

(42) "Record" means the documentation in the infant's or toddler's regional center client file and/or the LEA's cumulative file.

(43) "Regional center" means a diagnostic, counseling and service coordination center for persons with developmental disabilities and their families which is established and operated pursuant to Chapter 5 of Division 4.5 of the Welfare and Institutions Code, Sections 4620 through 4669, by a private nonprofit community agency/corporation acting as a contractor for the Department of Developmental Services.

(44) "Referral" means the receipt of oral or written information that causes a record to be opened for an infant or toddler who may be eligible for early intervention services.

(45) "Resources" means the strengths, abilities, formal and informal supports of the family available to meet the developmental needs of the infant or toddler.

(46) "Severe orthopedic impairment" means a condition which adversely affects an infant's or toddler's development. Such orthopedic impairments include impairments caused by congenital anomaly, impairments caused by disease and impairments from other causes which may affect functional movement and/or growth.

(47) "Social or emotional development" means the acquisition of capacities for human relationships, emotional expression, communication and learning. Social or emotional development is based on the motivation to engage in positive interaction and to sustain personal relationships and precedes the development of effective coping skills, self esteem and the ability to take advantage of opportunities for learning. Differences in temperament, self regulation, range and intensity of affect and modulating one's response to the environment are additional factors influencing social or emotional development.

(48) "Solely low incidence disability" means one or a combination of low incidence disabilities which are vision impairment, severe orthopedic impairment, and hearing impairment which is the primary disability and has a significant impact on learning and development of the infant or toddler as determined by the IFSP team of the LEA. The infant or toddler who has a solely low incidence disability shall not be eligible for services from a regional center.

(49) "Teratogen" means an agent or factor that causes the production of physical defects in the developing embryo.

(50) "Vision impairment" means a visual condition which, even with correction, adversely affects the infant's or

toddler's development.

[Authority cited: Sections 95009 and 95028, Government Code] [Reference: Sections 95014 and 95020, Government Code; Sections 3001(x) and 3030, Title 5 California Code of Regulations; Sections 1432, 1436, and 1440, Title 20 United States Code; Sections 303.12, 303.16, 303.17, 303.18, 303.21, 303.321, 303.322, 303.340, 303.345, 303.401, 303.402, 303.403, 303.406, 303.342, 303.343, 303.344, 303.420, 303.511, and 303.527, Title 34 Code of Federal Regulations]

Article 2. Eligibility for Calfiornia's Early Start Program

52020. General.

An infant or toddler shall be eligible for early intervention services if he or she is between birth up to thirty-six months of age and meets one of the criteria specified in Section 52022 as determined by means of evaluation pursuant to Section 52082 of these regulations and needs early intervention services.

- General Eligibility

[Authority cited: Sections 95009 and 95028, Government Code] [Reference: Section 1432(5), Title 20, United States Code; Sections 95014(a), and 95016, Government Code; Section 303.16, Title 34 Code of Federal Regulations]

52022. Eligibility Criteria.

(a) Developmental Delay

A developmental delay exists if there is a significant difference pursuant to 52082 between the infant's or toddler's current level of functioning and the expected level of development for his or her age in one or more of the following developmental areas:

(1) Cognitive;

(2) Physical: including fine and gross motor, vision, and hearing;

(3) Communication;

(4) Social or emotional;

(5) Adaptive.

(b) Established Risk

(1) An established risk condition exists when an infant or toddler has a condition of known ctiology which has a high probability of resulting in developmental delay; or

(2) An established risk condition exists when an infant or

- Eligibility Criteria
- Developmental Delay

- Established Risk

toddler has a solely low incidence disability.

(c) High Risk for Developmental Disability

- High Risk for Developmental Disability

(1) High risk for a developmental disability exists when a multidisciplinary team determines that an infant or toddler has a combination of two or more of the following factors that requires early intervention services based on evaluation and assessment pursuant to section 52082 and section 52084:

(A) Prematurity of less than 32 weeks gestation and/or low birth weight of less than 1500 grams.

(B) Assisted ventilation for 48 hours or longer during the first 28 days of life.

(C) Small for gestational age: below the third percentile on the National Center for Health Statistics growth charts.

(D) Asphyxia neonatorum associated with a five minute Apgar score of 0 to 5.

(E) Severe and persistent metabolic abnormality, including but not limited to hypoglycemia, acidemia, and hyperbilirubinemia in excess of the usual exchange transfusion level.

(F) Neonatal seizures or nonfebrile seizures the first three years of life.

(G) Central nervous system lesion or abnormality.

(H) Central nervous system infection.

(I) Biomedical insult including, but not limited to, injury, accident or illness which may seriously or permanently affect developmental outcome.

(J) Multiple congenital anomalies or genetic disorders which may affect developmental outcome.

(K) Prenatal exposure to known teratogens.

(L) Prenatal substance exposure, positive infant neonatal toxicology screen or symptomatic neonatal toxicity or withdrawal.

(M) Clinically significant failure to thrive, including, but not limited to, weight persistently below the third percentile for age on standard growth charts or less than 85% of the ideal weight for age and/or acute weight loss or failure to gain weight with the loss of two or more major percentiles on the growth curve.

(N) Persistent hypotonia or hypertonia, beyond that otherwise associated with a known diagnostic condition.

(2) High risk for a developmental disability also exists when a multidisciplinary team determines that the parent of the infant or toddler is a person with a developmental disability and the infant or toddler requires early intervention services based on evaluation and assessment as specified in

Section 52082 and Section 52084.

(d) A developmental delay shall not be determined based on:

(1) Temporary physical disability;

(2) Cultural or economic factors;

(3) The normal process of second language acquisition; or

(4) Manifestation of dialect and sociolinguistic variance.

[Authority cited: Sections 95009 and 95028, Government Code] [Reference: Sections 1432(5), 1432(3), and 1435(a)(1), Title 20 United States Code; Sections 303.10, 303.16, and 303.300, Title 34 Code of Federal Regulations; Sections 95014 and 95028(b)(2), Government Code; Section 4642, Welfare and Institutions Code]

Subchapter 2. Program and Service Components

Article 1. Child Find and Referral

52040. Child Find.   - Child Find

(a) Regional centers and LEAs shall conduct child find activities to locate all infants and toddlers who may be eligible for early intervention services.

(b) Child find activities may include:

(1) Assigning liaisons to local hospitals and hospitals with neonatal intensive care units;

(2) Contacting local parent organizations and support groups;

(3) Distributing early intervention materials to agencies and individuals providing medical, social and educational services in the community;

(4) Community-wide health and developmental screening;

(5) Producing and distributing public service announcements;

(6) Producing pamphlets, brochures and other written communication; and,

(7) Making presentations to local professional groups, philanthropic organizations and other organizations established to inform and/or to serve culturally diverse populations.

(c) Regional centers and LEAs shall coordinate local child find activities with each other and other public agencies.

(d) Primary referral sources include but are not limited to hospitals, including prenatal and postnatal care facilities, physicians, parents, child care programs, LEAs, public health facilities, other social services agencies and other health care providers.

(e) Regional centers and LEAs shall inform primary referral sources of the:

(1) Eligibility criteria for early intervention services;

(2) Types of early intervention services available through the Early Start Program;

(3) Contact persons and telephone numbers for regional centers and LEAs; and,

(4) Federal requirement that a referral shall be made to the regional center or LEA within two (2) working days of identification of an infant or toddler who is in need of early intervention services.

[Authority cited: Sections 95009 and 95028, Government Code] [Reference: Section 1435(a)(5), Title 20, United States Code; Section 303.321, Title 34 Code of Federal Regulations; and Section 95022(b) and (e), Government Code]

52060. Referral.

The regional center or LEA that receives an oral or written referral for early intervention services shall ensure that:

(a) The date of the referral is documented in the infant's or toddler's record;

(b) A service coordinator is assigned pursuant to Section 52120 of these regulations; and,

(c) Written notice is provided and consent is requested pursuant to Section 52161 and 52162 of these regulations.

- Referral for Early Intervention Services

[Authority cited: Sections 95009 and 95028, Government Code] [Reference: Section 303.321(d), Title 34 Code of Federal Regulations]

Article 2. Evaluation and Assessment

52082. Procedures for Evaluation and Assessment to Determine Eligibility.

- Procedures for Evaluation and Assessment

(a) The determination of eligibility for an infant or toddler shall be made by qualified personnel of the regional center or LEA. The determination shall be made with the participation of the multidisciplinary team including the parent.

(b) Evaluation and assessment shall be based on informed clinical opinion and include:

(1) A review of pertinent records related to the infant or toddler's health status and medical history provided by qualified health professionals who have evaluated or assessed the infant or toddler;

(2) Information obtained from parental observation and report; and,

(3) Evaluation by qualified personnel of the infant's or toddler's level of functioning in each of the following areas:

(A) Cognitive development;

(B) Physical and motor development, including vision and hearing;

(C) Communication development;

(D) Social or emotional development; and,

(E) Adaptive development.

(c) No single procedure shall be used as the sole criterion for determining an infant's or toddler's eligibility.

(d) Standardized tests or instruments may be used as part of the evaluation specified in 52082(b) above, and, if used, they shall:

(1) Be selected to ensure that, when administered to an infant or toddler with impaired sensory, motor or speaking skills, the tests produce results that accurately reflect the infant's or toddler's aptitude, developmental level, or any other factors the test purports to measure and not the infant's or toddler's impaired sensory, motor or speaking skills unless those skills are the factors the test purports to measure;

(2) Be validated for the specific purpose for which they are used.

(e) If standardized, normed or criterion referenced instruments are used as part of the evaluation specified in 52082(b) above, a significant difference between an infant's or toddler's current level of functioning and the expected level of development for his or her age shall be established when an infant's or toddler's age equivalent score falls one third below age expectation.

(f) Procedures and materials for evaluation and assessment of infants and toddlers shall be selected and administered so as not to be racially or culturally discriminatory.

(g) Infants or toddlers with solely low incidence disabilities shall be evaluated and assessed by qualified personnel of the LEA whose professional preparation, license or credential authorization are specific to the suspected disability.

(h) Regional centers, LEAs and multidisciplinary teams shall not presume or determine eligibility, including eligibility for medical services provided through the Department of

Health Services, for any other state or local government program or service when conducting evaluations or assessments of an infant or toddler or their family.

[Authority cited: Sections 95009 and 95028, Government Code] [Reference: Sections 303.300(b) and (c), 303.322, 303.344, and 303.323(b)and(c), Title 34 Code of Federal Regulations; Sections 95014(a)(1), and 95016, Government Code]

52084. Assessment for Service Planning.

(a) Assessment for service planning for eligible infants or toddlers shall identify all of the following:

(1) The infant's or toddler's unique strengths and needs in each of the five areas specified in Section 52082(b)(3);

(2) Early intervention and other services appropriate to meet the needs identified in (a)(1) of this subsection; and,

(3) If the family consents to a family assessment, the resources, priorities and concerns of the family and the supports and services necessary to enhance the family's capacity to meet the developmental needs of an infant or toddler with a disability.

(b) For purposes of service planning, regional centers and LEAs may use existing evaluation materials if the multidisciplinary team agrees that the existing materials adequately describe the levels of development and service needs for the infant or toddler.

(c) Assessment for service planning shall be based on age appropriate methods and procedures which may include any of the following:

(1) A review of information related to the infant's or toddler's health status and medical history provided by qualified health professionals who have evaluated or assessed the infant or toddler;

(2) Developmental observations by qualified personnel and the parent;

(3) Other procedures used by qualified personnel to determine the presence of a developmental delay, established risk condition, or high risk for a developmental disability; and,

(4) Standardized tests or instruments.

(d) Assessments of family resources, priorities and concerns related to enhancing the development of the infant or toddler shall be voluntary on the part of the family. The family assessment shall:

(1) Be conducted by qualified personnel trained to utilize appropriate methods and procedures;

(2) Be based on information provided by the family through a personal interview;

(3) Incorporate the family's description of its resources, priorities and concerns related to enhancing the development of the infant or toddler; and,

(4) Be conducted in the language of the family's choice or other mode of communication unless it is not feasible to do so.

(e) Evaluations pursuant to Section 52082 and assessments for service planning shall be conducted in natural environments whenever possible.

[Authority cited: Sections 95009 and 95028, Government Code] [Reference: Sections 1435(a)(3) and 1436(a)(1), Title 20 United States Code; Section 303.322, Title 34 Code of Federal Regulations; Sections 95014, and 95016, Government Code]

52086. Time Lines for Completion of Evaluation and Assessment.

- Time Lines for Completion of Evaluation and Assessment

(a) Except as provided in subsection (b), the initial evaluation and assessment for eligibility for each infant or toddler shall be completed within 45 days of the date that the regional center or LEA received the referral.

(b) In the event of exceptional circumstances which make it impossible to complete the initial evaluation and assessment for eligibility within 45 days of receiving a referral, the service coordinator shall:

(1) Document the exceptional circumstances in the infant's or toddler's record;

(2) Inform the parent of the reasons for the delay;

(3) Inform the parent of an alternative time line which includes a specific date for completing the evaluation as soon as possible; and,

(4) Document that the parent has been informed and is in agreement with the reasons documented for the extension beyond 45 days.

(c) If an infant or toddler has been determined eligible but the assessment required in Section 52082 has not been completed within 45 days of receiving a referral because of exceptional circumstances, the service coordinator shall:

(1) Document the exceptional circumstances in the infant's or toddler's record;

(2) Inform the parent of the reasons for the delay;

(3) Develop an interim IFSP pursuant to Section 52107 of these regulations; and,

(4) Provide the services agreed upon in the interim IFSP.

(d) At the parent's signed request, regional centers or LEAs may extend the 45 day time line for completion of evaluation and assessment. The request for an extension shall be documented in the infant's or toddler's record.

[Authority cited: Sections 95009 and 95028, Government Code] [Reference: Section 1435(a)(3), Title 20 United States Code; Sections 303.322(d), 303.322(e) and 303.345(b), Title 34 Code of Federal Regulations; Sections 95016(b) and 95020(b), Government Code]

Subchapter 3. Individualized Family Service Plan

Article 1. General

52100. Individualized Family Service Plan (IFSP).

Regional centers and/or LEAs shall ensure that a written IFSP is developed for providing early intervention services. The IFSP shall address the infant's or toddler's developmental needs and the needs of the family related to meeting the developmental needs of the infant or toddler. An IFSP shall be developed and implemented for each infant or toddler who has been evaluated, assessed and determined to be eligible for early intervention services.

- Individualized Family Service Plan

[Authority cited: Sections 95009 and 95028, Government Code] [Reference: Sections 1435(a)(4), and 1436(a)(2), Title 20 United States Code; Sections 303.14, 303.340, and 303.342, Title 34 Code of Federal Regulations Section 95020, Government Code]

Article 2. Content and Procedures for the IFSP

52102. Procedures for IFSP Development, Review and Evaluation.

(a) An initial IFSP shall be developed by the regional center and/or LEA for each eligible infant or toddler, who has been evaluated and assessed, within 45 days of the receipt, by either the regional center or LEA, of the oral or written referral except as provided for in Section 52107 of these regulations.

- Procedures for IFSP Development, Review, and Evaluation

(b) A periodic review of the IFSP for an infant or toddler and the infant's or toddler's family shall be conducted every six months, or more frequently if service needs change, or if the parent requests such a review.

(c) Documentation of each periodic review of the IFSP by the service coordinator shall include:

(1) The degree to which progress toward achieving the outcomes is being made; and

(2) All modifications or revisions of the outcomes or services as necessary.

(d) The periodic review of the IFSP may be carried out by a meeting or by another means that is acceptable to the parent and other participants.

(e) An annual meeting to review the IFSP shall be conducted to document the infant's or toddler's progress and revise its provisions and shall include team members as specified in Section 52104 of these regulations.

(f) Information obtained from ongoing assessment shall be used in reviewing and revising outcomes and determining the appropriate services that will be provided or continued.

(g) All IFSP meetings shall be conducted:

(1) In settings and at times or by means that are reasonably convenient to the parent; and

(2) In the language of parent's choice unless it is clearly not feasible to do so.

(h) Meeting arrangements shall be made with, and written notice provided to, the parent and other members of the multidisciplinary team in a timely manner to ensure attendance at the IFSP meeting pursuant to the general notice requirements contained in Section 52161 of these regulations.

(i) The contents of the initial and annual IFSP and changes to the IFSP resulting from the periodic review shall be fully explained and a legible copy of the document given to the parent. Written consent from the parent shall be obtained prior to the provision of early intervention services described in the IFSP as required in Section 52162(a) of these regulations.

(j) If the parent does not provide consent with respect to a particular early intervention service listed in the IFSP or withdraws consent after first providing it, that service shall not be provided. The early intervention services to which parental consent is obtained shall be provided.

[Authority cited: Sections 95009 and 95028, Government Code] [Reference: Sections 1435(a)(4), and 1436, Title 20

United States Code; Sections, 303.340, 303.342, 303.343, 303.344 and 303.403, Title 34 Code of Federal Regulations; Section 95020(b), Government Code]

52104. Participants in Initial and Annual IFSP Meeting and Periodic Reviews. - IFSP Meeting Participants

(a) Each initial IFSP meeting and each annual IFSP meeting shall include the following participants:

(1) The parent of the infant or toddler;

(2) The service coordinator who has been working with the family since the initial referral of the infant or toddler for evaluation and assessment or who has been designated by the regional center or LEA to be responsible for implementation of the IFSP; and,

(3) The person(s) who conducted the evaluations or assessments.

(b) If requested by the parent, each initial IFSP meeting and each annual IFSP meeting shall include the following participants:

(1) Other family members; and

(2) An advocate or person outside of the family.

(c) Each IFSP meeting shall include persons who will be providing services to the infant or toddler and family, as appropriate.

(d) Each periodic review of the IFSP shall include:

(1) The parent;

(2) The service coordinator;

(3) Service providers as appropriate; and,

(4) Other family members, an advocate or person outside of the family upon parent request.

(e) If either the evaluators or assessors are unable to attend an initial, or annual IFSP meeting, arrangements shall be made for the person's involvement through other means, including:

(1) Participating in a telephone conference call;

(2) Having a knowledgeable representative attend an IFSP meeting; and

(3) Making pertinent records available at the IFSP meeting.

[Authority cited: Sections 95009 and 95028, Government Code] [Reference: Sections, 1435(b)(4), and 1436(b), Title 20 United States Code; Section 95020(e), Government Code; Section 303.343, Title 34 Code of Federal Regulations]

52106. Content of the IFSP.

(a) For purposes of this Section: - Definition of Terms

(1) Duration means the period between the initiation date of services and the ending date of services in the IFSP.

(2) Frequency means the number of days or sessions that a service will be provided during a specified period of time, such as, two times each week or four times each month.

(3) Initiation means the beginning date of the service.

(4) Intensity means the length of time the service is provided during each session, and whether the service is provided in a group or individual setting.

(5) Location means the environment where early intervention services are provided.

(6) Method means how a service is provided, by qualified persons to accomplish a specified outcome.

(b) The IFSP shall include the following: - Content of the IFSP

(1) With the agreement of the parent, a statement of the family's resources, priorities, and concerns related to enhancing the development of the infant or toddler;

(2) A statement, based on evaluation and assessment information, of the infant's or toddler's present levels of:

(A) Physical development including fine and gross motor development, vision, hearing, and health status;

(B) Cognitive development;

(C) Communication development;

(D) Social or emotional development; and,

(E) Adaptive development;

(3) The statement of present levels of development required in subsection (b)(2) of this section shall be based on evidence that can be measured or observed by a qualified professional;

(4) A statement of the developmental outcomes expected for the infant or toddler and the criteria, procedures, and time lines used to determine the degree to which progress toward achieving outcomes is being made. Such outcomes shall be based on the identified needs of the infant or toddler and family pursuant to assessment;

(5) A statement about the outcomes for the family when services for the family are related to meeting the special developmental needs of the infant or toddler;

(6) Statements of the specific early intervention services necessary to meet the unique needs of the infant or toddler and the family to achieve the outcomes including:

(A) The frequency, intensity, and method of delivering the services;

(B) The location where the services will be delivered;

(1) The statements of location shall specify the natural environments such as home, child care, school program, or private program where early intervention services shall be provided; and,

(2) The statement shall include a justification of the extent, if any, to which the services will not be provided in a natural environment.

(C) The projected date for initiation of each service;

(D) The anticipated duration of the services;

(E) The scheduled days when services/programs will not be available when the service provider operates a program which has a fixed schedule which includes breaks in service for periods such as holidays or vacations; and,

(F) The name of the regional center, LEA or service provider providing each early intervention service.

(7) The funding source for other or non-required services provided by any entity other than regional centers or LEAs including the procedures that will be followed to obtain such funding;

(8) The name of the service coordinator; and,

(9) A statement of the transition steps, which are initiated when the toddler is two years nine months, or at the discretion of all parties, up to six months before the toddler turns three years old, that are necessary to ensure the transition of the toddler to:

(A) Preschool services under Part B of the Individuals with Disabilities Education Act, Title 20 United States Code Sections 1400 - 1420, if the toddler with a disability is eligible; or

(B) Other public and private services that may be needed by the toddler pursuant to Section 52112 of these regulations.

(c) Regional centers and LEAs shall not place an infant or toddler on a waiting list for early intervention services required by the IFSP.

- No Waiting List

(d) Regional centers and LEAs shall arrange, provide or purchase early intervention services required by the IFSP as soon as possible.

- Services Shall Be Provided as Soon as Possible

[Authority cited: Sections 95009 and 95028, Government Code] [Reference: Sections 1400 - 1420 and 1436(d), Title 20 United States Code; Sections 303.12, and 303.344, Title 34 Code of Federal Regulations and Section 95020, Government Code]

52107. Interim IFSP.

(a) An interim IFSP may be developed for an infant or toddler, who has been determined eligible for early intervention services. The early intervention services may begin before the completion of the assessment if there is an immediate need to provide services and the infant's or toddler's parent has given written consent.

(b) The interim IFSP shall include:

(1) Time lines for completing assessments;

(2) The name of the service coordinator responsible for completion of evaluation and assessment within the 45 day timeline and implementation of the interim IFSP;

(3) The services agreed upon at the interim IFSP meeting as necessary for the infant or toddler.

(c) An interim IFSP meeting shall provide for the participation of the parent and the service coordinator and the persons responsible for the assessment at a minimum pursuant to Section 52104(a) of these regulations. Provisions shall be made for the participation of other family members, an advocate or person outside of the family at the parent's request.

(d) The immediate need, the early intervention services needed and the name of the service coordinator must be documented in the infant's or toddler's interim IFSP.

(e) The existence of an interim IFSP does not absolve the regional center or LEA from complying with the 45-day time period to complete the initial assessment in all five areas of development.

(f) An interim IFSP developed to meet an immediate need shall be followed by an IFSP meeting within the 45-day period that commenced with the referral except as provided for in Section 52086(d) of these regulations.

(g) An interim IFSP may be developed for an infant or toddler who has been determined eligible when exceptional circumstances prevent the completion of assessment within 45 days.

[Authority cited: Sections 95009 and 95028, Government Code.] [Reference: Sections 303.322(e)(2)(ii) and 303.345, Title 34 Code of Federal Regulations]

52108. Designation of Services on the IFSP.

(a) Each service on the IFSP shall be designated as one of the following:

(1) A required early intervention service. These services

- Interim IFSP

- Content of Interim IFSP

- Meeting Participation

- Service Documentation

- Complying with Time Period

- Meeting Within 45-Day Period

- Interim IFSP for Eligible Infant or Toddler

- Designation of Services on the IFSP

shall be provided, purchased or arranged by a regional center or LEA; or

(2) Other public programs providing services that may benefit the infant, toddler and/or family which the eligible infant or toddler or his or her family may be eligible to receive, subject to the statutory, regulatory and other program criteria of those programs or agencies. These services may include but not be limited to: residential care; family reunification services, Head Start, Supplemental Security Income; Supplemental Security Programs; Temporary Assistance to Needy Families and food stamps; Medi-Cal; or

(3) A referral to a community service that may be provided to an eligible infant or toddler or his or her family but is not required under the California Early Intervention Services Act, Government Code Sections 95000-95030.

(A) A non-required service includes but is not limited to: employment; child care; housing; medical services such as surgery, or medication, hospitalization, medical devices necessary to control or treat a medical condition, or immunizations, well-baby care, income support, family or marital counseling unrelated to the infant or toddler's development, and substance abuse counseling.

(B) The IFSP shall, to the extent appropriate, include the steps and time lines for the service coordinator to assist the parent to secure those services through public or private sources.

(b) The receipt of required early intervention services listed on the IFSP, pursuant to Section 52108(a)(1) of these regulations, from other state or federal agencies such as California Children Services, is dependent on the infant or toddler and the infant's or toddler's parent meeting the statutory, regulatory, and other program criteria of the agency and/or program that provides those services. These criteria may include financial eligibility and medical condition eligibility as diagnosed by program certified personnel, and on the availability of funding for the program.

(1) In the event that the infant or toddler or infant's or toddler's parent is not eligible to receive those agency services, or funding for the program is unavailable, the required early intervention services shall be provided by the regional center or the LEA.

(2) The parent shall be informed in writing of this provision during the initial 45-day evaluation and assessment period and/or during the IFSP meeting.

[Authority cited: Sections 95009 and 95028, Government Code] [Reference: Section 1435(a)(4), Title 20 United States Code; Sections 303.12, 303.522 and 303.527(c), Title 34 Code of Federal Regulations; Section 95020(d), Government Code]

52109. Basis for the Provision of Services through Regional Centers.

(a) Regional centers shall provide, arrange, or purchase early intervention services, as required by the infant's or toddler's IFSP, and be payor of last resort for infants and toddlers determined eligible for early intervention services as:

(1) Developmentally delayed pursuant to 52022(a);

(2) Established risk pursuant to 52022(b)(1); or,

(3) High risk for developmental disability pursuant to 52022(c).

(b) Regional centers shall be the payor of last resort after all other public and private sources for payment have been reviewed to determine if a referral shall be made by the service coordinator and/or the parent. Referrals may include but not be limited to California Children Services, Medi-Cal, or private insurance providers that may have responsibility for payment. This review shall not delay the provision of early intervention services specified on the IFSP. Early intervention services specified on the IFSP shall begin as soon as possible.

[Authority cited: Sections 95009 and 95028, Government Code] [Reference: Sections 1435(a)(10) and (c), and 1440, Title 20 United States Code; Sections 303.520, and 303.527, Title 34 Code of Federal Regulations; Section 95004 and 95014(b), Government Code]

52110. Basis for the Provision of Services Through LEAs.

(a) LEAs shall provide, arrange, or purchase early intervention services, as required by the infant's or toddler's IFSP, and be payor of last resort for infants and toddlers with solely low incidence disabilities determined eligible for early intervention services under the category of established risk as specified in Section 52022(b)(2) of these regulations and who are not eligible for regional center services.

(b) LEAs, pursuant to Education Code Section 56425, shall provide services for infants and toddlers who are also eligible for regional center services when the infant or toddler

- Basis for Services Through Regional Centers

- Infants and Toddlers Determined Eligible

- Payor of Last Resort

- Basis for Services Through LEAs

is identified as an individual with exceptional needs pursuant to Education Code Section 56026 and Title 5 California Code of Regulations Section 3030 and who requires intensive special education services and:

(1) The infant or toddler is functioning at or below 50% of his or her chronological age level in any one of the following skill areas:

(A) Gross or fine motor development;

(B) Receptive or expressive language development;

(C) Social or emotional development;

(D) Cognitive development;

(E) Visual development; or,

(2) The infant or toddler is functioning between 51% and 75% of his or her age level in any two of the skill areas identified in (b)(1)(A) through (b)(1)(E) of this section; or,

(3) Has a condition of known etiology which has a high probability of resulting in developmental delay as specified in Section 52022(b)(1); and,

(4) The LEA is operating below the funded capacity as required by Government Code Section 95014(c).

[Authority cited: Sections 95009 and 95028, Government Code] [Reference: Section 1440, Title 20 United States Code; Sections 303.520, and 303.527, Title 34 Code of Federal Regulations; Section 95014(b) and (c), Government Code]

Article 3. Transfer and Transition Procedures

52111. Transfer.

(a) Regional centers and LEAs shall use existing information whenever possible to determine continued eligibility and to minimize delay in the provision of appropriate early intervention services when an eligible infant's or toddler's residence changes to another regional center or LEA.

(b) The procedures contained in Welfare and Institutions Code Section 4643.5, pertaining to transfers between regional centers, shall apply for an infant or toddler with an existing IFSP who moves from an area where he or she received early intervention services from a regional center into another regional center area.

(c) The procedures contained in Education Code Section 56325, pertaining to an IEP, shall apply instead for an infant or toddler with an existing IFSP who moves from an area where he or she received early intervention services from an

- Transfer

LEA into another LEA that provides early intervention services and the LEA is operating below the funded capacity, or for an infant or toddler with a solely low incidence disability.

(d) For an infant or toddler, with an existing IFSP, who is receiving early intervention services from an LEA :

(1) Who has not been determined eligible for regional center services; and,

(2) Who moves from an area where an LEA provides early intervention services to an area where there are no services available for the infant or toddler through the LEA,

(A) With parent consent, the sending LEA, if informed about the move by the family, shall notify the receiving regional center as soon as possible of a move to the new area and transmit the infant's or toddler's record to expedite service delivery in the new area; or

(B) With parent consent, the LEA shall transmit the infant or toddler's record upon request of the receiving regional center if the LEA was not previously informed of the move by the family.

(C) The receiving regional center shall:

1. Assign a service coordinator as specified in Section 52060; and,

2. Arrange, purchase or provide early intervention services to the extent possible within existing resources as specified on the infant's or toddler's current IFSP as soon as possible; and,

3. Within 30 days of receipt of evaluation and assessment materials from the LEA determine eligibility and conduct a periodic review of the IFSP.

[Authority cited: Sections 95009 and 95028, Government Code] [Reference: Section 4643.5, Welfare and Institutions Code; Section 56325, Education Code]

52112. Transition from Early Intervention Services.

(a) LEAs shall provide special education and related services to eligible children at age three. Pursuant to the requirements contained in Title 34 Code of Federal Regulations, Section 303.344, each LEA shall participate in the transition planning for toddlers served under the Early Intervention Services Act, Government Code Sections 95000-95030, who may be eligible for preschool programs under Part B of the Individuals with Disabilities Education Act, Title 20 United States Code Sections 1400 - 1420, before the

- Transition from Early Intervention Services

- Eligible Children at Age Three

toddler is two years nine months, or at the discretion of all parties up to six months before the child turns three to ensure that an IEP has been developed and is implemented by the toddler's third birthday.

(b) The service coordinator, six months before the third birthday of the toddler receiving early intervention services, shall:

- Service Coordinator Responsibilities

(1) Notify the parent of a toddler who may be eligible for special education and related services under Part B of the Individuals with Disabilities Education Act that transition planning will occur within the next three to six months;

(2) Notify the LEA where the toddler resides that there will be an IFSP meeting requiring the attendance of an LEA representative pursuant to 34 CFR 300.132, before the toddler is two years nine months, or at the discretion of all parties, up to six months before the toddler turns three years old to specify the transition steps necessary for movement into a services under Part B of the Individuals with Disabilities Education Act and,

(3) Within thirty days following notification of the parent and the LEA, the family, service coordinator, and LEA shall agree on the date for the IFSP to specify the transition steps necessary for movement into services under Part B.

(c) For all toddlers with an IFSP, the transition steps contained in the IFSP at two years nine months or earlier shall include all of the following:

- Transition Steps

(1) Discussions with and providing information to parents regarding:

(A) The toddler's transition to special education for a toddler with a disability who may be eligible for special education and related services under Part B of the Individuals with Disabilities Education Act, Title 20 United States Code Sections 1400 - 1420; and,

(B) Steps to prepare the toddler for changes in service delivery, including steps to help the toddler adjust to, and function in, a new setting;

(2) Provide information about community resources, such as Head Start, Child Development Preschools, private or public preschool, for a toddler who will not be eligible for special education services after thirty six months of age; and,

(3) A projected date for conducting a final review of the IFSP to review the early intervention services and the transition outcomes by age three.

(d) For toddlers who may be eligible for preschool services from the LEA under Part B of the Individuals with

- Toddlers Who May Be Eligible for Preschool Services

Disabilities Education Act, Title 20 United States Code Sections 1400 - 1420, the transition steps necessary for movement into services under Part B or other appropriate program, written at the IFSP meeting before the toddler is two years nine months, or, at the discretion of all parties, up to six months before the toddler's third birthday, shall include all of the following:

(1) With parental consent, the transmission of information about the toddler to the LEA including evaluation and assessment information and copies of IFSPs that have been developed and implemented;

(2) Identifying needed assessments to determine regional center and special education eligibility and determining the regional center or LEA responsible and time lines for completing the needed assessments;

(3) Statements of the steps necessary to ensure that the referral to an LEA is received by the LEA in a timely manner to ensure that assessments required under the provisions of Part B of the Individuals with Disabilities Education Act are completed and an IEP is implemented by the toddler's third birthday;

(4) A referral for evaluation and assessment for services under Part B of the Individuals with Disabilities Education Act, Title 20 United States Code Sections 1400 - 1420, no later than the time that the toddler is two years nine months of age or before the LEA's break in school services if the toddler will become three years of age during a break in school services. The transition IFSP shall contain steps necessary to satisfy the referral and IEP development requirements contained in Education Code Sections 56321 and 56344;

(5) Identification of the people responsible for convening an IEP and final IFSP meeting, and, the person responsible for convening an IPP meeting, if necessary, for a toddler by age three to:

(A) Review the progress toward meeting the early intervention services outcomes identified in the IFSP;

(B) Determine the eligibility for special education and develop the IEP and,

(C) Develop an IPP if the toddler is also eligible for services under the Lanterman Developmental Disabilities Services Act as required in Welfare and Institutions Code Section 4646.

(e) If a toddler is older than two years and six months on the date of the initial IFSP, the IFSP shall include steps to ensure transition to Special Education Services under Part B of the Individuals with Disabilities Education Act or other services that may be appropriate.

- If Toddler Is Older Than Two Years and Six Months on Date of Initial IFSP

(f) Regional centers may continue providing or purchasing services for a preschooler who has been determined eligible for regional center services:

- Regional Centers May Continue Services for Eligible Preschoolers

(1) Until the beginning of the next school term after the toddler's third birthday during a period when the LEA special education preschool program is not in session; and,

(2) When the multidisciplinary team determines that services are necessary until the LEA special education program resumes.

[Authority cited: Sections 95009 and 95028, Government Code] [Reference: Section 1436(d)(8), Title 20 United States Code; Sections 303.343, 303.344(h) 303.148, 303.322, 303.340, 303.342, and 303.346 Title 34 Code of Federal Regulations; Sections 56321, 56343 and 56344, Education Code]

Subchapter 4. Service Coordination and Interagency Agreements

Article 1. Service Coordinatrion

52120. General.

(a) Regional centers or LEAs shall assign a service coordinator under the following circumstances:

- Service Coordinator

(1) At the time that infants or toddlers are referred for evaluation and assessment; and,

(2) When infants or toddlers are determined eligible for early intervention services from regional centers and/or LEAs.

(b) A parent may perform service coordination activities for his or her own infant or toddler in collaboration with the service coordinator assigned by the regional center or LEA.

- Parent May Perform Service Coordination Activities

[Authority cited: Sections 95009 and 95028, Government Code] [Reference: Sections 303.22 and 303.344(g), Title 34 Code of Federal Regulations; Section 95018, Government Code]

52121. Service Coordination Responsibilities .

(a) The service coordinator shall:

(1)   Provide the initial notice to the parent pursuant to Section 52160 of these regulations;

(2)   Obtain consent pursuant to Section 52162 of these regulations and provide written notice pursuant to Section 52161;

(3) Serve as the primary point of contact for coordinating services and assistance for the infant's or toddler's parent, service providers and regional center and/or public agencies;

(4) Inform the parent of the availability of additional non-required services as specified in Section 52108(a)(3)(A) of these regulations which may provide assistance to the family;

(5) Facilitate the delivery of services on the initiation date identified in the IFSP;

(6) Continuously seek the appropriate services and service providers necessary to enhance the development of each infant or toddler being served for the duration of the infant's or toddler's eligibility;

(7) Coordinate the performance of initial and subsequent evaluations and assessments;

(8) Participate in the development and review of the IFSP;

(9) Monitor the delivery of services and the degree to which progress toward achieving outcomes is being made through the periodic review of the IFSP;

(10) Inform the parent of advocacy services and procedural safeguards contained in these regulations;

(11)   Facilitate the exchange of information between service providers including health providers, medical case managers, regional centers and LEAs; and

(12) Facilitate the development of transition steps in the IFSP.

(b)   Service coordination may include medical case management services provided by another agency such as High Risk Infant Follow-up Program, California Children Services or Medi-Cal Managed Care.

[Authority cited: Sections 95009 and 95028, Government Code] [Reference: Section 1436(d)(8) Title 20 United States Code; Sections 303.22 and 303.344(g), Title 34 Code of Federal Regulations. Section 95018, Government Code]

52122. Service Coordinator Qualifications.

Service coordinators shall have demonstrated knowledge about:

(a) Infants and toddlers who are referred for evaluation and assessment or who are eligible for early intervention services;

(b) Working with families and community resources; and

(c) Federal and State requirements related to California's Early Start Program including:

(1) Parent rights and responsibilities;

(2) Due process;

(3) Confidentiality;

(4) Required components of the IFSP;

(5) Time lines specified within these regulations beginning with Section 52000 et seq.; in Sections 52086(a), 52112(b), 52164(b), 52168(c), 52171(a) and 52174(c) of these regulations;

(6) Transition processes from the early intervention service system specified in section 52112 of these regulations; and,

(7) The system of payments for services identified in the IFSP.

[Authority cited: Sections 95009 and 95028, Government Code] [Reference: Section 1436(d)(8) Title 20 United States Code; Section 303.22(d), and 303.344(g), Title 34 Code of Federal Regulations. Section 95018, Government Code]

Article 2. Interagency Agreements

52140. Local Interagency Agreements.

- Local Interagency Agreements

(a) Regional centers and LEAs shall develop and maintain local interagency agreements

(b) Local interagency agreements shall include, but not be limited to, the following:

(1) The responsibilities of each LEA and regional center for meeting the terms of the agreement;

(2) Procedures for coordination of child find activities with local public agencies and regional centers to identify infants and toddlers who may be eligible for early intervention services;

(3) Specific procedures for coordination of referrals for evaluation and assessment;

(4) Procedures for the assignment of a service coordinator;

(5) Interagency procedures for identifying the responsibilities of the regional center and LEA for completing the evaluation and assessment and determining eligibility within the time requirements contained in Section 52086 of these regulations, when an infant or toddler may receive

services from both the regional center and LEA;

(6) Procedures for the timely exchange of information between regional centers and LEAs;

(7) Mechanisms for ensuring the availability of contacts at regional centers and LEAs at all times during the year;

(8) Procedures for interagency IFSP development when infants and toddlers may be eligible for early intervention services from the regional center and the LEA or other state or local programs or services;

(9) Procedures to ensure the provision of services during periods of school vacations when services are required on the IFSP;

(10) Transition planning procedures which begin at least six months prior to a toddler's third birthday pursuant to Section 52112 of these regulations;

(11) Procedures for resolving disputes between regional centers and LEAs;

(12) Procedures for the training and assignment of surrogate parents; and

(13) Procedures for accepting transfers of infants or toddlers with existing IFSPs.

(c) Local interagency agreements shall be dated, and signed by representatives of the regional center and LEA.

(d) Interagency agreements shall be reviewed by both parties annually, revised as necessary, dated, and signed by both parties.

[Authority cited: Sections 95009 and 95028, Government Code] [Reference: Section 1435(a)(10), Title 20 United States Code; Sections 303.1, 303.174, 303.523, and 303.524, Title 34 Code of Federal Regulations]

Subchapter 5. Procedural Safeguards

Article 1. Notice and Consent

52160. Initial and Annual Notice.
Prior to the initial evaluation and assessment to determine eligibility required in Section 52082 of these regulations and annually thereafter, service coordinators shall give written notice to the parent, which shall include:

(a) The personally identifiable information maintained by the regional center or LEA;

(b) The types of information used in the evaluation, assessment and IFSP development; and,

- Initial and Annual Notice

(c) The methods that regional centers and LEAs use to protect the confidentiality of personally identifiable information including:

(1) The sources from whom personally identifiable information is gathered;

(2) The uses to be made of the personally identifiable information;

(3) The policies and procedures which regional centers and LEAs follow regarding storage, disclosure to third parties, retention, and destruction of personally identifiable information as required in Title 34 Code of Federal Regulations, Sections 300.572 through 300.573; and,

(4) The rights of parents and infants and toddlers regarding access to information, including the rights accorded to families in these regulations and the rights under the Family Education Rights and Privacy Act of 1974, Title 20 United States Code, Section 1232(g) and implementing regulations in Title 34 Code of Federal Regulations, Section 99.

[Authority cited: Sections 95009 and 95028, Government Code] [Reference: Sections 99.7, 300.561(a)(4) and 303.460, Title 34 Code of Federal Regulations, Sections 1232(g), 1476(b)(12), and 1480(2) and (3), Title 20 United States Code;, Scction 95007(g), Government Code]

52161. General Notice Requirements.

(a) Written notice shall be given to the parent of an infant or toddler, eligible or suspected to be eligible to receive early intervention services, a reasonable time before a regional center or LEA proposes, or refuses, to initiate or change:

(1) The identification, evaluation, assessment or placement of the infant or toddler; or

(2) Early intervention services to the infant or toddler and the infant's or toddler's family.

(b) The notice shall be in sufficient detail to inform the parent about:

(1) The action that is being proposed or refused;

(2) The reasons for taking the action; and

(3) All procedural safeguards that are available under Title 34 Code of Federal Regulations, Sections 303.400 through 303.460.

(c) The notice shall be:

(1) Written using words that are understandable to the general public; and

(2) Provided in the language of the parent's choice, unless

it is clearly not feasible to do so. The regional center or LEA shall take steps to ensure that:

(A) The notice is translated;

(B) The parent understands the notice; and

(C) There is written evidence that the requirements of this subsection have been met.

[Authority cited: Sections 95009 and 95028, Government Code] [Reference: Section 95007(g), Government Code; Sections 1435(a)(13) and 1439(6)-(7), Title 20 United States Code; Sections 303.403(a), 303.403(b) and 303.403(c)(1)-(2), Title 34 Code of Federal Regulations]

52162. Consent.

(a) The service coordinator shall obtain written parental consent before:

(1) The initial evaluation and assessment of an infant or toddler is conducted; and

(2) Early intervention services are initiated.

(b) The infant's or toddler's record shall contain written evidence that the parent has been informed:

(1) Of information relevant to the evaluation, assessment, early intervention service, or exchange of records for which consent is sought, in the language of the parent's choice, and agrees to the completion of the evaluation or assessment and the provision of early intervention services;

(2) That consent is voluntary and may be revoked at any time;

(3) That he/she may accept or decline an early intervention service and may decline such service after first accepting it, and continue to receive other early intervention services; and,

(4) About who will receive the records and a listing of the records to be exchanged.

(c) If consent is not given or is withdrawn, the regional center or LEA service coordinator shall ensure:

(1) That the parent has been informed of the nature of the evaluation and assessment or the early intervention services that would have been provided;

(2) That the parent has been informed that the infant or toddler will not receive the evaluation and assessment or early intervention services unless consent is given; and,

(3) That the infant's or toddler's record contains documentation of the attempts to obtain consent.

[Authority cited: Sections 95009 and 95028, Government Code] [Reference: Section 1480, Title 20 United States Code; Sections 303.401(a)(1)-(3), 303.403(c)(2)(iii), 303.404(a), 303.404(b), and 303.405, Title 34 Code of Federal Regulations]

Article 2. Access Rights

52164. Access Rights.

- Access Rights

(a) A regional center and/or LEA shall permit the parent or authorized representative to inspect and review any record relating to their infant or toddler.

(b) The regional center and/or LEA shall comply with a request for access to records before any meeting regarding an IFSP or any hearing relating to the identification, evaluation, assessment, placement, or the provision of early intervention services to the infant or toddler and in no case more than 5 working days after the request has been made.

(c) A regional center and/or LEA shall respond to requests for explanations and interpretations of the content of a record from parents with the requested explanation or interpretation.

(d) A regional center and/or LEA may presume that the parent has authority to inspect and review records relating to their infant or toddler unless there is a court order, state statute, or legally binding document relating to such matters as divorce, separation or custody that specifically revokes those rights.

(e) Each service coordinator shall provide parents, on request, a list of the types and locations of records collected or used by the regional center or LEA.

[Authority cited: Sections 95009 and 95028, Government Code] [Reference: Section 1435(a)(13), and 1439(4), Title 20 United States Code; Sections 300.562, 300.565, 300.576, 303.402, and 303.460, Title 34 Code of Federal Regulations; Section 95007(g), Government Code]

52165. Documentation of Access .

- Documentation of Access

(a) The regional center and/or LEA providing early intervention services to the infant or toddler shall maintain documentation specifying to whom the record was disclosed, other than parents and authorized employees specified by the regional center or LEA. The parent may inspect the documentation.

(b) Documentation of access shall include:

(1) The name of the person to whom the record was disclosed;

(2) The date the record was disclosed; and

(3) The purpose for which the record was disclosed.

[Authority cited: Sections 95009 and 95028, Government Code] [Reference: Sections 1435(a)(13) and 1439(4), Title 20 United States Code; Sections 303.402, and 303.460, Title 34 Code of Federal Regulations; Section 95007(g), Government Code]

52166. Records On More Than One Infant or Toddler.

If a record includes information on more than one infant or toddler, the regional center or LEA shall provide, for the parent's inspection or review, only the information relating to their infant or toddler or inform the parent of that specific information.

[Authority cited: Sections 95009 and 95028, Government Code] [Reference: Section 1439(2) and (3), Title 20 United States Code; Sections 300.564 and 303.460, Title 34 Code of Federal Regulations]

52167. Fees For Copies Of Records.

(a) A regional center or LEA may charge a reasonable fee for copies of records in an amount not to exceed the actual cost of reproducing records.

(b) The amount of the fee shall not prevent the parents from exercising their right to inspect and review those records.

(c) A regional center or LEA may not charge a fee to search for or retrieve records requested by parents or an authorized representative.

[Authority cited: Sections 95009 and 95028, Government Code] [Reference: Section 1439 (3), Title 20 United States Code; Sections 300.566 and 303.460, Title 34 Code of Federal Regulations; Section 49065, Education Code]

52168. Amendment Of Records At Parental Request.

(a) A parent, who believes that information in a regional center's or LEA's records is inaccurate or misleading or violates the privacy or other rights of an infant or toddler or family, may request that the director of the regional center or the Superintendent of the LEA amend or remove the information over which the regional center or LEA has authority.

(b) The service coordinator, upon request, shall assist a parent in communicating with those persons who created information contained in the record, when the regional center or LEA did not originate the information which the parent believes is inaccurate, misleading, or violates the privacy or other rights of an infant or toddler or family.

(c) No later than 14 days after receipt of the request for amendment or removal of information from a record, the regional center or LEA shall notify the parent if the request has been denied and advise the parent of the right to a meeting with the Director of the regional center or the Superintendent of the LEA pursuant to Title 34 Code of Federal Regulations, Section 99.20(c).

(d) If the result of the meeting is that the record will not be amended, the regional center or LEA shall inform the parent of the right to place, in the record maintained on the infant or toddler, a statement commenting on the information contained in the record or setting forth any reasons for disagreeing with the contents of any document in the child's records, regardless of whether the document was created by the regional center or LEA or by any other agency or individual. Any statement placed in the record of the infant or toddler pursuant to Section (d) above shall:

(1) Be kept by the regional center or LEA as part of the record of the infant or toddler as long as the contested portion of the record is maintained by the regional center or LEA; and,

(2) Accompany the record of the infant or toddler if the contested portion is disclosed by the regional center or LEA.

[Authority cited: Sections 95009 and 95028, Government Code] [Reference: Sections 300.566, 300.567, 300.569, and 303.460, Title 34 Code of Federal Regulations]

52169. Consent for Release of Information.

Written parental consent shall be obtained before personally identifiable information is disclosed in writing or orally to anyone other than authorized employees specified by the regional center or LEA.

- Consent for Release of Information

[Authority cited: Sections 95009 and 95028, Government Code] [Reference: Sections 1435(a)(13) and 1439(2), Title

20 United States Code; Sections 300.571 and 303.460, Title 34 Code of Federal Regulations]

Article 3. Complaint Process

52170. Complaint Procedures.

(a) A complaint shall be a written and signed statement alleging that a regional center, LEA or any private service provider receiving funds under Part C of the Individuals with Disabilities Education Act, Title 20 United States Code, Sections 1431 - 1445, has violated a federal or state law or regulation governing the provision of early intervention services provided through Part C of the Individuals with Disabilities Education Act, Title 20 United States Code Sections 1431 - 1445, for infants or toddlers and their families.

(b) Any individual or organization may file a complaint.

(c) The procedures under Chapter 1, commencing with Section 4500 of Division 4.5 of the Welfare and Institutions Code or Part 30, commencing with Section 56500 of the Education Code, or Title 5 California Code of Regulations Section 4600 et seq., shall not be used for resolving complaints regarding California's Early Start Program.

(d) Each regional center and LEA shall inform the parent and other interested individuals or organizations of the right to file a complaint directly with the Department of Developmental Services at the following address:

Department of Developmental Services
Attention: Chief, Early Start Program Development Section
1600 Ninth Street,
Sacramento, CA 95814

(e) If the complainant is unable to provide the complaint in writing, the service coordinator shall directly assist the complainant or provide assistance to identify resources which can aid the complainant in completing the written complaint.

(f) The complaint shall include the following:

(1) The name, address and phone number of the complainant;

(2) A statement that a regional center, LEA or any private service provider receiving funds under Part C of the Individuals with Disabilities Education Act, Title 20 United States Code Sections 1431 - 1445, has violated a federal or state law or regulation governing the provision of early

- Complaint Procedures
- Written and Signed Statement

- Individual or Organization May File

- Procedures for Resolving Complaints

- Regional Centers and LEAs Shall Inform of Right to File

- Address

- Assistance in Filing

- Content of Complaint

intervention services for infants or toddlers and their families in California;

(3) A statement of facts upon which the alleged violation is based;

(4) The party allegedly responsible; and

(5) A description of the voluntary steps taken at the local level to resolve the complaint, if any.

[Authority cited: Sections 95009 and 95028, Government Code] [Reference: Sections 303.22, and 303.510-303.512, Title 34 Code of Federal Regulations; and Section 95007(f) Government Code]

52171. Complaint Investigation.

(a) Within 60 days of receipt of the complaint the Department of Developmental Services shall:

(1) Assign the investigation of the complaint to a state interagency team or to the appropriate state agency that is responsible for the administration of the regional center, LEA or any private service provider receiving funds under Part C of the Individuals with Disabilities Education Act, Title 20 United States Code Sections 1431 - 1445, named in the complaint, which shall:

(A) Conduct an investigation, on-site if necessary; and

(B) Give the complainant the opportunity to submit additional information, either orally or in writing, about the allegations in the complaint;

(2) Review all relevant information and make a determination as to whether there has been a violation of a statutory or regulatory requirement contained in:

(A) Part C of the Individuals with Disabilities Education Act, Title 20 United States Code Sections 1431 - 1445;

(B) The Federal regulations pertaining to Part C of the Individuals with Disabilities Education Act;

(C) The California Early Intervention Services Act, Government Code Sections 95000-95030;

(D) Regulations contained in this chapter;

(E) Welfare and Institutions Code, Division 4.5, Chapter 5, beginning with Section 4500; or,

(F) Education Code beginning with Sections 56425 through 56431.

(3) Provide a written decision to all parties which addresses each allegation and includes:

(A) Findings and conclusions;

(B) The reasons for the final decision;

I-54

(C) The required corrective actions;

(D) Time lines for completion of the corrective actions; and,

(E) Provisions for technical assistance.

(4) Inform all parties involved in the complaint that the final decision may be appealed to the U.S. Secretary of Education.

(b) An extension of the time limit under paragraph (a) of this Section shall be made by the Department of Developmental Services when events beyond the control of the Department of Developmental Services occur including but not limited to the complainant's illness, the complainant's absence from the geographical area, inability to locate the complainant, or a natural disaster.

[Authority cited: Sections 95009 and 95028, Government Code] [Reference: Section 303.512, Title 34 Code of Federal Regulations; Section 52007(g), Government Code]

Article 4. Mediation and Due Process Procedures

52172. Procedures that Apply to Both Mediation and Due Process.

(a) A parent may request a mediation conference and/or a due process hearing under any of the following circumstances:

(1) A regional center or LEA proposes to initiate or change the identification, evaluation, assessment, placement or provision of appropriate early intervention services;

(2) A regional center or LEA refuses to initiate or change the identification, evaluation, assessment, placement or provision of appropriate early intervention services; or,

(b) A regional center or LEA may request a mediation conference and/or a due process hearing when the parent refuses to consent to all or any part of an evaluation and assessment of the infant or toddler.

(c) All requests for a mediation conference and/or due process hearing shall be in writing and filed with the contractor that the Department of Developmental Services uses for mediation and due process hearings. If a parent is unable to make a request for mediation or a due process hearing in writing, the service coordinator shall assist the parent in filing the request.

(d) The duration for both mediation and due process hearing shall not exceed a total thirty day period from the

- Procedures for Requesting Mediation or Hearing

- Circumstances

receipt of the mediation or due process request to the mailing of the decision.

(e) The location of the mediation and/or due process hearing shall be at a time and place reasonably convenient to the parent.

(f) During the pendency of mediation and/or due process hearing procedures, the infant or toddler shall continue to receive the early intervention services listed on the IFSP they are currently receiving. If mediation and/or due process hearing involves the initiation of a service(s) the infant or toddler shall receive those services that are not in dispute.

(g) Mediation and due process hearings shall be conducted in English and interpreted in the language of the family's choice or other mode of communication.

[Authority cited: Sections 95009 and 95028, Government Code; and Section 4712(k), Welfare and Institutions Code] [Reference: Sections 1435(a)(13) and 1439(l), Title 20 United States Code; Sections, 303.420 and accompanying notes, 303.421, 303.423 and 303.425, Title 34 Code of Federal Regulations; Section 95007(g), Government Code]

52173. Mediation Procedures.   - Mediation Procedures

(a) Mediation shall be voluntary.

(b) The matter being mediated shall proceed to a scheduled due process hearing if either party waives mediation or if mediation fails in whole or in part. The mediator may assist the parties in specifying any unresolved issue(s) to be included in the hearing request.

(c) The mediation conference shall be conducted by a mediator who is an impartial, third party with no personal or professional interest that would conflict with his or her objectivity in mediating a disagreement.

(d) The due process hearing officer shall be a different person than the mediator when mediation does not resolve the disagreement.

(e) The mediator shall be trained in communication, mediation and problem solving and shall be knowledgeable about early intervention programs and the federal and state laws and regulations applicable to Part C of the Individuals with Disabilities Education Act, Title 20 United States Code Sections 1431 - 1445, and the California Early Intervention Services Act, Government Code Sections 95000-95030.

(f) The mediator shall be under contract with the Department of Developmental Services.

(g) A person who otherwise qualifies under Subsections (c) and (d) of this Section as a mediator is not an employee of the Department of Developmental Services solely because the person is paid by the Department of Developmental Services to conduct the mediation process.

(h) A parent may be accompanied by any representative at the mediation.

(i) The mediator shall ensure that written agreements from the mediation conference are signed and provided to all participants at the conclusion of the mediation conference.

[Authority cited: Sections 95009 and 95028, Government Code] [Reference: Section 1439(1), Title 20 United States Code; Sections 303.420(a)-(b) and accompanying notes, 303.421(a)-(b) and 303.422, Title 34 Code of Federal Regulations]

52174. Due Process Hearing Procedures. - Due Process Hearing Procedures

(a) The hearing shall be conducted by a due process hearing officer who is an impartial, third party with no personal or professional interest that would conflict with his or her objectivity in conducting the hearing.

(b) The due process hearing officer shall be knowledgeable about the federal and state laws and regulations applicable to Part C of the Individuals with Disabilities Education Act, Title 20 United States Code Sections 1431 - 1445 and the California Early Intervention Services Act, Government Code Sections 95000-95030, the Lanterman Developmental Disabilities Services Act, Welfare and Institutions Code Sections 4500 et seq.; and Part 30 of the California Education Code, commencing with Section 56500 et seq.

(c) The hearing officer shall:

(1) Listen to the presentation of relevant viewpoints about the issue of disagreement;

(2) Examine the evidence presented during the hearing;

(3) Issue a decision that is in compliance with federal and state law;

(4) Provide documentation of the proceedings, including findings of fact and a written decision; and

(5) Ensure that the decision is mailed to each party after completion of the hearing and within 30 days of receipt of the due process hearing request.

(d) A parent involved in a due process hearing shall have the right to:

(1) Be accompanied and advised by counsel and/or by an

individual with special knowledge and training with respect to early intervention services,

(2) Present evidence and confront, cross-examine, and compel the attendance of witnesses;

(3) Prohibit the introduction of any evidence at the proceeding that has not been disclosed to the parent or the other party at least five days before the proceeding;

(4) Obtain a written or electronic, verbatim transcription of the proceeding; and

(5) Obtain written findings of fact and decision.

(e) The hearing officer shall be under contract with the Department of Developmental Services. A person who otherwise qualifies under Subsection (a) or (b) of this Section is not an employee of a regional center or LEA solely because the person is paid by the agency to conduct the due process hearing.

(f) Disputes which occur related to an IEP meeting which may occur prior to the child's third birthday and which pertain to proposed Part B preschool placements or services shall be filed with and processed by the agent or division of the Department of Education which is responsible for administering due process mediations and hearings pursuant to Part B of the Individuals with Disabilities Education Act and Part 30 of the California Education Code, commencing with Section 56500 et seq.

[Authority cited: Sections 95009 and 95028, Government Code] [Reference: Section 1439(l), Title 20 United States Code; Sections 303.421(a)-(b), 303.422(b) and 303.423(b), Title 34 Code of Federal Regulations; Section 95007(g), Government Code]

Article 5. Surrogate Parents

52175. Surrogate Parents.

(a) Regional centers or LEAs shall assign an individual to act as a surrogate parent if:

(1) No parent can be identified;

(2) The infant or toddler is a dependent of the juvenile court and the parental rights of the parent have been limited by the court or relinquished; or

(3) The parent cannot be located, after reasonable efforts by the regional center or LEA.

(b) Interagency agreements as required in Section 52140(b)(12) shall include procedures for:

- Surrogate Parents

(1) Determining whether an infant or toddler needs a surrogate parent;

(2) Assigning a surrogate parent to the infant or toddler consistent with the provisions of this Article and Government Code Section 7579.5;

(3) Ensuring that surrogates have no interest that conflicts with the interests of the infant or toddler he or she represents;

(4) Ensuring that surrogates have knowledge and skills that ensure adequate representation of the infant or toddler;

(5) Ensuring that the surrogate parent is not an employee of any regional center, LEA or service provider involved in the provision of early intervention services to the infant or toddler.   A person who otherwise qualifies as a surrogate parent is not an employee solely because he or she is paid by a regional center or LEA to serve as a surrogate parent.

(c) A surrogate parent may represent an infant or toddler in all matters related to:

(1) The evaluation and assessment of the infant or toddler;

(2) Development and implementation of the infant's or toddler's IFSP including annual evaluations, assessments and periodic reviews;

(3) The ongoing provision of early intervention services to the infant or toddler;

(4) Requesting mediation or due process hearings; and,

(5) Any other early intervention service established under Part C of the Individuals with Disabilities Education Act, Title 20 United States Code Sections 1431 - 1445.

(d) A surrogate parent may not provide consent for medical services for which consent by a parent or legal guardian is required.

[Authority cited: Sections 95009 and 95028 Government Code]   [Reference: Section 1439(5), Title 20 United States Code; Sections 303.18, and   303.406(a-e), Title 34Code of Federal Regulations; Section 95022(f), Government Code]

NOTE

The permanent Title 17 regulations implementing California's Early Intervention Services Act became effective in August 1998.

BUDGET ACT OF 2001-2002
SPECIAL EDUCATION BUDGET ITEMS
(Senate Bill 739, Chapter 106 , Statutes of 2001)
(Approved by the Governor on July 26, 2001)

STATE PROPOSITION 98 FUNDS FOR SPECIAL EDUCATION

6110-161-0001--For local assistance, Department of Education (Proposition 98), Program 10.60--Special Education Programs for Exceptional Children.. $2,607,658,000
Schedule:
(1)   10.60.050.003-Special education instruction..... ....$2,553,391,000
(2)   10.60.050.080-Early Education Program for Individuals with Exceptional
Needs..$ 68,662,000
(3)   Reimbursements for Early Education Program, Part C..............................$ -14,395,000
Provisions:
1.   Funds appropriated by this item are for transfer by the Controller to Section A of the State School Fund, in lieu of the amount that otherwise would be appropriated for transfer from the General Fund in the State Treasury to Section A of the State School Fund for the 2001-02 fiscal year pursuant to Sections 14002 and 41301 of the Education Code, for apportionment pursuant to Part 30 (commencing with Section 56000) of the Education Code, superseding all prior law.
2.   Of the funds appropriated in Schedule (1) of this item, $10,107,000, plus the COLA, shall be available for the purchase, repair, and inventory maintenance of specialized books, materials, and equipment for pupils with low-incidence disabilities, as defined in Section 56026.5 of the Education Code.
3.   Of the funds appropriated in Schedule (1) of this item, $7,829,000, plus the COLA, shall be available for the purposes of vocational training and job placement for special education pupils through Project Workability I pursuant to Article 3 (commencing with Section 56470) of Chapter 4.5 of Part 30 of the Education Code. As a condition of receiving these funds, each local educational agency shall certify that the amount of nonfederal resources, exclusive of funds received pursuant to this provision, devoted to the provision of vocational education for special education pupils shall be maintained at or above the level provided in the 1984-85 fiscal year.   The Superintendent of Public Instruction may waive this requirement for local educational agencies that demonstrate that the requirement would impose a severe hardship.
4.   Of the funds appropriated in Schedule (1) of this item, $4,084,000, plus the COLA, shall be available for regional occupational centers and programs that serve pupils having disabilities, and $68,974,000, plus the COLA, shall be available for regionalized program specialist services, including $1,660,000 for small special education local plan areas (SELPAs) pursuant to Section 56836.24 of the Education Code.
5.   Of the funds appropriated in Schedule (1), $5,856,000, plus the COLA is provided for an adjustment for low-incidence disabilities, based on the results of the study required by Section 67 of Chapter 854 of the Statutes of 1997.

6. Of the funds appropriated in Schedule (1), $1,000,000 is provided for extraordinary costs associated with single placements in nonpublic, nonsectarian schools, pursuant to Section 56836.21 of the Education Code.

7. Of the funds appropriated in Schedule (1), a total of $6,942,000 is available for equalization funding pursuant to Section 56836.14 of the Education Code.

8. Of the funds appropriated in Schedule (1), a total of $120,154,000, plus the COLA, is available to fully fund the costs of children placed in licensed children's institutions who attend nonpublic schools.

9. Of the amount appropriated in Schedule (2) of this item, $1,007,000, plus the COLA, shall be available for infant program growth units (ages birth-two years). Funds for infant units shall be allocated pursuant to Provision 11 of this item, with the following average number of pupils per unit:
    (a) For special classes and centers -- 16.
    (b) For resource specialist programs -- 24.
    (c) For designated instructional services -- 16.

10. Notwithstanding any other provision of law, early education programs for infants and toddlers shall be offered for 200 days. Funds appropriated in Schedule (2) shall be allocated by the State Department of Education for the 2001-02 fiscal year to those programs receiving allocations for instructional units pursuant to Section 56432 of the Education Code for the Early Education Program for Individuals with Exceptional Needs operated pursuant to Chapter 4.4 (commencing with Section 56425) of Part 30 of the Education Code, based on computing 200-day entitlements. Notwithstanding any other provision of law, funds in Schedule (2) shall be used only for the purposes specified in Provisions 10 and 11 of this item.

11. Notwithstanding any other provision of law, state funds appropriated in Schedule (2) of this item in excess of the amount necessary to fund the deficited entitlements pursuant to Section 56432 of the Education Code and Provision 10 of this item shall be available for allocation by the State Department of Education to local educational agencies for the operation of programs serving solely low-incidence infants and toddlers pursuant to Title 14 (commencing with Section 95000) of the Government Code. These funds shall be allocated to each local educational agency for each solely low-incidence child through age two in excess of the number of solely low-incidence children through age two served by the local educational agency during the 1992-93 fiscal year and reported on the April 1993, pupil count. These funds shall only be allocated if the amount of reimbursement received from the State Department of Developmental Services is insufficient to fully fund the costs of operating the Early Intervention Program, as authorized by Title 14 (commencing with Section 95000) of the Government Code.

12. The State Department of Education, through coordination with the SELPAs, shall ensure local interagency coordination and collaboration in the provision of early intervention services, including local training activities, child find activities, public awareness, and the family resource center activities.

13. Of the amount provided in Schedule (1), $122,866,000 is provided for a COLA at a rate of 3.87 percent.

14. Of the amount provided in Schedule (2), $2,549,000 is provided for a COLA at a rate of 3.87 percent.

15. Of the funds appropriated in Schedule (1) of this item, $97,874,000 shall be appropriated for the following priority sequence:

(a) The Superintendent of Public Instruction shall allocate the additional amount needed, if any, to augment the amounts appropriated in this item to ensure the full funding in the 2001-02 fiscal year of the equalization adjustments pursuant to Section 56836.14 of the Education Code.

(b) Of the remaining amount, the Superintendent of Public Instruction shall allocate any additional amount needed, if any, to augment the amounts appropriated in this item to ensure the full funding for the special disabilities adjustment pursuant to Section 56836.155 of the Education Code for the 2001-02 fiscal year.

(c) Of the remaining amount, the Superintendent of Public Instruction shall allocate 50 percent for the purposes of Section 56836.158 of the Education Code and the other 50 percent for the purposes of Section 56836.159 of the Education Code.

16. Funds appropriated in this item are available for the sole purpose of funding 2001-02 special education program costs and shall not be used to fund any prior year adjustments, claims or costs.

FEDERAL FUNDS FOR SPECIAL EDUCATION

6110-161-0890--For local assistance, Department of Education, payable from the Federal Trust Fund, Program 10.60--Special Education Programs for Exceptional Children.......................$664,818,000
Schedule:
(1)   10.60.050.012-Local Agency Entitlements, IDEA Special Education...............$545,340,000
(2)   10.60.050.013- State Agency Entitlements, IDEA Special Education................$ 1,541,000
(3)   10.60.050.015-IDEA, Local Entitlements, Preschool Program.........................$ 34,792,000
(4)   10.60.050.021-IDEA, Capacity Building, Special Education............................ $ 41,456,000
(5)   10.60.050.030-PL 99-457, Preschool Grant. Program...................................$ 39,849,000
(6)   10.60.050.031-IDEA, State Improvement Grant, Special Education............ ......$ 1,840,000
Provisions:
1. If the funds for Part B of the federal Individuals with Disabilities Education Act that are actually received by the state exceed $650,018,000, at least 95 percent of the funds received in excess of that amount shall be allocated for local entitlements and to state agencies with approved local plans. Five percent of the amount received in excess of $650,018,000 may be used for state administrative expenses. If the funds for Part B of the federal Individuals with Disabilities Education Act that are actually received by the state are less than $650,018,000, the reduction shall be taken in capacity building.

2. The funds appropriated in Schedule (2) shall be distributed to state-operated programs serving disabled children from 3 to 21 years of age, inclusive. In accordance with federal law, the funds appropriated in Schedules (1) and (2) shall be distributed to local and state agencies on the basis of an equal amount per eligible, identified pupil.

3. Of the funds appropriated in Schedule (4) of this item, up to $1,000,000 may be used to fund licensed children's institution growth pursuant to Section 56836.18 of the Education Code.

4. Pursuant to Section 56427 of the Education Code, of the funds appropriated in Schedule (4) of this item, up to $2,324,000 may be used to provide funding for infant programs, and may be used for those programs that do not qualify for funding pursuant to Section 56432 of the Education Code.

5. Of the funds appropriated in Schedule (4) of this item, $29,475,000 shall be allocated to local education agencies for the purposes of Project Workability I.

6. Of the funds appropriated in Schedule (4) of this item, $1,700,000 shall be used to provide specialized services to pupils with low-incidence disabilities, as defined in Section 56026.5 of the Education Code.

7. Of the funds appropriated in Schedule (4) of this item, up to $3,617,000 shall be used for a personnel development program. This program shall include state-sponsored staff development, local in-service components, bilingual, student study team, and core curriculum components. Of this amount, a minimum of $2,500,000 shall be allocated directly to special education local plan areas. The local in-service programs shall include a parent training component and may include a staff training component. Use of these funds shall be described in the local plans. These funds may be used to provide training in alternative dispute resolution and the local mediation of disputes. All programs are to include evaluation components.

8. Of the funds appropriated in Schedule (4) of this item, up to $200,000 shall be used for research and training in cross-cultural assessments.

9. Of the funds appropriated in Schedule (4) of this item, up to $300,000 shall be used to develop and test procedures, materials, and training for alternative dispute resolution in special education.

10. Of the funds appropriated by Schedule (5) for the Preschool Grant Program, $1,228,000 shall be used for in-service training programs and shall include a parent training component and may, in addition, include a staff training program. These funds may be used to provide training in alternative dispute resolution and the local mediation of disputes. This program shall include state-sponsored and local components.

11. Of the funds appropriated in this item, $1,420,000 is available for local assistance grants in third year of the Quality Assurance and Focused Monitoring Pilot Program to monitor local education agency compliance with state and federal laws and regulations governing special education. This funding level is to be used to continue the third year of facilitated reviews and, to the extent consistent with the key performance indicators developed by the State Department of Education, these activities focus on local education agencies identified by the United States Department of Education's Office of Special Education Programs.

13. Notwithstanding the notification requirements listed in Section 26.00 (d) of this act, the Department of Finance is authorized to approve intraschedule transfers of funds within this item submitted by the State Department of Education for the purposes of ensuring that special education funding provided in this item is appropriated in accordance with the statutory funding formula required federal IDEA and the special education funding formula required pursuant to Chapter 7.2 (commencing with Section 56836) of Part 30 of Division 4 of Title 2 of the Education Code, without waiting 30 days, but shall provide a notice to the Legislature each time a transfer occurs.

14. Of the funds appropriated in Schedule (4), up to $1 million shall be available in fiscal year 2001-02 for a special education local plan area that may apply for emergency impaction funds under this provision and pursuant to Section 56836.18 of the Education Code in the event a court of appropriate jurisdiction orders or advises the closure of a nonpublic, nonsectarian school operating at a licensed children's institution and the special education local plan area, in which the licensed children's institution is located, is required to provide for special education and related services to individuals with exceptional needs who had been enrolled in the nonpublic, nonsectarian school at the time of closure. For pupils placed in the LCI/NPS pursuant to a court order, the special education local plan area shall be eligible to apply for reimbursement of actual costs under this provision for up to one-half of the costs per pupil for which the nonpublic, nonsectarian school was previously reimbursed in the most recent fiscal year for which data is available. This provision shall apply to a maximum of one nonpublic, nonsectarian school operating at a licensed children's institution, and shall apply only to a school which closes as a result of a court order or advisory. Any special education local plan area receiving funds appropriated pursuant to this provision shall report to the State Department of Education, the Department of Finance, and the Legislative Analyst's office by April 15, 2002, regarding the services provided to students through this pilot and the performance outcomes for students, including, but not limited to, a summary of STAR test scores for students and any alternate assessments used to measure the achievement of special education students.

15. Of the funds appropriated in Schedule (4) of this item, $420,000 is provided for LCI and NPS mediated settlements covering fiscal years 1993-94 through 1996-97 and 2000-01 revisions to NPS/LCI claims by local education agencies.

REAPPROPRIATION TO FULLY FUND SPECIAL EDUCATION ADA INCREASE

6110-485-0001--Reappropriation (Proposition 98), Department of Education. The sum of $466,102,000 is reappropriated from the Proposition 98 Reversion Account, for the following purposes:
(3) $12,005,000 for transfer by the Controller to Section A of the State School Fund, for allocation by the Superintendent of Public Instruction to SELPAs to fully fund the 2000-01 Special Education average daily attendance increase.

STATE SPECIAL SCHOOLS

6110-005-0001--For support of Department of Education, as allocated by the Department of Education to the State Special Schools, Program 10.60.040...................................$30,595,000
Schedule:
(1)   10.60.040 – Instruction..$31,182,000
     (a) 10.60.040.001 - School for the Blind, Fremont.....................................$ 4,521,000
     (b) 10.60.040.002 - School for the Deaf, Fremont.....................................$13,416,000
     (c) 10.60.040.003 - School for the Deaf, Riverside....................................$13,245,000
(2)   Reimbursements...$ -587,000
Provisions:
1.   The State Special Schools for the Deaf in Fremont and Riverside and the State Special

Schools for the Blind in Fremont shall provide a four-week extended session.

2. Of the amount appropriated in this item, up to $13,000 is provided for payment of energy service contracts in connection with the issuance of Energy Conservation Efficiency Revenue Bonds.

3. Of the amount appropriated in Schedule (c) of this item, $1,121,000 shall be available on a one-time basis for the purpose of renovating 16 restrooms.

4. Of the amount appropriated in Schedule (c) of this item, $349,000 shall be available on a one-time basis for the purpose of installing air conditioning in the social hall.

5. Of the amount appropriated in Schedule (c) of this item, $159,000 shall be available on a one-time basis for the purpose of replacing nine hot water tanks.

STATE PROPOSITION 98 FUNDS FOR STATE SPECIAL SCHOOLS AND CENTERS

6110-006-0001--For support of Department of Education (Proposition 98), as allocated by the Department of Education to the State Special Schools..$33,483,000

Schedule:
(1) 10.60.040 - Instruction, State Special Schools...$38,370,000
        (a) 10.60.040.001 - School for the Blind, Fremont.................................$ -4,911,000
        (b) 10.60.040.002 - School for the Deaf, Fremont.................................$13,347,000
        (c) 10.60.040.003 - School for the Deaf, Riverside..............................$11,198,000
        (d) 10.60.040.007 - Diagnostic Centers...$ 8,914,000
(2) Reimbursements...$ -4,747,000
(3) Amount payable from the California State Lottery Education Fund
        (Item 6110-006-0814)..$ -140,000

Provisions:
1. On or before September 15 of each year, the superintendent of each State Special School shall report to each school district the number of pupils from that district who are attending a State Special School and the estimated payment due on behalf of the district for those pupils pursuant to Section 59300 of the Education Code. The Controller shall withhold from the State School Fund in the first principal apportionment of that fiscal year the amount due from each school district, as reported to the Controller by the Superintendent of Public Instruction. The amount withheld shall be transferred from the State School Fund to this item. The Superintendent of Public Instruction is authorized to adjust the estimated payments required after the close of the fiscal year by reporting to the Controller the information needed to make the adjustment. The payments by the Controller that result from this year-end adjustment shall be applied to the current year.

2. The State Special Schools for the Deaf in Fremont and Riverside and the State Special School for the Blind in Fremont shall provide a four-week extended session.

LOTTERY EDUCATION FUND/STATE SPECIAL SCHOOLS

6110-006-0814--For support of Department of Education, for payment to Item 6110-006-0001, payable from the California State Lottery Education Fund......................................$ 140,000

Provisions:
1. All funds received pursuant to Chapter 12.5 of Division 1 of Title 2 of the Government Code that are allocable to the State Special Schools pursuant to Section 8880.5 of the Government

Code, and that are in excess of the amount appropriated in this item, are hereby appropriated in augmentation of this item.

STATE SPECIAL SCHOOLS TRANSPORTATION

6110-008-0001--For support of Department of Education, as allocated by the Department of Education to the State Special Schools for student transportation allowances, Program 10.60.040..$ 1,064,000
Provisions:
1.   Funds appropriated in this item are in lieu of funds that otherwise would be transferred from the General Fund to Section A of the State School Fund in accordance with Sections14007 and 41301.5 of the Education Code.

STATE SPECIAL SCHOOLS CAPITAL OUTLAY

6110-301-0001--For capital outlay, Department of Education.................................$2,568,000
Schedule:
California School for the Blind, Fremont:
(1) 80.60.025- Young Children's Housing—Construction....................................$ 351,000
California School for the Deaf, Fremont:
(2) 80.75.020- Pupil Personnel Services—Construction.....................................$2,124,000
California School for the Deaf, Riverside:
(3) 80.80.010-Middle School Facility—Equipment..$ 93,000

STATE OPERATIONS - FEDERAL TRUST FUND

6110-001-0890--For support of Department of Education, for payment to Item 6110-001-0001, payable from the Federal Trust Fund.. $109,361,000
(SPECIAL EDUCATION & RELATED ITEMS ONLY)
(The operations of the Department's Special Education Division are also funded from this item.)
Provisions:
2.   Of the funds appropriated by this item, $96,000 is available to the Advisory Commission on Special Education for the in-state travel expenses of the commissioners and the secretary to the commission.
4.   Of the funds appropriated by this item, up to $364,000 shall be used to provide in-service training for special and regular educators and related persons, including, but not limited to, parents, administrators, and organizations serving severely disabled children. These funds are also to provide up to four positions for this purpose.
5.   Of the funds appropriated by this item, $318,000 shall be used to provide training in culturally nonbiased assessment and specialized language skills to special education teachers.
10.   Of the funds appropriated by this item, $7,952,000 is for dispute resolution services, including mediation and fair hearing services, provided through contract for the Special Education Program.

11. Of the amount provided in this item, $843,000 is provided for staff for the Special Education Focused Monitoring Pilot Program to be established by the State Department of Education for the purpose of monitoring local education agency compliance with state and federal laws and regulations governing special education.

19. Of the funds appropriated in this item, $250,000 shall be allocated by the Department of Education to the California State University, San Bernardino, Center for the Study of Correctional Education, for special education monitoring of and technical assistance for the California Youth Authority pursuant to legislation as enacted during the 2001-02 Regular Session. If this legislation is not enacted, the $250,000 shall be used for the purposes of implementing the interagency agreement between the Department of Education and the California Youth Authority, which shall be revised to require onsite, full reviews of each institution and each camp operated by the California Youth Authority once every two years and to require that the onsite, full reviews include, but not be limited to, observation of service delivery, file reviews, and interviews with wards, teachers, parents or surrogate parents, and institutional staff.

STATE SUPPORT OF DEPARTMENT OF EDUCATION

6110-001-0001--For support of Department of Education.....................................$50,445,000
(SPECIAL EDUCATION & RELATED ITEM ONLY)
Provision:
9. Of the funds appropriated in this item, $206,000 shall be available as matching funds for the Department of Rehabilitation and provide coordinated services to disabled pupils. Expenditure of the funds shall be identified in the memorandum of understanding or other written agreement with the Department of Rehabilitation to ensure an appropriate match to federal vocational rehabilitation funds.

The following is a list of special education code sections and the most recent legislative bills which affected them. See Page K-3 for year bills were enacted.

EDUCATION CODE SECTION	LEGISLATIVE BILL NUMBER	EDUCATION CODE SECTION	LEGISLATIVE BILL NUMBER	EDUCATION CODE SECTION	LEGISLATIVE BILL NUMBER
56000	AB 369	56132	AB 598	56195.10	AB 598
56000.5	AB 1836	56133	AB 3075	56200	AB 804
56001	SB 1686	56134	AB 369	56201	SB 2059
56020	SB 1870	56135	AB 369	56202	AB 602
56021	SB 1870	56136	AB 598	56203	AB 1115
56022	SB 1870	56137	AB 1892	56205	SB 1686
56023	SB 1870	56140	SB 933	56206	AB 602
56024	SB 1870	56145	SB 1686	56207	AB 804
56025	SB 1870	56146	SB 1686	56207.5	AB 1115
56026	AB 804	56150	AB 456	56208	AB 602
56026.2	AB 1836	56155	AB 817	56211	AB 598
56026.5	SB 181	56155.5	SB 1686	56212	AB 598
56027	SB 998	56156	AB 1528	56213	AB 303
56028	AB 1528	56156.4	AB 598	56240	SB 998
56029	AB 804	56156.5	AB 598	56241	SB 1870
56030	SB 1870	56156.6	AB 598	56243	SB 2403
56030.5	AB 1248	56157	SB 998	56244	SB 2194
56031	SB 1686	56159	SB 998	56245	AB 1487
56032	SB 1686	56162	SB 1345	56300	SB 998
56033	SB 1870	56163	AB 817	56301	SB 1686
56034	AB 3601	56164	AB 817	56302	AB 1060
56035	AB 2355	56165	AB 817	56302.5	SB 1686
56040	AB 3075	56166	AB 817	56303	SB 1870
56041	AB 2773	56166.5	AB 817	56320	AB 3188
56041.5	SB 1686	56167	AB 602	56320.1	AB 369
56042	AB 2355	56167.5	AB 3246	56321	AB 2773
56043	SB 1686	56168	AB 575	56321.5	AB 2267
56045	SB 662	56169.5	AB 3246	56322	SB 998
56048	AB 598	56169.7	AB 3246	56323	SB 1870
56050	SB 1686	56170	SB 1686	56324	AB 3075
56055	AB 804	56171	SB 1686	56325	AB 598
56060	SB 1870	56172	SB 1686	56326	AB 1248
56061	SB 1870	56173	SB 1686	56327	AB 2652
56062	SB 1870	56174	SB 1686	56328	SB 998
56063	SB 1870	56175	SB 1686	56329	SB 1686
56100	AB 602	56176	SB 1686	56333	AB 3075
56101	AB 369	56177	SB 1686	56337	SB 1870
56120	SB 1870	56190	AB 602	56337.5	AB 2773
56121	SB 1870	56191	AB 1055	56338	AB 3075
56122	SB 1870	56192	AB 1248	56339	AB 2773
56123	SB 1870	56193	SB 1870	56340	SB 998
56124	SB 1870	56194	SB 998	56340.1	AB 369
56125	SB 1870	56195	AB 602	56341	SB 1105
56126	SB 1870	56195.1	AB 1115	56341.1	SB 1105
56127	SB 1870	56195.3	AB 602	56341.5	SB 1086
56128	SB 1870	56195.5	AB 602	56342	AB 602
56129	SB 998	56195.7	AB 598	56342.5	SB 1686
56130	SB 1870	56195.8	AB 602	56343	SB 1686
56131	AB 598	56195.9	AB 602	56343.5	AB 456

EDUCATION CODE SECTION	LEGISLATIVE BILL NUMBER	EDUCATION CODE SECTION	LEGISLATIVE BILL NUMBER	EDUCATION CODE SECTION	LEGISLATIVE BILL NUMBER
56344	AB 2773	56414	SB 511	56490	AB 2321
56345	SB 1686	56425	AB 602	56491	AB 2321
56345.1	SB 1686	56425.5	AB 602	56492	AB 2321
56345.5	SB 998	56426	SB 1686	56493	AB 2321
56346	AB 3235	56426.1	AB 602	56494	AB 2321
56347	SB 2403	56426.2	AB 602	56495	AB 2321
56350	AB 2445	56426.25	AB 602	56500	AB 602
56351	AB 2445	56426.3	AB 3246	56500.1	AB 2773
56351.5	AB 306	56426.4	AB 602	56500.2	AB 2773
56352	AB 306	56426.5	AB 369	56500.3	AB 2773
56360	AB 602	56426.6	AB 369	56501	SB 1686
56361	SB 1686	56426.7	AB 3235	56502	AB 369
56361.2	AB 3246	56426.8	AB 3235	56503	AB 2773
56361.5	SB 998	56426.9	AB 967	56504	SB 1345
56362	AB 602	56427	AB 602	56504.5	AB 2773
56362.1	AB 1055	56428	AB 1564	56505	SB 1686
56362.5	SB 1634	56429	AB 602	56505.1	SB 1686
56362.7	SB 386	56430	AB 602	56505.2	AB 2355
56363	AB 205	56431	AB 3246	56506	SB 1686
56363.1	SB 1686	56432	AB 602	56507	SB 1686
56363.3	SB 998	56435	AB 1539	56508	AB 2773
56363.5	SB 998	56440	SB 975	56520	AB 1248
56364	SB 1686	56441	AB 369	56521	AB 1248
56364.1	SB 1686	56441.1	AB 2666	56523	AB 2586
56364.2	SB 1686	56441.2	AB 2666	56524	AB 2586
56364.5	SB 998	56441.3	AB 2666	56600	SB 2059
56365	AB 598	56441.4	AB 1248	56600.5	SB 2059
56366	SB 933	56441.5	AB 1248	56601	AB 2773
56366.1	AB 804	56441.6	AB 2666	56602	AB 1250
56366.2	AB 602	56441.7	AB 2666	56603	SB 1870
56366.3	AB 992	56441.8	AB 675	56604	SB 2059
56366.4	SB 1686	56441.9	AB 2666	56605	SB 2059
56366.5	SB 998	56441.11	AB 3235	56606	SB 998
56366.6	AB 2355	56441.13	AB 2666	56836	AB 602
56366.7	SB 989	56441.14	AB 602	56836.01	AB 598
56366.8	SB 933	56442	AB 2666	56836.02	AB 804
56366.9	AB 602	56443	AB 2666	56836.03	AB 598
56367	AB 369	56445	AB 2666	56836.04	AB 602
56368	AB 1248	56446	AB 598	56836.05	AB 598
56369	AB 998	56447.1	AB 2666	56836.06	AB 1115
56370	AB 602	56449	AB 1539	56836.08	AB 1115
56380	SB 998	56452	AB 2386	56836.09	SB 1564
56381	SB 1686	56453	AB 3075	56836.095	SB 735
56382	AB 369	56454	AB 2386	56836.10	AB 2907
56390	AB 2907	56456	AB 2386	56836.11	AB 2907
56391	AB 804	56460	AB 2386	56836.12	SB 1468
56392	AB 2907	56461	AB 2386	56836.13	AB 598
56393	AB 2907	56462	AB 3562	56836.14	AB 602
56400	SB 511	56463	AB 2386	56836.15	AB 1115
56402	SB 511	56470	AB 2386	56836.155	SB 1564
56404	SB 511	56471	SB 2059	56836.156	SB 982
56406	SB 511	56472	AB 2386	56836.157	SB 982
56408	SB 511	56473	AB 2386	56836.158	SB 982
56410	SB 511	56474	AB 2386	56836.159	SB 735
56412	SB 511	56475	AB 369	56836.16	AB 598

EDUCATION CODE SECTION	LEGISLATIVE BILL NUMBER	EDUCATION CODE SECTION	LEGISLATIVE BILL NUMBER
56836.17	AB 602	56857	SB 679
56836.18	AB 602	56857.5	SB 1345
56836.20	AB 602	56858	AB 982
56836.21	AB 598	56858.5	SB 1345
56836.22	AB 602	56858.7	SB 1345
56836.23	AB 602	56859	AB 369
56836.24	SB 1468	56860	SB 1345
56836.25	AB 602	56862	SB 679
56837	SB 1686	56863	AB 369
56838	SB 1686	56864	AB 598
56839	SB 1686	56865	SB 1345
56840	SB 1686	56867	SB 505
56841	SB 1686	56875	AB 817
56842	SB 1686	56876	AB 369
56845	SB 662	56877	AB 817
56850	AB 369	56878	AB 817
56851	AB 369	56879	AB 817
56852	AB 369	56881	AB 817
56852.5	SB 1345	56882	AB 817
56853	AB 369	56883	AB 817
56854	SB 1345	56884	AB 817
56855	AB 1202	56885	SB 1191
56856	AB 1345		

EDUCATION CODE - PART 30. SPECIAL EDUCATION PROGRAMS

See Pages L-1 - L-9 for more information on the following bills:

Bills Enacted in 1980: SB 1870, AB 1202, AB 3075
Bills Enacted in 1981: AB 817, AB 1055
Bills Enacted in 1982: SB 386, SB 1345, AB 2652
Bills Enacted in 1983: SB 679, AB 1892
Bills Enacted in 1984: SB 1634
Bills Enacted in 1985: AB 456, AB 982
Bills Enacted in 1986: SB 2403, AB 3246
Bills Enacted in 1987: SB 998, AB 2386, AB 2666
Bills Enacted in 1988: SB 2059
Bills Enacted in 1990: SB 2194, AB 1528, AB 2586
Bills Enacted in 1991: AB 675, AB 1060, AB 1487
Bills Enacted in 1992: AB 1248, AB 2267, AB 2773
Bills Enacted in 1993: AB 369, AB 2355
Bills Enacted in 1994: AB 1250, AB 1836, AB 2445, AB 3235, AB 3562, AB 3601
Bills Enacted in 1995: SB 181, SB 975, AB 575, AB 967
Bills Enacted in 1996: SB 989, AB 3188
Bills Enacted in 1997: AB 602
Bills Enacted in 1998: SB 933, SB 1193, SB 1468, SB 1564, SB 1686, AB 205, AB 598
Bills Enacted in 1999: AB 1062, AB 1115, AB 1600
Bills Enacted in 2000: SB 1843, AB 2321, AB 2907
Bills Enacted in 2001: SB 505, SB 511, SB 662, SB 735, SB 982, SB 1105, SB 1191,
              AB 303, AB 306, AB 804, SB 992, AB 1539

BILL/AUTHOR   **CHAPTER NUMBER/EFFECTIVE DATE**

1980

Senate Bill 1870 (Rodda)
- Chapter 797 - Statutes of 1980
  July 28, 1980

Assembly Bill 3075 (Papan)
- Chapter 1353 - Statutes of 1980
  September 30, 1980

Assembly Bill 507 (Chacon)
- Chapter 1339 - Statutes of 1980
  January 1, 1981

Assembly Bill 1202 (Hart)
- Chapter 1191 - Statutes of 1980
  September 29, 1980

Assembly Bill 2286 (Kapiloff)
- Chapter 1325 - Statutes of 1980
  January 1, 1981

Assembly Bill 2394 (Egeland)
- Chapter 1276 - Statutes of 1980
  January 1, 1981

Assembly Bill 3043 (Vasconcellos)
- Chapter 1373 - Statutes of 1980
  January 1, 1981

Assembly Bill 3269 (Hart)
- Chapter 1329 - Statutes of 1980
  January 1, 1981

Senate Bill 1616 (Watson)
- Chapter 1218 - Statutes of 1980
  January 1, 1981

1981

Senate Bill 769 (Sieroty)
- Chapter 1094 - Statutes of 1981
  January 1, 1982, With Computation
  or Recomputations of Allowances
  Deemed Operative for Entire 1981-82
  Fiscal Year

Senate Bill 1192 (Rains)
- Chapter 714 - Statutes of 1981
  January 1, 1982

Assembly Bill 61 (L. Greene)
- Chapter 1093 - Statutes of 1981
  January 1, 1982

Assembly Bill 92 (Lehman)
- Chapter 1176 - Statutes of 1981
  January 1, 1982

Assembly Bill 159 (Kapiloff)
- Chapter 149 - Statutes of 1981
  January 1, 1982

Assembly Bill 817 (Papan)   - Chapter 1044 - Statutes of 1981
                                      January 1, 1982/July 1, 1982

Assembly Bill 933 (Kapiloff)   - Chapter 893 - Statutes of 1981
                                      January 1, 1982

Assembly Bill 1055 (Farr)   - Chapter 972 - Statutes of 1981
                                      January 1, 1982

1982

Senate Bill 386 (Stiern)   - Chapter 866 - Statutes of 1982
                                      September 9, 1982

Senate Bill 1345 (Sieroty)   - Chapter 1201 - Statutes of 1982
                                      September 22, 1982

Senate Bill 2058 (Rains)   - Chapter 466 - Statutes of 1982
                                      January 1, 1983

Assembly Bill 1124 (Hughes)   - Chapter 11 - Statutes of 1982
                                      January 27, 1982

Assembly Bill 1253 (Vasconcellos)   - Chapter 115 - Statutes of 1982
                                      March 12, 1982

Assembly Bill 2652 (Moore)   - Chapter 1334 - Statutes of 1982
                                      January 1, 1983

Assembly Bill 3049 (Kapiloff)   - Chapter 644 - Statutes of 1982
                                      January 1, 1983

1983

Senate Bill 679 (Seymour)   - Chapter 922 - Statutes of 1983
                                      September 20, 1983

Senate Bill 813 (Hart)   - Chapter 498 - Statutes of 1983
                                      July 28, 1983

Assembly Bill 1063 (Hughes)   - Chapter 501 - Statutes of 1983
                                      July 28, 1983

Assembly Bill 1892 (Felando)   - Chapter 1099 - Statutes of 1983
                                      January 1, 1984

BILL/AUTHOR	CHAPTER NUMBER/EFFECTIVE DATE

1984

Senate Bill 585 (Seymour)	- Chapter 1668 - Statutes of 1984 January 1, 1985
Senate Bill 1379 (Alquist)	- Chapter 268 - Statutes of 1984 June 29, 1984
Senate Bill 1634 (Keene)	- Chapter 144 - Statutes of 1984 January 1, 1985
Assembly Bill 2841 (Felando)	- Chapter 1677 - Statutes of 1984 September 30, 1984
Assembly Bill 3007 (Mountjoy)	- Chapter 1717 - Statutes of 1984 September 30, 1984

1985

Senate Bill 1264 (Seymour)	- Chapter 1603 - Statutes of 1985 October 2, 1985
Assembly Bill 72 (Felando)	- Chapter 55 - Statutes of 1985 June 4, 1985
Assembly Bill 456 (Papan)	- Chapter 795 - Statutes of 1985 January 1, 1986
Assembly Bill 982 (O'Connell)	- Chapter 1546 - Statutes of 1985 January 1, 1986
Assembly Bill 1537 (Farr)	- Chapter 999 - Statutes of 1985 September 26, 1985
Assembly Bill 1807 (Harris)	- Chapter 106 - Statutes of 1985 January 1, 1986
Assembly Bill 2557 (Papan)	- Chapter 115 - Statutes of 1985 June 28, 1985

1986

Senate Bill 656 (Seymour)	- Chapter 7 - Statutes of 1986 February 18, 1986
Senate Bill 2403 (Seymour)	- Chapter 233 - Statutes of 1986 July 2, 1986

BILL/AUTHOR	CHAPTER NUMBER/EFFECTIVE DATE

Assembly Bill 3011 (Farr)
- Chapter 374 - Statutes of 1986
  July 16, 1986

Assembly Bill 3246 (Papan)
- Chapter 1296 - Statutes of 1986
  January 1, 1987/July 1, 1987

Assembly Bill 3263 (O'Connell)
- Chapter 1124 - Statutes of 1986
  January 1, 1987

Assembly Bill 4074 (Allen)
- Chapter 703 - Statutes of 1986
  January 1, 1987

1987

Senate Bill 998 (Hart)
- Chapter 1452 - Statutes of 1987
  January 1, 1988

Assembly Bill 93 (O'Connell)
- Chapter 917 - Statutes of 1987
  January 1, 1988

Assembly Bill 1155 (Johnston)
- Chapter 393 - Statutes of 1987
  September 2, 1987

Assembly Bill 2386 (Allen)
- Chapter 1484 - Statutes of 1987
  January 1, 1988

Assembly Bill 2666 (Hannigan)
- Chapter 311 - Statutes of 1987
  July 30, 1987

1988

Senate Bill 2059 (Seymour)
- Chapter 1508 - Statutes of 1988
  January 1, 1989

Assembly Bill 2658 (Speier)
- Chapter 35 - Statutes of 1988
  March 17, 1988

Assembly Bill 3513 (N. Waters)
- Chapter 449 - Statutes of 1988
  January 1, 1989

1989

(No Bills Amending Part 30 of the Education Code)

1990

Senate Bill 823 (Bergeson)
- Chapter 1135 - Statutes of 1990
  January 1, 1991

Senate Bill 1320 (Seymour)
- Chapter 523 - Statutes of 1990
  January 1, 1991

BILL/AUTHOR	CHAPTER NUMBER/EFFECTIVE DATE
Senate Bill 2194 (Morgan)	- Chapter 1596 - Statutes of 1990 January 1, 1991
Assembly Bill 812 (Campbell)	- Chapter 118 - Statutes of 1990 January 1, 1991
Assembly Bill 1528 (Farr)	- Chapter 182 - Statutes of 1990 January 1, 1991
Assembly Bill 2586 (Hughes)	- Chapter 959 - Statutes of 1990 January 1, 1991
Assembly Bill 2875 (O'Connell)	- Chapter 1263 - Statutes of 1990 January 1, 1991
Assembly Bill 3040 (Speier)	- Chapter 1501 - Statutes of 1990 January 1, 1991
Assembly Bill 3057 (Polanco)	- Chapter 1623 - Statutes of 1990 January 1, 1991
Assembly Bill 3451 (Hannigan)	- Chapter 184 - Statutes of 1990 June 29, 1990
Assembly Bill 3880 (Farr)	- Chapter 1234 - Statutes of 1990 January 1, 1991

1991

Assembly Bill 675 (O'Connell)	- Chapter 756 - Statutes of 1991 October 9, 1991
Assembly Bill 1060 (Farr)	- Chapter 223 - Statutes of 1991 January 1, 1992
Assembly Bill 1134 (Campbell)	- Chapter 325 - Statutes of 1991 January 1, 1992
Assembly Bill 1487 (Horcher)	- Chapter 1091 - Statutes of 1991 January 1, 1992
Assembly Bill 1845 (Gotch)	- Chapter 109 - Statutes of 1991 July 11, 1991

1992

Senate Bill 807 (McCorquodale)	- Chapter 1361 - Statutes of 1992 January 1, 1993
Assembly Bill 1248 (Alpert)	- Chapter 759 - Statutes of 1992 September 21, 1992

Assembly Bill 1446 (Quackenbush)	- Chapter 90 - Statutes of 1992 January 1, 1993
Assembly Bill 2267 (Hannigan)	- Chapter 106 - Statutes of 1992 January 1, 1993
Assembly Bill 2773 (Farr)	- Chapter 1360 - Statutes of 1992 January 1, 1993
Assembly Bill 2925 (Eastin)	- Chapter 1213 - Statutes of 1992 January 1, 1993
Assembly Bill 3783 (Farr)	- Chapter 1061 - Statutes of 1992 January 1, 1993

1993

Senate Bill 896 (McCorquodale)	- Chapter 984 - Statutes of 1993 January 1, 1994
Assembly Bill 369 (O'Connell)	- Chapter 1296 - Statutes of 1993 October 11, 1993
Assembly Bill 599 (Speier)	- Chapter 1295 - Statutes of 1993 January 1, 1994
Assembly Bill 1242 (V. Brown)	- Chapter 688 - Statutes of 1993 January 1, 1994
Assembly Bill 1891 (Polanco)	- Chapter 51 - Statutes of 1993 June 30, 1993
Assembly Bill 2211 (Goldsmith)	- Chapter 589 - Statutes of 1993 January 1, 1994
Assembly Bill 2355 (Eastin)	- Chapter 939 - Statutes of 1993 October 8, 1993

1994

Senate Bill 732 (Bergeson)	- Chapter 936 - Statutes of 1994 September 28, 1994
Senate Bill 1347 (Russell)	- Chapter 333 - Statutes of 1994 January 1, 1995
Assembly Bill 1250 (Campbell)	- Chapter 921 - Statutes of 1994 January 1, 1995

BILL/AUTHOR	CHAPTER NUMBER/EFFECTIVE DATE
Assembly Bill 1836 (Eastin)	- Chapter 1126 - Statutes of 1994 September 30, 1994
Assembly Bill 2445 (Conroy)	- Chapter 998 - Statutes of 1994 January 1, 1995
Assembly Bill 2587 (Eastin)	- Chapter 922 - Statutes of 1994 January 1, 1995
Assembly Bill 2798 (Bronshvag)	- Chapter 513 - Statutes of 1994 January 1, 1995
Assembly Bill 2971 (O'Connell)	- Chapter 1172 - Statutes of 1994 January 1, 1995
Assembly Bill 3235 (Solis)	- Chapter 1288 - Statutes of 1994 January 1, 1995
Assembly Bill 3562 (Eastin)	- Chapter 840 - Statutes of 1994 January 1, 1995
Assembly Bill 3601 (Committee on Judiciary)	- Chapter 146 - Statutes of 1994 January 1, 1995
Assembly Bill 3793 (Eastin)	- Chapter 661 - Statutes of 1994 January 1, 1995

1995

Senate Bill 181 (Ayala)	- Chapter 203 - Statutes of 1995 January 1, 1996
Senate Bill 975 (Committee on Judiciary)	- Chapter 91 - Statutes of 1995 January 1, 1996
Assembly Bill 575 (Knox)	- Chapter 976 - Statutes of 1995 January 1, 1996
Assembly Bill 825 (W. Brown)	- Chapter 308 - Statutes of 1995 August 3, 1995
Assembly Bill 967 (Ducheny)	- Chapter 530 - Statutes of 1995 January 1, 1996

1996

Senate Bill 210 (Solis)	- Chapter 208 - Statutes of 1996 January 1, 1997
Senate Bill 989 (Polanco)	- Chapter 944 - Statutes of 1996 January 1, 1997

BILL/AUTHOR	CHAPTER NUMBER/EFFECTIVE DATE
Assembly Bill 1438 (Campbell)	- Chapter 233 - Statutes of 1996 July 22, 1996
Assembly Bill 3188 (House)	- Chapter 661 - Statutes of 1996 January 1, 1997
Assembly Bill 3488 (Ducheny)	- Chapter 204 - Statutes of 1996 July 22, 1996

1997

Senate Bill 1015 (Schiff)	- Chapter 545 - Statutes of 1997 January 1, 1998
Senate Bill 1261 (Sher)	- Chapter 30 - Statutes of 1997 June 30, 1997
Assembly Bill 602 (Davis)	- Chapter 854 - Statutes of 1997 January 1, 1998
Assembly Bill 1578 (Migden)	- Chapter 299 - Statutes of 1997 August 18, 1997

1998

Senate Bill 933 (M. Thompson)	- Chapter 311 - Statutes of 1998 August 19, 1998
Senate Bill 1193 (Peace)	- Chapter 313 - Statutes of 1998 August 19, 1998
Senate Bill 1468 (Rosenthal)	- Chapter 846 - Statutes of 1998 September 25, 1998
Senate Bill 1564 (Schiff)	- Chapter 330 - Statutes of 1998 August 21, 1998
Senate Bill 1686 (Solis)	- Chapter 691 - Statutes of 1998 January 1, 1999
Assembly Bill 205 (Machado)	- Chapter 1058 - Statutes of 1998 January 1, 1999
Assembly Bill 598 (Davis)	- Chapter 89 - Statutes of 1998 June 30, 1998

1999

Assembly Bill 1062 (Margett)	- Chapter 392 - Statutes of 1999 January 1, 2000
Assembly Bill 1115 (Strom-Martin)	- Chapter 78 - Statutes of 1999 July 7, 1999

Assembly Bill 1600 (Committee on Education)   - Chapter 646 - Statutes of 1999
January 1, 2000

2000

Senate Bill 1843 (Solis)   - Chapter 286 – Statutes of 2000
January 1, 2001

Assembly Bill 2321 (Mazzoni)   - Chapter 591 – Statutes of 2000
January 1, 2001

Assembly Bill 2907 (Committee on Education   - Chapter 1058 – Statutes of 2000
January 1, 2001

2001

Senate Bill 505 (Perata)   - Chapter 536 – Statutes of 2001
October 5, 2001

Senate Bill 511 (Alpert)   - Chapter 690 – Statutes of 2001
January 1, 2002

Senate Bill 662 (Committee on Judiciary)   - Chapter 159 – Statutes of 2001
August 9, 2001

Senate Bill 735 (Committee on Budget and Fiscal Review)   - Chapter 891 – Statutes of 2001
October 14, 2001

Senate Bill 982 (O'Connell)   - Chapter 203 – Statutes of 2001
August 13, 2001

Senate Bill 1105 (Margett)   - Chapter 405 – Statutes of 2001
January 1, 2002

Senate Bill 1191 (Speier)   - Chapter 745 – Statutes of 2001
October 12, 2001

Assembly Bill 303 (Dickerson)   - Chapter 551 – Statutes of 2001
January 1, 2002

Assembly Bill 306 (Frommer)   - Chapter 736 – Statutes of 2001
January 1, 2002

Assembly Bill 804 (Committee on Education)   - Chapter 734 – Statutes of 2001
October 11, 2001

Assembly Bill 992 (Papan)   - Chapter 215 – Statutes of 2001
January 1, 2002

Assembly Bill 1539 (Pavley)   - Chapter 629 – Statutes of 2001
January 1, 2002

--- INDEX ---

TOPICAL & CODE REFERENCE

The page number is where the section begins and is not necessarily the page where the word or phrase is located.

A

DEFINITIONS (GENERALLY) - - Cont'd.

DEFINITIONS (GENERALLY) Cont'd.

DEFINITIONS (GENERALLY) Cont'd.

E

G

I

L

N

O

Q

R

M-52

S

T

U

V

W

XYZ

California Special Education Programs
A Composite of Laws
(Twenty-fourth edition)

Note: Parents of children with a disability are eligible to receive one complimentary copy of this publication.

☐ **I am a parent of a child with a disability.**

Parent Signature   **Date**

Name of school child attends

Order Form

BUSINESS HOURS: 8:00 A.M.–4:30 P.M., PST

To order call: 1-800-995-4099

MONDAY THROUGH FRIDAY • FAX 916-323-0823

FROM:

SCHOOL/DISTRICT (if applicable)   ☐ PUBLIC   ☐ PRIVATE

NAME/ATTENTION

ADDRESS

CITY   COUNTY   STATE   ZIP CODE

(   )

DAYTIME TELEPHONE

PAYMENT METHOD: ☐ CHECK (Payable to California Department of Education)
☐ VISA
☐ MASTERCARD
☐ PURCHASE ORDER

CREDIT CARD NUMBER

EXPIRATION DATE

AUTHORIZED SIGNATURE

Item No.	Title	Quantity	Price each	Total
1557	California Special Education Programs: A Composite of Laws (Twenty-fourth edition)		$20.00	$

SUBTOTAL	$
California residents add sales tax. For county sales tax rates see <www.boe.ca.gov/rates/citycnty.htm>.	$
Shipping and handling charges (See chart at left.)	$
TOTAL	$

SHIPPING AND HANDLING CHARGES

Purchase amount	Add
0 - $15	$ 5.95
$15.01 - $30	7.95
$30.01 - $50	9.95
$50.01 - $100	11.95
$100.01 - $150	13.95
$150.01 - $200	15.95
$200.01 - $250	17.95
$250.01 - $300	19.95
$300.01 - $350	21.95
$350.01 and up	6% of subtotal

Mail completed order form to:

California Department of Education
CDE Press Sales Office
P.O. Box 271
Sacramento, CA 95812-0271

Or fax completed order form to: **916-323-0823**

Visit our Web site <*http://www.cde.ca.gov/cdepress*>.

☐ **Please send me a free copy of the current *Educational Resources* catalog.**

Note: Mail orders must be accompanied by a check, a purchase order, or a VISA or MasterCard credit card number, including expiration date and your signature. Purchase orders without checks are accepted from educational institutions, businesses, and governmental agencies. Purchase orders and credit card orders may be placed by FAX (916) 323-0823. Telephone orders will be accepted toll-free (1-800-995-4099) for credit card purchases. Please do not send cash. Stated prices are subject to change. Please order carefully; include correct item number and quantity for each publication ordered. *All sales are final.*

PRICES AND AVAILABILITY OF PUBLICATIONS ARE SUBJECT TO CHANGE WITHOUT NOTICE.